Programming *and* Problem Solving

with Java™

Nell Dale
University of Texas, Austin

Chip Weems
University of Massachusetts, Amherst

Mark Headington
University of Wisconsin – La Crosse

JONES AND BARTLETT PUBLISHERS
Sudbury, Massachusetts
BOSTON   TORONTO   LONDON   SINGAPORE

World Headquarters

Jones and Bartlett Publishers
40 Tall Pine Drive
Sudbury, MA 01776
978-443-5000
info@jbpub.com
www.jbpub.com

Jones and Bartlett Publishers
Canada
2406 Nikanna Road
Mississauga, ON L5C 2W6
CANADA

Jones and Bartlett Publishers
International
Barb House, Barb Mews
London W6 7PA
UK

Cover image © Peter J. Robinson/Photolibrary/PictureQuest

Text photo credits follow the index, which constitutes a continuation of the copyright page. Unless otherwise acknowledged, all photographs are the property of Jones and Bartlett Publishers.

Library of Congress Cataloging-in-Publication Data

Dale, Nell B.
 Programming and problem solving with Java / Nell Dale, Chip Weems, Mark Headington.
  p. cm.
 Includes index.
 ISBN 0-7637-0490-3
  1. Java (Computer program language) I. Weems, Chip. II. Headington, Mark R. III.
Title.

QA76.73.J38D346 2003
005.13'3--dc21

2002043476

Production Credits
Chief Executive Officer: Clayton Jones
Chief Operating Officer: Don W. Jones, Jr.
Executive V.P. and Publisher: Robert W. Holland, Jr.
V.P., Design and Production: Anne Spencer
V.P., Manufacturing and Inventory Control: Therese Bräuer
V.P., Sales and Marketing: William Kane
Editor-in-Chief, College: J. Michael Stranz
Production Manager: Amy Rose
Senior Marketing Manager: Nathan Schultz
Associate Production Editor: Karen C. Ferreira
Associate Editor: Theresa DiDonato
Production Assistant: Jenny McIsaac
Cover Design: Kristin Ohlin
Composition: Northeast Compositors
Illustrations and Technical Art: Smolinski Studios
Copyediting: Jill Hobbs
Proofreading: Trillium Project Management
Text Design: Anne Spencer
Printing and Binding: Courier Kendallville
Cover Printing: Lehigh Press

This book was typeset in QuarkXPress 4.1 on a Macintosh G4. The font families used were Caecilia, Myria, and Letter Gothic. The first printing was printed on 45# Utopia GW Matte.

Printed in the United States of America
07 06 05 04 10 9 8 7 6 5 4 3 2

This book is dedicated to you, and to all of our other students for whom it was begun and without whom it would never have been completed.

To quote Mephistopheles, one of the chief devils, and tempter of Faust,

> *…My friend, I shall be pedagogic,*
> *And say you ought to start with Logic…*
> *…Days will be spent to let you know*
> *That what you once did at one blow,*
> *Like eating and drinking so easy and free,*
> *Can only be done with One, Two, Three.*
> *Yet the web of thought has no such creases*
> *And is more like a weaver's masterpieces;*
> *One step, a thousand threads arise,*
> *Hither and thither shoots each shuttle,*
> *The threads flow on, unseen and subtle,*
> *Each blow effects a thousand ties.*
> *The philosopher comes with analysis*
> *And proves it had to be like this;*
> *The first was so, the second so,*
> *And hence the third and fourth was so,*
> *And were not the first and second here,*
> *Then the third and fourth could never appear.*
> *That is what all the students believe,*
> *But they have never learned to weave.*

J. W. von Goethe, *Faust*, Walter Kaufman trans., New York, Anchor/Doubleday: 1963.

As you study this book, do not let the logic of algorithms bind your imagination, but rather make it your tool for weaving masterpieces of thought.

Contents

Chapter 4   Selection and Encapsulation   152

Chapter 9   Exceptions and Additional Control Structures   430

Chapter 10   One-Dimensional Arrays   478

Preface

Programming and Problem Solving with Java™ represents a significant transition in the development of the Dale series, with much that is new. Here we briefly summarize the features of this new text.

The most obvious new feature is the beautiful full-color design, which allows us to use colored code displays that follow conventions similar to the editors found in integrated development environments. The code coloring conventions also make syntax stand out from the text more effectively. For the first time, we are able to show realistic full-color screen images of program output. Color is used extensively to enhance the clarity and improve overall readability of illustrations, feature boxes, and other elements of the text. We're very excited to add this new dimension to our pedagogical toolkit.

This book has been developed from the ground up to be a Java text. It is not a "Java translation" of our previous texts. We have, however, retained our familiar easy-to-read style and clear approach to introducing new topics. Each chapter has the same overall organization as in our previous books, with a full problem-solving case study, testing and debugging hints, summary, and five types of exercises. Also, some topics, such as problem solving, are independent of the programming language and thus contain familiar discussions.

An exciting new feature in each chapter is the division of the learning goals into knowledge goals and skill goals. Each chapter thus addresses specific concepts that students should understand as distinct from skills that they should develop. For example, in the chapter that covers inheritance, students are expected to understand the concept of a class hierarchy, and to be able to implement a derived class.

In every regard, this new book is object-oriented in its presentation of the fundamental concepts of computing. From the very first chapter we use object-oriented terminology to describe the software development process. Classes are covered extensively in Chapter 2, where we first encounter Java syntax. Over the course of the next several chapters, students learn to build separately compiled classes representing realistic objects and to add to their sophistication gradually. In Chapter 6, we present the CRC card technique for object-oriented design, and in Chapter 7 we formalize the earlier coverage of classes and introduce inheritance.

Unlike our other Java text, *Introduction to Java™ and Software Design,* here we save the introduction of graphical user interface components for Chapter 8. These are used only sparingly in the remaining chapters, so that instructors who do not wish to focus on GUI and event programming do not have to do so. We use a modest subset of the Swing library components that is appropriate to a course at this level. Event driven I/O is the dominant model not only in Java, but in the modern world of programming in general. Students come to our classes with prior familiarity of event-driven interfaces and expect to learn how to write programs containing them. In this book, we have thus strived to strike a balance between covering the more complex style of I/O with which students are familiar, and the more traditional console I/O that is simpler to use for early applications.

The text uses real Java I/O classes rather than ones we supply. It would have made our job much easier to supply a streamlined set of I/O classes to simplify Java I/O. We have seen many books that introduce either C or Pascal-like command-line I/O classes or simplified windowing classes that automatically handle events. However, our view is that using such libraries produces students who still do not know how to write real Java programs at the end of the course, leaving them to learn the Java I/O library on their own, without help or guidance. Instead, we have carefully chosen a subset of the console I/O and Swing packages that is within their grasp, and that covers all of the essential concepts necessary for them to explore additional features of the library on their own.

All of the programs have been tested with Metrowerks CodeWarrior® or the Apple OSX version of the Sun SDK. The program code is included on the Student Resource Disk for Java, which accompanies your new book.

Chapter Coverage

Chapter 1 begins with basic definitions, computer concepts, software life cycle, compilation versus interpretation, problem solving techniques including object-oriented problem solving, and a problem-solving case study resulting in an object-oriented algorithm. We introduce objects from the very beginning, defining them in this first chapter, and consistently using object-oriented terminology throughout the book.

In Chapter 2, we examine the char type, the String class, and concatenation expressions. We also examine the process of declaring a reference variable, instantiating an object, assigning its address to the variable, and using the object. These are difficult but essential concepts for beginners to grasp. Chapter 2 further covers sequential control flow, simple output to System.out, and string input via System.in. This gets students off to a quick start with a simple working program and past the mechanics of program entry and execution.

Because the input operation is a value-returning method and the output operation is a void method, we take the opportunity in the second major portion of Chapter 2 to explain these concepts. We close the chapter with a discussion of class and method construction, including writing a very simple value-returning method. The case study results in a Java application that contains a class for a name object, including several simple methods.

In Chapter 3, we turn to the numeric types and expression syntax. We cover type conversions, precedence rules, and the use of numeric types with String objects. We also reinforce the distinction between the reference and primitive types in this chapter. We then see how to develop an application with separately compiled classes, using the default anonymous package. The case study then develops an employee object that imports a revised version of the name class developed in Chapter 2. The result is a fairly sophisticated application that appears simple and requires noticeably less work as a result of reuse.

With Chapter 4, we introduce the first variation in control flow, branching. The *if-else* statement is introduced first as the general case and the *if* statement is then a special instance of it. The Boolean type and expressions are covered extensively in preparation for branching. The concepts of encapsulation and abstraction are then introduced and motivate an example in which the name class from the preceding two chapters is made more broadly applicable. It is then used in the case study, as part of developing a student record class that is then used in a grade-notices application. This layered development of the name class, together with its use in yet another context, helps to drive home the importance of object-oriented design. The chapter closes with a discussion of testing strategies and formal test plans.

Chapter 5 brings us to file I/O and loops. As in our other texts, we introduce all of the basic loop algorithms with one loop construct, the *while* loop. We prefer to focus on how loops are used in algorithms, while introducing only the minimum syntax necessary to illustrate the concepts: count-controlled, event controlled, and various loop processes together with a loop design methodology. In that way, students don't develop the misperception that the different forms of control structures are bound to the different syntactic structures in a language. This approach also avoids the situation that we commonly see in which students are focused on their confusion over choosing among different looping statements when they are really still unsure of the underlying algorithmic mechanism that they wish to express. Chapter 9 compares and contrasts the remaining looping structures with the *while* loop, once students have gained enough experience to be confident in their understanding of how loops work. Chapter 5 also includes a discussion of mutable and immutable objects, and this is then reinforced in the case study where we build a gender class that is mutable and use it in an application.

Chapter 6 takes a break from the introduction of significant amounts of new syntax and focuses on object-oriented design using the CRC-card technique, which is one of the simpler representations recognized by UML. The students learn how to brainstorm initial classes, filter the initial list, then develop the responsibilities and collaborations for these and other classes that they discover through a series of scenarios. During this process, we give the students an initial taste of the concept of inheritance. The only new Java syntax that we introduce in Chapter 6 is the named package. The chapter also explores ethical issues in computing before closing with a case study that builds two new classes, and reuses the name class in order to construct an application that does the initial data entry for an address book.

Chapter 7 is, in a sense, the core of the text. In this chapter, we bring together all of the discussion of classes and objects in the context of an object hierarchy with inheritance and polymorphism. Students learn how to read the documentation for a class hierarchy and how to determine the inherited members of a class. They also see how the classes are related through Java's scope rules. The students are thus brought to the point of being armed with essentially all of Java's object-oriented tools with the exception of abstract classes and interfaces.

With Chapter 8, we take a break from our steady uphill climb through the landscape of object-oriented programming, and look at a topic that many students find fascinating and fun: graphical user interfaces. The GUI also provides excellent examples of using objects from a library. We use just a few Swing components to construct all of the GUI interfaces in the text. A JFrame provides the basic output window, JLabel is used for output, and JTextField is used for input. GUI programming requires handling of events, and here we also keep things simple, using the window's default exit-on-close handler to terminate execution, and a JButton to signal when input is ready. These constructs enable us to build typical user interfaces while we focus on the algorithmic issues of event loops. Chapter 8 develops two case-study applications that reinforce the object-oriented design approaches in Chapters 6 and 7.

Chapter 9 is the "ice cream and cake" section of the book, covering the additional control structures that make the coding of certain algorithms easier. In addition to the `switch`, do, and for statements, Chapter 9 introduces the concept of exception handling. We show students how to use a `try-catch` statement to catch exceptions. Because we've already covered inheritance, it is a simple matter to define new exception classes that can be thrown between sections of user code. Students are then able to write code that is robust in the face of errors that cannot be handled directly with testing and branching.

Chapters 10, 11, and 12 are devoted to composite data structures. In Chapter 10, the basic concept of a composite structure is introduced and illustrated with the Java array. In Chapter 11, we show how an array can be used to implement a general-purpose list class. Our prior class designs have been in the context of specific applications, and this provides experience in developing an object-oriented design that does not have a predefined client. Then in Chapter 12, we extend the discussion of arrays to multiple dimensions, and through a case study we show how they can be used to represent mathematical matrices. Given this numerically motivated case study, it is also natural to review the limitations of floating-point numbers as they are represented in the computer.

Chapter 13 provides a quick tour of the concept of recursion and some example algorithms. As in our previous texts, this chapter is designed so that it can be assigned for reading along with earlier chapters. The first half of the chapter can be covered after Chapter 5, The second half of the chapter can be read after Chapter 10, as it applies recursion to arrays.

The book closes with Chapter 14, devoted to the implementation of Java applets. We specifically chose to use only applications in the first part of the text because of their more general applicability, their ability to use console I/O, and to avoid various issues with portability across browsers in different environments. We recognize, however, that many students are interested in web programming, and are curious to learn how to write applets. Chapter 14 thus serves this interest.

Chapter Features

■ Goals

Each chapter begins with a list of learning objectives for the student, divided into knowledge goals and skill goals. These goals are reinforced and tested in the end-of-chapter exercises.

■ Timeline

An illustrated timeline on computer history develops throughout the course of the book, on the opening pages of each chapter. This timeline highlights important moments in computer history and identifies key players in the development of computer technology.

■ Problem-Solving Case Studies

A full development of a problem from its statement to a working Java application is developed in each case study. In chapters beginning with 6, the CRC Card design strategy is employed to develop object-oriented designs that are then translated into code. Test plans and sample test data are also presented for many of these case studies.

■ Testing and Debugging

These sections consider the implications of the chapter material with regard to testing of applications or classes. They conclude with a list of testing and debugging hints.

■ Quick Checks

These questions test the student's recall of major points associated with the chapter goals. Upon reading each question, students should immediately know the answer, which they can verify by glancing at the answer at the end of the section. The page number on which the concept is discussed appears at the end of each question so that students can review the material in the event of an incorrect response.

■ Exam Preparation Exercises

To help students prepare for tests, the Exam Preparation questions usually have objective answers. They are designed to be answerable with a few minutes of work. Answers to selected questions are given in the back of the book, and the remaining questions are answered in the Instructor's Guide.

■ Programming Warm-Up Exercises

These questions provide students with experience in writing Java code fragments. Students can practice the syntactic constructs in each chapter without the burden of writing a complete program.

■ Programming Problems

These exercises require students to design solutions and write complete Java applications.

■ Case Study Follow-Up Exercises

Much of modern programming practice involves reading and modifying existing code. These exercises provide students with an opportunity to strengthen this critical skill by answering questions about the case study code, or making changes to it.

Supplements

■ Online Instructor's ToolKit

Also available to adopters on request from the publisher is a powerful teaching tool entitled "Instructor's ToolKit." These downloadable files contain an electronic version of the Instructor's Guide, a Brownstone Diploma computerized test bank, PowerPoint lecture presentations, and the complete programs from the text. To download your copy visit **http://computer-science.jbpub.com/ppsjava.**

■ Programs

The programs contain the source code for all of the complete Java applications and stand-alone classes that are found within the textbook. They are included in the Student Resource Disk for Java and are available as a free download for instructors and students from the publisher's web site: **http://computerscience.jbpub.com/ppsjava**. The programs from all of the Case Studies, plus several programs that appear in the chapter bodies, are included. Fragments or snippets of code are not included, nor are the solutions to the chapter-ending "Programming Problems." These application files can be viewed or edited using any standard text editor, but in order to compile and run the applications, a Java compiler must be used.

■ Student Resource Disk for Java

The Student Resource Disk for Java contains Borland® JBuilder™ 7 Personal, the Sun Java™ 2 SDK Standard edition v. 1.4.1, the Sun Java™ SDK Standard Edition Documentation, and program files for the Java applications and stand-alone classes in your textbook. This CD also contains the program files for *A Laboratory Course for Programming with Java*. Your copy of the Student Resource Disk for Java is included free of charge with the purchase of your new textbook.

■ Student Lecture Companion: A Note-Taking Guide ISBN : 076372372X

Designed from the PowerPoint presentation developed for this text, the Student Lecture Companion is an invaluable tool for learning. The notebook is designed to encourage students to focus their energies on listening to the lecture as they fill in additional details. The skeletal outline concept helps students organize their notes and readily recognize the important concepts in each chapter.

◼ A Laboratory Course for Programming with Java™ ISBN : 0763724637

Written by Nell Dale, this lab manual follows the organization of the text. The lab manual is designed to allow the instructor maximum flexibility and may be used in both open and closed laboratory settings. Each chapter contains three types of activities: Prelab, Inlab, and Postlab. Each lesson is broken into exercises that thoroughly demonstrate the concept covered in the chapter. The applications, application shells (partial applications), and data files are available online, and also on the Student Resource Disk for Java that accompanies your textbook.

Acknowledgements

We would like to thank the many individuals who have helped us in the preparation of this text. We are indebted to the members of the faculties of the Computer Science Departments at the University of Texas at Austin, The University of Massachusetts at Amherst, and the University of Wisconsin – Lacrosse.

We extend special thanks to Jeff Brumfield for developing the syntax template metalanguage and allowing us to use it in this text.

For their many helpful suggestions, we thank the lecturers, teaching assistants, consultants, and student proctors who run the courses for which this book was written, and the students themselves.

We are grateful to the following people who took the time to review the manuscript at various stages in its development: Rama Chakrapani, Tennessee Technological University; Ilyas Cicekli, University of Central Florida; Jose Cordova, University of Louisiana at Monroe; Mike Litman, Western Illinois University; and Rathika Rajaravivarma, Central Connecticut State University.

We also thank Mike and Sigrid Wile, along with the many people at Jones and Bartlett who contributed so much, especially J. Michael Stranz, Amy Rose, Theresa DiDonato, and Anne Spencer.

Anyone who has ever written a book – or is related to someone who has – can appreciate the amount of time involved in such a project. To our families – all the Dale clan and the extended Dale Family (too numerous to name); to Lisa, Charlie, and Abby; to Anne, Brady, and Kari – Thanks for your tremendous support and indulgence.

N.D.
C.W.
M.H.

Introduction to Object-Oriented Programming

goals

Knowledge Goals

- To understand what a computer program is
- To know the three phases of the software life cycle
- To understand what an algorithm is
- To learn what a high-level programming language is
- To understand the difference between machine code and Bytecode
- To understand the compilation, execution, and interpretation processes
- To learn what the major components of a computer are and how they work together
- To understand the concept of an object in the context of computer problem solving

Skill Goals

To be able to:

- List the basic stages involved in writing a computer application
- Distinguish between hardware and software
- List the ways of structuring code in a Java application
- Name several problem-solving techniques
- Choose a problem-solving technique to apply
- Identify the objects in a problem statement

timeline

3000 BC
The precursor to today's wire-and-bead abacus was invented in Babylonia

1612-1614
John Napier conceives "Napier's Bones," ivory rods that serve as an early calculator

1622
The slide rule is invented by the great mathematician William Oughtred

1642-1643
Blaise Pascal invents one of the first mechanical calculators, the Pascalene

1801
Punch-card-controlled Jacquard's Loom is invented. Uses binary automation

1820
The first mass-produced calculator, the Thomas Arithmometer, is introduced to the world

introduction

DIGITAL COMPUTERS

PEOPLE WHO COUNT ON THEIR FINGERS

THE BOOK OF PHRASES

By permission of Johnny Hart and Creators Syndicate, Inc.

com·put·er \kəm-pyōō′tər\ *n. often attrib* (1646): one that computes; specif: a programmable electronic device that can store, retrieve, and process data[1]

What a brief definition for something that has, in just a few decades, changed the way of life in industrialized societies! Computers touch all areas of our lives: paying bills, driving cars, using the telephone, shopping. In fact, it might be easier to list those areas of our lives in which we do *not* use computers. You are probably most familiar with computers through the use of games, word processors, Web browsers, and other applications. Be forewarned: This book covers more than just using computers. This text teaches you how to program them.

---

[1]By permission. From *Merriam-Webster's Collegiate Dictionary*, tenth edition © 1994 by Merriam-Webster Inc.

1822
Charles Babbage formulates his design for the Difference Engine

1842-1843
Augusta Ada Byron earns her designation as the first computer programmer with her notes on the Analytical Engine

1844
Samuel F.B. Morse successfully transmits a telegraph message across a wire from Washington to Baltimore

1854
George Boole's famous paper "An Investigation of the Laws of Thought" is published

1858
The first transatlantic telegraphic communication takes place

1868
Christopher Sholes creates the QWERTY keyboard for the early typewriter

1.1 Overview of Object-Oriented Programming

Learning to program a computer is a matter of training yourself to solve problems in a very detailed and organized manner. You are already experienced in solving problems intuitively, but now you must develop the skill of writing a problem solution in terms of objects and actions that are appropriate for a computer. In this chapter we begin developing this skill by answering some of the most commonly asked questions about programming and computers, and we then look at some formal techniques for solving problems.

■ What Is Programming?

Much of human behavior and thought is characterized by logical sequences of actions involving objects. Since infancy, you have been learning how to act, how to do things. And you have learned to expect certain behaviors from everything you encounter in the world around you.

A lot of what you do every day you do automatically. Fortunately, you do not need to consciously think of every step involved in a process as simple as turning a page by hand:

1. Lift hand.
2. Move hand to right side of book.
3. Grasp top-right corner of page.
4. Move hand from right to left until page is positioned so that you can read what is on the other side.
5. Release page.

Think how many neurons must fire and how many muscles must respond, all in a certain order or sequence, to move your arm and hand. Yet you move them unconsciously.

Much of what you now do quite naturally you once had to learn. Watch how a baby concentrates on putting one foot before the other while learning to walk. Then watch a group of three-year-olds playing tag. How far they have come!

On a broader scale, mathematics never could have been developed without logical sequences of steps for manipulating symbols to solve problems and prove theorems. Mass production never would have worked without operations taking place on component parts in a certain order. Our entire civilization is based on the order of actions, the logical arrangement of things, and their interactions.

Programming Developing instructions for carrying out a task involving a set of objects

Computer A programmable device that can store, retrieve, and process data

We create order, both consciously and unconsciously, through a process called programming. This book is concerned with the programming of one particular tool—the computer.

Notice that the key word in the definition of a computer is *data*. Computers manipulate data. When you write a program (a plan) for a computer, you specify the properties of the data and the operations that can be applied to it. The combination of the data and operations serves to represent objects. The objects we represent can be either physical objects from the real world, such as products in an inventory, or abstract objects, such as mathematical constructs. Our computer representations of objects are then programmed to interact as necessary to solve a problem. Data is information in a form that the computer can use—for example, numbers and letters. Information is any knowledge that can be communicated, including abstract ideas and concepts such as "the Earth is round."

Data come in many different forms: letters, words, integer numbers, real numbers, dates, times, coordinates on a map, and so on. In the absence of operations that manipulate the data, however, these forms are essentially meaningless. For example, the number 7.5 has no meaning out of context. In the context of an operation that computes it from a measurement of a person's head, however, it becomes a hat size. The combination of data with related operations, in the form of an object, makes it possible to represent information in the computer. Virtually any kind of information can be represented as an object.

Just as a concert program lists the pieces to be performed in the order that the players will perform them, a computer program lists the objects needed to solve a problem and orchestrates their interactions. From now on, when we use the words *programming* and *program*, we mean computer programming and computer program.

The computer allows us to perform tasks more efficiently, quickly, and accurately than we could by hand—if we could do them by hand at all. For this powerful machine to be a useful tool, however, it must first be programmed. That is, we must specify what we want done and how. We do so through programming.

Data Information in a form that a computer can use

Information Any knowledge that can be communicated

Object A collection of data values and associated operations

Computer programming The process of specifying objects and the ways in which those objects interact to solve a problem

Computer program Instructions defining a set of objects and orchestrating their interactions to solve a problem

How Do We Write a Program?

A computer is not intelligent. It cannot analyze a problem and come up with a solution. A human (the *programmer*) must analyze the problem, develop the objects and instructions for solving the problem, and then have the computer carry out the instructions. What's the advantage of using a computer if it can't solve problems? Once we have written a solution for the computer, the computer can repeat the solution very quickly and consistently, again and again. In this way, the computer frees people from repetitive and boring tasks.

To write a program for a computer to follow, we must go through a two-phase process: *problem solving* and *implementation* (see Figure 1.1).

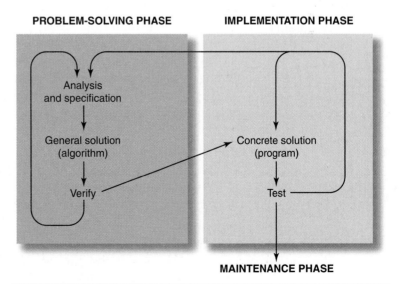

Figure 1.1   Programming Process

Problem-Solving Phase

1. *Analysis and specification.* Understand (define) the problem and identify what the solution must do.
2. *General solution (algorithm).* Specify the objects and their interactions that solve the problem.
3. *Verify.* Follow the steps exactly to see if the solution really does solve the problem.

Implementation Phase

1. *Concrete solution (program).* Translate the object specifications and algorithms (the general solution) into a programming language.
2. *Test.* Have the computer carry out the program and then check the results. If you find errors, analyze the program and the general solution to determine the source of the errors, and then make corrections.

Once a program has been written, it enters a third phase: *maintenance.*

Maintenance Phase

1. *Use.* Use the program.
2. *Maintain.* Modify the program to meet changing requirements or to correct any errors that show up in using it.

Class A description of the representation of a specific kind of object, in terms of data and operational behaviors

Algorithm Instructions for solving a problem in a finite amount of time using a finite amount of data

The programmer begins the programming process by analyzing the problem, identifying the objects that collaborate to solve the problem, and developing a specification for each kind of object, called a class. The objects work together to create an application that solves the original problem. Understanding and analyzing a problem take up much more time than Figure 1.1 implies. These tasks form the heart of the programming process.

A program is an algorithm that is written for a computer. When we define classes of objects and orchestrate their interactions to solve a problem, we are writing an algorithm. We generally refer to Java programs as *applications.*[2]

More generally, an algorithm is a verbal or written description of a logical set of actions involving objects. We use algorithms every day. Recipes, knitting instructions, and driving directions are all examples of algorithms that are not programs.

When you start your car, for example, you follow a step-by-step set of actions involving various objects. The algorithm might look something like this:

Objects: Key, Transmission, Gas Pedal, Engine, Phone

1. Insert the key.
2. Make sure the transmission is in Park (or Neutral).

---

[2]Java supports two types of programs, applications and applets. An *applet* is a restricted form of application that can be executed by a Web browser. We do not use applets in most of this book, but Chapter 14 explains how applications and applets differ and shows how to convert an application into an applet.

3. Depress the gas pedal.
4. Turn the key to the start position.
5. If the engine starts within six seconds, release the key to the ignition position.
6. If the engine doesn't start within six seconds, release the key and gas pedal, wait ten seconds, and repeat Steps 3 through 6, but not more than five times.
7. If the car doesn't start, phone the garage.

Without the phrase "but not more than five times" in Step 6, you could be stuck trying to start the car forever. Why? Because if something is wrong with the car, repeating Steps 3 through 6 over and over will not start it. This kind of never-ending situation is called an *infinite loop*. If we leave the phrase "but not more than five times" out of Step 6, the procedure doesn't fit our definition of an algorithm. An algorithm must terminate in a finite amount of time for all possible conditions.

Suppose a programmer needs an algorithm to determine an employee's weekly wages. The algorithm reflects what would be done by hand:

Objects: Employee Record, Personnel Database, Employee ID, Time Card, Pay Rate, Hours Worked, Regular Wages, Overtime Wages, Total Wages

1. Get the Employee Record from the Personnel Database, using the Employee ID from the Time Card.
2. Get the Pay Rate from the Employee Record.
3. Get the Hours Worked during the week from the Time Card.
4. If the number of Hours Worked is less than or equal to 40, multiply by the Pay Rate to calculate the Regular Wages.
5. If the number of Hours Worked is greater than 40, multiply 40 by the Pay Rate to calculate the Regular Wages, and then multiply the Hours Worked minus 40 by $1\frac{1}{2}$ times the Pay Rate to calculate the Overtime Wages.
6. Add the Regular Wages to the Overtime Wages (if any) to determine the Total Wages for the week.

The steps the computer follows are often the same steps you would use to do the calculations by hand.

After developing a general solution, the programmer tests the algorithm by "walking through" each step mentally or manually with paper and pencil. If the algorithm doesn't work, the programmer repeats the problem-solving process, analyzing the problem again and coming up with another algorithm. Often the second algorithm is simply a variation of the first. When the programmer is satisfied with the algorithm, he or she translates it into a programming language. This book focuses on the Java programming language.

Programming language A set of rules, symbols, and special words used to construct a computer program

A programming language is a simplified form of English (with math symbols) that adheres to a strict set of grammatical rules. English is far too complicated a language for today's computers to follow. Programming languages, because they have a limited vocabulary and grammar, are much simpler.

Although a programming language is simple in form, it is not always easy to use. Try giving someone directions to the nearest airport using a vocabulary limited to no more than 25 words, and you begin to see the problem. Programming forces you to write very simple, exact instructions.

Code Instructions for a computer that are written in a programming language

Translating an algorithm into a programming language is called *coding* the algorithm. **Code** is the product of translating an algorithm into a programming language. The term *code* can refer to a complete program or to any portion of a program. A program is tested by running (*executing*) it on the computer. If the program fails to produce the desired results, the programmer must *debug* it—that is, determine what is wrong and then modify the program, or even revise the algorithm, to fix it. The process of coding and testing the algorithm takes place during the implementation phase.

There is no single way to implement an algorithm. For example, an algorithm can be translated into more than one programming language. Each translation produces a different implementation (see Figure 1.2a). Even when two people translate an algorithm into the same programming language, they often come up with different implementations (see Figure 1.2b). Why? Because every programming language allows the programmer some flexibility in terms of how an algorithm is translated. Given this flexibility, people adopt their own *styles* in writing programs, just as they do in writing short stories or essays. Once you have some programming experience, you will develop a style of your own. Throughout this book, we offer tips on good programming style.

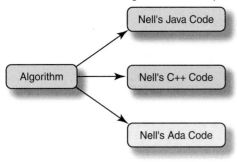

a. Algorithm translated into different languages

Some people try to speed up the programming process by going directly from the problem definition to coding (see Figure 1.3). Taking such a shortcut is very tempting and, at first glance, seems to save a lot of time. However, for many reasons that will become obvious as you read this book, this kind of shortcut actually consumes *more* time and requires more effort. Developing a general solution before you write Java code will help you manage the problem, keep your thoughts straight, and avoid mistakes. If you don't take the time at the beginning to think out and polish your algorithm, you'll spend a lot of extra time debugging and revising your code. So think first and code later! The sooner you start coding, the longer it takes to write an application that works.

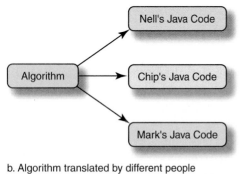

b. Algorithm translated by different people

Figure 1.2 Differences in Implementation

Once a Java application has been put into use, it often becomes necessary to modify it later. Modification may involve fixing an error that is discovered during use of the application or changing the code in response to changes in the user's requirements. Each time the code is modified, the programmer should repeat the problem-solving and implementation phases for those aspects of the application that change.

This phase of the programming process, known as maintenance, actually accounts for the majority of the effort expended on most applications. For example, an application that is implemented in a few months may need to be maintained over a period of many years. For this reason, it is a cost-effective investment of time to carefully develop the initial problem solution and algorithm implementation. Together, the problem-solving, implementation, and maintenance phases constitute the application's *life cycle*.

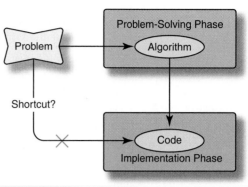

Figure 1.3   Programming Shortcut?

In addition to solving the problem, implementing the algorithm, and maintaining the code, documentation is an important part of the programming process. Documentation includes written explanations of the problem at hand and the organization of the solution, comments embedded within the code itself, and user manuals that describe how to use the program. Many different people are likely to work on an application over its lifetime. Each of those individuals must be able to read and understand the code.

Documentation   The written text and comments that make an application easier for others to understand, use, and modify

Binary Representation of Data

In a computer, data are represented electronically by pulses of electricity. Electric circuits, in their simplest form, are either on or off. A circuit that is on is typically represented by the number 1; a circuit that is off is represented by the number 0. Any kind of data can be represented by combinations of enough 1s and 0s. We simply have to choose which combination represents each piece of data we are using. For example, we could arbitrarily choose the pattern 1101000110 to represent the name "Java."

Data represented by 1s and 0s are in binary form. The binary, or base–2, number system uses only 1s and 0s to represent numbers. (The decimal, or base–10, number system uses the digits 0 through 9.) The word *bit* (short for <u>bi</u>nary digi<u>t</u>) refers to a single 1 or 0. Thus the pattern 1101000110 has 10 bits. A binary number with 10 bits can represent 2^{10} (1,024) different patterns. A *byte* is a group of 8 bits; it can represent 2^8 (256) patterns. Inside the computer, each character (such as the letter A, the letter *g*, or a question mark) is usually represented by either one or two bytes.[3] Groups of 16, 32, and 64 bits are generally referred to as *words* (the terms *short word* and *long word* are sometimes used to refer to 16-bit and 64-bit groups, respectively).

The process of assigning bit patterns to pieces of data is called *coding*—the same name we give to the process of translating an algorithm into a programming language. The names are the same because the first computers recognized only one language—which was binary in form. Thus, in the early days of computers, programming meant translating both data and algorithms into patterns of 1s and 0s.

Theoretical Foundations

---

[3]Most programming languages use the American Standard Code for Information Interchange (ASCII) to represent the English alphabet and other symbols. Each ASCII character is stored in a single byte. Java recognizes both ASCII and a newer standard called Unicode, which includes the alphabets of many other languages. A single Unicode character takes up two bytes in the computer's memory.

Binary coding schemes are still used inside the computer to represent both the instructions that it follows and the data that it uses. For example, 16 bits can represent the decimal integers from 0 to $2^{16} - 1$ (65,535). More complicated coding schemes are necessary to represent negative numbers, real numbers, and numbers in scientific notation. Characters also can be represented by bit combinations. In one coding scheme, 01001101 represents M and 01101101 represents *m* (look closely—the third bit from the left is the only difference).

The patterns of bits that represent data vary from one family of computers to another. Even on the same computer, different programming languages may use different binary representations for the same data. A single programming language may even use the same pattern of bits to represent different things in different contexts. (People do this, too: The four letters that form the word *tack* have different meanings depending on whether you are talking about upholstery, sailing, sewing, paint, or horseback riding.) The point is that patterns of bits by themselves are meaningless. Rather, it is the way in which the patterns are used that gives them their meaning. That's why we combine data with operations to form meaningful objects.

Fortunately, we no longer have to work with binary coding schemes. Today, the process of coding is usually just a matter of writing down the data in letters, numbers, and symbols. The computer automatically converts these letters, numbers, and symbols into binary form. Still, as you work with computers, you will continually run into numbers that are related to powers of 2—numbers like 256, 32,768, and 65,536. They are reminders that the binary number system is lurking somewhere nearby.

1.2 How Is Java Code Converted into a Form That a Computer Can Use?

In the computer, all data, whatever their form, are stored and used in binary codes, consisting of strings of 1s and 0s. Instructions and data are stored together in the computer's memory using these binary codes. If you looked at the binary codes representing instructions and data in memory, you could not tell the difference between them; they are distinguished only by the manner in which the computer uses them. This fact enables the computer to process its own instructions as a form of data.

Machine language The language, made up of binary-coded instructions, that is used directly by the computer

Assembly language A low-level programming language in which a mnemonic represents each machine language instruction for a particular computer

When computers were first developed, the only programming language available was the primitive instruction set built into each machine—the machine language (also known as machine code).

Even though most computers perform the same kinds of operations, their designers choose different sets of binary codes for each instruction. As a result, the machine code for one family of computers is not the same as that for another family of computers.

When programmers used machine language for programming, they had to enter the binary codes for the various instructions, a tedious process that was prone to error. Moreover, their programs were difficult to read and modify. In time, assembly languages were developed to make the programmer's job easier.

Instructions in an assembly language are in an easy-to-remember form called a *mnemonic* (pronounced "ni-'män-ik"). Typical instructions for addition and subtraction might look like this:

Assembly Language	Machine Language
ADD	100101
SUB	010011

Although humans find it easier to work with assembly language, the computer cannot directly execute the instructions. Because a computer can process its own instructions as a form of data, it is possible to write a program to translate assembly language instructions into machine code. Such a program is called an assembler.

Assembly language represents a step in the right direction, but it still forces programmers to think in terms of individual machine instructions. Eventually, computer scientists developed high-level programming languages. These languages are easier to use than assembly languages or machine code because they are closer to English and other natural languages (see Figure 1.4 on page 12).

A program called a compiler translates algorithms written in certain high-level languages (Java, C++, Visual Basic, and Ada, for example) into machine language. If you write an application in a high-level language, you can run it on any computer that has the appropriate compiler. This portability is possible because most high-level languages are standardized, which means that an official description of the language exists.

Assembler   A program that translates an assembly language program into machine code

Compiler   A program that translates code written in a high-level language into machine code

Source code   Instructions written in a high-level programming language

Object code   A machine language version of a source code

FOXTROT © 2000 Bill Amend. Reprinted with Permission of UNIVERSAL PRESS SYNDICATE. All Rights Reserved.

The text of an algorithm written in a high-level language is called source code. To the compiler, source code is just input data—letters and numbers. It translates the source code into a machine language form called object code (see Figure 1.5 on page 13).

Figure 1.4 Levels of Abstraction

As noted earlier, standardized high-level languages allow you to write *portable* (or *machine-independent*) code. As Figure 1.5 emphasizes, the same C++ application can be run on different machines, whereas a program written in assembly language or machine language is not portable from one computer to another. Because each computer family has its own machine language, a machine language program written for computer A may not run on computer B.

Java takes a somewhat different approach to achieve even greater portability. Java source code is translated into a standard machine language called Bytecode.

Bytecode A standard machine language into which Java source code is compiled

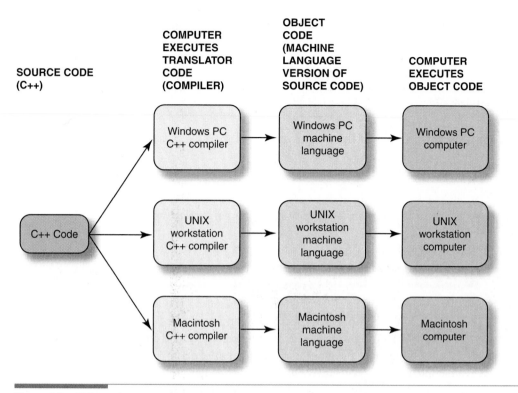

Figure 1.5   High-Level Programming Languages Allow Applications to Be Compiled on Different Systems

No computers actually use Bytecode as their machine language. Instead, for a computer to run Bytecode, it must have another program called the Java Virtual Machine (JVM) that serves as a language interpreter for the Bytecode (we will explain the meaning of the term "virtual machine" shortly). Just as an interpreter of human languages listens to words spoken in one language and then speaks a translation of them in a language that another person understands, so the JVM reads the Bytecode instructions and translates them into machine language operations that the particular computer executes. Interpretation takes place as the Bytecode is running, one instruction at a time. This process is not the same as compilation, which is a separate step that translates all of the source code instructions in a program prior to execution. Figure 1.6 shows how the Java translation process achieves greater portability.

As Figure 1.6 illustrates, the compiled Java code can run on any computer that has the JVM program available to interpret for it, which means that the Java application does not have to be compiled for each type of computer. This level of portability has grown in importance as computers across the globe are connected by the World Wide Web (also called the Web: a part of the Internet). For example, a programmer can write a Java application and make its Bytecode available to the public via the Web without having to recompile it for the many different types of computers that may be used to run it.

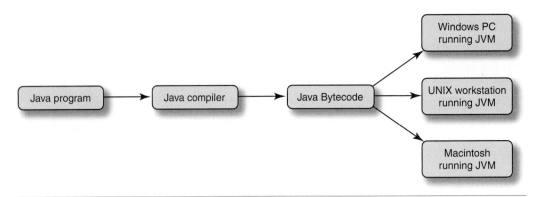

Figure 1.6 A Java Compiler Produces Bytecode that Can Be Run on Any Machine with the JVM

1.3 How Does Interpreting Code Differ from Executing It?

Direct execution of code differs significantly from interpretation of code. A computer can directly execute a program that is compiled into machine language. The JVM, for example, is a machine language program that is directly executed. The computer cannot directly execute Bytecode, however. Instead, it must execute the JVM to interpret each Bytecode instruction so as to run the compiled Java source code. The JVM does not produce machine code, like a compiler, but rather it reads each Bytecode instruction and gives the computer a corresponding series of operations to perform. Because each Bytecode instruction must first be interpreted, the computer cannot run Bytecode as quickly as it can execute machine language. Slower execution is the price we pay for increased portability.

Direct execution The process by which a computer performs the actions specified in a machine language program

Interpretation The translation, while a program is running, of nonmachine-language instructions (such as Bytecode) into executable operations

1.4 How Is Compilation Related to Interpretation and Execution?

It is important to understand that *compilation* and *execution* are two distinct processes. During compilation, the computer runs the compiler. During execution, the object code is loaded into the computer's memory unit, replacing the compiler. The computer then directly executes the object code, doing whatever it is instructed to do (see Figure 1.7).

We can use the JVM as an example of the process shown in Figure 1.7. The JVM is written in a high-level programming language such as C++ and then compiled into machine language. This machine language is loaded into the computer's memory, and the JVM is executed. Its input consists of Java Bytecode. Its results are the series of actions that would take place if the computer could directly execute Bytecode. Figure 1.8 on page 16 illustrates this process.

In looking at Figure 1.8, it is important to understand that the output from the compilers can be saved for future use. Once the JVM and the Java application have been compiled, they can be used repeatedly without being recompiled. You never need to compile the JVM, in fact, because that step has already been done for you. Figure 1.8 shows its compilation sim-

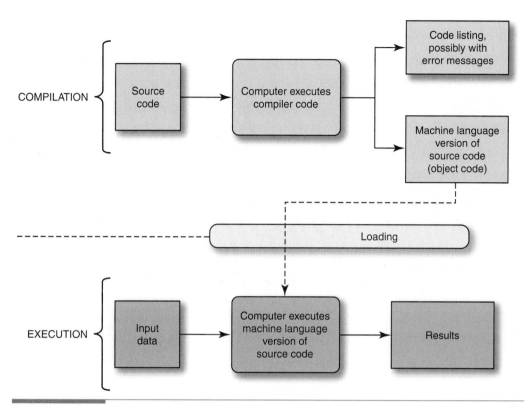

Figure 1.7   Compilation/Execution

ply to illustrate the difference between the traditional compile–execute steps and the compile–interpret steps used with Java.

Viewed from a different perspective, the JVM makes the computer look like a different computer, one that has Bytecode as its machine language. The computer itself hasn't changed—it remains the same collection of electronic circuits—but the JVM makes it *appear* to be a different machine. When a program is used to make one computer act like another computer, we call it a **virtual machine**. For convenience, we may refer to the computer as "executing a Java application," but keep in mind this is just shorthand for saying that "the computer is executing the JVM running a Java application."

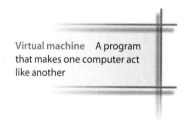

Virtual machine   A program that makes one computer act like another

1.5   What Kinds of Instructions Can Be Written in a Programming Language?

The instructions in a programming language reflect the operations a computer can perform:

- A computer can transfer data from one place to another.
- A computer can input data from an input device (a keyboard or mouse, for example) and output data to an output device (a screen, for example).

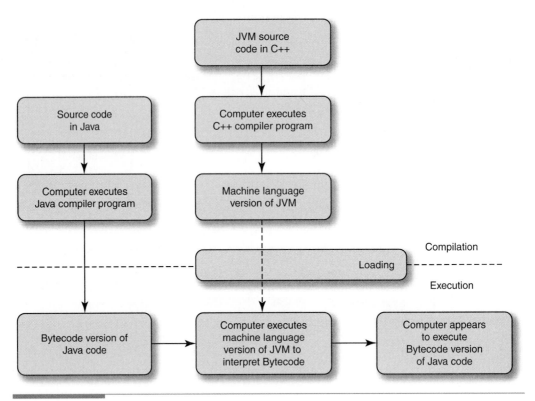

Figure 1.8 Compilation and Execution of JVM Combined with Compilation and Interpretation of Bytecode

- A computer can store data into and retrieve data from its memory and secondary storage (parts of a computer that we discuss in the next section).
- A computer can compare data values for equality or inequality and make decisions based on the result.
- A computer can perform arithmetic operations (addition and subtraction, for example) very quickly.
- A computer can branch to a different section of the instructions.

In addition, a programming language contains instructions, called declarations, which we use to specify the data and operations in classes. Programming languages require that we use certain *control structures* to organize the instructions that specify the behaviors of objects. Instructions that describe behavior can be organized in four ways in most programming languages: sequentially, conditionally, repetitively, and with subprograms. Java adds a fifth way: asynchronously (see Figure 1.9).

- A sequence is a series of operations that are executed one after another.
- Selection, the conditional control structure, executes different operations depending on certain conditions.

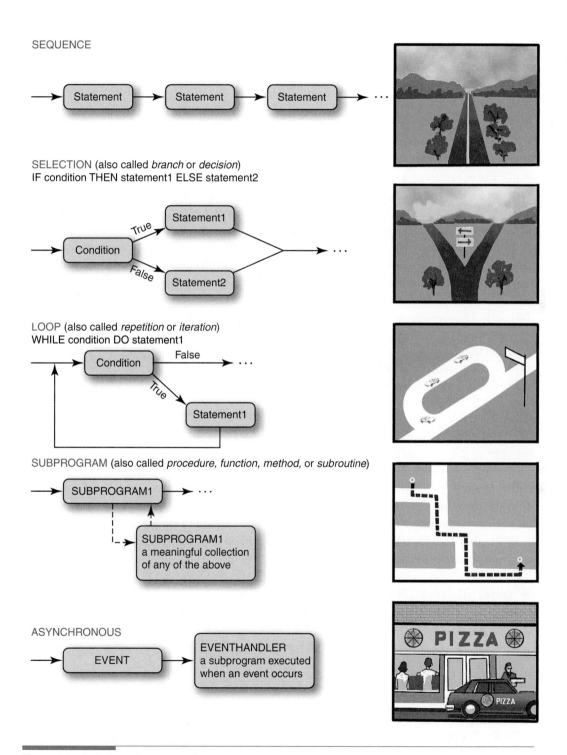

SEQUENCE

SELECTION (also called *branch* or *decision*)
IF condition THEN statement1 ELSE statement2

LOOP (also called *repetition* or *iteration*)
WHILE condition DO statement1

SUBPROGRAM (also called *procedure, function, method,* or *subroutine*)

ASYNCHRONOUS

Figure 1.9   Basic Control Structures of Programming Languages

- The repetitive control structure, the *loop*, repeats operations while certain conditions are met.
- The subprogram allows us to organize our code into units that correspond to specific object behaviors; Java calls these units *methods*.
- Asynchronous control lets us write code that handles events, such as the user clicking a button on the screen with the mouse.

Each of these ways of structuring operations controls the order in which the computer executes the operations, which is why they are called control structures.

Suppose you're driving a car. Going down a straight stretch of road is like following a *sequence* of instructions. When you come to a fork in the road, you must decide which way to go and then take one or the other branch of the fork. The computer does something similar when it encounters a *selection* control structure (sometimes called a *branch* or *decision*) in a program. Sometimes you have to go around the block several times to find a place to park. The computer does the same sort of thing when it encounters a loop.

A subprogram is a named sequence of instructions written as a separate unit. When the computer executes an instruction that refers to the name of the subprogram, the code for the subprogram executes. When the subprogram finishes, execution resumes at the instruction that originally referred to the subprogram. Suppose, for example, that every day you go to work at an office. The directions for getting from home to work form a method called "Go to the office." It makes sense, then, for someone to give you directions to a meeting by saying, "Go to the office, then go four blocks west"—without listing all the steps needed to get to the office.

Responding to asynchronous events is like working as a pizza delivery person. You wait around the dispatch station with all of the other delivery people. The dispatcher calls your name and gives you some pizzas and a delivery address. You deliver the pizzas and return to the dispatch station. At the same time, other delivery people may be out driving.[4] The term *asynchronous* means "not at the same time." In this context, it refers to the fact that the user can, for example, click the mouse on the screen at any time while the application is running. The mouse click does not have to happen at some particular time corresponding to certain instructions within the code.

■ Object-Oriented Programming Languages

Early programming languages focused their attention on the operations and control structures of programming. These *procedural* languages paid little explicit attention to the relationships between the operations and the data. At that time, a typical computer program used

---

[4]Java actually allows us to write more general asynchronous programs using a construct called a *thread*. Threaded programs are beyond the scope this text. We restrict our use of asynchronous structures to handling events.

only simple data types such as integers and real numbers, which have obvious sets of operations defined by mathematics. Those operations were built directly into early programming languages. Each kind of data in the computer was said to have a specific data type. For example, if we say that two data items are of type int (a name that Java uses for integer numbers), we know how they are represented in memory and that we can apply arithmetic operations to them.

As people gained experience with the programming process, they realized that in solving complex problems, it is helpful to define new types of data, such as dates and times, which aren't a standard part of a programming language. Each new type of data typically has an associated set of operations, such as determining the number of days between two dates.

Procedural languages thus evolved to include the feature of *extensibility*: the capability to define new data types. However, they continued to treat the data and operations as separate parts of the program. A programmer could define a data type to represent the data values making up the time of day and then write a subprogram to compute the number of minutes between two times, but could not explicitly indicate that the two were related.

Modern programming languages such as Java allow us to collect data and its associated operations into objects. For this reason, they are called *object-oriented* programming languages. The advantage of an object is that it makes the relationships between the data and operations explicit. Each object is a complete, self-contained unit that can be reused again in other applications. This reusability enables us to write a significant portion of our code using existing objects, thereby saving a considerable amount of time and effort.

Most modern programming languages, Java included, retain vestiges of their procedural ancestors in the form of a small set of primitive data types. These usually include integer and real numbers, characters, and a type representing the values true and false. Java also defines the object as one of its primitive data types. In Java, all objects are said to be of the same data type—the type that lets us represent any object. We distinguish among different kinds of objects by referring to the classes that define them. For example, we may refer to an object of the class String. Sometimes we may refer to objects as being of different types, which is common terminology in the computer industry. In such a case, we really mean objects of different classes, as there is strictly just one type of object in Java.

As noted earlier, a class is a description of an object. When we need an object in an application, we must create one from such a description. Java provides an operation to let us do so, and we say that the operation instantiates the class. That is, we write an instruction in Java that provides us with an instance of the object described by the specified class.

One characteristic of an object-oriented programming language is the presence of a large library of classes. Within the library, classes are usually collected into groups called packages.

In this book we present only a small subset of the many classes that are available in the Java library. It is easy to become overwhelmed by the sheer size of Java's library, but many of those thousands of objects are highly specialized and unnecessary for learning the essen-

> **Data type**   The specification in a programming language of how information is represented in the computer as data and the set of operations that can be applied to it
>
> **Instantiate**   To create an object based on the description supplied by a class.
>
> **Package**   A collection of related classes

tial concepts of programming.

In the next few chapters, we consider how to write simple code that instantiates just a few of the classes in Java's library. We first learn how to write a specific form of class, called an application. Then we write some simple classes of our own. Once we gain some experience with these essentials, in Chapter 6 we see how to organize a solution to a complex problem in a manner that takes full advantage of the features of classes and objects. In Chapter 7, we explore the aspects of the Java language that enable us to extend existing classes with new features.

1.6   What's Inside the Computer?

You can learn how to use a programming language, write applications, and run (execute) these applications without knowing much about computers. If you know something about the parts of a computer, however, you can better understand the effect of each instruction in a programming language.

Most computers have six basic components: the memory unit, the arithmetic/logic unit, the control unit, input devices, output devices, and auxiliary storage devices. Figure 1.10 shows a stylized diagram of the basic components of a computer.

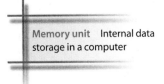

Memory unit   Internal data storage in a computer

The **memory unit** is an ordered sequence of storage cells, each capable of holding a piece of data. Each memory cell has a distinct address to which we refer to store data into it or retrieve data from it. These storage cells are called *memory cells*, or *memory locations*.[5] The memory unit holds data (input data or the product of computation) and instructions (programs), as shown in Figure 1.11.

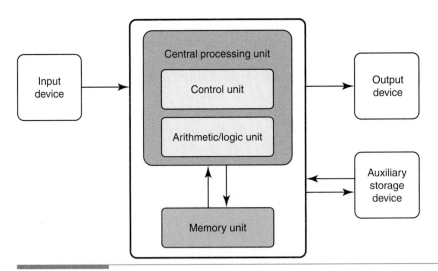

Figure 1.10   Basic Components of a Computer

---

[5]The memory unit is also referred to as RAM, an acronym for random access memory (because we can access any location at random).

The part of the computer that follows instructions is called the central processing unit (CPU). The CPU usually has two components. The arithmetic/logic unit (ALU) performs arithmetic operations (addition, subtraction, multiplication, and division) and logical operations (comparing two values). The control unit manages the actions of the other components so that program instructions execute in the correct order.

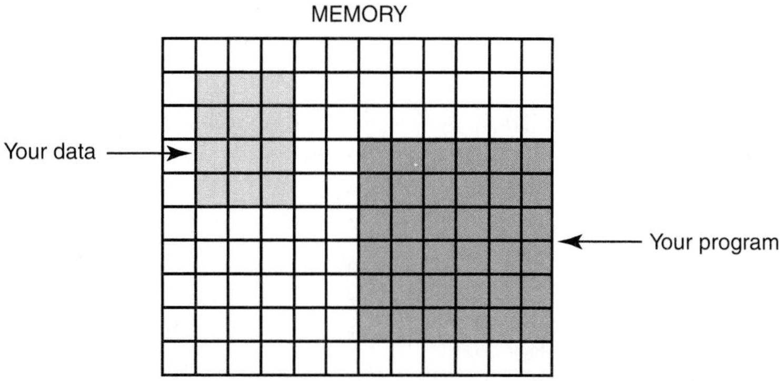

To use computers, we must have some way of getting data into and out of them. Input/output (I/O) devices accept data to be processed (input) and present data that have been processed (output). A keyboard is a common input device, as is a *mouse*, a "pointing" device. A video display is a common output device, as are printers and liquid crystal display (LCD) screens.

For the most part, computers simply move and combine data in memory. The many types of computers differ primarily in terms of the size of their memory, the speed with which data can be recalled, the efficiency with which data can be moved or combined, and limitations on I/O devices.

When a program is executing, the computer proceeds through a series of steps, making up the *fetch-execute cycle*:

1. The control unit retrieves (*fetches*) the next coded instruction from memory.
2. The instruction is translated into control signals.
3. The control signals tell the appropriate unit (arithmetic/logic unit, memory, I/O device) to perform (*execute*) the instruction.
4. The sequence is repeated beginning from Step 1.

Computers can support a wide variety of peripheral devices. An auxiliary storage device, or *secondary storage device*, holds coded data for the computer until we actually want to use the data. Instead of inputting data every time, we can input it once and have the computer store it onto an auxiliary storage device. Whenever we need to use the data, we simply tell the computer to transfer the data from the auxiliary storage device to its memory. An auxiliary storage device therefore serves as both an input device and an output device.

Typical auxiliary storage devices include disk drives and magnetic tape drives. A disk drive is like a cross between a compact disc player and a tape recorder. It uses a thin disk made out of magnetic material. A read/write head (similar to the

MEMORY

Your data

Your program

Figure 1.11   Memory

Central processing unit (CPU) The part of the computer that executes the instructions (object code) stored in memory; made up of the arithmetic/logic unit and the control unit

Arithmetic/logic unit (ALU) The component of the central processing unit that performs arithmetic and logical operations

Control unit The component of the central processing unit that controls the actions of the other components so that instructions (the object code) execute in the correct sequence

Input/output (I/O) devices The parts of the computer that accept data to be processed (input) and present the results of that processing (output)

Peripheral device An input, output, or auxiliary storage device attached to a computer

Auxiliary storage device A device that stores data in encoded form outside the computer's main memory

record/playback head in a tape recorder) travels across the spinning disk, retrieving or recording data. A CD-ROM or DVD-ROM drive uses a laser to read information stored optically on a plastic disk. Some forms of CDs and DVDs can also be used to store (write) data. A *magnetic tape drive* is like a tape recorder and is most often used to back up (make a copy of) the data on a disk in case the disk becomes damaged.

Hardware The physical components of a computer

Together, all of these physical components are known as hardware. The programs that allow the hardware to operate are called software. Hardware usually is fixed in design; in contrast, software is easily changed. In fact, the ease with which software can be manipulated is what makes the computer such a versatile, powerful tool.

Software Computer programs; the set of all programs available on a computer

Interface A connecting link at a shared boundary that allows independent systems to meet and act on or communicate with each other

In addition to the software that we write or purchase, some programs in the computer are designed to simplify the user/computer interface, making it easier for humans to use the machine. The interface between the user and the computer consists of a set of I/O devices—for example, the keyboard, mouse, and screen—that allows the user to communicate with the computer. We work with the keyboard, mouse, and screen on our side of the interface boundary; wires attached to the keyboard and the screen carry the electronic pulses that the computer manipulates on its side of the interface boundary. At the boundary itself is a mechanism that translates information for the two sides.

Interactive system A system that supports direct communication between the user and the computer

When we communicate directly with the computer through an interface, we use an interactive system. Interactive systems allow direct entry of source code and data and provide immediate feedback to the user. In contrast, *batch systems* require that all data be entered before an application runs and provide feedback only after an application has been executed. In this book we focus largely on interactive systems, although in Chapter 5 we discuss file-oriented applications, which share certain similarities with batch systems.

Operating system A set of programs that manages all of the computer's resources

Editor An interactive program used to create and modify source programs or data

The set of programs that simplifies the user/computer interface and improves the efficiency of processing is called *system software*. It includes the JVM and the Java compiler as well as the operating system and the editor (see Figure 1.12). The operating system manages all of the computer's resources. It can input programs, call the compiler, execute object code, and carry out any other system commands. The editor is an interactive program used to create and modify source programs or data.

1.7 Problem-Solving Techniques

We solve problems every day, often while remaining unaware of the process we are going through. In a learning environment, we usually are given most of the information we need: a clear statement of the problem, the necessary input, and the required output. In real life, of course, the process is not always so simple. We often have to define the problem ourselves and then decide what information we have to work with and what the results should be.

After we understand and analyze a problem, we must come up with a potential solution—an algorithm. Earlier, we defined an algorithm as a step-by-step procedure for solving a problem in a finite amount of time with a finite amount of data. Although we work with algorithms

Program entry
Data entry

INPUT

COMPUTER

System software: operating system,
compiler, editor

Reports, lists

OUTPUT

Figure 1.12 User/Computer Interface

all the time, most of our experience with them comes in the context of *following* them. We follow a recipe, play a game, assemble a toy, or take medicine. In the problem-solving phase of computer programming, however, we actually *design* algorithms. This means we must be conscious of the strategies we use to solve problems so that we can apply them to programming problems effectively.

■ Ask Questions

If you are given a task orally, you ask questions—When? Why? Where?—until you understand exactly what you have to do. If your instructions are written, you might put question marks in the margin, underline a word or a sentence, or indicate in some other way that the task is not clear. Your questions may be answered by a later paragraph, or you might have to discuss them with the person who assigned you the task.

Here are some of the questions you might ask in the context of programming:

- What do I have to work with—that is, what objects does the problem require?
- What do the objects look like?
- What tasks do the objects perform on their data?
- How much input is there?
- How do I know when I have input the last value?
- What should my output look like?
- How do the objects work together to solve the problem?
- What special error conditions might come up?

Look for Things That Are Familiar

Never reinvent the wheel. If a solution already exists, use it. If you've solved the same or a similar problem before, just repeat your solution. In fact, people are good at recognizing similar situations. We don't have to learn how to go to the store to buy milk, then to buy eggs, and then to buy candy. We know that "going to the store" is always the same; only what we buy differs on each trip.

In programming, certain problems occur again and again in different guises. A good programmer immediately recognizes a subtask that he or she has solved before and plugs in the solution. For example, finding the daily high and low temperatures is really the same problem as finding the highest and lowest grades on a test. You want the largest and smallest values in a set of numbers (see Figure 1.13).

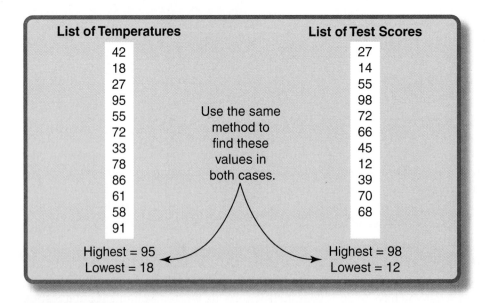

List of Temperatures

42
18
27
95
55
72
33
78
86
61
58
91

Highest = 95
Lowest = 18

Use the same method to find these values in both cases.

List of Test Scores

27
14
55
98
72
66
45
12
39
70
68

Highest = 98
Lowest = 12

Figure 1.13   Look for Things that Are Familiar

We also apply this strategy by using classes from the Java library. When we recognize an object that we've seen before, we reuse it in the new problem. Even if an existing class isn't quite what we need, it can serve as the starting point for a new class. In Chapter 7, we see how we can implement this problem-solving strategy in Java by using a mechanism called *inheritance*, which allows us to define a new object that adds to the capabilities of an existing object.

Solve by Analogy

Often a problem may remind you of one you have seen before. You may find solving the problem at hand easier if you remember how you solved the other problem. In other words, you can draw an analogy between the two problems. For example, a solution to a perspective projection problem from an art class might help you figure out how to compute the distance to a landmark when you are on a cross-country hike. As you work your way through the new problem, you may come across things that are different than they were in the old problem, but usually you can deal with these minor details one at a time.

Analogy is really just a broader application of the strategy of looking for things that are familiar. When you are trying to find an algorithm for solving a problem, don't limit yourself to computer-oriented solutions. Step back and try to get a larger view of the problem. Don't worry if your analogy doesn't match perfectly—the only reason for starting with an analogy is that it gives you a place to start (see Figure 1.14). The best programmers are people who have broad experience solving all kinds of problems.

Means-Ends Analysis

Often the beginning state and the ending state are given; the problem requires you to define a set of interactions between objects that takes you from one state to the other. Suppose you want to go from Boston, Massachusetts, to Austin, Texas. You know the beginning state (you are in Boston) and the ending state (you want to be in Austin). The problem is how to get from one place to the other.

A library catalog system can give insight into how to organize a parts inventory.

Figure 1.14   Analogy

Start: Boston **Goal**: Austin	**Means**: *Fly*, walk, hitchhike, bike, drive, sail, bus
Start: Boston **Goal**: Austin	**Revised Means**: Fly to Chicago and then to Austin; *fly to Newark and then to Austin:* fly to Atlanta and then to Austin
Start: Boston **Intermediate Goal**: Newark **Goal**: Austin	**Means to Intermediate Goal**: *Commuter flight*, walk, hitchhike, bike, drive, sail, bus
Solution: Take commuter flight to Newark and then catch cheap flight to Austin	

Figure 1.15   Means-Ends Analysis

In this example, you have lots of options. You can take a plane, walk, hitchhike, ride a bike, or whatever. The method you choose depends on your circumstances. If you're in a hurry, you'll probably decide to fly.

Once you've identified the essential objects and their capabilities (airplane; fly between cities), you have to work out the details. It may help to establish intermediate goals that are easier to meet than the overall goal. Suppose a really cheap, direct flight to Austin goes out of Newark, New Jersey. You might decide to divide the trip into legs: Boston to Newark, and then Newark to Austin. Your intermediate goal is to get from Boston to Newark. Now you merely have to examine the means of meeting that intermediate goal (see Figure 1.15). Is there an object (airplane) that has the necessary capabilities (fly between Boston and Newark)?

The overall strategy of means-ends analysis is to define the ends and then to analyze your means of achieving them. The process translates easily to computer programming. That is, you begin by writing down what the input is and what the output should be. Then you consider the available objects and the actions they can perform and choose a sequence of those actions that can transform the input into the desired results. If no appropriate object is available, then you may have to create a new one.

■ Divide and Conquer

We often break up large problems into smaller units that are easier to handle. Cleaning the whole house may seem overwhelming; cleaning each room, one at a time, seems much more manageable. The same principle applies to programming. We break up a large problem into smaller pieces that we can solve individually (see Figure 1.16). A problem is divided into its component objects, and for each class of objects we define a set of capabilities.

The Building-Block Approach

Another way of attacking a large problem is to see if any solutions for smaller pieces of the problem exist. It may be possible to combine these solutions to solve most of the big problem. This strategy is just a combination of the look-for-familiar-things and divide-and-conquer approaches. You look at the big problem and see that it can be divided into smaller problems for which solutions already exist. Solving the big problem is just a matter of putting the existing solutions together, like mortaring together blocks to form a wall (see Figure 1.17).

With an object-oriented programming language, the building blocks are classes. We often solve a problem by looking in the class library to see which solutions have been developed previously; we then write a small amount of additional code to put the pieces together. As we will see later, this problem-solving technique forms the basis for the methodology called *object-based design*.

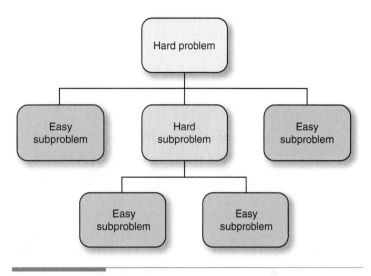

Figure 1.16   Divide and Conquer

Merging Solutions

Another way to combine existing solutions is to merge them on a step-by-step basis. For example, to compute the average of a list of values, we must both sum and count the values. If we already have separate solutions for summing values and for counting the number of

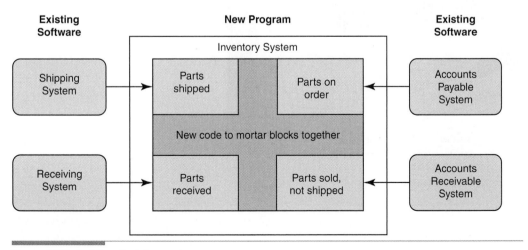

Figure 1.17   Building-Block Approach

values, we can combine them. If we first do the summing and then do the counting, however, we have to read the list twice. We can save steps by merging these two solutions: read a value and then add it to the running total and add 1 to our count before going on to the next value. When you're writing a method for a class, and existing methods can be used but partially duplicate each other's actions, think about merging the steps they perform instead of simply calling them one after the other.

Mental Blocks: The Fear of Starting

Writers are all too familiar with the experience of staring at a blank page, not knowing where to begin. Programmers often have the same difficulty when they first tackle a big problem. They look at the problem and it seems overwhelming (see Figure 1.18).

Figure 1.18   Mental Block.

Remember that you always have a place to begin when trying to solve any problem: Write it down on paper in your own words so that you understand it. Once you paraphrase the problem, you can focus on each of the subparts individually instead of trying to tackle the entire problem at once. This process gives you a clearer picture of the overall problem. It helps you see pieces of the problem that look familiar or that are analogous to other problems you have solved in the past. It also pinpoints areas where something is unclear, where you need more information.

As you write down a problem, you tend to group things together into small, understandable chunks of data and operations, which may be natural candidates for objects. Your description of the problem may collect all of the information about data and results into one place for easy reference. Then you can see the beginning and ending states necessary for means-ends analysis.

Most mental blocks are caused by not really understanding the problem. Writing down the problem in your own words is a good way to focus on the subparts of the problem, one at a time, and to understand what is required for a solution.

■ Object-Oriented Problem Solving

The initial step in solving many problems is to identify the obvious objects in the problem description. If you are given a recipe, for example, the first thing you do is to identify the ingredients. Some may already be in your cupboard or refrigerator. For others, you may have to go shopping. Object-oriented problem solving involves much the same process. You look at a problem statement and make a list of the objects in it. Some of those objects are already available in the Java library, just waiting to be used. Other objects you may have to write yourself.

Remember that the computer can do only certain things. Your primary concern, then, is making the computer coordinate the actions of objects to produce the desired effects. If you keep in mind the objects, operations, and data types available in Java, you won't design an algorithm that is difficult or impossible to code.

In this book, we introduce you to these object classes and operations in a gradual manner. In each chapter, we add to our knowledge of Java and programming techniques so that we can tackle a growing range of problems. At first the problems may seem trivial because we have so much to learn before we can write even a simple program. Soon, however, we encounter problems that require thoughtful use of these problem-solving techniques. In Chapter 6, we introduce an object-oriented design technique that helps us to organize our problem solving for even larger programs.

Coming up with an algorithm for solving a particular problem is not always a cut-and-dried process. Just the opposite, in fact—it is usually a trial-and-error process requiring several attempts and refinements. We test each attempt to see if it really solves the problem. If it does, that's great. If it doesn't, we try again. You typically use a combination of the techniques we've described to solve any nontrivial problem.

PARTY PLANNING

Problem: You and some friends want to have a party on Saturday night, and you need to plan and prepare for it.

Discussion: You're familiar with the problem from having attended many parties. Parties can be fun or they can turn into disasters. You know that it takes a great deal of preparation to throw a party that everyone enjoys. Let's start with some means-ends analysis. The starting state is that you want to have a party, and the goal state is that your party ends with everyone having had a good time. Your means are you and your friends—you need to examine their capabilities more closely.

One of your friends, Sally, has a car. Another, James, has a stereo and a large music collection. You have an apartment with a big living room. All of you know people who you want to invite, and you all have ideas about what makes a great party. You collaborate with your friends to develop a guest list. From your experience with parties that have gone well (looking for things that are familiar), you and your friends identify the major steps in the process: invite people, get food, choose music and set up the stereo, clean the apartment and move furniture, welcome guests, have snacks available and some background music playing while people arrive, dance for most of the evening, wind down with some party games, and say goodbye to guests as they leave.

Now it's time to divide and conquer all of this work. Sally can help James deliver the stereo and can get the food. James can set up the stereo and select the music. You can clean the apartment and move the furniture (with everyone's help). Each of you can call and invite some of the people, keeping a count of the ones who can come. Sally can then get those counts from you and James, and figure out how much food to buy. On the evening of the party, you can answer the doorbell, James can run the stereo and help lead the games, and Sally can take care of the food. After the party, everyone can help clean up, and Sally can help James take the stereo back to his apartment.

Here is a list of the "objects" we've identified and their responsibilities:

```
You
Call guests and keep a count of the ones who can come.
Clean apartment.
Move furniture.
Answer doorbell.
Say goodbye to leaving guests.
Clean up apartment and move furniture back.
```

```
Sally
Call guests and keep a count of the ones who can come.
Get counts from you and James and sum them.
Make a shopping list and buy food.
Help James deliver the stereo.
Take care of food at party.
Clean up apartment and move furniture back.
Help James return the stereo.
```

```
James
Call guests and keep a count of the ones who can come.
Select music and gather it together.
Deliver and set up stereo.
Run stereo.
Help lead games.
Clean up apartment and move furniture back.
Return stereo and put away music.
```

Each of these responsibilities requires further expansion. For example, in making up the food list, Sally needs to take into account any food allergies among the guests. It takes James several steps to set up the stereo, and he has to develop a play-list of the music so that people won't have to wait between dances while he chooses the next song. Calling the guests involves keeping track of who answered the phone and who needs another call. This algorithm is just a top-level solution. Developing a complete solution would require you to work out and write down all of the details. Computers require such complete solutions. Fortunately, for a problem like party planning, you can count on your friends to work out the details themselves. (If you were planning a flight of the space shuttle, where any misstep could have serious consequences, you'd work out every step that everyone needs to do. Such life-critical tasks are often programmed with the same precision that a computer requires.)

Because the number of potential guests to call is limited, you decide that it would be easier to merge this part of the solution into a single responsibility that you handle. Often, when we first write down a problem solution, we notice things that we want to change. Our solutions are not written in stone—we can modify them as necessary. However, it is helpful in programming to settle on a solution and avoid making unnecessary changes once we begin coding.

Our collection of objects needs to be coordinated in carrying out their responsibilities. We don't just perform these steps in random fashion. In programming, such a coordinating plan is called a *driver*. In our driver, we write a series of steps that refers to each object and its responsibility as necessary. For example:

```
You: Call guests and keep a count of the ones who can come.
Sally: Use count to write shopping list and buy food.
James: Select music.
James: Deliver stereo (collaborate with Sally for delivery).
You: Clean apartment.
You: Move furniture (collaborate with Sally and James on moving heavy pieces).
You: Welcome guests.
Sally: Take care of food.
James: Run stereo.
James: Help lead games.
You: Say goodbye to guests.
You: Clean apartment and move furniture back (collaborate with Sally and James).
James: Return stereo (collaborate with Sally).
```

As we will see, Java uses a similar mechanism (known as a *method call*) for naming an object and one of its responsibilities in order to get the object to carry out an action. Many of the statements we write in our Java programs are of this sort. Over the next few chapters you will gain a great deal of experience with writing and calling methods.

We've illustrated the use of problem solving in a noncomputer context to show that these techniques are very general. Even if your career takes you in a direction that doesn't require computer programming, the organizational and problem-solving skills that you learn in this course can be applied in many different situations. By learning to program a computer, which requires very precise instructions, you can hone your problem-solving skills to a much higher degree.

1.8 Testing and Debugging

Even the best-laid plans sometimes go awry. Along the way, we will offer tips on what to do when things don't work as expected. We will also offer advice on how to avoid problems (programming bugs) in the first place.

Testing and Debugging Hints

1. Be sure to understand the problem before you start trying to solve it.
2. Note anything that is unclear and ask questions to clarify the problem.
3. Rewrite the problem statement in your own words.
4. Identify the objects required and their capabilities.
5. Use the problem-solving techniques discussed in this chapter to help develop your solution.
6. Keep in mind the actions that a computer can perform when developing solutions for it.

Summary

We think nothing of turning on a television and sitting down to watch it. Television is simply a complex communication tool that we use easily. Today computers are becoming as common as televisions—that is, just a normal part of our lives. Like televisions, computers are based on complex principles but are designed for easy use.

Computers are dumb; they must be told what to do. A true computer error is extremely rare (and usually crops up because of a component malfunction or an electrical fault). Because we tell the computer what to do, most errors in computer-generated output are really human errors.

Computer programming is the process of developing a problem solution for a computer to execute. It encompasses a problem-solving phase as well as an implementation phase. After analyzing a problem, we develop and test a general solution (an algorithm). This general solution becomes a concrete solution—a program—when we write it in a high-level programming language. A program coordinates the interactions of a collection of objects that collaborate to solve the problem. Objects are an assemblage of data and operations that can be applied to those data. They are often

Learning Portfolio

designed to represent real objects in the problem and are described by a class. The instructions that make up the program (the source code) are either compiled into machine code (the language used by the computer) or Bytecode (the language used by the Java Virtual Machine). After correcting any errors or "bugs" that show up during testing, the program is ready to use.

Once we begin to use the program, it enters the maintenance phase. Maintenance involves correcting any errors discovered by users and changing the program to reflect changes in the users' requirements.

Data and instructions are represented as binary numbers (numbers consisting of just 1s and 0s) in electronic computers. The process of converting data and instructions into a form usable by the computer is called coding.

A programming language reflects the range of operations that a computer can perform. In this book, you will learn to write application programs in the high-level programming language called Java. The basic control structures in the Java programming language—sequence, selection, loop, subprogram, and asynchronous control—are based on the fundamental operations of the computer. Java provides the ability to collect data and operations into self-contained units called objects, as specified by classes, which other applications can then reuse.

Computers are composed of six basic parts: the memory unit, the arithmetic/logic unit, the control unit, input devices, output devices, and auxiliary storage devices. The arithmetic/logic unit and control unit together form the central processing unit. The physical parts of the computer constitute hardware. The programs that are executed by the computer are called software. System software is a set of programs designed to simplify the user/computer interface. It includes the compiler, the operating system, the JVM, and the editor.

The most important phase of any programming project is the development of the initial solution to the problem. We use problem-solving techniques such as analogy, means-ends analysis, divide and conquer, building blocks, and merging solutions to help us organize our efforts in this phase. Object-oriented problem solving focuses on the objects in the problem statement, trying to save effort by reusing existing classes of objects.

The computer is widely used today in science, engineering, business, government, medicine, production of consumer goods, and the arts. Learning to program in Java can help you use this powerful tool more effectively. In addition, the problem-solving skills that you develop through programming can be applied in many noncomputer contexts.

Quick Check

Quick Check exercises are intended to help you decide whether you've met the goals set forth at the beginning of each chapter. If you understand the material in the chapter, the answer to each question should be fairly obvious. After reading a question, check your response against the answers listed at the end of the Quick Check. If you don't know an answer or don't understand the answer that's provided, turn to the page(s) listed at the end of the question to review the material.

1. What is a computer program? (p. 5)

2. What are the three phases in a program's life cycle? (pp. 5–9)

3. Is an algorithm the same as a program? (p. 6)

4. What are the advantages of using a high-level programming language? (pp. 10–11)

5. What is the difference between machine code and Bytecode? (pp. 12–13)

6. What part does the Java Virtual Machine play in the compilation and interpretation process? (pp. 14–15)

7. What are the six basic components of a computer? (pp. 20–22)

8. What is meant by the term *object*, in the context of programming? (pp. 5, 18–20)

9. What should you do before you begin to code a problem solution in Java? (pp. 22–24, 28–29)

10. Name the five basic ways of structuring statements in Java. (pp. 15–18)

11. What is the difference between hardware and software? (p. 22)

12. Name the problem-solving technique in which we break the problem into more manageable chunks. (pp. 24–28)

13. Which problem-solving technique would be a natural choice in planning a hike between two campgrounds? (pp. 24–28)

14. In the following problem statement, what are the objects: "Compute the area of a circle, given its radius." (pp. 5, 18–20, 29)

Answers

1. A computer program is a list of instructions performed by a computer. 2. The three phases of a program's life cycle are problem solving, implementation, and maintenance. 3. No. A program is an algorithm written in a programming language. All programs are algorithms, but not all algorithms are programs. 4. A high-level programming language is easier to use than an assembly language or a machine language. Also, programs written in a high-level language can be run on many different computers. 5. Machine code is the native binary language that is directly executed by any particular computer. Bytecode is a standard portable machine language that is executed by the Java Virtual Machine, but it is not directly executed by the computer. 6. It translates the Bytecode instructions into operations that are executed by the computer. 7. The basic components of a computer are the memory unit, arithmetic/logic unit, control unit, input devices, output devices, and auxiliary storage devices. 8. A collection of data and associated operations that can be applied to the data. 9. Understand the problem and develop an algorithmic solution to the problem. 10. Sequence, selection, loop, subprogram, and asynchronous. 11. Hardware is the physical components of the computer; software is the collection of programs that run on the computer. 12. Divide and conquer. 13. Means-ends analysis. 14. Area, circle, and radius are the obvious objects.

Exam Preparation Exercises

1. Explain why the following series of steps is not an algorithm, then rewrite the series so that it is.

   Shampooing

   1. Rinse.
   2. Lather.
   3. Repeat.

2. Describe the input and output files used by a compiler.

3. In the following recipe for chocolate pound cake, identify the steps that are branches (selection) and loops, and the steps that make references to subalgorithms outside the algorithm.

   ```
   Preheat the oven to 350 degrees
   Line the bottom of a 9-inch tube pan with wax paper
   Sift 2 ¾ c flour, ¾ t cream of tartar, ½ t baking soda, 1½ t salt, and 1¾ c
       sugar into a large bowl
   Add 1 c shortening to the bowl
   If using butter, margarine, or lard, then
     add 2/3 c milk to the bowl,
   else
     (for other shortenings) add 1 c minus 2 T of milk to the bowl
   Add 1 t vanilla to the mixture in the bowl
   If mixing with a spoon, then
     see the instructions in the introduction to the chapter on cakes
   else
     (for electric mixers) beat the contents of the bowl for 2 minutes at medium
         speed, scraping the bowl and beaters as needed
   Add 3 eggs plus 1 extra egg yolk to the bowl
   Melt 3 squares of unsweetened chocolate and add it to the mixture in the bowl
   Beat the mixture for 1 minute at medium speed
   Pour the batter into the tube pan
   Put the pan into the oven and bake for 1 hour 10 minutes
   Perform the test for doneness described in the introduction to the chapter on
       cakes
   Repeat the test once each minute until the cake is done
   Remove the pan from the oven and allow the cake to cool for 2 hours
   Follow the instructions for removing the cake from the pan, given in the
       introduction to the chapter on cakes
   Sprinkle powdered sugar over the cracks on top of the cake just before serving
   ```

4. Put a check next to each of the following items that is a peripheral device.

_____ a. Disk drive

_____ b. Arithmetic/logic unit

_____ c. Magnetic tape drive

_____ d. Printer

_____ e. CD-ROM drive

_____ f. Memory

_____ g. Auxiliary storage device

_____ h. Control unit

_____ i. LCD display

_____ j. Mouse

5. Next to each of the following items, indicate whether it is hardware (H) or software (S).

_____ a. Disk drive

_____ b. Memory

_____ c. Compiler

_____ d. Arithmetic/logic unit

_____ e. Editor

_____ f. Operating system

_____ g. Object program

_____ h. Java Virtual Machine

_____ i. Central processing unit

6. Distinguish between information and data.

7. You are planning a trip. Which problem-solving strategy would you use?

8. You are designing a house. Which problem-solving strategy would you use?

9. You are lost on a hike. Which problem-solving strategies would you use?

10. Identify the obvious objects in the recipe in Exercise 3.

Programming Warm-Up Exercises

1. Look up a recipe for angel food cake in a cookbook. Identify the obvious objects in the recipe. Then identify which portions of this algorithm consist of a sequence of instructions, where branches occur, where loops occur, and where subprograms are called.

2. Find a set of instructions for operating an appliance that requires you to set the date and time, such as a VCR, microwave oven, clock radio, or a computer.

Identify the obvious objects in the instructions. Then identify which portions of this algorithm consist of a sequence of instructions, where branches occur, where loops occur, and where subprograms are called.

3. Music notation works much like a programming language. Identify the symbols and notation in music that indicate a unit of music in a sequence of such units, that indicate repetition of a section of music, that indicate a choice between endings of a song, and that indicate a separate section to be played or sung at a given point. If you aren't familiar with musical notation, you'll need to do some research in books on basic musicianship.

4. Browse through the next several chapters of this book and identify Java statements that are used for branching and looping. (*Hint:* Look in the table of contents.)

Programming Problems

1. Write an algorithm for driving from where you live to the nearest airport that has regularly scheduled flights. Restrict yourself to a vocabulary of 20 words plus numbers and place names. You must select the appropriate set of words for this task. The purpose of this exercise is to give you practice in writing simple, exact instructions with a small vocabulary, just as a computer programming language requires you to do.

2. Write an algorithm for making a peanut butter and jelly sandwich, using a vocabulary of just 20 words (you choose the words). Assume that all ingredients are available in the cabinet or refrigerator and that the necessary tools are in a drawer under the kitchen counter. The instructions must be very simple and exact because the person making the sandwich has no knowledge of food preparation and takes every word literally.

3. Write an algorithm for doing your laundry, using a vocabulary of just 20 words (you choose the words). Assume that you have the detergent, bleach, fabric softener, and any other objects needed to do the laundry, and that the starting state is you standing before a washing machine with your laundry and these objects. The ending state is a set of clean, neatly folded laundry items (no starch in the socks, please).

Case Study Follow-Up

1. Expand the instructions for Sally's responsibility to make the shopping list. It may help to imagine that you are writing the instructions for someone else to follow.

2. You have another friend who plays guitar and sings. How might you change the plan for the party and reassign the responsibilities?

3. This occasion marks the first time you've ever given a party, and you're unsure of your plans. How could you check them out before the party to confirm that you've covered everything that needs to be done?

Java Syntax and Semantics, Classes, and Objects

goals

Knowledge Goals

- To understand the difference between syntax and semantics
- To see why it is important to use meaningful identifiers in Java
- To understand the distinction between built-in types and objects
- To appreciate the difference between a class in the abstract sense and a class as a Java construct
- To see the difference between objects in general and their use in Java
- To recognize how the char type and String objects are related and differ
- To understand the difference between a named constant and a variable
- To know how assignment of an object differs from assignment of a standard type
- To understand what happens when a method is invoked
- To understand how a Java application is composed of a class with one or more methods
- To appreciate the differences between void and value-returning methods

Skill Goals

To be able to:

- Read and understand the formal syntax rules governing Java programs
- Create and recognize legal Java identifiers
- Declare fields of type char and String
- Assign values to variables
- Construct string expressions
- Declare a class
- Write a method declaration and invocation
- Invoke a method
- Use a constructor to instantiate an object
- Use comments to clarify your programs
- Write simple input and output statements using the System class
- Determine what is displayed by a given code segment

timeline

1876

Alexander Graham Bell invents the telephone, and obtains one of the most valuable patents in history

1882

William S. Burroughs leaves his job at a bank to pursue the invention of an accurate and efficient adding machine

1889

Herman Hollerith patents his Tabulating Machine, which is used to expedite the processing of census data in 1890

1895

Italian inventor Guglielmo Marconi sends and receives his first radio signal, demonstrating the feasibility of wireless communication

1901

The keypunch, which cuts holes or notches in a punch card, emerges in the form it remains for the next 50 years

1904

John A. Fleming builds on Thomas Edison's work, and invents the diode vacuum tube, which converts AC signals to DC signals

introduction

Programmers develop solutions to problems using a programming language. In this chapter, we look at some of the rules and symbols that make up the Java programming language. We also review the steps required to create an application and make it work on a computer.

1906
The National Electrical Signaling Company's radio station in Massachusetts hosts the first broadcasted radio program of speech and music on Christmas Eve

1911
The Calculating, Tabulating, and Recording Company (CTR) is established

1915
Physicist Manson Benedicks discovers that AC can be converted to DC using the germanium crystal, providing the basis for microchips

1919
W.H. Eccles and F. W. Jordan invent the electronic trigger circuit, or today's flip-flop switching circuit

1920-1921
Playwright Karl Capek introduces the word "robot" in his work "Rossum's Universal Robots"

1924
The Calculating, Tabulating, and Recording Company is renamed by T.J. Watson to International Business Machines, or IBM

2.1 The Elements of Java Programs

In this section we examine in turn each of the components that are needed to write a program that can perform simple actions, including input and output. In Section 2.2 we see how to assemble these components into a complete program.

■ Syntax and Semantics

A programming language is a set of rules, symbols, and special words used to construct a program. Rules apply to both syntax (grammar) and semantics (meaning).

Syntax is a formal set of rules that defines exactly which combinations of letters, numbers, and symbols can be used in a programming language. The syntax of a programming language leaves no room for ambiguity because the computer can't think; it doesn't "know what we mean." To avoid ambiguity, syntax rules themselves must be written in a very simple, precise, formal language called a metalanguage.

Syntax The formal rules governing how valid instructions are written in a programming language

Semantics The set of rules that determines the meaning of instructions written in a programming language

Metalanguage A language that is used to write the syntax rules for another language

Learning to read a metalanguage is like learning to read the playbook for a sport. Once you understand the notation, you can learn the plays that give a team its competitive edge. It's true that many people learn a sport simply by watching others play, but what they learn is usually just enough to allow them to take part in casual games. You could learn Java by following the examples in this book, but a serious programmer, like a serious athlete, must take the time to read and understand the rules and to recognize how they are applied.

Syntax rules are the blueprints we use to "build" instructions in a program. They allow us to take the elements of a programming language—the basic building blocks of the language—and assemble them into *constructs*, or syntactically correct structures. If our code violates any of the rules of the language—by misspelling a crucial word or leaving out an important comma, for instance—the program is said to have *syntax errors* and cannot compile correctly until we fix them.

■ Syntax Templates

The following Theoretical Foundations feature describes notations (called metalanguages) that have long been used to define the syntax of programming languages. In this book we write the syntax rules for Java using a metalanguage called a *syntax template*. A syntax template is a generic example of the Java construct being defined. Graphic conventions show which portions are optional and which can be repeated. A color word or symbol is written in the Java construct just as it is in the template. A black word can be replaced by another template. A square bracket indicates a set of items from which you can choose.

Metalanguages

Metalanguage is the word *language* with the prefix *meta*, which means "beyond" or "more comprehensive." In other words, a metalanguage is a language that goes beyond a normal language by allowing us to speak precisely about that language. It is a language for talking about languages.

One of the oldest computer-oriented metalanguages is the *Backus-Naur Form* (BNF), which is named for John Backus and Peter Naur, who developed it in 1960. BNF syntax definitions are written out using letters, numbers, and special symbols. For example, an *identifier* (a name for something) in Java must be at least one letter, underscore, or dollar sign, which may or may not be followed by additional letters, underscores, dollar signs, or digits. The BNF definition of an identifier in Java is

<identifier> ::= <letter> | <letter> <letter-digit-sequence>

< letter-digit-sequence > ::= <letter-or-digit> | <letter-or-digit>< letter-digit-sequence >

<letter-or-digit> ::= <letter> | <digit>

<letter> ::= _ | $ | A | B | C | D | E | F | G | H | I | J | K | L | M | N | O | P | Q | R | S | T | U | V | W | X | Y | Z

           | a | b | c | d | e | f | g | h | i | j | k | l | m | n | o | p | q | r | s | t | u | v | w | x | y | z

<digit> ::= 0 | 1 | 2 | 3 | 4 | 5 | 6 | 7 | 8 | 9

where the symbol ::= is read "is defined as," the symbol | means "or," and the symbols < and > are used to enclose words called *nonterminal symbols* (symbols that still need to be defined). Everything else is called a *terminal symbol*.

The first line of the definition reads as follows: "An identifier is defined as a letter or a letter followed by a letter-digit-sequence." This line contains nonterminal symbols that must be defined. In the second line, the nonterminal symbol <letter-digit-sequence> is defined as a <letter-or-digit> or as a <letter-or-digit> followed by another <letter-digit-sequence>. The self-reference in the definition is a roundabout way of saying that a <letter-digit-sequence> can be a series of one or more letters or digits. In the third line, a <letter-or-digit> is defined as either a <letter> or a <digit>. In the fourth and last lines, we finally encounter terminal symbols that define <letter> to be an underscore, dollar sign, or any of the uppercase or lowercase letters and <digit> as any one of the numeric characters 0 through 9.

BNF is an extremely simple language, but that simplicity leads to syntax definitions that can be long and difficult to read. An alternative metalanguage, the *syntax diagram*, is easier to follow. It uses arrows to indicate how symbols can be combined. The following syntax diagrams define an identifier in Java:

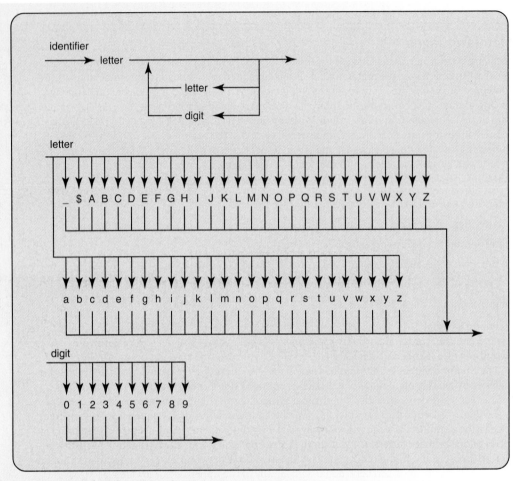

To read the diagrams, start at the left and follow the arrows. When you come to a branch, take any one of the branch paths. A lowercase word is a nonterminal symbol.

The first diagram shows that an *identifier* can consist of a letter and, optionally, any number of letters or digits. The nonterminal symbols *letter* and *digit* are then defined to be any one of the alphabetic or numeric characters. Here, we have eliminated the BNF nonterminal symbols <letter-digit-sequence> and <letter-or-digit> by using arrows in the first syntax diagram to allow a sequence of consecutive letters or digits.

Syntax diagrams are easier to interpret than BNF definitions, but they still can be difficult to read. In this book, we introduce another metalanguage, called a *syntax template*. Syntax templates show at a glance the form of a Java construct.

One final note: Metalanguages show only how to write instructions that the compiler can translate. They do not define what those instructions can do (their semantics). Formal languages for defining the semantics of a programming language exist, but they are beyond the scope of this text. Throughout this book, we will describe the semantics of Java in English.

Let's look at an example. This template defines a Java identifier, which is Java's way of naming something in a program:

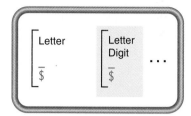

The shading indicates the optional part of the definition. The three dots (...) mean that the preceding symbol or shaded block can be repeated. Thus an identifier in Java is a letter, an underscore, or dollar sign that may be optionally followed by one or more letters, digits, underscores, or dollar signs.

Remember that a word not in color can be replaced with another template. Consider the templates for a letter and a digit:

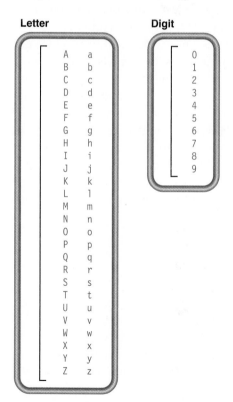

In these templates, the brackets again indicate lists of items from which you can choose any one. Thus a letter can be any one of the uppercase or lowercase letters, and a digit can be any of the numeric characters 0 through 9.

Now let's look at the syntax template for a Java application:

```
Import-Declaration;   • • •

Class-Modifier • • •      class  Identifier
{
    Class-Declaration   • • •
}
```

A Java application may optionally begin with a series of import declarations. As we noted in Chapter 1, an object-oriented language such as Java provides a very large library of ready-made objects that are available for us to use in our programs. Java's library contains so many, in fact, that they must be organized into smaller groups called **packages**. Import declarations are statements that tell the Java compiler which library packages our program uses. We will look at how to write import declarations shortly, but first let's continue our examination of this syntax template.

Package   A named collection of object classes in Java that can be imported by a program

Class   A definition for an object or an application in Java

Identifier   A name associated with a package, class, method, or field and used to refer to that element

Method   A subprogram in Java

The next line may optionally begin with a series of class modifiers, which are then followed by the word *class*, and an identifier. This line is called the *heading* of the class. An application in Java is a collection of elements that are grouped together into a **class**. The heading gives the class a name (the identifier) and may optionally specify some general properties of the class (the class modifiers). You've already seen what an identifier is, and we define class modifiers later in this chapter.

The heading is followed by an open brace, a series of class declarations, and a closing brace. These three elements make up the *body* of the class. The braces indicate where the body begins and ends, and the class declarations contain all of the statements that tell the computer what to do. The simplest Java program we can write would look like this:

```
class DoNothing
{
}
```

As its name implies, this program does absolutely nothing. It is simply an empty shell of an application. Our job as programmers is to add useful instructions to this shell.

When you finish this chapter, you should know enough about the syntax and semantics of statements in Java to be able to write simple applications. But before we can talk about writing statements, we must understand how names are defined in Java and become familiar with some of the elements of Java code.

■ Naming Program Elements: Identifiers

As we noted in our discussion of metalanguages, we use an **identifier** in Java to name something. For example, an identifier could be the name of a class, a subprogram (called a **method** in Java), or a place in the computer's memory that holds data (called a field in Java). Identifiers are made up of letters (A–Z, a–z), digits (0–9), the underscore character (_), and the dollar sign ($), but each *must* begin with a letter, underscore, or dollar sign:

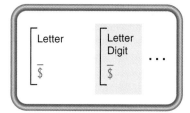

Identifiers beginning with an underscore have special meaning in some Java systems, so it is best to begin an identifier with a letter. Similarly, the dollar sign has special meaning in some Java systems and should not be used in identifiers that you write. We have included it in the syntax template so that you can recognize its use if you encounter it in Java code that someone else has written.

Here are some examples of valid identifiers:

```
sum_of_squares  J9  box_22A  GetData  Bin3D4  count   Count
```

> **Field** A named place in memory that holds a data object
>
> **Reserved word** A word that has special meaning in Java; it cannot be used as a programmer-defined identifier

Note that the last two identifiers (count and Count) are considered completely different names by the Java compiler. That is, the uppercase and lowercase forms of a letter are two distinct characters to the computer. Here are some examples of invalid identifiers and the reasons why they are invalid:

Invalid Identifier	Explanation
40Hours	Identifiers cannot begin with a digit
Get Data	Blanks are not allowed in identifiers
box–22	The hyphen (–) is a math symbol (minus) in Java
empty_?	Special symbols such as ? are not allowed
int	The word int is predefined in the Java language

The last identifier in the table, int, is an example of a reserved word. Reserved words have specific uses in Java; you cannot use them as programmer-defined identifiers. Appendix A lists all of the reserved words in Java. In the code in this book, they are colored red.

Now that we've seen how to write identifiers, let's look at some of the things that Java allows us to name.

■ Built-in Types in Java

A computer program operates on data. In Java, each piece of data must be of a specific data type. The data type determines how the data is represented in the computer and the kinds

Matters of Style

Using Meaningful, Readable Identifiers

The names we use to refer to things in our code are totally meaningless to the computer. The computer behaves in the same way whether we call a value 3.14159265, pi, or cake, as long as we always call it the same thing. Of course, it is much easier for a person to figure out how your code works if the names you choose for elements actually tell something about them. When ever you make up a name for something in your code, try to pick one that is meaningful to a human reader.

Java is a *case-sensitive* language, which means that it sees uppercase letters as different from lowercase letters. The identifiers

```
PRINTTOPPORTION   printtopportion   pRiNtToPpOrTiOn   PrintTopPortion
```

are four distinct names and are not interchangeable in any way. As you can see, the last of these forms is the easiest to read. In this book, we use combinations of uppercase letters, lowercase letters, and underscores in identifiers. Many Java programmers use different capitalizations of identifiers as a way to indicate what they represent. Later in this chapter, we show you the conventions that we, and many other Java programmers, use.

---

of processing the computer can perform on it. Recall from Chapter 1 that all objects are of the same type, but differ in their class. Java includes types other than `Object`, each of which has its own name.

Because some types of data are used very frequently, Java provides them for us. These are called **standard** (or **built-in**) **types**. You are already familiar with most of them from everyday life: integer numbers, real numbers, and characters. In Chapter 3, we examine the integer types `int` and `long`, and the real types `float` and `double`. By the end of Chapter 4, you'll be equally familiar with one more type, `boolean`.

> **Standard (built-in) type** A data type that is automatically available for use in every Java program

In this chapter we look first at the built-in type `char` and then later at the class `String` that Java provides for us to manipulate character data.

The char Data Type The built-in type `char` describes data consisting of one alphanumeric character—a letter, a digit, or a special symbol. Java uses a particular *character set*, or set of alphanumeric characters that it can represent. Java's character set, which is called Unicode, includes characters for many written languages. In this book, we use a subset of Unicode that corresponds to an older character set called the American Standard Code for Information Interchange (ASCII). ASCII consists of the alphabet for the English language, plus numbers and symbols.

Here are some example values of type `char`:

```
'A'   'a'   '8'   '2'   '+'   '-'   '$'   '?'   '*'   ' '
```

Data Storage

Where does our code get the data it needs to operate? Data is stored in the computer's memory. Recall that memory is divided into a large number of separate locations or cells, each of which can hold a piece of data. Each memory location has a unique address we refer to when we store or retrieve data. We can visualize memory as a set of post office boxes, with the box numbers serving as the addresses used to designate particular locations.

Of course, the actual address of each location in memory is a binary number in a machine language code. In Java, we use identifiers to name memory locations; the compiler and the JVM then translate those identifiers into binary form for us. This translation represents one of the advantages provided by a high-level programming language: It frees us from having to keep track of the numeric addresses of the memory locations in which our data and instructions are stored.

Notice that each character is enclosed in single quotes (apostrophes). The Java compiler needs the quotes to be able to differentiate between the character data and other Java elements. For example, the quotes around the characters `'A'` and `'+'` distinguish them from the identifier A and the addition sign. Notice also that the blank, `' '`, is a valid character.

How do we write the single quote itself as a character? If we write `'''`, Java complains that we have made a syntax error. The second quote indicates the end of the (empty) character value, and the third quote starts a new character value. To deal with this problem, Java provides a special *escape sequence* that allows us to write a single quote as a character. That is, Java treats the sequence of two characters \' as a single character representing the quote. When we want to write the quote as a character in Java, we thus write

'\''

Notice that we use the backward slash, or backslash (\), as the escape character rather than the regular, forward slash (/). As we will see in Chapter 3, Java uses the regular slash as a division sign, so it is important to recognize that the two slashes are different. A moment's thought reveals that this scheme introduces a new problem: How do we write the backslash as a character? The answer is that Java provides a second escape sequence, \\, that allows us to write a backslash. Thus we write the char value of backslash in Java as follows:

'\\'

Be careful that you don't confuse this sequence with the // sequence, which begins a comment in Java (we look at comments a little later in this chapter).

Java provides operations that allow us to compare data values of type char. The Unicode character set has a *collating sequence*, a predefined ordering of all the characters. In Unicode, 'A' compares as less than 'B', 'B' as less than 'C', and so forth. Also, '1' compares as less than '2', '2' as less than '3', and so on.

The type char is one of Java's primitive types. The String class, which allows us to work with collections of characters, such as words and sentences, is one of the Object types in Java. We've discussed classes and objects in the abstract sense as part of the problem-solving process. Now we must further explore what classes and objects are in Java before we move on to strings.

■ Classes and Objects

In Chapter 1, we identified two phases of programming: the problem-solving phase and the implementation phase. Often the same vocabulary is used in different ways in the two phases.

In the problem-solving phase, for example, an object is an entity or some *thing* that makes sense in the context of the problem at hand. A group of objects with similar properties and behaviors is described by an *object class*, or *class* for short. Object-oriented problem solving involves isolating the objects that make up the problem. Objects interact with one another by sending messages.

In the implementation phase, a class is a Java construct that allows the programmer to describe an object. A class contains fields (data values) and methods (subprograms) that define the behavior of the object. Think of a class in the general sense as a pattern for what an object looks like and how it behaves, and a Java class as the construct that allows you to simulate the object in code. If a class is a description of an object, how do we get an object that fits the description? We use an operator called new, which takes the class name and returns an object of the class type. The object that is returned is an *instance* of the class. The act of creating an object from a class is called *instantiation*.

The following definitions provide new meanings for the terms *object* and *class* in addition to how we defined them in Chapter 1:

Class (general sense)   A description of the behavior of a group of objects with similar properties and behaviors

class (Java construct)   A pattern for an object

Object (general sense)   An entity or thing that is relevant in the context of a problem

Object (Java)   An instance of a class

Instantiation   Creating an object, which is an instance of a class

Method   A subprogram that defines one aspect of the behavior of a class

Here is the syntax diagram for a class:

Class

```
Import-Declaration;  • • •

Class-Modifiers  • • •  class  Identifier
{
    Class-Declaration  • • •
}
```

Class-Modifiers

```
private

public
```

Our class declaration template looks identical to the template for a Java application because a Java application is just a class that has a method called main. We look specifically at construction of an application later in this chapter. Here we are interested in those aspects of defining a class that apply to all Java classes.

When we first showed the syntax template for a Java application, we mentioned that the application can optionally include an import declaration. Import declarations can start any class declaration. Here is the syntax diagram for such a declaration:

Import-Declaration

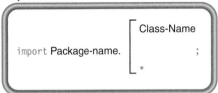

As the template shows, an import declaration begins with the keyword `import`, the name of a package, and a dot (period). Following the period, we can either write the name of a class in the package or type an asterisk (*). The declaration ends with a semicolon. If we want to use exactly one class in a particular package, then we can simply give its name (Class-name) in the import declaration. More often, however, we want to use multiple classes in a package, and the asterisk is a shorthand notation to the compiler that says, "Import whatever classes from this package that this class uses."

Why would we ever want to use the first form, when the asterisk has the same effect and is easier to type? The first form documents the specific class that we intend to use, and it causes the compiler to warn us if we mistakenly attempt to use another class from the package. In this book, we typically use the asterisk instead of the Class-Name, but we document the class(es) we are importing by including a comment.

Access modifiers Reserved words in Java that specify where a class, method, or field may be accessed; two examples are `public` and `private`

The next line, the class heading, begins with zero or more class modifiers, which are Java reserved words. The syntax diagram includes two of Java's modifiers that are relevant here: `public` and `private`. They are called **access modifiers** because they specify whether elements outside of the class can use the class. What's outside of the class? Any of the packages that we list in `import` declarations. Also, every application class actually resides within a package called `java` that is part of the JVM. Thus, if we declare an identifier to be `public`, we allow the JVM and all imported packages to make use of it. Because we want the JVM to be able to execute our application class, we specify that its name be `public`.

The heading is followed by the body of the class: an open brace, a series of class declarations, and a closing brace. The braces indicate where the body begins and ends, and the class declarations contain all of the statements that tell the computer what to do. Here's an example of a Java class:

```
private class Example
{
   char someLetter = 'A';
   System.out.println("someLetter is " + someLetter);
}
```

Don't worry if you don't understand everything shown here. This code includes some elements of Java that we have not yet explained. By the end of the chapter, it should all be clear to you.

The String Class   Whereas a value of type char is limited to a single character, a *string* (in the general sense) is a sequence of characters, such as a word, name, or sentence, enclosed in double quotes. In Java, a string is an object, an instance of the String class. For example, the following are strings in Java:

```
"Introduction to "    "Programming and Problem Solving"    " with Java "    "."
```

A string must be typed entirely on one line. For example, the string

```
"This string is invalid because it
is typed on more than one line."
```

is not valid because it is split across two lines before the closing double quote. In this situation, the Java compiler will issue an error message at the first line. The message may say something like QUOTE EXPECTED, depending on the particular compiler.

The quotes are not considered to be part of the string but are simply there to distinguish the string from other parts of a Java class. For example, "amount" (in double quotes) is the character string made up of the letters $a, m, o, u, n,$ and t in that order. On the other hand, amount (without the quotes) is an identifier, perhaps the name of a place in memory. The symbols "12345" represent a string made up of the characters 1, 2, 3, 4, and 5 in that order. If we write 12345 without the quotes, it is an integer quantity that can be used in calculations.

A string containing no characters is called the *empty string*. We write the empty string using two double quotes with nothing (not even spaces) between them:

```
""
```

The empty string is not equivalent to a string of spaces; rather, it is a special string that contains no characters.

To write a double quote within a string, we use another escape sequence, \". Here is a string containing both quotation marks and the escape sequence for a backslash:

```
"She said, \"Don't forget that \\ is not the same as the / character.\""
```

The value of this string is

```
She said, "Don't forget that \ is not the same as the / character."
```

Notice that within a string we do not have to use the escape sequence \' to represent a single quote. Similarly, we can write the double quote as a value of type char ('"') without using an escape sequence. In contrast, we have to use \\ to write a backslash as a char value or within a string.

Java provides operations for joining strings, comparing strings, copying portions of strings, changing the case of letters in strings, converting numbers to strings, and converting strings to numbers. We will look at some of these operations later in this chapter and cover the remaining operations in subsequent chapters.

■ Defining Terms: Declarations

How do we tell the computer what an identifier represents? We use a declaration, a statement that associates a name (an identifier) with a description of an element in a Java program (just as a dictionary definition associates a name with a description of the thing being named). In a declaration, we name both the identifier and what it represents.

> **Declaration**   A statement that associates an identifier with a field, a method, a class, or a package so that the programmer can refer to that item by name

When we declare an identifier, the compiler picks a location in memory to be associated with it. We don't have to know the actual address of the memory location because the computer automatically keeps track of it for us.

To see how this process works, suppose that when we mail a letter, we have to put only a person's name on it and the post office will look up the address. Of course, everybody in the world would need a different name with such a system; otherwise, the post office wouldn't be able to figure out whose address was whose. The same is true in Java. Each identifier can represent just one thing (except under special circumstances, which we talk about later). Every identifier you use in your code must be different from all others.

■ Field Declarations

Classes are made up of methods and fields. We've seen that methods are the operations that are associated with the data in an object. Fields are the components of a class that represent the data. Data in a class can be of any type, including the primitive types or objects. It's important to grasp the significance of being able to have objects within objects, as it allows us to gradually build up objects of great complexity.

We use identifiers to refer to fields. In Java you must declare every identifier before it is used. The compiler can then verify that the use of the identifier is consistent with its declaration. If you declare an identifier to be a field that can hold a `char` value and later try to store a number into the field, for example, the compiler will detect this inconsistency and issue an error message.

A field can be either a constant or a variable. In other words, a field identifier can be the name of a memory location whose contents are not allowed to change or it can be the name of a memory location whose contents can change. There are different forms of declaration statements for variables and constants in Java. First we look at variables, then consider constants, and finally look at fields in general. Declarations for methods and classes are covered later in the chapter.

Variables   Data is stored in memory. While an application is executing, different values may be stored in the same memory location at different times. This kind of memory location is called a **variable**, and its contents are the *variable value*. The symbolic name that we associate with a memory location is the *variable name* or *variable identifier*. In practice, we often refer to the variable name more briefly as the *variable*.

Declaring a variable means specifying both its name and its data type or class. This specification tells the compiler to associate a name with a memory location and informs it that the values to be stored in that location are of a specific type or class (for example, char or String). The following statement declares myChar to be a variable of type char:

```
char myChar;
```

> **Variable** A location in memory, referenced by an identifier, that contains a data value that can be changed
>
> **Strongly typed** A property of a programming language in which the language allows variables to contain only values of the specified type or class

Notice that the declaration does not specify what value is stored in myChar. Rather, it specifies that the name myChar can hold a value of type char. At this point, myChar has been reserved as a place in memory but it contains no data. Soon, we will see how to actually put a value into a variable. (See Figure 2.1.)

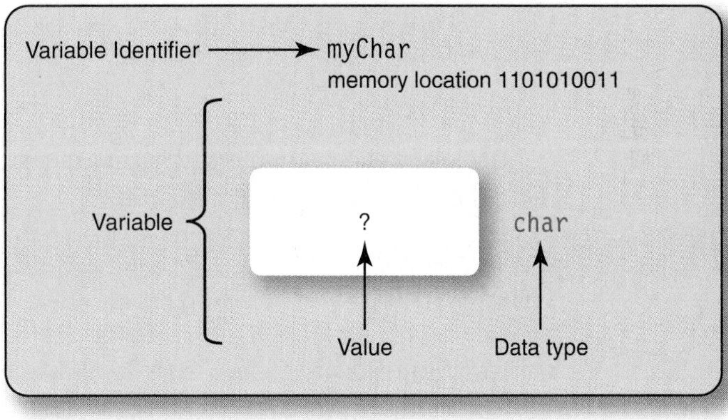

Java is a **strongly typed** language, which means that a variable can contain a value only of the type or class specified in its declaration.[1] Because of the above declaration, the variable myChar can contain *only* a char value. If the Java compiler comes across an instruction that tries to store a value of the wrong type, it gives an error message, usually something like "Cannot assign String to char."

Figure 2.1 Variable

Here's the syntax template for a variable declaration:

Variable-Declaration

```
Modifiers  Type-Name Identifier , Identifier • • • ;
```

---

[1]Many early programming languages, some of which are still in use today, allow a value of any type to be stored in a variable. This weak typing was inherited from assembly language programming and has been a source of many programming errors. Modern languages check that variables contain proper values, thereby helping us to avoid such errors.

Here, Modifiers are like the modifiers for the class declarations (`public` and `private`), and Type-Name is the name of a type or class such as `char` or `String`. We will introduce additional modifiers as we need them in later chapters. Note that the modifiers are optional—we can write a declaration without using any of them. Notice also that a declaration always ends with a semicolon.

From the syntax template, you can see that we can declare several variables in one statement:

```
char letter, middleInitial, ch;
```

Here, all three variables are declared to be `char` variables. Our preference, though, is to declare each variable with a separate statement:

```
char letter;
char middleInitial;
char ch;
```

Declaring each variable with a separate statement allows you to attach comments to the right of each declaration. For example:

```
String firstName;       // A person's first name
String lastName;        // A person's last name
String title;           // A person's title, such as Dr.
char middleInitial;     // A person's middle initial
char myChar;            // A place to store one letter
```

These declarations tell the compiler to reserve memory space for three `String` variables—`firstName`, `lastName`, and `title`—and two `char` variables—`middleInitial` and `myChar`. The comments explain to someone reading the program what each variable represents.

We saw earlier that the syntax template for a class contains a set of class declarations, and that some of those declarations can be variables. For example, the following class has two variable declarations and shows how we might use a `private` modifier as part of a declaration:

```
public class Sample          // The start of a public class called Sample
{
  private char   myChar;     // A private char type variable declared in class Sample
         String myString;    // A String object variable declared in class Sample
}                            // The end of class Sample
```

Now that we've seen how to declare variables in Java, let's look at how to declare constants.

Constants All single characters (enclosed in single quotes) and strings (enclosed in double quotes) are constants.

```
'A'   '@'   "Howdy boys"   "Please enter an employee number:"
```

In Java, as in mathematics, a constant is something whose value never changes. When we use the actual value of a constant in a program, we are using a literal value (or *literal*).

An alternative to the literal constant is the named constant (or symbolic constant), which is introduced in a declaration statement. A named constant is just another way of representing a literal value. Instead of using the literal value directly our code, we give the literal value a name in a declaration statement, then use that name in the code. For example, we can write an instruction that prints the title of this book using the literal string `"Introduction to Programming and Problem Solving with Java"`. Or we can declare a named constant called `BOOK_TITLE` that equals the same string and then use the constant name in the instruction. That is, we can use either

```
"Introduction to Programming and Problem Solving with Java "
```

or

```
BOOK_TITLE
```

in the instruction.

> **Literal value** Any constant value written in Java
>
> **Named constant (symbolic constant)** A location in memory, referenced by an identifier, that contains a data value that cannot be changed

Using the literal value of a constant may seem easier than giving it a name and then referring to it by that name. In fact, named constants make a program easier to read, because they make the meaning of literal constants clearer. Also, named constants make it easier to change a program later on.

The syntax template for a constant declaration is similar to the template for a variable declaration:

Constant-Declaration

Modifiers `final` Type-Name Identifier = Literal-Value ;

The only difference is that we must include the modifier `final`, a reserved word, and follow the identifier with an equals sign (=) and the value to be stored in the constant. The `final` modifier tells the Java compiler that this value is the last and only value that this field should have.

The following are examples of constant declarations:

```
final String STARS = "********";
final char   BLANK = ' ';
final String BOOK_TITLE =
      "Introduction to Programming and Problem Solving with Java";
final String MESSAGE = "Error condition";
```

As shown in the preceding code, many Java programmers capitalize the entire identifier of a named constant and separate the English words with an underscore. The idea is to help the reader quickly distinguish between variable names and constant names when they appear in the middle of code. In one case, we split the declaration across two lines, placing the string literal on the line following the definition of the identifier. This kind of break works in Java, but remember that we cannot split the string literal itself across two lines.

It's a good idea to add comments to constant declarations as well as variable declarations. For example:

```
final String STARS = "********";    // Row of stars to use as a separator
final char   BLANK = ' ';           // A single blank
```

Fields   The similar appearance of variable and constant declarations in Java is no coincidence. Java doesn't actually distinguish between the declarations of named constants and variables because both are considered just different kinds of fields. A named constant is merely a field that is given an initial value, together with the modifier final, which says that the value can never change. If we extend the template for a variable declaration to include the syntax necessary to give the variable an initial value and add the keyword final to the list of modifiers, then we have a generic template for a field declaration in Java:

Field-Declaration

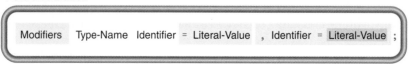

Modifiers

The following declarations are legal:

```
final String WORD1 = "Introduction to ";
      String word3 = "Programming and Problem Solving ";
final String WORD5 = "with Java";
```

Capitalization of Identifiers

Programmers often use capitalization to provide a quick, visual clue as to what an identifier represents. Different programmers adopt different conventions for using uppercase letters and lowercase letters. Some use only lowercase letters, separating the English words in an identifier with the underscore character:

```
pay_rate   emp_num  pay_file
```

The convention used by many Java programmers and the one we use in this book is the following:

- Variables and methods begin with a lowercase letter and capitalize each successive English word.

  ```
  lengthInYards  middleInitial   hours
  ```

- Class names begin with an uppercase letter but are capitalized the same as variable names thereafter.

  ```
  PayRollFrame   Sample   MyDataType   String
  ```

  Capitalizing the first letter allows a person reading the code to tell at a glance that an identifier represents a class name rather than a variable or method. Java's reserved words use all lowercase letters, so the type char is lowercase. String is a class, so it begins with a capital letter.

- Identifiers representing named constants are all uppercase with underscores used to separate the English words.

  ```
  BOOK_TITLE   OVERTIME   MAX_LENGTH
  ```

These conventions are simply that—conventions. Java does not require this particular style of capitalizing identifiers. You may wish to write your identifiers in a different fashion. But whatever method you use, it is essential that you maintain a consistent style throughout your code. A person reading your code will be confused or misled if you use a random style of capitalization.

They store `"Introduction to "` as the value for constant `WORD1`. The string `"Programming and Problem Solving "` is stored in the variable `word3`, and we store `"with Java"` in the constant `WORD5`.

■ Assignment and Expressions

Up to this point, we've looked at ways of declaring fields in a class. As part of the declaration, we can give an initial value to a field. Now we turn our attention to ways of acting, or performing operations, on values in fields.

Assignment   We can set or change the value of a variable through an assignment statement. For example,

```
lastName = "Lincoln";
```

assigns the string value "Lincoln" to the variable lastName (that is, it stores the sequence of characters "Lincoln" into the memory associated with the variable named lastName).

Here's the syntax template for an assignment statement:

Assignment-Statement

Variable = Expression ;

Assignment statement A statement that stores the value of an expression into a variable

Expression An arrangement of identifiers, literals, and operators that can be evaluated to compute a value of a given type

Evaluate To compute a new value by performing a specified set of operations on given values

The semantics (meaning) of the assignment operator (=) are "is set equal to" or "gets"; the variable is *set equal to* the value of the expression. Any previous value in the variable is destroyed and replaced by the value of the expression. If you look back at the syntax for a field declaration, you can see that it uses the same syntax to assign an initial value to a field.

Only one variable can appear on the left side of an assignment statement. An assignment statement is *not* like a math equation ($x + y = z + 4$). Instead, the expression (what is on the right side of the assignment operator) is evaluated, and the resulting value is stored into the single variable on the left side of the assignment operator. A variable keeps its assigned value until another statement stores a new value into it.

Because you are accustomed to reading from left to right, the way that the assignment operator moves a value from right to left may at first seem awkward. Just remember to read the = as "is set equal to" or "gets"—then the process seems more natural.

The value assigned to a variable must be of the same type as the variable. Given the declarations

```
String  firstName;
String  middleName;
String  lastName;
String  title;
char    middleInitial;
char    letter;
```

the following assignment statements are valid:

```
firstName = "Abraham";       // String literal assigned to string variable
middleName = firstName;      // String variable assigned to string variable
middleName = "";             // String literal assigned to string variable
```

```
lastName = "Lincoln";        // String literal assigned to string variable
title = "President";         // String literal assigned to string variable
middleInitial = ' ';         // char literal assigned to char variable
myChar = 'B';                // char literal assigned to char variable
```

The following assignments are *not* valid:

Invalid Assignment Statement	Explanation
`middleInitial = "A.";`	`middleInitial` is of type `char`; `"A."` is a string
`myChar = firstName;`	`myChar` is of type `char`; `firstName` is of type `String`
`myChar = " ";`	`myChar` is of type `char`; `" "` is a one-character literal string
`firstName = Thomas;`	`Thomas` is an undeclared identifier
`"Edison" = lastName;`	Only a variable can appear to the left of =
`lastName = ;`	The expression to the right of = is missing

Figure 2.2 shows the variable `myChar` with the letter B stored in it.

String Expressions   Although we can't perform arithmetic on strings, Java provides the `String` class with a special string operation, called *concatenation*, that uses the + operator. Concatenating (joining) two strings yields a new string containing the characters from both strings. For example, given the statements

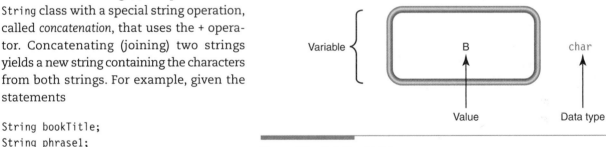

Figure 2.2   Variable with Value

```
String bookTitle;
String phrase1;
String phrase2;
```

```
phrase1 = "Introduction to Programming and Problem Solving ";
phrase2 = "with Java";
```

we could write

```
bookTitle = phrase1 + phrase2;
```

which results in `bookTitle` being set equal to the character string

```
"Introduction to Programming and Problem Solving with Java"
```

The order of the strings in the expression determines how they appear in the resulting string. If, for example, we write

```
bookTitle = phrase2 + phrase1;
```

then `bookTitle` is set equal to the string

```
"with JavaIntroduction to Programming and Problem Solving "
```

Concatenation works with named `String` constants and literal strings as well as `String` variables. For example, suppose we have declared the following constants:

```
final String WORD1 = "Introduction";
final String WORD3 = "Programming";
final String WORD5 = "with Java";
```

Then we could write the following statement to assign the title of this book to the variable `bookTitle`:

```
bookTitle = WORD1 + " to " + WORD3 + " and Problem Solving " + WORD5;
```

As a result, `bookTitle` is assigned the following string:

```
"Introduction to Programming and Problem Solving with Java"
```

The preceding example demonstrates how we can combine identifiers and literal strings in a concatenation expression. Of course, if we simply want to assign the complete string to `bookTitle`, we can do so directly:

```
bookTitle = "Introduction to Programming and Problem Solving with Java";
```

Occasionally, however, we need to assign a string literal that is too long to fit on one line. Then a concatenation expression is necessary, as in the following statement:

```
longSentence = "The Red-Wing Blackbird hovered precariously in the gusty " +
               "breeze as he tried to display his brilliant red and " +
               "yellow epaulets to his rival suitor. ";
```

Sometimes we may encounter a situation in which we want to add some characters to an existing string value. Suppose that `bookTitle` already contains `"Introduction to Programming"` and that we wish to complete the title. We could use a statement of the form

```
bookTitle = bookTitle + " and Problem Solving with Java";
```

This statement retrieves the value of `bookTitle` from memory, concatenates the string `" and Problem Solving with Java"` to form a new string, and then assigns the new string back to `bookTitle`. The new string replaces the old value of `bookTitle` (which is destroyed).

Concatenation works only with values of the class `String`. If we try to concatenate a value of one of Java's built-in types with a string, Java will automatically convert the value into an equivalent string and perform the concatenation. For example, the code segment

```
String result;
result = "The square of 12 is " + 144;
```

assigns the string `"The square of 12 is 144"` to the variable `result`. Java converts the integer literal 144 into the string `"144"` before performing the concatenation.

Initializer Expressions Now that we have defined expressions, we can generalize the field declaration syntax to allow for the use of an expression in initializing the field.

Field-Declaration

| Modifiers | Type-Name | Identifier | = | Expression | , | Identifier | = | Expression | ; |

The following declarations are, therefore, legal:

```
final String WORD1 = "Introduction";
final String WORD3 = "Java " + WORD1;
final String WORD5 = "Design " + WORD3;
```

They store `"Design Java Introduction"` as the value of the constant `WORD5`.

Assignment of Primitive Types Versus Objects

After reading the preceding discussion of assignment statements and expressions, you may wonder what really happens inside the computer when assignment occurs. For Java's primitive types that represent simple data values such as characters and numbers, the answer is straightforward: The value on the right side of the equals sign is stored in the memory location corresponding to the identifier on the left-hand side.

But what about objects such as strings? Surely they can't fit into a single memory location? The answer is no, they can't. So how does assignment work in that case?

Assignment of objects is done indirectly. A variable of the object data type contains a value that is the memory address where the actual object is stored. When Java needs to operate on an object, it uses the value stored in the variable to find the object in memory. This process takes place automatically, so we don't have to worry about it. With respect to assignment, however, it means that assigning one object variable to another works just the same as assigning one integer variable to another. The value contained in one variable is copied from its memory location into the location associated with the other variable. For an object, this value is an address in memory.

In later chapters we will return to this topic and note that it has some additional consequences. In the meantime, we will avoid situations where this issue might cause problems.

Background Information

◼ Beyond Minimalism: Adding Comments to Code

All you need to create a working application is the correct combination of declarations and executable statements. The compiler ignores comments, but this kind of documentation is of enormous help to anyone who must read the code. Comments can appear anywhere in your code except in the middle of an identifier, a reserved word, or a literal constant.

Java comments come in two forms. The first is any sequence of characters enclosed by the /*   */ pair. The compiler ignores anything within the pair. Here's an example:

```
String idNumber;    /* Identification number of the aircraft */
```

One special note about using this form of comment: When the first character of the comment is an asterisk, the comment has a special meaning that indicates it should be used by an automatic documentation generation program called *javadoc*. For the time being, as we do not discuss javadoc in this text, we recommend that you avoid comments that start with /**.

The second, and more common, form begins with two slashes (//) and extends to the end of that line of the program:

```
String idNumber;    // Identification number of the aircraft
```

The compiler ignores anything after the two slashes to the end of the line.

Writing fully commented code is good programming style. A comment should appear at the beginning of an application or class to explain what it does:

```
// This application computes the weight and balance of a Beechcraft
// Starship-1 airplane, given the amount of fuel, number of
// passengers, and weight of luggage in fore and aft storage.
// It assumes that there are two pilots and a standard complement
// of equipment, and that passengers weigh 170 pounds each.
```

Another good place for comments is in field declarations, where comments can explain how each identifier is used. In addition, they should introduce each major step in a long code segment and should explain anything that is unusual or difficult to read (for example, a lengthy formula).

You should keep your comments concise and arrange them in the code so that they are easy to see and it is clear what they document. If comments are too long or crowd the statements, they make the code more difficult to read—just the opposite of what you intended! In this text we use color to make the comments stand out from the rest of the Java code in our examples.

◼ Output

Have you ever asked someone, "Do you know what time it is?", only to have the person smile smugly and say, "Yes, I do"? This situation is like the one that currently exists between you and the computer. You now know enough Java syntax to tell the computer to assign values to variables and to concatenate strings, but the computer won't give you the results until you tell it to display them.

Early computers used printers to display their output. Older programming languages had output statements, such as *print* or *write*, that would type the contents of a variable or a constant on the printer. As technology advanced, printers were replaced by display screens, but output still appeared on the screen as if it was being typed by a printer, line by line. In the 1970s, computer scientists at the Xerox Palo Alto Research Center developed a new approach to output in which a program could display separate panels on the screen and print or draw on each panel independently. The panels, which were called windows, opened a new era in the design of user interfaces for computer programs.

Today, virtually every computer operating system supports a graphical user interface (GUI) based on windows. Such interfaces make it much easier for people to use programs, but they require more work on the part of the programmer than did the old-fashioned printer-style output. Because Java was developed after the GUI became the standard mechanism for interactive input and output, it includes built-in features that support the programming of a user interface. Even so, the programming of such a user interface can still be rather complicated, so we defer coverage of this topic until after we've explored more of the basics of programming. If you are curious about what is involved in GUI programming, you may peek ahead to Chapter 8.

Here we introduce a very simple way of writing messages on the screen that is similar to the technique used in older languages. To do so, we use a method call statement.

Calling Methods Methods (the operators associated with objects in the abstract sense) are implemented as subprograms that are called upon to perform some predefined set of actions. A **call** to a method is another form of executable statement in Java. We write the call statement simply by specifying the name of the method, followed by a list of **arguments** enclosed in parentheses. The call causes control of the computer to jump to the instructions in the method, which may use the values given to it as arguments. When the method has completed its task, control of the computer returns to the statement following the call.

Call A statement that causes a method to be executed; in Java we call a method by writing its name, followed by a list of arguments enclosed in parentheses

Argument An expression used for communicating values to a method

Here is the syntax template for a call statement:

Call

Method-Name (Argument , Argument ···) ;

As you examine the template, note that the arguments in a call are optional, but the parentheses are required. We often write call statements of the following form:

```
methodName();
```

A synonym for the term *call* is *invoke*. Saying that a method is invoked is another way of saying that it is called.

`print` and `println` Methods   Java provides an object that represents an output device—by default, the screen. We can send messages to this object, asking it to print something on the screen. The name of the object is `System.out` and the messages that we can send (the methods that we can apply) are `print` and `println`. For example,

```
System.out.print("Susy" + "  " + "Sunshine");
```

prints

```
Susy  Sunshine
```

in a window on the screen. There are several things to notice about this statement. The method is invoked (the message sent) by placing the method name next to the object name with a dot in between. The "something" to be printed is a string expression that serves as an argument to the method. Notice that the string appears within the parentheses. What do you think the next code fragment prints?

```
System.out.print("Susy");
System.out.print("  ");
System.out.print("Sunshine");
```

If you said that the two code fragments print the same thing, you would be correct. Successive messages sent via the `print` method print the strings next to each other on the same line. If you want to go to the next line after the string is printed, you use the `println` method. For example, the code fragment

```
System.out.println("Susy");
System.out.println("  ");
System.out.println("Sunshine");
```

prints

```
Susy

Sunshine
```

Note that the `println` method does not go to the next line until *after* the string is printed. The second line contains two blanks—it is not the empty string. We can print variables as well as literals. For example,

```
String myName = "Susy  Sunshine";
System.out.println(myName);
```

prints exactly the same thing on the screen as the statement

```
System.out.print("Susy  Sunshine");
```

There is a difference, however. If the latter statement (which uses the print method) is followed by another message to System.out, the next string would begin on the same line. If the former code (which uses the println method) is followed by another message to System.out, the next string would begin on the next line.

Input

An application needs data on which to operate. So far, we have written all of the data values into the code itself, in literal and named constants. If this technique was the only way we could enter data, we would have to rewrite our code each time we wanted to apply it to a different set of values. In this section we look at ways of entering data into an application while it is running.

One of the biggest advantages associated with computers is that an application can be used with many different sets of data. To do so, the data must be kept separate from the code until the code executes. Then method calls in the code can copy values from the data set into variables in the application. After storing these values in the variables, the code can perform calculations with them (see Figure 2.3).

The process of placing values from an outside data set into variables in an application is called input. The data for the application can come from an input device or from a file on an auxiliary storage device. We will look at file input in detail in Chapter 5; here we consider only the standard input window, represented by the object System.in.

Unfortunately, Java doesn't make it quite as simple to input data from System.in as it does to output data to System.out. System.in is a very primitive object that is designed to serve as the basis for building more sophisticated objects. With System.in, we can

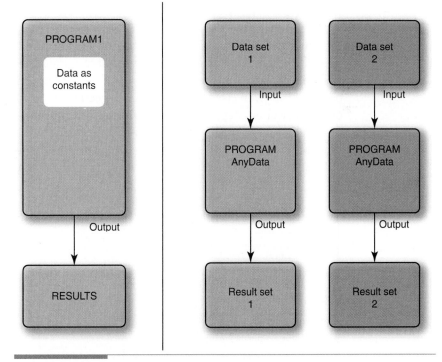

Figure 2.3 Separating the Data from Code

input a single byte or a series of bytes (recall from Chapter 1 that a byte is eight binary bits). To be useful to us, this data must be converted to a string.

This problem sounds like a good opportunity to apply means-ends analysis. We look through the Java library documentation and find a class called `BufferedReader` that provides a method called `readLine`, which returns a string that it gets from an object of the class `Reader`. However, `System.in` is an object of the class `InputStream`. We're part of the way to our solution; now we just have to find a way to convert the input from an `InputStream` object so that it acts like a `Reader` object. Further searching in the library reveals a class called `InputStreamReader` that does precisely this.

Why do we need to take these steps? What do these conversions actually accomplish? `System.in` returns raw binary bytes of data. An `InputStreamReader` converts these bytes to the Unicode character set that Java uses. Because we don't want our input to be in the form of individual characters, we use a `BufferedReader` to convert the characters into a `String` value. Figure 2.4 illustrates this layering of classes.

In Figure 2.4, `System.in` is an object of the class `InputStream`—an instance of this class. What we need is an object of the class `InputStreamReader`. That is, we need to instantiate an object of the class `InputStreamReader`. Earlier we said that we use the `new` operator to instantiate objects. To do so, we write the reserved word `new`, followed by the name of a class, followed by an argument list. For example:

```
InputStreamReader inStream;              // A variable of class InputStreamReader
inStream = new InputStreamReader(System.in);
```

The code following `new` looks very much like a method call. In fact, it is a call to a special kind of method called a constructor. Every class has at least one constructor method. The purpose of a constructor is to prepare a new object for use. The `new` operator creates an empty object of the given class and then calls the constructor, which can fill in fields of the object or take any other steps needed to make the object usable. For example, the preceding code first creates an object of the class `InputStreamReader` that is prepared to use `System.in` as its input source. The new object is then assigned to the variable `inStream`. Constructors are called only via the `new` operator; we cannot write them as normal method calls.

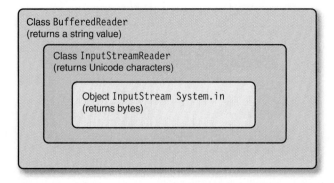

Figure 2.4 Layering of Classes for Java Input

Constructors have a special feature that requires some further explanation. The call to the constructor method isn't preceded by an object name or a class name as in the case for `System.out.print`, for example. If you stop to consider that the constructor creates an object *before* it is assigned to a field, you realize that it can't be associated with a particular object name. We don't have to precede the constructor name with the class name because its name already tells Java to which class it belongs.

The capitalization of a constructor doesn't follow our usual rule of starting each method name with a lowercase letter. By convention, all class names in the Java library begin with an uppercase letter, and the constructor name *must* be spelled exactly the same as the name of the class that contains it.

The `BufferedReader` class has a constructor that takes an `InputStreamReader` object as an argument and prepares a `BufferedReader` object that uses the `InputStreamReader` object as its input source. Thus we can write

```
BufferedReader in;          // A variable of class BufferedReader
in = new BufferedReader(inStream);
```

We now have an object, assigned to the variable `in`, which is a `BufferedReader` that takes its input from `inStream`, which in turn takes its input from `System.in`.

We can shorten this process by nesting the constructor calls as follows:

```
in = new BufferedReader(new InputStreamReader(System.in));
```

This one statement has the same effect as writing

```
InputStreamReader inStream;          // A variable of class InputStreamReader
inStream = new InputStreamReader(System.in);
in = new BufferedReader(inStream);
```

Anonymous object An object that is instantiated but not assigned to an identifier and, therefore, lacks a name

It also avoids the need to declare a separate variable to hold the `InputStreamReader` object. The inner `new` operator still creates the object, but it is not assigned to a variable and, therefore, has no name. Objects that lack a name are said to be anonymous.

readLine   The class `BufferedReader` gives us another useful method, called `readLine`. Its name is descriptive of its function: The computer "reads" what we type into it on one line and returns the characters we type as a string. Here is an example of using `readLine`:

```
String oneLineOfTyping;                 // A variable of class String
oneLineOfTyping = in.readLine();
```

Notice that a call to `readLine` is quite different from a call to `println`. We call `println` as a separate statement:

```
System.out.println("A line of text to output.");
```

Value-returning method A method that is called from within an expression and returns a value that can be used in the expression

Void method A method that is called as a separate statement; when it returns, processing continues with the next statement

In contrast, readLine is called from within an expression. Java supports two kinds of methods: value-returning methods and void methods. They are distinguished by how they are called. readLine, a value-returning method, is called within an expression. When it returns, a value that it has computed takes its place in the expression and can be used for assignment or further computation. println, a void method, doesn't return a value. We call it as a separate statement and, when it has finished, execution picks up with the statement that follows it.

◼ Interactive Input and Output

When an application inputs and outputs values that a human user supplies and reads, it performs interactive input/output. To make the application more user-friendly, the programmer has to consider additional information that the user needs beyond the raw input and output. For example, the user must be prompted to enter values; otherwise, he or she won't know when or where to type the input. When the application outputs its results, it must label them so that they are meaningful. Labeling output also helps the user to distinguish among different values displayed by the application.

The following code segment inputs the three parts of a name, using System.out.print to display a prompting message for each input value:

```
System.out.print("Enter first name: ");       // Prompt for first name
first = in.readLine();                         // Get first name
System.out.print("Enter last name: ");         // Prompt for last name
last = in.readLine();                          // Get last name
System.out.print("Enter middle initial: ");    // Prompt for middle initial
middle = in.readLine();                        // Get middle initial
```

The next code segment outputs the name with System.out.println, using a label to indicate what is displayed:

```
System.out.println("You entered the name: " +
                first + " " + middle + ". " + last);
```

When an application outputs data that has just been entered, it confirms to the user that the data was typed correctly or indicates that an error occurred. This kind of input–output sequence is known as *echo printing.*

2.2 Application Construction

So far in this chapter, we have looked at the basic elements of Java code: identifiers, declarations, variables, constants, expressions, assignment statements, method calls, input, output, and comments. Now let's see how to collect these elements into an application. A Java application is a class containing class declarations: fields and methods. For the class to be a Java application, one of the methods must be named main. Execution of the Java application begins in the main method.

We have already shown the template for a field declaration, so let's look at the declaration of a method. A method declaration consists of the method heading and its body, which is delimited by left and right braces. The following syntax template represents the declaration of a void method (the kind that main must be). We examine the declaration of value-returning methods later in this chapter.

Method-Declaration

Modifiers void Identifier (Parameter List)
{
    Statement ...
}

Here's an example of an application with just one method, the main method. Note that the programmer selects the name for the application class; we chose PrintName. Because an application is a class, we begin the name with an uppercase P.

```java
//*************************************************************************
// PrintName application
// This application inputs a name and prints it in two different formats
//*************************************************************************
import java.io.*;                    // Package for stream readers
public class PrintName
{
  public static void main(String[] args) throws IOException
  {
    String first;                    // Person's first name
    String last;                     // Person's last name
    String middle;                   // Person's middle initial
    String firstLast;                // Name in first-last format
    String lastFirst;                // Name in last-first format
    BufferedReader in;               // Input stream for strings

    in = new BufferedReader(new InputStreamReader(System.in));
    System.out.print("Enter first name: ");        // Prompt for first name
    first = in.readLine();                          // Get first name
    System.out.print("Enter last name: ");         // Prompt for last name
    last = in.readLine();                           // Get last name
    System.out.print("Enter middle initial: ");    // Prompt for middle initial
    middle = in.readLine();                         // Get middle initial
    firstLast = first + " " + last;                 // Generate first format
    System.out.println("Name in first-last format is " + firstLast);
    lastFirst = last + ", " + first + ", ";         // Generate second format
    System.out.println("Name in last-first-initial format is " +
                  lastFirst + middle + ".");
  }
}
```

The application begins with a comment that explains what it does. Next comes an import declaration that tells the compiler we will use input and output classes (for example, BufferedReader) from the java.io package.

The import declaration is followed by the class heading, which begins with the modifier public. Recall that we use public to make the class accessible to the JVM. If you look a little farther down in the application, you see that the heading of the main method also begins with public. The JVM must also be able to find main to start execution there. In later chapters, we will encounter situations where we want to limit access to a field, method, or class. We do so by using the modifier private. If we used the private modifier with main, then the method would be invisible to the JVM and it wouldn't know where to start.

The class heading is followed by an open brace that begins the body of the class. The class contains the method declaration for the main method. The first line of the method is its heading. There are several points to emphasize regarding the method heading. Let's take another look.

```
public static void main(String[] args) throws IOException
```

We've already said that the public modifier is needed to make main visible to the JVM. The keyword static is another modifier that we will wait to explain more fully. The keyword void identifies main as a void method rather than a value-returning method. Of course, main is just the name of the method. Between the parentheses are the method's parameters. Parameters are declarations of special variables to which arguments are passed when the method is called. That is, the values we place in the argument list of a method call are copied to the parameter variables in the method.

The parameter to main is an array of strings called args. (We explain arrays in Chapter 10.) If we omitted the brackets following String, then the parameter would just be a string called args. Adding the brackets tells Java that multiple strings may be passed to main. Who would call main, and what values would they pass to it? When PrintName is run as an application, the operating system calls it. Some operating systems (such as Unix) allow the user to enter argument values that are passed to the application when it begins execution. In that case, the application finds those values stored in the array of strings called args. We do not use such arguments in this book, but Java still requires us to supply this specific parameter in the heading of main. For now, you can just memorize this part of the heading and use it in your applications.

At the end of the heading is a throws clause. In many Java methods, when an unusual situation arises that cannot be handled within the method, the application indicates the situation to the caller by throwing an **exception**. In Chapter 9, we will explore how to throw exceptions and see how to use a catch statement to respond to an exception. For example, if readLine finds too many characters on one line to store into a string, it throws an IOException. Java requires that whenever a method can throw an exception, we must either catch it or explicitly throw it to the next level. For this reason, main must explicitly indicate, using a throws clause, that it is using a method that can throw an IOException. Then, if such an exception occurs, the exception is passed up to the JVM and eventually the operating system outputs a message saying that the application terminated with an unusual condition.

Exception An unusual condition that is indicated by a method using a throw statement; the method's caller must either catch the exception or explicitly throw it to the next level

The body of the method contains declarations of five `String` variables (`first`, `last`, `middle`, `firstLast`, and `lastFirst`), a `BufferedReader` variable (`in`), and a list of executable statements. The compiler translates these executable statements into Bytecode instructions. During the execution phase, these instructions are executed.

Note that neither the `public` nor the `private` modifier precedes the fields declared within `main`. Fields declared inside the body of a method are *local* to that method, which means that they are accessible only within the method. Thus there is no need to explicitly specify that they are `private`, and they cannot be made `public`. In fact, the only modifier allowed in a local declaration is `final`.

Notice how we use spacing in the `PrintName` application to make it easy for someone else to read. We use blank lines to separate statements into related groups, and we indent the entire body of the class and the `main` method. The compiler doesn't require us to format the code this way; we do so only to make it more readable. We will have more to say in subsequent chapters about formatting code.

Here is what the program displays on the screen when it executes:

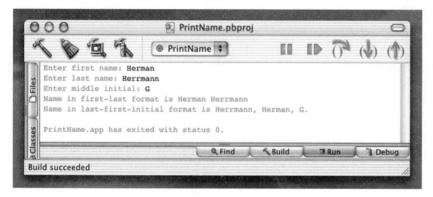

Blocks

The body of a method is an example of a *block*. The syntax template for a block is as follows:

Block

A block is just a sequence of zero or more statements enclosed (delimited) by a {} pair. Now we can redefine a method declaration as a heading followed by a block:

Method-Declaration

```
Heading
Block
```

In later chapters, we will define the syntax of a heading in greater detail. In the case of the `main` method, Heading is simply

```
public static void main(String[] args)
```

and may include a `throws` clause, such as

```
throws IOException
```

if the body contains exception-throwing method calls.

Here is the syntax template for a statement, limited to the Java statements discussed in this chapter:

Statement

```
┌─ Null-Statement
│  Local-Field-Declaration
│  Assignment-Statement
│  Method-Call
└─ Block
```

A statement can be empty (the *null statement*). The null statement is just a semicolon (;) and looks like this:

```
;
```

It does absolutely nothing at execution time; execution just proceeds to the next statement. It is rarely used.

As the syntax template shows, a statement also can be a field declaration, an executable statement, or even a block. In the latter case, we see that we can use an entire block wherever a single statement is allowed. In later chapters, when we introduce the syntax for branching and looping structures, this fact will prove very important.

We use blocks often, especially as parts of other statements. Leaving out a {} pair can dramatically change the meaning as well as the execution of an application. That explains why we always indent the statements inside a block—the indentation makes a block easy to spot in a long, complicated section of code.

Notice that the syntax templates for the block and the statement do not mention semicolons. Yet the `PrintName` application contains many semicolons. If you look back at the templates for a field declaration, assignment statement, and method call, you can see that a semicolon is required at the end of each kind of statement. The syntax template for a block, however, shows no semicolon after the right brace. The rule for using semicolons in Java, then, is quite simple: Terminate each statement *except* a block with a semicolon.

One more thing about blocks and statements: According to the syntax template for a statement, a field declaration is officially considered to be a statement. A declaration, therefore, can appear wherever an executable statement can. In a block, we can mix declarations and executable statements if desired, but the declaration of any item must come before the item is used.

```
{
  char ch;                        // Declaration
  ch = 'A';
  System.out.println(ch);
  String str;                     // Declaration
  str = "Hello";
  System.out.println(str);
}
```

In this book, we group the declarations together because we think it is easier to read and, therefore, better style.

```
{
  // Declarations
  char  ch;
  String str;
  // Executable statements
  ch = 'A';
  System.out.println(ch);
  str = "Hello";
  System.out.println(str);
}
```

2.3 Application Entry, Correction, and Execution

Once you have an application written down on paper, you must enter it into the computer on the keyboard. In this section, we examine the code entry process in general. You should consult the manual for your particular computer to learn any computer-specific details.

■ Entering Application Code

The first step in entering code is to get the computer's attention. With a personal computer, this usually means turning it on. Workstations connected to a network are usually left running all the time. You must *log on* to such a machine to get its attention, which involves entering a user name and a password. The password system protects information that you've stored in the computer from being tampered with or destroyed by someone else.

Once the computer is ready to accept your commands, you tell it that you want to enter code by running the editor. The editor is an application that allows you to create and modify code by entering information into an area of the computer's secondary storage called a file.

File A named area in secondary storage that is used to hold a collection of data; the collection of data itself

A file in a computer system is like a file folder in a filing cabinet—a collection of data that has a name associated with it. You usually choose the name for the file when you create it with the editor. From that point on, you refer to the file by the name you've given it. The Java compiler requires that files containing Java code have the suffix .java.

So many different types of editors exist, each with different features, that we can't begin to describe them all here. We can, however, describe some of their general characteristics.

The basic unit of information in an editor is a display screen full of characters. The editor lets you change anything that you see on the screen.

When you create a new file, the editor clears the screen to show you that the file is empty. You then enter your program, using the mouse and keyboard to go back and make corrections as necessary. Figure 2.5 shows an example of an editor's display screen.

```
//**********************************************************
// NameDriver application
// This application inputs a name and prints it in
// two different formats
//**********************************************************
import java.io.*;                    //Package for stream readers
public class NameDriver
{
  static class Name
  {
    String first;                    // Person's first name
    String last;                     // Person's last name
    String middle;                   // Person's middle initial

    public Name() throws IOException //Gets a name from System.in
    {
      BufferedReader in;                        //Input stream for strings
      //Instantiate in using System.in
      in = new BufferedReader(new InputStreamReader(System.in));
      System.out.print("Enter first name: ");   //Prompt for first name
      first = in.readLine();                     //Get first name
      System.out.print("Enter last name: ");     //Prompt for last name
      last = in.readLine();                      //Get last name
      System.out.print("Enter middle initial: "); //Prompt for middle initial
      middle = in.readLine();                    //Get middle initial
    }
```

Figure 2.5 Display Screen for an Editor

Compiling and Running an Application

Once your application is stored in a file, you compile it by issuing a command to run the Java compiler. The compiler translates the application and then stores the Bytecode version into a new file. Sometimes, the compiler may display a window with messages indicating errors in the application. Some systems let you click on an error message to automatically position the cursor in the editor window at the point where the error was detected.

If the compiler finds errors in your application (*syntax errors*), you must determine their cause, return to the editor and fix them, and then run the compiler again. Once your application compiles without errors, you can run (execute) it.

Some systems automatically run an application when it compiles successfully. On other systems, you must issue a separate command to run the application. Whatever series of commands your system uses, the result is the same: Your application is loaded into memory and executed by the JVM.

Even though an application runs, it still may have errors in its design. After all, the computer does exactly what you tell it to do, even if that's not what you intended. If your application doesn't do what it should (a *logic error*), you must revise the algorithm, and then go to the editor and fix the code. Finally, you compile and run the code again. This *debugging* process is repeated until the application works as planned (see Figure 2.6).

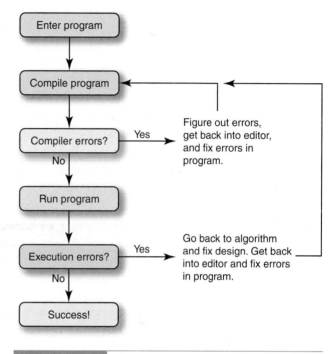

Figure 2.6 The Debugging Process

Finishing Up

On a workstation, once you finish working on your code, you have to *log off* by typing the appropriate command. This practice frees up the workstation so that someone else can use it. It also prevents someone from walking up after you leave and tampering with your files.

On a personal computer, when you're done working, you save your files and quit the editor. Turning off the power wipes out what's in the computer's short-term memory, but your files remain stored safely on disk. It is a wise precaution to periodically make a copy of your code files on a removable diskette. When a disk in a computer suffers a hardware failure, it is impossible to retrieve your files. Having a backup copy on a diskette enables you to restore your files to the disk once it is repaired.

Be sure to read the manual for your particular system and editor before you enter your first application. Don't panic if you have trouble at first—almost everyone does. The process becomes much easier with practice. That's why it's a good idea to practice first with an application such as PrintName, where mistakes don't matter—unlike in homework programming assignments!

2.4 Classes and Methods

We've now seen how to write an application class that has just the required method, main. This kind of coding resembles the process of coding programs that were written in older languages that lacked support for object-oriented programming. Of course, as problem complexity grows, the number of declarations and executable statements also grows. Eventually, applications may become so immense that it is nearly impossible to maintain them. To avoid this complexity, we can break the problem up into classes that are small enough to be easily understood and that we can test and debug independently. In this section we see how to declare classes other than an application class, and methods other than main.

■ User Classes

All of the syntax that we've seen for declaring application classes applies for declaring non-application classes as well. The only differences are that the latter classes do not contain a main method, and for now we won't use the public modifier. Java permits an application to have just one public class. In a later chapter we will see how to create our own packages, like java.io; with such packages, we can bundle together a collection of public classes. Within a single application, however, the only class that can be public is the one that contains main.

As an example, let's consider creating a class called Name that provides the responsibilities needed by the PrintName application. Then we can simplify main, gaining some experience with object-oriented programming style along the way. What would we like Name to do? It would be nice to have it get a name from the user, store the name internally, and provide methods that return the name in the different formats.

From our prior experience (looking for things that are familiar), we know that the class needs fields to hold the parts of the name. Here's what we now know we need:

```
class Name
{
  String first;          // Person's first name
  String last;           // Person's last name
  String middle;         // Person's middle initial
}
```

The class should have a method for each of its responsibilities. In this case, we need a method to get a name from the user, another to return the name in the first format, and a third to return the name in the second format. It looks as though we're ready to take a closer look at writing methods.

Methods

We've already seen that a method consists of a method heading plus a block that can contain declarations and executable statements. Between the parentheses in a method heading are the method's parameters. We will examine the syntax of parameters in more detail in a later chapter. For now, simply recognize that a parameter is made up of two parts: a data type or class name, and an identifier (just like a field declaration).

Whereas field declarations end with a semicolon, parameters are listed between the parentheses with commas separating them. For now, we can think of the parameters as a special kind of local field within the method. When a method is called, the arguments from the method call are copied into the method's parameters.

Here's an example of a method heading, showing a list of three parameters.

```
void prepareName(String arg1, String arg1, char arg3)
```

A call to such a method would contain three arguments: two strings and a character, in that order. For example:

```
prepareName("Herrmann", "Herman", 'G')
```

The arguments are copied into the parameter variables one-for-one, in the order listed, as shown here:

```
void prepareName(String arg1, String arg1, char arg3)
```

```
             prepareName("Herrmann", "Herman", 'G')
```

Method Call or Invocation   Let's take a closer look at how we call a method and what happens when we do so. We've already used the `print` and `println` methods to display strings on the screen. Using object-oriented terminology, we sent messages to `System.out`. Technically, we *called* the methods. A method call may or may not have to be appended to an object or class identifier with a dot in between. (We will explain these different forms of a call statement shortly.) The arguments to `print` and `println` were the strings to be displayed; the method names were appended to the object identifier `System.out`.

A call causes control of the computer to jump to the instructions in the method, which may make use of the argument values that are copied into its parameters. When the method completes its task, control of the computer returns to the statement following the call.

Here is the syntax template for a call statement:

Call

Object-Name . Method-Name (argument , argument···) ;

In Java, methods come in four flavors: instance methods, class methods, helper methods, and constructors. Instance methods are associated with individual objects. Class (`static`) methods, like `main`, are associated with classes. Helper, or auxiliary, methods are subprograms within a class that help other methods in the class. Constructors, as discussed earlier, are used with the `new` operator to prepare an object for use.

Instance Methods   When we create an object of a given class, it usually has several fields associated with it. Each object of the class has its own set of these fields, called instance fields. Because we can have more than one object of a given class, we must designate to which object the method will be applied, so that the method can access the fields of that particular object. Stated in object-oriented terms, we must designate to which object the message is being sent. The object name is appended in front of the method name with a dot in between. In the call

```
System.out.println("Good morning.");
```

`System.out` is the name of the object to which the `println` method is applied.

Most of our methods are instance methods. Their headings are written without any special modifiers. For example:

```
public void updateLastName(String lastName)
```

The use of `public` here indicates that we can use the method outside of its class. Because the class is declared within an application class, "outside" means that it can be accessed by `main`. It is not public beyond the application class, so it is not visible to the JVM.

Class Methods   When we declare a method with the `static` modifier, it belongs to the class rather than to objects of that class. Hence it is called a **class method**. Here's an example of a class method heading:

Class method   A method that belongs to a class rather than its object instances; identified as such with the `static` modifier

Class field   A field that belongs to a class rather than its object instances; identified as such with the `static` modifier

```
public static void setNameFormat(String format)
```

What does it mean for a method to belong to a class? Such a method is independent of all objects instantiated from the class. It does not have access to the fields of the objects, but rather has access only to those fields that are likewise declared with the `static` modifier. Such fields are called **class fields**. Instance methods have access to both instance fields (fields declared without the `static` modifier) and class fields.

To call a class method, we append its name to the class identifier instead of an object identifier. We can use a class method to specify properties that are common to all objects. For example, in a Date class, where we can format a date for output in multiple ways, we might have a method that specifies the format to use for all date objects:

```
Date.setDefaultFormat(Date.MONTH_DAY_YEAR);
```

You may have noticed that the argument in this call is a constant that is also appended to the class name. This argument exemplifies the use of a class field. The Date class provides us with constants representing the different date formats that we can use as arguments to its methods.

Helper Methods   Helper methods are declared privately within a class. They are used in complex classes to help organize the code or to provide operations that are used only internally to the class. Thus helper methods are called from within other methods of the class. A call to a helper method is not appended to an object or class identifier because it is clear which class it is in, and it is not associated with any specific object. We won't use helper methods until much later in this book.

Constructors   We use essentially the same syntax for a constructor as for any other method, but with two special differences: (1) the method name is identical to the class name and (2) there is no void keyword. Constructors are almost always declared as public; a private constructor would be nearly useless because it could be called only from within the class. Here is an example constructor heading for a class called Name:

```
public Name(String firstName, String lastName, String middleInit)
```

Value-Returning Methods   All of the method headings we've examined so far have been for void methods or constructors. Java also supports value-returning methods. Let's see how they differ from void methods.

Value-returning methods are called from within expressions and can be instance methods, class methods, or helper methods. Constructors are neither void methods nor value-returning methods; they are a special case that is separate from the other kinds of methods.

The same rules apply for writing a method call, whether it is void or value-returning. The only difference relates to where the call appears (in an expression or as a separate statement). For an instance method, we append the method name to the object name with a dot in between. For a class method, we append the method name to the class name with a dot separating them. We call a helper method simply by using its name. Here are example calls:

```
nameString = myName.firstLast();   // Instance call; myName in an object
formatString = Name.getFormat();   // Class call; Name is the class name
initialchar = getInitial(middle);  // Helper call; used inside of Name class only
```

As you might guess, the heading for a value-returning method omits the reserved word void. In its place we write the name of a class or a primitive type. Here is an example of a heading for a value-returning instance method called firstLast that takes no parameters and returns a string. Notice that the absence of the static modifier makes it be an instance method.

```
public String firstLast() // Public method; returns a string; has no parameters
```

There is one other difference between value-returning and void methods that appears in the method body. We must indicate the value to be returned through the use of a return statement. The syntax of the return statement is simple:

Return-Statement

```
return expression ;
```

Let's look at a complete value-returning method by finishing the definition of the instance method firstLast. The following code assumes that the fields first, last, and middle are string variables declared as instance fields in the enclosing Name class:

```
public String firstLast() // Returns name in first-last format
{
    return first + " " + last;
}
```

Is that it? Yes, matters really are that simple. In fact, many value-returning methods are equally as simple. They are often used as a way to provide a shorthand notation for a formula. One characteristic of the object-oriented programming style is that we use many short methods as a means of building up a level of abstraction that simplifies the coding of larger problems. If we hide all of the details within classes and their methods, then the final solution can be coded in a way that is simple and easy to understand, and thus easy to debug and maintain. We call this kind of hiding *encapsulation,* and we discuss the underlying concepts further in Chapter 4.

Now that we've seen how to write methods and classes, let's go through the process of building an object-oriented version of PrintName. We'll do so in the context of a case study.

DISPLAY A NAME IN MULTIPLE FORMATS

Problem: You are beginning to work on a problem that needs to output names in several formats. To start, you decide to write a short Java application that inputs a single name and displays it in a variety of formats, so you can be certain that all of your string expressions are correct.

Input: The name in three parts, as input via System.in:
    First
    Last
    Middle Initial

Output: The input name in two formats:
    First Last
    Last, First, Middle Initial.

Discussion: You could easily just type the name in the two formats as string literals in the code, but the purpose of this exercise is to develop and test the string expressions you need for the larger problem. We also know that a Name is an object in that problem, so we should develop such an object from the beginning.

Because you plan to use the same expressions in the full application, you decide that this preliminary application should implement a Name class that provides a constructor to input the name as well as value-returning methods that provide the name in the two formats. Then you can reuse the class in the full application, which will keep this application very simple.

A name consists of three parts: first name, last name, and middle initial. These parts become the fields in the class. Here is the algorithmic solution:

```
Define Fields
String first
String last
String middle
```

As we noted in our earlier discussion, three methods are associated with this class: a constructor and two value-returning methods. Let's look first at the constructor. We know that it must be called Name. Its job is to input the name from System.in. To do so, it must first instantiate a BufferedReader, then prompt for input of each of the three parts and read each part via the BufferedReader.

CASE STUDY

Name Constructor

```
Define a BufferedReader in
Instantiate a BufferedReader using an InputStreamReader using System.in, and
    assign it to in
Prompt for first name on System.out
Get first name from in
Prompt for last name on System.out
Get last name from in
Prompt for middle initial on System.out
Get middle initial from in
```

Our two value-returning methods use straightforward string expressions that are identical to those in the original problem.

First Last Format

```
return first + " " + last
```

Last First Middle Format

```
return last + ", " + first + ", " + middle + "."
```

We are now ready to write the code for the class. What about the application? Our application is really just meant to test the class. Software engineers refer to such a test application as a *driver*.

Name Driver

```
Define a Name testName
Instantiate a Name object and assign it to testName
Print First Last Format
Print Last First Middle Format
```

It's hard to believe that the `main` method has been reduced to just four steps, but that's the beauty of object-oriented programming.

Now we're ready to write the whole application. We also include comments as necessary.

```java
//*****************************************************************
// NameDriver application
// This application inputs a name and prints it in
// two different formats
//*****************************************************************
import java.io.*;                        // Package for stream readers
public class NameDriver
{
  static class Name
  {
    String first;                        // Person's first name
```

```
    String last;                        // Person's last name
    String middle;                      // Person's middle initial

    public Name() throws IOException    // Gets a name from System.in
    {
      BufferedReader in;                           // Input stream for strings
      // Instantiate in using System.in
      in = new BufferedReader(new InputStreamReader(System.in));
      System.out.print("Enter first name: ");      // Prompt for first name
      first = in.readLine();                        // Get first name
      System.out.print("Enter last name: ");        // Prompt for last name
      last = in.readLine();                         // Get last name
      System.out.print("Enter middle initial: ");   // Prompt for middle initial
      middle = in.readLine();                        // Get middle initial
    }

    public String firstLastFormat ()              // Returns name in first-last format
    {
      return first + " " + last;
    }

    public String lastFirstMiddleFormat()         // Returns name as last, first, m.
    {
      return last + ", " + first + ", " + middle + ".";
    }
  } // End of Name Class

  // Driver for testing Name class
  public static void main(String[] args) throws IOException
  {
    Name testName;                                     // Declare a name
    testName = new Name();                             // Instantiate a name
    System.out.println("Name in first-last format is " +
                  testName.firstLastFormat());         // First format
    System.out.println("Name in last-first-initial format is " +
                  testName.lastFirstMiddleFormat());   // Second format
  }
}
```

The output from the program follows:

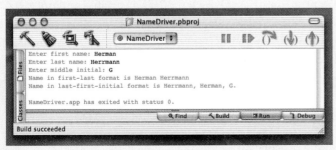

This application does exactly what the original version did, yet it is longer. In some ways it seems like a waste to make this extra effort. The advantage, however, is that now we have a Name class that we can use in other applications. We also have the ability to instantiate multiple names just by adding declarations and constructor calls to the application. To add another format, we could simply write another method as part of the class and add another statement to the driver. The object-oriented version is much easier to reuse, to maintain, and to extend. The original version had fewer lines of code, but was monolithic in its construction, and thus solved one specific problem. The object-oriented version is divided into useful pieces that can be applied to solve many different problems. We've done a little more work now, but have potentially saved much more work in the future.

2.5 Testing and Debugging

Testing and Debugging Hints

1. You must declare every identifier that isn't a Java reserved word. If you use a name that hasn't been declared, you will receive an error message.

2. If you try to declare an identifier that is the same as a reserved word in Java, you will receive an error message from the compiler. See Appendix A for a list of reserved words.

3. Java is a case-sensitive language, so two identifiers that are capitalized differently are treated as different identifiers. The word main and all Java reserved words use only lowercase letters.

4. Check for mismatched quotes in char and String literals. Each char literal begins and ends with an apostrophe (single quote). Each String literal begins and ends with a double quote.

5. Use only the apostrophe (') to enclose char literals. Most keyboards include a reverse apostrophe (`) that is easily confused with the apostrophe. If you use the reverse apostrophe, the compiler will issue an error message.

6. To use a double quote within a literal string, use the two symbols \" in a row. If you use just a double quote, it ends the string, and the compiler then sees the remainder of the string as an error. Similarly, to write a single quote in a char literal, use the two symbols \' without any space between them (that is, '\'' is the char literal for a single quote).

7. In an assignment statement, make sure that the identifier to the left of = is a variable and not a named constant.

8. In assigning a value to a String variable, the expression to the right of = must be a String expression or a literal string.

9. In a concatenation expression, at least one of the two operands of + must be of the class String.

10. Make sure your statements end with semicolons (except blocks, which do not have a semicolon after the right brace).

11. On most Java systems, the file name that holds the program must be the same as the name of the class, but with the extension .java. For example, the program NameDriver is stored in a file called NameDriver.java. Using another name will produce an error message from the compiler.

12. Be careful when using the /* */ pair to delimit comments. If you forget the */, then everything that follows until the end of the next /* */ comment (or the end of your program) will be treated as a comment. Also, remember to avoid starting comments of this form with two asterisks (/**) because comments of that form are used by the javadoc program.

13. Confirm that every open brace ({) in your program is matched by a close brace (}) in the appropriate place. Braces determine the beginning and end of blocks in Java, and their placement affects the structure of the program. Similarly, it is always wise to confirm that parentheses are used in matched pairs in your program.

14. Instantiate instances of every class variable by using new.

15. When instantiating an object in an argument list, include the new operator before the class name.

16. Objects to which methods are being applied must have the method name appended to the object name with a dot in between.

17. Be clear about which methods are class methods and which are instance methods. When you call a class method, its name is appended to the name of the class. When you call an instance method, its name is appended to an object identifier.

18. Make sure that the application class and main are public, and that any user classes are not public.

19. Include the throws clause in the heading of any method that uses readLine.

Summary

The syntax (grammar) of the Java language is defined by a metalanguage. In this book, we use a form of metalanguage called syntax templates. We describe the semantics (meaning) of Java statements in English.

Identifiers are used in Java to name things. Some identifiers, called reserved words, have predefined meanings in the language; others are created by the programmer. The identifiers you invent are restricted to those *not* reserved by the Java language. (Reserved words are listed in Appendix A.)

Identifiers are associated with memory locations through declarations. A declaration may give a name to a location whose value does not change (a constant)

Learning Portfolio

or to a location whose value can change (a variable). Every constant and variable has an associated data type or class. Java provides many predefined data types and classes. In this chapter, we examined the `char` type and the `String` class. A class contains fields and methods that describe the behavior of an object. An object is an instance of the class that describes it.

You use the assignment operator to change the value of a variable by assigning the value of an expression to it. At execution time, the expression is evaluated and the result is stored into the variable. With the `String` class, the plus sign (+) is an operator that concatenates two strings. A string expression can concatenate any number of strings to form a new `String` value.

Simple output to the screen is accomplished by using the `System.out` object that is provided in Java. Two methods are defined on this object: `print` and `println`. `System.out.print("A string")` prints whatever is between the parentheses on the screen. `println` behaves in exactly the same way as `print`, except that `println` goes to the next line after it finishes the printing. Simple input is not so simple in Java, however; it requires that we filter the input from `System.in` first through an `InputStreamReader` and then a `BufferedReader`, which enables us to input a line of typing as a string value. (We defer the use of a graphical user interface until Chapter 8.)

A Java application is a `public` class containing one or more class declarations, which are fields and methods. One of the methods *must* be named `main`. Execution of an application class always begins with the `main` method. User classes may also be included in the application class, but cannot be `public`.

A class begins with `import` declarations and a heading, then a block containing class declarations of fields and methods. Methods are declared with a heading and a block. Four types of methods exist: instance methods, class methods, helper methods, and constructors. Each type of method is called with its name and an argument list, but preceded by an object name, a class name, nothing, or `new`, respectively. A constructor is called when an object is instantiated via the `new` operator, and its name is the same as the name of the class.

Quick Check

1. What is syntax? (p. 42)
2. Why do we write meaningful identifiers in our code? (p. 48)
3. What is stored in a variable that is of a primitive type? (p. 63)
4. How does a class in Java differ from a class in the abstract sense? (pp. 50–51)
5. How do objects in the general sense differ from objects in Java? (pp. 50–51)
6. Is `char` an object or a primitive type? (pp. 48–50)
7. What distinguishes a named constant from a variable field? (pp. 57–58)
8. When an object is assigned to a variable, what is actually stored there? (p. 63)

9. What happens when a void method is called? (pp. 65–66)

10. What are the essential components of a Java application? (pp. 70–75)

11. What distinguishes the heading of a void method from a value-returning method syntactically? (pp. 81–82)

12. Use the following syntax template to decide whether your last name is a valid Java identifier. (pp. 46–47)

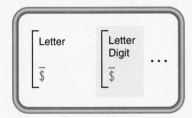

13. Write a Java constant declaration that gives the name ZED to the value 'Z'. (pp. 57–58)

14. Declare a char variable named letter and a String variable named street. (pp. 54–56)

15. Assign the value "Elm" to the String variable street. (pp. 59–63)

16. Add the value " Street" to the value in street. (pp. 59–63)

17. What are the heading and body of a class? (pp. 70–75)

18. What are the heading and body of a void method? (pp. 78–79)

19. Write an output statement that displays the title of this book (*Introduction to Programming and Problem Solving with Java*) on System.out. (pp. 64–67)

20. Write a call to a constructor for the class Name. (pp. 68–69)

21. The following code is incorrect. Rewrite it, using correct comment syntax. (p. 64)

```
String address;    / Employee's street address,
                   / including apartment
```

22. What does the following code segment output on the screen? (pp. 64–67)

```
String str;
str = "Abraham";
System.out.println("The answer is " + str + "Lincoln");
```

Answers

1. Syntax is the set of rules that defines valid constructs in a programming language. **2.** Meaningful identifiers make the code easier to debug and maintain. **3.** The actual value of the primitive type is stored in the variable. **4.** A class in Java defines an object that can be instantiated. In the abstract sense, a class describes an object in a problem. **5.** Objects in Java represent objects in the general sense through code that simulates their behavior. **6.** It is a primitive type. **7.** The use of the reserved word `final`. **8.** The memory address where the object's data is stored. **9.** The argument values are copied into the parameter variables of the method and the method is executed. When it returns, execution resumes with the next statement. **10.** A public class containing a method named `main`. **11.** The use of the reserved word `void` instead of a class name or type name. **12.** Unless your last name is hyphenated, it probably is a valid Java identifier. **13.** `final char ZED = 'Z';`

14. `char letter;`
  `String street;`

15. `street = "Elm";` **16.** `street = street + " Street";` **17.** A class heading consists of modifiers, the reserved word `class`, and a name. The body is a block. **18.** A method heading consists of modifiers, the reserved word `void`, a name, and a parameter list. The body is a block.

19. `System.out.print("Introduction to Programming and Problem Solving with Java");`

20. `new Name()`

21. `String address;   // Employee's street address,`
  `                   // including apartment`

  or

  `String address;   /* Employee's street address,`
  `                      including apartment        */`

22. The answer is Abraham Lincoln

Exam Preparation Exercises

1. Mark the following identifiers either valid or invalid.

		Valid	Invalid
a.	item#1	_____	_____
b.	data	_____	_____
c.	y	_____	_____
d.	3Set	_____	_____
e.	PAY_DAY	_____	_____
f.	bin-2	_____	_____
g.	num5	_____	_____
h.	Sq Ft	_____	_____

2. Given these four syntax templates:

Dwit   Twitnit   Twit   Nit

mark the following "Dwits" as either valid or invalid.

		Valid	Invalid
a.	XYZ	_____	_____
b.	123	_____	_____
c.	X1	_____	_____
d.	23Y	_____	_____
e.	XY12	_____	_____
f.	Y2Y	_____	_____
g.	ZY2	_____	_____
h.	XY23X1	_____	_____

3. Match each of the following terms with the correct definition (1 through 15) given below. There is only one correct definition for each term.

_____ **a.** program   _____ **g.** variable

_____ **b.** algorithm   _____ **h.** constant

_____ **c.** compiler   _____ **i.** memory

_____ **d.** identifier   _____ **j.** syntax

_____ **e.** compilation phase   _____ **k.** semantics

_____ **f.** execution phase   _____ **l.** block

(1) A symbolic name made up of letters, digits, underscores, and dollar signs, but not beginning with a digit

(2) A place in memory where a data object that cannot be changed is stored

(3) A program that takes a program in a high-level language and translates it into machine code or Bytecode

(4) An input device

(5) The time spent planning a program

(6) Grammar rules

(7) A sequence of statements enclosed by braces

(8) Meaning

    (9) A program that translates assembly language instructions into machine code

   (10) When the compiled version of a program is being run

   (11) A place in memory where a data value that can be changed is stored

   (12) When a program in a high-level language is converted into machine code or Bytecode

   (13) A part of the computer that can hold both program and data

   (14) Instructions for solving a problem in a finite amount of time with a finite amount of data

   (15) Data type specifications and instructions used by a computer to solve a problem

4. Which of the following are reserved words and which are programmer-defined identifiers?

		Reserved	Programmer-Defined
a.	char	_____	_____
b.	sort	_____	_____
c.	INT	_____	_____
d.	new	_____	_____
e.	Public	_____	_____

5. Reserved words can be used as variable names. (True or False)?

6. In a Java application containing just one method, that method can be named either `main` or `Main`. (True or False?)

7. If `s1` and `s2` are `String` variables containing `"blue"` and `"bird"`, respectively, what does each of the following statements print?

   a. `System.out.println("s1 = " + s1 + "s2 = " + s2);`

   b. `System.out.println("Result:" + s1 + s2);`

   c. `System.out.println("Result:   " + s1 + s2);`

   d. `System.out.println("Result:   " + s1 + ' ' + s2);`

8. Show precisely what is output by the following statement:

```
System.out.println("A rolling" +
    "stone" +
    "gathers" +
    "no" +
    "moss");
```

9. How many characters can be stored into a variable of type `char`?

10. How many characters are in the empty string?

11. A variable of the class String can be assigned to a variable of type char. (True or False?)

12. A literal string can be assigned to a variable of the class String. (True or False?)

13. What is the difference between the literal string "computer" and the identifier computer?

14. What is output by the following code segment? (All variables are of the class String.

```
street = "Elm St.";
address = "1425B";
city = "Amaryllis";
state = "Iowa";
streetAddress = address + " " + street;
System.out.println(streetAddress);
System.out.println(city);
System.out.println(", " + state);
```

15. Correct the following program so that it displays "Martin Luther King Jr."

```
// This application is full of errors
class LotsOfErrors;
{
    void main (string args[]);
    {
        constant String FIRST : Martin";
        constant String MID : "Luther;
        constant String LAST : King

        String name;
        character initial;
        name = Martin + Luther + King;
        initial = MID;
        LAST = "King Jr.";
           System.out.println('Name = ' + name));
           System.out.println(mid
    }
```

16. What does a constructor do?

17. Name three kinds of methods other than a constructor.

18. How do you invoke an instance method?

19. Name two instance methods associated with the System.out object.

20. What does the expression "sending a message to" mean?
21. Describe the role of a parameter list.
22. What do we call a public class that contains a method called `main`?
23. What is the function of the `readLine` method of the class `BufferedReader`?
24. Do we use a `return` statement with a void method?
25. We have used the convention that method names begin with a lowercase letter. Why does a constructor have to begin with an uppercase letter?

Programming Warm-Up Exercises

1. Write the output statement that prints your name.
2. Write three consecutive output statements that print the following three lines.

   ```
   The moon
   is
   blue.
   ```

3. Write declaration statements to declare three variables of the class `String` and two variables of type `char`. The `String` variables should be named `make`, `model`, and `color`. The `char` variables should be named `plateType` and `classification`.
4. Write a series of output statements that display the values in the variables declared in Exercise 3. Each value should be preceded by an identifying message.
5. Change the `PrintName` application (pages 71–72) so that it also prints the name in the following format

   First-name Middle-initial. Last-name

   Define a new `String` variable to hold the name in the new format and assign it the string using the existing variables, any literal strings that are needed for punctuation and spacing, and concatenation operations. Print the string, labeled appropriately.
6. Print the following groups of text.
   a. ```
      Four score
      and seven years ago
      ```
   b. ```
      Four score
      and seven
      years ago
      ```
   c. ```
      Four score
      and
      seven
      years ago
      ```
      ```

    d. Four

       score

       and

       seven

       years

       ago

7. Write the declarations and statements necessary to input a string from `System.in`.

8. Write a class that represents a date, with the month, day, and year represented by strings. The class should have a constructor that takes the three parts of the date as parameters, and value-returning methods that return the date in mm/dd/yyyy format and in yyyy-mm-dd format. (*Hint:* The general structure of this class is very similar to `Name`.)

9. Enter and run the following application. Be sure to type it exactly as it appears here.

```
//*****************************************************************
// HelloWorld application
// This application displays two simple messages
//*****************************************************************
public class HelloWorld
{
  public static void main(String args[])
  {
    final String MSG1 = "Hello world.";
    String msg2;

    System.out.println(MSG1);
    msg2 = MSG1 + " " + MSG1 + " " + MSG1;
    System.out.println(msg2);
  }
}
```

Programming Problems

1. Write a Java application that displays a series of Haiku poems. A Haiku poem is written in three phrases. The first phrase has five syllables, the second has seven syllables, and the third phrase has five syllables. For example:

Bright flash then silence

My expensive computer

Has gone to heaven

Your program should input three strings with five syllables and two strings of seven syllables. Output every possible 5–7–5 permutation of these phrases. Do not use the same phrase twice in any poem. See if you can create phrases that make sense together in every permutation. Be sure to include appropriate comments in your code, choose meaningful identifiers, and use indentation as shown in the code in this chapter.

2. Write a program that simulates the children's game called "My Grandmother's Trunk." In this game, the players sit in a circle, and the first player names something that goes in the trunk: "In my grandmother's trunk, I packed a pencil." The next player restates the sentence and adds something new to the trunk: "In my grandmother's trunk, I packed a pencil and a red ball." Each player in turn adds something to the trunk, attempting to keep track of all the items that are already there.

   Your program should simulate just five turns in the game. Starting with the empty string, simulate each player's turn by reading and concatenating a new word or phrase to the existing string, and print the result.

3. Write a program that prints its own grading form. The program should output the name and number of the class, the name and number of the programming assignment, your name and student number, and labeled spaces for scores reflecting correctness, quality of style, late deduction, and overall score. Have the program input the name, ID number, and assignment number as strings. An example of such a form is the following:

```
CS–101 Introduction to Programming and Problem Solving


Programming Assignment 1


Sally A. Student    ID Number 431023877


Grade Summary:


Program Correctness:     Quality of Style:
Late Deduction:          Overall Score:
Comments:
```

Case Study Follow-Up

1. Change the NameDriver application so that the two formats are shown in the opposite order on the screen.

2. In the NameDriver application, explain what takes place in the return statement in the method FirstLastFormat.

3. Change the NameDriver application so that it also prints the name in the following format:

   First-name Middle-initial. Last-name
   Make the change by adding a method to the class Name.

4. Change the NameDriver application so that it inputs two names and displays them in the different formats.

Arithmetic Expressions

goals

Knowledge Goals
- To understand the relationship between primitive and reference classes
- To see why different numeric types have different ranges of values
- To understand the differences between integral and floating-point types
- To see how precedence rules affect the order of evaluation in an expression
- To understand implicit type conversion and explicit type casting
- To be able to use additional operations associated with the `String` type
- To understand how a value-returning method works

Skill Goals
To be able to:
- Declare named constants and variables of type `int` and `double`
- Construct simple arithmetic expressions
- Evaluate simple arithmetic expressions
- Construct and evaluate expressions that include multiple arithmetic operations
- Use Java math methods in expressions
- Format the statements in a class in a clear and readable fashion
- Write a simple value-returning method
- Develop a simple class representing an object
- Place classes in separate files and import them into an application

timeline

1927
First public demonstration of television in the U.S. takes place: a speech in D.C. is broadcast in New York

1929
Experimentation with color television begins; Bell Laboratories is the first in the U.S. to demonstrate the technology

1935
The IBM 601 punch-card machine and the electric typewriter are introduced

1935
IBM graduates its first class of female service technicians

1936
Konrad Zuse begins developing the first binary digital computer to help automate engineering and architectural drawing

1937
Howard Aiken proposes a calculating machine that can carry out operations in a predetermined sequence

introduction

In Chapter 2, we examined enough Java syntax to be able to construct application classes using assignment and simple input and output, and to write a user class within an application. In that chapter, we focused on the char and String types and saw how to construct expressions using the concatenation operator. In this chapter, we continue to write applications that use assignment and simple I/O, but we concentrate on additional built-in data types: int, long, float, and double. These numeric types include multiple operators that enable us to construct complex arithmetic expressions. We show how to make expressions even more powerful by using calls to Java's value-returning math methods. In addition, we return to the topics of classes and methods and see how to write a non-application class that includes a class as well as instance fields and methods. Such classes can be stored in files separate from the application and imported into it.

1937

George Stibitz develops the "Model K," the prototype binary adder circuit

1937

Alan Turing introduces the idea of his "Turing Machine" a theoretical model for a general purpose computer

1938

Bill Hewlett and Dave Packard begin Hewlett-Packard in a garage with $538 in capitol

1939

John Vincent Atanasoff and Cliff Berry create a model for the electronic-digital computer

1943

Construction of the ENIAC (Electronic Numerical Integrator and Computer) begins at the Moore School of Electrical Engineering in Philadelphia

1943

Invention of the first all-electronic calculating device, the Collosus, used by England during World War II to decrypt secret messages

3.1 Overview of Java Data Types

In Chapter 2, we informally discussed the distinctions among Java's data types. Now it is time to make this intuitive understanding formal. Java's built-in data types are organized into primitive types and reference types (see Figure 3.1).

You might have noticed that String isn't listed in Figure 3.1. In Chapter 2, we noted that String is an example of a class construct, which falls under the category of reference types. We also used classes such as BufferedReader, InputStreamReader, and System. Recall that our naming convention is to capitalize the first letter of all classes in this manner, so as to help us identify them in our code.

The division of Java's data types into *primitive* and *reference* types stems from the way that Java stores values of each type in memory. We briefly discussed the distinction between these types in Chapter 2, and now we are ready to take a deeper look at them. Recall that Java stores each primitive value at the memory address it chooses for it. When we assign a value to a variable of a primitive type, Java copies the value into the address that has been chosen for the variable. This procedure is possible because each primitive type takes a specified amount of space.

Because reference types can contain different numbers of fields and methods, they consume different amounts of the computer's memory. Most are too large to fit into a single memory location, so Java stores the *address* of the memory location where the object can be found. That is, the chosen location contains a binary number that tells the computer where the object is stored. When Java assigns an object to a variable, it copies this address into the variable.

Let's look at a pair of examples that demonstrate the difference between primitive values and reference values.

```
char letter;
String title;
String bookName;
```

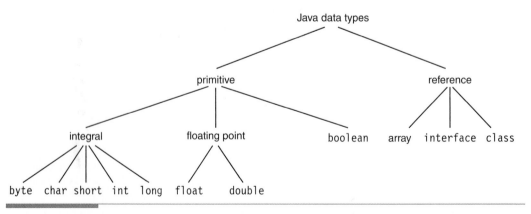

Figure 3.1 Java data types

```
letter = 'J';
title = "Programming and Problem Solving with Java";
bookName = title;
```

When we declare the variables letter, title, and bookName, addresses are assigned to these variables. When we assign the value 'J' to the char variable letter, Java stores the value 'J' into it. When we assign the string "Programming and Problem Solving with Java" to the String variable title, Java chooses locations into which to store the string, and it stores the *address* of the first location into title. If we assign the value of title to another String variable called bookName, then Java simply copies the value stored in title (the address) to the place it chose for bookName.

Figure 3.2 illustrates the difference between primitive and reference types. It also demonstrates that a reference type offers the advantage of saving memory space when copying values that take up multiple locations in memory. The lengthy value is stored just once, and each of the variables assigned that value takes up just one location. If Java stored reference types the same way it stores primitive types, it would have to store a copy of the whole value in each variable, which would consume more space.

The fact that only one copy of an object exists is, however, a double-edged sword. If you assign an integer value to several variables and then change the value in one of those variables, the change doesn't affect any of the other copies. With a reference type, in contrast, each variable stores a reference to the single copy of the object. Thus, if you change the object through one of the references, then it affects all of the other references.

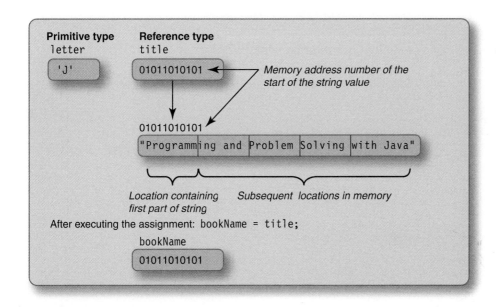

Figure 3.2 Primitive types and reference types

For example, you could declare a variable of the class `PrintStream` (which is the class that defines `System.out`), called `output`, and assign `System.out` to it:

```
PrintStream output;
output = System.out;
```

Both variables refer to the same object representing the standard I/O window on the screen. Printing with either one of them causes the output to appear in the same window, as shown in Figure 3.3.

Having variables that are synonyms for the same object can occasionally be useful, but often it leads to mystifying behavior. When the value in an object can be changed through different variables, it becomes more difficult to keep track of the source of the changes. You may spend a long time trying to figure out how an assignment statement could possibly have produced the erroneous value in an object, only to discover that an entirely different assignment to a synonym for the object caused the problem. At this stage in your programming career, it is best to avoid the use of synonyms.

You should understand that assigning a new object to a variable doesn't change the object that was previously assigned to it. Instead, the variable now refers to the new object; the

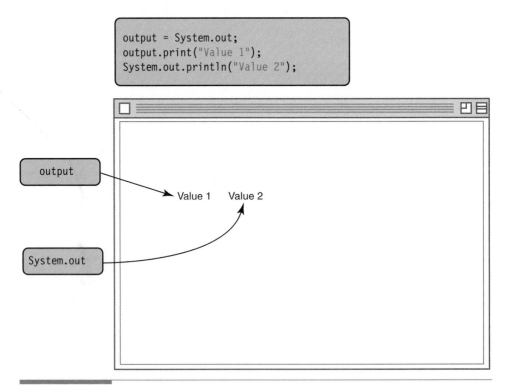

Figure 3.3   An object may be changed through any of its references

old object remains unchanged. It's like when you move to a new house or apartment. Your old residence still exists, but you go home to the new place each day. To stretch this analogy a bit farther, if no one else is living in your old residence, and it remains abandoned for long enough, it may be demolished and the land reused. The same thing happens in Java. If no variable refers to an object, then eventually the JVM notices this lack of a reference and reclaims its memory space so that it can be reused.

The name "reference," by the way, comes from the fact that the contents of a reference variable *refer* to another place in memory. You can also think of a reference type as being analogous to the call number of a library book. Armed with the call number, you can go into the library and find the book. If a friend wants to find the same book, you can give a copy of the call number to him or her, which is much easier than giving your friend a copy of the book.

Do not feel overwhelmed by the quantity of data types shown in Figure 3.1. Its purpose is simply to give you an overall picture of what is available in Java. Except for the String and I/O classes, this chapter focuses mainly on the primitive types. First we look at the primitive integral types (used primarily to represent integers), and then we consider the floating-point types (used to represent real numbers containing decimal points). We postpone detailed coverage of the remaining primitive type, boolean, until Chapter 4.

3.2 Numeric Data Types

You already are familiar with the basic concepts of integers and real numbers in mathematics. However, as used on a computer, the corresponding data types have certain limitations, which we now examine.

■ Integral Types

The data types byte, short, int, and long are known as integral types (or integer types) because they refer to integer values—whole numbers with no fractional part. In Java, the simplest form of integer value is a sequence of one or more digits:

```
22   16   1   498   0   4600
```

Commas are not allowed.

A minus sign preceding an integer value makes the integer negative:

```
−378   −912
```

The data types byte, short, int, and long are intended to represent different sizes of integers, from smaller (fewer bits) to larger (more bits), as shown in Figure 3.4.

The Java language specifies the sizes of the integral types to match those shown in the figure. The more bits in the type, the larger the integer value that can be stored.

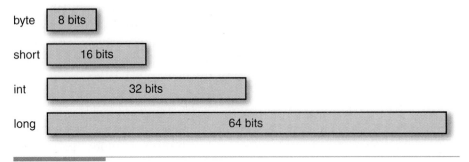

Figure 3.4 TheIntegral types in Java

The `int` type is, by far, the most common data type for manipulating integer data. The `byte` and `short` types are used far less frequently. In Java you nearly always use `int` for manipulating integer values, but sometimes you may use `long` if your application requires values larger than the maximum `int` value. The range of `int` values is from –2147483648 through +2147483647. As noted in Chapter 1, numbers like these remind us that the binary number system is working in the background.

A variable of type `int` can hold any value with up to 9 decimal digits, such as a Social Security number. For values with more digits, such as a telephone number with country and area codes, this type isn't large enough. Such numbers require the `long` type, which can hold any integer up to 18 digits in length.

When you write a literal integer value, Java automatically assumes that it is of type `int`. To write a literal of type `long`, you must follow the last digit of the number with the letter "L". You may also use the lowercase "l", but it looks so much like the digit "1" that it may be impossible for a person to recognize the literal as `long` when reading your code. We use only the uppercase "L" in this text. Here are some examples of literals of type `int` and `long`:

Literal	Type
0	int
0L	long
2001	int
18005551212L	long
18005551212	invalid (11 digits are too many for the type int)

If your code tries to compute a value larger than a type's maximum value, it results in *integer overflow*. Some programming languages give you an error message when overflow occurs, but Java doesn't. If a computation in Java produces a value that is too large for the type to represent, you simply get an erroneous result.

One caution about integer literals in Java: A literal constant beginning with a zero is assumed to be an octal (base–8) number instead of a decimal (base–10) number. For example, if you write

015

the Java compiler takes it to mean the decimal number 13. If you aren't familiar with the octal number system, don't worry about why an octal 15 is the same as a decimal 13. The important thing to remember is not to start a decimal integer literal with a zero (unless you want the number 0, which is the same in both octal and decimal).

■ Floating-Point Types

We use floating-point types (or floating types) to represent real numbers. Floating-point numbers have an integer part and a fractional part, with a decimal point in between. Either the integer part or the fractional part, but not both, may be missing. Here are some examples:

18.0   127.54   0.57   4.   193145.8523   .8

Starting 0.57 with a 0 does not make it an octal number. Only with integer values does a leading 0 indicate an octal number.

Just as the integral types in Java come in different sizes (byte, short, int, and long), so do the floating-point types. In increasing order of size, the floating-point types are float and double (meaning double precision). The double type gives us a wider range of values and more precision (the number of significant digits in the number) than the float type, but at the expense of twice the memory space to hold the number. In Java, int and float values take up 32 bits of memory space, whereas both long and double take up 64 bits of memory space.

Floating-point values also can have an exponent, as in scientific notation. (In scientific notation, a number is written as a value multiplied by 10 to some power.) Instead of writing 3.504×10^{12}, in Java we would write 3.504E12. The E (you can also use e) means "exponent of base 10." The number preceding the letter E doesn't need to include a decimal point. Here are some examples of floating-point numbers in scientific notation:

1.74536E–12   3.652442E4   7E20   –8.01994E–23

A float value can represent any 7-digit decimal number with an exponent in the range of –45 through 38. A double value can represent any 15-digit decimal number with an exponent ranging from –324 to 308.

In Java, the compiler automatically assumes that floating-point literals of the form shown here are of type double. To write a literal of type float, you must end the number with the letter F (or f). Here are some examples of floating-point literals:

Literal	Type
0.0	double
0.0f	float
2.001E3	double
2.001E3F	float
1.8E225F	invalid (the exponent 225 is too large for the type float)

We'll discuss floating-point numbers in more detail in Chapter 12, but there is one more thing you should know about them now. Computers cannot always represent floating-point numbers exactly. In Chapter 1, you learned that the computer stores all data in binary (base–2) form. Many decimal floating-point values can only be approximated in the binary number system. Don't be surprised if your application prints out the number 4.8 as 4.799998. In most cases, slight inaccuracies in the rightmost fractional digits are to be expected and are not the result of programmer error.

3.3 Declarations for Numeric Types

Just as with the types char and String, we can declare fields of type int, long, float, and double. Such declarations use the same syntax introduced earlier, except that the literals and the names of the data types are different.

Named Constant Declarations

In the case of named constant declarations, the literal values in the declarations are numeric instead of being characters in single or double quotes. For example, here are some constant declarations that define int, long, float, and double values. For comparison, declarations of char and String values are included.

```
final double  PI = 3.14159;
final float   E = 2.71828F;
final long    MAX_TEMP = 1000000000L;
final int     MIN_TEMP = -273;
final char    LETTER = 'W';
final String  NAME = "Elizabeth";
```

Although we put character and string literals in quotes, we do not follow this approach with literal integers and floating-point numbers, because there is no chance of confusing them with identifiers. Why? Because identifiers must start with a letter or underscore, and numbers must start with a digit or sign.

Using Named Constants Instead of Literals

It's a good idea to use named constants instead of literals in your code. In addition to making your code more readable, named constants can make your applications easier to modify. Suppose you wrote an application last year to compute taxes. In several places you used the literal 0.05, which was the sales tax rate at the time. Now the rate has gone up to 0.06. To change your code, you must locate every mention of the literal 0.05 and change it to 0.06. If 0.05 is used for some other reason—to compute deductions, for example—you also need to find each place where it is used, figure out its purpose, and then decide whether to change it.

This process becomes much simpler if you use a named constant. Instead of using the literal constant 0.05, suppose you had declared a named constant TAX_RATE with a value of 0.05. To change your code, you would simply change the declaration, setting TAX_RATE equal to 0.06. This one modification changes all of the tax rate computations without affecting the other places where 0.05 is used.

Java allows us to declare constants with different names but the same value. If a value has different meanings in different parts of an application, it makes sense to declare and use a constant with an appropriate name for each meaning.

Named constants are also reliable—they protect us from mistakes. If you mistype the name PI as PO, for example, the Java compiler will tell you that the name PO has not been declared. On the other hand, even though we recognize that the number 3.14149 is a mistyped version of pi (3.14159), the number is perfectly acceptable to the compiler. It won't warn us that anything is wrong.

■ Variable Declarations

We declare numeric variables the same way that we declare char and String variables, except that we use the names of numeric types. Here are some example declarations:

```
int     studentCount;     // Number of students
int     sumOfScores;      // Sum of their scores
long    sumOfSquares;     // Sum of squared scores
double  average;          // Average of the scores
float   deviation;        // Standard deviation of scores
char    grade;            // Student's letter grade
String  stuName;          // Student's name
```

Given these declarations

```
int    num;
int    alpha;
double rate;
char   ch;
```

the following are appropriate assignment statements:

Variable	Expression
alpha =	2856;
rate =	0.36;
ch =	'B';
num =	alpha;

In each of these assignment statements, the data type of the expression matches the data type of the variable to which it is assigned. Later in this chapter, we will see what happens when the data types do not match.

3.4 Simple Arithmetic Expressions

Now that we have looked at declarations and assignments, we can consider how to use values of numeric types in our calculations. Calculations are performed with expressions. Here we look first at simple expressions that involve at most one operator so that we may examine each operator in detail. Then we move on to compound expressions that combine multiple operations.

Arithmetic Operators

Expressions are made up of constants, variables, and operators. The following are all valid expressions:

```
alpha + 2     rate - 6.0     4 - alpha     rate     alpha * num
```

The operators allowed in an expression depend on the data types of the constants and variables in the expression. The *arithmetic operators* are

- \+   Unary plus
- \-   Unary minus
- \+   Addition
- \-   Subtraction
- *   Multiplication
- /   { Floating-point division (floating-point result) / Integer division (no fractional part) }
- %   Modulus (remainder from division)

The first two operators are unary operators—they take just one operand. The last five are binary operators—they take two operands. Unary plus and minus are used as follows:

```
-54     +259.65     -rate
```

Unary operator   An operator that has just one operand

Binary operator   An operator that has two operands

Programmers rarely use the unary plus. Without any sign, a numeric constant is assumed to be positive anyway.

You may be less familiar with integer division and modulus (%), so let's look at them more closely. Note that % can be used with both integers and floating-point numbers. When you divide one integer by another, you get an integer quotient and a remainder. Integer division gives only the integer quotient, and % gives only the remainder.

```
  3  ← 6 / 2        3  ← 7 / 2
2)6              2)7
  6                6
  0  ← 6 % 2        1  ← 7 % 2
```

In Java, the sign of the remainder is the same as the sign of the dividend. For example:

```
  3 %  2 =  1
  3 % -2 =  1
 -3 %  2 = -1
 -3 % -2 = -1
```

In contrast to integer division, floating-point division yields a floating-point result. For example, the expression

```
7.2 / 2.0
```

yields the value 3.6.

The floating-point remainder operation returns the remainder after dividing the dividend by the divisor a whole number of times. For example,

```
7.2 % 2.1
```

yields the value 0.9 because 2.1 goes into 7.2 exactly 3 times (3 * 2.1 = 6.3), with 0.9 remaining.

Here are some expressions using arithmetic operators and their values:

Expression	Value
3 + 6	9
3.4 − 6.1	−2.7
2 * 3	6
8 / 2	4
8.0 / 2.0	4.0
8 / 8	1
8 / 9	0
8 / 7	1

8 % 8	0
8 % 9	8
8 % 7	1
0 % 7	0
5.0 % 2.3	0.4

Be careful with division and modulus calculations. For instance, the expressions 7 / 0 and 7 % 0 will produce error messages, because the computer cannot divide an integer by zero. With floating-point values, however, the expressions 7.0 / 0.0 and 7.0 % 0.0 do not result in error messages. The result of the expression 7.0 / 0.0 is a special value representing *infinity*. The result of 7.0 % 0.0 is another special value called *not a number* (NaN).

Calculations involving these special values produce unusual results. For example, the result of any arithmetic operation involving NaN is also NaN. If you encounter such results, they indicate that you need to carefully reexamine the expressions in your code to confirm that division and remainder cannot have a zero divisor.

Because variables are allowed in expressions, the following are valid assignments:

```
alpha = num + 6;
alpha = num / 2;
num = alpha * 2;
num = 6 % alpha;
alpha = alpha + 1;
num = num + alpha;
```

As we saw with assignment statements involving String expressions, the same variable can appear on both sides of the assignment operator. In the case of

```
num = num + alpha;
```

the value in num and the value in alpha are added together, and then the sum of the two values is stored into num, replacing the value previously stored there. This example shows the difference between mathematical equality and assignment. The mathematical equality

num = num + alpha

is true only when *alpha* equals zero. The assignment statement

```
num = num + alpha;
```

is valid for *any* value of alpha.

Here's a simple application that uses arithmetic expressions:

```
//*****************************************************************
// FreezeBoil application
// This application computes the midpoint between
// the freezing and boiling points of water
//*****************************************************************

public class FreezeBoil
{
  public static void main(String[] args)
  {
    final double FREEZE_PT = 32.0;          // Freezing point of water
    final double BOIL_PT = 212.0;           // Boiling point of water
    double avgTemp;                         // Holds the result of averaging
                                            // FREEZE_PT and BOIL_PT

    // Display initial data
    System.out.print("Water freezes at " + FREEZE_PT);
    System.out.println(" and boils at " + BOIL_PT + " degrees.");
    // Calculate and display average
    avgTemp = FREEZE_PT + BOIL_PT;
    avgTemp = avgTemp / 2.0;
    System.out.println("Halfway between is " + avgTemp + " degrees.");
  }
}
```

The application begins with a comment that explains what the application does. Inside the class is a declaration section where we declare the main method, which includes declarations of the constants FREEZE_PT and BOIL_PT and the variable avgTemp and then a sequence of executable statements. These statements display the initial data, add FREEZE_PT and BOIL_PT, divide the sum by 2, and then show the result. Here is the output from the application:

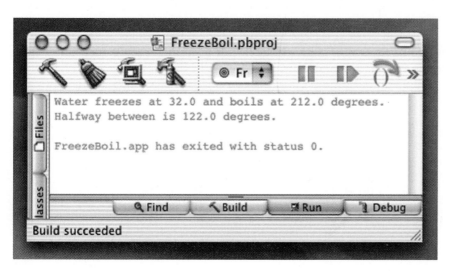

■ Increment and Decrement Operators

In addition to the familiar arithmetic operators, Java provides *increment* and *decrement operators*:

++   Increment

--   Decrement

These unary operators take a single variable name as an operand. For integer and floating-point operands, the effect is to add 1 to (or subtract 1 from) the operand. If num currently contains the value 8, for example, the statement

```
num++;
```

causes num to contain 9. You can achieve the same effect by writing the assignment statement

```
num = num + 1;
```

Java programmers, however, typically prefer the increment operator.

The ++ and -- operators can be either *prefix operators*

```
++num;
```

or *postfix operators*

```
num++;
```

Both of these statements behave in exactly the same way; that is, they add 1 to whatever is in num. The choice between the two is a matter of personal preference, although most Java programmers favor the latter form.

Java allows you to use ++ and -- in the middle of a larger expression:

```
alpha = num++ * 3;
```

In this case, the postfix form of ++ gives a different result from the prefix form. In Chapter 10, we examine the ++ and -- operators in more detail. In the meantime, you should use them only to increment or decrement a variable as a separate, stand-alone statement:

Increment-Statement

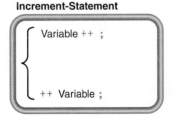

```
Variable ++ ;
```

```
++ Variable ;
```

Decrement-Statement

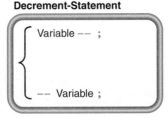

```
Variable -- ;
```

```
-- Variable ;
```

The Origins of Java

If we were to chart the history of programming languages, we would find several distinct families of languages that have their origins in the early days of computing. When the idea of high-level languages first arose, it seemed that everyone had his or her own notion of the ideal form for a programming language. The result—the *Tower of Babel* period of programming languages. As more programs were written, the cost of rewriting them to use the features of a new language increased, so the computing world began to concentrate on a few languages. These included Fortran, Algol, COBOL, Basic, PL/1, Lisp, and BCPL.

As computers were used in more sophisticated ways, it became necessary to create more powerful languages. In many cases, these new languages were just expanded versions of older languages. Expanding a language allows older applications to be used unchanged, but enables programmers to add to applications using the language's new features. This strategy is known as *upward compatibility*. A good example is the Fortran series that began with Fortran, then Fortran II, Fortran IV, Fortran 77, Fortran 90, and High-Performance Fortran.

Sometimes, however, extensions to a language result in excess complexity. The solution is to redesign the language to eliminate conflicting features while preserving its desirable qualities. For example, Pascal replaced the Algol language series and was itself superseded by the Modula series of languages. Java is a redesign of languages derived from BCPL (Basic Combined Programming Language).

In the 1960s BCPL had a small but loyal following, primarily in Europe. It spawned another language with the abbreviated name of B. In the early 1970s, Dennis Ritchie, working on a new language at AT&T Bell Labs, adopted features from the B language and decided that the successor to B naturally should be named C.

In 1985, Bjarne Stroustrup, also of Bell Labs, invented the C++ programming language by adding features for object-oriented programming to the C language. Instead of naming the new language D, the Bell Labs group named it C++ in a humorous vein: ++ is the increment operation in C, so the name C++ suggests it is the successor of the C language.

C includes many features that are close to the level of machine code, allowing programmers to write detailed instructions for the computer. C++ adds features that enable programmers to write instructions at a very powerful and abstract level that is far removed from machine language. If used with care, this combination of features enables programmers to "shift gears" between easily programming complex operations and writing instructions that are close to machine code. Many people find it difficult to keep the features separate, however, and view the combination as fraught with potential for introducing errors.

In the early 1990s, James Gosling, working at Sun Microsystems, needed a language for programming the microprocessors being used in consumer electronics (for example, digital cameras). Like Stroustrup, he began with C. Gosling, however, decided to eliminate features that would conflict with the structures that he was adding. The Algol family of languages as well as several experimental programming languages inspired some of the new features. Gosling called his language Oak, and he spent several years experimenting with it and refining it. When the popularity of the Internet began to grow, Gosling worked with a team of designers at Sun to adapt Oak for writing applications that could operate over the network. The revised language was renamed Java and released to the public in May 1996.

Java offers many of the capabilities of C++, albeit in a less complicated fashion. It supports programming for the Internet and writing applications with graphical user interfaces that are now the standard for interactive I/O. In addition, Java applications are highly portable. These features combined to cause the popularity of Java to skyrocket in the first year after it was released. It is very rare for a new programming language to appear and achieve success so quickly. Because Java is powerful yet simple, it has also become popular as a language for teaching programming.

Background Information

3.5 Compound Arithmetic Expressions

The expressions we've used so far have contained at most a single arithmetic operator. We also have been careful not to mix integer and floating-point values in the same expression. Now we look at more complicated expressions—ones that are composed of several operators and ones that contain mixed data types.

Precedence Rules

Arithmetic expressions can be made up of many constants, variables, operators, and parentheses. In what order are the operations performed? For example, in the assignment statement

```
avgTemp = FREEZE_PT + BOIL_PT / 2.0;
```

is FREEZE_PT + BOIL_PT calculated first or is BOIL_PT / 2.0 calculated first?

The five basic arithmetic operators (+ for addition, − for subtraction, * for multiplication, / for division, and % for modulus) and parentheses are ordered the same way mathematical operators are, according to *precedence rules*:

Highest precedence: ()

++ (postfix increment)   -- (postfix decrement)

++ (prefix increment)   -- (prefix decrement)

unary +   unary -

*   /   %

Lowest precedence: +   -

In the preceding example, we first divide BOIL_PT by 2.0 and then add FREEZE_PT to the result.

You can change the order of evaluation by using parentheses. In the statement

```
avgTemp = (FREEZE_PT + BOIL_PT) / 2.0;
```

FREEZE_PT and BOIL_PT are added first, and then their sum is divided by 2.0. We evaluate subexpressions in parentheses first and then follow the precedence of the operators.

When multiple arithmetic operators have the same precedence, their *grouping order* (or *associativity*) is from left to right. Thus the expression

```
int1 − int2 + int3
```

means (int1 − int2) + int3, not int1 − (int2 + int3). As another example, we would use the expression

```
(double1 + double2) / double1 * 3.0
```

to evaluate the expression in parentheses first, then divide the sum by `double1`, and multiply the result by `3.0`. Here are some more examples:

Expression	Value
10 / 2 * 3	15
10 % 3 – 4 / 2	−1
5.0 * 2.0 / 4.0 * 2.0	5.0
5.0 * 2.0 / (4.0 * 2.0)	1.25
5.0 + 2.0 / (4.0 * 2.0)	5.25

■ Type Conversion and Type Casting

Integer values and floating-point values are stored differently inside a computer's memory. The pattern of bits that represents the constant 2, for example, does not look at all like the pattern of bits that represents the constant 2.0. (In Chapter 12, we examine why floating-point numbers need a special representation inside the computer.) What happens if we mix integer and floating-point values together in an assignment statement or an arithmetic expression? Let's look first at assignment statements.

Assignment Statements   If you make the declarations

```
int    someInt;
double someDouble;
```

then `someInt` can hold *only* integer values, and `someDouble` can hold *only* double-precision floating-point values. The assignment statement

```
someDouble = 12;
```

may seem to store the integer value 12 into `someDouble`, but this is not true. The computer refuses to store anything other than a `double` value into `someDouble`. The compiler inserts extra Bytecode instructions that first convert 12 into 12.0 and then store 12.0 into `someDouble`. This implicit (automatic) conversion of a value from one data type to another is known in Java as **type conversion**.

> Type conversion   The implicit (automatic) conversion of a value from one data type to another

The statement

```
someInt = 4.8;
```

also causes type conversion. When a floating-point value is assigned to an `int` variable, the fractional part is truncated (cut off). As a result, `someInt` is assigned the value 4.

With both of the preceding assignment statements, the code would be less confusing for someone to read if we avoided mixing data types:

```
someDouble = 12.0;
someInt = 4;
```

More often, it is not just constants but entire expressions that are involved in type conversion. For example, both of the assignments

```
someDouble = 3 * someInt + 2;
someInt = 5.2 / someDouble - anotherDouble;
```

lead to type conversion. Storing the result of an int expression into a double variable doesn't cause loss of information; a whole number such as 24 can be represented in floating-point form as 24.0. In the Java language, a type conversion that does not result in a loss of information is known as a **widening conversion**. Assigning int values to long variables or float values to double variables are also examples of widening conversions.

However, storing the result of a floating-point expression into an int variable can cause a loss of information because the fractional part is truncated. Java refers to such a conversion as a **narrowing conversion**. It is easy to overlook the assignment of a floating-point expression to an int variable, a double value to a float variable, or a long value to an int variable when we try to discover why our code is producing the wrong answers.

To make our code as clear (and error-free) as possible, we should use explicit **type casting**. A Java *cast operation* consists of a data type name within parentheses, followed by the expression to be converted:

```
someDouble = (double)(3 * someInt + 2);
someInt = (int)(5.2 / someDouble - anotherDouble);
```

Both of the statements

```
someFloat = someInt + 8;
someFloat = (float)(someInt + 8);
```

produce identical results; the only difference is in their clarity. With the cast operation, it is perfectly clear to the programmer and to others reading the code that the mixing of types is intentional, not an oversight. Countless errors have resulted from unintentional mixing of types.

There is a nice way to round off rather than truncate a floating-point value before storing it into an int variable:

```
someInt = (int)(someDouble + 0.5);
```

With pencil and paper, see for yourself what gets stored into someInt when someDouble contains 4.7. Now try it again, assuming someDouble contains 4.2. (This technique of rounding by adding 0.5 assumes that someDouble is a positive number.)

---

[1]In non-Java terminology, implicit conversions are called *coercions* and explicit conversions are called *casts*.

Arithmetic Expressions   So far we have discussed mixing data types across the assignment operator (=). It's also possible to mix data types within an expression:

```
someInt * someDouble
4.8 + someInt - 3
```

Such expressions are called mixed type (or mixed mode) expressions.

> **Mixed type expression** An expression that contains operands of different data types; also called a mixed mode expression

Whenever an integer value and a floating-point value are joined by an operator, implicit type conversion occurs as follows:

1. The integer value is temporarily converted to a floating-point value.
2. The operation is performed.
3. The result is a floating-point value.

Let's examine how the computer evaluates the expression `4.8 + someInt - 3`, where `someInt` contains the value 2. First, the operands of the + operator have mixed types, so the value of `someInt` is converted to 2.0. (This conversion is merely temporary; it does not affect the value that is currently stored in `someInt`.) The addition takes place, yielding a value of 6.8. Next, the subtraction (-) operator joins a floating-point value (6.8) and an integer value (3). The value 3 is converted to 3.0, the subtraction takes place, and the result is the floating-point value 3.8.

Just as with assignment statements, you can use explicit type casts within expressions to lessen the risk of errors. Writing expressions such as

```
(double)someInt * someDouble
4.8 + (double)(someInt - 3)
```

makes it clear what your intentions are.

Not only are explicit type casts valuable for code clarity, but in some cases they are mandatory for correct programming. To see why this is so, given the declarations

```
int     sum;
int     count;
double  average;
```

suppose that `sum` and `count` currently contain 60 and 80, respectively. Assuming that `sum` represents the sum of a group of integer values and `count` represents the number of values, let's find the average value:

```
average = sum / count;     // Gives the wrong answer
```

Unfortunately, this statement stores the value 0.0 into `average`. Here's why: The expression to the right of the assignment operator is not a mixed type expression. Instead, both operands of the / operator are of type `int`, so integer division is performed. Dividing 60 by 80 yields the integer value 0. Next, the machine implicitly converts 0 to the value 0.0 before storing it into average. The correct (and clear) way to find the average is

```
average = (double)sum / (double)count;
```

This statement gives us floating-point division instead of integer division. It results in the value 0.75 being stored into average.

As a final remark about type conversion and type casting, you may have noticed that we have concentrated only on the `int` and `double` types. It is also possible to stir `byte`, `long`, `short`, and `float` values into the pot. The results can be confusing and unexpected. You should avoid unnecessarily mixing values of these types within an expression. Whenever it becomes necessary to do so, you should use explicit type casting to clarify your intentions.

String Conversion Just as Java attempts to convert between numeric types when we mix them in expressions, so it also tries to convert numeric values to strings when we mix them into expressions with the string concatenation operator. For instance, if we declare a `String` object called answer, we can write an assignment expression of the following form:

```
answer = "The average is: " + average;
```

If average contains the value 27.65, then the outcome of this assignment is that answer contains the following string:

```
"The average is: 27.65"
```

When one of the operands of the + operator is a string and the other operand is a numeric type, the numeric type is converted to a string prior to concatenation. The + operator has the same precedence whether it is adding numeric values or concatenating strings. Java's string conversion is a useful feature for formatting output in which we mix numeric values with text that explains their meaning. For example, we might use the preceding expression in a call to `println` as follows:

```
System.out.println("The average is: " + average);
```

You can use a series of concatenation operators to create complex strings. For example,

```
answer = "The results are: " + 27 + 18 + " and " + 9;
```

produces the string

```
"The results are: 2718 and 9"
```

Notice, however that the values 27 and 18 were concatenated without any spaces between them. String conversion of numeric values doesn't add any space around the digits of the number. Instead, we must explicitly include any spaces that we need as part of the expression:

```
answer = "The results are: " + 27 + ", " + 18 + ", and " + 9;
```

It is also important to note that the result of the original expression wasn't

```
"The results are: 45 and 9"
```

Why doesn't the subexpression 27 + 18 perform an integer addition? The answer lies in the precedence rules. Let's take a closer look at the evaluation of this expression. All of the operators in the expression have the same precedence and thus are evaluated left to right. The first operand is a string, so the first + is a concatenation. The second operand is converted to a string and concatenated, giving the string

```
"The results are: 27"
```

as the result. This string becomes the first operand of the second + operator, so it is also a concatenation. The number 18 is thus converted to a string and concatenated with the result of the first operator to produce a new string:

```
"The results are: 2718"
```

The third operator has two strings as its operands, so no conversion is necessary. It produces

```
"The results are: 2718 and "
```

The last operator then has a string as its first operand and an integer as its second operand. The integer is converted to a string and concatenated to form the final result, which is assigned to answer.

As you can see from the preceding discussion, when an expression mixes strings and numeric types, you must consider the entire expression in light of the precedence rules. Take a look at the following expression and see if you can determine what its result is:

```
answer = 27 + 18 + 9 + " are the results."
```

If you think it is

```
"27189 are the results."
```

then you are forgetting the effect of the left-to-right evaluation precedence rule. Its actual result is

```
"54 are the results."
```

The first two + operators are integer additions because neither of their operands are strings. Only the last + operation is a concatenation; its left operand is the sum of the three numbers, which it converts into a string. If a chain of + operators begins with a concatenation, then the succeeding operators are concatenations as well. The following is an invalid assignment:

```
answer = 27 + 18 + 9;              // Invalid; expression type is int
```

String conversion occurs only with the concatenation operator, not with assignment. The result of this expression is an `int` value, which can't be assigned to a string. However, we can use a trick to turn this expression into a series of string concatenations. That is, we can concatenate the values with the empty string:

```
answer = "" + 27 + 18 + 9;         // Valid; expression is a String
```

The value stored in `answer` is then `"27189"`. But what if we want `answer` to contain the string representing the sum of these integers? That is, how do we get Java to first compute the integer sum before applying string conversion? We do so in the same way that we change the order of evaluation of any expression: We use parentheses.

```
answer = "" + (27 + 18 + 9);
```

Now the expression 27 + 18 + 9 is evaluated first and, because all of the operands are integers, the + operators perform addition. Once the sum is computed, it is converted to a string and concatenated with the empty string. The assignment then stores `"54"` into `answer`.

To summarize, Java's string conversion is a useful feature for formatting numeric output. But keep in mind that it works only as part of string concatenation. Also, remember that you must consider the precedence rules whenever you write a complex expression containing multiple numeric values.

3.6 Additional Mathematical Methods

Certain computations, such as taking square roots or finding the absolute value of a number, are very common in programming. It would be an enormous waste of time if every programmer had to start from scratch and create methods to perform these tasks. To help make the programmer's life easier, Java's `Math` class provides a number of useful methods, shown in Table 3.1. Note that the class name must precede each of these methods with a dot in between.

Blaise Pascal

One of the great historical figures in the world of computing was the French mathematician and religious philosopher Blaise Pascal (1623–1662), the inventor of one of the earliest known mechanical calculators.

Pascal's father, Etienne, was a noble in the French court, a tax collector, and a mathematician. His mother died when Pascal was three years old. Five years later, the family moved to Paris, where Etienne took over the education of the children. Pascal quickly showed a talent for mathematics. When he was only 17, he published a mathematical essay that earned the jealous envy of René Descartes, one of the founders of modern geometry. (Pascal's work actually had been completed before he was 16.) It was based on a theorem, which he called the *hexagrammum mysticum* (mystic hexagram) that described the inscription of hexagons in conic sections (parabolas, hyperbolas, and ellipses). In addition to the theorem (now called Pascal's theorem), his essay included more than 400 corollaries.

When Pascal was about 20, he constructed a mechanical calculator that performed addition and subtraction of eight-digit numbers. That calculator required the user to dial in the numbers to be added or subtracted; the sum or difference then appeared in a set of windows. His motivation for building this machine may have been to aid his father in collecting taxes. The earliest version of the machine does, indeed, split the numbers into six decimal digits and two fractional digits, as would be used for calculating sums of money. It was hailed by his contemporaries as a great advance in mathematics, and Pascal built several more forms of his calculator. It achieved such popularity that many fake, nonfunctional copies were built by others and displayed as novelties. Several of Pascal's calculators still exist in various museums.

Pascal's box, as it is called, was long believed to be the first mechanical calculator. However, in 1950, a letter from Wilhelm Shickard to Johannes Kepler written in 1624 was discovered. This letter described an even more sophisticated calculator built by Shickard 20 years prior to Pascal's box. Unfortunately, the machine was destroyed in a fire and never rebuilt.

During his twenties, Pascal solved several difficult problems related to the cycloid curve, indirectly contributing to the development of differential calculus. Working with Pierre de Fermat, he laid the foundation of the calculus of probabilities and combinatorial analysis. One result of this work came to be known as Pascal's triangle, which simplifies the calculation of the coefficients of the expansion of $(X + Y)^N$, where N is a positive integer.

Pascal also published a treatise on air pressure and conducted experiments showing that barometric pressure decreases with altitude, helping to confirm theories that had been proposed by Galileo and Torricelli. His work on fluid dynamics forms a significant part of the foundation of that field. Among the most famous of his contributions is Pascal's law, which states that pressure applied to a fluid in a closed vessel is transmitted uniformly throughout the fluid.

When Pascal was 23, his father became ill, and the family was visited by two disciples of Jansenism, a reform movement in the Catholic Church that had begun six years earlier. The family converted, and five years later one of his sisters entered a convent. Initially, Pascal was not so taken with the new movement, but by the time he was 31, his sister had persuaded him to abandon the world and devote himself to religion. His religious works are considered no less brilliant than his mathematical and scientific writings. Some consider *Provincial Letters*, his series of 18 essays on various aspects of religion, to be the beginning of modern French prose.

Pascal returned briefly to mathematics when he was 35, but a year later his health, which had always been poor, took a turn for the worse. Unable to perform his usual work, he devoted himself to helping the less fortunate. Three years later, he died while staying with his sister, having given his own house to a poor family.

May We Introduce

Method	Argument Type(s)	Result Type	Result
Math.abs(x)	int, long, float, or double	same as argument	absolute value of x
Math.cos(x)	double	double	cosine of x (x is in radians)
Math.sin(x)	double	double	sine of x (x is in radians)
Math.log(x)	double	double	natural logarithm of x
Math.pow(x,y)	double	double	x raised to the power y (if x = 0.0, y must be positive; if x ≤ 0.0, y must be a whole number)
Math.min(x,y)	int, long, float, or double	same as argument	smaller of x and y
Math.max(x,y)	int, long, float, or double	same as argument	larger of x and y
Math.random()	none	double	a random number greater than or equal to 0.0 and less than 1.0
Math.round(x)	double	long	the argument rounded up to the nearest integer
Math.round(x)	float	int	the argument rounded up to the nearest integer
Math.sqrt(x)	double	double	square root of x (x ≥ 0.0)

Table 3.1 Math Methods

3.7 Value-Returning Class Methods

The calls to the Math methods like those in Table 3.1 are value-returning class methods. For example, the statement

```
rootX = Math.sqrt(x);
```

calls the sqrt method associated with the Math class, which returns the square root of x that is then assigned to rootX. The third column in Table 3.1 tells you the type of the value that is returned by each of the Math methods.

Notice that these arithmetic value-returning methods (such as Math.abs and Math.sqrt) are called with the name of their class rather than the name of a specific object. Recall from Chapter 2 that methods can be instance methods or class methods. The Math methods are class methods because they are associated with the class itself rather than a particular instance of the class. They belong to the class java.lang.Math, which is automatically imported into every application by the Java compiler.

In Chapter 2, we saw how easy it is to write our own value-returning instance methods. Value-returning class methods are just as easy to write. For example, suppose we want to write a `public` class method that has no parameters and returns an `int` result. We would write the heading this way:

```
public static int myMethod()
```

The only difference between this heading and the ones we wrote in Chapter 2 is the use of the reserved word `static`. We follow the heading with the body of the method enclosed in braces, just as we did for instance methods. Within the body, when our computation is finished, we write a `return` statement.

Let's look at an example of a value-returning class method declaration. The method should return a random integer in the range of 1 to 10. We call the `Math.random` method, which returns a value that is greater than or equal to 0.0 and less than 1.0. We must change this value into our desired range, so we multiply it by 10.0 and convert the result to an `int`. The `int` will then be in the range of 0 to 9, so we add 1 to get a number in the desired range. Here's the expression that does the job:

```
(int) (Math.random() * 10.0) + 1
```

Now we're ready to write the method. Let's call it `random1to10`.

```
public static int random1to10()
{
  return (int) (Math.random() * 10.0) + 1;
}
```

Is that it? Our new method is just like the value-returning methods that we wrote in Chapter 2, except that the heading includes `static`. Of course, we call it by using the name of the class in which we declare it rather than an object name. It also bears repeating that class methods can access class fields, but not instance fields. Many value-retuning methods are self-contained, as in the case of the preceding example. That is, they don't need to access any fields. As a consequence, they can be either class methods or instance methods. However, the advantage of a class method is that we can use it even when we haven't instantiated any objects of the class. For example, we don't have to instantiate an object of the class `Math` to be able to use its class methods. Instance methods must be used in conjunction with an object, so we have to instantiate the class to make use of them.

As noted in Chapter 2, we will defer looking closely at the parameter list syntax until later. But from what we've already said about writing parameters, you could easily extend this approach to write a method that takes numeric arguments. For example, suppose you want a method that computes the hypotenuse of a right triangle from its other two sides. You could write the following:

```
public static double hypotenuse(double side1, double side2)
{
  return Math.sqrt(side1 * side1 + side2 * side2);
}
```

If we call this method in the following assignment statement, which is within the same class as the method declaration, then answer is assigned the value 5.0:

```
answer = hypotenuse(3.0, 4.0);
```

Working anywhere outside of the class that contains the method declaration, we need to precede the method name with the class name in a call. Within the same class, we can refer directly to our method. If we wanted it to be a helper method, we could use the private modifier in place of public. In Chapters 6 and 7 we explore all of the different rules regarding accessibility and the other modifiers that Java supports.

Matters of Style

Code Formatting

As far as the compiler is concerned, Java statements are *free format:* They can appear anywhere on a line, more than one can appear on a single line, and one statement can span several lines. The compiler needs only blanks (or comments or new lines) to separate important symbols, and it needs semicolons to terminate statements. Of course, it is extremely important that your code be readable, both for your sake and for the sake of anyone else who has to examine it.

When you write an outline for an English paper, you follow certain rules of indentation to make it readable. The same kinds of rules can make your code easier to read. In addition, it is much easier to spot a mistake in a neatly formatted class than in a messy one. For these reasons, you should keep your code neatly formatted while you are working on it. If you've gotten lazy and let your code become messy while making a series of changes, take the time to straighten it up. Often the source of an error becomes obvious during the process of formatting the code.

Take a look at the following application for computing the cost per square foot of a house. Although it compiles and runs correctly, it does not conform to any formatting standards.

```java
// HouseCost application This application computes the cost per square foot of
// living space for a house, given the dimensions of the house, the number
// of stories, the size of the nonliving space, and the total cost less land
public class HouseCost { public static void main(String[] arg){
final double WIDTH = 30.0; final double LENGTH = 40.0; //Length of the house
final double STORIES = 2.5; //Number of full stories
final double NON_LIVING_SPACE = 825.0; //Garage, closets, etc.
final double PRICE = 150000.0; //Selling price less land
     double grossFootage; //Total square footage
double livingFootage; //Living area
double costPerFoot; //Cost/foot of living area
grossFootage = LENGTH * WIDTH * STORIES; //Compute gross footage
     livingFootage = grossFootage - NON_LIVING_SPACE; //Compute net footage
  costPerFoot = PRICE / livingFootage; //Compute cost per usable foot
      System.out.println("Cost per square foot is " + costPerFoot);}}
```

Now look at the same class with proper formatting:

```java
//*********************************************************************
// HouseCost application
// This application computes the cost per square foot of
// living space for a house, given the dimensions of
// the house, the number of stories, the size of the
// nonliving space, and the total cost less land
//*********************************************************************

public class HouseCost
{
  public static void main(String[] args)
  {
    final double WIDTH = 30.0;                // Width of the house
    final double LENGTH = 40.0;               // Length of the house
    final double STORIES = 2.5;               // Number of full stories
    final double NON_LIVING_SPACE = 825.0;    // Garage, closets, etc.
    final double PRICE = 150000.0;            // Selling price less land

    double grossFootage;                      // Total square footage
    double livingFootage;                     // Living area
    double costPerFoot;                       // Cost/foot of living area

    grossFootage = LENGTH * WIDTH * STORIES;  // Compute gross footage
    livingFootage = grossFootage - NON_LIVING_SPACE;  // Compute net footage
    costPerFoot = PRICE / livingFootage;      // Compute cost per usable foot

    System.out.println("Cost per square foot is " +  // Output result
        costPerFoot);
  }
}
```

Need we say more?

Appendix F discusses coding style. We suggest you use it as a guide when you are writing your own code.

3.8 Additional String Operations

Now that we have introduced numeric types, we can take advantage of additional features of the `String` data type. Here we introduce three useful methods that operate on strings: `length`, `indexOf`, and `substring`. All three are value-returning instance methods.

■ The length Method

The `length` method, when applied to a `String`, returns an `int` value that equals the number of characters in the string. If `myName` is a `String` object, a call to the `length` method looks like this:

```
myName.length()
```

The `length` method requires no arguments to be passed to it, but you still must use parentheses to signify an empty argument list. Also, `length` is a value-returning method, so the method call must appear within an expression:

```
String firstName;                 // Local declarations
String fullName;
int    len;

firstName = "Alexandra";
len = firstName.length();         // Assigns 9 to len
fullName = firstName + " Jones";
len = fullName.length();          // Assigns 15 to len
```

■ The indexOf Method

The `indexOf` method searches a string to find the first occurrence of a particular substring and returns an `int` value indicating the point where the substring was found. The substring, passed as an argument to the method, can be a literal string or a `String` expression. If `str1` and `str2` are of type `String`, the following are valid method calls, each of which returns an integer:

```
str1.indexOf("the")        str1.indexOf(str2)          str1.indexOf(str2 + "abc")
```

In each case, `str1` is searched to see if the specified substring appears within it. If so, the method returns the position in `str1` where the match begins. (Positions are numbered starting at 0, so the first character in a string is in position 0, the second is in position 1, and so on.) For a successful search, the match must be exact, including identical capitalization. If the substring could not be found, the method returns the value −1.

Given the code segment

```
String phrase;
int    position;

phrase = "The dog and the cat";
```

then the statement

```
position = phrase.indexOf("the");
```

assigns to position the value 12. In contrast, the statement

```
position = phrase.indexOf("rat");
```

assigns to position the value −1, because no match was found.

The argument to the indexOf method can also be a char value. In this case, indexOf searches for the first occurrence of that character within the string and returns its position (or –1, if the character was not found). For example, the code segment

```
String theString;

theString = "Abracadabra";
position = theString.indexOf('a');
```

assigns the value 3 to position, which is the position of the first occurrence of a lowercase *a* in theString.

Following are more examples of calls to the indexOf method, assuming the following code segment has been executed:

```
String str1;
String str2;

str1 = "Programming and Problem Solving";
str2 = "gram";
```

Method Call	Value Returned by Method
str1.indexOf("and")	12
str1.indexOf("Programming")	0
str2.indexOf("and")	−1
str1.indexOf("Pro")	0
str1.indexOf("ro" + str2)	1
str1.indexOf("Pr" + str2)	−1
str1.indexOf(' ')	11

In the fourth example, str1 contains two copies of the substring "Pro", but indexOf returns only the position of the first copy. Also notice that the matches can be either separate words or parts of words—indexOf merely tries to match the sequence of characters given in the argument list. The final example demonstrates that the argument can be as simple as a single character, even a single blank.

■ The substring Method

The substring method returns a particular substring of a string. Assuming myString is of type String, a method call has the following form:

```
myString.substring(5, 20)
```

The arguments are integers that specify positions within the string. The method returns the piece of the string that starts with the position specified by the first argument and continues to the position given by the second argument minus 1. Thus the length of the substring returned by the example call is 20 − 5 = 15 characters. Note that substring doesn't change myString; instead, it returns a new String value that is a copy of a portion of the string. The following examples assume that the statement

```
myString = "Programming and Problem Solving";
```

has been executed:

Method Call	String Contained in Value Returned by Method
myString.substring(0, 7)	"Program"
myString.substring(7, 15)	"ming and"
myString.substring(10, 10)	""
myString.substring(24, 31)	"Solving"
myString.substring(24, 25)	"S"

In the third example, specifying the second argument to be the same as the first produces the empty string as the result. The last example illustrates how to obtain a single character from a given position in the string.

If either of the arguments specifies a position beyond the end of the string, or if the second argument is smaller than the first, then the call to substring results in an error message. One way to avoid such errors is to write the call to substring in the following form. Here, start is an int variable containing the starting position, and len is another int variable containing the length of the desired substring.

```
myString.substring(start, Math.min(start+len, myString.length()))
```

Recall from our discussion of Java's math methods that Math.min returns the smaller of its two arguments. If, by accident, start+len is greater than the length of the string, then min returns the length of myString instead. In this way, we ensure that the second argument in the call to substring can be no greater than the length of myString. We assume that start is less than the length of the string, but we can use the same sort of formula as the first argument if we aren't certain that this assumption is valid.

Because substring returns a value of type String, you can use it with the concatenation operator (+) to copy pieces of strings and join them together to form new strings. The indexOf and length methods can be useful in determining the location and end of a piece of a string passed to substring as an argument.

Here is a code segment that uses several of the String operations:

```
fullName = "Jonathan Alexander Peterson Jr.";
startPos = fullName.indexOf("Peterson");
name = "Mr. " + fullName.substring(startPos, fullName.length());
```

This code assigns "Mr. Peterson Jr." to name. First, it stores a string into the variable fullName. Then, it uses indexOf to locate the start of the name Peterson within the string. Next, it builds a new string by concatenating the literal "Mr. " with the characters "Peterson Jr.", which are copied from the original string. As we will see in later chapters, string operations are an important aspect of many computer applications.

Understanding Before Changing

When you are trying to get an application to run and you come across an error, it's tempting to start changing parts of the code in an attempt to make it work. *Don't!* You'll nearly always make matters worse. It's essential that you understand what is causing the error and that you carefully think through the solution. The only thing you should try is running the application with different data to determine the pattern of the unexpected behavior.

No magic trick—inserting an extra semicolon or right brace, for example—can automatically fix a coding error. If the compiler tells you that a semicolon or a right brace is missing, you need to examine the code in light of the syntax rules and determine precisely what the problem is. Perhaps you accidentally typed a colon instead of a semicolon. Or maybe you included an extra left brace.

If the source of a problem isn't immediately obvious, a good rule of thumb is to leave the computer and go somewhere where you can quietly look over a printed copy of the code. Studies show that people who do all of their debugging away from the computer actually get their code to work in less time *and ultimately produce better code* than those who continue to work on the machine—more proof that there is still no mechanical substitute for human thought.[*]

Software Engineering Tip

---

[*]Basili, V. R., and Selby, R. W., "Comparing the Effectiveness of Software Testing Strategies," *IEEE Transactions on Software Engineering*, Vol. SE–13, No. 12, pp. 1278–1296, Dec. 1987.

■ Converting Strings to Numeric Values

Many of the problems that we use computers to solve involve the entry of numerical data—that is, values of the types `int`, `long`, `float`, and `double`. A `BufferedReader` object enables us to enter a `String`. How, then, do we input a number? The answer is that we can't—at least not directly. Java provides only for the input of strings. We must enter a number as a string and then convert the string into one of the numeric types using methods from Java's library.

Java's standard library includes a set of classes that correspond to the built-in numeric types. These classes provide methods and constants that are useful in working with the numeric types. Like the `Math` class, they are automatically imported to every Java class. Table 3.2 lists these predefined classes and the built-in type to which each one corresponds.

As you can see, the general rule is that the class name is the same as the name of the built-in type except that its first letter is capitalized. The lone exception is that the class corresponding to `int` is called `Integer`.

Built-in Type	Object Type
int	Integer
long	Long
float	Float
double	Double

Table 3.2 Predefined Classes Corresponding to Built-in Numeric Types

Among the methods associated with each of these classes is one that takes a string as its argument and returns a value of the corresponding type. Table 3.3 shows the relevant methods.

For example, we can write

```
number = Double.parseDouble("-435.82E27");
```

Object Type	Method	Argument	Returns
Integer	parseInt	String	int
Long	parseLong	String	long
Float	parseFloat	String	float
Double	parseDouble	String	double

Table 3.3 String-to-Numeric Type Conversion Methods

to convert `"-435.82E27"` into a value of type `double` and store it in `number`. Of course, what we really want to do is convert an input string into a number. We can replace the string `"-435.82E27"` in the preceding statement with a call to the `readLine` method associated with a `BufferedReader`:

```
number = Double.parseDouble(in.readLine());
```

Let's look at an example of inputting an integer value:

```
int intNumber;
intNumber = Integer.parseInt(in.readLine());
```

We now have a single statement that reads a numerical value from the screen. What if the user types something other than a number? At this point in our knowledge of Java, the result is that the application halts and displays a message such as "Number Format Error." In Chapter 9, we will see how an application can catch such an error (another example of an *exception*) and respond to it without stopping.

◼ Noninteractive Input/Output

Although we tend to use examples of interactive I/O in this book, many applications work with noninteractive I/O. A common example of noninteractive I/O on large computer systems is batch processing. In batch processing (introduced in Chapter 1), the user and the computer do not interact while the application is running. This method is most effective when an application will input or output large amounts of data. An example of batch processing is an application that takes as input a file containing semester grades for thousands of students and prints grade reports to be mailed out.

When an application must read in many data values, the usual practice is to prepare them ahead of time, storing them into a disk file. The user can then make changes or corrections to the data as necessary before running the application. When an application is designed to print lots of data, the output can be sent directly to a high-speed printer or another disk file. After the application has been run, the user can examine the data at leisure.

Most Java applications are written for interactive use, but the flexibility of the language allows you to write noninteractive applications as well. The biggest difference relates to the input/output requirements. Noninteractive applications are generally more rigid about the organization and format of the input and output data.

Applications can also combine interactive input and output with file input and output. In Chapter 5, we will discuss input and output with disk files.

3.9 Applications with Multiple Class Files

An application with multiple classes can be implemented with those classes stored in separate files. With each Java class stored in its own file, the code is divided into smaller chunks that are easier to work with. Keeping classes in separate files also makes it easier to import them into other applications. In addition, most Java development environments keep track of which files have been changed, and do not recompile unchanged files. Thus, when you're debugging just one of the classes, you don't have to wait for compilation of the other ones. Using multiple files has a further advantage in that it provides us with more flexibility in developing the classes of an application. Team programming projects, in which multiple programmers work together to solve a problem, would be very cumbersome if all of the programmers had to share a single file.

Java systems require that we name each file using the name of the class it contains. This approach allows the Java compiler to use file names to locate the classes. For example, a class called Name would be stored in a file called Name.java. Other classes that wish to use this class would include the following statement:

```
import Name;
```

The class files should all reside in the same directory on the disk. The Java compiler automatically searches this directory for related files.[2] For example, we might have the

---

[2]There are ways of indicating to the compiler that it should search other directories, but such a strategy is mainly useful for much larger programming projects than we use in this book.

following three files in a single application directory. The ellipsis (…) between the braces indicates the code for the class.

```
class Name { ... }

class Address { ... }

public class MailList { ... }    // Imports Name and Address
```

The application class MailList then has access to the other two classes, and all these classes have access to one another's nonprivate members. Two of the classes, Name and Address, are not public, so they are not visible to the JVM. However, they are also not private. Recall that we use public to make a class visible outside of itself, and that the JVM is outside of an application. Classes in the same directory are considered to be like a family, so that they can access one another's nonprivate members without being public. Later, when we explore Java's package construct in more detail, we will see that this kind of access is called package access. If we make these classes private, then they will have access only to one another's public members.

As an example, let's see how we can turn the Name class from the application in Chapter 2 into a class that we could import into an application. At the same time, let's enhance the class to make it more general. In its original form, it has just one constructor that goes to the screen to get the parts of a name. We'll add a constructor that accepts the three strings as arguments. The constructor then assigns the values of its arguments to the corresponding fields in the class. It's such a simple method that we can code it directly:

```
public Name(String firstName, String lastName, String middleName)
{
  first = firstName;                      // Assign parameters to fields
  last = lastName;
  middle = middleName;
}
```

Let's also add a method that returns the full name in the usual format of first, then middle, then last name. This method is equally simple, as it just returns the concatenation of the three strings:

```
public String full()
    {
      return first + " " + middle + " " + last;
    }
```

All we have to do besides adding these methods is to place the class code in a separate file called Name.java within the directory that has the application, and omit access modifiers from the class heading. Here is the Name class, with the new methods:

```java
//*******************************************************************
// This class provides a basic name object. The default constructor
// requests that a name be entered from System.in. A second constructor
// allows creation of a name from strings. Methods return the name
// in various formats.
//*******************************************************************
import java.io.*;                        // Package for stream readers
class Name
  {
     String first;                       // Person's first name
     String last;                        // Person's last name
     String middle;                      // Person's middle name

     // Gets a name from System.in
     public Name() throws IOException
     {
       BufferedReader in;                          // Input stream for strings
       // Instantiates in using System.in
       in = new BufferedReader(new InputStreamReader(System.in));
       System.out.print("Enter first name: ");     // Prompt for first name
       first = in.readLine();                       // Get first name
       System.out.print("Enter last name: ");       // Prompt for last name
       last = in.readLine();                        // Get last name
       System.out.print("Enter middle name: ");     // Prompt for middle name
       middle = in.readLine();                      // Get middle name
     }

     // Builds a name from string parameters
     public Name(String firstName, String lastName, String middleName)
     {
       first = firstName;                           // Assign parameters to fields
       last = lastName;
       middle = middleName;
     }

     // Returns name in first last format
     public String firstLast()
     {
       return first + " " + last;
     }

     // Returns full name in usual format
     public String full()
     {
       return first + " " + middle + " " + last;
     }
```

```
// Returns name as last, first, m.
public String lastFirstMI()
{
  return last + ", " + first + ", " + middle.substring(0, 1) + ".";
}
}
```

To show how we would use this package, we can rewrite the NameDriver application. We simply remove the class from the application itself and include an import declaration for the name package. Let's call the application NewNameDriver.

```
//*************************************************************
// NewNameDriver application
// This application inputs a name and prints it in
// two different formats
//*************************************************************
import java.io.*;                    // Package for stream readers
import Name;                         // Name class
public class NewNameDriver
{
  public static void main(String[] args) throws IOException
  {
    Name testName;                                  // Declare a name
    testName = new Name();                           // Instantiate a name
    System.out.println("Name in first-last format is " +
                  testName.firstLast());             // First format
    System.out.println("Name in last-first-initial format is " +
                  testName.lastFirstMI());           // Second format
  }
}
```

Now we can really see how object-oriented programming helps simplify application development. The NewNameDriver application is very short and easy to understand because we've separated the details of how a name is created and accessed into a class. What's more, we can now use Name objects in other problems merely by importing the Name class. In fact, that's precisely what we will do in the Case Study.

SMALL COMPANY PAYROLL

Problem: You're running a small company with just a few part-time employees, and you want an application that computes their week's pay.

Input: The hours worked for each employee, entered as real numbers via `System.in`.

Output: The pay for each employee, and the company's total pay for the week.

Discussion: This calculation would be easy to do by hand, but it is a good exercise for exploring the use of numerical input and object-oriented problem solving.

The objects in our problem are employees, so we would like to define a class for an employee. An employee in this case has a name, a pay rate, a number of hours worked, and wages earned. These items can be instance fields in our class. For each employee, we need to input the hours worked and compute the pay. This task can be a responsibility of the constructor.

Once we have an employee object, we need to get the name of the employee, the amount of pay for the employee, and the total pay for all employees. The name and pay for the employee are associated with each instance of an employee, while the total pay is a property of the entire class of employees. Thus we need instance methods to return the employee's name and pay, and a class method to return the total pay, which should be kept in a class field. Let's look at each of these methods in turn.

The constructor must get the employee name and pay rate, which can be passed in as arguments and stored in the instance fields. Because the employees change infrequently, we can encode these arguments as literal constants in the constructor calls. The hours worked are different each time we run the application, so we need to input them. The constructor must prompt the user via `System.out` and read the response via `System.in`. As we've seen, data is input as a string, which we must convert to a `double` value using the `parseDouble` method.

Once we have the hours, computing the pay is quite easy: We simply multiply the pay rate times the hours worked. The only tricky part is rounding the result to the nearest cent. Without this step, we are likely to get results that include fractions of cents. In this chapter, we showed how to round a floating-point value to the nearest integer by adding 0.5 and using a type cast to truncate the result:

```
(int)((double)Value + 0.5))
```

To round to the nearest cent, we first multiply the value by 100, round the result to the nearest integer, and then divide by 100 again. For example, if `doubleValue` contains 5.162, then

```
(double)((int)(doubleValue * 100.0 + 0.5)) / 100.0
```

gives 5.16 as its result. Here is the algorithmic solution:

```
Class Fields
Name myName
double rate
double hours
double wages
static double total
```

```
Employee Constructor
Parameters: first, last, middle names, all String; payrate, double

Declare a BufferedReader in
Create a new Name, myName, using first, last, middle
Copy payrate parameter into rate field
Instantiate in using System.in
Prompt for hours worked, using myName firstLast format
Get hours worked from in, and convert to double, storing in hours field
Compute wages and round to cents
Add wages to total
```

The method to return the name just calls the Name method that provides the name in the necessary format.

```
name value-returning instance method
return myName in last, first, MI format
```

Because the pay was computed and stored when the employee object was instantiated, we return the field value.

```
pay value-returning instance method
return wages
```

The total is updated by each instantiation, so again we can just return the field value.

```
totalPay value-returning class method
return total
```

That's all there is to the employee class responsibility algorithms. As you can see, most of the methods are trivial in their design. This simplicity is a common characteristic of object-oriented problem solutions. To hide the implementation details in a consistent manner, we turn accesses to internal fields into value-returning methods. Software engineers refer to such methods as *observers*, and we will have more to say about their role in a later chapter. Now, let's look at the code for the Employee class, which we store in a file called Employee.java.

```
//**************************************************************
// This class provides an employee record object. The provided
// constructor takes the employee name as three strings and
// creates a Name field. It also takes the pay rate as a double
// value. It then inputs the hours for the week from System.in.
// Instance methods return the name formatted as a string and
// the pay for the employee. A class method returns the total pay.
// Constructor throws IOException.
//**************************************************************
import java.io.*;                    // Package for IOException
import Name;                         // Class for names
class Employee
{
  Name myName;                       // Employee name field
  double rate;                       // Pay rate
  double hours;                      // Hours worked
  double wages;                      // Simple wages (rate * hours)
  static double total = 0.0;         // Total pay for all employees

  // Builds an employee record
  public Employee (String first, String last, String middle,
                   double payrate) throws IOException
  {
    BufferedReader in;               // Input stream for strings
    // Initialize fields
    myName = new Name(first, last, middle);
    rate = payrate;
    // Instantiate input stream in using System.in
    in = new BufferedReader(new InputStreamReader(System.in));
    // Prompt for hours worked
    System.out.print("Enter hours worked by " + myName.firstLast() + ": ");
    // Get hours worked and convert from string to double
    hours = Double.parseDouble(in.readLine());
    wages = (double)((int)(hours * rate * 100.0 + 0.5))/100.0;
    total = total + wages;
  }

  // Returns employee name
  public String name()
  {
    return myName.lastFirstMI();
  }

  // Returns employee wages
  public double pay()
  {
    return wages;
  }
```

```
// Returns total wages for all employees
public static double totalPay()
{
  return total;
}
}
```

We now have a simulation of the object on which our application depends, so we can solve the payroll problem in terms of what the object can do for us. The first task is to create an object for each employee. In the process, the constructor takes care of inputting the hours worked, computing the pay, and adding it to the total. Once the objects are created, all of the work is done, and we just need to report the results. For each employee object, we print out a message indicating the name and the pay. Finally, we print the total pay. Here is the algorithm for a payroll with three employees:

```
Payroll Application

Instantiate emp1 (first, last, middle, rate)
Instantiate emp2 (first, last, middle, rate)
Instantiate emp3 (first, last, middle, rate)
Print "Pay " emp1 name " $" emp1 pay
Print "Pay " emp2 name " $" emp2 pay
Print "Pay " emp3 name " $" emp3 pay
Print Employee total pay
```

Of course, we also need to declare three Employee variables: emp1, emp2, and emp3. In addition, we need to wrap all of this in main, inside of a class called Payroll. We need to remember to import the Employee class. We do not need to import Name, however, because we don't use it directly; Employee imports it for its own use. We still need to import java.io, even though we don't directly use the BufferedReader class. The reason is that the Employee constructor can throw an IOException, so we need to explicitly throw this exception to the next level in the heading of main—and the IOException object is defined in java.io. If we forget to import java.io, the compiler will complain that IOException isn't defined.

We now have three classes in three different files involved in this application: Name, Employee, and Payroll. How do we get them to find one another? We place the three class files in the same directory and let Payroll import Employee, which in turn imports Name. In Chapter 6, we will show an even better solution: bundling related classes into a user-defined package.

Now we're ready to write the application. We've added comments where needed. Here is the code:

```
//****************************************************************
// Payroll application
// This application computes the pay for three employees
// and also outputs the total pay
//****************************************************************
```

```
import java.io.*;                      // Package for IOException
import Employee;                       // Employee class

public class Payroll
{
  public static void main(String[] args) throws IOException
  {
    // Declare employees
    Employee emp1;
    Employee emp2;
    Employee emp3;
    // Instantiate employees
    emp1 = new Employee("Herman", "Herrmann", "George", 14.95);
    emp2 = new Employee("Clara", "Eames", "Julia", 16.28);
    emp3 = new Employee("Matilda", "Hagen", "Louise", 12.73);
    // Output pay for each employee
    System.out.println("Pay " + emp1.name() + " $" + emp1.pay());
    System.out.println("Pay " + emp2.name() + " $" + emp2.pay());
    System.out.println("Pay " + emp3.name() + " $" + emp3.pay());
    // Output total pay for all employees
    System.out.println("Total pay is $" + Employee.totalPay());
  }
}
```

The output from the application follows:

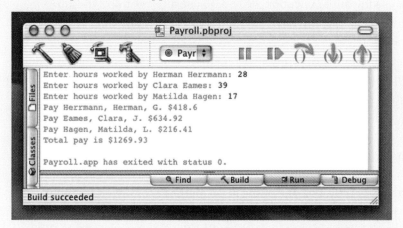

As you can see, the application code is short and simple. It includes basically just three statements that are each repeated for the three employees. This is the goal of object-oriented design—to produce applications that seem simple on the surface because the complexity is hidden in the objects. Nor are the objects themselves especially complex. If the algorithm for an object grows in complexity to the point that it becomes difficult to understand, it likely contains other objects that should be identified and developed separately. In such a case, we can then simplify the object's algorithms.

3.10 Testing and Debugging

Testing and Debugging Hints

1. An `int` literal other than 0 should not start with a zero. If it starts with zero, it is an octal (base–8) number.

2. Watch out for integer division. The expression `47 / 100` yields 0, the integer quotient. This is one of the major sources of wrong output in Java code.

3. When using the / and % operators with integers, remember that division by zero is not allowed.

4. Double-check every expression according to the precedence rules to confirm that the operations are performed in the desired order, especially with expressions involving string conversion.

5. Avoid mixing integer and floating-point values in expressions. If you must mix them, use explicit type casts to reduce the chance of mistakes.

6. For each assignment statement, verify that the expression result has the same data type as the variable to the left of the assignment operator (=). If not, use an explicit type cast for clarity and safety. Also, remember that storing a floating-point value into an `int` variable truncates the fractional part.

7. If an application is producing erroneous results and all of its expressions appear to be correct, check whether any of them can result in integer overflow. Also, check whether they contain any unintentional type conversions.

8. For every library package you use in your application, be sure to use an `import` declaration.

9. Examine each method call to confirm that you have the right number of arguments and that the data types of the arguments are correct.

10. Remember to return an expression from a value-returning method. The expression must produce the same type as the result type specified in the method heading.

11. Keep your code neatly formatted so that it is easier to read.

12. If the cause of an error in your code is not obvious, leave the computer and study a printed listing. Change your code only after you understand the source of the error.

13. Remember to use a class name with a class method, and an object name with an instance method.

14. You cannot input numeric values directly. Use one of the `parse` methods to convert an input string to a numeric value.

15. Be careful to type valid numeric values as input to an application that reads numbers. At this point in our knowledge of Java, entering an incorrectly formed number will cause the application to crash with an error message.

Summary

Java provides several built-in numeric data types, of which the most commonly used are `int` and `double`. The integral types are based on the mathematical integers, but the computer limits the range of integer values that can be represented. The floating-point types are based on the mathematical notion of real numbers. As with integers, the computer limits the range of floating-point numbers that can be represented. In addition, it limits the number of digits of precision in floating-point values. We can write literals of type `double` in several forms, including scientific (E) notation. Java provides the standard mathematical operations to go with these data types: addition (+), subtraction (-), multiplication (*), division (/), and remainder (%). Java also provides an increment operation (++) and a decrement operation (--).

Mixing values of the integer and floating-point types in an expression results in automatic type conversion to achieve compatibility between the operands of all of the operators. If you aren't careful, these automatic conversions can have unanticipated results. It is best to explicitly use type cast operations whenever you need to mix types within expressions.

Much of the computation of an application is performed in arithmetic expressions. Expressions can contain more than one operator. The order in which the operations are performed is determined by precedence rules. In arithmetic expressions, the unary operators (such as negation) are performed first; then type casts; then multiplication, division, and modulus; and finally addition and subtraction. Multiple arithmetic operations of the same precedence are grouped from left to right. You can use parentheses to override the precedence rules.

Not only should the output produced by an application be easy to read, but the format of the code itself should also be clear and readable. A consistent style that uses indentation, blank lines, and spaces within lines helps you (and other programmers) understand and work with your code.

Value-returning class methods are another way of implementing the behaviors of objects. They are written by specifying `static` in the heading. The call appends the method name to the name of its class, separated by a period.

A `BufferedReader` object returns a string. To input numerical data, we must use other Java-supplied classes corresponding to the numeric types. These classes provide methods to parse a string and convert it to a value of the corresponding numeric type.

We can save our class code in separate files and import the class into our applications. Separating the class code makes it easier to manage the files, makes the classes easier to reuse, and makes it easier to divide a large project among a team of programmers.

Quick Check

1. When you assign one reference variable to another, how many copies of the object are there? (pp. 100–103)

Learning Portfolio

2. Which integer and real types take up the same number of bits in the computer's memory? (pp. 103–106)

3. What syntactic parts do floating-point values have that integral types lack? (pp. 105–106)

4. If you want to change the precedence of operations in an expression, what symbols do you use? (p. 114)

5. Add type casts to the following statements to make the type conversions clear and explicit. Your answers should produce the same results as the original statements. (pp. 115–118)

   a. `someDouble = 5 + someInt;`

   b. `someInt = 2.5 * someInt / someDouble;`

6. If the `String` variable str contains the string "Now is the time", what is the result of the following expression? (pp. 126–129)

   `str.length() + " " + str.substring(1, 3)`

7. A value-returning method can be called either within an expression or as a separate statement. (True or False?) (pp. 122–123)

8. Write a local Java constant declaration that gives the name PI to the value 3.14159. (p. 106)

9. Declare a local `int` variable named count and a local `double` variable named sum. (pp. 107–108)

10. You want to divide 9 by 5.

    a. How do you write the expression if you want the result to be the floating-point value 1.8?

    b. How do you write the expression if you want only the integer quotient? (pp. 108–111)

11. What is the value of the following Java expression? (pp. 108–109)

    `5 % 2`

12. What is the result of evaluating the following expression? (pp. 114–115)

    `(1 + 2 * 2) / 2 + 1`

13. How would you write the following formula as a Java expression that produces a floating-point value as a result? (pp. 115–118)

    $$\frac{9}{5}c + 32$$

14. You want to compute the square roots and absolute values of some floating-point numbers. Which Java methods would you use? (pp. 120–122)

15. Who needs to have code formatted in a clear and readable manner—the Java compiler, the human reader, or both? (pp. 124–125)

16. What distinguishes the heading of a value-returning method from a method that doesn't return a value? (pp. 122–123)

17. What features distinguish class methods from instance methods, both syntactically and semantically? (pp. 122–123)

18. When saving a class called `Animals` in a separate file, what should you name the file? (pp. 131–134)

Answers

1. There is only one copy, with two references to it. **2.** `int` and `float` are both 32 bits. `long` and `double` are both 64 bits. **3.** A decimal point, a fractional part, and an exponent. **4.** Parentheses ( )
5. a. `someDouble = (double)(5 + someInt);`
   b. `someInt = (int)(2.5 * (double)(someInt) / someDouble);`
6. `15` ow **7.** False. It can be called only within an expression. **8.** `final double PI = 3.14159;`
9. `int     count;`
   `double sum;`
10. a. `9.0 / 5.0` or `(double) 9 / (double) 5` **b.** `9 / 5`
11. The value is 1. **12.** The result is 3. **13.** `9.0 / 5.0 * c + 32.0` **14.** `Math.sqrt` and `Math.abs` **15.** The human reader. The compiler ignores code formatting. **16.** It has a type or class name in place of the keyword `void`. **17.** Class methods are static. They exist in only one place, yet are accessible to all objects of the class. In referring to a class method, we precede its name with the class name and a period. Instance methods are not static, and they are associated with each object. In referring to an instance method, we precede its name with the object name and a period. **18.** `Animals.java`.

Exam Preparation Exercises

1. Mark the following constructs either valid or invalid. Assume all variables are of type `int`.

	Valid	Invalid
a. `x * y = c;`	_____	_____
b. `y = con;`	_____	_____
c. `private static final int x : 10;`	_____	_____
d. `int x;`	_____	_____
e. `a = b % c;`	_____	_____

2. If `alpha` and `beta` are `int` variables with `alpha = 4` and `beta = 9`, what value is stored into `alpha` in each of the following? Answer each part independently of the others.

   a. `alpha = 3 * beta;`

   b. `alpha = alpha + beta;`

   c. `alpha++;`

   d. `alpha = alpha / beta;`

   e. `alpha--;`

   f. `alpha = alpha + alpha;`

   g. `alpha = beta % 6;`

3. Compute the value of each legal expression. Indicate whether the value is an integer or a floating-point value. If the expression is not legal, explain why.

	Integer	Floating Point
a. 10.0 / 3.0 + 5 * 2	_____	_____
b. 10 % 3 + 5 % 2	_____	_____
c. 10 / 3 + 5 / 2	_____	_____
d. 12.5 + (2.5 / (6.2 / 3.1))	_____	_____
e. −4 * (−5 + 6)	_____	_____
f. 13 % 5 / 3	_____	_____
g. (10.0 / 3.0 % 2) / 3	_____	_____

4. What value is stored into the `int` variable result in each of the following?

   a. `result = 15 % 4;`

   b. `result = 7 / 3 + 2;`

   c. `result = 2 + 7 * 5;`

   d. `result = 45 / 8 * 4 + 2;`

   e. `result = 17 + (21 % 6) * 2;`

   f. `result = (int)(4.5 + 2.6 * 0.5);`

5. If a and b are `int` variables with a = 5 and b = 2, what output does each of the following statements produce?

   a. `System.out.println("a = " + a + "b = " + b);`

   b. `System.out.println("Sum:" + a + b);`

   c. `System.out.println("Sum:   " + a + b);`

   d. `System.out.println(a / b + " feet");`

6. What does the following application print?

```
public class ExamPrep
{
    public static void main(String[] args)
    {
        final int LBS = 10;
        int   price;
        int   cost;
        char ch;
        price = 30;
        cost = price * LBS;
        ch = 'A';
        System.out.println("Cost is ");
        System.out.println(cost);
```

```
System.out.println("Price is " + price + "Cost is " + cost);
System.out.println("Grade " + ch + " costs ");
System.out.println(cost);
    }
}
```

7. Translate the following Java code into algebraic notation. (All variables are `double` variables.)

```
y = -b + Math.sqrt(b * b - 4.0 * a * c);
```

8. Given the code fragment:

```
int    i;
int    j;
double z;


i = 4;
j = 17;
z = 2.6;
```

determine the value of each of the following expressions. If the result is a floating-point value, include a decimal point in your answer.

a. `i / (double)j`

b. `1.0 / i + 2`

c. `z * j`

d. `i + j % i`

e. `(1 / 2) * i`

f. `2 * i + j - i`

g. `j / 2`

h. `2 * 3 - 1 % 3`

i. `i % j / i`

j. `(int)(z + 0.5)`

9. Evaluate the following expressions. If the result is a floating-point number, include a decimal point in your answer.

a. `Math.abs(-9.1)`

b. `Math.sqrt(49.0)`

c. `3 * (int)7.8 + 3`

d. `Math.pow(4.0, 2.0)`

e. `Math.sqrt((double)(3 * 3 + 4 * 4))`

f. `Math.sqrt(Math.abs(-4.0) + Math.sqrt(25.0))`

10. Given the statements

```
String heading;
String str;

heading = "Exam Preparation Exercises";
```

what is the output of each of the following code segments?

a. `System.out.println(heading.length());`

b. `System.out.println(heading.substring(6, 16));`

c. `System.out.println(heading.indexOf("Ex"));`

d. `str = heading.substring(2, 26);`
   `System.out.println(str.indexOf("Ex"));`

e. `str = heading.substring(heading.indexOf("Ex") + 2, 24);`
   `System.out.println(str.indexOf("Ex"));`

f. `str = heading.substring(heading.indexOf("Ex") + 2, heading.length());`
   `System.out.println(str.indexOf("Ex"));`

11. Incorrectly formatting an application causes an error. (True or False?)

Programming Warm-Up Exercises

1. Change the application in Exam Preparation Exercise 6 so that it prints the cost for 15 pounds.

2. Write an assignment statement to calculate the sum of the numbers from 1 through n using Gauss's formula:

$$sum = \frac{n(n + 1)}{2}$$

Store the result into the `int` variable sum.

3. Given the declarations

```
int     i;
int     j;
double  x;
double  y;
```

write a valid Java expression for each of the following algebraic expressions.

a. $\dfrac{x}{y} - 3$ e. $\dfrac{i}{j}$ (the floating-point result)

b. $(x + y)(x - y)$ f. $\dfrac{i}{j}$ (the integer quotient)

c. $\dfrac{1}{x+y}$ **g.** $\dfrac{\dfrac{x+y}{3} - \dfrac{x-y}{5}}{4x}$

d. $\dfrac{1}{x} + y$

4. Given the declarations

```
int    i;
long   n;
double x;
double y;
```

write a valid Java expression for each of the following algebraic expressions. Use calls to math methods wherever they are useful.

a. $|i|$ **e.** $\dfrac{x^3}{x+y}$

b. $|n|$ **f.** $\sqrt{x^6 + y^5}$

c. $|x+y|$ **g.** $(x + \sqrt{y})^7$

d. $|x| + |y|$

5. Write expressions to compute both solutions for the quadratic formula. The formula is

$$\dfrac{-b \pm \sqrt{b^2 - 4ac}}{2a}$$

The $\pm$ symbol means "plus or minus" and indicates that the equation has two solutions: one in which the result of the square root is added to $-b$ and one in which the result is subtracted from $-b$. Assume all variables are `float` variables.

6. Enter the following application into your computer and run it. In the initial comments, replace the items within parentheses with your own information. (Omit the parentheses.)

```
//*********************************
// Programming Assignment One
// (your name)
// (date application was run)
// (description of the problem)
//*********************************
```

```java
public class WarmUp
{
  public static void main(String[] args)
  {
    final double DEBT = 300.0;        // Original value owed
    final double PMT = 22.4;          // Payment
    final double INT_RATE = 0.02;     // Interest rate
    double charge;                    // Interest times debt
    double reduc;                     // Amount debt is reduced
    double remaining;                 // Remaining balance
    // Compute values for output
    charge = INT_RATE * DEBT;         // Compute interest charge
    reduc = PMT - charge;             // Compute debt reduction
    remaining = DEBT - reduc;         // Compute remaining balance
    // Output result
    System.out.println("Payment: " + PMT + " Charge: " + charge +
                       " Balance owed: " + remaining);

  }
}
```

7. Enter the following application into your computer and run it. Add comments, using the pattern shown in Exercise 6. (Notice how difficult it is to tell what the code does without the comments.)

```java
public class WarmUp2
{
  public static void main(String[] args)
  {
    final int TOT_COST = 1376;
    final int POUNDS = 10;
    final int OUNCES = 12;
    int    totOz;
    double uCost;
    totOz = 16 * POUNDS;
    totOz = totOz + OUNCES;
    uCost = TOT_COST / totOz;
    System.out.println("Cost per unit: " + uCost);
  }
}
```

Learning Portfolio

8. Complete the following Java application. The application should find and output the perimeter and area of a rectangle, given the length and the width. Be sure to label the output. Don't forget to use comments.

```
//************************************************
// Rectangle application
// This application finds the perimeter and the area
// of a rectangle, given the length and width
//************************************************
public class Rectangle
{
  public static void main(String[] args)
  {
    double length;          // Length of the rectangle
    double width;           // Width of the rectangle
    double perimeter;       // Perimeter of the rectangle
    double area;            // Area of the rectangle

    length = 10.7;
    width = 5.2;
```

9. Write an expression whose result is the position of the first occurrence of the characters "res" in a String variable named sentence. If the variable contains the first sentence of this question, then what is the result? (Look at the sentence carefully!)

10. Write a sequence of Java statements to output the positions of the second and third occurrences of the characters "res" in the String variable named sentence. You may assume that there are always at least three occurrences in the variable. (*Hint:* Use the substring method to create a new string whose contents are the portion of sentence following an occurrence of "res".)

11. Reformat the following application to make it clear and readable.

```
//****************************************************************
  // This application computes the sum and product of two integers
//****************************************************************
public class SumProd {  public static void main(String[] args){
final int INT2=8;   final int INT1=20; System.out.println(
"The sum of " + INT1 + " and "
+ INT2 + " is " + (INT1+INT2)); System.out.println (
"Their product is " + (INT1*INT2)); }}
```

Programming Problems

1. Java systems provide a set of user-defined types that duplicate the names of primitive types except that the first letter of the type name is capitalized (for example, Double and Long instead of double and long). The one exception is that the type corresponding to int is called Integer. Each of these types contains declarations of constants related to the corresponding primitive type. Two of these constants are Integer.MAX_VALUE and Integer.MIN_VALUE, the largest and smallest int values that Java allows. Write an application to display the values of Integer.MAX_VALUE and Integer.MIN_VALUE. The output should identify which value is Integer.MAX_VALUE and which value is Integer.MIN_VALUE. Be sure to include appropriate comments in your code, and use indentation as we do in the code in this chapter. Each of these types defines similar constants, so you may want to extend your application to display Long.MIN_VALUE, and so on, just to learn what the actual maximum and minimum numbers are for each of the primitive types.

2. Write an application that outputs three lines as follows:

   ```
   7 / 4 using integer division equals  <result>

   7 / 4 using floating-point division equals  <result>

   7 modulo 4 equals  <result>
   ```

   where *<result>* stands for the result computed by your application. Use named constants for 7 and 4 everywhere in your application (including the output statements) to make the application easy to modify. Be sure to include appropriate comments in your code, choose meaningful identifiers, and use indentation as we do in the code in this chapter.

3. Write a Java application that takes an integral Celsius temperature as input and converts it to its Fahrenheit equivalent. The formula is

   $$\text{Fahrenheit} = \frac{9}{5}\,\text{Celsius} + 32$$

   After the Celsius temperature is input, it should be displayed along with the corresponding Fahrenheit equivalent. The application should include appropriate messages identifying each value. Be sure to include appropriate comments in your code, choose meaningful identifiers, and use indentation as we do in the code in this chapter.

4. Write an application to calculate the diameter, circumference, and area of a circle with a radius input by the user. Assign the radius to a float variable, and then output the radius with an appropriate message. Declare a named constant PI with the value 3.14159. The application should output the diameter, circumference, and area, each on a separate line, with identifying labels. Be sure to include appropriate comments in your code, choose meaningful identifiers, and use indentation as we do in the code in this chapter.

Case Study Follow-Up

1. Modify the Payroll application to handle a fourth employee. Use your own name, and be generous with your pay.

2. Change the Employee class to also return the hours worked, and modify the Payroll application to echo-print the hours that were entered for each employee.

3. Modify the Payroll application to also calculate and print the average pay.

4. Change the Employee class to also compute the average pay and provide a method that returns it, and then modify the Payroll application to display the average using the new method.

5. If you did Exercises 3 and 4, compare the different versions of Payroll. Which do you think is simpler?

Selection and Encapsulation

goals

Knowledge Goals

- To understand the Boolean operators AND, OR, and NOT
- To understand the concept of control flow with respect to selection statements
- To understand how nested control flow works
- To know the differences between the *if-else* and *if-else-if* selection structures
- To understand the differences between a nested *if* structure and a series of *if* structures
- To know when each form of selection structure is appropriate
- To know what an algorithm walk-through is and how it is used
- To understand the purpose of tracing the execution of Java code
- To become familiar with the design concepts of encapsulation and abstraction

Skill Goals

To be able to:

- Construct a simple logical (Boolean) expression to evaluate a given condition
- Construct a complex Boolean expression to evaluate a given condition
- Construct an *if-else* statement to perform a specific task
- Construct an *if* statement to perform a specific task
- Construct a set of nested *if* statements to perform a specific task
- Test and debug a Java application

timeline

1943

The first "Walkie-Talkie" is invented by Dan Nobel. This portable FM two-way radio uses 35 lb. backpacks

1945

J. Presper Eckert and John Mauchly join forces to develop the Electronic Discrete Variable Automatic Computer (EDVAC)

1945

John von Neumann outlines the principles of a stored-program computer

1945

Grace Murray Hopper discovers a moth in her computer: the first computer "bug"

1946

The ENIAC is unveiled at the Moore School of Electrical Engineering at UPENN and is accepted by the U.S. Army Ordnance Corps

1947

Magnetic drum memory is introduced

introduction

So far, the statements in our code have always executed in the same order in which we write them. The first statement executes, then the second, and so on. One variation on this ordering is the method call, which executes a separate sequence of statements. But what if we want the computer to execute the statements in an order other than sequentially? For example, suppose we want to check the validity of input data and then perform a calculation *or* display an error message, but not both. To do so, we must be able to ask a question and then, based on the answer, choose one or another course of action.

The *if* statement allows us to execute statements in an order that differs from their physical order. We can ask a question with this kind of statement and do one thing if the answer is yes (true) or another if the answer is no (false). In the first part of this chapter, we deal with asking questions; in the second part, we examine the *if* statement itself. We then use the *if* statement to handle multiple event sources, and apply what we've seen in the Case Study.

1948

Researchers at the University of Manchester develop the Manchester Mark I, a computer with all the main components of today's computers that can store data and user programs in electronic memory

1947

The world's first transistor is developed at Bell Labs

1949

Jay Forrester refines magnetic core memory in his work on the Whirlwind computer

1949

John Mauchly creates the first high-level programming language: Short Order Code

1950

Alan Turing asks "Can Machines Think?" and outlines criteria for the Turing Test of machine intelligence

1951

The UNIVAC (Universal Automatic Computer) I is completed

4.1 Flow of Control

The order in which statements execute is called the **flow of control**. In a sense, the computer is under the control of one statement at a time. After a statement executes, control turns over to the next statement (like a baton being passed in a relay race).

The flow of control is normally sequential (see Figure 4.1). That is, when one statement is finished executing, control passes to the next statement in the code. Where we want the flow of control to be nonsequential, we use **control structures**, or special statements that transfer control to a statement other than the one that physically comes next. As we saw earlier, method calls are control structures that alter the flow of control so that a separate sequence of statements can be executed.

> **Flow of control** The order in which the computer executes statements
>
> **Control structure** A statement used to alter the normally sequential flow of control

Selection

We use a selection (or branching) control structure when we want the computer to choose between alternative actions. To do so, we make an assertion, a claim that is either true or false. If the assertion is true, the computer executes one statement. If it is false, it executes another (see Figure 4.2). The computer's ability to solve practical problems is a product of its ability to make decisions and execute different sequences of instructions.

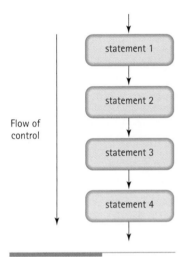

Flow of control

Figure 4.1   Sequential Control

The `Payroll` application in Chapter 3 is unable to recognize an invalid amount of hours worked, such as a negative number. How can the computer respond to erroneous input? It can decide whether a negative number has been entered. It does so by testing the assertion that the number is less than zero. If the assertion is true, the computer follows the instructions for displaying an error message. If the assertion is false, the computer simply computes the pay. Before we examine selection control structures in Java, let's look closely at how we get the computer to make decisions.

4.2 Conditions and Logical Expressions

To ask a question in Java, we don't phrase it as a question; rather, we state it as an assertion. If our assertion is true, the answer to the question is yes. If our assertion is false, the answer to the question is no. The need to simplify assertions to true-false form stems from the fact that it is easiest for the computer to work with answers that can be represented by the 1s and 0s of the binary number system. For example, to ask, "Are we having spinach for dinner tonight?" we would say, "We are having spinach for dinner tonight." If the assertion is true, the answer to the question is yes. If it is false, the answer is no.

Thus asking questions in Java means making an assertion that is either true or false. The computer *evaluates* the assertion, checking it against some internal condition (the values stored in certain variables, for instance) to see whether it is true or false.

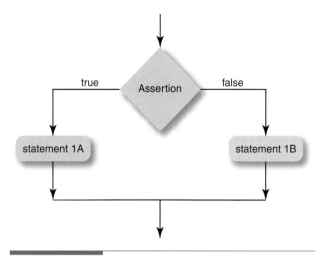

Figure 4.2 Selection (branching) Control Structure

■ The boolean Data Type

The boolean data type consists of just two values, the constants true and false. The reserved word boolean is pronounced "bool-e-un."[1] Boolean data is used for testing conditions in code so that the computer can make decisions (as in a selection control structure).

We declare variables of type boolean in the same way that we declare variables of other standard types—by writing the name of the data type and then an identifier:

```
boolean dataOK;    // True if the input data is valid
boolean done;      // True if the process is done
boolean taxable;   // True if the item has sales tax
```

Each variable of type boolean can contain one of two values: true or false. It's important to understand right from the beginning that true and false are neither variable names nor strings. Rather, they are special constants in Java and, in fact, are reserved words.

■ Logical Expressions

In programming languages, assertions take the form of *logical expressions* (also called *Boolean expressions*). Just as an arithmetic expression is made up of numeric values and operations, a logical expression is made up of logical values and operations. Every logical expression has one of the two boolean values: true or false.

Here are some examples of logical expressions:

- A boolean variable or constant
- An arithmetic expression followed by a relational operator followed by an arithmetic expression
- A logical expression followed by a logical operator followed by a logical expression

---

[1]The name boolean is a tribute to George Boole, a nineteenth-century English mathematician who described a system of logic using variables with just two values, true and false. (See the May We Introduce box on page 164.)

Let's look at each of these possibilities in detail.

`boolean` Variables and Constants   As we have seen, a `boolean` variable is a variable declared to be of type `boolean`, which can contain either the value `true` or the value `false`. For example, if `dataOK` is a `boolean` variable, then

```
dataOK = true;
```

is a valid assignment statement.

Relational Operators   Another way of assigning a value to a `boolean` variable is to set it equal to the result of comparing two expressions with a *relational operator*. Relational operators test a relationship between two values.

Let's look at an example. In the following code fragment, `lessThanZero` is a `boolean` variable and `i` and `j` are `int` variables:

```
lessThanZero = (i < 0);    // Compare i and 0 with the "less than"
                           // operator, and assign the value to lessThanZero
```

By comparing two values, we assert that a relationship (such as "less than") exists between them. If the relationship does exist, the assertion is true; if not, it is false. We can test for the following relationships in Java:

Operator	Relationship Tested
==	Equal to
!=	Not equal to
>	Greater than
<	Less than
>=	Greater than or equal to
<=	Less than or equal to

An expression followed by a relational operator followed by an expression is called a *relational expression*. The result of a relational expression is of type `boolean`. For example, if x is 5 and y is 10, the following expressions all have the value `true`:

```
x != y
y > x
x < y
y >= x
x <= y
```

If x and y are instead of type `char`, and x contains the character `'M'` and y holds `'R'`, the values of the expressions are still `true` because the relational operator <, when used with letters, means "comes before in the alphabet" or, more properly, "comes before in the collating sequence of the character set." For example, in the ASCII subset of the Unicode character set, all of the uppercase letters are in alphabetical order, as are the lowercase letters, but all of the uppercase letters come before the lowercase letters. So the expressions

```
'M' < 'R'
```

and

```
'm' < 'r'
```

have the value `true`, but

```
'm' < 'R'
```

has the value `false`. All uppercase letters come before any of the lowercase letters.

Of course, we have to be careful about the data types of things that we compare. The safest approach is to compare identical types: `int` with `int`, `double` with `double`, `char` with `char`, and so on. If you mix data types in a comparison, implicit type conversion takes place just as it does in arithmetic expressions. If you try to compare an `int` value and a `double` value, for example, the computer temporarily converts the `int` value to its `double` equivalent before making the comparison. As with arithmetic expressions, it's wise to use explicit type casting to make your intentions known:

```
someDouble >= (double)someInt
```

If you try to compare a `boolean` value with a numeric value (probably by mistake), the compiler will display an error message. Values of type `boolean` cannot be converted to any type other than `String`. When a `boolean` variable is concatenated with a string, its value is automatically converted to either `"true"` or `"false"`. No type can be converted to `boolean`.

Be careful to compare `char` values only with other `char` values. For example, the comparisons

```
'0' < '9'
```

and

```
0 < 9
```

are appropriate, but comparing a digit in quotes (a character) and a digit, such as

```
'0' < 9
```

generates an implicit type conversion and a result that probably isn't what you expect. The character for the digit `'0'` is converted to its Unicode `int` value, which is 79, and the comparison returns `false` because 79 is greater than 9.

We can use relational operators to compare not only variables or constants, but also the values of arithmetic expressions. In the following table, we compare the results of adding 3 to x and multiplying y by 10 for different values of x and y:

Value of x	Value of y	Expression	Result
12	2	x + 3 <= y * 10	true
20	2	x + 3 <= y * 10	false
7	1	x + 3 != y * 10	false
17	2	x + 3 == y * 10	true
100	5	x + 3 > y * 10	true

Caution: It's easy to confuse the assignment operator (=) and the relational operator (==). These two operators have very different effects in your code, however. Some people pronounce the relational operator as "equals-equals" to remind themselves of the difference.

Comparing Strings   You cannot compare strings using the relational operators. Syntactically, Java lets you write the comparisons for equality (==) and inequality (!=) between values of class String, but such a comparison is not what you typically want. Recall from Chapter 2 that String is a reference type. That is, the content of a String variable is the memory address for the beginning of the string object. When you assign one string to another, Java simply copies this address. Similarly, when you compare two strings, Java checks whether they have the same address. It does *not* check whether they contain the same sequence of characters.

Forgetting that Java makes comparisons involving strings in this manner, and mistakenly using the == or != operator, is a source of some insidious errors. Sometimes, the comparison seems to work; at other times it fails. The reason is that most Java compilers are quite clever about how they store String literals. If you type the same literal in two different places in your code, the compiler recognizes their equality and stores the character sequence just once; it then uses the same address in the Bytecode. Thus, comparing a String literal to a variable that has been assigned an identical literal elsewhere in the program is likely to indicate that they are equal (if the Java compiler is well designed).

On the other hand, if you get a string from a BufferedReader object and compare it to a String literal, the two must always compare as unequal, even when they contain the exact same sequence of characters. The string from the BufferedReader and the String literal are stored in different places in memory, which means that their addresses compare as unequal.

Rather than using the relational operators, we compare strings with a set of value-returning instance methods that Java supplies as part of the String class. Because they are instance methods, the method name is written following a String object, separated by a dot. The string to which the method name is appended is one of the strings in the comparison, and the string in the argument list is the other string to be compared. Because we sometimes want to compare strings ignoring capitalization, the String class provides methods called toLowerCase and toUpperCase that convert all the characters of a string to lowercase or up-

Method Name	Argument Type	Returns	Operation Performed
`equals`	`String`	`boolean`	Tests for equality of string contents.
`equalsIgnoreCase`	`String`	`boolean`	Returns `true` if the strings are equal, ignoring the case of the letters. Returns `false` if they are unequal.
`compareTo`	`String`	`int`	Returns 0 if equal, a positive integer if this string comes after the string in the argument, and a negative integer if it comes before the argument string.
`toLowerCase`		`String`	Returns a new identical string except that the characters are all lowercase.
`toUpperCase`		`String`	Returns a new identical string except that the characters are all uppercase.

Table 4.1   Java Comparison and Case-Conversion Methods

percase, respectively. The three most useful comparison methods are summarized in Table 4.1, along with `toLowerCase` and `toUpperCase`.

Many of Java's classes support a method called `compareTo`. As we will see in later chapters, this common use of `compareTo` enables the same piece of code to compare objects of different classes. With strings, we often combine the use of `compareTo` with either `toLowerCase` or `toUpperCase`, as we show below. Note that `equals` and `equalsIgnoreCase` test only for equality. We must use the `compareTo` method to test for relationships such as "greater than" or "less than."

Let's look at some examples. If `lastName` is a `String` variable, we can write

```
lastName.equals("Olson")        // Tests whether lastName equals "Olson"
```

Because every `String` literal is also a `String` object, Java lets us append the method call to a literal, if we so choose.

```
"Olson".equals(lastName)        // Tests whether lastName equals "Olson"
```

As another example, we might write

```
lastName.compareTo("Olson") > 0   // Tests if lastName comes after "Olson"
```

Comparison of strings in Java follows the collating sequence used in the Unicode character set. When the computer tests a relationship between two strings, it begins with the first character of each one, compares the characters according to the collating sequence, and if they are the same, repeats the comparison with the next character in each string. The character-by-character test continues until either a mismatch is found or the final characters have been compared and are equal. If all their characters are equal, then the two strings are equal. If a mismatch is found, then the string with the character that comes before the other is the "lesser" string.

For example, given the statements

```
String word1;
String word2;

word1 = "Tremendous";
word2 = "Small";
```

the following relational expressions have the values shown:

Expression	Value	Reason
word1.equals(word2)	false	They are unequal in the first character.
word1.compareTo(word2) > 0	true	'T' comes after 'S' in the collating sequence.
word1.compareTo("Tremble") < 0	false	The fifth characters don't match, and 'e' comes after 'b'.
word2.equals("Small")	true	They are equal.
"cat".compareTo("dog") == 0	false	They are unequal.

Remembering the way that `compareTo` works can be a bit challenging at first. A convention that helps overcome this confusion is to write the relational expression with zero on the right side of the operator. Then the operator has the same meaning as if we were able to substitute it for the method name. That is, writing

```
word1.compareTo(word2) > 0
```

has the same effect as if Java allowed us to write

```
word1 > word2
```

In most cases, the ordering of strings corresponds to alphabetical ordering. When strings have mixed-case letters, however, we can get nonalphabetical results. For example, in a phone book we would expect to see "Macauley" before "MacPherson." The Unicode collating sequence places all English uppercase letters before the lowercase letters, so the string "MacPherson" compares less than "Macauley" in Java. To compare strings for strict alphabetical ordering, all the characters must be in the same case. In the following examples, `toLowerCase` and `toUpperCase` are used to convert strings to a single case:

```
lowerCaseString = myString.toLowerCase();
upperCaseString = myString.toUpperCase();
```

We can use these methods directly in a comparison expression. For example, the following expressions convert word1 and word2 to the same case before comparing them. It doesn't matter whether the strings are both converted to uppercase or both converted to lowercase, as long as they are both converted using the same method.

```
word1.toLowerCase().compareTo(word2.toLowerCase()) > 0
word1.toUpperCase().compareTo(word2.toUpperCase()) > 0
```

If two strings with different lengths are compared and the comparison is equal up to the end of the shorter string, then the shorter string compares as less than the longer string. For example, if word2 contains "Small", the expression

```
word2.compareTo("Smaller") < 0
```

yields true, because the strings are equal up to their fifth character position (the end of the string on the left), and the string on the right is longer.

If you are just interested in testing the equality of strings, ignoring their case, then equalsIgnoreCase method is a perfect choice. For example, the following expression returns true:

```
"MacPherson".equalsIgnoreCase("macpherson")
```

Logical Operators In mathematics, the *logical* (or *Boolean*) *operators* AND, OR, and NOT take logical expressions as operands. Java uses special symbols for the logical operators: && (for AND), || (for OR), and ! (for NOT). By combining relational operators with logical operators, we can make more complex assertions. For example, suppose we want to determine whether a final score is greater than 90 *and* a midterm score is greater than 70. In Java, we would write the expression this way:

```
finalScore > 90 && midtermScore > 70
```

The AND operation (&&) requires both relationships to be true for the overall result to be true. If either or both of the relationships are false, then the entire result is false.

The OR operation (||) takes two logical expressions and combines them. If *either* or *both* are true, the result is true. Both values must be false for the result to be false. Now we can determine whether the midterm grade is an A *or* the final grade is an A. If either the midterm grade or the final grade equals A, the assertion is true. In Java, we write the expression like this:

```
midtermGrade == 'A' || finalGrade == 'A'
```

The && and || operators always appear between two expressions; they are binary (two-operand) operators. The NOT operator (!) is a unary (one-operand) operator. It precedes a single logical expression and gives its opposite as the result. For example, if (grade == 'A') is false, then `!(grade == 'A')` is true. NOT gives us a convenient way of reversing the meaning of an assertion. For example,

```
!(hours > 40)
```

is the equivalent of

```
hours <= 40
```

In some contexts, the first form is clearer; in others, the second makes more sense.

The following pairs of expressions are equivalent:

Expression	Equivalent Expression
`!(a == b)`	`a != b`
`!(a == b || a == c)`	`a != b && a != c`
`!(a == b && c > d)`	`a != b || c <= d`

Take a close look at these expressions to be sure you understand why they are equivalent. Try evaluating them with some values for a, b, c, and d. Notice the pattern: The expression on the left is just the one to its right with `!` added and the relational and logical operators reversed (for example, `==` instead of `!=` and `||` instead of `&&`). Remember this pattern. It allows you to rewrite expressions in the simplest form.[2]

You can apply logical operators to the results of comparisons. You can also apply them directly to variables of type `boolean`. For example, instead of writing

```
isElector = (age >= 18 && district == 23);
```

to assign a value to the `boolean` variable `isElector`, we could use two intermediate `boolean` variables, `isVoter` and `isConstituent`:

```
isVoter = (age >= 18);
isConstituent = (district == 23);
isElector = isVoter && isConstituent;
```

The following tables summarize the results of applying `&&` and `||` to a pair of logical expressions (represented here by the `boolean` variables x and y).

Value of x	Value of y	Value of (x && y)
true	true	true
true	false	false
false	true	false
false	false	false

---

[2]In Boolean algebra, the pattern is formalized by a theorem called *DeMorgan's law*.

Value of x	Value of y	Value of (x || y)
true	true	true
true	false	true
false	true	true
false	false	false

The following table summarizes the results of applying the ! operator to a logical expression (represented by the boolean variable x).

Value of x	Value of !x
true	false
false	true

Short-Circuit Evaluation Consider the logical expression

```
i == 1 && j > 2
```

Some programming languages use *full evaluation* to parse such a logical expression. With full evaluation, the computer first evaluates both subexpressions (both i == 1 and j > 2) before applying the && operator to produce the final result.

In contrast, Java uses **short-circuit** (or **conditional**) **evaluation** of logical expressions. That is, evaluation proceeds from left to right, and the computer stops evaluating subexpressions as soon as possible—as soon as it knows the Boolean value of the entire expression. How can the computer know if a lengthy logical expression yields true or false if it doesn't examine all the subexpressions? Let's look first at the AND operation.

> **Short-circuit (conditional) evaluation** Evaluation of a logical expression in left-to-right order with evaluation stopping as soon as the final Boolean value can be determined

An AND operation yields the value true only if both of its operands are true. In the preceding expression, suppose that the value of i is 95. The first subexpression yields false, so it isn't necessary to even look at the second subexpression. The computer stops evaluation and produces the final result of false.

With the OR operation, the left-to-right evaluation stops as soon as a subexpression yielding true is found. Recall that an OR produces a result of true if either one or both of its operands are true. Given the expression

```
c <= d || e == f
```

if the first subexpression is true, then evaluation stops and the entire result is true. The computer doesn't waste time evaluating the second subexpression.

Java provides a second set of logical operators that result in full evaluation of Boolean expressions. The single & and | perform logical AND and OR operations, respectively, with full evaluation. We don't recommend their use at this stage in your experience with programming. In Java these operators have another meaning with variables or constants of type byte, short, int, or long, which can lead to errors that may prove difficult to find.

George Boole

Boolean algebra is named for its inventor, English mathematician George Boole, who was born in 1815. Boole's father, a tradesman, began teaching him mathematics at an early age. But Boole initially was more interested in classical literature, languages, and religion—interests that he maintained throughout his life. By the time he was 20, he had taught himself French, German, and Italian. He was well versed in the writings of Aristotle, Spinoza, Cicero, and Dante, and wrote several philosophical papers himself.

At 16, to help support his family, Boole took a position as a teaching assistant in a private school. His work there and a second teaching job left him little time to study. A few years later, he opened his own school and began to study higher mathematics independently. Despite his lack of formal training, his first scholarly paper was published in the *Cambridge Mathematical Journal* when he was just 24. Boole went on to publish more than 50 papers and several major works before he died in 1864, at the peak of his career.

Boole's *The Mathematical Analysis of Logic* was published in 1847. It would eventually form the basis for the development of digital computers. In the book, Boole set forth the formal axioms of logic (much like the axioms of geometry) on which the field of symbolic logic is built.

Boole drew on the symbols and operations of algebra in creating his system of logic. He associated the value 1 with the universal set (the set representing everything in the universe) and the value 0 with the empty set, restricting his system to just these two values. He then defined operations that are analogous to subtraction, addition, and multiplication. Variables in the system have symbolic values. For example, if a Boolean variable P represents the set of all plants, then the expression $1 - P$ refers to the set of all things that are not plants. We can simplify the expression by using $-P$ to mean "*not* plants." ($0 - P$ is simply 0 because we can't remove elements from the empty set.) The subtraction operator in Boole's system corresponds to the ! (NOT) operator in Java. In Java code, we might set the value of the Boolean variable `plant` to `true` when the name of a plant is entered, so that `!plant` is `true` when the name of anything else is input.

The expression $0 + P$ is the same as P. However, $0 + P + F$, where F is the set of all foods, is the set of all things that are either plants or foods. So the addition operator in Boole's algebra is the same as the Java `||` (OR) operator.

The analogy can be carried to multiplication as well: $0 \times P$ is 0, and $1 \times P$ is P. But what is $P \times F$? It is the set of things that are both plants and foods. In Boole's system, the multiplication operator is the same as the Java `&&` (AND) operator.

In 1854, Boole published *An Investigation of the Laws of Thought, on Which Are Founded the Mathematical Theories of Logic and Probabilities*. In the book, he described theorems built on his axioms of logic and extended the algebra to show how probabilities could be computed in a logical system. Five years later, Boole published *Treatise on Differential Equations*, then *Treatise on the Calculus of Finite Differences*. The latter is one of the cornerstones of numerical analysis, which deals with the accuracy of computations. (In Chapter 12, we examine the important role that numerical analysis plays in computer programming.)

During his lifetime, Boole received recognition and honors for his work on differential equations. But the importance of Boolean algebra for computer and communication technology was not recognized until the early twentieth century. George Boole was truly one of the founders of computer science.

■ Precedence of Operators

In Chapter 3, we discussed the rules of precedence, which govern the evaluation of complex arithmetic expressions. Java's rules of precedence also apply to relational and logical operators. The following list shows the order of precedence for the arithmetic, relational, and logical operators (with the assignment operator thrown in as well):

```
()                                          Highest precedence
!   unary –   unary +  ++  -- (post)
++  --  (pre)
*   /   %
+   -
<   <=   >   >=
==    !=
&&
||
=                                           Lowest precedence
```

Operators on the same line in the list have the same precedence. If an expression contains several operators with the same precedence, most of the operators group (or *associate*) from left to right. For example, the expression

```
a / b * c
```

means (a / b) * c, not a / (b * c). However, the ! operator groups from right to left. Although you'd never have occasion to use the expression

```
!!badData
```

It means !(!badData) rather than the useless (!!)badData. Appendix B gives the order of precedence for all operators in Java. In skimming the appendix, you can see that a few of the operators associate from right to left (for the same reason we just described for the ! operator).

You can use parentheses to override the order of evaluation in Boolean expressions. If you're not sure whether parentheses are necessary, use them anyway. The compiler disregards unnecessary parentheses. So, if they clarify an expression, use them. Some programmers like to include extra parentheses when assigning a relational expression to a boolean variable:

```
dataInvalid = (inputVal == 0);
```

The parentheses are not needed; the assignment operator has the lowest precedence of all the operators we've just listed. So we could write the statement as

```
dataInvalid = inputVal == 0;
```

The parenthesized version, however, is more readable.

One final comment about parentheses: Java, like other programming languages, requires that you always use parentheses in pairs. Whenever you write a complicated expression, take a minute to go through and pair up all of the opening parentheses with their closing counterparts.

PEANUTS reprinted by permission of United Features Syndicate, Inc.

//te1 Software Engineering Tip

Changing English Statements into Logical Expressions

In most cases, you can write a logical expression directly from an English statement or mathematical term in an algorithm. But you have to watch out for some tricky situations. Recall our example logical expression:

```
midtermGrade == 'A' || finalGrade == 'A'
```

In English, you would be tempted to write this expression: "Midterm grade or final grade equals A." In Java, you can't write the expression as you would in English. That is,

```
midtermGrade || finalGrade == 'A'
```

won't work because the || operator connects a char value (midtermGrade) and a logical expression (finalGrade == 'A'). The two operands of || must both be logical expressions. This example will generate a syntax error message.

A variation of this mistake is to express the English assertion "i equals either 3 or 4" as

```
i == 3 || 4
```

This syntax is incorrect. In the second subexpression, 4 is an int rather than a boolean value. The || operator (and the && operator) can only connect two boolean expressions. Here's what we want:

```
i == 3 || i == 4
```

In math books, you might see notation like this:

```
12 < y < 24
```

It means "y is between 12 and 24." This expression is illegal in Java. First, the relation 12 < y is evaluated, giving a boolean result. Next, the computer tries to compare it with the number 24. Because a boolean value cannot be converted to any type other than String, the expression is invalid. To write this expression correctly in Java, you must use the && operator:

```
12 < y && y < 24
```

Relational Operators with Floating-Point Types

So far, we've talked only about comparing int, char, and String values. Here we look at float and double values.

Do not compare floating-point numbers for equality. Because small errors in the rightmost decimal places are likely to arise when calculations are performed on floating-point numbers, two float or double values rarely are exactly equal. For example, consider the following code that uses two double variables named oneThird and x:

```
oneThird = 1.0 / 3.0;
x = oneThird + oneThird + oneThird;
```

We would expect x to contain the value 1.0, but it probably doesn't. The first assignment statement stores an *approximation* of 1/3 into oneThird, perhaps 0.333333. The second statement stores a value like 0.999999 into x. If we now ask the computer to compare x with 1.0, the comparison will yield false.

Instead of testing floating-point numbers for equality, we can test them for *near* equality. To do so, we compute the difference between the two numbers and see whether the result is less than some maximum allowable difference. For example, we often use comparisons such as the following:

```
Math.abs(r - s) < 0.00001
```

where Math.abs is the absolute value method from the Java library. The expression Math.abs(r - s) computes the absolute value of the difference between two variables r and s. If the difference is less than 0.00001, the two numbers are close enough to call them equal. We discuss this problem with floating-point accuracy in more detail in Chapter 12.

4.3 The if Statement

Now that we've seen how to write logical expressions, let's use them to alter the normal flow of control in our code. The *if statement* is the fundamental control structure that allows branches in the flow of control. With it, we can ask a question and choose a course of action: *If* a certain condition exists, perform one action; *else* perform a different action.

The computer performs just one of the two actions under any given set of circumstances. Yet we must write *both* actions into the code. Why? Because, depending on the circumstances, the computer can choose to execute *either* of them. The *if* statement gives us a way of including both actions in our code and gives the computer a way of deciding which action to take.

■ The if-else Form

In Java, the *if* statement comes in two forms: the *if-else* form and the *if* form. Let's look first at *if-else*. Here is its syntax template:

If-Statement (the *if-else* form)

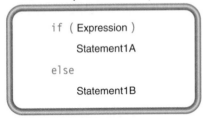

```
if ( Expression )
        Statement1A
else
        Statement1B
```

The expression in parentheses must produce a `boolean` result. At run time, the computer evaluates the expression. If the value is `true`, the computer executes Statement1A. If the value of the expression is `false`, it executes Statement1B. Statement1A is often called the *then clause*; Statement1B is the *else clause*. Figure 4.3 illustrates the flow of control of the *if-else* statement. In the figure, Statement2 is the next statement in the code after the entire *if* statement.

Notice that a Java *if* statement uses the reserved words `if` and `else` but the *then* clause does not include the word *then*. The following code fragment shows how to write an *if* statement. Observe the indentation of the *then* clause and the *else* clause, which makes the statement easier to read. Also notice the placement of the statement following the *if* statement.

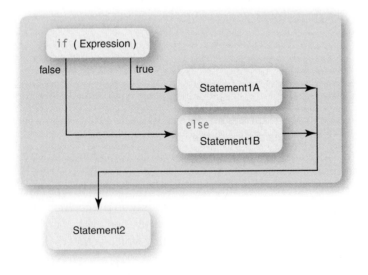

Figure 4.3 *if-else* Flow of Control

```
if (hours <= 40.0)
  pay = rate * hours;
else
  pay = rate * (40.0 + (hours — 40.0) * 1.5);
System.out.println("Pay is " + pay);
```

In terms of instructions to the computer, this code fragment says, "If hours is less than or equal to 40.0, compute the regular pay and then go on to execute the output statement. But if hours is greater than 40, compute the regular pay and the overtime pay, and then go on to execute the output statement." Figure 4.4 shows the flow of control of this if statement.

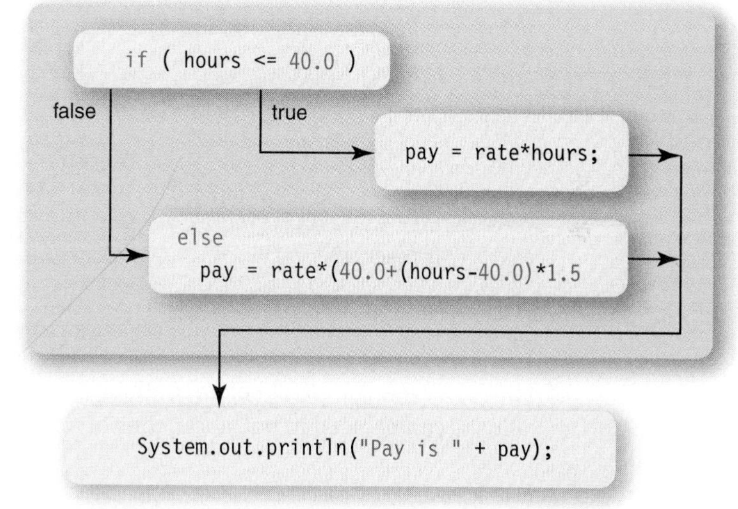

If-else statements are often used to check the validity of input. For example, before we ask the computer to divide by a data value, we should be sure that the value is not zero. (Even computers can't divide something by zero. If you try it with int values, the computer will halt the execution of your application. With floating-point types, you get the special infinity value.) If the divisor is zero, our code should display an error message. Here's an example that prints an error message:

Figure 4.4   Flow of Control for Calculating Pay

```
if (divisor != 0)
  result = dividend / divisor;
else
  System.out.println("Division by zero is not allowed.");
```

Before we examine if statements further, let's take another look at the syntax template for if-else. According to the template, no semicolon appears at the end of an if statement. In both of the preceding code fragments—the worker's pay and the division-by-zero examples—there seems to be a semicolon at the end of each if statement. In reality, the semicolons belong to the statements in the *then* clause and the *else* clause in those examples; assignment statements end in semicolons, as do method calls. The if statement doesn't have its own semicolon at the end.

Blocks (Compound Statements)

In our division-by-zero example, suppose that when the divisor is equal to zero we want to do *two* things: write the error message *and* set the variable named result equal to a special value such as Integer.MAX_VALUE. We would need two statements in the same branch to do so, but the syntax template seems to limit us to one.

What we really want to do is turn the *else* clause into a *sequence* of statements. This is easy. Recall from Chapter 2 that the compiler treats the block (compound statement)

```
{
  .
  .
  .
}
```

as a single statement. If you put a { } pair around the sequence of statements you want in a branch of the *if* statement, the sequence of statements becomes a single block. For example:

```
if (divisor != 0)
  result = dividend / divisor;
else
{
  System.out.println("Division by zero is not allowed.");
  result = Integer.MAX_VALUE;
}
```

If the value of divisor is zero, the computer both displays the error message and sets the value of result to Integer.MAX_VALUE before continuing with whatever statement follows the *if* statement.

Blocks can be used in both branches of an *if-else* statement. For example:

```
if (divisor != 0)
{
  result = dividend / divisor;
  System.out.println("Division performed.");
}
else
{
  System.out.println("Division by zero is not allowed.");
  result = Integer.MAX_VALUE;
}
```

When you use blocks in an *if* statement, you must remember a rule of Java syntax: *Never use a semicolon after the right brace of a block.* Semicolons are used only to terminate simple statements such as assignment statements and method calls. If you look at the earlier examples, you won't see a semicolon after the right brace that signals the end of each block.

■ The if Form

Sometimes you run into a situation where you want to say, "*If* a certain condition exists, perform some action; otherwise, don't do anything." In other words, you want the computer

Braces and Blocks

Java programmers use different styles when it comes to locating the left brace of a block. The style used in this book puts the left and right braces directly below the words if and else, with each brace on its own line:

```java
if (n >= 2)
{
   alpha = 5;
   beta = 8;
}
else
{
   alpha = 23;
   beta = 12;
}
```

Another popular style is to place the statements following if and else on the same line as the left brace; the right braces still line up directly below the left braces.

```java
if (n >= 2)
{ alpha = 5;
   beta = 8;
}
else
{ alpha = 23;
   beta = 12;
}
```

It makes no difference to the Java compiler which style you use (and other styles exist as well, such as placing the left braces at the ends of the lines containing if and else). It's a matter of personal preference. Whichever style you use, though, you should maintain it throughout the entire application. Inconsistency can confuse a person reading your code and give the impression of carelessness.

Matters of Style

to skip a sequence of instructions if a certain condition isn't met. You could do so by leaving the else branch empty, using only the null statement:

```java
if (a <= b)
   c = 20;
else
   ;
```

Better yet, you could simply leave off the `else` part. The resulting statement is the *if* form of the *if* statement. Here is its syntax template:

If-Statement (the *if* form)

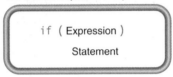

```
if ( Expression )
    Statement
```

Here's an example of an *if* form. Notice the indentation and the placement of the statement that follows the *if*.

```
if (age < 18)
   System.out.print("Not an eligible ");
System.out.println("voter.");
```

This statement means that if age is less than 18, first print `"Not an eligible "` and then print `"voter."` If age is not less than 18, skip the first statement and go directly to printing `"voter."` Figure 4.5 shows the flow of control for an *if* form.

Like the two branches in an *if-else*, the one branch in an *if* can be a block. For example, suppose you are writing an application to compute income taxes. One of the lines on the tax form says, "Subtract line 23 from line 17 and enter the result on line 24; if the result is less than zero, enter zero and check box 24A." You can use an *if* to perform this task in Java:

```
result = line17 - line23;
if (result < 0.0)
{
   System.out.println("Check box 24A");
   result = 0.0;
}
line24 = result;
```

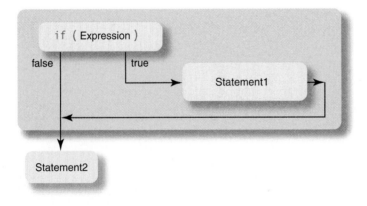

Figure 4.5   *if* Flow of Control

This code does exactly what the tax form says it should: First it computes the result of subtracting line 23 from line 17. Then it checks whether result is less than zero. If it is, the fragment displays a message telling the user to check box 24A and sets result to zero. Finally, the calculated result (or zero, if result is less than zero) is stored into a variable named line24.

What happens if we leave out the left and right braces in the code fragment? Let's look at it:

```
result = line17 − line23;                // Incorrect version
if (result < 0.0)
  System.out.println("Check box 24A");
  result = 0.0;
line24 = result;
```

Despite the way we have indented the code, the compiler assumes that the first clause is a single statement—the output statement. If result is less than zero, the computer executes the output statement, sets result to zero, and then stores result into line24. So far, so good. But if result is initially greater than or equal to zero, the computer skips the first clause and proceeds to the statement following the *if* statement—the assignment statement that sets result to zero. The unhappy outcome is that result ends up as zero no matter what its initial value was! The moral here is not to rely on indentation alone; you can't fool the compiler. If you want a compound statement for either clause, you must include the left and right braces.

4.4 Nested if Statements

Java does not place any restrictions on what the statements in an *if* can be. Therefore, an *if* within an *if* is okay. In fact, an *if* within an *if* within an *if* is legal. The only limitation here is that people cannot follow a structure that is too involved. Of course, readability is one of the hallmarks of a good program.

When we place an *if* within an *if*, we are creating a *nested control structure*. Control structures nest much like mixing bowls do, with smaller ones tucked inside larger ones. Here's an example, written in pseudocode:

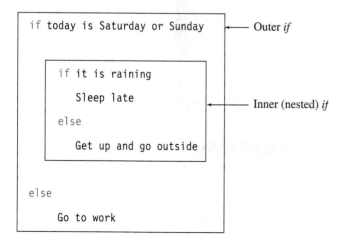

In general, any problem that involves a *multiway branch* (more than two alternative courses of action) can be coded using nested *if* statements. For example, to store the name of a month into a string variable, given its number, we could use a sequence of *if* statements (unnested):

```
if (month == 1)
  monthName = "January";
if (month == 2)
  monthName = "February";
if (month == 3)
 monthName = "March";
   ⋮
if (month == 12)
  monthName = "December";
```

The equivalent nested *if* structure,

```
if (month == 1)
  monthName = "January";
else
  if (month == 2)                 // Nested if
    monthName = "February";
  else
    if (month == 3)               // Nested if
      monthName = "March";
    else
      if (month == 4)             // Nested if
                  ⋮
```

is actually more efficient because it makes fewer comparisons. The first version—the sequence of independent *if* statements—always tests every condition (all 12 of them), even if the first one is satisfied. In contrast, the nested *if* solution skips all remaining comparisons after one alternative has been selected. As fast as modern computers are, many applications require so much computation that an inefficient algorithm can waste hours of computer time. Always be on the lookout for ways to make your code more efficient, as long as doing so doesn't make it difficult for other programmers to understand. It's usually better to sacrifice a little efficiency for the sake of readability.

In the last example, notice how the indentation of the *then* and *else* clauses causes the statements to move continually to the right. Alternatively, we can use a special indentation style with deeply nested *if-else* statements to indicate that the complex structure is just choosing one of a set of alternatives. This general multiway branch is known as an *if-else-if* control structure:

```
if (month == 1)
  monthName = "January";
else if (month == 2)            // Nested if
  monthName = "February";
```

```
else if (month == 3)          // Nested if
  monthName = "March";
else if (month == 4)          // Nested if
  ⋮
else
  monthName = "December";
```

This style prevents the indentation from marching continuously to the right. Even more importantly, it visually conveys the idea that we are using a 12-way branch based on the variable month.

It's important to note one difference between the sequence of *if* statements and the nested *if* structure: More than one alternative can be taken by the sequence of *if* statements, but the nested *if* can select only one choice. To see why this difference is important, consider the analogy of filling out a questionnaire. Some questions are like a sequence of *if* statements, asking you to check all the items in a list that apply to you (such as all of your hobbies). Other questions ask you to select only one item in a list (your age group, for example) and thus are like a nested *if* structure. Both kinds of questions occur in programming problems. Being able to recognize which type of question is being asked permits you to immediately select the appropriate control structure.

Another particularly helpful use of the nested *if* is when you want to select from a series of consecutive ranges of values. For example, suppose that we want to display a message indicating an appropriate activity for the outdoor temperature, given the following table:

Activity	Temperature
Swimming	Temperature > 85
Tennis	70 < Temperature ≤ 85
Golf	32 < Temperature ≤ 70
Skiing	0 < Temperature ≤ 32
Dancing	Temperature ≤ 0

At first glance, you may be tempted to write a separate *if* statement for each range of temperatures. On closer examination, however, it becomes clear that these conditions are interdependent. That is, if one of the statements executes, none of the others should execute. We really are selecting one alternative from a set of possibilities—just the sort of situation in which we can use a nested *if* structure as a multiway branch. The only difference between this problem and our earlier example of printing the month name from its number is that we must check ranges of numbers in the *if* expressions of the branches.

With consecutive ranges, we can take advantage of that fact to make our code more efficient. To do so, we arrange the branches in consecutive order by range. Then, if a particular branch has been reached, we know that the preceding ranges have been eliminated from consideration. Thus, the *if* expressions must compare the temperature to only the lowest value of each range.

```
message = "The recommended activity is ";
if (temperature > 85)
  message = message + "swimming.";
```

```
else if (temperature > 70)
  message = message + "tennis.";
else if (temperature > 32)
  message = message + "golf.";
else if (temperature > 0)
  message = message + "skiing.";
else
  message = message + "dancing.";
System.out.println(message);
```

To see how this *if-else-if* structure works, consider the branch that tests for temperature greater than 70. If it has been reached, we know that temperature must be less than or equal to 85 because that condition causes this particular else branch to be taken. Thus, we need to test only whether temperature is above the bottom of this range (> 70). If that test fails, then we enter the next *else* clause knowing that temperature must be less than or equal to 70. Each successive branch checks the bottom of its range until we reach the final *else*, which takes care of all the remaining possibilities.

If the ranges aren't consecutive, of course, we must test the data value against both the highest and lowest value of each range. We still use an *if-else-if* because it is the best structure for selecting a single branch from multiple possibilities, and we may arrange the ranges in consecutive order to make them easier for a human reader to follow. But, in fact, we cannot reduce the number of comparisons when there are gaps between the ranges.

■ The Dangling else

When *if* statements are nested, you may find yourself confused about the *if-else* pairings. That is, to which *if* does an *else* belong? For example, suppose that if a student's average is below 60, we want to display "Failing"; if it is at least 60 but less than 70, we want to display "Passing but marginal"; and if it is 70 or greater, we don't want to display anything.

We code this information with an *if-else* nested within an *if*:

```
if (average < 70.0)
  if (average < 60.0)
    System.out.println("Failing");
  else
    System.out.println("Passing but marginal");
```

How do we know to which *if* the *else* belongs? Here is the rule that the Java compiler follows: In the absence of braces, an *else* is always paired with the closest preceding *if* that doesn't already have an *else* paired with it. We indented the code to reflect this pairing.

Suppose we write the fragment like this:

```
if (average >= 60.0)                        // Incorrect version
  if (average < 70.0)
    System.out.println("Passing but marginal");
else
  System.out.println("Failing");
```

Here we want the *else* branch attached to the outer *if* statement, not the inner one, so we indent the code as shown here. But indentation does not affect the execution of the code. Even though the *else* aligns with the first *if*, the compiler pairs it with the second *if*. An *else* that follows a nested *if* is called a *dangling else*. It doesn't logically belong with the nested *if* but is attached to it by the compiler.

To attach the *else* to the first *if*, not the second, you can turn the outer *then* clause into a block:

```
if (average >= 60.0)                              // Correct version
{
  if (average < 70.0)
    System.out.println("Passing but marginal")
}
else
  System.out.println("Failing");
```

The { } pair indicates that the first *if* statement has a compound first clause that contains an *if* statement (with no *else* clause), so the *else* must belong to the outer *if*.

4.5 Encapsulation

Prior to this chapter we have written Java classes without considering the larger issues of their design and reusability. For example, we developed an initial version of the Name class in Chapter 2 that was just sufficient for the purposes of the NameDriver application. In Chapter 3, we found that we needed to add a constructor to the Name class to make it usable for the Payroll application. By following some common design principles and using a little forethought, we can develop classes that are much more broadly useful, and that don't require modification for each new application.

In this section we consider the principles that result in a well-designed and general class implementation. Primary among these is the concept of encapsulation. The dictionary provides several definitions of the word *capsule*. For example, it can mean a sealed gelatin case that holds a dose of medication. Early spacecraft were called capsules because they were sealed containers that carried passengers through space. A capsule protects its contents from outside contaminants or harsh conditions. To encapsulate something is to place it into a capsule.

> **Encapsulation** Designing a class so that its implementation is protected from the actions of external code except through the formal interface

> **Abstraction** The separation of the logical properties of an object from its implementation

What does encapsulation have to do with classes and object-oriented programming? One goal in designing a class is to protect its contents from being damaged by the actions of external code. If the contents of a class can be changed only through a well-defined interface, then it is much easier to use the class and to debug errors in an application.

Why is it important to encapsulate a class? Encapsulation is the basis for abstraction in programming. Consider, for example, that abstraction lets us use a BufferedReader without having to know the details of its operation.

Abstraction is how we simplify the design of a large application. We design classes that can be described in simple terms. Some implementation details of each class are irrelevant to using it, so those details are hidden by encapsulation. As a consequence, the programmer who implements the class doesn't have to understand how the larger application uses it, and the programmer who uses the class doesn't have to think about how it is implemented.

Even when you are the programmer in both cases, abstraction simplifies your job because it allows you to focus on different parts of the implementation in isolation from each other. What seems like a huge programming problem at first becomes much more manageable when you break it into little pieces that you can solve separately (the divide-and-conquer strategy introduced in Chapter 1).

Separating a class into a logical description (an interface) and an encapsulated implementation has two additional benefits: modifiability and reuse.

Encapsulation enables us to modify the implementation of a class after its initial development. Perhaps we are rushing to meet a deadline, so we create a simple but inefficient implementation. Later, we can replace the implementation with a more efficient version. The modification is undetectable by users of the class with the exception that their applications run faster and require less memory.

If we write a class in a manner that exposes implementation details, user code may try to exploit some of those details. If we later change the implementation, the user code would stop working. Figure 4.6 illustrates an encapsulated implementation versus one that is exposed to external code.

Encapsulation also allows us to use a class in other applications. An encapsulated class is self-sufficient so that it doesn't depend on declarations in the application. It can thus be imported into different applications without requiring changes to either the class or the application.

As we will see in Chapter 7, reuse also means that an encapsulated class can be easily extended to form new related classes. For example, suppose you work for a utility company and are developing software to manage its fleet of vehicles. As shown in Figure 4.7, an encapsulated class that describes a vehicle could be used in the applications that schedule its use and keep track of maintenance as well as the tax accounting application that computes its operating cost and depreciation. Each of those applications could add extensions to the vehicle class to suit its particular requirements.

Reuse is a way to save programming effort. It also ensures that objects have the same behavior every place that they are used. Consistent behavior helps us to avoid and detect programming errors.

Of course, preparing a class that is suitable for wider reuse requires us to think beyond the immediate situation. The class should provide certain basic services that enable it to be used more generally. We will look at some of these properties later in this chapter where we revisit the design of the Name class. Not every class needs to be designed for general reuse. In many cases, we merely need a class that has specific properties for the problem at hand, and that won't be used elsewhere.

Modifiability The property of an encapsulated class definition that allows the implementation to be changed without having an effect on code that uses it (except in terms of speed or memory space)

Reuse The ability to import a class into code that uses it without additional modification to either the class or the user code; the ability to extend the definition of a class

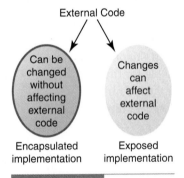

Figure 4.6 Encapsulated versus Exposed Implementation

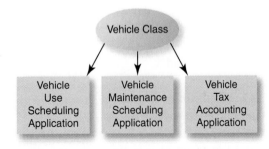

Figure 4.7 Reuse

It is important to understand that encapsulation isn't a Java language construct. We achieve encapsulation by carefully designing the class interface. Once that task is complete, we take advantage of Java features that simplify implementation of an encapsulated class.

4.6 Abstraction

How do we design a class with an encapsulated implementation? We begin with an abstraction for the real-world object. That way, we can focus on the class interface independently of how we may implement it. As a result, the implementation is automatically separated from the interface. We therefore begin with a discussion of abstraction in programming.

■ Data and Control Abstraction

Creation of a new class begins when we need a new kind of object. We create a list of the responsibilities associated with the class. (In Chapter 6, we will formalize a process that helps us do this; for now, however, we will just work with classes in which it is easy to identify some obvious responsibilities.) Some responsibilities require us to supply data to the class (for example, constructors or `void` methods), while others return data (value-returning methods such as `readLine`). Each responsibility has a control component (what it does) and a data component (the information it needs or returns). Encapsulation allows us to create an abstraction of either or both of these components.

Data abstraction is the separation of the external representation of an object's values from their internal implementation. For example, the external representation of a date might be integer values for the day and year, and a string that specifies the name of the month. But we might implement the date within the class using a standard value that calendar makers call the Julian day, which is the number of days since January 1, 4713 BC.

The advantage of using the Julian day is that it simplifies arithmetic on dates, such as computing the number of days between dates. All of the complexity of dealing with leap years and the different number of days in the months is captured in formulas that convert between the conventional representation of a date and the Julian day. From the user's perspective, however, the methods of a `Date` object receive and return a date as two integers and a string.[3]

In many cases, the external representation and the implementation of the values are identical. However, we won't tell that to the user, in case we decide to change the implementation in the future.

Control abstraction is the separation of the logical properties of the actions of a responsibility from their implementation. For example, the documentation for the `Date` class says that it takes into account all of the special leap-year rules. In the implementation, only the Julian

> **Data abstraction** The separation of the logical representation of an object's range of values from their implementation
>
> **Control abstraction** The separation of the logical properties of the operations on an object from their implementation

---

[3]The Java library includes a `Date` class, `java.util.Date`. However, the familiar properties of dates make them a natural example to use in explaining the concepts of class interface design. We ignore the existence of the library class in the discussion that follows, as if we must design our own `Date` class. In writing real programs, however, you would probably use the `GregorianCalendar` library class that replaced `Date` in Java 1.2.

day conversion formulas handle those rules; the other responsibilities merely perform simple arithmetic on the Julian day number.

A user can simply imagine that every Date responsibility is separately computing leap years. Control abstraction lets us actually program a more efficient implementation and then hide that complexity from the user.

To see how we can apply these principles, let's revisit our design for the Name class, making it more general, and thus making it a more complete abstraction of a real Name object. In terms of data abstraction, a typical name consists of three parts: first name, middle name, and last name. Less typical name structures include having two middle names or having no middle name. Many names also have a prefix, such as "Dr." or "Rev."; others have suffixes such as "Jr." or "III". Adding these possibilities to our existing Name class abstraction merely requires us to provide more fields to hold the values and some methods to access them. We might also extend the methods that format the name to include the new information as appropriate. We won't change the data abstraction of the Name class here, because it just makes the example code longer without demonstrating any new concepts. The Case Study Follow-Up exercises include some problems that ask you to make these additions.

Now let's turn our attention to the control abstraction of Name. Here are the responsibilities that Name currently supports:

```
new Name()
new Name(first, last, middle)
firstLast() returns String
full() returns String
lastFirstMI() returns String
```

We have two ways to create a new Name: one that hides a series of interactions with the user via the System class, and another that merely copies the arguments to its internal fields. Abstraction allows us to make these constructors do very different things, while presenting similar functionality through the interface. As far as the user code is concerned, calling a Name constructor builds a new Name object. How it happens doesn't matter.

A Name can return its contents in three specific formats. But what if we want a Name in a different format? We could try to create a method for every imaginable format, but that would be a lot of work and we'd still undoubtedly miss at least one format that a user would want. Alternatively, we can let the user construct any name formats that aren't provided, if we provide methods that return the parts of the name as strings. So we should add the following responsibilities to our design for Name:

```
knowFirstName() returns String
knowMiddleName() returns String
knowLastName() returns String
```

As we saw earlier in this chapter, we often want to compare objects so that we can make decisions based on their values. Thus we should add responsibilities that compare two names for equality or inequality. Inequality is based on alphabetical ordering by last name, first name, and middle name.

```
equals(Name otherName) returns boolean
compareTo(Name otherName) returns int
```

Now that we've defined a more general set of responsibilities for the Name class, we have a class that can be imported and reused by a wide range of user code. The abstraction is reasonably complete, and we've identified some features that could be added to extend it even further. The use of methods to implement the entire interface encapsulates the abstraction so that user code cannot take advantage of special features of the implementation.

Here is an implementation of the new Name class. It looks like quite a bit of code, but if you focus on each method separately, you can see that the class is broken into many pieces, each of which is quite simple. Pay especially close attention to the methods that implement the comparisons. They use the equals and compareTo methods associated with the String class to compare the names. Recall that the == operator tests whether reference variables refer to the same place in memory. To compare the actual contents of two objects, we use methods such as these. Also note that our comparison methods convert the names to all uppercase letters as discussed previously.

```java
import java.io.*;                      // Package for stream readers

//*****************************************************************
// This class provides a basic name object. The default constructor
// requests that a name be entered from System.in. A second constructor
// allows creation of a name from strings. Methods return the name
// in various formats.
//*****************************************************************
class Name
// This class defines a name consisting of three parts
{
  String first;                 // Person's first name
  String last;                  // Person's last name
  String middle;                // Person's middle name

  // Gets a name from System.in
  public Name() throws IOException
  {
    BufferedReader in;                          // Input stream for strings
    // Instantiate in using System.in
    in = new BufferedReader(new InputStreamReader(System.in));
```

```
    System.out.print("Enter first name: ");      // Prompt for first name
    first = in.readLine();                        // Get first name
    System.out.print("Enter last name: ");        // Prompt for last name
    last = in.readLine();                         // Get last name
    System.out.print("Enter middle name: ");      // Prompt for middle name
    middle = in.readLine();                       // Get middle name
  }

  // Builds a name from string parameters
  public Name(String firstName, String lastName, String middleName)
  {
    first = firstName;                            // Assign parameters to fields
    last = lastName;
    middle = middleName;
  }

  // Basic observer methods that return the value of each field

  public String knowFirstName()
  {
    return first;
  }

  public String knowMiddleName()
  {
    return middle;
  }

  public String knowLastName()
  {
    return last;
  }

  // Additional observer methods that return a formatted name

  // Returns name in first last format
  public String firstLast()
  {
    return first + " " + last;
  }

  // Returns full name in usual format
  public String full()
  {
    return first + " " + middle + " " + last;
  }
```

```java
// Returns name as last, first, m.
public String lastFirstMI()
{
  return last + ", " + first + ", " + middle.substring(0, 1) + ".";
}


// Additional observer methods that compare an instance to another name

// Tests for equality
public boolean equals(Name otherName)
{
  return first.equals(otherName.knowFirstName()) &&
         middle.equals(otherName.knowMiddleName()) &&
         last.equals(otherName.knowLastName());
}


// Tests for inequality
public int compareTo(Name otherName)
{
  String ourFullName;
  String otherFullName;
  ourFullName = (last + first + middle).toUpperCase();
  otherFullName = (otherName.knowLastName() + otherName.knowFirstName() +
              otherName.knowMiddleName()).toUpperCase();
  return ourFullName.compareTo(otherFullName);
}
}
```

WARNING NOTICES

Problem: Many universities send warning notices to freshmen who are in danger of failing a class. Your application should calculate the average of three test grades and print out a student's name, average, and an indication of whether the student is passing. Passing is a 60-point average or better. If the student is passing with less than a 70 average, the program should indicate that he or she is marginal.

Input: Student name followed by three test grades (of type `int`).

Output:

Prints prompts for input of each value.

The input values (echo print).

Student name, average grade, passing/failing message, marginal indication, and error message if any of the test scores are negative.

Discussion: Looking for things that are familiar, we notice that the name can be of class `Name`. However, we are dealing with an object that is more than a name—it is a record for a student's grades. We'd like the class to take care of creating the record, and then tell us the student's status so that we can print the proper message. Thus, the object needs to average the student's scores and compare them to the ranges of values for passing, marginal, and failing. How should we have it return the status? The object could provide one of three strings to output. For example:

```
"Passing"
"Passing but marginal"
"Failing"
```

Let's think about the reusability of this class. What if we want to output a different message from the application? We would have to compare the string returned from the class to literals with exactly the same contents to determine the status of the student. This approach could work, but it's clumsy and prone to error. And what if we want to use the student's status in another way in another application, such as sending a report to his or her faculty advisor? We need a more general way to indicate the status.

We could simply return an `int` value with a coded meaning:

0 = Failing

1 = Passing but marginal

2 = Passing

This strategy exposes the internal implementation of the status to the user code. Knowing that the values are of type `int`, a programmer might write user code to compare them directly. If we later change the representation (perhaps by using type char to save space), the modification could cause the dependent user code to fail. Instead, we need a way to indicate a status that is encapsulated. (Notice how we're applying means-ends analysis in this problem-solving process.)

What means do we have for representing a set of values that the user cannot change, and that the class can make available to the user without exposing the type? It sounds like a set of public named constants. Would this approach work? Well, the user needs to know only the names and which methods use them. The type doesn't need to be specified. We could tell the user that it is okay to compare the constants with the relational operators, but we would retain more control if we provide equals and compareTo methods for this purpose. That way, if we change the representation later, we don't have to preserve the property of being comparable using relational operators. Also, if we use comparison methods that compare a class constant with the status field of the object, we don't even have to return the status value to the user code. In this way, we avoid having to write a separate knowStatus method. Let's give the constants the following names:

```
FAILING
MARGINAL
PASSING
```

The class should provide methods that return the values that the user code stores in a record. We can simply return a Name, and the user code can use the methods in Name that return the parts of the name. To return a score, we could use a separate method to return each score, or we could use a method that takes a score number as a parameter and returns the corresponding value. Let's try the latter strategy. If we ever want to change the record to include more scores, we wouldn't have to keep adding a method for each one. Instead, we could just change the one method to accept a wider range of score numbers. Let's list the responsibilities of this class:

```
new Student (student name, score1, score2, score3)
knowName() returns Name
knowScore(int number) returns int
equalStatus(class constant) returns Boolean
```

Now we have a class with an interface that presents an abstraction of a student record object. Next, we turn to the algorithms for the individual responsibilities. Let's begin with the constructor. First we assign the values of the parameters to the fields of the object. Then we compute the average and determine the student's status.

To calculate the average, we must add the three test scores and divide by 3. To assign the appropriate status, we must determine whether the average is at least 70 for passing or at least 60 for marginal; otherwise, it is failing. We can use a nested *if* control structure to test these conditions.

```
constructor Student (Name student name, int score1, score2, score3)
Set my name to student name
Set my score1 to score1
Set my score2 to score2
Set my score3 to score3
Set average to (score1 + score2 + score3)/3
if average >= 70
    Set status to PASSING
else
    if average >= 60
        Set status to MARGINAL
    else
        Set status to FAILING
```

The method that returns the name is trivial.

```
knowName() returns Name
return my name
```

The method that returns a score requires some thought. We receive an integer in the range of 1 to 3, and use this value to select the score to return. The key word here is "select." We use a selection control structure to make the choice. As we're selecting just one item from a list, a nested *if* structure is appropriate.

```
if score number is 1
    return score1
else if score number is 2
    return score2
else if score number is 3
    return score3
else ????
```

Oh! What do we do if the score number isn't an acceptable value? This spot would be a good place to throw an exception, but we haven't seen how to do that yet. Instead, let's return an invalid score value, such as −1.

```
knowScore(int score number) returns int
if score number is 1
    return my score1
else if score number is 2
    return my score2
else if score number is 3
    return my score3
else
    return −1
```

The equalStatus method for the status field is quite simple. We just compare the parameter to the field and return the boolean result, as both are simple types.

```
equalStatus (int test status) returns boolean
return status == test status
```

Now that we've designed this class, we can easily write its Java implementation.

```java
//*******************************************************************
// This class provides a student record object. The constructor
// requires a name and three integer scores. Observers permit the
// user to retrieve these values. A method is provided to compare
// student status with the class constants FAILING, MARGINAL,
// and PASSING.
//*******************************************************************

import Name;                              // Our Name class
class Student
{
  // Class constants for use in comparisons
  public static final int FAILING = 0;
  public static final int MARGINAL = 1;
  public static final int PASSING = 2;

  Name myName;                            // Student name field
  int myScore1;                          // First score
  int myScore2;                          // Second score
  int myScore3;                          // Third score
  int average;                           // Average score
  int status;                            // Status based on average

  // Constructor
  public Student(Name studentName, int score1, int score2, int score3)
  {
    myName = studentName;
    myScore1 = score1;
    myScore2 = score2;
    myScore3 = score3;
    average = (score1 + score2 + score3)/3;
    if (average >= 70)
      status = PASSING;
    else
      if (average >= 60)
        status = MARGINAL;
      else
        status = FAILING;
  }

  // Returns name field
  public Name knowName()
  {
    return myName;
  }
```

```
// Returns one of the three score fields based on parameter value
// Returns -1 if parameter value is invalid
public int knowScore(int scoreNumber)
{
  if (scoreNumber == 1)
    return myScore1;
  else if (scoreNumber == 2)
    return myScore2;
  else if (scoreNumber == 3)
    return myScore3;
  else
    return -1;
}


// Test for equality of status with a class constant
public boolean equalStatus(int testStatus)
{
  return status == testStatus;
}
}
```

Next, we turn our attention to the application that solves our particular problem. We need to input the data and instantiate a Student object. For input, we can use the Name constructor that gets a name, and we can input the three scores separately. Then we compare the student's status to the status constants provided by the Student class and output an appropriate message. To simplify echo-printing of the data, we first create a string that holds that part of the message and just add the status to it in the appropriate branch of a nested *if* structure. Here's the algorithm:

```
Student Status

inputName = new Name()
print "Enter first score: "
score1 = Integer.parseInt(in.readLine())
print "Enter second score: "
score2 = Integer.parseInt(in.readLine())
print "Enter third score: "
score3 = Integer.parseInt(in.readLine())
the student = new Student(inputName, score1, score2, score3)
message = inputName.full() + " with scores of " + score1 + ", " + score2 +
    ", and " + score3 + " is "
if the student.equalStatus(Student.FAILING)
    message = message + "failing."
else if the student.equalStatus(Student.MARGINAL)
    message = message + "marginally passing."
else
    message = massage + "passing."
println message
```

We need to declare variables to hold the name, the scores, the Student object, and the message. We also need to import Student, Name, and java.io.*. Now that we have designed the algorithm for our application, we are ready to implement it in Java.

```java
//********************************************************************
// This application determines whether a student is passing,
// marginally passing, or failing, based on three test scores.
//********************************************************************
import java.io.*;              // For IOException, BufferedReader
import Student;                // Represents a student
import Name;                   // A basic representation of a name
public class StudentStatus
{
  public static void main(String[] args) throws IOException
  {
    Name inputName;            // Place to hold input name
    int score1;                // First test score
    int score2;                // Second test score
    int score3;                // Third test score
    Student theStudent;        // Student record
    String message;            // Output message
    BufferedReader in;         // Input source
    // Input name and three scores
    in = new BufferedReader(new InputStreamReader(System.in));
    inputName = new Name();
    System.out.print("Enter first score: ");
    score1 = Integer.parseInt(in.readLine());
    System.out.print("Enter second score: ");
    score2 = Integer.parseInt(in.readLine());
    System.out.print("Enter third score: ");
    score3 = Integer.parseInt(in.readLine());
    // Create a student record
    theStudent = new Student(inputName, score1, score2, score3);
    // Create basic message with echo print of input
    message = inputName.full() + " with scores of " + score1 + ", " +
            score2 + ", and " + score3 + " is ";
    // Determine status and finish building message
    if (theStudent.equalStatus(Student.FAILING))
      message = message + "failing.";
    else if (theStudent.equalStatus(Student.MARGINAL))
      message = message + "marginally passing.";
    else
      message = message + "passing.";
    System.out.println(message); // Output final message
  }
}
```

CASE STUDY

Here is a sample output from running the program:

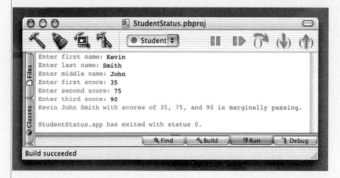

Here is another sample run:

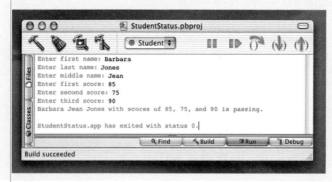

4.7 Testing and Debugging

In Chapter 1, we discussed the problem-solving and implementation phases of computer programming. Testing is an integral part of both phases. Testing in the problem-solving phase occurs after the solution is developed but before it is implemented. In the implementation phase, we test after the algorithm is translated into code, and again after the code has compiled successfully. The compilation itself constitutes another stage of testing that is performed automatically.

Testing Strategies

When an individual programmer is designing and implementing an application, he or she can find many software errors with pencil and paper. Desk checking the design solution is a very common method of manually verifying a design or code. The programmer writes down essential data (variables, input values, parameters of methods, and so on) and walks through the design, manually simulating the actions of the computer and recording changes in the data on paper. Portions of the design or code that are complex or that are a source of concern should be double-checked.

Desk checking Tracing an execution of a design or code on paper

Desk checking can be done by an individual, but most sizable applications are developed by *teams* of programmers. Two extensions of desk checking that are used effectively by programming teams are the design or code walk-through and the code inspection. The intention of these formal team activities is to move the responsibility for uncovering bugs from the individual programmer to the group. Because testing is time-consuming and errors cost more the later they are discovered, the goal is to identify errors before testing begins.

In a *walk-through*, the team performs a manual simulation of the design or code with sample test inputs, keeping track of the code's data by hand. Unlike thorough testing, the walk-through is not intended to simulate all possible test cases. Instead, its purpose is to stimulate discussion about the way the programmer chose to design or implement the code's requirements.

At an *inspection*, a reader (typically not the code's author) goes through the design or code line by line. Inspection participants point out errors, which are recorded on an inspection report. Some errors are uncovered just by the process of reading aloud. Others may have been noted by team members during their preinspection preparation. As with the walk-through, the chief benefit of the team meeting is the discussion that takes place among team members. This interaction among programmers, testers, and other team members can uncover many errors long before the formal testing stage begins.

> **Walk-through** A verification method in which a team performs a manual simulation of the code or design
>
> **Inspection** A verification method in which one member of a team reads the code or design line by line and the other team members point out errors
>
> **Execution trace** Going through the code with actual values, recording the state of the variables

At the high-level design stage, the design should be compared to the application requirements to confirm that all required responsibilities have been included and that this application or class correctly "interfaces" with other software in the system. At the low-level design stage, when the design has been filled out with more details, it should be reinspected before its implementation begins.

After the code is written, you should go over it line by line to verify that you've faithfully reproduced the algorithm—a process known as a *code walk-through*. In a team-programming situation, you could ask other team members to walk through the algorithm and code with you, to double-check the design and code.

You also should take some actual values and hand-calculate what the output should be by doing an execution trace (or *hand trace*). When the code is executed, you can use these same values as input and check the results. The computer is a very literal device—it does exactly what we tell it to do, which may or may not be what we want it to do. To make sure that our code does what we want, we trace the execution of the statements.

When code contains branches, it's a good idea to retrace its execution using different input data so that each branch is traced at least once. In the next section, we describe how to develop data sets that test each branch.

To test an application or method with branches, we need to execute each branch at least once and verify the results. For example, the constructor of the class Name includes a nested *if* statement that selects among three possible conditions. Overall, the application thus executes three different sections of code depending on the values in its score arguments.

We need at least three data sets to test the different branches. For example, the following sets of argument values cause all of the branches to be executed:

	Score 1	Score 2	Score 3
Set 1	75	75	75
Set 2	65	65	65
Set 3	50	50	50

Every branch in the code is executed at least once through this series of test runs. Eliminating any of the test data sets would leave at least one branch untested. This series of data sets provides what is called *minimum complete coverage* of the application's branching structure. Whenever you test an application containing branches, you should design a series of tests that cover all of the branches. Because an action in one branch often affects processing in a later branch, it is critical to test as many *combinations of branches*, or paths, through the code as possible. By doing so, we can be sure that no interdependencies will cause problems. Shouldn't we try all possible paths? Yes, in theory. However, the number of paths in even a small application can be very large.

The approach to testing that we've used here is called *code coverage* because the test data are designed by looking at the code. Code coverage is also called *white-box* (or *clear-box*) *testing* because we are allowed to see the application code while designing the tests. Another approach to testing, called *data coverage*, attempts to test as many allowable data values as possible without referencing the code. Because we need not see the code in this form of testing, it is also called *black-box testing*—we would design the same set of tests even if the code were hidden in a black box. Complete data coverage is as impractical as complete code coverage for many applications. For example, the Student constructor bases the student's status on the average of three int values in the range of 0 to 100 and thus has more than 1,000,000 possible input values.

Often, testing combines these two strategies. Instead of trying every possible data value (data coverage), we examine the code (code coverage) and look for ranges of values for which processing is identical. Then we test the values at the boundaries and, sometimes, a value in the middle of each range. For example, a simple condition such as

```
alpha < 0
```

divides the integers into two ranges:

1. Integer.MIN_VALUE through −1
2. 0 through Integer.MAX_VALUE

Thus, we should test the four values Integer.MIN_VALUE, −1, 0, and Integer.MAX_VALUE. A compound condition such as

```
alpha >= 0 && alpha <= 100
```

divides the integers into three ranges:

1. `Integer.MIN_VALUE` through –1
2. 0 through 100
3. 101 through `Integer.MAX_VALUE`

Thus, we have six values to test. In addition, to verify that the relational operators are correct, we should test for values of 1 (> 0) and 99 (< 100).

Conditional branches are merely one factor in developing a testing strategy. We consider more of these factors in later chapters.

■ The Test Plan

We've discussed strategies and techniques for testing applications, but how do you approach the testing of a specific application? You design and implement a test plan—a document that specifies the test cases that should be tried, the reason for each test case, and the expected output. In Chapter 3, we briefly and informally discussed the idea of a test plan. Now we take a closer look at what makes up a formal test plan. Implementing a test plan involves running the application using the data specified by the test cases in the plan and checking and recording the results.

The test plan should be developed together with the design. The following table shows a partial test plan for the StudentStatus application. The first test case involves a passing set of scores. The second test case is a marginal set, and the third test case is a failing set. The last set checks what happens when we input invalid data. Our program treats negative values as valid scores and merely computes an average with them, so in this case the result should be failing. A Case Study Follow-Up exercise asks you to add a test for invalid data.

Test plan A document that specifies how an application is to be tested

Test plan implementation Using the test cases specified in a test plan to verify that an application outputs the predicted results

Test Plan for the StudentStatus Application

Reason for Test Case	Input Values	Expected Output	Observed Output
Test passing	`70, 80, 90`	`passing`	
Test marginal	`65, 75, 55`	`marginally passing`	
Test failing	`45, 55, 65`	`failing`	
Test invalid data	`-10, -10, -10`	`failing`	

Implementing a test plan does not guarantee that your code is completely correct. It means only that a careful, systematic test of the code has not demonstrated any bugs. The situation shown in Figure 4.8 is analogous to trying to test a program without a plan—depending only on luck, you may completely miss the fact that a program contains numerous errors. Developing and implementing a written test plan, on the other hand, casts a wide net that is much more likely to find errors.

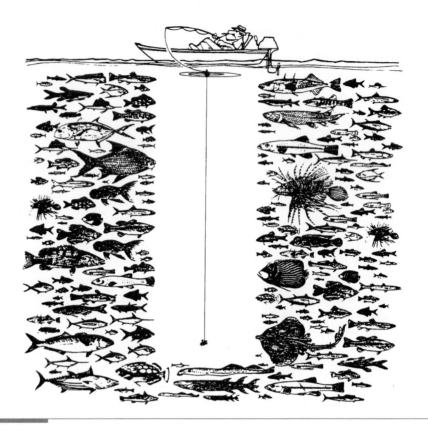

Figure 4.8   When You Test a Program without a Plan, You Never Know What You Might Be Missing

■ Tests Performed Automatically During Compilation and Execution

Once a design is coded and test data have been prepared, the application is ready for compiling. The compiler has two responsibilities: to report any errors and, if there are no errors, to translate the source code into object code or Bytecode.

Errors can be either syntactic or semantic. The compiler finds *syntactic errors*. For example, the compiler warns you when reserved words are misspelled, identifiers are undeclared, semicolons are missing, and operand types are mismatched. But it won't find all of your typing errors. If you type > instead of <, you won't receive an error message; instead, you will get erroneous results when you test the code. It's your responsibility to design a test plan and carefully check the code to detect errors of this type.

Semantic errors (also called *logic errors*) are mistakes that give you the wrong answer. They are more difficult to locate than syntactic errors and usually surface when code is executing. Java detects only the most obvious semantic errors—those that result in an invalid operation (dividing by zero, for example). Although typing errors sometimes cause semantic errors, they are more often a product of a faulty algorithm design. By walking

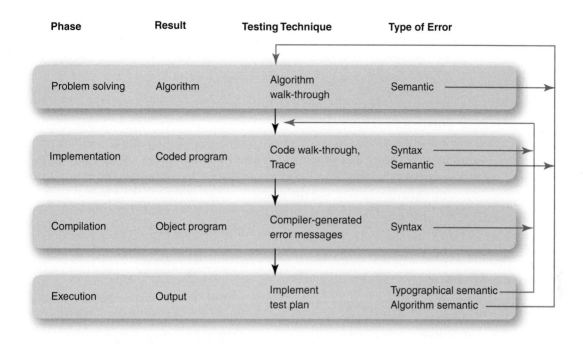

Figure 4.9   Testing Process

through the algorithm and the code, tracing the execution of the application, and developing a thorough test strategy, you should be able to avoid, or at least quickly locate, semantic errors in your code.

Figure 4.9 illustrates the testing process we've been discussing. It shows where syntax and semantic errors occur and in which phase they can be corrected.

Testing and Debugging Hints

1. Java has three pairs of operators that are similar in appearance but different in effect: == and =, && and &, and || and |. Double-check all of your logical expressions to make sure you're using the "equals-equals," "and-and," and "or-or" operators. Then check them again to confirm that you didn't double type the < or > operators.

2. If you use extra parentheses for clarity, make sure that the opening and closing parentheses match up. To verify that parentheses are properly paired,

start with the innermost pair and draw a line connecting them. Do the same for the others, working your way out to the outermost pair. For example:

```
if (((total/scores) > 50) && ((total/(scores - 1)) < 100))
```

3. Here is a quick way to tell whether you have an equal number of opening and closing parentheses. The scheme uses a single number (the "magic number"), whose initial value is 0. Scan the expression from left to right. At each opening parenthesis, add 1 to the magic number; at each closing parenthesis, subtract 1. At the final closing parenthesis, the magic number should be 0. For example,

```
if (((total/scores) > 50) && ((total/(scores - 1)) < 100))
0   123                 2    1    23        4        32      10
```

4. Don't use =< to mean "less than or equal to"; only the symbol <= works. Likewise, => is invalid for "greater than or equal to"; you must use >= for this operation.

5. Don't compare strings with the == operator. Use the associated instance methods such as `equals` and `compareTo`. When testing for alphabetical order, remember to convert the strings to the same case before making the comparison.

6. When comparing values of different types, use explicit casting to clarify how the values should be converted before comparison.

7. Don't compare floating-point types for exact equality. Check that the difference between the values is less than some small amount.

8. In an *if* statement, remember to use a { } pair if the first clause or the *else* clause is a sequence of statements. Also, don't put a semicolon after the right brace.

9. Test for bad data. If a data value must be positive, use an *if* statement to test the value. If the value is negative or 0, an error message should be displayed; otherwise, processing should continue.

10. Take some sample values and try them by hand. Develop a test plan before you start testing your code.

11. If your application produces an answer that does not agree with a value you've calculated by hand, try these suggestions:
    - Redo your arithmetic.
    - Recheck your input data.
    - Carefully go over the section of code that performs the calculation. If you're in doubt about the order in which the operations are performed, insert clarifying parentheses.

12. Check for integer overflow. The value of an `int` variable may have exceeded `Integer.MAX_VALUE` in the middle of a calculation. Java doesn't display an error message when this problem happens.

13. Check the conditions in branching statements to confirm that the correct branch is taken under all circumstances.

14. Design your classes to be encapsulated so they can be tested independently of user code.

Summary

Using logical expressions is a way of asking questions while code is executing. The computer evaluates each logical expression, producing the value `true` if the expression is true or the value `false` if the expression is not true.

The *if* statement allows you to take different paths through the code based on the value of a logical expression. The *if-else* statement is used to choose between two courses of action; the *if* statement is used to choose whether to take a particular course of action. The branches of an *if* or *if-else* can be any statement, simple or compound. They can even be another *if* statement.

Encapsulation is an approach to implementing a class that is reusable in other contexts. By starting with an abstraction of an object and then designing an interface that is a general representation of the object, we create a design that is logically complete and that hides its implementation details from the user.

The algorithm walk-through is a manual simulation of the algorithm at the design phase. By testing our design in the problem-solving phase, we can eliminate errors that can be more difficult to detect in the implementation phase.

An execution trace allows us to find errors once we've entered the implementation phase. It's a good idea to trace your code before you run it, so that you have some sample results against which to check the output. A written test plan is an essential part of any application development effort.

Quick Check

1. Given that A holds `true` and B holds `false`, what are the values of A && B, A || B, and !A? (pp. 161–163)

2. How does an *if* statement let us affect the flow of control? (pp. 167–169)

Learning Portfolio

3. If an *if-else* structure contains a nested *if-else* in each of its branches, as shown below, how many different paths can be taken through the whole structure? (pp. 173–176)

```
if
    if
    else
else
    if
    else
```

4. What is the difference between the *if* and the *if-else* control structures? (pp. 170–173)

5. Which actions below are more like a sequence of *ifs*, and which are more like nested *ifs* (mark the questions with S or N) (pp. 173–176)

   a. Indicating your age in a list of ranges?

   b. Marking all of your hobbies in a list

   c. Checking off in a list all of the magazines you receive

   d. Marking the items you want to order on a menu

   e. Checking the box that indicates your marital status on a tax form

6. In a problem where you are determining the grade for a test score, given a series of score ranges and corresponding grades, would it be more appropriate to use a nested *if* structure or a sequence of *ifs*? (pp. 173–176)

7. What is the purpose of an algorithm walk-through? (pp. 190–193)

8. In what phase of the program development process should you carry out an execution trace? (pp. 190–193)

9. How does encapsulation make a class reusable? (pp. 177–179)

10. Write a Java expression that compares the variable `letter` to the constant `'Z'` and yields `true` if `letter` is less than `'Z'`. (pp. 156–158)

11. Write a Java expression that yields `true` if `letter` is between `'A'` and `'Z'`, inclusive. (pp. 156–158)

12. Write a Java statement that sets the variable `value` to its negative if it is greater than zero. (pp. 170–173)

13. Extend the statement in Question 12 so that it sets `value` to 1 if it is less than or equal to 0. (pp. 168–169)

14. On a telephone, each of the digits 2 through 9 has a segment of the alphabet associated with it. What kind of control structure would you use to decide which segment a given letter falls into and to display the corresponding digit? (pp. 173–176)

15. You've written an application that displays the corresponding digit on a phone, given a letter of the alphabet. Everything seems to work right except that you can't get the digit 5 to display; you keep getting the digit 6. What steps would you take to find and fix this bug? (pp. 190–195)

Answers

1. `false`, `true`, `false` **2.** It enables us to choose one course of action (control flow path) or another. **3.** Four paths. **4.** The *if* lets us choose whether to perform an action; the *if-else* allows us to choose between two courses of action. **5.** a. N, b. S, c. S, d. S, e. N **6.** A nested *if* structure **7.** To have a team verify the algorithm through hand-simulation **8.** The implementation phase **9.** By making the class self-contained and independent of the code that uses it **10.** `letter < 'Z'` **11.** `letter >= 'A' && letter <= 'Z'` **12.** `if (value > 0) value = -value;` **13.** `if (value > 0) value = -value; else value = 1;` **14.** A nested *if* statement **15.** Carefully review the section of code that should display 5. Check the branching condition and the output statement there. Try some sample values by hand.

Exam Preparation Exercises

1. What is the purpose of a control structure?
2. What is a logical expression?
3. Given the following relational expressions, state in English what they say.

Expression	Meaning in English
`one == two`	
`one != two`	
`one > two`	
`one < two`	
`one >= two`	
`one <= two`	

4. Given these values for the `boolean` variables x, y, and z:

```
x = true
y = false
z = true
```

   evaluate the following logical expressions. In the blank next to each expression, write a T if the result is `true` or an F if the result is `false`.

   _____ **a.** `x && y || x && z`
   _____ **b.** `(x || !y) && (!x || z)`
   _____ **c.** `x || y && z`
   _____ **d.** `!(x || y) && z`

5. Given these values for variables i, j, p, and q:

```
i = 10
j = 19
p = true
q = false
```

add parentheses (if necessary) to the expressions below so that they evaluate to true.

a. `i == j || p`

b. `i >= j || i <= j && p`

c. `!p || p`

d. `!q && q`

6. Given these values for the `int` variables i, j, m, and n:

```
i = 6
j = 7
m = 11
n = 11
```

what is the output of the following code?

```
System.out.print("Madam");
if (i < j)
  if (m != n)
    System.out.print("How");
  else
    System.out.print("I'm");
if (i >= m)
  System.out.print("Cow");
else
  System.out.print("Adam");
```

7. Given the `int` variables x, y, and z, where x contains 3, y contains 7, and z contains 6, what is the output of each of the following code fragments?

a.
```
if (x <= 3)
   System.out.print ("x" + "y");
 System.out.print("x" + "y");
```

b.
```
if (x != -1)
   System.out.print("The value of x is " + x);
 else
   System.out.print("The value of y is " + y);
```

```
c. if (x != -1)
   {
     System.out.print(x);
     System.out.print(y);
     System.out.print(z);
   }
   else
     System.out.print("y");
     System.out.print("z");
```

8. Given this code fragment:

```
if (height >= minHeight)
  if (weight >= minWeight)
    System.out.print("Eligible to serve.");
  else
    System.out.print("Too light to serve.");
else
  if (weight >= minWeight)
    System.out.print("Too short to serve.");
  else
    System.out.print("Too short and too light to serve.");
```

   a. What is the output when `height` exceeds `minHeight` and `weight` exceeds `minWeight`?

   b. What is the output when `height` is less than `minHeight` and `weight` is less than `minWeight`?

9. Match each logical expression in the left column with the logical expression in the right column that tests for the same condition.

   ____ **a.** x < y && y < z   (1) !(x != y) && y == z

   ____ **b.** x > y && y >= z   (2) !(x <= y || y < z)

   ____ **c.** x != y || y == z   (3) (y < z || y == z) || x == y

   ____ **d.** x == y || y <= z   (4) !(x >= y) && !(y >= z)

   ____ **e.** x == y && y == z   (5) !(x == y && y != z)

10. The following expressions make sense but are invalid according to Java's rules of syntax. Rewrite them so that they are valid logical expressions. (All the variables are of type `int`.)

    a. x < y <= z

    b. x, y, and z are greater than 0

    c. x is equal to neither y nor z

    d. x is equal to y and z

11. Given these values for the `boolean` variables x, y, and z,

    ```
    x = true
    y = true
    z = false
    ```

    indicate whether each expression is `true` (T) or `false` (F).

    _____ **a.** !(y || z) || x

    _____ **b.** z && x && y

    _____ **c.** ! y || (z || !x)

    _____ **d.** z || (x && (y || z))

    _____ **e.** x || x && z

12. For each of the following problems, decide which is more appropriate, an *if-else* or an *if*. Explain your answers.

    a. Students who are candidates for admission to a college submit their SAT scores. If a student's score is equal to or above a certain value, print a letter of acceptance for the student. Otherwise, print a rejection notice.

    b. For employees who work more than 40 hours per week, calculate overtime pay and add it to their regular pay.

    c. In solving a quadratic equation, whenever the value of the discriminant (the quantity under the square root sign) is negative, print out a message noting that the roots are complex (imaginary) numbers.

    d. In a computer-controlled sawmill, if a cross section of a log is greater than certain dimensions, adjust the saw to cut 4-inch by 8-inch beams; otherwise, adjust the saw to cut 2-inch by 4-inch studs.

13. What causes the error message "UNEXPECTED ELSE" when this code fragment is compiled?

    ```
    if (mileage < 24.0)
    {
      System.out.print("Gas ");
      System.out.print("guzzler.");
    };
    else
      System.out.print("Fuel efficient.");
    ```

14. The following code fragment is supposed to print "Type AB" when `boolean` variables typeA and typeB are both `true`, and to print "Type 0" when both variables are `false`. Instead, it prints "Type 0" whenever just one of the variables is `false`. Insert a { } pair to make the code segment work the way it should.

```
if (typeA || typeB)
  if (typeA && typeB)
    System.out.print("Type AB");
else
  System.out.print("Type O");
```

15. The nested *if* structure below has five possible branches depending on the values read into char variables ch1, ch2, and ch3. To test the structure, you need five sets of data, each set using a different branch. Create the five test data sets.

```
if (ch1 == ch2)
  if (ch2 == ch3)
    System.out.print("All initials are the same.");
  else
    System.out.print("First two are the same.");
else if (ch2 == ch3)
  System.out.print("Last two are the same.");
else if (ch1 == ch3)
  System.out.print("First and last are the same.");
else
  System.out.print("All initials are different.");
```

   a. Test data set 1: ch1 = _____ ch2 = _____ ch3 = _____
   b. Test data set 2: ch1 = _____ ch2 = _____ ch3 = _____
   c. Test data set 3: ch1 = _____ ch2 = _____ ch3 = _____
   d. Test data set 4: ch1 = _____ ch2 = _____ ch3 = _____
   e. Test data set 5: ch1 = _____ ch2 = _____ ch3 = _____

16. If x and y are boolean variables, do the following two expressions test the same condition?

```
x != y
(x || y) && !(x && y)
```

17. The following *if* condition is made up of three relational expressions:

```
if (i >= 10 && i <= 20 && i != 16)
    j = 4;
```

   If i contains the value 25 when this *if* statement is executed, which relational expression(s) does the computer evaluate? (Remember that Java uses short-circuit evaluation.)

18. **a.** If strings cannot be compared using the relational operators in Java, how can you compare two strings?

b. Fill in the following table that describes methods that can be applied to string objects.

Method Name	Argument	Returns	English Description
equals			
equalsIgnoreCase			
compareTo			
toUpperCase			
toLowerCase			

Programming Warm-Up Exercises

1. Declare `eligible` to be a `boolean` variable, and assign it the value `true`.

2. Write a statement that sets the `boolean` variable `available` to `true` if `numberOrdered` is less than or equal to `numberOnHand` minus `numberReserved`.

3. Write a statement containing a logical expression that assigns `true` to the `boolean` variable `isCandidate` if `satScore` is greater than or equal to 1100, `gpa` is not less than 2.5, and `age` is greater than 15. Otherwise, `isCandidate` should be `false`.

4. Given the declarations

   ```
   boolean leftPage;
   int     pageNumber:
   ```

   write a statement that sets `leftPage` to `true` if `pageNumber` is even. (*Hint:* Consider what the remainders are when you divide different integers by 2.)

5. Write an *if* statement (or a series of *if* statements) that assigns to the variable `biggest` the greatest value contained in variables `i`, `j`, and `k`. Assume the three values are distinct.

6. Rewrite the following sequence of *if-(then)* as a single *if-else*.

   ```
   if (year % 4 == 0)
     System.out.print(year + " is a leap year.");
   if (year % 4 != 0)
   {
     year = year + 4 - year % 4;
     System.out.print(year + " is the next leap year.");
   }
   ```

7. Simplify the following code segment, taking out unnecessary comparisons. Assume that `age` is an `int` variable.

```
if (age > 64)
   System.out.print("Senior voter");
if (age < 18)
   System.out.print("Under age");
if (age >= 18 && age < 65)
   System.out.print("Regular voter");
```

8. The following code fragment is supposed to print out the values 25, 60, and 8, in that order. Instead, it prints out 50, 60, and 4. Why?

```
length = 25;
width = 60;
if (length = 50)
   height = 4;
else
   height = 8;
System.out.print("" + length + " " + width + " " + height);
```

9. The following Java code segment is almost unreadable because of the inconsistent indentation and the random placement of left and right braces. Fix the indentation and align the braces properly.

```
// This is a nonsense program segment
if (a > 0)
if (a < 20)
        {
 System.out.print("A is in range.");
b = 5;
    }
        else
            {
    System.out.print("A is too large.");
    b = 3;
}
    else
System.out.print("A is too small.");
System.out.print("All done.")
```

10. Given the float variables x1, x2, y1, y2, and m, write a code segment to find the slope of a line through the two points (x1, y1) and (x2, y2). Use the formula

$$m = \frac{y2 - y1}{x2 - x1}$$

to determine the slope of the line. If x1 equals x2, the line is vertical and the slope is undefined. The segment should display the slope with an appropriate label. If the slope is undefined, it should display the message "Slope undefined."

11. Given the `float` variables a, b, c, root1, root2, and `discriminant`, write a code segment to determine whether the roots of a quadratic polynomial are real or complex (imaginary). If the roots are real, find them and assign them to root1 and root2. If they are complex, write the message "No real roots."

The formula for the solution to the quadratic equation is

$$\frac{-b \pm \sqrt{b^2 - 4ac}}{2a}$$

The ± means "plus or minus" and indicates that the equation has two solutions: one in which the result of the square root is added to $-b$ and one in which the result is subtracted from $-b$. The roots are real if the discriminant (the quantity under the square root sign) is not negative.

Programming Problems

1. Design and write a Java application that takes as input a single letter and displays the corresponding digit on the telephone. The letters and digits on a telephone are grouped this way:

2 = ABC	4 = GHI	6 = MNO	8 = TUV
3 = DEF	5 = JKL	7 = PRS	9 = WXY

No digit corresponds to either Q or Z. For these two letters, your application should display a message indicating that they are not used on a telephone.

The screen dialog might look like this:

```
Enter a single letter, and I will tell you what the corresponding
digit is on the telephone.
R
The digit 7 corresponds to the letter R on the telephone.
```

Here's another example:

```
Enter a single letter, and I will tell you what the corresponding
digit is on the telephone.
Q
There is no digit on the telephone that corresponds to Q.
```

Your code should display a message indicating that there is no matching digit for any nonalphabetic character entered by the user. Also, the application should recognize only uppercase letters. Include the lowercase letters with the invalid characters.

Prompt the user with an informative message for the input value, as shown above. The application should include the input letter as part of the output.

Use proper indentation, appropriate comments, and meaningful identifiers throughout the code.

2. People who deal with historical dates use a number called the *Julian day* to calculate the number of days between two events. The Julian day is the number of days that have elapsed since January 1, 4713 B.C. For example, the Julian day for October 16, 1956, is 2435763.

There are formulas for computing the Julian day from a given date, and vice versa. One very simple formula computes the day of the week from a given Julian day:

Day of the week = (Julian day + 1) % 7

where % is the Java modulus operator. This formula gives a result of 0 for Sunday, 1 for Monday, and so on, up to 6 for Saturday. For Julian day 2435763, the result is 2 (Tuesday). Your job is to write a Java application that requests and inputs a Julian day, computes the day of the week using the formula, and then displays the name of the day that corresponds to that number.

Your output might look like this:

```
Enter a Julian day number and press Enter.
2451545
Julian day number 2451545 is a Saturday.


Enter a Julian day number and press Enter.
2451547
Julian day number 2451547 is a Monday.
```

3. You can compute the date for any Easter Sunday from 1982 to 2048 as follows (all variables are of type `int`):

a is year % 19
b is year % 4
c is year % 7
d is (19 * a + 24) % 30
e is (2 * b + 4 * c + 6 * d + 5) % 7

Easter Sunday is March $(22 + d + e)$ [4]

For example, Easter Sunday in 1985 is April 7.

Write an application that inputs the year and outputs the date (month and day) of Easter Sunday for that year.

---

[4] Notice that this formula can give a date in April.

4. The algorithm for computing the date of Easter can be extended easily to work with any year from 1900 to 2099. There are four years—1954, 1981, 2049, and 2076—for which the algorithm gives a date that is seven days later than it should be. Modify the application for Programming Problem 3 to check for these years and subtract 7 from the day of the month. This correction does not cause the month to change. Be sure to change the documentation for the code to reflect its broadened capabilities.

5. Write a Java application that calculates and prints the diameter, the circumference, or the area of a circle, given the radius. The application should input a character corresponding to one of three actions: D for diameter, C for circumference, and A for area. The user should be prompted to enter the radius in floating-point form and then the appropriate letter. The output should be labeled appropriately. For example, if the input is 6.75 and A, your application should print something like this:

```
The area of a circle with radius 6.75 is 143.14.
```

Here are the formulas you need:

Diameter = $2r$

Circumference = $2\pi r$

Area of a circle = πr^2

where r is the radius. Use 3.14159265 for π.

6. The factorial of a number n is $n * (n - 1) * (n - 2) * \ldots * 2 * 1$. Stirling's formula approximates the factorial for large values of n:

$$\frac{n^n \sqrt{2\pi n}}{e^n}$$

where $\pi = 3.14159265$ and $e = 2.718282$.

Write a Java application that inputs an integer value (but stores it into a double variable n), calculates the factorial of n using Stirling's formula, assigns the (rounded) result to a long integer variable, and then displays the result appropriately labeled.

Depending on the value of n, you should obtain one of these results:

■ A numerical result.

■ If n equals 0, the factorial is defined to be 1.

■ If n is less than 0, the factorial is undefined.

■ If n is too large, the result exceeds Long.MAX_VALUE.

Because Stirling's formula is used to calculate the factorial of very large numbers, the factorial approaches Long.MAX_VALUE quickly. If the factorial exceeds Long.MAX_VALUE, it causes an arithmetic overflow in the computer, in which case the program continues with a strange-looking integer result, perhaps a negative value. Before you write the application, then, you first must write a small application that lets you determine, by trial and error, the largest value of n for which Java can compute a factorial using Stirling's formula. After you've determined this value, you can write the application using nested *if*s that display different messages depending on the value of n. If n is within the acceptable range, output the number and the result with an appropriate message. If n is 0, write the message, "The number is 0. The factorial is 1." If the number is less than 0, write "The number is less than 0. The factorial is undefined." If the number is greater than the largest value of n for which Java can compute a factorial, write "The number is too large."

Hint: Don't compute Stirling's formula directly. The values of n^n and e^n can be huge, even in floating-point form. Take the natural logarithm of the formula and manipulate it algebraically to work with more reasonable floating-point values. If r is the result of these intermediate calculations, the final result is e^r. Make use of the standard library methods Math.log and Math.exp. These methods compute the natural logarithm and natural exponentiation, respectively.

Case Study Follow-Up

1. Add support for a second middle name, a prefix, and a suffix to the Name class. The full method should now include these parts of the name. You should add know methods to return these new parts. You may optionally provide methods for different name formats based on the extended Name class.

2. Change the Student class to include an INVALID status constant, and set it to invalid when any of the scores are outside of the range of 0 to 100.

3. Change the StudentStatus application so that it prints an appropriate message when the input data are invalid.

4. Write a test plan to fully test the StudentStatus application and implement the test plan.

5. Write a driver application that is designed specifically to test all aspects of the Student class, and implement the test plan associated with the driver.

6. Add a method to the Student class that enables it to compare the status of two students in the same manner that compareTo does for names or string. Call the method compareStatusTo, and have it take another Student object as an argument. It should return −1 if the other student's status is greater, 0 if it is equal, and 1 if it is less than the instance's status.

7. Add equals and compareTo methods to the Student class that compare two student records. In the case of equals, the method should return true if the names and scores are equal. The compareTo method should test for alphabetical ordering of the student names. (*Hint:* You'll be glad we implemented compareTo for the Name class.)

File Objects and Looping Statements

goals

Knowledge Goals

- To recognize when noninteractive input/output is appropriate and how it differs from interactive input/output
- To know how to read from a text file
- To know how to write to a text file
- To know how to read a numeric value from a file
- To understand the semantics of a *while* loop
- To understand when a count-controlled loop is appropriate
- To understand when an event-controlled loop is appropriate
- To recognize how mutable and immutable objects differ

Skill Goals

To be able to:

- Write applications that use data files for input and output
- Construct syntactically correct *while* loops
- Construct count-controlled loops with a *while* statement
- Construct event-controlled loops with a *while* statement
- Use the end-of-file condition to control the input of data
- Use flags to control the execution of a *while* statement
- Construct counting loops with a *while* statement
- Construct summing loops with a *while* statement
- Choose the correct type of loop for a given problem
- Construct nested *while* loops
- Choose data sets that test a looping application comprehensively

timeline

1951
Admiral Grace Murray Hopper invents the first compiler

1952
The EDVAC, the first stored-program computer, is operational

1952
IBM introduces the IBM 701

1953
The IBM 650 Magnetic Drum Calculator is introduced, mass produced, and becomes the best selling computer of the 1950s

1954
Earl Masterson at Univac introduces his Uniprinter, a line printer that prints 600 lines per minute

1954
Texas Instruments develops the world's first silicon transistor

introduction

In Chapters 2, 3, and 4, we used `System.in` for input and `System.out` for output. With these classes, all input is from the keyboard and output is to the screen. In this chapter, we look at input that can be prepared ahead of time on a file and output that can be written to a file for later use. We also examine another of Java's control structures, the *loop*. In Chapter 4, we saw how the flow of control in an application can be altered to select among different actions with the *if* statement. In this chapter, we work with a statement that allows us to repeat actions: the *while* statement.

1957
The concept of artificial intelligence is developed at Dartmouth College

1956-57
The RAMAC, random-access method of accounting and control, is introduced by IBM for hard disk data storage

1957
John Backus debuts the first Fortran compiler

1957
John McCarthy founds MIT's Artificial Intelligence Department

1957
The first computer-controlled launch of the Atlas missile takes place

1957
Russia launches Sputnik I into orbit

5.1 File Input and Output

In everything we've done so far, we've assumed that input occurs via the screen. We have read input typed on the screen and sent messages to the screen. We look now at input/output (I/O) using files.

Files

Earlier we defined a *file* as a named area in secondary storage that holds a collection of information (for example, the Java code we have typed into the editor). The information in a file usually is stored on an auxiliary storage device, such as a disk (see Figure 5.1).

Reading and writing data on files is similar to input and output on the screen, but it differs in some important ways. A file contains a sequence of values, and it has a distinct beginning and end—that is, a first value and a last value. You may think of reading a file as analogous to reading a book in that it is read from the front to the back. Just as you might use a bookmark to keep track of your place in a book, Java uses a *file pointer* to remember its place in a file. Each time some data are read from the file, the file pointer advances to the point where reading should resume next. Each read operation copies a value from the file into a variable in the code and advances the file pointer. A series of read operations eventually reaches the last value in the file, and the pointer is then said to be at end-of-file (EOF).

Writing data on a file is like writing in an empty notebook. At the beginning, the file is empty. Then data are written onto it from front to back. The file pointer always indicates the end of the last value written so that writing can resume after that point. In effect, the file

Figure 5.1   Disks Used for File Storage

pointer is always at EOF when a file is being written. The size of the file increases with each write operation. The only limit placed on the size of a file is the amount of disk space available to the application.

Why would we want an application to read data from a file instead of the user interface? If an application will read a large quantity of data, it is easier to enter the data into a file with an editor than to enter it while the application is running. With the editor, we can go back and correct mistakes. Also, we do not have to enter the data all at once; we can take a break and come back later. If we want to rerun the application at some point, having the data stored in a file allows us to do so without retyping the data.

Why would we want the output from an application to be written to a disk file? The contents of a file can be displayed on a screen or printed. This ability gives us the option of looking at the output over and over again without having to rerun the application. Also, the output stored in a file can be read into another application as input. For example, an application that calculates a payroll could write its output to a file that could then be input to an application that prints checks.

Using Files

If we want an application to use file I/O, we have to do five things:

1. Import the library package `java.io.*`.
2. Use declaration statements to declare the file variable identifiers we will use.
3. Instantiate each file object.
4. Use methods associated with the file object to read or write it.
5. Call a method to close the file when we are done with it.

Import the Package `java.io.*`   The first thing we must do is import the package containing the classes that define a file:

```
import java.io.*;
```

Through the package `java.io.*`, Java defines many classes for different forms of I/O. In the case of our applications, we use just four of these classes: `FileReader`, `FileWriter`, `BufferedReader`, and `PrintWriter`. The `FileReader` and `FileWriter` classes are like the `InputStreamReader` class that we've been using with `System.in`. We won't use them directly, but we do need them as part of instantiating the `BufferedReader` and `PrintWriter` classes. The reason is that the Java library builds the abstraction for the file classes in layers. The `FileReader` and `FileWriter` classes provide only the basic file object functionality of reading and writing one character at a time. On top of this abstraction, Java builds another layer of objects that are more convenient for input and output of different kinds of data. Figure 5.2 shows the relationships among these classes. We explore how we can create our own Java layering of abstractions in Chapter 7.

`PrintWriter` is the file class that is most similar to `System.out`. Of course, we've been using `BufferedReader` on top of `System.in` all along, and now we see how to apply it to a file. Thus, many of the operations that we use with files should already be familiar to you.

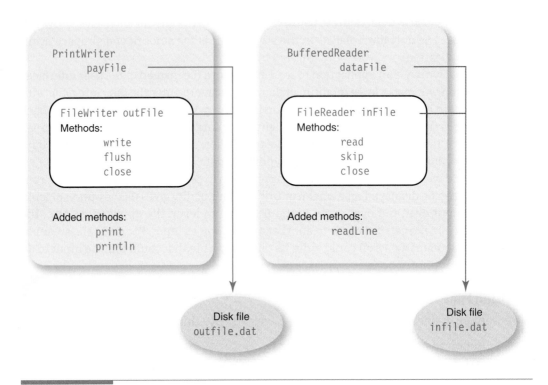

Figure 5.2 Relationships between FileWriter and PrintWriter, and between FileReader and BufferedReader

Declare the File Identifier In Java, you declare file identifiers in the same way that you declare any variable—you specify the class and then the name:

```
PrintWriter outFile;
BufferedReader inFile;
```

Character stream file A file that is stored as a sequence of characters

Note that BufferedReader is used for input files only, and PrintWriter is used for output files only. With these classes, you cannot read from and write to the same file. These classes work with what Java calls **character stream files**. In a later chapter, we will encounter other kinds of files that allow us to output and input whole objects. The advantage of a character stream file is that we work with this kind of file in the editor. Thus, we can prepare an input file with the editor, process it with an application, and then view the output with the editor.

The data in character stream files are organized into lines. A line is a string of characters that ends with a special character called an end-of-line (EOL) mark. When you examine such a file with an editor, each line in the file appears as a line of text on the screen. The editor doesn't display the EOL mark. Rather, the EOL mark simply tells the editor when to go to the next line as it places the characters on the screen.

Instantiate the File Objects   The third thing we have to do is to instantiate the file objects. Part of instantiating a file object involves telling the operating system the name of the file on the disk. Thus, we pass the file's name on the disk to the constructor for the object. That way, the JVM and operating system know which disk file to use when the code performs an operation on the file. As we've done with System.in, we nest the instantiation of the simpler class inside of the class that we actually use. Here's what we've been doing:

```
BufferedReader in;
in = new BufferedReader(new InputStreamReader(System.in));
```

In using BufferedReader with a file, we write the following instead:

```
inFile = new BufferedReader(new FileReader("infile.dat"));
```

where the operating system uses the string "infile.dat" to identify the actual disk file we wish to use. We instantiate a PrintWriter in much the same way. For example, we can write the following statement:

```
outFile = new PrintWriter(new FileWriter("outfile.dat"));
```

Exactly what do these statements do? The constructors create file objects for use in your code and associate them with physical files on disk. The object is then assigned to a file variable that you can reference in other statements in your code. The first statement creates a connection between the file variable inFile and the disk file named infile.dat. (Names of file variables must be Java identifiers, but many computer systems do not use Java syntax for file names on disk. For example, file names can include dots and slashes (/) but file variable identifiers cannot.) Similarly, the second statement associates the identifier outFile with the disk file outfile.dat.

The constructor performs additional operations depending on whether the file is an input file or an output file. With an input file, the constructor places the file pointer at the first piece of data in the file. (Each input file has its own file pointer.) With an output file, the constructor checks whether the file already exists. If the file doesn't exist, it creates a new empty file. If the file does exist, it erases the old contents of the file. Then the file pointer is placed at the beginning of the empty file (see Figure 5.3).

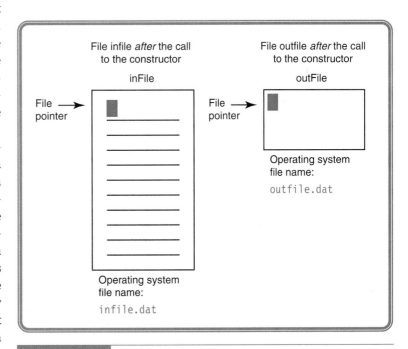

Figure 5.3   The Effect of Calling a Constructor for a Character Stream File Object

As output proceeds, each successive output operation advances the file pointer to add data to the end of the file.

Because calling the constructor creates a file object and prepares the file for reading or writing, you must call it before you can use any input or output methods that refer to the file. It's a good habit to call the constructor early in the application to be sure that the files are prepared before any attempts to perform file I/O are made.

```java
public static void main(String[] args)
{
  PrintWriter outFile;
  BufferedReader inFile;
  // Instantiate the file objects
  outFile = new PrintWriter(new FileWriter("outfile.dat"));
  inFile = new BufferedReader(new FileReader("infile.dat"));
  .
  .
  .
}
```

Use Methods Associated with the File Object to Read or Write It   Once a file has been declared and instantiated, we are ready to use it. The main operation that we can perform on a file of the class PrintWriter is to print a value onto it. The print method can be passed a value of any of Java's primitive types. We typically pass it a string, using string conversion to convert other types such as int or double to be part of the string. For example:

```java
outFile.print("The answer is " + 49);
```

We could also write

```java
outFile.print("The answer is ");
outFile.print(49);
```

and the output would be identical to that produced by the preceding version. The int value 49 is converted to a string for output.

If you print a floating-point value that has been calculated within an application, you have no control over the number of digits printed. For example, if you divide 1 by 3, you get 0.333333333 .... To gain control over the appearance of such numbers, you can use the String class valueOf method, which takes a value of a numeric type as an argument and returns a string representation of the value. Then you can use the String methods indexOf and substring to select only the characters representing the digits you wish to output. We ask you to explore this technique in the exercises at the end of this chapter.

PrintWriter also provides a println method that works in the same way as the println method associated with System.out. The only difference between print and println is that println automatically adds the EOL mark at the end of whatever it writes. For example, the following method call first writes its argument to the file payFile, and then writes an EOL mark to start a new line in the file:

```
payFile.println("Rate = " + rate);
```

Now we turn our attention to file input. The BufferedReader class provides the readLine method with which we're already familiar from reading lines entered via System.in. Recall that readLine is a value-returning method that returns the input line as a string. This method actually reads the EOL mark at the end of the line, but then discards it instead of storing it in the string. As a consequence, the file pointer advances to the start of the next line. If we read a line from one file, we can write it out to another file with println. For example, if dataLine is a String object, we can write

```
dataLine = dataFile.readLine();
payFile.println(dataLine);
```

When println outputs the string in dataLine, it appends an EOL mark that replaces the one discarded by readLine. The advantage of having readLine discard the EOL mark is that it is easier to work with the input string. For example, if we want to add some characters to the end of the string before we write it to payFile, we can simply use string concatenation:

```
dataLine = dataFile.readLine();
dataLine = dataLine + "***";
payFile.println(dataLine);
```

If readLine did *not* discard the EOL mark, then after the concatenation an EOL mark would appear between the last character from the input line and the appended stars. The call to println would then output two lines on payFile.

What happens when we call readLine and the file pointer is at EOF? At EOF, there's no valid value to return as a string. Java defines a special value called null that signifies that a reference type variable contains an invalid value. When readLine discovers that the file pointer is already at EOF, it returns the value null. Note that null is not the same as the empty string. Rather, it is a unique value in Java that does not correspond to any valid object value. We will see later how we can test for null in a Boolean expression.

If readLine always returns a string, how do we get numbers into our application? Exactly the same way we did with System.in. We must convert the string to a numeric value using one of the parse methods. As a reminder, here is how we have been getting a floating-point value from System.in:

```
double number;
number = Double.parseDouble(in.readLine());
```

Using this code as a model, we can input a floating-point value from a file as follows:

```
double floatNumber;
floatNumber = Double.parseDouble(dataFile.readLine());
```

Likewise, an integer value can be read as shown here:

```
int intNumber;
intNumber = Integer.parseInt(dataFile.readLine());
```

Reading data from a file does *not* destroy the data on the file. Because the file pointer moves in just one direction, however, we cannot go back and reread data that has been read from the disk file unless we return the pointer to the beginning of the file and start over. As we will see in the next section, closing a file and reassigning it to a file object with new causes the file pointer to return to the beginning of the file.

Another method associated with objects of the class BufferedReader is called skip. When we pass a long value to skip, it causes the file pointer to skip over that many characters in the file. Recall that we write a literal value of type long with an L at the end. For example, the statement

```
inFile.skip(100L);
```

skips the next 100 characters in the file. Reading can then resume at the new file pointer's position. If skip reaches EOF before it has skipped the specified number of characters, then the application halts with an error message because an IOException is thrown. When we put all of this together in an application, we see that, just as happened when we used System.in, file input requires us to include the throws IOException clause in the heading for main; it lets Java know that such an exception should be passed to the JVM. The FileWriter class similarly includes methods that can throw an IOException. Thus, for any application that uses file I/O, the heading for main should include the throws clause.

```
public static void main(String[] args) throws IOException
```

We will return to the subject of reading data from files later in this chapter. Except for some trivial cases, we must combine reading operations with loops to read through all of the data on a file.

Call a Method to Close the File When Done with It   After we have finished reading from or writing to a file, we must close the file. Closing a file tells the operating system that we no longer need the file, and it makes the file available for use by another application. Once a file is closed, it is no longer associated with the corresponding identifier in our code. Each of the file classes that we have discussed in this chapter has a void method called close associated with it. The close method does not take any arguments. The following code segment closes the files that we have been using in our discussions:

```
inFile.close();
outFile.close();
```

Although most Java systems automatically close every file when an application exits, it is good programming practice to explicitly close each file. Also, once an application has finished using a file, it should be closed immediately. You don't have to wait until the end of an application to close a file.

Once a file is closed, it can again be assigned to a file object with a call to new. For example, if the file infile.dat is associated with the file object inFile, we can write the following:

```
inFile.close();
inFile = new BufferedReader(new FileReader("infile.dat"));
```

The effect of these two statements is to temporarily break the association between the disk file (infile.dat) and the file identifier (inFile), and then to restore their connection. A side effect of these operations is that the file pointer is reset to the beginning of the file as part of the constructor call. After the call to close, it would also be possible to assign a different disk file to inFile or to assign infile.dat to a different file identifier. Here's an example that does both:

```
inFile.close();
inFile = new BufferedReader(new FileReader("somefile.dat"));
differentFile = new BufferedReader(new FileReader("infile.dat"));
```

■ An Example Application Using Files

Now let's pull our discussion of file I/O together by writing a simple application. The application should read three lines from an input file, display each line on System.out, and write the lines in reverse order onto an output file. We use BufferedReader and PrintWriter file objects that we associate with files called infile.dat and outfile.dat. Let's name the three lines of input lineOne, lineTwo, and lineThree. Because readLine returns a string, we can invoke it as we instantiate each string object. Once the lines have been read, we close the input file.

```
import java.io.*;                            // File classes
public class UseFile
{
  public static void main(String[] args) throws IOException
  {
    PrintWriter outFile;          // Output data file
    BufferedReader inFile;        // Input data file
    String lineOne;               // Strings to hold data lines
    String lineTwo;
    String lineThree;
    // Prepare input and output files
    inFile = new BufferedReader(new FileReader("infile.dat"));
    outFile = new PrintWriter(new FileWriter("outfile.dat"));
    // Read in three lines from infile.dat
    lineOne = new String(inFile.readLine());
    lineTwo = new String(inFile.readLine());
    lineThree = new String(inFile.readLine());
    inFile.close();                          // Finished reading
    // Write three lines to screen
    System.out.println(lineOne);
    System.out.println(lineTwo);
```

```
    System.out.println(lineThree);
    // Write three lines to outFile in reverse order
    outFile.println(lineThree);
    outFile.println(lineTwo);
    outFile.println(lineOne);
    outFile.close();                                    // Finished writing
  }
}
```

Here are the input file, output file, and screen:

File `infile.dat`:

File `outfile.dat`:

On `System.out`:

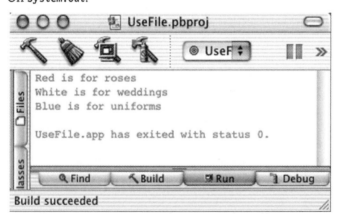

5.2 Looping

In Chapter 4, we introduced a statement that allows us to explicitly change the order in which statements execute within a method. With this strategy, the flow of control within a method can differ from the physical order of the statements. The *physical order* is the order in which the statements appear in the code; the *logical order* is the order in which we want the statements to be executed.

The *if* statement is one way of making the logical order differ from the physical order. Looping control structures are another way. A loop executes the same statement (simple or compound) over and over, as long as a condition or set of conditions is satisfied.

In this chapter, we discuss different kinds of loops and consider how they are constructed using the *while* statement. We also discuss *nested loops* (loops that contain other loops).

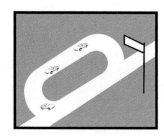

Loop A control structure that causes a statement or group of statements to be executed repeatedly

The while Statement

The *while* statement, like the *if* statement, tests a condition. Here is the syntax template for the *while* statement:

While-Statement

```
while ( Expression )
    Statement
```

Here is an example of one:

```
count = 1;
while (count <= 25)
  count = count + 1;
```

The *while* statement is a looping control structure. The statement to be executed each time through the loop is called the *body* of the loop. In the preceding example, the body of the loop is a statement that adds 1 to the value of count. This *while* statement says to execute the body repeatedly as long as count is less than or equal to 25. The *while* statement is completed (and hence the loop stops) when count is greater than 25. The effect of this loop, then, is to count through the int values from 1 to 25.

Just like the condition in an *if* statement, the condition in a *while* statement must be an expression of type boolean. The *while* statement says, "If the value of the expression is true, execute the body and then go back and test the expression again. If the value of the expression is false, skip the body." Thus the loop body is executed over and over as long as the expression remains true when it is tested. When the expression is false, the code skips the body and execution continues at the statement immediately following the loop. Of course, if the expression is false initially, the body never executes. Figure 5.4 shows the flow of control of the *while* statement, where Statement1 is the body of the loop and Statement2 is the statement following the loop.

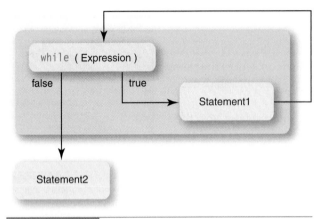

The body of a loop can consist of a block of statements, which allows us to execute any group of statements repeatedly. Typically, we use *while* loops in the following form:

```
while (Expression)
{
    .
    .
    .
}
```

Figure 5.4 *while* Statement Flow of Control

In this structure, if the expression is true, the entire sequence of statements in the block is executed, and then the expression is checked again. If it is still true, the statements are executed again. The cycle continues until the expression becomes false.

Although in some ways the *if* and *while* statements are alike, there are fundamental differences between them (see Figure 5.5). In the *if* structure, Statement1 is either skipped or executed exactly once. In the *while* structure, Statement1 can be skipped, executed once, or executed over and over. The *if* is used to *choose* a course of action; the *while* is used to *repeat* a course of action.

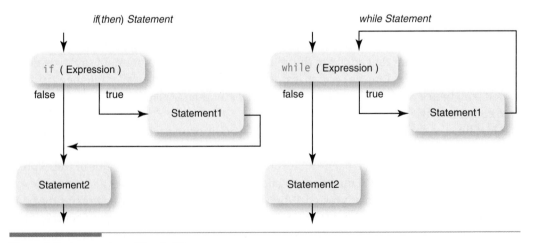

Figure 5.5 A comparison of *if* and *while*

Phases of Loop Execution

The body of a loop is executed in several phases:

- The moment that the flow of control reaches the first statement inside the loop body is the loop entry.

- Each time the body of a loop is executed, a pass is made through the loop. This pass is called an iteration.

- Before each iteration, control is transferred to the loop test at the beginning of the loop.

- When the last iteration is complete and the flow of control has passed to the first statement following the loop, the code has exited the loop. The condition that causes a loop to be exited is the termination condition. In the case of a *while* loop, the termination condition is that the *while* expression becomes false.

Notice that the loop exit occurs at only one point: when the loop test is performed. Even though the termination condition may become satisfied midway through the execution of the loop, the current iteration is completed before the computer checks the *while* expression again.

The concept of looping is fundamental to programming. In this chapter, we will spend some time looking at typical kinds of loops and ways of implementing them with the *while* statement. These looping situations come up again and again when you are analyzing problems and designing algorithms.

Loop entry The point at which the flow of control reaches the first statement inside a loop

Iteration An individual pass through, or repetition of, the body of a loop

Loop test The point at which the *while* expression is evaluated and the decision is made either to begin a new iteration or to skip to the statement immediately following the loop

Loop exit The point at which the repetition of the loop body ends and control passes to the first statement following the loop

Termination condition The condition that causes a loop to be exited

Count-controlled loop A loop that executes a specified number of times

Event-controlled loop A loop that terminates when something happens inside the loop body to signal that the loop should be exited

Loops Using the while Statement

In solving problems, you will encounter two major types of loops: count-controlled loops, which repeat a specified number of times, and event-controlled loops, which repeat until something happens within the loop. In the context of a loop, we use the word *event* to mean a specific condition that we expect to occur during some iteration of the loop, and that can be tested by a Boolean expression.

If you are making an angel food cake and the recipe reads, "Beat the mixture 300 strokes," you are executing a count-controlled loop. If you are making a pie crust and the recipe reads, "Cut with a pastry blender until the mixture resembles coarse meal," you are executing an event-controlled loop; you don't know ahead of time the exact number of loop iterations.

Count-Controlled Loops

A count-controlled loop uses a variable called the *loop control variable* in the loop test. Before we enter a count-controlled loop, we must *initialize* (set the initial value of) the loop control variable and then test it. Then, as part of each iteration of the loop, we must *increment* (increase by 1) the loop control variable. Here's an example:

```
loopCount = 1;                          // Initialization
while (loopCount <= 10)                 // Test
{
    .
    .                                   // Repeated actions
    .
    loopCount = loopCount + 1;          // Incrementation
}
```

Here loopCount is the loop control variable. It is set to 1 before loop entry. The *while* statement tests the expression

```
loopCount <= 10
```

and executes the loop body as long as the expression is true. The dots inside the compound statement represent a sequence of statements to be repeated. The last statement in the loop body increments loopCount by adding 1 to it.

Look at the statement in which we increment the loop control variable. Notice its form:

```
variable = variable + 1;
```

This statement adds 1 to the current value of the variable, and the result replaces the old value. Variables that are used this way are called *counters*. In our example, loopCount is incremented with each iteration of the loop—we use it to count the iterations. The loop control variable of a count-controlled loop is always a counter.

We've encountered another way of incrementing a variable in Java. The incrementation operator (++) increments the variable that is its operand. Thus the statement

```
loopCount++;
```

has precisely the same effect as the assignment statement

```
loopCount = loopCount + 1;
```

From here on, we will typically use the ++ operator, as do most Java programmers.

When designing loops, it is the programmer's responsibility to see that the condition to be tested is set correctly (initialized) before the *while* statement begins. The programmer also must make sure that the condition changes within the loop so that it eventually becomes false; otherwise, the loop will never be exited.

```
loopCount = 1;  // Variable loopCount must be initialized
while (loopCount <= 10)
{
    .
    .
    .
    loopCount++;  // loopCount must be incremented
}
```

A loop that never exits is called an *infinite loop* because, in theory, the loop executes forever. In the preceding code, omitting the incrementation of loopCount at the bottom of the loop leads to an infinite loop; the *while* expression is always true because the value of loopCount is forever 1. If your application runs for much longer than expected, chances are that you've created an infinite loop. In such a case, you may have to issue an operating system command to stop the application.

How many times does the loop in our example execute—9 or 10? To answer this question, we must look at the initial value of the loop control variable and then at the test to see its final value. Here we've initialized loopCount to 1, and the test indicates that the loop body is executed for each value of loopCount up through 10. If loopCount starts at 1 and runs up to 10, the loop body is executed 10 times. If we want the loop to execute 11 times, we must either initialize loopCount to 0 or change the test to

```
loopCount <= 11
```

Event-Controlled Loops

There are several kinds of event-controlled loops; we examine two of them here: sentinel-controlled and end-of-file-controlled. In all event-controlled loops, the termination condition depends on some event occurring while the loop body is executing.

Sentinel-Controlled Loops Loops often are used to read in and process long lists of data. Each time the loop body is executed, a new piece of data is read and processed. Often a special data value, called a *sentinel* or *trailer value*, is used to signal the code that no more data remain to be processed. Looping continues as long as the data value read is *not* the sentinel; the loop stops when the code recognizes the sentinel. In other words, reading the sentinel value is the event that controls the looping process.

A sentinel value must be something that never shows up in the normal input to an application. For example, if an application reads calendar dates, we could use February 31 as a sentinel value:

```
// This code is incorrect
while ( !date.equals("0231") )
{
  date = dataFile.readLine();          // Get a date
  .                                     // Process it
  .
  .
}
```

There is a problem in the loop this example. The value of date is not defined before the first pass through the loop. Somehow we have to initialize this String. We could assign an arbitrary value to it, but then we would run the risk that the first value input will be the sentinel value, which would then be processed as data. Also, it's inefficient to initialize a variable with a value that is never used.

We can solve the problem by reading the first data value *before* entering the loop. This is called a *priming read*. (The idea is similar to priming a pump by pouring a bucket of water into the mechanism before starting it.) Let's add the priming read to the loop:

```
// This is still incorrect
date = dataFile.readLine();              // Get a date--priming read
while ( !date.equals("0231") )
{
  date = dataFile.readLine();            // Get a date
      .                                  // Process it
      .
      .
}
```

With the priming read, if the first value input is the sentinel value, then the loop correctly does not process it. We've solved one problem, but now a problem crops up when the first value input is valid data. The first thing the code does inside the loop is to get a date, destroying the value obtained by the priming read. Thus, the first date in the data list is never processed. Given the priming read, the *first* thing that the loop body should do is process the data that's already been read. But at what point do we read the next input value? We do so *last* in the loop. In this way, the *while* condition is applied to the next input value before it is processed. Here's how it looks:

```
// This version is correct
date = dataFile.readLine();              // Get a date--priming read
while ( !date.equals("0231") )
{
      .                                  // Process it
      .
      .
  date = dataFile.readLine();            // Get a date
}
```

This segment works correctly. The first value is read in; if it is not the sentinel, it is processed. At the end of the loop, the next value is read in, and we return to the beginning of the loop. If the new value is not the sentinel, it is processed just like the first value. When the sentinel value is read, the *while* expression becomes false, and the loop exits (*without* processing the sentinel).

Many times the problem dictates the value of the sentinel. For example, if the problem does not allow data values of 0, then the sentinel value should be 0. Sometimes a combination of values is invalid. The combination of February and 31 as a date is such a case. Sometimes a range of values (negative numbers, for example) is the sentinel.

When you are choosing a value to use as a sentinel, what happens if no invalid data values exist? Then you may have to input an extra value in each iteration: a value whose only purpose is to signal the end of the data. For example, look at this code segment:

```
data = dataFile.readLine();          // Get first data line
sentinel = data.substring(0, 1);     // Extract sentinel character
while (sentinel.equals("Y"))
{
  // Extract data value from line and convert to double
  value = Double.parseDouble(data.substring(1, data.length()));
    .                                  // Process data value

    .

    .
  data = dataFile.readLine();         // Get next data line
  sentinel = data.substring(0, 1);    // Extract sentinel character
}
```

The first value on each line of the following data set is used to indicate whether more data are present. In this data set, when the sentinel value is anything other than Y, no more data remain; when it is Y, more data should be processed.

Sentinel Values	Data Values
Y	12.78
Y	−47.90
Y	5.33
Y	21.83
Y	−99.01
N	

What happens if you forget to include the sentinel value? Once all the data have been read from the file, the loop body is executed again. However, there aren't any data left—because the computer has reached the end of the file. In the next section, we describe a way to use the end-of-file situation as an alternative to a sentinel.

End-of-File-Controlled Loops   After an application has read the last piece of data from an input file, the computer is at the end of the file (EOF, for short). The next time that we attempt to read from the file, there is nothing to read and thus nothing for the readLine method to return. What happens? The readLine method normally returns a String value that holds the contents of the line, so it returns null as its sentinel.

Thus, to read and process lines from a file, we can write a sentinel-controlled loop like the following:

```
line = dataFile.readLine();          // Get a line--priming read
while ( line != null )
{
    .                                  // Process it

    .

    .
  line = dataFile.readLine();         // Get the next line
}
```

The test in this *while* statement uses the relational operator != instead of the equals method. The reason is that equals compares the contents of two strings, but the meaning of null is that the String variable doesn't even contain the address of a String object. Thus, a null String has no contents to compare with anything. Be sure that you understand the distinction between a null String and an empty string (""). If the empty string is assigned to a String variable, then the variable contains the address of a place in memory where a String object of length 0 is stored. When null is assigned to a String variable, it has an invalid address value that refers to nowhere in memory. The comparison

```
line.equals(null)
```

always returns false, because the null String has no contents that can be compared to line. When

```
line == null
```

returns true, the equals method in the preceding example throws a NullPointerException. Because it is an uncaught exception, the application crashes.

Java provides a convenient way of avoiding the need to separately write the priming read and the read that gets the next value. When the input operation consists of a simple assignment statement, we can instead write the loop as follows:

```
while ((line = dataFile.readLine()) != null )    // Get a line
{
    .                                            // Process it
    .
    .
}
```

At first glance, the expression in this *while* statement looks rather strange. The reason for its strangeness is that there is an aspect of the assignment operator that we haven't discussed yet. In the past, we have written the assignment operator in assignment statements:

```
x = 2;
```

The assignment operator can also appear in expressions, where it has both a value and a side effect. The side effect is the action we normally associate with assignment statements: The result of the expression to the right of = is assigned to the variable to its left. The value that = returns is the same as the value that is assigned to the variable. An assignment statement is really just a special form of assignment expression where the side effect (the assignment) takes place and then the value returned by the expression is discarded. For example, in the comparison

```
(x = 2 + 2) == 5
```

the value 4 is assigned to the `int` variable x as a side effect, and the subexpression (x = 2 + 2) has the result 4, which is compared to the literal 5, giving a final result of `false`. When we use the result of an assignment expression in a comparison, we must enclose the assignment expression in parentheses because = has the lowest precedence of all the operators. This example demonstrates why you must be careful not to confuse the = and == operators in writing a comparison!

In the *while* statement

```
while ((line = dataFile.readLine()) != null )    // Get a line
{
    .                                            // Process it
    .
    .
}
```

`line` is assigned the value returned by `readLine`, and the `!=` operator compares that same value (the result of the assignment expression) to `null`.

Because the parentheses force the input operation to happen before the comparison, the effect is the same as using a separate priming read. When the flow of control reaches the end of the loop, it returns to the test in the *while* statement. There another input operation takes place before the comparison, with the same effect as using a separate input operation at the end of the loop body. Thus, the input operation in the assignment expression, within the *while* statement's comparison, takes the place of two separate input operations.

If we can write the *while* statement in this manner, why would we ever need the longer form with the two separate input operations? When the test in the *while* statement depends on something other than the value returned by the input operation, we need to use the longer form. For example, if an input line contains three numbers that must be converted to `int` values and their sum is then compared to zero to decide whether the loop should exit, we can't use a simple assignment expression within the *while*. Whenever the condition in the *while* depends on performing multiple operations on the input value, it is best to code the input and the operations as separate priming and updating statements before and within the loop.

▇ Looping Subtasks

We have been looking at ways to use loops to affect the flow of control in code. But looping by itself does nothing. The loop body must perform a task for the loop to accomplish something. In this section, we look at two tasks—counting and summing—that often are used in loops.

Counting   A common task in a loop is to keep track of the number of times the loop has been executed. For example, the following code fragment reads and counts integer input values until it comes to a zero. (Both `number` and `count` are of type `int`.) The loop in the following example has a counter variable, but it is not a count-controlled loop because the variable is not used as a loop control variable:

```
count = 0;                                         // Initialize counter
number = Integer.parseInt(inFile.readLine());      // Read a number
while (number != 0)                                // Test the number
{
   count++;                                        // Increment counter
   number = Integer.parseInt(inFile.readLine());   // Read a number
}
```

The loop continues until a zero is read. After the loop is finished, `count` contains one less than the number of values read. That is, it counts the number of values up to, but not including, the sentinel value (the zero). If a zero is the first value, the loop body is not entered and `count` contains a zero, as it should. We use a priming read here because the loop is sentinel-controlled, and because it is easier to understand the intent of the loop test than if we write it using our shortcut. Here's how the loop looks if we use an assignment in the comparison:

```
count = 0;                                               // Initialize counter
while ((number = Integer.parseInt(inFile.readLine())) != 0)
   count++;                                               // Increment counter
```

Iteration counter A counter variable that is incremented in each iteration of a loop

As you can see, this code is shorter, but its meaning is not nearly as obvious to the reader. A good Java compiler generates Bytecode that is equally efficient in both cases, so it is better to use the version that is easier to understand.

The counter variable in this example is called an **iteration counter** because its value equals the number of iterations through the loop. According to our definition, the loop control variable of a count-controlled loop is an iteration counter. However, as you've just seen, not all iteration counters are loop control variables.

What happens if our example loop encounters EOF before it reads a zero? It crashes with a `NumberFormatException`. The reason is that `readLine` returns `null` when the file pointer is at EOF. The `parseInt` method cannot convert this value to a number, so it throws an exception. The loop is thus more properly written as follows:

```
count = 0;                                            // Initialize counter
inLine = inFile.readLine();                           // Read a number string
if (inLine == null)                                   // If EOF
   number = 0;                                        // Set number to 0
else
{
   number = Integer.parseInt(inFile.readLine());      // Convert string to int
   while (number != 0)                                // Test the number
   {
      count++;                                         // Increment counter
      inLine = inFile.readLine();                      // Read a number string
```

```
    if (inLine == null)                          // If EOF
      number = 0;                                // Set number to 0
    else
      number = Integer.parseInt(inFile.readLine()); // Convert number
  }
}
```

We've used parseInt previously but we haven't included NumberFormatException in the throws clause of main. Why is it different from the IOException that we must list in a throws clause when we use file I/O? The reason is that Java defines two kinds of exceptions, checked and unchecked. **Checked exceptions** must be caught or explicitly forwarded with a throws clause. **Unchecked exceptions** may be optionally caught, or they can be allowed to pass automatically to the JVM. NumberFormatException is an unchecked exception so it does not have to be listed in a throws clause, while IOException is an example of a checked exception that must be explicitly thrown.

Checked exceptions usually indicate error conditions that are unlikely to occur, while unchecked exceptions are intended for errors that every good programmer is careful to avoid, such as division by zero. If we had to list every possible unchecked exception in the heading of main, then it would be several lines long. Instead of making us do so, the designers of the Java library simply assume that our code is carefully written to avoid these common errors. If one of them does occur, the error is automatically forwarded to the JVM, and our application crashes. In response, we identify the source of the error, and then we correct the algorithm and the corresponding code to avoid further crashes.

To keep our examples short and understandable, we often omit tests for unchecked exceptions in this book. However, in writing code for actual applications, you should always try to avoid such potential sources of crashes.

> **Checked exception** An exception in Java that must either be caught with a *catch* statement or explicitly thrown to the next level
>
> **Unchecked exception** An exception in Java that can optionally be caught or allowed to propagate automatically to the next level

Summing   Another common looping task is to sum a set of data values. Notice in the following example that the summing operation is written the same way, regardless of how the loop is controlled:

```
sum = 0;                                         // Initialize sum
count = 1;
while (count <= 10)
{
  number = Integer.parseInt(dataFile.readLine());  // Input a value
  sum = sum + number;                            // Add value to sum
  count++;
}
```

We initialize sum to 0 before the loop starts so that the first time the loop body executes, the statement

```
sum = sum + number;
```

adds the current value of sum (0) to number to form the new value of sum. After the entire code fragment has executed, sum contains the total of the 10 values read, count contains 11, and number contains the last value read.

In the preceding code, count is incremented in each iteration. For each new value of count, there is a new value for number. Does this mean we could decrement count by 1 and inspect the previous value of number? No. Once a new value has been read into number, the previous value is gone forever unless we've saved it in another variable (or we reset the file and reread the data).

Let's look at another example. This time, let's also check for EOF. We want to count and sum the first 10 odd numbers in a data set. To do so, we need to test each number to see whether it is even or odd. (We can use the modulus operator to find out. If number % 2 equals 1, number is odd; otherwise, it's even.) If the input value is even, we do nothing. If it is odd, we increment the counter and add the value to our sum. We use a *flag* (a boolean variable) to control the loop because this is not a normal count-controlled loop. In the following code segment, all variables are of type int except the String line and the boolean flag, notDone.

```
count = 0;                          // Initialize event counter
sum = 0;                            // Initialize sum
notDone = true;                     // Initialize loop control flag
while (notDone)
{
  line = dataFile.readLine();       // Get a line
  if (line != null)                 // Got a line?
  {
    number = Integer.parseInt(line);  // Convert line to an int
    if (number % 2 == 1)            // Is the int value odd?
    {
      count++;                      // Yes--increment counter
      sum = sum + number;           // Add value to sum
      notDone = (count < 10);       // Update loop control flag
    }
  }
  else                              // Hit EOF unexpectedly
  {
    errorFile.println("EOF reached before ten odd values read.");
    notDone = false;                // Update loop control flag
  }
}
```

We control the loop with the flag notDone, because the loop exits when either of two events occurs: reading and processing 10 odd values or reaching EOF. Because we use a Boolean flag to control the loop, this type of loop is often called a *flag-controlled loop*.

In this example, there is no relationship between the value of the counter variable and the number of times that the loop is executed. Note that count is incremented only when an odd number is read; it is an event counter. We initialize an event counter to 0 and increment it only when a certain event occurs. The counter in the previous example was an *iteration counter*; it was initialized to 1 and incremented during each iteration of the loop.

> **Event counter** A variable that is incremented each time a particular event occurs

How to Design Loops

It's one thing to understand how a loop works when you look at it and something else again to design a loop that solves a given problem. In this section, we look at how to design loops. We can divide the design process into two tasks: designing the flow of control and designing the processing that takes place in the loop. Each task consists of three parts: the task itself, initialization, and updating. It's also important to specify the state of the code when it exits the loop, because a loop that leaves variables and files in a mess is not well designed.

There are seven different points to consider in designing a loop:

1. What condition ends the loop?
2. How should the condition be initialized?
3. How should the condition be updated?
4. What is the process being repeated?
5. How should the process be initialized?
6. How should the process be updated?
7. What is the state of the code on exiting the loop?

We can use these questions as a checklist. The first three help us design the parts of the loop that control its execution. The next three help us design the processing within the loop. The last question reminds us to make sure that the loop exits in an appropriate manner.

Designing the Flow of Control

The most important step in loop design is deciding what should make the loop stop. If the termination condition isn't well thought out, infinite loops and other mistakes could potentially occur. Here is our first question:

- What condition ends the loop?

We can usually answer this question by closely examining the problem statement. For example:

Key Phrase in Problem Statement	Termination Condition
"Sum 365 temperatures"	The loop ends when a counter reaches 365 (count-controlled loop)
"Process all data in the file"	The loop ends when EOF occurs (EOF-controlled loop)
"Process until 10 odd integers have been read"	The loop ends when 10 odd numbers have been input (event counter)
"The end of the data is indicated by a negative test score"	The loop ends when a negative input value is encountered (sentinel-controlled loop)

Now we need statements that make sure the loop starts correctly and statements that allow the loop to reach the termination condition. We need to ask the next two questions:

- How should the condition be initialized?
- How should the condition be updated?

The answers to these questions depend on the type of termination condition.

Count-Controlled Loops   If the loop is count-controlled, we initialize the condition by giving an initial value to the loop control variable. For count-controlled loops in which the loop control variable is also an iteration counter, the initial value is usually 1. If the process requires the counter to run through a specific range of values, the initial value should be the lowest value in that range.

The condition is updated by increasing the value of the counter by 1 for each iteration. (Occasionally, you may come across a problem that requires a counter to count from some value *down* to a lower value. In this case, the initial value is the greater value, and the counter is *decremented* by 1 for each iteration.) For count-controlled loops that use an iteration counter, these are the answers to the two questions:

- Initialize the iteration counter to 1.
- Increment the iteration counter at the end of each iteration.

If the loop is controlled by a variable that counts an event within the loop, the control variable usually is initialized to 0 and incremented each time the event occurs. For count-controlled loops that use an event counter, here are the answers to the two questions:

- Initialize the event counter to 0.
- Increment the event counter each time the event occurs.

Sentinel-Controlled Loops   In sentinel-controlled loops, a priming read may be the only initialization required. You may also need to open the file in preparation for reading. To update the condition, a new value is read at the end of each iteration. For sentinel-controlled loops, we answer our two questions this way:

- Open the file, if necessary, and input a value before entering the loop (priming read).
- Input a new value for processing at the end of each iteration.

EOF-Controlled Loops   EOF-controlled loops require the same initialization as sentinel-controlled loops. You must open the file, if necessary, and perform a priming read. Updating the loop condition happens implicitly; the input value reflects the success or failure of the operation. However, if the loop doesn't read any data, it never reaches EOF, so updating the loop condition means the loop must keep reading data.

Flag-Controlled Loops   In flag-controlled loops, the Boolean flag variable must be initialized to `true` or `false` and then updated when the condition changes. Here are the answers to the two questions:

- Initialize the flag variable to `true` or `false`, as appropriate.
- Update the flag variable as soon as the condition changes.

In a flag-controlled loop, the flag variable essentially remains unchanged until it is time for the loop to end. Then the code detects some condition within the process being repeated that changes the value of the flag (through an assignment statement). Because the update depends on what the process does, sometimes we have to design the process before we can decide how to update the condition.

Designing the Process Within the Loop

Once we've decided on the appropriate looping structure, we can fill in the details of the process. In designing the process, we must first decide what a single iteration should do. Assume for a moment that the process will execute only once. What tasks must it perform?

- What is the process being repeated?

To answer this question, we have to take another look at the problem statement. The definition of the problem may require the process to sum up data values or to keep a count of data values that satisfy some test. For example:

Count the number of integers in the file `howMany`.

This statement tells us that the process to be repeated is a counting operation.

Here's another example:

Read a stock price for each business day in a week and compute the average price.

In this case, part of the process involves reading a data value. We conclude from our knowledge of how an average is computed that the process also involves summing the data values.

In addition to counting and summing, another common loop process is reading data, performing a calculation, and writing out the result. Many other operations can appear in looping processes. We've mentioned only the simplest here; we will look at some other processes later on.

After we've determined the operations to be performed if the process is executed only once, we can design the parts of the process that are necessary for it to be repeated correctly. We often have to add some steps to account for the fact that the loop executes more than once. This part of the design typically involves initializing certain variables before the loop begins and then reinitializing or updating them before each subsequent iteration.

- How should the process be initialized?
- How should the process be updated?

For example, if the process within a loop requires that several different counts and sums be performed, each must have its own statements to initialize variables, increment counting variables, or add values to sums. Just deal with each counting or summing operation by itself—that is, first write the initialization statement, and then write the incrementing or summing statement. After you've handled this task for one operation, go on to the next operation.

The Loop Exit

When the termination condition occurs and the flow of control passes to the statement following the loop, the variables used in the loop still contain values. Also, if an input file has been used, the reading marker has been left at some position in the file. Or maybe an output file has new contents. If these variables or files are used later in the application, the loop must leave them in an appropriate state. For this reason, the final step in designing a loop is answering this question:

■ What is the state of the code on exiting the loop?

Now we have to consider the consequences of our design and double-check its validity. For example, suppose we've used an event counter and later processing depends on the number of events. It's important to confirm (with an algorithm walk-through) that the value left in the counter is the exact number of events—that it is not off by 1.

Look at this code segment:

```
lineCount = 1;                    // This code is incorrect
while ((inLine = inFile.readLine()) != null)
   lineCount++;
System.out.println("There are " + lineCount + " lines in the file.");
```

This loop reads lines from an input file and counts the number of lines in the file. However, when the loop terminates, lineCount equals the actual number of lines plus 1 because the loop initializes the event counter to 1 before any events take place. By determining the state of lineCount at loop exit, we've detected a flaw in the initialization. lineCount should be initialized to zero. Note that this code segment also demonstrates the use of an assignment expression within a loop test. Because the loop contains just a single statement (the increment statement), there is no need for the usual braces to enclose a block of statements.

Designing correct loops depends as much on experience as it does on the application of design methodology. At this point, you may want to read through the Problem-Solving Case Study at the end of the chapter to see how the loop design process is applied to a real problem.

Nested Loops

In Chapter 4, we described nested *if* statements. It's also possible to nest *while* statements. Both *while* and *if* statements contain statements and are themselves statements. So the body of a *while* statement or the branch of an *if* statement can contain other *while* and *if* statements. By nesting, we can create complex control structures.

Suppose we want to count the commas in each line, repeating this operation for all the lines in a file. We put an event-controlled loop within the main loop. The inner loop uses the charAt method of the String class, which returns the character at a given position in the string. The loop scans the line, position by position, searching for commas.

```
lineCount = 0;                    // Initialize iteration count
inLine = inFile.readLine();       // Priming read
while (inLine != null)            // Outer loop test for EOF
{
   lineCount++;                   // Update outer iteration count
```

```
commaCount = 0;                          // Initialize event counter
index = 0;                               // Initialize loop control count
while (index < inLine.length())          // Inner loop test
{
  if (inLine.charAt(index) == ',')
    commaCount++;                         // Update inner event count
  index++;                               // Update inner exit condition
}
System.out.println("Found " + commaCount + " commas on line " + lineCount);
inLine = inFile.readLine();              // Update outer exit condition
}
System.out.println("There are " + lineCount " lines in the file.");
```

The outer loop is EOF-controlled, and its process is to count input lines and run the inner loop. The inner loop is count-controlled, and its process is to count the commas that it finds on a line. Note the unusual starting and ending values for this inner count-controlled loop. We usually begin at 1, and our ending condition is <= the maximum value. However, the positions in a String are numbered starting at 0 and go up to length() − 1. In this case, because the iteration counter is also used as the position number within the string, it is more natural to start at 0.

General Pattern

Let's examine the general pattern of a simple nested loop. Here the dots represent places where the processing and updating may take place in the outer loop:

```
Initialize outer loop
while ( Outer loop condition )
{

    ⋮

    Initialize inner loop
    while ( Inner loop condition )
    {
        Inner loop processing and update
    }

    ⋮

}
```

Notice that each loop has its own initialization, test, and update steps. An outer loop could potentially do no processing other than to execute the inner loop repeatedly. On the other hand, the inner loop might be just a small part of the processing done by the outer loop; many statements could precede or follow the inner loop.

Let's look at another example. For nested count-controlled loops, the pattern looks like this (where outCount is the counter for the outer loop, inCount is the counter for the inner loop, and limit1 and limit2 are the number of times each loop should be executed):

```
outCount = 1;                    // Initialize outer loop counter
while (outCount <= limit1)
{
  ⋮
  inCount = 1;                   // Initialize inner loop counter
  while (inCount <= limit2)
  {
    ⋮
    inCount++;                   // Increment inner loop counter
  }
  ⋮
  outCount++;                    // Increment outer loop counter
}
```

Here, both the inner and outer loops are count-controlled loops, but the pattern can be used with any combination of loops. The following code fragment shows a count-controlled loop nested within an EOF-controlled loop. The outer loop inputs an integer value telling how many asterisks to print on each line of an output file. (We use the numbers to the right of the code to trace the execution of the code.)

```
line = dataFile.readLine();                        1
while (line != null)                               2
{
  starCount = Integer.parseInt(line);              3
  loopCount = 1;                                   4
  while (loopCount <= starCount)                   5
  {
    outFile.print('*');                            6
    loopCount++;                                   7
  }
  outFile.println();                               8
  line = dataFile.readLine();                      9
}
outFile.println("End");                            10
```

To see how this code works, let's trace its execution with these data values (<EOF> denotes end-of-file):

```
3
1
<EOF>
```

We'll keep track of the variables line, starCount, and loopCount, as well as the logical expressions. To do so, we've numbered each line (except lines containing only a brace). As we trace the code, we indicate the first execution of line 3 by 3.1, the second by 3.2, and so on. Each loop iteration is enclosed by a large brace, and true and false are abbreviated as T and F (see Table 5.1).

| | Variables | | | Logical Expressions | | |
Statement	line	starCount	loopCount	line != null	loopCount <= starCount	Output
1.1	'3'	—	—	—	—	—
2.1	'3'	—	—	T	—	—
3.1	'3'	3	—	—	—	—
4.1	'3'	3	1	—	—	—
5.1	'3'	3	1	—	T	—
6.1	'3'	3	1	—	—	*
7.1	'3'	3	2	—	—	—
5.2	'3'	3	2	—	T	—
6.2	'3'	3	2	—	—	*
7.2	'3'	3	3	—	—	—
5.3	'3'	3	3	—	T	—
6.3	'3'	3	3	—	—	*
7.3	'3'	3	4	—	—	—
5.4	'3'	3	4	—	F	—
8.1	'3'	3	4	—	—	\n (newline)
9.1	'1'	3	4	—	—	—
2.2	'1'	3	4	T	—	—
3.2	'1'	1	4	—	—	—
4.2	'1'	1	1	—	—	—
5.5	'1'	1	1	—	T	—
6.4	'1'	1	1	—	—	*
7.4	'1'	1	2	—	—	—
5.6	'1'	1	2	—	F	—
8.2	'1'	1	2	—	—	\n (newline)
9.2	null	1	2	—	—	—
2.3	null	1	2	F	—	—
10.1	null	1	2	—	—	End

Table 5.1   Code Trace

Here's the output on outFile from the code given the input used for our trace:

```
***
*
End
```

Because starCount and loopCount are variables, their values remain the same until they are explicitly changed, as indicated by the repeating values in Table 5.1. The values of the logical expressions line != null and loopCount <= starCount exist only when the test is made. We indicate this fact with dashes in those columns at all other times.

Designing Nested Loops

To design a nested loop, we begin with the outer loop. The process being repeated includes the nested loop as one of its steps. Because that step is complex, we defer designing it; we will come back to it later. Then we can design the nested loop just as we would any other loop.

As an example, here's the design process for the outer loop in the preceding code segment:

1. *What condition ends the loop?* EOF is reached in the input.
2. *How should the condition be initialized?* A priming read should be performed before the loop starts.
3. *How should the condition be updated?* An input statement should occur at the end of each iteration.
4. *What is the process being repeated?* Using the value of the current input integer, the code should print that many asterisks across one output line.
5. *How should the process be initialized?* No initialization is necessary.
6. *How should the process be updated?* A sequence of asterisks is output and then a newline character is output. There are no counter variables or sums to update.
7. *What is the state of the code on exiting the loop?* The file dataFile is at EOF, starCount contains the last integer read from the input stream, and the rows of asterisks have been printed along with a concluding message.

From the answers to these questions, we can write this much of the algorithm:

```
Read line from dataFile
while NOT EOF
    Set starCount to the integer equivalent of the string in line
    Print starCount asterisks
    Output newline on outFile
    Read line from dataFile
Print "End"
```

After designing the outer loop, it's obvious that the process in its body (printing a sequence of asterisks) is a complex step that requires us to design an inner loop. So we repeat the methodology for the corresponding lower-level module:

1. *What condition ends the loop?* An iteration counter exceeds the value of starCount.

2. *How should the condition be initialized?* The iteration counter should be initialized to 1.

3. *How should the condition be updated?* The iteration counter is incremented at the end of each iteration.

4. *What is the process being repeated?* The code should print a single asterisk on the output file.

5. *How should the process be initialized?* No initialization is needed.

6. *How should the process be updated?* No update is needed.

7. *What is the state of the code on exiting the loop?* A single row of asterisks has been printed, the writing marker is at the end of the current output line, and loopCount contains a value one greater than the current value of starCount.

Now we can write the full algorithm:

```
Read line from dataFile
while NOT EOF
    Set starCount to the integer equivalent of the string in line
    Set loopCount = 1
    while loopCount <= starCount
        Print '*' on outFile
        Increment loopCount
    Output newline on outFile
    Read line from dataFile
Print "End"
```

Of course, nested loops themselves can contain nested loops (called *doubly nested loops*), which can contain nested loops (*triply nested loops*), and so on. You can use this design process for any number of levels of nesting. The trick is to defer details—that is, focus on the outermost loop first, and treat each new level of nested loop as a single step within the loop that contains it.

It's also possible for the process within a loop to include more than one loop. For example, here's an algorithm that reads students' test and homework scores from a file and prints their average on another file:

```
while NOT EOF
    Input line with name
    Print name
    Read and average test scores until a negative score is input
    Print average test score
    Read and average homework scores until a negative score is input
    Print average homework score
    Output newline
```

The steps for reading and averaging the scores require us to design two separate loops. All of these loops are sentinel-controlled.

This kind of complex control structure would be difficult to read if written out in full. It contains too many variables, conditions, and steps to remember at one time. When an algorithm becomes so complex, it is an indication that we failed to identify objects that would naturally hide some of this complexity via abstraction. In this case, we could create a new class with methods that get the scores of one type for a student and return their average. We could call the new class `ScoreFileReader`. The individual loops would then be hidden in the class, and the application would look essentially like the algorithm above.

5.3 Mutable and Immutable Objects

In this section, we see how objects are divided into two distinct categories, *mutable* and *immutable*. The distinction determines their behavior when they are passed as arguments to methods. When a method is executed, it uses copies of the values of the arguments. Because of how reference types are stored, however, the effect of passing mutable or immutable arguments varies. Thus far, most of our objects have been immutable, but in the Case Study we will create a class with mutable objects. First we review how arguments and parameters work in general.

With primitive types, such as `int`, `double`, and `boolean`, the parameter receives a copy of the value of the argument. The method can freely use and change the copy in the parameter. When we pass a variable as an argument to a parameter, it is easy to think that the two identifiers are connected in some way, as if the parameter becomes a synonym for the argument. In reality, their only connection occurs at the moment when the value of the argument is copied to the parameter. Otherwise, they remain independent of each other. That is, operations on the parameter do not affect the argument.

When the method returns, whatever value is in the parameter is discarded. It is not copied back into a variable in the argument. Thus, values of primitive types may be passed into methods, but changes to those values aren't returned. Figure 5.6 illustrates the passing of primitive types. Keep in mind that we are referring here only to the parameters, not to the return value of a value-returning method.

With reference types such as `String` and other classes, a variable contains the address where an object's fields are stored in memory. This address is the value copied from the argument to the parameter. Only one copy of the object's fields exists, which both the calling code and the method use. Figure 5.7 illustrates the difference between passing primitive and reference types to a method.

Changes to the primitive type parameters don't affect the argument. But in the situation pictured in Figure 5.7, wouldn't the changes to a reference type parameter, such as `String`, also change the argument? For many reference types the answer would be yes, but `String` is an **immutable** class.

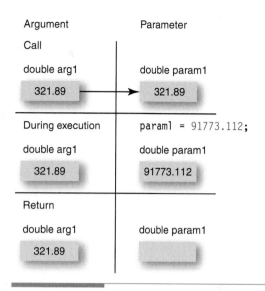

Figure 5.6 Passing a Primitive Type as an Argument to a Parameter

Any object that stores information is said to have **state**. The object's state is the current set of values that it contains. An object is instantiated with an initial state. If any of its methods can subsequently change its state, then the object is said to be **mutable**. `System.out`, for example, is a mutable object: Its `print` method changes its state—it makes the appearance of the window change by adding text to it. If an object doesn't have any methods that can change its state, it is immutable. A `String` is an immutable object; we can merely retrieve its contents.

> **Immutable object**   An object whose state cannot be changed once it is created
>
> **State**   The information stored in an object at any given time
>
> **Mutable object**   An object whose state can be changed after it is created

Thus there is no way to change a `String` object; we can only assign a new value to a `String` variable. Because each string value occupies a different place in memory, the effect of assigning a new value to a `String` variable is to store a different address in it. A parameter of type `String` is initially given a copy of the address of the string argument. When we assign a new value to it, the address is replaced by the address of the new value. The argument itself is left unchanged. Figure 5.8 illustrates what happens when we change the value of a parameter of type `String`.

In contrast to the primitive types and immutable classes like `String`, some classes provide methods for directly changing instance fields. For example, we could write a method that takes `System.out` as a parameter and uses `System.out.print` to display the string `"Java"`. The method's parameter receives the address where `System.out` is stored. Calling `print` with the parameter directly changes the same window that the argument refers to.

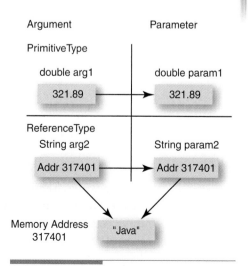

Figure 5.7 Passing Primitive and Reference Types

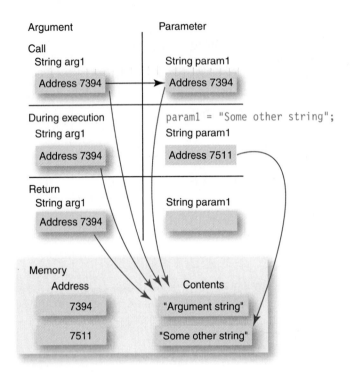

Figure 5.8 The Effect of Assigning a New Value to a Reference Type Parameter

Figure 5.9 shows this process, and you should carefully compare it to Figure 5.8 to be sure that you understand the difference. Assigning a new value (the address of a different object) to a reference type parameter does not change the object to which the argument refers. But changes to the fields of the object referred to by the parameter are made to the argument object.

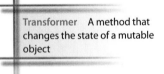

Transformer A method that changes the state of a mutable object

When you need to change the contents of an argument's object, you should make it clear in the documentation that the method changes the object. Software engineers refer to a method that changes the state of a mutable object as a *transformer*. We will have more to say about this issue in Chapter 7.

■ A Parameter-Passing Analogy

To help you remember the behavior of simple and reference parameters, we offer another analogy. Suppose you have a slip of paper in your hand, and you are talking to someone who has another slip of paper. You are like the call and the other person is like the method. You read to the person what's written on your paper and he or she writes it down. If your slip contains a simple type, such as a number representing the current temperature, the other party

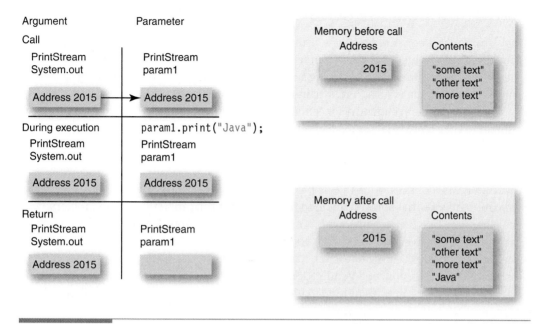

Figure 5.9   The Effect of Changing the Fields of a Reference Type Parameter

can use his or her copy of that number to perform some task. The person could also replace the number with a different one. When done, the individual throws away that paper and your paper remains unchanged.

Now suppose your slip of paper contains the address of a house (a reference type). The other person can use his or her copy of the address to go look at the house. If the person changes the address on that slip of paper (assigns a new value to the reference type parameter), then he or she can go to a different house, but would no longer have the address of the first house. When the other person is done, he or she throws away the paper. Your slip of paper still has the original address, so you can go and look at the house; you find it unchanged.

Finally, suppose that you again have an address on your slip of paper, but this time the person goes to the house and, instead of just looking at it, goes inside and rearranges the furniture. When done, the other party throws away his or her paper, but your paper still has the address of the house. When you go to the house, you find that its contents have changed.

In every case, your slip of paper remained unchanged. In Java, the argument is never affected by a method call. But in the last situation, the method changed the object at the address it was given. So even though the address in the argument remained untouched, the object to which it refers was altered. Whenever you are writing a method that changes a reference parameter, and you are unsure about how the operation will behave, stop and ask yourself, "Am I going inside the house, or am I going to a different address?"

AVERAGE INCOME BY GENDER

Problem: You've been hired by a law firm that is working on a sex discrimination case. Your firm has obtained a file of incomes, gender.dat, which contains the salaries for every employee in the company being sued. Each salary amount is preceded by "F" for female or "M" for male. As a first pass in the analysis of these data, you've been asked to compute the average income for females and the average income for males. The number of males and the number of females should be output as well. The output should be saved on a file for later review.

Discussion: Most of the nouns in this problem statement (which are usually good indicators of potential objects) relate to the reason for the problem, not the problem itself. There are two file objects: one for input and one for output. The result of the application is a pair of averages and a pair of counts, one of each for males and for females. These averages are double values, not classes. However, male and female are two instances of a single concept: gender. Sometimes a problem statement may list specific instances of objects, and it's our job to identify the class that describes those instances in general. We will begin by creating a Gender class.

What state and responsibilities do we need to support for a Gender object? Well, we need to provide a count of the number of this particular gender and the average salary. That task can be handled via value-returning methods. The average is the total salary divided by the count, so we need to keep a running total along with the count. We also need a constructor to create an object and initialize those values. The only responsibility left is to update the values each time this particular gender is input. Because we're changing the initial state of the object, we know that the object is mutable and this responsibility is a transformer. Let's list the state and responsibilities of a Gender object:

State
count (initially 0)
total salary (initially 0.0)

Responsibilities
constructor
update (double salary)
knowCount returns int
knowAverage returns double

Next, we go through the responsibilities, one by one, designing their algorithms. The constructor needs no arguments, as it merely initializes the fields. In fact, if the declarations for the fields include initialization, then the constructor doesn't have to do anything. In such a case, Java lets us omit the constructor, and it provides a default constructor for the class that does nothing. We can just strike the constructor off our list. That's about as easy as it can get!

Updating is very simple. This operation just increments the count and adds its argument to the total salary. Note that it is a void method.

> void update (double salary)
>
> ```
> increment count
> add salary to total salary
> ```

The knowCount responsibility just returns the count field.

> knowCount () returns int
>
> ```
> return count
> ```

For the knowAverage responsibility, we need to return the result of dividing the total salary by the count, remembering to cast the value of the count to type `double`.

> knowAverage () returns double
>
> ```
> return total salary / (double) count
> ```

That completes the design for the Gender class. Now we're ready to implement it in Java.

```java
//*****************************************************
// This class keeps the statistics for an individual
// gender in processing a set of incomes.
//*****************************************************
class Gender
{
  int count = 0;
  double totalSalary = 0.0;

  // Transformer to update state
  public void update(double salary)
  {
    count++;
    totalSalary = totalSalary + salary;
  }

  // Returns count of salary values added with update
  public int knowCount()
  {
    return count;
  }
```

```
// Returns average of salary values added with update
public double knowAverage()
{
    return totalSalary / (double)count;
}
}
```

Now we can turn to the processing for this application and its main method; let's call this class Incomes. We need to prepare the files for input and output, then process the data on the input file. After the last value has been input, we write the output to its file. Of course, we also need to close the files when we're finished with them.

We must write the file processing as a loop that involves two subtasks, because we must process two genders instead of just one. We use our checklist of questions to develop these subtasks in detail.

1. *What condition ends the loop?* The termination condition is EOF on the file inFile. It leads to the following loop test (in pseudocode):

   ```
   while NOT EOF on inFile
   ```

2. *How should the condition be initialized?* A priming read must take place to enter a gender code and amount.

3. *How should the condition be updated?* We must input a new data line with a gender code and amount at the end of each iteration.

   We must input each data line as a string. Then we need to extract the gender code and salary from the string. Because the input of the line is a single operation, we can combine the priming read and the updating read using Java's assignment expression shortcut. Here's the resulting algorithm:

   ```
   while Reading inLine from inFile does not return EOF
       Extract gender code and amount from inLine
       :   (Process being repeated)
   ```

4. *What is the process being repeated?* We need to update the appropriate Gender object with the input data.

5. *How should the process be initialized?* female and male objects need to be instantiated.

6. *How should the process be updated?* When a female income is input, female.update is called. Otherwise, an income is assumed to be for a male, so male.update is called.

7. *What is the state of the code on exiting the loop?* The file inFile is at EOF; female contains the number of input values preceded by 'F' and their total salary; male contains the number of values not preceded by 'F' and the sum of those values.

From the description of how the process is updated, we can see that the loop must contain an *if* structure, with one branch for female incomes and one branch for male incomes. Each branch must call the correct update method. After the loop has exited, we use the know methods associated with each gender to output the count and average.

Now we're ready to write the complete algorithm:

```
main method
Instantiate inFile
Instantiate outFile
Instantiate female
Instantiate male
while Reading inLine from inFile does not return EOF
    Extract gender code and salary from inLine
    if gender code == 'F'
        female.update(salary)
    else
        male.update(salary)
close inFile
Print female.knowCount() and female.knowAverage()
Print male.knowCount() and male.knowAverage()
close outFile
```

We can use the charAt method to extract the gender code from the first position (position 0) of the input line:

```
genderCode = inLine.charAt(0);
```

Then we use substring to retrieve the remainder of the line for conversion by parseDouble:

```
salary = Double.parseDouble(inLine.substring(1, inLine.length()));
```

All of these algorithms depend on the file being created in a certain way. These assumptions should be stated in a special section of the design as follows.

Assumptions: There is at least one male and one female among the data sets. The data sets are entered properly in the input file, with the gender code in the first character position on each line and a floating-point number starting in the second character position. The only gender codes in the file are 'M' and 'F'—any other codes are counted as 'M'. (This last assumption invalidates the results if the data contain any illegal codes. Case Study Follow-Up Exercise 1 asks you to change the application as necessary to address this problem.)

Here is the code for the application.

```
//*********************************************************
// This application reads a file of income amounts classified by
// gender and computes the average income for each gender.
//*********************************************************
```

CASE STUDY

```java
import java.io.*;                                          // File types

public class Incomes
{
  public static void main(String[] args) throws IOException
  {
    Gender female;                          // Females
    Gender male;                            // Males
    String inLine;                          // A line from the file
    char genderCode;                        // Indicates gender
    double salary;                          // Salary amount
    BufferedReader inFile;                  // Input data file
    PrintWriter outFile;                    // Output data file

    // Prepare files for reading and writing
    inFile = new BufferedReader(new FileReader("gender.dat"));
    outFile = new PrintWriter(new FileWriter("results.dat"));

    // Initialize process
    female = new Gender();
    male = new Gender();

    while ((inLine = inFile.readLine()) != null)
    {
      // Update process
      // Extract gender code and amount from input line
      // Gender is the first character
      genderCode = inLine.charAt(0);
      // Amount begins in the second position
      salary = Double.parseDouble(inLine.substring(1, inLine.length()));
      // Process amount based on gender code
      if (genderCode  == 'F')
        // Female
        female.update(salary);
      else
        // Male
        male.update(salary);
    }
    inFile.close();                         // Done reading
    // Write results
    outFile.println("For " + female.knowCount() + " females, the average income is "
      +  female.knowAverage()  + ".");
    outFile.println("For " + male.knowCount() + " males, the average income is " +
      male.knowAverage() + ".");
    outFile.close();
  }
}
```

Testing: Given the following data on the file `gender.dat`

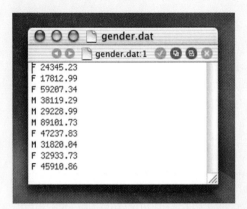

the application `Incomes` writes the following on the file `results.dat`:

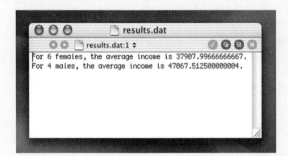

With an EOF-controlled loop, the obvious test cases are a file with data (as that shown above) and an empty file. We should test input values of both 'F' and 'M' for the gender, and try some typical data (so that we can compare the results with our hand-calculated values) and some atypical data (to see how the process behaves). An atypical data set for testing a counting operation is an empty file, which should result in a count of zero. Any other result for the count indicates an error. For a summing operation, atypical data might include negative or zero values.

The `Incomes` application is not designed to handle empty files or negative income values; the assumption that the file was not empty and contained at least one male and one female was written into the design. An empty file causes both `female` and `male` to have count equal to zero at the end of the loop. Although this result is correct, the statements that compute the average income cause the application to produce invalid results (infinity) because they divide by zero. A negative income would be treated like any other value, even though it is probably a mistake.

To correct these problems, we should insert *if* statements to test for the error conditions at appropriate points in the application. When an error is detected, the application should either display an error message or write an error report to a file instead of carrying out the usual computation.

5.4 Testing and Debugging

Loop-Testing Strategy

Even if a loop has been properly designed, it is still important to test it rigorously, because the chance of an error creeping in during the implementation phase is always present. To test a loop thoroughly, we must check for the proper execution of both a single iteration and multiple iterations.

Remember that a loop has seven parts (corresponding to the seven questions in our checklist). A test strategy must test each part. Although all seven parts aren't implemented separately in every loop, the checklist reminds us that some loop operations serve multiple purposes, each of which should be tested. For example, the incrementing statement in a count-controlled loop may update both the process and the ending condition. It's important to verify that it performs both actions properly with respect to the rest of the loop.

Consider what the acceptable ranges of variables are and what sorts of I/O operations you expect see in the loop. Try to devise data sets that could cause the variables to go out of range or leave the files in unexpected states.

It's also good practice to test a loop for four special cases:

1. When the loop is skipped entirely
2. When the loop body is executed just once
3. When the loop executes some normal number of times
4. When the loop fails to exit

Statements following a loop often depend on its processing. If a loop can be skipped, those statements may not execute correctly. If it's possible to execute a single iteration of a loop, the results can show whether the body performs correctly in the absence of the effects of previous iterations, which can prove very helpful when you're trying to isolate the source of an error. Obviously, it's important to test a loop under normal conditions, with a wide variety of inputs. If possible, you should test it with real data in addition to mock data sets. Count-controlled loops should be tested to confirm that they execute exactly the right number of times. Finally, if there is any chance that a loop might never exit, your test data should try to make that happen.

Testing an application can be as challenging as writing it. To test an application, you need to step back, take a fresh look at what you've written, and then attack it in every way possible to make it fail. This isn't always easy to do, but it's necessary to make your applications be reliable. (A *reliable application* works consistently and without errors regardless of whether the input data is valid or invalid.)

Test Plans Involving Loops

In Chapter 4, we introduced formal test plans and discussed the testing of branches. Those guidelines still apply to applications with loops, but here we provide some additional guidelines that are specific to loops. In general, the goal of testing a loop is to verify that it behaves as expected.

Unfortunately, when a loop is embedded in a larger application, it sometimes is difficult to control and observe the conditions under which the loop executes using test data and output alone. In some cases we must use indirect tests. For example, if a loop reads floating-point values from a file and prints their average without echo-printing them, you cannot tell directly that the loop processes all of the data. If the data values in the file are all the same, for example, then the average will appear correct if even one of them is processed. You must construct the input file so that the average is a unique value that can be arrived at only by processing all the data.

To simplify our testing of such loops, we would like to observe the values of the variables involved in the loop at the start of each iteration. How can we observe the values of variables while an application is running? Two common techniques are the use of the system's *debugger* application and the use of extra output statements designed solely for debugging purposes. We discuss these techniques in Testing and Debugging Hints.

Now let's look at some test cases that are specific to the different types of loops that we've examined in this chapter.

Count-Controlled Loops When a loop is count-controlled, you should include a test case that specifies the output for all the iterations. It may help to add an extra column to the test plan that lists the iteration number. If the loop reads data and outputs a result, then each input value should produce a different output to make it easier to spot errors. For example, in a loop that is supposed to read and print 100 data values, it is easier to tell that the loop executes the correct number of iterations when the values are 1, 2, 3 … , 100 than if they are all the same.

If the application takes as input the iteration count for the loop, you need to test the cases in which the count is invalid. For example, when a negative number is input, an error message should be output and the loop should be skipped. You should also test various valid cases. When a count of 0 is input, the loop should be skipped; when a count of 1 is input, the loop should execute once; and when some typical number of iterations is input, the loop should execute the specified number of times.

Event-Controlled Loops In an event-controlled loop, you should test the situation in which the event occurs before the loop, in the first iteration, and in a typical number of iterations. For example, if the event is that EOF occurs, then try an empty file, a file containing one data set, and another containing several data sets. If your testing involves reading from test files, you should attach printed copies of the files to the test plan and identify each in some way so that the plan can refer to them. It also helps to identify where each iteration begins in the Input and Expected Output columns of the test plan.

When the event is the input of a sentinel value, you need the following test cases:

1. The sentinel is the only data set.
2. The sentinel follows one data set.
3. The sentinel follows a typical number of data sets.

Given that sentinel-controlled loops involve a priming read, it is especially important to verify that the first and last data sets are processed properly.

Testing and Debugging Hints

---

1. For each file that an application uses, check that all five of the required steps are performed: import the package `java.io.*`, declare a variable of the given file class, instantiate the file object, use the methods associated with the file object to perform input or output operations, and close the file when you are done using it.

2. Remember that the constructor for a `FileReader` or a `FileWriter` can be passed the name of the disk file, but the constructor for a `BufferedReader` must be passed an object of type `FileReader` and the constructor for a `PrintWriter` must be passed a `FileWriter` object.

3. If you use file I/O, remember that `main` must have the `throws IOException` clause appended to its heading.

4. Plan your test data carefully to test all sections of an application.

5. Beware of infinite loops, where the expression in the *while* statement never becomes false. The symptom: the application doesn't stop.

6. If you have created an infinite loop, check your logic and the syntax of your loops. Be sure no semicolon follows immediately after the right parenthesis of the *while* condition:

   ```
   while (Expression);        // Wrong
       Statement
   ```

   This semicolon causes an infinite loop in most cases; the compiler thinks the loop body is the null statement (the do-nothing statement composed only of a semicolon). In a count-controlled loop, make sure the loop control variable is incremented within the loop. In a flag-controlled loop, make sure the flag eventually changes.

7. Check the loop termination condition carefully, and verify that something in the loop causes it to be met. Watch closely for values that cause one iteration too many or too few (the "off-by-one" syndrome).

8. Write out the consistent, predictable part of a loop's behavior in each iteration. Look for patterns that it establishes. Are they just what you want? Perform an algorithm walk-through to verify that all of the appropriate conditions occur in the right places.

9. Trace the execution of the loop by hand with a code walk-through. Simulate the first few passes and the last few passes very carefully to see how the loop really behaves.

10. Use a *debugger* if your system provides this kind of application. A debugger runs your application in "slow motion," allowing you to execute one instruction at a time and to examine the contents of variables as they change. If you haven't already done so, find out whether a debugger is available on your system.

11. If all else fails, use *debug output statements*—output statements inserted into an application to help debug it. They output a message to a separate file that indicates the flow of execution in the application or reports the values of variables at certain points in the application.

    For example, if you want to know the value of variable beta at a certain point in an application, you could insert this statement:

    ```
    logFile.println("beta = " + beta);
    ```

    If this output statement appears in a loop, you will get as many values of beta on the file associated with logFile as there are iterations of the body of the loop.

    After you have debugged your application, you can remove the debug output statements or just precede them with // so that they'll be treated as comments. (This practice is referred to as *commenting out* a piece of code.) You can remove the double slashes if you need to use the statements again.

12. An ounce of prevention is worth a pound of debugging. Use the checklist questions, and design your loop correctly at the outset. It may seem like extra work, but it pays off in the long run.

Summary

Applications operate on data. If data and applications are kept separate, the data are available to use with other applications, and the same application can be run with different sets of data. Noninteractive input/output allows data to be prepared before an application is run and allows the application to be run again with the same data in the event that a problem crops up during processing.

Data files are often used for noninteractive processing and to permit the output from one application to be used as input to another application. In Java, we use four file classes to read and write text data: FileReader, FileWriter, BufferedReader, and PrintWriter. FileReader and FileWriter work with individual characters, and we use

Learning Portfolio

them in the instantiation of objects of the other two classes. BufferedReader provides a readLine method that inputs an entire line as a string. PrintWriter provides the print and println methods that enable the output of the standard Java primitive types and the String class.

To use files, you must do five things: (1) import the package java.io.*, (2) declare the file variables along with your other variable declarations, (3) instantiate each file object, (4) use methods associated with each file object to read or write it, and (5) call the close method associated with each file object when you are finished with it. When using files, we must forward exceptions to the JVM by adding a throws IOException clause to the heading of main.

The *while* statement is a looping construct that allows the application to repeat a statement as long as the value of an expression remains true. When the value of the expression becomes false, the statement is skipped, and execution continues with the first statement following the loop.

With the *while* statement, you can construct several types of loops that you can use again and again. These types of loops are classified into two categories: count-controlled loops and event-controlled loops.

In a count-controlled loop, the loop body is repeated a specified number of times. You initialize a counter variable immediately before the *while* statement. This variable is the loop control variable. The control variable is tested against the limit in the *while* expression. The last statement in the loop body increments the control variable.

Event-controlled loops continue executing until something inside the body signals that the looping process should stop. Event-controlled loops include those that test for a sentinel value in the data, end-of-file, or a change in a flag variable.

Sentinel-controlled loops are input loops that use a special data value as a signal to stop reading. EOF-controlled loops are loops that continue to input (and process) data values until no more data remain. To implement them with a *while* statement, you must test the value returned by the input method. The readLine method returns null. Sentinel-controlled loops usually require a priming read just before entry into the loop and an updating read at the end of the loop. You can use Java's assignment expression as a shortcut to combine these two input operations into one within the loop test. The assignment expression shortcut should be used only in simple cases where the intent is clear to a human reader. Otherwise, it is preferable to write a sentinel-controlled loop in the usual manner.

Counting is a looping operation that keeps track of how many times a loop is repeated or how many times some event occurs. This count can be used in computations or to control the loop. A counter is a variable that is used for counting. It may be the loop control variable in a count-controlled loop, an iteration counter in a counting loop, or an event counter that counts the number of times a particular condition occurs in a loop.

Summing is a looping operation that keeps a running total of certain values. It is like counting in that the variable that holds the sum is initialized outside the loop. The summing operation, however, adds up unknown values; the counting operation adds a constant to the counter (or decrements it by a constant) each time.

When you design a loop, there are seven points to consider: how the termination condition is initialized, tested, and updated; how the process in the loop is initialized, performed, and updated; and the state of the code upon loop exit. By answering the checklist questions, you can bring each of these points into focus.

To design a nested loop structure, begin with the outermost loop. When you get to the point where the inner loop must appear, make it a separate module and come back to its design later.

Objects have state. If an object's initial state can be changed by any of its methods, it is said to be mutable. Otherwise, it is immutable. When a mutable object is passed as an argument, changes made by the method to its corresponding parameter can affect the state of the object. Immutable objects are protected from such changes.

Quick Check

1. If an application will have input consisting of 1,000 integer numbers, is interactive input appropriate? (pp. 212–213)

2. What does a constructor for an input file do? (pp. 215–216)

3. What does the following series of statements write on the file fileOut?
   (pp. 216–218)

   ```
   fileOut.print('W');
   fileOut.print(88);
   fileOut.print("  What comes next?");
   ```

4. What is the statement that reads in a string and stores the integer equivalent into number? (pp. 217–218)

5. Write the first line of a *while* statement that loops until the value of the boolean variable done becomes true. (pp. 221–222)

6. What are the four parts of a count-controlled loop? (pp. 223–225)

7. Should you use a priming read with an EOF-controlled loop? (pp. 227–229)

8. How is a flag variable used to control a loop? (pp. 232–233)

9. What is the difference between a counting operation in a loop and a summing operation in a loop? (pp. 229–233)

10. What is the difference between a loop control variable and an event counter? (pp. 229–233)

11. What kind of loop would you use in an application that reads the closing price of a stock for each day of the week? (pp. 233–236)

12. How would you extend the loop in Question 11 to make it read prices for 52 weeks? (pp. 236–242)

13. What distinguishes a mutable object from an immutable object? (pp. 242–245)

14. Describe the data sets you would use to test an EOF-controlled loop that averages test scores. (pp. 252–255)

Answers

1. No. File input is more appropriate for applications that input large amounts of data.
2. The constructor associates the name of the disk file with the file variable used in the code, and places the file pointer at the first piece of data in the file.
3. W88 What comes next?
4. `number = Integer.parseInt(infile.readLine());`
5. `while ( !done )` 6. The process being repeated, plus initializing, testing, and incrementing the loop control variable 7. Yes 8. The flag is set outside the loop; the expression checks the flag; and an *if* inside the loop resets the flag when the termination condition occurs. 9. A counting operation increments by a fixed value with each iteration of the loop; a summing operation adds unknown values to the total. 10. A loop control variable controls the loop; an event counter simply counts certain events during execution of the loop. 11. Because there are five days in a business week, you would use a count-controlled loop that runs from 1 to 5. 12. Nest the original loop inside a count-controlled loop that runs from 1 to 52. 13. The state of a mutable object can be changed after instantiation; an immutable object cannot be changed. 14. Normal data, data with erroneous values such as negative test scores, a set with a single input value, and an empty file

Exam Preparation Exercises

1. What are the five steps in using file input?

2. What is the meaning of the argument to the constructor for file types `FileReader` and `FileWriter`?

3. Where should the file declarations and the calls to the appropriate constructors be placed in an application? Why?

4. What does the following statement do?

   ```
   inFile.skip(1000L);
   ```

5. What does the `readLine` method for the class `BufferedReader` return?

6. a. What value does the `readLine` method return at end-of-file?

   b. Does the `readLine` method include the newline character in its return value?

   c. Distinguish between a `null` value and an empty string.

7. Explain the difference between a loop and a branch.

8. What does the following loop print out? (`number` is of type `int`.)

   ```
   number = 1;
   while (number < 11)
   ```

```
{
    number++;
    out.println(number);
}
```

9. By rearranging the order of the statements (don't change the way they are written), make the loop in Exercise 8 print the numbers from 1 through 10.

10. When the following code is executed, how many iterations of the loop are performed?

```
number = 2;
done = false;
while ( !done )
{
    number = number * 2;
    if (number > 64)
        done = true;
}
```

11. What is the output of this nested loop structure?

```
i = 4;
while (i >= 1)
{
    j = 2;
    while (j >= 1)
    {
        out.print(j +  " ");
        j--;
    }
    out.println(i);
    i--;
}
```

12. The following code segment is supposed to write out the even numbers between 1 and 15. (n is an int variable.) It has two flaws in it.

```
n = 2;
while (n != 15)
{
    n = n + 2;
    out.print(n + " ");
}
```

    a. What is the output of the code as written?
    b. Correct the code so that it works as intended.

13. The following code segment is supposed to copy one line from the file inFile to the file outFile.

```
inLine = inFile.readLine();
count = 1;
while (count < inLine.length())
{
  outFile.print(inLine.charAt(count));
  count++;
}
outFile.println();
```

a. What is the output if the input line consists of the characters ABCDE?

b. Rewrite the code so that it works properly.

14. Does the following code segment need any priming reads? If not, explain why. If so, add the input statement(s) in the proper place. (letter is of type char.)

```
while (datum != null)
{
  letter = datum.charAt(0);
  count = 0;
  while (count < datum.length())
  {
    outFile.print(letter);
    count++;
    letter = datum.charAt(count);
  }
  outFile.println();
  datum = inFile.readLine();
  outFile.println("Another line read ...");
}
```

15. What sentinel value would you choose for an application that reads telephone numbers as integers?

16. Consider the following code segment:

```
sum = 0;
i = 1;
limit = 8;
finished = false;
```

```
while (i <= limit && !finished)
{
  number = Integer.parseInt(dataFile.readLine());
  if (number > 0)
    sum = sum + number;
  else if (number == 0)
    finished = true;
  i++;
}
out.print("End of test. " + sum + " " + number);
```

and these data values:

```
5  6  –3  7  –4  0  5  8  9
```

   a. What are the contents of sum and number after exit from the loop?

   b. Does the data fully test the code? Explain your answer.

17. What is the output of the following code segment? (All variables are of type int.)

```
i = 1;
while (i <= 5)
{
  sum = 0;
  j = 1;
  while (j <= i)
  {
    sum = sum + j;
    j++;
  }
  System.out.print(sum + " ");
  i++;
}
```

18. The physical order of the statements in an application is the order in which the statements are _____ (written, executed).

19. The logical order of the statements in an application is the order in which the statements are _____ (written, executed).

20. **a.** What are the two major types of loops?

    b. Distinguish between a count-controlled loop and an event-controlled loop.

    c. What happens if you forget to increment the loop control variable in a count-controlled loop?

    d. What happens if you forget to change the event within the body of an event-controlled loop?

    e. Name three kinds of event-controlled loops.

21. Distinguish between an iteration counter and an event counter.

22. **a.** What is an assignment expression?

    b. Write the assignment expression that can be used to control a reading loop with the method `readLine`.

23. Which of the following, when passed as an argument to a method, can have its value changed as a result of the method changing its parameters?

    a. Variable of primitive type

    b. Immutable object

    c. Mutable object

24. What is a method called that changes the state of a mutable object?

Programming Warm-Up Exercises

1. Write the statements that associate an object of the class `FileReader` with the file `infile.dat`.

2. Write the statements that associate an object of the class `BufferedReader` with the file `infile.dat`.

3. Write the statements that associate an object of the class `PrintWriter` with the file `outfile.dat`.

4. What does the following series of statements write on the file `fileOut`?

```
fileOut.print('W');
fileOut.print('\n');
fileOut.print(88);
fileOut.print('\n');
fileOut.println("  This is a string.");
```

5. What is printed by the following series of statements?

```
fileOutPr.println('W');
fileOutPr.println(88);
fileOutPr.println("  This is a string");
```

6. Write a code fragment that reads a line from `fileIn` and stores the first two characters into two `char` variables `first` and `second`. (`fileIn` is of the class `BufferedReader` and has been declared and assigned.)

7. Write a code fragment that reads a line from `fileInBuf` and prints it on `fileOutPr` with blank lines before and after it.

8. Write the statements that close `fileOut` and then associate it with the file `dataOut.dat`.

9. Write an application segment that sets a `boolean` variable `dangerous` to `true` and stops reading data if `pressure` (a `float` variable being read in) exceeds 510.0. Use `dangerous` as a flag to control the loop.

10. Here is a simple count-controlled loop:

```
count = 1;
while (count < 20)
   count++;
```

   a. List three ways of changing the loop so that it executes 20 times instead of 19.

   b. Which of those changes makes the value of `count` range from 1 through 21?

11. Write an application segment that counts the number of times the integer 28 occurs in a file of 100 integers.

12. Write a nested loop code segment that produces this output:

```
1
1 2
1 2 3
1 2 3 4
```

13. Write a code segment that reads a file of student scores for a class (any size) and finds the class average.

14. Write a code segment that reads in integers and then counts and prints the number of positive integers and the number of negative integers. If a value is zero, it should not be counted. The process should continue until end-of-file occurs.

15. Write a code segment that adds the even integers from 16 through 26, inclusive.

16. Write a statement(s) that increments `count` by 1 and sets it back to 0 when it reaches 13.

17. Write an application segment that prints out the sequence of all the hour and minute combinations in a day, starting with 1:00 A.M. and ending with 12:59 A.M.

18. Rewrite the code segment for Exercise 17 so that it prints the times in 10-minute intervals.

19. Write a loop or loops to count the number of not-equal operators (!=) in a file that contains a Java application. Your algorithm should count the number of times an exclamation mark (!) followed by an equals sign (=) appears in the input. Process the input file one character at a time, keeping track of the two most recent characters (the current value and the previous value). In each iteration of the loop, a new current value is extracted from the input line with charAt and the old current value becomes the previous value. When EOF is reached, the loop is finished.

20. Write statements that print a floating-point number on the file outfile, with four digits after the decimal point. Use the String.valueOf method to convert the floating-point value to a string. (It is a value-returning class method that takes the floating-point value as an argument.) Then use indexOf to locate the decimal point. After the decimal point, select the next four digits using the substring method. Note that fewer than four digits may follow the decimal point. You can check this by comparing the result of indexOf with the length of the string. When there are fewer than four digits to the right of the decimal point, you should concatenate "0" characters to the string to fill it out to the correct number of places.

Programming Problems

1. Design and write a Java application that takes as input an integer and a character from the screen. The output should be a diamond on the screen composed of the character and extending for the width specified by the integer. For example, if the integer is 11 and the character is an asterisk (*), the diamond would look like this:

```
     *
    ***
   *****
  *******
 *********
***********
 *********
  *******
   *****
    ***
     *
```

If the input integer is an even number, it should be increased to the next odd number. Use meaningful variable names, proper indentation, appropriate comments, and good prompting messages. Use `System.in` for input and a `PrintWriter` object for output.

2. Design and write a Java application that takes as input an integer larger than 1 and calculates the sum of the squares from 1 to that integer. For example, if the integer equals 4, the sum of the squares is 30 (1 + 4 + 9 + 16). The output should be the value of the integer and the sum, properly labeled on the screen. The application should repeat this process for several input values. Use a sentinel value to end processing, and use screen input and output.

3. You are burning some music CDs for a party. You've arranged a list of songs in the order in which you want to play them. You would like to maximize your use of space on the CD, which holds 80 minutes of music. To do so, you want to figure out the total time for a group of songs and see how well they fit. Design and write a Java application to help you do this. The data is on the file `songs.dat`. The time is entered as seconds. For example, if a song takes 7 minutes and 42 seconds to play, the data entered for that song would be

462

After all the data has been read, the application should print a message indicating the time remaining on the CD.

The output should be in the form of a table with columns and headings written on a file. For example:

```
Song            Song Time             Total Time
Number     Minutes    Seconds     Minutes    Seconds
------     -------    -------     -------    -------
  1           5         10           5         10
  2           7         42          12         52
  5           4         19          17         11
  3           4         33          21         44
  4          10         27          32         11
  6           8         55          41          6
There are 38 minutes and 54 seconds of space left on the 80 minute CD.
```

Note that the output converts the input from seconds to minutes and seconds.

4. Design and write an application that prints out the approximate number of words in a file of text. For our purposes, this number is the same as the number of gaps following words. A *gap* is defined as one or more spaces in a row, so a sequence of spaces counts as just one gap. The newline character also counts as a gap. Anything other than a space or newline is considered to be part of a word. For example, there are 13 words in this sentence, according to our definition. The application should echo-print the data.

Use meaningful variable names, proper indentation, and appropriate comments. Thoroughly test the application with your own data sets.

Case Study Follow-Up

1. Change the Incomes application so that it does the following:

   a. Prints an error message when a negative income value is input and then goes on to process any remaining data. The erroneous data should not be included in any of the calculations. Thoroughly test the modified application with your own data sets.

   b. Does not produce infinity values when the input file contains no males or no females (or the file is empty). Instead, it should print an appropriate error message. Test the revised application with your own data sets.

   c. Rejects data sets that are coded with a letter other than 'F' or 'M' and prints an error message before continuing to process the remaining data. The application also should print a message indicating the number of erroneous data sets encountered in the file.

2. Develop a thorough set of test data for the Incomes application as modified in Exercise 1.

3. Rather than having the application class responsible for extracting the gender code and salary from the input line, redesign this problem to extend Gender with two new methods: `char getGender(String inLine)` and `double getSalary(String inLine)`.

   Code and test your redesign.

4. Use the String methods `valueOf`, `indexOf`, and `substring` to print only two decimal places for all floating-point output values in the Incomes application. To accomplish this conversion, you must perform the following tasks:

   a. Convert the floating-point value to a string using the `valueOf` method.

   b. Find the location of the decimal point using the `indexOf` method.

   c. Create a new string that is a substring of the original with only two characters following the decimal point using the `substring` method.

Object-Oriented Software Design and Implementation

goals

Knowledge Goals

- To understand the basic principles of object-oriented design
- To know what distinguishes a class member from an instance member
- To understand what a responsibility is
- To understand how objects collaborate
- To understand the concept of inheritance
- To understand the concept of a compilation unit
- To understand how using a package facilitates information hiding
- To know some aspects of ethics as related to computing
- To appreciate the differences between programming projects at different scales

Skill Goals

To be able to:

- Develop an initial set of objects for solving a problem, using brainstorming
- Filter an initial set of objects
- Write a CRC card for an object
- Conduct scenarios using CRC cards
- Identify collaborations between objects
- Identify responsibilities for classes and objects
- Convert a CRC card into a Java class
- Convert responsibilities into methods
- Distinguish between superclass and subclass relationships in a design
- Write a compilation unit
- Create and use a package

timeline

1958
Kenneth Olsen, Stan Olsen, and Harlan Anderson form the Digital Equipment Corp.

1958
Jack Kilby at Texas Instruments invents the integrated circuit

1958
Bell Labs' modem data phone makes possible the transmission of binary data through phone lines

1959
The language Cobol, Common Business Oriented Language, is developed

1959
John McCarthy at M.I.T. develops the language Lisp on the IBM 704 for artificial intelligence applications

1959
Japan introduces its first commercial transistor computer

introduction

In Chapter 1, we introduced some general techniques for solving simple problems. In the real world, many programming problems are collections of multiple problems that must be solved in a coordinated manner. We now know enough Java syntax to solve many such problems, but we need to learn how to organize our problem solving to achieve success in the face of greater complexity.

In this chapter, we reexamine the programming process and introduce a software design strategy that helps us tame the seemingly vast array of details that accompany a larger problem. In particular, we formalize the concepts of object-oriented design and present the CRC card design technique.

We revisit the class construct, the implementation structure that we use to code our object-oriented design. Once we have a design in the form of CRC cards, we see how to convert it into a class. As part of this process, we look at the user interface, the implementation of the responsibility algorithms, and the testing of the class. Then we explore how to use Java packages to organize groups of classes.

Finally, we take the opportunity to emphasize that professional responsibility comes with the skills that this book teaches.

1959
Xerox debuts the first commercial copy machine

1959
General Electric develops the GE ERMA, the first machine that can process checks encoded with magnetic ink

1960
Digital Equipment Corporation debuts the PDP-1, which has a monitor and keyboard input

1961
The first robot patent is obtained by Georg Devol whose "Unimates" are the first modern industrial robots

1961
Computer capabilities launch forward with the IBM 7030, which runs 30 times faster than the 704

1962
The first computer science departments are established at Stanford University and Purdue University

6.1 Software Design Strategies

As we have stressed several times, the programming process consists of a problem-solving phase and an implementation phase. The problem-solving phase includes *analysis* (analyzing and understanding the problem to be solved) and *design* (designing a solution to the problem). Given a complex problem—one that results in a 10,000-line program, for example—it's simply not reasonable to skip the design process and go directly to writing Java code. What we need is a systematic way of designing a solution to a problem, no matter how complicated the problem is.

> **Object-oriented design** A technique for developing software in which the solution is expressed in terms of objects—self-contained entities composed of data and operations on that data that interact by sending messages to one another
>
> **Functional decomposition** A technique for developing software in which the problem is divided into more easily handled subproblems, the solutions to which create a solution to the overall problem

We've used the term **object-oriented design (OOD)** frequently throughout this book, and we have employed OOD in an intuitive manner in the Case Studies. In this chapter, we describe in a more methodical way and see how OOD can be used in designing solutions to more complex problems. This methodology helps you create solutions that can be easily implemented as Java applications. The resulting applications are readable, understandable, and easy to debug and modify. Java was developed in part to facilitate the use of the OOD methodology. In the next two sections, we present the essential concepts of OOD; throughout the rest of the book, we will expand our treatment of this approach. At times OOD is used in conjunction with a second, older methodology, which we also discuss in this chapter—**functional decomposition**.

OOD focuses on the entities (objects) in a problem. Using this approach, we solve a problem by identifying the components that make up a solution and determining how those components interact. The result is a design for a set of objects that cooperate to solve a problem.

In contrast, functional decomposition views the solution to a problem as a task to be accomplished. It focuses on the sequence of operations that are required to complete the task. When the problem requires a series of steps that is long or complex, we divide it into easier-to-solve subproblems. Functional decomposition is the method that we have used to this point to break our simple problems into sequences of steps that the computer can follow. This strategy can be used to develop algorithms for an object's methods.

In most large problems, we naturally find entities that we wish to represent in our code. For example, in designing an application that manages a checking account, we might identify checks, deposits, account balances, and account statements as entities. These entities interact through messages. For example, a check could send a message to the balance entity that tells it to deduct an amount from itself. We didn't list the amount in our initial set of objects, but it may be another entity that we need to represent.

This example illustrates a common approach to OOD. We begin by identifying a set of objects that we think are important in a problem. Then we consider some scenarios in which the objects interact to accomplish a task. In the process of envisioning how a scenario happens, we identify additional objects and messages. We keep trying new scenarios until we find that our set of objects and messages is sufficient to accomplish any task required by the problem.

6.2 Objects and Classes Revisited

Let's review what we have said about objects and see how they work in the context of programming. Then we can more effectively explore how to solve a problem with OOD.

What is an object? We have defined an *object* in three ways: as a collection of data together with associated operations, as an entity or thing that is relevant in the context of a problem, and as an instance of a class. What is a class? We have also defined a *class* in three ways: as a description of an object that specifies the types of data values that it can hold and the operations that it can perform, as a description of the behavior of a group of objects with similar properties, and as a pattern for an object.

Although varied, these definitions are complementary rather than contradictory. In the problem-solving phase, we look for objects (things) that are relevant to the problem at hand. We analyze these objects and see how they interact. We abstract the common properties and behaviors from these real objects and define classes that describe this behavior. In the implementation phase, we then use these descriptions (classes) and the syntax of our programming language to define classes (in the Java sense) that describe the data values that an object can have and the operations that it can perform. Our application instantiates objects of these classes that interact to solve the original problem.

Several *object-oriented programming languages* have been created specifically to support OOD. Examples include Java, C++, Visual Basic.NET, Ada 95, C#, Smalltalk, CLOS, Eiffel, and Object-Pascal. In these languages, a *class* is the construct used to define the pattern employed when instantiating an object. Let's look first at this construct in a little more depth; in the next section, we outline a strategy for finding objects and classes in the problem-solving phase.

As you should recognize by now, a class isn't an object, but rather specifies a pattern to use in creating a specific kind of object. For example, in Chapter 2 we defined a Name class. Once we define the class, we can declare a variable of the class Name, such as testName, instantiate an object with new, and assign the object's address to testName. Here is some example code that illustrates the process:

```
// Define a class
class Name
{
    .
    .
    .
}
// End of Name class definition
    .
    .
    .
// Now that we have defined the class, we can declare a variable of
//the class Name
Name testName;
```

.
.
.

```
//Then we can instantiate an object of the class Name with new
//and assign it to the variable
testName = new Name();
```

Think of the class definition as analogous to a set of blueprints. A blueprint isn't a house, but it tells you how to construct a house. A class isn't an object, but it tells the computer how to construct an object. Declaring a variable is like putting an empty page in your address book in anticipation of having an address for the house. You don't yet have the address because the house hasn't been built.

The new operator invokes the constructor method for the class; it is analogous to calling in a construction crew to interpret the blueprints and actually build the house. Once the house is built on a lot, it has an address, and you can then write this address on the blank page in your address book (assign the address of the object to the variable). Figure 6.1 illustrates this analogy.

Class definition

Variable declaration

Instantiating the object

Assigning the address of the new object to the variable

Figure 6.1 An Analogy Illustrating the Relationships among a Class, a Variable, and an Object

In Chapter 2, we saw that a class declaration is a collection of field and method declarations. The fields and methods in a class are called the members of the class. As we have also seen, members can be public or private, and they can be static (or not static) and final (or not final). The public members of a class combine to specify its public interface. Here we use *interface* in the general sense of the word, in contrast to the Java interface construct, which we introduce later. When a programmer wishes to employ a predefined class in writing a program, he or she looks up its interface to see what fields and methods it makes available for use.

What do we mean by "modes of access" in our definition of interface? In Chapter 2, we defined the access modifiers as reserved words and explained their effects. Here we are interested in how they relate to the public interface of a class. Recall our earlier discussion of instance methods and class methods. We invoke a class method by writing the class name, a period, and then the method name. We invoke an instance method by writing the object name, a period, and then the method name. In a class declaration, the two types of methods look exactly the same except that class method declarations include the static modifier. In other words, the static modifier specifies this aspect of how we access the method. Consider these statements:

```
value = Double.parseDouble(inFile.readLine());
System.out.println("Value input is: " + value);
```

parseDouble is a class method and is prefaced by the name of the class Double. It takes a string and converts it into a value of type double. readLine is an instance method and is prefaced by inFile, an instance of the class BufferedReader. The third method call in these two statements is a call to println. From its call, can you tell whether println is an instance method or a class method?[1]

The public and private modifiers determine whether a member can be accessed outside of a class. The final modifier specifies whether a member can be changed. There are eight combinations of these modifiers, each of which effectively defines a mode of access. Only the public members are part of the public interface, however. From code that is outside of the class definition, we cannot access members that are private.

For example, the public interface for the class Double includes some final fields, such as the maximum and minimum double values. It provides a set of class (static) methods that includes parseDouble, and a set of instance methods that includes a version of compareTo. All of these members are public. We can also surmise that the definition of Double includes a private field of type double that is used to store a numerical value. Later in this chapter and in Chapter 7, we introduce additional access modifiers.

> **Member** A field or method within a class
>
> **Public interface** The members of a class that can be accessed outside of the class, together with the modes of access that are specified by other modifiers

---

[1]It is an instance method.

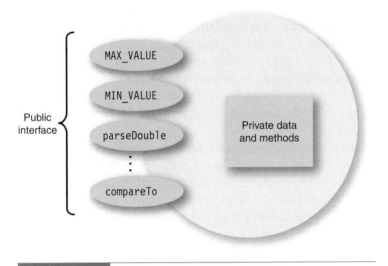

Figure 6.2   An Object and Its Public Interface

In Figure 6.2, we picture a Double object as having a private part and a public part. The private part includes fields and methods that the user cannot access and doesn't need to know about to use the object. The public part, shown as ovals in the side of the object, represents its public interface: values and operations that are available to programmers wishing to use the object.

6.3 Object-Oriented Design

Now we turn to the process of developing a problem solution using OOD. Our goal is to develop a design that captures the information needed to program a solution to a problem. Our design should not be at the level of detail of an actual program, however. That is, we want a way to write out a solution without becoming distracted by programming language syntax. As we have said before, it is important to think first and code later. In this section, we introduce an informal technique for developing object-oriented designs, known as CRC cards.[2]

The first step in OOD is to identify the major objects in the problem. We identify the abstract properties of each object, and use these to define the classes that we need. Each class

---

[2]Originally published in: Kent Beck and Ward Cunningham, "A Laboratory for Teaching Object-Oriented Thinking," *OOPSLA '89 Proceedings, SIGPLAN Notices* 24(10): 1–6, October 1989.

specifies a set of responsibilities, which are the actions that its objects support. Objects collaborate with each other by sending messages. A message is a request for an object to carry out one of its responsibilities. The collection of Classes, Responsibilities, and Collaborations (CRC) works together to solve a problem.

> **Responsibility** An action that an implementation of an object must be capable of performing
>
> **Collaboration** An interaction between objects in which one object requests that another object carry out one of its responsibilities

OOD thus leads to programs that are collections of objects. Each object is responsible for one part of the entire solution, and the objects send messages to one another in a collaborative manner. Many libraries of prewritten classes are available, including the standard Java library. In many cases, it is possible to browse through a library, choose classes you need for a problem, and assemble them to form a substantial portion of your application. Putting existing pieces together in this fashion is an excellent example of the building-block approach discussed in Chapter 1.

Let's briefly return to the more general topic of problem solving before we look at CRC cards in depth.

Object-Oriented Problem Solving

As we discuss OOD, keep in mind that there are many different correct solutions to most problems. The techniques we use may seem imprecise, especially when contrasted with the precision required by the computer. In fact, the computer merely demands that we express (code) a particular solution precisely. The process of deciding which particular solution to use involves the skills of judgment and reasoning. It is our human ability to make choices without having complete information that enables us to solve problems. Different choices naturally lead to different solutions to a problem.

For example, in developing a simulation of an air traffic control system, we might decide that airplanes and control towers are objects that communicate with each other. Or we might decide that pilots and controllers are the objects that communicate. This choice affects how we subsequently view the problem and the responsibilities that we assign to the objects. Either choice can lead to a working application. We may simply prefer the one with which we are most familiar (recall the "Look for things that are familiar" strategy from Chapter 1).

Some of our choices lead to designs that are more or less efficient than others. For example, keeping a list of names in alphabetical order rather than random order makes it possible for the computer to find a particular name much faster. However, choosing to leave the list randomly ordered still produces a valid (but slower) solution.

Other choices affect the amount of work that is required to develop the remainder of a problem solution. In creating an application for choreographing ballet movements, we might begin by recognizing the dancers as the important objects and then create a class for each dancer. In doing so, we discover that all of the dancers have certain common responsibilities. Rather than repeat the definition of those responsibilities for each class of dancer, we can change our initial choice: we can define a class for a generic dancer that includes all the common responsibilities and then develop subclasses (the subject of Chapter 7) that add responsibilities specific to each individual.

The point is this: Don't hesitate to begin solving a problem because you are waiting for some flash of genius that leads to the perfect solution. There is no such thing. It is better to jump in and try something, step back and see if you like the result, and then either proceed in the same direction or make changes. The CRC card technique is a way to easily explore different design choices and keep track of them.

■ Software Engineering

Humans have come to depend greatly on computers in many aspects of their lives. That reliance is fostered by the perception that computers function reliably; that is, they work correctly most of the time. However, the reliability of a computer depends on the care that is taken in writing its software.

Errors in code can have serious consequences. Here are a few examples of real incidents involving software errors. An error in the control software of the F–18 jet fighter caused it to flip upside down the first time it flew across the equator. A rocket launch went out of control and had to be blown up because a comma was typed in place of a period in its control software. A radiation therapy machine killed several patients because a software error caused the machine to operate at full power when the operator typed certain commands too quickly.

Even when the software is used in less critical situations, errors can have significant effects. Examples of such errors include the following:

- An error in your word processor that causes your term paper to be lost just hours before it is due
- An error in a statistical package that causes a scientist to draw a wrong conclusion and publish a paper that must later be retracted
- An error in a tax preparation application that produces an incorrect return, leading to a fine

Programmers have a responsibility to develop software that is free from errors. The process that is used to develop correct software is known as software engineering.

Software engineering has many aspects. The software life cycle described in Chapter 1 outlines the stages in the development of software. Different techniques are used at each of these stages. We address many of these techniques in this text. In this chapter we introduce methodologies for developing object-oriented designs. We discuss strategies for testing and validating programs in every chapter. We use a modern programming language that enables us to write readable, well-organized code, and so on. Some aspects of software engineering, such as the development of a formal, mathematical specification for an application, are beyond the scope of this text.

> **Software engineering** The application of traditional engineering methodologies and techniques to the development of software

6.4 The CRC Card Design Process

There are three basic steps in developing an OOD using CRC cards. We've actually been using these steps in the Case Studies without naming them. The first step is to identify an initial set of object classes that seem to be relevant to the problem. In previous Case Studies, we looked at the nouns in a problem statement as a source of possible objects. The second step is to filter this list, eliminating duplicates or objects that aren't really appropriate for the computer to implement. The third step is to identify the responsibilities for the reduced list of objects. In the Case Studies, we've merely listed the responsibilities, but the methodology we present uses scenarios to determine and refine the responsibilities.

In moving to problems that involve multiple classes, however, these steps become more complex. We must explore how the objects interact. In the CRC card design process, we do so through role-playing under a variety of scenarios. That is, we pretend to be the objects, and we go through the steps required to carry out some portion of the problem's solution. Along the way, we identify new objects or responsibilities that are needed. We also note special relationships between classes, such as the subclasses mentioned earlier. After gaining some experience with a few initial scenarios, we identify additional scenarios that should be tried. We repeat the last step until we run out of ideas for scenarios or are convinced that we've covered all of the necessary objects and responsibilities in our design.

Now we look at each of these steps in turn.

■ Identifying the Initial Classes Through Brainstorming

The first step in solving a problem with OOD is to identify the classes of objects that are found in the problem. There is no foolproof technique for doing this; we just have to start brainstorming ideas and see where they lead us. A large program is typically written by a team of programmers, so the brainstorming process often occurs in a team setting. Team members identify whatever objects they see in the problem and then propose classes to represent them. The proposed classes are written on a board. None of the ideas for classes are discussed or rejected in this first stage.

For example, suppose we have the following problem statement: Create an application that mimics a physical address book for holding names, addresses, and other information about friends, relatives, and business contacts.

We begin by looking at a physical address book and then brainstorm with our teammates about what we see there. We decide that our application has the following potential objects:

Cover
Pages
Address
Name
Home phone number
Work phone number
E-mail
Fax number
Pager number
Cell phone number
Birthday
Company name
Work address
Calendar
Time zone map
Owner information
Emergency numbers
User

Some of these items are clearly not a part of our solution, such as the user. The purpose of brainstorming, however, is to generate ideas without any inhibitions. Once we've run out of ideas, we move on to critiquing them.

◼ Filtering

After brainstorming, we filter the classes. First, we eliminate duplicates. Next, we decide whether each class really represents an object in the problem. The team then looks for classes that seem to be related. Perhaps they aren't duplicates, but they have much in common, and so they are grouped together on the board. At the same time, the discussion may reveal some classes that were overlooked.

For each class that survives the filtering stage, we create a CRC card. The CRC card is just an index card with a line drawn vertically down the middle. The name of the class is written at the top and the two columns have the headings *Responsibilities* and *Collaborations*. Figure 6.3 shows a blank CRC card.

We have added spaces at the top of the CRC card for naming the superclass and subclasses of the class. These items are discussed in Chapter 7. Recalling our example of the

Class Name:	Superclass:	Subclasses:
Responsibilities	Collaborations	

Figure 6.3   A Blank CRC Card

choreography application, the different kinds of dancers would be subclasses of the generic dancer class. Each specific dancer class would have the generic dancer class listed as its superclass. Filling in these spaces helps us to keep track of these relationships between our classes.

Let's filter the list we just generated for the address book. Our application doesn't need to represent the physical parts of an address book, so we can delete Cover and Pages. However, we need something analogous to a page that holds the same sort of information. Let's call it an Entry. The different telephone numbers can all be represented by the same kind of object. Thus we can combine Home, Work, Fax, Pager, and Cell Phone into a Phone number class. We decide that the electronic address book doesn't need the special pages that are often found in a printed address book, so we delete Calendar, Time Zone Map, Owner Information, and Emergency Numbers.

Of course, the User isn't part of the application, although its identification does point to the need for a User interface that we did not originally list. A Work Address is a specific kind of address that has additional fields, so we can make it a subclass of Address. Company Names are just strings, so there is no need to distinguish them, but Names have a first, last, and middle part. Our filtered list of classes now looks like this:

For each of these classes, we create a CRC card. In the case of a Work Address, we list Address as its Superclass and on the Address card we list Work Address in its Subclasses space.

In doing coursework, you may be asked to work individually rather than in a collaborative team. You can still do your own brainstorming session and filtering. However, we recommend that you take a break after the brainstorming session and do the filtering once you have let your initial ideas rest for a while. An idea that seems brilliant in the middle of brainstorming may lose some of its attraction after a day or even a few hours.

■ Determining Responsibilities

Initial Responsibilities   Once you (or your team) have identified the classes and created CRC cards for them, go over each card and write down any responsibilities that are obvious. For example, a Name class has a responsibility to know its first name, its middle name, and its last name. We would list these three responsibilities in the left column of its card as shown in Figure 6.4. In an implementation, they become methods that return the corresponding part of the name. For many classes, the initial responsibilities include knowing some value or set of values. We call these *knowledge responsibilities*. We indicate the type or object that the responsibility returns on the CRC card.

Scenario Walk-Through   To further expand the responsibilities of the classes and see how they collaborate, we must pretend to carry out various processing scenarios by hand. This kind of role-playing is known as a *walk-through*. It is a different process than the algorithm walk-through discussed in Chapter 4. An algorithm walk-through is intended to verify an algorithm.

Class Name: *Name*	Superclass:	Subclasses:
Responsibilities		**Collaborations**
Know first *return String*		*None*
Know middle *return String*		*None*
Know last *return String*		*None*
. . .		

Figure 6.4 A CRC Card with Initial Responsibilities

A scenario walk-through is intended to explore potential solutions to a problem. We ask a question such as, "What happens when the user wants to find an address that's in the book?" We then answer the question by explaining how each object is involved in accomplishing this task. In a team setting, the cards are distributed among the team members. When an object of a class is doing something, its card is held in the air to visually signify that it is active.

For the preceding question, we might pick up the User Interface card and say, "I have a responsibility to get the person's name from the user." That responsibility is written down on the card. Once the name is input, the User Interface must collaborate with other objects to look up the name and get the corresponding address. With which objects should it collaborate?

We've found a hole in our list of classes! The Entry objects should be organized into a Book object. We quickly write out a Book CRC card. The User Interface card-holder then says, "I'm going to collaborate with the Book class to get the address." "Book" is written in the right column of the User Interface card, which remains in the air. The owner of the Book card holds it up, saying, "I have a responsibility to find an Entry in the list of Entry objects that I keep, given a name from User Interface." That responsibility gets written on the Book card, whose owner says, "I have to collaborate with each Entry to compare its name with the name sent to me by the User Interface." Figure 6.5 shows a team in the middle of a walk-through.

Now comes a decision. What are the responsibilities of Book and Entry for carrying out the comparison? Should Book get the name from Entry and do the comparison, or should Book send the name to Entry and receive an answer that indicates whether they are equal? The team decides that Book should do the comparing, so the Entry card is held in the air, and its owner says, "I have a responsibility to return a copy of my Name object." The responsibility is recorded and the Entry card is lowered.

Figure 6.5 A Scenario Walk-through in Progress

Book says, "I need to collaborate with Name." Name says, "I have the responsibilities to know my first, middle, and last names. These are already on my card, so I'm done." The Name card is then lowered. Book says, "I keep collaborating with Entry, getting a new Name object until I find the matching name. Then I must return the entry from which the name came to User Interface." Now the Book card is lowered. Next, the User Interface says, "I need to get the address from Entry." This collaboration is placed on its card and the Entry card is held up again, with its holder saying "I have a responsibility to provide an address. I'm not going to collaborate with Address, but am just going to return the Address object to User Interface." The Entry card has this responsibility added and then goes back on the table. Figure 6.6 shows User Interface's, Book's, and Entry's CRC cards after this scenario. Notice that we have included Entry's knowledge responsibilities.

At this point, the holder of User Interface (whose arm is getting very tired) says, "I need to collaborate with Address to get each line of the address as a string that I can place in a pair of labels." Address is raised, with its holder saying, "I have responsibilities to know my street,

Class Name: *User Interface*	Superclass:	Subclasses:
Responsibilities		**Collaborations**
Find address for (name)		Entry, Address
. . .		

Class Name: *Book*	Superclass:	Subclasses:
Responsibilities		**Collaborations**
Find entry with (name) return Entry		Entry, Address
. . .		

Class Name: *Entry*	Superclass:	Subclasses:
Responsibilities		**Collaborations**
Know name return Name		None
Know address return Address		None
Know phone number return Phone		None
Know birthday return Date		None

Figure 6.6 The CRC Cards for Entry, Book, and User Interface

city, state, and ZIP code, and those are already on my list." User Interface says, "I can concatenate the last three to form the second line, so that satisfies the collaboration." The collaboration is recorded, and User Interface says, "Now I display the information, and I'm done." The last card is lowered and the scenario ends.

Reading about the scenario makes it seem longer and more complex than it really is. Once you get used to role-playing, the scenarios move quickly and the walk-through becomes more like a game. However, to keep things moving, it is important to avoid becoming bogged down with implementation details. Book should not be concerned with how the Entry objects are organized on the list. Address doesn't need to think about whether the ZIP code is stored as an int or a String. Merely explore each responsibility in enough depth to decide whether a further collaboration is needed or if it can be solved with the available information.

Subsequent Scenarios We began the first scenario with a "What happens when…" question for the most obvious case. The next step is to brainstorm some additional questions that produce new scenarios. Consider the following list of some further scenarios for our address book example:

> What happens when the user
> asks for a name that's not in the book?
> wants to add an entry to the book?
> deletes an entry?
> tries to delete an entry that isn't in the book?
> wants a phone number?
> wants a business address?
> wants a list of upcoming birthdays?

We walk through each of the scenarios, adding responsibilities and collaborations to the CRC cards as necessary. After several scenarios have been tried, the number of additions decreases. When one or more scenarios take place without adding to any of the cards, we brainstorm further to see if we can come up with new scenarios that may not have been covered yet. When all of the scenarios that we can envision seem to be doable with the existing classes, responsibilities, and collaborations, then the design is finished.

When our design is complete, we can implement the responsibilities for each class. The implementation may reveal details of a collaboration that weren't obvious in the walk-through. Of course, knowing the collaborating classes makes it easy to change their corresponding responsibilities. The implementation phase should also include a search of available class libraries to see if any existing classes can be used. For example, the java.util.GregorianCalendar class represents a date that can be used to implement Birthday.

■ Inheritance

In walking through the scenario in which the user requests a business address, we notice that the Work Address class is nearly identical to the Address class, except that it also provides a Work Name and a Second Address Line. Rather than copy all of the responsibilities and collaborations from the Address card to this one, we can list Address as the superclass of Work Address.

Because Business Address is a subclass of Address, it *inherits* all of the responsibilities that are in Address. A subclass is automatically able to use the responsibilities of its superclass and also add its own unique responsibilities. In addition, a subclass can replace an inherited responsibility with a new definition of the responsibility. The new definition provides a way to retain the same form of interface, but customize its implementation to reflect the differences between the superclass and the subclass. In OOD, this concept is called inheritance, and it allows you to adapt an existing class to satisfy additional responsibilities.

> Inheritance A mechanism that enables us to define a new class by adapting the definition of an existing class

All classes in Java are actually subclasses of a master class called Object. They form a hierarchy of subclasses and superclasses that may be many levels deep. As we will see in Chapter 7, looking at the definition of a class in the Java library may reveal only a small portion of its capabilities, like the tip of an iceberg. Its superclasses may define many more features that it inherits. The inheritance mechanism is a very powerful tool in object-oriented design, enabling us to reuse existing code easily and flexibly. In this way, we can gradually build up classes, one on top of another, until we have classes with very extensive capabilities. Yet at each stage, the capabilities are added in a clear and simple manner, making the code easy to manage and maintain.

To summarize the CRC card process, we brainstorm the objects in a problem and abstract them into classes. Then we filter the list of classes to eliminate duplicates and unnecessary items. For each class, we create a CRC card and list any obvious responsibilities that it should support. We then walk through a common scenario, recording responsibilities and collaborations as they are discovered. Next, we walk through additional scenarios, moving from common cases to special and exceptional cases. When it appears that we have all of the scenarios covered, we brainstorm additional scenarios that may need more responsibilities and collaborations. When our ideas for scenarios are exhausted and all the scenarios are covered by the existing CRC cards, the design is done.

6.5 Functional Decomposition

The second design technique we use is functional decomposition (also called *structured design*, *top-down design*, *stepwise refinement*, and *modular programming*). It allows us to use the divide-and-conquer approach, which we presented in Chapter 1. We apply this technique to designing the algorithms that implement the responsibilities for an object-oriented design.

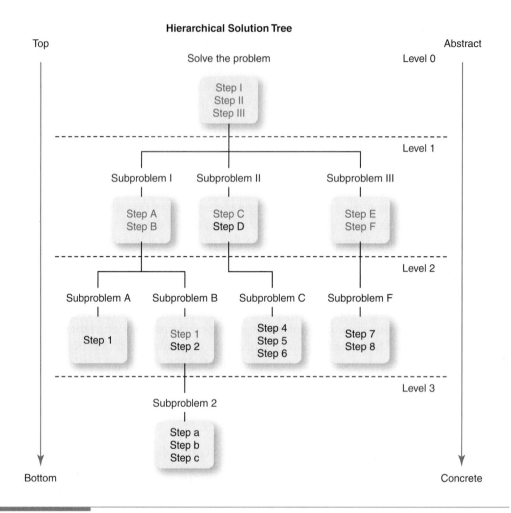

Figure 6.7 Hierarchical Solution Tree

When a responsibility clearly involves a series of major steps, we break it down (decompose it) into pieces. In the process, we move to a lower level of abstraction—that is, some of the implementation details (but not too many) are now specified. Each of the major steps becomes an independent subproblem that we can tackle separately. The process continues until each subproblem cannot be divided further or has an obvious solution.

By subdividing the problem, you create a hierarchical structure called a *tree structure*. Each level of the tree is a complete solution to the problem that is less abstract (more detailed) than the level above it. Figure 6.7 shows a generic solution tree for a problem. Steps shown in black type have enough implementation details to be translated directly into Java statements; they are concrete steps. Those shown in colored type are abstract steps; they reappear as subproblems in the next level down. Each box in the figure represents a module. Modules are the basic building blocks in a functional decomposition. The diagram in Figure 6.7 is, therefore, also called a *module structure chart*.

◾ Writing Modules

Here's one approach to writing modules:

> **Concrete step** A step for which the implementation details are fully specified
>
> **Abstract step** A step for which some implementation details remain unspecified
>
> **Module** A self-contained collection of steps that solves a problem or subproblem; it can contain both concrete and abstract steps

1. Think about how you would solve the subproblem by hand.
2. Begin writing down the major steps.
3. If a step is simple enough that you can see how to implement it directly in Java, it is at the concrete level; it doesn't need any further refinement.
4. If you have to think about implementing a step as a series of smaller steps or as several Java statements, it is still at an abstract level.
5. If you are trying to write a series of steps and start to feel overwhelmed by details, you are probably bypassing one or more levels of abstraction. Stand back and look for pieces that you can write as more abstract steps.

We could call this approach the "procrastinator's technique." If a step is cumbersome or difficult, put it off to a lower level; don't think about it today, think about it tomorrow. Of course, tomorrow does come eventually, but the whole process can be applied again to the subproblem. A trouble spot often seems much simpler when you can focus on it. Ultimately, the entire problem is broken up into manageable units.

As you work your way down the solution tree, you inevitably make a series of design decisions. If a decision proves awkward or wrong (and many times it does!), you can backtrack (go back up the tree to a higher-level module) and try something else. You don't have to scrap the entire design—only the small part you are working on. You may make many intermediate steps and try many trial solutions before you reach a final design.

Before OOD was developed, functional decomposition was used to solve entire problems. However, by itself, it results in designs that lack flexibility. Applications developed entirely this way are hierarchical in nature, and often we find that at the bottom of the hierarchy we are implementing multiple versions of the same responsibility. With OOD, we would define a superclass and a set of subclasses to organize these responsibilities and save ourselves programming effort. But functional decomposition doesn't allow for this kind of organization.

Today, we typically use functional decomposition as a way to design the algorithm for a complex responsibility. For example, in a class that supports image processing, a morphing responsibility that distorts part of an image might have no need of any other collaboration. Yet the algorithm that transforms the image data may include many mathematically sophisticated steps. Functional decomposition provides a way to break such a problem down into simpler pieces that are easier to solve.

Pseudocode You'll find it easier to implement a design if you write the steps in pseudocode. *Pseudocode* is a mixture of English statements and Java-like control structures that can be translated readily into Java. (We've been using pseudocode in the algorithms in the Problem-Solving Case Studies.) When a concrete step is written in pseudocode, it should be possible to rewrite it directly as a Java statement in a program.

Always remember that the problem-solving phase of the programming process takes time. If you spend the bulk of your time analyzing and designing a solution, coding (implementing) the program should take relatively little time.

Constructor An operation that creates a new instance of a class

Transformer An operation that changes the internal state of an object

Observer An operation that allows us to observe the state of an object without changing it

Copy constructor An operation that creates a new instance of a class by copying an existing instance, possibly altering some or all of its state in the process

Iterator An operation that allows us to process—one at a time—all the components in an object

---

Theoretical Foundations

Categories of Responsibilities

Class instance responsibilities generally fall into three categories: constructors, transformers, and observers.

A constructor is an operation that creates a new instance of a class. Operators that modify the state of an object are transformers. For example, an operation that changes the year of a Date object is a transformer. The knowFirstName method of a Name class is an example of an observer.

Some operations are combinations of observers and constructors. An operation that takes a Date object and an integer value and returns a new Date object that is the original date plus that number of days is an example of an observer (of the original Date object) and a constructor (of the new Date object). This particular case is an example of a copy constructor.

In addition to the three basic categories of responsibility, there is a fourth category that is less common: iterators.

In later chapters we will examine classes that are made up of multiple values, all of the same type. An iterator allows us to observe each of these components one at a time. For example, given a class representing a list of names, an iterator would enable us to go through the list, observing or transforming each of the names one by one.

6.6 Object-Oriented Implementation

Our design is now represented in a set of CRC cards. In general, each CRC card becomes a Java class and the responsibilities become methods of the class. This translation begins by replacing the expressions used to describe a responsibility with properly formed method names. If the responsibility returns a value, the method should be a value-returning method. If the responsibility requires information, the information becomes a parameter in the method. This information is available on the CRC card.

The next step is to write the algorithms to implement the responsibilities. In many cases the algorithms are very simple, requiring only the return of a value. In other cases the algorithms are more complex, requiring a further functional design.

Class Interface Design

Let's begin our discussion of designing the class interface by looking at the CRC card for a new class, Phone, with two fields: one for the area code and one for the digits in the number.

Class Name: *Phone*	Superclass:	Subclasses:
Responsibilities	**Collaborations**	
Create itself (areaCode, digits)	None	
Know area code return int	None	
Know digits return int	None	
Number as digits return int	None	
Number in print form return int	None	
Are two numbers equal? return boolean	String Phone	

We know that "Create itself" must be a constructor that uses new to instantiate itself. The remaining responsibilities all return information about a phone number, so they are observers.

The responsibilities do not include any transformers, so an instance of this class is an *immutable* object; once created, it doesn't change. How do we know that the instance doesn't change? No transformer methods are defined for the class.

Now let's look at how we turn this CRC card into a design for a class. The data abstraction of an object can be provided to the user in two ways: in the fields that it makes publicly accessible and in the parameters of its methods. We briefly consider `public` field values, and then look at methods and parameters. The data fields are `areaCode` and `digits`.

```
int areaCode;
int digits;
```

Because the observer responsibilities return the values of these fields, we might consider simply declaring the corresponding fields to be `public` and letting the user access them directly. However, this approach defeats the purpose of encapsulating the class by revealing its internal representation to the user. We can achieve encapsulation by making each of these responsibilities be a method. If we later change the internal representation, the methods can be rewritten to convert the new internal representation into the existing external form.

Would we ever want to declare a `public` data field in a class? Yes. Sometimes it's useful to provide constants that a collaborator can pass to responsibilities. For example, the names of the primary colors for a `Spectrum` object could be represented by public constants. The constant `RED` could be an `int` with a value of 1 or a `String` with a value of `"RED"`. The collaborator doesn't know how the class represents the constant. It merely passes the class-supplied constant as an argument to a method, as in this example:

```
colorObject.mixWith(RED);
```

In Java, such constants are declared `static`; that is, they belong to the class rather than to an instance. We want every object of a given class to use the same set of constants, so they should be kept centrally located in the class. The `Phone` class doesn't have any such constants on its CRC card. Normally, they would be identified during the scenario phase, when we would note that some responsibilities receive one value from among a small set. Here's part of the CRC card for `Spectrum` that illustrates the need for constants.

Class Name: *Spectrum*	Superclass:	Subclasses:
Responsibilities	**Collaborations**	
mixWith (a color, one of red, orange, yellow, green, blue, indigo or violet)	None	
. . .		

Internal Data Representation

The first implementation step for a class is to decide on the internal representation of data. Then we can use the means-ends analysis technique from Chapter 1 to design the algorithms for translating between the abstract and internal representations. These algorithms form the basis for the constructor and observer methods, as well as parts of some transformer and iterator methods.

As we saw with our example of a Date object, the internal representation (Julian day) and the abstract representation (month, day, year) can be quite different. In other cases, such as the Name class, the internal representation may be exactly the same as the abstract form of the data. We choose the internal form to be useful for the programmer rather than the user.

Our goal in selecting an internal representation should be to simplify our task and to make the object efficient in terms of storage space and execution time. These goals sometimes come in conflict, and we must balance simplicity against efficiency.

Two problem-solving strategies that are valuable in designing the internal data representation are looking for things that are familiar and solving by analogy. In the case of the Date class, you can go to the library and research calendars. For the Name class, you already know how to write a name.

Rarely will you have to invent an entirely new data representation. Most programs are written to solve problems with which people have dealt in the past. Consider who would normally use such data, and consult with those people or look in books that they would use (Figure 6.8). For example, astronomers use dates in computing the positions of planets over the centuries. You can find the formulas for computing the Julian day in some astronomy texts.

As another example, a geography professor gave an assignment to draw a map showing nearby airports with their elevations and the lengths of their runways. Most students spent hours poring through almanacs and topographic maps to gather the data. Even so, their maps were inaccurate. One student, however, got a perfect grade because she stopped to consider who would use such data. She went to a pilot supply shop and bought a precise map of nearby airports. While there, she noticed a book that listed information for airports using an especially efficient representation. If she ever had to develop a computerized version of the map, she would start with that representation.

From the preceding discussion, it should be clear that we can't give you a set of rules that will automatically lead you to an internal data representation for a class. Each situation you encounter is different. Be prepared to give this part of your design some careful thought, to go to a library and do some research, to consult with other people, and to trade off issues of efficiency and complexity.

Sometimes you may discover that no one representation is always best. Or there may not be enough information to choose among several options. In those cases, you simply have to pick a representation and use it. In the end, it may not turn out to be the best choice. But remember the beauty of encapsulation—you can go back later and change to a better internal representation!

Now back to our Phone class. The CRC card for Phone assumed that the area code and number would be kept as numeric values. These fields could just as easily be kept as strings.

```
Julian Day Formula

intRes1 = 2-year/100+year/400
intRes2 = (int) (365.25*year)
intRes3 = (int) (30.6001*(month+1))
julianDay = intRes1+intRes2+intRes3+day+1720994.5
```

Figure 6.8 Who Would Use Similar Data?

Is one representation better than another? We can't answer that question without knowing how the class might be used in a problem. However, the beauty of abstraction and encapsulation is that the internal representation of the fields can be changed and the program that uses the class remains oblivious to the modification.

■ Responsibilities as Methods

Each responsibility on the CRC card can be implemented by a method in the class. If we know the information that is needed and what is returned by each one, then the design is straightforward. An observer naturally returns a value, so we implement observers as Java value-returning methods. A transformer is typically a void method. Iterators may be either value-returning or void, but we won't consider them until we introduce arrays in Chapter 11.

If a responsibility implicitly refers to an object, then it should be implemented as an instance method. Observers, transformers, and iterators are always instance methods. They implicitly take their associated object as an argument and have access to its fields. In addition, they can receive values through the parameter list, as noted on the CRC card.

Class methods are used to implement responsibilities that are not associated with a particular object, such as the Math.abs method. They may also affect all the instances of a class. For example, we can set the maximum score for all TestScore objects so that they can be checked for errors. None of the responsibilities of the Phone class is appropriate for a class method implementation.

We are ready to write the responsibilities of the Phone class as methods. We must convert the responsibility names written as phrases into Java method identifiers. "Create itself" becomes the class constructor Phone. "Know area code" becomes knowAreaCode, and "Know digits" becomes knowDigits. "Number as digits" becomes asDigits, and "Number in print form" becomes asString. "Are two numbers equal" becomes equals(Phone secondNumber).

The algorithms for knowledge responsibilities are so simple that we can go straight to writing code. What about asDigits, the method that returns the number as 10 digits? We can multiply the area code by 10,000,000 to shift the digits over and add the result to the number. How do we convert the area code and number to strings and insert hyphens as separators? *Hyphens!* Exactly how is the number as a string supposed to look? We often see a telephone number written with two hyphens as follows: 512–441–2323. Thus we have to break the number portion into two pieces: the first three digits and the last four digits. We can use integer division and remainder to accomplish this separation. To compare two phone numbers, we first compare the area codes. If they are not the same, the numbers are not equal. If the area codes are the same, we then compare the numbers. If both the area codes and the numbers are the same, the method returns the value true.

```java
public class Phone
{
  private int areaCode;
  private int digits;

  public Phone(int area, int number)
  // Constructor
  {
    areaCode = area;
    digits = number;
  }

  public int knowAreaCode()
  {
    return areaCode;
  }

  public int knowDigits()
  {
    return digits;
  }
```

```java
public long asDigits()
// Returns area code and number as a sequence of 10 digits
{
  return (long)(areaCode * 10000000L + digits);
}

public String asString()
// Returns area code, hyphen, first three digits of the number, hyphen,
//   and last four digits of the number
{
  String result;
  long firstThree;                          // First three digits of the number
  long lastFour;                            // Last four digits of the number
  firstThree = digits / 10000;
  lastFour = digits % 10000;
  result = new String(areaCode + "-" + firstThree + "-" + lastFour);
  return result;
}

public boolean equals(Phone secondNumber)
// Returns true if the phone numbers are the same; false otherwise
{
  if (areaCode != secondNumber.knowAreaCode())
    return false;
  if (digits != secondNumber.knowDigits())
    return false;
  else
    return true;
}
}
```

6.7 Packages

As we noted previously, Java lets us group related classes together into a unit called a *package*. Classes within a package can access each other's nonprivate members, which can save us programming effort and make it more efficient to access their data. The other advantage of packages is that they can be compiled separately and imported into our code. Together with the access modifiers, packages provide the means for implementing encapsulation because they allow us to distribute our classes as Bytecode files. The unreadable nature of Bytecode prevents users from seeing the implementation details.

■ Package Syntax

The syntax for a package is extremely simple. We've been writing our separate classes as unnamed packages all along, so we merely have to specify the package name at the start of the class. The first line of a package consists of the keyword package followed by an identifier and a semicolon. By convention, Java programmers start a package identifier with a lowercase letter to distinguish it from class identifiers.

```
package someName;
```

Next, we can write our import declarations and then one or more class declarations. Java calls this a *compilation unit*. Its syntax diagram is shown here:

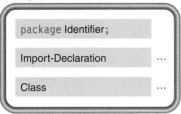

Compilation-Unit

```
package Identifier;

Import-Declaration          ...

Class                       ...
```

As you can see from the syntax diagram, we can write a series of class declarations following the import declarations. These classes are members of the package. All of the package members (the classes) have access to each other's nonprivate members. We say "nonprivate" because, in addition to using the keywords `public` or `private` with fields and methods, we can write member declarations without any modifiers. When we do so, then the field or method is neither `public` nor `private`, but rather it is something in between—it can be accessed by any member of the package.

When we use `public`, then a field or method can be used outside of the class and by any class that imports its package. When we use `private`, then the field or method can be accessed only within the class itself. When we use neither, the field or method can be used within the class and within other classes in the same package, but not by classes outside of the package. As an analogy, you can think of packages as being like a family. Some things are yours alone (`private`), some things you share with your family (package), and some things anyone can use (`public`).

Classes that are imported into the package can be used by any of the classes declared in the package. From the perspective of the imported classes, the declared classes are user code and thus can access only their `public` members. Note that imported classes are not members of the package. You can think of an imported package as a guest in your house. Your guest may share some things (`public`) with your family, but the things that you share only with your family are not shared with the guest, and the things that the guest shares only with his or her family aren't shared with you.

Although we can declare multiple classes in a compilation unit, only one class can be declared `public`. The others must have package-level access; that is, they are written without an access modifier. If a compilation unit can hold at most one `public` class, how do we create packages with multiple `public` classes? We use multiple compilation units, as we describe next.

▓ Packages with Multiple Compilation Units

Each Java compilation unit is stored in its own file. Java systems name the file using a combination of the package name and the name of the `public` class in the compilation unit. Java restricts us to having a single `public` class in a file so that it can use file names to locate all `public` classes. Thus, a package with multiple `public` classes must be implemented with multiple compilation units, each placed in a separate file.

Using multiple compilation units has the further advantage that it provides us with more flexibility in developing the classes of a package. Team programming projects would be very cumbersome if Java made multiple programmers share a single package file.

We split a package among multiple files simply by placing its members into separate compilation units with the same package name. For example, we can create one file containing the following code (the … between the braces represents the code for each class):

```
package someName;
public class One { ... }
class Two { ... }
```

A second file contains the following code:

```
package someName;
class Three { ... }
public class Four { ... }
```

The result is that the package `someName` contains four classes, all of which have access to each other's nonprivate members. Two of the classes, `One` and `Four`, are `public`, and so are available to be imported by user code.

Many programmers simply place every class in its own compilation unit. Others gather the nonpublic classes into one unit, separate from the `public` classes. How you organize your packages is up to you, but you should use a consistent approach to make it easy to find the members of the package among all of its files.

How does the Java compiler find these separate pieces and put them together? The answer is that the compiler requires all of the compilation unit files for a package to reside in a single directory or folder. For our preceding example, a Java system would store the source code in files called `One.java` and `Four.java` in a directory called `someName`.

Splitting a package among multiple files has one other benefit. Each compilation unit can have its own set of import declarations. Thus, if the classes in a package need to use different sets of imported classes, you can place them in separate compilation units, each with just the import declarations that are required.[3]

---

[3]In addition to following the naming conventions, most Java systems require that you specify that the compiler should include this directory among the set that it examines when it compiles your code. With an integrated development environment, this specification can be as simple as dragging the file into a window that lists all of the files for the project. In a command-line environment, you may have to enter an operating system command that defines a value called a class path. Check the documentation for your system, or ask your instructor whether something like this needs to be done.

Package Example

If the class Phone must be made available for others to use, we need to be sure that it has been thoroughly tested. Let's write and implement a test plan to test Phone. We must test five methods plus the constructor. The knowledge methods need to be tested with only one case: Do they return the proper fields? Likewise, do the two conversion methods return the data in the proper format? The sixth method compares two instances of the class Phone. This method must be tested several times: once when the area codes are not equal, once when the area codes are equal but the numbers are not, and once when both are equal.

Reason for Test Case	Input Values	Expected Output	Observed Output
Phone	523, 3733344		
knowAreaCode		523	
knowDigits		3733344	
asDigits		5233733344	
asString		523–373–3344	
equal	523, 3774433	Numbers are not equal	
	521, 3733344	Numbers are not equal	
	523, 3733344	Numbers are equal	

This test plan is implemented in the following application class:

```java
import java.io.*;
import Phone;
public class TestPhone
{
  public static void main(String[] args) throws IOException
  {
    Phone firstPhone;
    Phone secondPhone;
    Phone thirdPhone;
    Phone fourthPhone;
    PrintWriter outFile;
    outFile = new PrintWriter(new FileWriter("phoneOut"));
    outFile.println("Test results for class Phone");
    firstPhone = new Phone(523, 3733344);
    secondPhone = new Phone(523, 3774433);
    thirdPhone = new Phone(521, 3733344);
    fourthPhone = new Phone(523, 3733344);
    outFile.println("knowAreaCode: " + firstPhone.knowAreaCode());
    outFile.println("knowDigits: " + firstPhone.knowDigits());
    outFile.println("asDigits: " + firstPhone.asDigits());
    outFile.println("asString: " + firstPhone.asString());
    outFile.print("equal: Is firstPhone equal to secondPhone? ");
    if (firstPhone.equals(secondPhone))
```

```
      outFile.println(" Yes.");
    else
      outFile.println(" No.");
    outFile.print("equal: Is firstPhone equal to thirdPhone? ");
    if (firstPhone.equals(thirdPhone))
      outFile.println(" Yes.");
    else
      outFile.println(" No.");
    outFile.print("equal: Is firstPhone equal to fourthPhone? ");
    if (firstPhone.equals(fourthPhone))
      outFile.println(" Yes.");
    else
      outFile.println(" No.");
    outFile.close();
  }
}
```

We have a public class `Phone` and a public class `TestPhone`, which includes several variables of the class `Phone`. How do we get these two classes to interact? Until now, we have simply put them in the same directory and had the driver import the class. We promised a better way to do this; here it is. We declare the class `Phone` to be in the package `phone` and store it in the file `Phone.java` in the directory `phone`. The class `TestPhone` then imports the package `phone`. That is, in the file `Phone.java` in the directory `phone`, we have

```
package phone;
public class Phone { ... }
```

In the file `TestPhone.java`, we have

```
import phone.*;
public class TestPhone { ... }
```

Here is a copy of the file `phoneOut`:

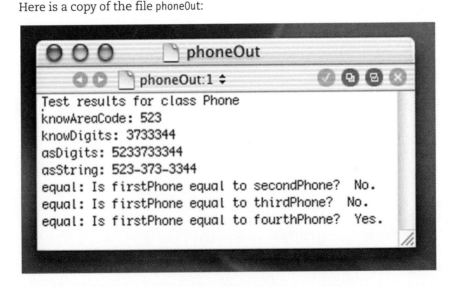

Why is putting a class in a package and importing the package a better strategy than putting the class in the same directory as the importing class? There are two reasons. First, any number of compilation units can be put in a package and imported with one statement. Second, a package can be imported from anywhere. That is, a package is stored in a directory named after the package, so it can be imported by any application, not just one in the same directory.

Self-documenting code Program code containing meaningful identifiers as well as judiciously used clarifying comments

Documentation

As you create your object-oriented design, you are developing documentation for your code. *Documentation* includes the written problem specifications, design, development history, and actual code.

Good documentation helps other programmers read and understand your code and can prove invaluable when software is being debugged and modified (maintained). If you haven't looked at your code for six months and need to change it, you'll be happy that you documented it well. Of course, if someone else has to use and modify your program, good documentation is indispensable.

Documentation is both external and internal to the code. External documentation includes the specifications, the development history, and the design documents, such as CRC cards. Internal documentation includes code formatting and self-documenting code—meaningful identifiers and comments. You can use the pseudocode from your design as comments in your code.

This kind of documentation may be sufficient for someone reading or maintaining your applications. However, if an application will be used by people who are not programmers, you must provide a user's manual as well.

Be sure to keep your documentation up-to-date. Indicate any changes you make in the code in all of the pertinent documentation. Use self-documenting code to make your programs more readable.

Software Engineering Tip

Programming at Many Scales

To help you put the topics in this book into context, we describe in broad terms the way programming in its many forms is done in "the real world." Obviously, we can't cover every possibility, but we can try to give you a flavor of the state of the art.

Programming projects range in size from the small scale, in which a student or computer hobbyist writes a short application to try out something new, to large-scale multicompany programming projects involving hundreds of people. Between these two extremes are efforts of many other sizes. Some people use programming in their professions, even though it isn't their primary job. For example, a scientist might write a special-purpose application to analyze data from a particular experiment.

Even among professional programmers, many specialized programming areas exist. An individual might have a specialty in business data processing, in writing compilers or developing word processors (an area known as "tool making"), in research and development support, in graphical display development, in writing entertainment software, or in one of many other areas. However, one person can produce only a fairly small application (a few tens of thousands of lines of code at best). Work of this kind is called *programming in the small*.

A larger application, such as the development of a new operating system, might require hundreds of thousands or even millions of lines of code. Such large-scale projects require teams of programmers, many of them specialists, who must be organized in some manner. If left unorganized, they may waste valuable time just trying to communicate with one another.

Usually, a hierarchical organization is set up to handle this kind of project. One person, the *chief architect* or *project director*, determines the basic structure of the application and then delegates the responsibility of implementing the major components. The components may be implemented by either teams or individual programmers. This sort of organization is called *programming in the large*.

Programming languages and software tools can help a great deal in supporting programming in the large. For example, if a programming language lets programmers develop, compile, and test parts of an application independently before they are put together, then several people can work on the code simultaneously. Of course, it is hard to appreciate the complexity of programming in the large when you are writing a small application for a class assignment. However, the experience you gain in this course will be valuable as you begin to develop larger applications.

The following story is a classic example of what happens when a large project is developed without careful organization and proper language support. In the 1960s, IBM developed a major new operating system called OS/360, which was one of the first true examples of programming in the large. After the operating system was written, more than 1,000 significant errors were found. Despite years of trying to fix these errors, the programmers never did get the number of errors below 1,000, and sometimes the "fixes" produced far more errors than they eliminated.

What led to this situation? Hindsight analysis showed that the code was badly organized and that different pieces were so interrelated that no one could keep all of it straight. A seemingly simple change in one part of the code caused several other parts of the system to fail. Eventually, at great expense, an entirely new system was created using better organization and tools.

In those early days of computing, everyone expected occasional errors to occur, and it was still possible to get useful work done with a faulty operating system. Today, however, computers are used increasingly more often in critical applications such as medical equipment and aircraft control systems, where errors can prove fatal. Many of these applications depend on large-scale programming. If you were stepping onto a modern jetliner right now, you might well pause and wonder, "Just what sort of language and tools did they use when they wrote the code for this thing?" Fortunately, most large, life-critical, software development efforts today use a combination of good methodology, appropriate language, and extensive organizational tools—that is, *software engineering*.

6.8 Ethics and Responsibilities in the Computing Profession

Every profession operates with a set of ethics that help to define the responsibilities of the people who practice that profession. For example, medical professionals have an ethical responsibility to keep information about their patients confidential. Engineers have an ethical responsibility to their employers to protect proprietary information, but they also have a responsibility to protect the public and the environment from harm that may result from their work. Writers are ethically bound not to plagiarize the work of others, and so on.

The computer presents us with a vast new range of capabilities that can affect people and the environment in dramatic ways. As a consequence, it challenges society with many new ethical issues. Some of our existing ethical practices apply to the computer, whereas other situations require new ethical rules. In some cases, no guidelines have been established, but it is up to you to decide what is ethical. In this section, we examine some common situations encountered in the computing profession that raise particular ethical issues.

A professional in the computing industry, like any other professional, has knowledge that enables him or her to do certain things that others cannot do. Knowing how to access computers, how to program them, and how to manipulate data gives the computer professional the ability to create new products, solve important problems, and help people to manage their interactions with the ever more complex world in which we all live. Knowledge of computers can be a powerful means to effecting positive change.

Of course, knowledge can also be used in unethical ways. A computer can be programmed to trigger a terrorist's bomb, to sabotage a competitor's production line, or to steal money. Although these blatant examples make an extreme point and are unethical in any context, some more subtle examples are unique to computers.

Software Piracy

Computer software is easy to copy. But just like books, software is usually copyrighted—it is illegal to copy software without the permission of its creator. Such copying is called software piracy.

> **Software piracy** The unauthorized copying of software for either personal use or use by others

Copyright laws exist to protect the creators of software (and books and art) so that they can make a profit from their effort and money spent developing the software. A major software package can cost millions of dollars to develop, and this cost (along with the cost of producing the package, shipping it, supporting customers, and allowing for retailer markup) is reflected in the purchase price. If people make unauthorized copies of the software, then the company loses those sales and either has to raise its prices to compensate for the loss or spend less money to develop improved versions of the software. In either case, a desirable piece of software becomes more difficult to obtain.

Software pirates sometimes rationalize their theft with the excuse that they're just making one copy for their own use. It's not that they're selling a bunch of bootleg copies, after all. But if thousands of people do the same thing, the company's revenue losses add up to millions of dollars, which leads to higher prices for everyone.

Computing professionals have an ethical obligation to not engage in software piracy and to try to stop it from occurring. You never should copy software without permission. If someone asks you for a copy of a piece of software, you should refuse to supply it. If someone says that he or she just wants to "borrow" the software to "try it out," tell the person that he or she is welcome to try it out on your machine (or at a retailer's shop) but not to make a copy.

This rule isn't restricted to duplicating copyrighted software; it includes plagiarism of all or part of code that belongs to anyone else. If someone gives you permission to copy some of his or her code, then, just like any responsible writer, you should acknowledge that person with a citation in the code.

Privacy of Data

The computer enables the compilation of databases containing useful information about people, companies, geographic regions, and so on. These databases allow employers to issue payroll checks, banks to cash a customer's check at any branch, the government to collect taxes, and mass merchandisers to send out junk mail. Even though we may not care for every use of databases, they generally have positive benefits. However, they can also be used in negative ways.

For example, a car thief who gains access to the state motor vehicle registry could print out a "shopping list" of valuable car models together with their owners' addresses. An industrial spy might steal customer data from a company database and sell it to a competitor. Although these are obviously illegal acts, computer professionals face other situations that are not so obviously unethical.

Suppose your job includes managing the company payroll database, which includes the names and salaries of the firm's employees. You might be tempted to poke around in the database and see how your salary compares to your associates—but this act is unethical and an invasion of your associates' right to privacy. The information is confidential. Any information about a person that is not clearly public should be considered confidential. An example of public information is a phone number listed in a telephone directory. Private information includes any data that has been provided with an understanding that it will be used only for a specific purpose (such as the data on a credit card application).

A computing professional has a responsibility to avoid taking advantage of special access that he or she may have to confidential data. The professional also has a responsibility to guard that data from unauthorized access. Guarding data can involve such simple things as shredding old printouts, keeping backup copies in a locked cabinet, not using passwords that are easy to guess (such as a name or word), and more complex measures such as *encryption* (keeping data stored in a secret coded form).

Use of Computer Resources

If you've ever bought a computer, you know that it costs money. A personal computer can be relatively inexpensive, but it is still a major purchase. Larger computers can cost millions of dollars. Operating a PC may cost a few dollars per month for electricity and an occasional outlay for paper, disks, and repairs. Larger computers can cost tens of thousands of dollars per month to operate. Regardless of the type of computer, whoever owns it has to pay these costs. They do so because the computer is a resource that justifies its expense.

A computer is an unusual resource because it is valuable only when code is running. Thus, the computer's time is really the valuable resource. There is no significant physical difference between a computer that is working and one that is sitting idle. By contrast, a car is in motion when it is working. Thus, unauthorized use of a computer is different from unauthorized use of a car. If one person uses another's car without permission, that individual must take possession of it physically—that is, steal it. If someone uses a computer without permission, the computer isn't physically stolen, but just as in the case of car theft, the owner is deprived of a resource for which he or she is paying.

For some people, theft of computer resources is a game—like joyriding in a car. The thief doesn't really want the resources, but rather seeks out the challenge of breaking through a computer's security system and seeing how far he or she can get without being caught. Success gives a thrilling boost to this sort of person's ego. Many computer thieves think that their actions are acceptable if they don't do any harm. Whenever real work is displaced from the computer by such activities, however, harm is clearly being done. If nothing else, the thief is trespassing in the computer owner's property. By analogy, consider that even though no physical harm may be done by someone who breaks into your bedroom and takes a nap while you are away, such an action is certainly disturbing to you because it poses a threat of potential physical harm. In this case, and in the case of breaking into a computer, mental harm can be done.

Other thieves have malicious intentions. Like a joyrider who purposely crashes a stolen car, these people destroy or corrupt data to cause harm. They may feel a sense of power from being able to hurt others with impunity. Sometimes these people leave behind programs that act as time bombs, causing harm long after they have gone. Another kind of program that may be left is a **virus**—a program that replicates itself, often with the goal of spreading to other computers. Viruses can be benign, causing no other harm than to use up some resources. Others can be destructive, causing widespread damage to data. Incidents have occurred in which viruses have cost millions of dollars in lost computer time and data.

> **Virus** Code that replicates itself, often with the goal of spreading to other computers without authorization, and possibly with the intent of doing harm

Computing professionals have an ethical responsibility never to use computer resources without permission. This guideline includes activities such as doing personal work on an employer's computer. We also have a responsibility to help guard resources to which we have access—by using unguessable passwords and keeping them secret, by watching for signs of unusual computer use, by writing applications that do not provide loopholes in a computer's security system, and so on.

ADDRESS BOOK

Problem: Create an address book application that creates entries and writes them to the file bookFile.

Brainstorming: We've already started this process, having brainstormed the initial set of classes and filtered them. After the initial scenario walk-through, we have the following list:

Entry
Name
Address
Work address
Phone number
E-mail
Birthday
User interface

We also have the following *what-if* questions left unresolved:

What happens when the user
    asks for a name that's not in the book?
    wants to add an entry to the book?
    deletes an entry?
    tries to delete an entry that isn't in the book?
    wants a phone number?
    wants a business address?
    wants a list of upcoming birthdays?

Filtering: All of this information is important, but let's begin small. This application only needs to create a file of entries, not process them. Let's limit ourselves to an application that creates an address book with just a name, an address, and a phone number in each entry. We can add more information as we go on. Here then is our filtered list of classes for this application:

Entry
Name
Address
Phone number
User interface

Determining Responsibilities: Let's look at the Entry class as it was left when we stopped the scenarios.

Class Name: *Entry*	Superclass:	Subclasses:
Responsibilities	**Collaborations**	
Know name return Name	None	
Know address return Address	None	
Know phone number return Phone	None	
Know birthday return Date	None	

We can omit the "Know birthday" responsibility for the time being. Our driver needs to create one instance of Entry at a time and write it to a file. *Create!* We forgot to list Create as a responsibility. Because each class should be as encapsulated as possible, let's have two constructors: one that inputs values into its own fields and one that takes the values as arguments and stores the values into its fields. Have we forgotten anything else? The entry is to be written to a file. Should the Entry class be responsible for writing itself to a file or should the driver provide this function? Encapsulation dictates that the Entry should bear this responsibility. Here, then, is our revised CRC card for Entry:

Class Name: Entry	Superclass:	Subclasses:
Responsibilities	**Collaborations**	
Create (name, address, phone)	Name, Address, Phone	
Create( )	Name, Address, Phone, BufferedReader	
Know name return Name	None	
Know address return Address	None	
Know phone number return Phone	None	
Write entry to a file (outfile)	PrintWriter	

The knowledge responsibilities give us at least a partial list of the instance variables of the Entry class: a Name, an Address, and a Phone. There may be other internal fields. If so, we can add them later. We have a Name class and a Phone class. The only classes left to write are Address, Entry, and a driver.

In Chapter 7, we will examine several different versions of addresses. For this application, let's just use the street, city, state, and ZIP code. We should have one constructor that takes these attributes as parameters. Let's include another constructor that reads values into its fields. There should be four knowledge responsibilities, one for each of these fields. The first three fields should be strings. What about the ZIP code? If the ZIP code is just the standard five digits, we could use an integer. However, many ZIP codes now use five digits, plus a hyphen and four more digits. To cover both cases, let's use a string to represent the ZIP code. Should this class provide the values in these fields in a variety of formats like the Name class does? Not at this stage. We are only creating the address book now, not processing the information in some way.

Class Name: *Address*	Superclass:		Subclasses:
Responsibilities		**Collaborations**	
Create (street, city, state, zip)		String	
Create( )		String. BufferedReader	
Know street return String		None	
Know city return String		None	
Know state return String		None	
Know zip return String		None	

What are the responsibilities of the driver? To create instances of the class Entry and write them to a file. Entry has a responsibility that writes itself to a file, so that responsibility is implemented by sending a message to Entry. We have two possibilities for creating instances of the class: We can use the nonparameterized version of the constructor for Entry and let it be responsible for instantiating Name, Address, and Phone, or we can let the driver input the values and use Entry's parameterized constructor. Because this is a special-purpose driver whose only function is to create entries, let's centralize the input for the fields of Entry in the driver. We should also use the parameterized constructors for Name and Address. Phone doesn't have a nonparameterized constructor, so there is no choice. Here, then, is the CRC card for the driver:

Class Name: *AddressDr*	Superclass:		Subclasses:
Responsibilities		**Collaborations**	
Prepare input file		BufferedReader	
Prepare output file		PrintWriter	
Process entries		Name, Address, Phone, Entry	
Close files		BufferedReader, PrintWriter	

CASE STUDY

Responsibility Algorithms for `AddressDr`: We have prepared enough files for both input and output by now to consider these responsibilities concrete. "Process entries" implies more than one entry, which implies a loop. Let's instruct the user to enter "Quit" for the first name when all of the entries have been processed.

```
Process entries
Write "Quit entered for the first name ends the application."
Write "Enter first name: "
Read first
while (name is not equal to "quit")
   Enter rest of name
   name = new Name(first, last, middle)
   Enter address
   address = new Address(street, city, state, zip)
   Enter phone
   phone = new Phone(areaCode, number)
   entry = new Entry(name, address, phone)
   entry.writeToFile(outFile)
   Read first
close files
```

```
Enter rest of name
Write "Enter last name: "
Read last
Write "Enter middle name: "
Read middle
```

```
Enter address
Write "Enter street address: "
Read street
Write "Enter city: "
Read city
Write "Enter state: "
Read state
Write "Enter ZIP code: "
Read zip
```

```
Enter phone
Write "Enter area code: "
Read and convert area code to int
Write "Enter number: "
Read and convert number to int
```

Now all of the steps in "Process entries" are concrete.

Responsibility Algorithms for Address and Entry: This application is not using the nonparameterized constructors of the classes Address and Entry. Instead, we leave their implementations as a Case Study Follow-Up exercise. The remaining responsibilities are knowledge responsibilities that need no further refinement. However, we do need to decide what the file that Entry is writing should look like. We have two choices: (1) We can make it look like an address by printing the name on the first line, the address on two lines, and the phone number as a string with hyphens or (2) we can print each string or number on a line by itself. The address format is easy to create—so why would we even consider the one string per line format? The address format is easy to write, but it is not easy for another application to read. If we write the name all on one line, we must read the string back in and break the name apart. The same is true of the address and the phone number. Because the intent of this application is to create the beginnings of an address book that will be processed on the computer, we know that the values will be read in at a later time. Here we write them out one string per line for ease of subsequent input. In the next chapter, we introduce an even easier way to read the values into an object.

Implementation: Now we are ready to code these classes. The only question is whether to code "Process entries" as one method or to break up the subalgorithms into helper methods. It would be better style to make use of helper methods. However, this special-purpose driver probably will not be used again, so let's simply code it in main.

Here is the code for Address, Entry, and AddressDr. Name and Phone were defined previously. A copy of the input screen and the output file follow the code.

```
//*****************************************************************
// This class provides a basic address object. The constructor
// takes the state variables as strings. Four knowledge
// methods return the state values.
//*****************************************************************

package addressBook;
// Includes Name, Address, Phone, and Entry
public class Address
{
  // Instance variables
  String street;
  String city;
  String state;
  String zipCode;

  public Address(String newStreet, String newCity, String newState,
    String zip)
  {
```

```
    street = newStreet;
    city = newCity;
    state = newState;
    zipCode = zip;
  }

  // Knowledge methods
  public String knowStreet()
  {
    return street;
  }
  public String knowCity()
  {
    return city;
  }
  public String knowState()
  {
    return state;
  }
  public String knowZip()
  {
    return zipCode;
  }
}

//*************************************************************
// This class provides a basic entry object. The constructor
// takes the state variables as class objects. Three
// knowledge methods return the state objects. An observer
// writes the contents of the state objects on the file passed
// as a parameter.
//*************************************************************

package addressBook;
// Includes Name, Address, Phone, and Entry
import java.io.*;
public class Entry
{
  // Instance variables
  Name name;
  Address address;
  Phone phone;

  public Entry(Name newName, Address newAddress, Phone phoneNumber)
  {
    name = newName;
    address = newAddress;
    phone = phoneNumber;
  }
```

```
    // Knowledge responsibilities
    public Name knowName()
    {
      return name;
    }
    public Address knowAddress()
    {
      return address;
    }
    public Phone knowPhone()
    {
      return phone;
    }

    public void writeToFile(PrintWriter outFile)
    // State variables are written on file outFile
    {
      outFile.println(name.knowFirstName());
      outFile.println(name.knowLastName());
      outFile.println(name.knowMiddleName());
      outFile.println(address.knowStreet());
      outFile.println(address.knowCity());
      outFile.println(address.knowState());
      outFile.println(address.knowZip());
      outFile.println(phone.knowAreaCode());
      outFile.println(phone.knowDigits());
    }
}

//**************************************************************
// This class is a driver that creates entries made up of a
// name, an address, and a phone number.  Data are read
// from the screen.  Each entry is written to the file Entries.
//**************************************************************
import java.io.*;
import addressBook.*;
public class AddressDr
{
  public static void main(String[] args) throws IOException
  {
    // Declare local variables
    Name name;
    Address address;
    Phone phone;
    Entry entry;
    // String and integer variables used for input
    String first, last, middle, street, city, state, zip;
    int areaCode, number;
```

```java
// Set up input file
BufferedReader in;                              // Input stream for strings
// Instantiate in using System.in
in = new BufferedReader(new InputStreamReader(System.in));

// Set up output file
PrintWriter outFile;
outFile = new PrintWriter(new FileWriter("Entries"));

System.out.println("Quit entered for the first name ends the " +
  "application.");
// Prompt for and read first name
System.out.print("Enter first name: ");
first = in.readLine();

while (first.compareTo("Quit") != 0)
{
  // Prompt for and read the rest of the name
  System.out.print("Enter last name: ");
  last = in.readLine();
  System.out.print("Enter middle name: ");
  middle = in.readLine();
  name = new Name(first, last, middle);

  // Prompt for and read the address
  System.out.print("Enter street address: ");
  street = in.readLine();
  System.out.print("Enter city: ");
  city = in.readLine();
  System.out.print("Enter state: ");
  state = in.readLine();
  System.out.print("Enter ZIP code: ");
  zip = in.readLine();
  address = new Address(street, city, state, zip);

  // Prompt for and read the phone number
  System.out.print("Enter areaCode: ");
  areaCode = Integer.parseInt(in.readLine());
  System.out.print("Enter number: ");
  number = Integer.parseInt(in.readLine());
  phone = new Phone(areaCode, number);

  // Instantiate and output entry
  entry = new Entry(name, address, phone);
  entry.writeToFile(outFile);
  // Prompt for and read first name
```

```
        System.out.print("Enter first name: ");
        first = in.readLine();
    }
    outFile.close();
  }
}
```

File Entries:

6.9 Testing and Debugging

In addition to providing a design that is easy to implement, the CRC card process makes it easy to create an initial test plan. The scenario walk-throughs naturally correspond to test cases in our plan. We simply need to note an example of typical data and expected results from each walk-through. For example, in the walk-through for displaying an entry, we could write down a set of typical values that the user might enter for a name, and we could specify that the address book must contain the corresponding entry. We could also indicate what other information we expect to be returned with the entry.

The scenarios produce a plan that combines aspects of both code and data coverage. At the level of collaborations, we cover the structure of the code. That is, our test plan naturally covers the pattern of method calls corresponding to the collaborations that implement each responsibility.

If we think a little bit about the range of values that could be present as arguments in each call during a scenario walk-through, then we can also include data coverage in our plan. As you go through a scenario, each time a collaboration invokes a responsibility of another class, record the range of values that could appear in the arguments, as well as an example value and its expected result. For example, in walking through the addition of an entry, we collaborated with methods to create each of the objects contained within the entry. In each of these cases, we can also record the range of values that are acceptable and unacceptable as test cases.

Remember, however, that our CRC cards do not develop the algorithms for the individual responsibilities. Thus, we must extend the test plan with cases that exercise the paths found within each responsibility. Once the responsibility algorithms are written, review the test cases that were recorded during the scenario walk-throughs. In each case, consider whether your knowledge of the algorithm indicates control-flow paths that should be tested specifically.

It may be easiest to test individual classes with a separate driver application class, as we did with the Phone class. The purpose of the driver is to provide a very simple environment that allows us to directly test the methods of a class, explicitly controlling the argument values that are passed to them. When a class is part of a complex design that involves many different collaborations, it can be difficult to constrain the testing to just the one class, and to ensure that errors in other classes do not affect its arguments.

Testing and Debugging Hints

1. Use the design methodologies presented in this chapter to carefully design a complete OOD solution to a problem before you start writing any Java code. The design should be sufficiently detailed that converting it to Java becomes almost a mechanical process.

2. During brainstorming, don't try to filter ideas while they are being generated. It is the free flow of ideas that often produces the most innovative approaches.

3. If you are developing a design by yourself, wait to start filtering until the next day, or at least after a few hours of doing something different. It takes some mental distance to give the necessary perspective for successful filtering.

4. Pick a simple initial scenario, and then work your way into the more complex scenarios. Otherwise, the number of new classes that you have to create initially can be overwhelming.

5. Don't hesitate to write down additional useful information that is identified during the scenario walk-throughs. At the same time, don't get bogged down in writing responsibility algorithms during the walk-through process.

6. Use the package level of access for each data field unless your design specifically calls for it to be `public` or `private`.

7. Store multifile packages in the same directory. Otherwise, you will get an error message saying that the classes in the package can't be found.

Summary

Object-oriented design (OOD) and functional decomposition are methods for tackling nontrivial programming problems. The two methodologies are often used in combination, and experienced programmers often switch back and forth between them in solving a problem. We use OOD to design the overall solution to a complex problem, and then apply functional decomposition to aid in writing the algorithms for the individual responsibilities of each object.

Object-oriented design produces a problem solution by focusing on objects, their associated operations, and their interactions. The first step is to identify the major objects in the problem and create classes that are abstract descriptions of them. Next, we filter the initial classes, eliminating duplicate and inappropriate classes. We then walk through a series of scenarios, working from common cases to exceptional cases to determine the responsibilities and collaborations of the classes. The use of CRC cards helps us to keep track of this information as we explore the scenarios. The result of this process is a design consisting of self-contained objects that have responsibilities

Learning Portfolio

for managing their own data and collaborating with other objects by invoking each other's methods.

Functional decomposition begins with an abstract solution that then is divided into major steps. Each step becomes a subproblem that is analyzed and subdivided further. A concrete step is one that can be translated directly into Java; abstract steps need more refining. A module is a collection of concrete and abstract steps that solves a subproblem.

A package collects a set of related classes into a common structure that can be imported by other classes. The Java compiler allows just one `public` class per compilation unit, so a package consists of multiple files, all of which begin with identical `package` statements.

Careful attention to algorithm design, code formatting, and documentation produces well-organized and readable programs that are easy to debug and maintain.

Quick Check

1. Object-oriented design focuses on the _____ (nouns, verbs) when identifying potential objects in a problem statement. (p. 270)

2. (True or False?) A class field is distinguished from an instance field by having the modifier `static` in its declaration (p. 273)

3. What Java construct do we typically use to implement a responsibility in a class? (p. 280)

4. How do objects collaborate with each other? (p. 275)

5. A subclass may _____ (import, inherit, construct) methods from its superclass. (p. 285)

6. How many public classes may a compilation unit contain? (p. 295)

7. Can classes within the same package access each other's fields that are at the package level of access? (p. 295)

8. Name three ways that you can help to protect confidential data. (p. 302)

9. Class assignments are examples of programming in the _____ (small, large). (p. 300)

10. (True or False?) In the initial brainstorming for an object-oriented design, as we are generating ideas for candidate classes, we can simultaneously critique and filter them. (pp. 277–278)

11. What happens in the filtering stage of a design? (pp. 278–280)

12. What do we write on a CRC card? (pp. 277–285)

13. Should the first scenario that you explore be a common case or one of the exceptional cases? (pp. 280–285)

14. What is a collaboration between classes? (p. 275)

15. In what stage of the CRC card process do we identify responsibilities for classes? (pp. 280–285)

16. Does each CRC card result in the creation of a new class? (pp. 274–275)

17. Suppose you want to create a class that has all of the responsibilities of an existing class, but adds some new responsibilities. Would the new class be a superclass or a subclass of the existing class? (p. 285)

18. What should be the file name for a compilation unit that has a `public` class called `SomeClass`? (pp. 295–299)

19. What is the Java syntactic construct that bundles related classes? (pp. 295–299)

Answers

1. Nouns **2.** True **3.** A method **4.** By sending messages in the form of method calls **5.** Inherit **6.** One **7.** Yes **8.** Use passwords that are difficult to guess, encrypt the data, store backup copies of the data securely, use or develop well-engineered software that avoids security loopholes **9.** Small **10.** False **11.** We eliminate candidate classes that are duplicates, or clearly not part of the problem. **12.** The name of the class, its superclass and subclass relationships, its responsibilities, and its collaborators **13.** A common case **14.** A message passed between them, which is usually a method call, but can also involve the use of `public` fields **15.** During the scenario walk-through **16.** No. A CRC card may refer to an existing class that can be used directly. **17.** A subclass **18.** `SomeClass.java` **19.** `package`

Exam Preparation Exercises

1. Distinguish between the OOD and functional decomposition methodologies in terms of what aspect of a problem each focuses on.

2. Distinguish between the OOD and functional decomposition methodologies in terms of what kind of design each produces.

3. If it is natural to think of the solution to a problem in terms of a collection of component parts, which design technique is more appropriate?

4. If a method is modified by `static`, is it a class method or an instance method?

5. What are class members?

6. What is the public interface to a class?

7. Why would we want to have a private part of a class?

8. Name four responsibilities that might be associated with a class that represents a date.

9. Name two responsibilities that could be associated with a class that represents an exam score.

10. What are the responsibilities of the `BufferedReader` class that we have discussed in this text?

11. What are the responsibilities of the `PrintWriter` class that we have discussed in this text?

12. To have a value entered on the screen and provide it as a value of type `double`, with what classes do we collaborate?

13. What is the goal of the brainstorming phase of the CRC card design process?

14. If you are working by yourself, how long should you wait to begin filtering after you've completed brainstorming a CRC card design?

15. Do we need to identify all of the classes for solving a problem in the brainstorming stage? Explain.

16. Is there a CRC card for every class identified during brainstorming? Explain.

17. At what point do you add initial responsibilities to the CRC cards?

18. During a scenario walk-through, how do you indicate that a class is active?

19. When does a class become inactive in a scenario?

20. What happens when the need for a new class is identified in the middle of a scenario?

21. Inheritance enables us to create what kinds of classes?

22. What special notation do you make on a CRC card when you recognize that a new class is just a variation of an existing class that adds some new responsibilities?

23. Give some examples of additional information that you might add to a CRC card to enhance it.

24. How many levels of abstraction are present in a functional decomposition before you reach the point at which you can begin coding?

25. Is it software piracy if you make a copy of a commercial application for your own use without paying for it?

26. Give an example of data that is public and an example of data that is confidential.

27. Hacking into somebody else's computer and using it to send e-mail is obviously unethical. But what about using an employer's computer for personal work? Explain your answer.

28. What is a computer virus?

29. Why is it unethical to write an application for public use without using proper software engineering methodology?

30. What is self-documenting code?

31. a. What is a compilation unit?
    b. Can one compilation unit include multiple `public` classes?
    c. Where is each compilation unit stored?
    d. How is the file containing a compilation unit named?
    e. Can multiple `public` classes appear in the same package?

32. a. What are the two places in which data abstraction is visible to the user?

   b. Should `public` constants be initialized in their declarations or in assignment statements?

   c. Can variables be marked as `public` in Java?

Programming Warm-Up Exercises

1. Write a CRC card for a class, Car, representing an automobile with its make, model, color, and license plate number.

2. Write a CRC card for a subclass of the automobile class in Exercise 1, called RentalCar, that adds a responsibility for taking trip mileage and rental days values and computing a rental cost. Extend the responsibility for creating an object of this class to include specification of the cost per mile and cost per day.

3. Write a CRC card for a class, Book, representing a library book. It should support creating a book with a title, author, and call number, and knowing each of these values.

4. Write a CRC card that is a subclass of the Book class developed in Exercise 3, called LoanRecord. It adds the capability to record a patron ID number and a due date for the book, and to determine whether the book is overdue.

5. Write a CRC card for a subclass of LoanRecord (Exercise 4) that allows the inclusion of library ID number for interlibrary loans. Also add the ability to indicate, when an object is created, if it is not available for interlibrary lending. Provide a responsibility to test for this property of an object.

6. Write a CRC card for a class, Cow, representing a cow in a dairy herd. The class should include a name, an ID number, a date of birth, and a date of most recent calving.

7. Write a CRC card for a subclass of Cow (Exercise 6) that adds the ability to keep a total of milk output, to enter a value for a milking, and to compute average milk production. The subclass should also support the ability to reset the total milk output value to zero.

8. Brainstorm a set of classes for the following problem statement: You are creating an application that records progress in a fitness program. For each user of the program, you should keep track of the person's initial weight, quarter-mile jog time, standing long-jump distance, and bench-press weight. After each training session, new values are entered for each of these measurements, and the difference from the original values is displayed. The total number of sessions should also be counted.

9. Filter the classes that were brainstormed in Exercise 8.

10. Write CRC cards for the classes that remain after the filtering in Exercise 9. Include the initial responsibilities.

11. Conduct a first scenario walk-through of the CRC cards from Exercise 10, for recording a training session, and indicate any additional classes or responsibilities that you find.

12. Brainstorm a list of additional scenarios for the problem given in Exercises 8–11.

13. Use the scenario in Exercise 11 as the basis for the first test case in a test plan for the application.

14. Declare a package named `somePackage` with headings for the public classes `AddressLabel` and `PrintLabel`.

15. How does Java manage to put all the pieces of a package together?

Programming Problems

1. Use the CRC card process to design a game application that simulates a roulette table. The roulette table has 36 numbers (1–36) that are arranged in three columns of 12 rows. The first row has the numbers 1 through 3, the second row contains 4 through 6, and so on. The number 0 is outside of the table of numbers. The numbers in the table are colored red and black (0 is green). The red numbers are 1, 3, 5, 7, 9, 12, 14, 16, 18, 19, 21, 23, 25, 27, 30, 32, 34, and 36. The other half of the numbers are black. In a simplified set of rules, players can bet on an individual number (including 0), the red numbers, the black numbers, the even numbers, the odd numbers, the numbers 1–18, the numbers 19–36, and any of the columns or rows in the table.

The user should be allowed to enter one of the bets, and the application should use the Math.random method as the basis for computing the number that would be rolled on the wheel. It should then compare this number to the bet, and report whether it won or lost. The process repeats until the user closes the application window.

2. Develop the responsibility algorithms for the CRC card design of Programming Problem 1 and code the application. Use the scenarios to design the test plan.

3. Use the CRC card process to design an extension to the application of Programming Problem 1. The new application should allow the user to enter an initial amount of money into an account. In addition to placing a bet, the user should be able to specify an amount to go with the bet; this amount should be deducted from the account. Any winnings should be added to the account. The current winnings or losses (difference from the original amount) should be displayed as well as the value of the account. Winnings are computed as follows:

Single-number bets pay 36 times the amount placed.

Row bets pay 12 times.

Column bets pay 3 times.

Odd/even, red/black, and high/low half-bets pay 2 times the amount.

The user should not be allowed to bet more than the total in the account.

4. Develop the responsibility algorithms for the CRC card design of Programming Problem 3 and code the application. Use the scenarios to design the test plan.

5. Use the CRC card process to design a game application that plays the children's game of rock, paper, scissors. The user enters a letter, indicating a choice. The Math.random method is then used to pick a value in the range of 1 through 3, with 1 corresponding to rock, 2 corresponding to paper, and 3 corresponding to scissors. The computer's choice is compared to the user's choice according to the rules: rock breaks scissors, scissors cut paper, paper covers rock. Choices that match are ties. Display a count of the wins by the user and the computer, and the number of ties. The application ends when the user enters an invalid choice.

6. Develop the responsibility algorithms for the CRC card design of Programming Problem 5 and code the application. Use the scenarios to design the test plan.

Before paper and scissors

Case Study Follow-Up

1. Enhance the Address class with a constructor that reads values from the screen and stores them into its own fields.

2. Enhance the Entry class with a constructor that reads values from the screen and stores them into its own fields.

3. Enhance the Phone class with a constructor that reads values from the screen and stores them into its own fields.

Inheritance, Polymorphism, and Scope

goals

Knowledge Goals
- To understand the hierarchical nature of classes in object-oriented programming
- To understand the concept of inheritance in a class hierarchy
- To recognize the distinction between overriding and hiding in Java
- To understand the concept of polymorphism
- To recognize the difference between deep and shallow copying of objects
- To know and understand the access rules for Java classes
- To know and understand the assignment compatibility rules for objects
- To understand the concept of overloading in Java

Skill Goals
To be able to:
- Identify the interface components of a class in a hierarchy
- Design a derived class to extend an existing class hierarchy
- Implement a derived class using inheritance
- Use the keywords super and this to disambiguate references
- Create, write, and read files of objects

timeline

1962

MIT grad student Steve Russell uses the DEC computer PDP-1 to create Spacewar, the first video game

1962

The Bell Labs Telstar communications satellite makes possible the first transatlantic television pictures

1963

Joseph Weizenbaum develops "Eliza," a program that acts like a psychotherapist by following a script, but appears to have intelligence

1963

The ASCII character code, largely the work of Bob Bemer, is accepted by the American National Standards Institute

1963

The Semi-Automatic Ground Environment (SAGE) system, a real-time computer-based command and control defense system, is fully deployed

1964

John Kemeny and Thomas Kurtz develop the programming language BASIC

introduction

In Chapter 6, you saw how to create an object-oriented design through the use of CRC cards and how to translate a CRC card description into a Java class. At that time, we pointed out that classes can be related to each other through a hierarchy of properties. The relationship between derived classes (subclasses) and their superclass is defined by Java's rules of inheritance, which tell us the parts of the superclass that are automatically included in the derived classes. Java also provides a set of rules that determine the fields and methods of a class that can be accessed by derived classes, classes in the same package, user code, and so on. We examine these rules in this chapter.

Also in this chapter, we describe a class within the input/output hierarchy that allows us to write and read objects as a whole rather than having to read them field by field.

1964

Control Data Corporation presents Seymour Cray's CDC 6600, the first commercial supercomputer

1964

IBM develops a computer-aided design (CAD) system

1964

Douglas Engelbart invents the computer mouse

1965

J.A. Robinson sets the stage for logic programming with the development of unification

1967

Ole-Johan Dahl and Kristen Nygaard create Simula, the first object-oriented programming language

1967

The first hand-held electronic calculator that can add, subtract, multiply, and divide is created by Jack Kilby, Jerry Merryman, and James Van Tassel at Texas Instruments

7.1 Inheritance

Let's look at an analogy between the work of an architect and the work of a programmer. The way that an architect handles the complexity of a large building design sheds some light on how we can organize our own programming work. This analogy lets us consider the same concepts but without the distraction of Java syntax and semantics.

■ An Analogy

The architect begins by considering the overall requirements for a building: square footage, number of occupants, types of usage, size of the building lot, height limits, and so on. After making some initial decisions, the architect faces a basic aspect of any design: The building is composed of floors. In many buildings, the floors all have common characteristics: the same size and shape; the same number and locations for elevator shafts, stairways, and utility trunks; and so on. The architect could begin by designing a basic empty floor with all of these common elements in place. Once she installs this plan in the library of her computer aided design (CAD) program, she can then use it repeatedly as the starting point for designing each floor of the building.

The architect may further decide that the building has two main types of floors: office floors and mechanical equipment floors. The office floors might be of two types: executive office space and standard office space. Starting from the basic empty floor design, the architect adds components such as lavatories and hallways to make an empty office floor. She can then add offices and conference rooms to the empty space. Each of the four types of floor is thus derived from the basic empty floor and added to the library (see Figure 7.1). Drawing the entire building then becomes simply a matter of creating an instance of one of these four floor plans for each story.

The architect uses the same process to design the components that make up the floors. She might design a basic type of office, with a door, windows, lights, heating, wiring, and so forth, and then derive several types of offices from that one design. From a given type of office, such as secretarial, she might further refine the design into subtypes such as general secretarial, secretary/receptionist, and executive secretary.

Creating hierarchies of designs simplifies the architect's job. She begins each hierarchy with the most general form of a building component, such as the basic empty floor, and then derives new designs by adding details to the more general forms. The new designs *inherit* all of the characteristics of the general form, saving the architect from having to redraw those pieces they share in common. In some cases she replaces existing parts of a design, as when she substitutes a wider door for a reception area than appears in the basic secretarial office. The replacement part *overrides* what was originally specified in the more general form.

In addition to the components of individual floors, the architect can specify characteristics that are common to all floors, such as a color scheme. Each floor will then inherit these general properties. Sometimes she *hides* or deletes portions of the general properties, as when she customizes the color scheme for a particular floor that has been rented in advance by a company with its own corporate colors. We will see later how inheritance, overriding, and hiding are formally defined mechanisms in Java.

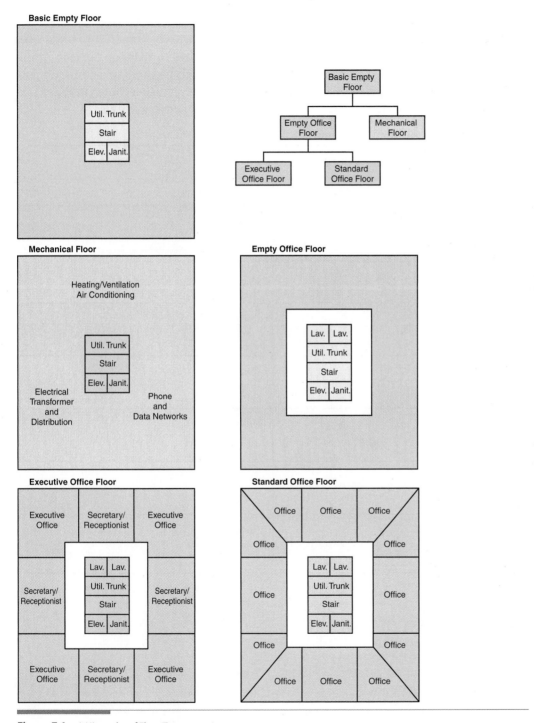

Figure 7.1 A Hierarchy of Floor Types

7.2 Inheritance and the Object-Oriented Design Process

Now let's consider how a class hierarchy originates in the CRC card design process. At the end of the filtering phase, we sometimes discover that several classes are similar. For example, in the address book example of Chapter 6, our filtered list of classes included Address and Work Address. Let's look at the CRC cards for some different address objects.

Class Name: *WorkAddress*	Superclass:		Subclasses:
Responsibilities		**Collaborations**	
Create itself (name, company, street, city, state, ZIP code)		Name	
Know its name return String		Name	
Know its company return String		None	
Know its street return String		None	
Know its city return String		None	
Know its state return String		None	
Know its ZIP code return String		None	

Class Name: HomeAddress	Superclass:	Subclasses:
Responsibilities	**Collaborations**	
Create itself (name, street, apartment, city, state, ZIP code)	Name	
Know its name return String	Name	
Know its street return String	None	
Know its apartment return String	None	
Know its city return return String	None	
Know its state return String	None	
Know its ZIP code return String	None	

Class Name: *BoxAddress*	Superclass:	Subclasses:
Responsibilities		**Collaborations**
Create itself (name, company, box, city, state, ZIP code)		*Name*
Know its name *return String*		*Name*
Know its company *return String*		*None*
Know its box *return String*		*None*
Know its city *return String*		*None*
Know its state *return String*		*None*
Know its ZIP code *return String*		*None*

Superclass A class that is extended by one or more derived classes (its subclasses)

Subclass A class that is derived from another class (its superclass)

These CRC cards might originate in the brainstorming phase, or they could result from a series of scenarios. No matter how they arise, it is quite obvious that they have several responsibilities in common: "Know its name", "Know its city", "Know its state", and "Know its ZIP code". We can save ourselves duplicate effort by defining a superclass, Address, that has the common responsibilities. In addition, two of the classes share the "Know its company" responsibility. We can thus define a subclass of Address called Company Address that becomes the superclass of these two. The third class directly extends Address with its specific responsibilities. Here are the revised CRC cards:

Class Name: Address	Superclass:	Subclasses: Home Address, Company Address
Responsibilities	**Collaborations**	
Create itself (name, city, state, ZIP code)	Name	
Know its name return String	Name	
Know its city return String	None	
Know its state return String	None	
Know its ZIP code return String	None	

Class Name: Company Address	Superclass: Address	Subclasses: Work Address, Box Address
Responsibilities	**Collaborations**	
Create itself (name, company, city, state, ZIP code)	Name	
Know its company return String	None	

Class Name: Work Address	Superclass: Company Address	Subclasses:
Responsibilities	**Collaborations**	
Create itself (name, company, street, city, state, ZIP code)	Name	
Know its street return String	None	

Class Name: Box Address	Superclass: Company Address	Subclasses:
Responsibilities	**Collaborations**	
Create itself (name, company, box, city, state, ZIP code)	Name	
Know its Box return String	None	

Class Name: Home Address	Superclass: Address	Subclasses:
Responsibilities: Create	**Collaborations**	
Create itself (name, street, apartment, city, state, ZIP code)	Name	
Know its street return String	None	
Know its apartment return String	None	

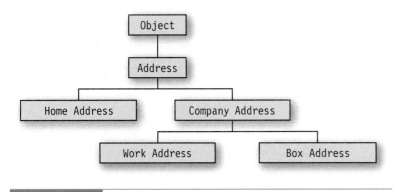

Figure 7.2 Address Object Hierarchy

Figure 7.2 shows the relationships among these classes. Address, the most general form, appears at the top of its hierarchy, just below Object, which is at the top of any hierarchy.

The ability of a programming language to support the creation of superclasses and subclasses is known as **inheritance**. Each subclass inherits the responsibilities that are defined by its superclass, including all of the responsibilities that the superclass has inherited. In addition, subclasses are assignment-compatible with the superclasses above them in the hierarchy. That is, we can assign a Work Address object to a Work Address variable, a Company Address variable, an Address variable, or an Object variable.

Periodically in the CRC card design process, it is useful to look for similarities among the cards and decide whether a superclass should be created. Inheritance is also used when we start to create a new class and realize that it is just a variation of an existing class. In this situation, there is no need to define an entirely new

Inheritance A mechanism by which one class acquires the properties—the data fields and methods—of another class

class when we can simply extend an existing class. As you look for things that are familiar in solving a problem, keep in mind the existing classes.

In our address book example, we collected responsibilities from similar classes to form a superclass. If we need to represent international telephone numbers, we could create a completely new class, but a better solution is create a subclass of Phone with a field for the country code. Whenever you encounter such a situation, you should immediately consider how you can take advantage of it through inheritance.

7.3 How to Read a Class Hierarchy

In Java, all classes can eventually trace their roots back to the Object class, which is so general that it does almost nothing: Objects of type Object are nearly useless by themselves. But Object does define several basic methods: comparison for equality, conversion to a string, and so on.

The Java library defines numerous classes that directly extend the Object class and thus inherit all of its methods. For example, a class called Component extends Object with the basic operations needed to display something in a window on the screen. We can't instantiate objects of the class Component directly, however, because they are incomplete. Java calls such classes **abstract**. Returning to our analogy, the architect would never include the basic empty floor in a building plan, but uses it instead to design floors that are complete. Similarly, we would never instantiate an object of an abstract class in our code, but we can use it as the superclass for defining new subclasses that are complete.

> **Abstract** A modifier of a class or field that indicates it is incomplete and must be fully defined in a derived class
>
> **Derived class** A class that is created as an extension of another class in the hierarchy

In Chapter 8, we will see how to create a graphical user interface consisting of a window on the screen, with buttons, labels that hold output, and boxes in which a user can enter data values. As a preview of the graphical user interface we introduce in Chapter 8, and because it provides a good example of the use of inheritance, let's look at the hierarchy of a class that allows us to create a data entry field within a window.

Being familiar with how Java functions, you should not be surprised to learn that Java provides a class called JTextField that is used to create input fields in a window. JTextField is **derived** from a class called JTextComponent, which is in turn derived from a class called JComponent, which is in turn derived from a class called Container, which is in turn derived from Component. As you can see, the hierarchy of classes can be many levels in depth, so it can become difficult to keep track of which class is descended from which class. Figure 7.3 shows how these classes are related. We use boxes with their corners cut out to represent the incomplete nature of an abstract class.

When the architect looks at a floor plan with her CAD program, she sees all of its parts, including those that are derived from the basic empty floor. When we look at the documentation for a Java class, however, we see only those fields that are added by that specific class and the name of its superclass.

As an example, let's look at a summary of the methods in the JTextField class. Java class summaries (documentation) are typically written as method headings. This summary includes a modifier, protected, that we have not yet

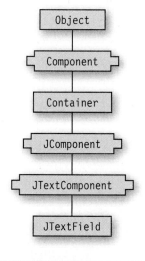

Figure 7.3 Hierarchy of Component Classes above JTextField

discussed. We will explain its meaning later in this chapter. Don't worry—you don't need to learn how any of these methods work! We're just illustrating how Java library classes are documented.

```
public class JTextField extends JTextComponent
{
  JTextField()
  JTextField(Document doc, String text, int columns)
  JTextField(int columns)
  JTextField(String text)
  JTextField(String text, int columns)
  void addActionListener(ActionListener l)
  protected void configurePropertiesFromAction(Action a)
  protected PropertyChangeListener createActionPropertyChangeListener(Action a)
  protected Document createDefaultModel()
  protected void fireActionPerformed()
  AccessibleContext getAccessibleContext()
  Action getAction()
  ActionListener[] getActionListeners()
  Action[] getActions()
  int getColumns()
  protected int getColumnWidth()
  int getHorizontalAlignment()
  BoundedRangeModel getHorizontalVisibility()
  Dimension getPreferredSize()
  int getScrollOffset()
  String getUIClassID()
  boolean isValidateRoot()
  protected String paramString()
  void postActionEvent()
  void removeActionListener(ActionListener l)
  void scrollRectToVisible(Rectangle r)
  void setAction(Action a)
  void setActionCommand(String command)
  void setColumns(int columns)
  void setDocument(Document doc)
  void setFont(Font f)
  void setHorizontalAlignment(int alignment)
  void setScrollOffset(int scrollOffset)
}
```

A first glance at the class is somewhat disappointing. If this class is used to create input boxes in a window, shouldn't it list methods to retrieve what the user inputs? None of these methods have identifiers that indicate they input values. But wait! The class header says that JTextField *extends* JTextComponent. That little bit of code tells us that this definition is just part of the story. We have to look at the documentation for JTextComponent to determine what JTextField inherits from it. In fact, JTextComponent defines 68 additional methods that are inherited by JTextField. We won't list them here, but among them is getText. We also see other methods in JTextComponent whose names imply that they manipulate text within the field.

The class heading for JTextComponent indicates that the story continues, because it extends the class JComponent. If we look at the documentation for that class, we find that it defines 138 more methods. We'll look at just one of them here, together with its heading:

```
public abstract class JComponent extends Container
{
    public void setVisible(boolean flag);
    .
    .
    .
}
```

Notice the use of the abstract modifier in the class heading. Whenever you see the keyword abstract in a class declaration, it tells you that the class being defined is incompletely specified and cannot be instantiated.

When a class is declared as abstract, its purpose is to provide a placeholder for a definition to be supplied in a derived class. The class JComponent doesn't have any constructors. It doesn't define the structure of a useful object that we can instantiate. Instead, it defines a collection of methods that are common to various objects that can appear in a window. By deriving classes for those objects from this common class, Java makes it easy to ensure that they all behave in a consistent manner.

As we can see from its definition, JComponent extends Container. Looking at Container, we see that it defines another 51 methods; it also extends Component, which in turn supplies another 138 methods. Finally, Component extends Object, which is the top of the entire hierarchy and supplies another 10 methods. We rarely use Object's methods directly, and several of them are related to features of Java that are beyond the scope of this text. Here we list just the ones that are familiar:

```
public class Object
{
    public Object();                    // Constructor
    public boolean equals(Object obj);
    public String toString();
    .
    .
    .
}
```

Now that we have the specification for every class that is an ancestor of JTextField, we can determine the methods that it has available. There are more than 400 methods that it may inherit. We could begin at the bottom of the hierarchy (JTextField) and write a list of all of its members as a column on one side of the page. In the next column, we would write the members of its superclass (excluding its constructors, because constructors technically aren't members and aren't inherited). We repeat this process in the third column, adding the members of `JComponent`. The process continues until finally, we write the members of `Object` (excluding its constructors) in the last column. Of course, with more than 400 methods, this process is quite tedious, especially given that we aren't interested in the vast majority of them. In practice, we just write down the ones that pertain to the problem at hand.

■ Overriding

A careful examination of the `JComponent` class reveals that it defines a method called `getUIClassID`. We don't use this method in this book, but it illustrates another aspect of Java class hierarchies. Looking back down the hierarchy, we find that `JTextField` redefines (**overrides**) `getUIClassID`, substituting its own version of `getUIClassID`. Thus, in our lists of methods, we would cross off the `JComponent` member name to indicate that it is redefined by `JTextField`.

Together, the columns in the complete table would tell us every member that is available in the class `JTextField`. When we first looked at the documentation for `JTextField`, it appeared that the class had just 33 members. Now, however, we can identify more than 400 members. This example illustrates the power of using inheritance in a hierarchy of classes. Just as the architect can save effort by defining a hierarchy of building parts, we can save ourselves a lot of work by using inheritance.

Override To provide an instance method in a derived class that has the same form of heading as an instance method in its superclass. The method in the derived class redefines (overrides) the method in its superclass. We cannot override class methods.

Hide To provide a field in a derived class that has the same name as a field in its superclass; to provide a class method that has the same form of heading as a class method in its superclass. The field or class method is said to hide the corresponding component of the superclass.

■ Hiding

In our `JTextField` example, we considered only inheritance of methods. In reality, fields may also be inherited through the hierarchy. When a derived class defines a field with the same name as one in its superclass, the field in the derived class **hides** the one in the superclass. Java also distinguishes the case of overriding a `static` (class) method with another class method as a form of hiding. The term *overriding* technically applies only to instance methods.

If you look at the `JTextField` hierarchy carefully, you would notice that nothing is deleted as a result of inheritance (except constructors). Java does not provide any way to remove a member that is inherited. We can cover over a member with a replacement member, but we can't delete it. This is an aspect of the philosophy of object-oriented design: As we go deeper in the hierarchy, we add or change functionality, but we do not lose functionality. In object-oriented design, a derived class is always an extension of its superclass.

For example, we would say that a `JTextField` *is a* `JTextComponent`. In object-oriented design, a fundamental concept is the "is a" relationship between a derived class and its superclass. A derived class *is a* form of its superclass. The closest that we can get to deleting a member of a superclass in a derived class is to override it or hide it with a member of the same name that does nothing. For example, we could override a method with a version that simply returns null. This approach would be considered poor programming practice, however.

■ Polymorphism

Let's take a closer look at the mechanism that allows getUIClassID to have two different implementations. When it is applied to a JTextField, it has one implementation; when applied to a JComponent, it has another. In object-oriented terms, we say that getUIClassID is polymorphic. That is, it has multiple forms. Java decides which form to use depending on the class of the object.

> **Polymorphic operation** An operation that has multiple meanings depending on the class of object to which it is bound

Together with inheritance and encapsulation, polymorphism gives us the ability to flexibly implement a hierarchy of objects. We use polymorphism to substitute different implementations of a responsibility as required by variations in the internal representation of classes at different levels of the hierarchy. For example, Address might represent a ZIP code as a single string, but then we might redefine its representation in the CompanyAddress class so that the four-digit extension is kept separately. Thus, the "Know ZIP code" responsibility would be implemented differently in CompanyAddress than in Address.

7.4 Derived Class Syntax

The declaration of a derived class looks very much like the declaration of any other class. Here is the syntax template for a declaring class:

```
Class-Modifiers  ···  class Identifier    extends Classname
{
    Class-Declaration  ···
}
```

The only difference between this template and the one in Chapter 2 is that we've added the optional extends clause that allows us to indicate the superclass from which our new class is derived. Here's an example declaration:

```
public class BusinessPhone extends Phone
{
    // Declare new data fields and methods as needed
}
```

This new class inherits all of the fields and methods of Phone (including anything Phone has inherited) and then adds some of its own. Is that all there is to implementing a derived class? In terms of syntax, yes. But in terms of semantics, there is more we need to know.

In Chapters 2 and 3, we learned how to create individual classes that are fully encapsulated. With inheritance and polymorphism, we are beginning to create related sets of classes.

Ada Lovelace

On December 10, 1815 (the same year that George Boole was born), a daughter—Augusta Ada Byron—was born to Anna Isabella (Annabella) Byron and George Gordon, Lord Byron. In England at that time, Byron's fame derived not only from his poetry but also from his wild and scandalous behavior. The marriage was strained from the beginning, and Annabella left Byron shortly after Ada's birth. By April 1816, the two had signed separation papers. Byron left England, never to return. Throughout the rest of his life he regretted that he was unable to see his daughter. At one point he wrote of her,

I see thee not. I hear thee not.

But none can be so wrapt in thee.

Before he died in Greece, at age 36, he exclaimed,

Oh my poor dear child! My dear Ada!

My God, could I but have seen her!

Meanwhile, Annabella, who eventually became a baroness in her own right, and who was educated as both a mathematician and a poet, carried on with Ada's upbringing and education. Annabella gave Ada her first instruction in mathematics, but it soon became clear that Ada was gifted in the subject and should receive more extensive tutoring. Ada received further training from Augustus DeMorgan, today famous for one of the basic theorems of Boolean algebra. By age eight, Ada had demonstrated an interest in mechanical devices and was building detailed model boats.

When she was 18, Ada visited the Mechanics Institute to hear Dr. Dionysius Lardner's lectures on the Difference Engine, a mechanical calculating machine being built by Charles Babbage. She became so interested in the device that she arranged to be introduced to Babbage. It was said that, upon seeing Babbage's machine, Ada was the only person in the room to understand immediately how it worked and to recognize its significance. Ada and Charles Babbage became lifelong friends. She worked with him, helping to document his designs, translating writings about his work, and developing programs for his machines. In fact, Ada today is recognized as history's first computer programmer.

When Babbage designed his Analytical Engine, Ada foresaw that it could go beyond arithmetic computations and become a general manipulator of symbols, and thus would have far-reaching capabilities. She even suggested that such a device eventually could be programmed with rules of harmony and composition so that it could produce "scientific" music. In effect, Ada foresaw the field of artificial intelligence more than 150 years ago.

In 1842, Babbage gave a series of lectures in Turin, Italy, on his Analytical Engine. One of the attendees was Luigi Menabrea, who was so impressed that he wrote an account of Babbage's lectures. At age 27, Ada decided to translate the account into English, with the intent to add a few of her own notes about the machine. In the end, her notes were twice as long as the original material, and the document, "The Sketch of the Analytical Engine," became the definitive work on the subject.

It is obvious from Ada's letters that her "notes" were entirely her own and that Babbage was acting as a sometimes unappreciated editor. At one point, Ada wrote to him,

> I am much annoyed at your having altered my Note. You know I am always willing to make any required alterations myself, but that I cannot endure another person to meddle with my sentences.

Ada gained the title Countess of Lovelace when she married Lord William Lovelace. The couple had three children, whose upbringing was left to Ada's mother while Ada pursued her work in mathematics. Her husband was supportive of her work, but for a woman of that day, such behavior was considered almost as scandalous as some of her father's exploits.

Ada died in 1852, just one year before a working Difference Engine was built in Sweden from one of Babbage's designs. Like her father, Ada lived only to age 36. Even though they led very different lives, she undoubtedly had admired him and took inspiration from his unconventional and rebellious nature. In the end, Ada asked to be buried beside him at the family's estate.

May We Introduce

Java lets us group related classes in a package so that encapsulation protects the whole collection. Within the package, it allows the related classes to communicate directly. Direct access is more efficient than converting back and forth between external and internal representations when classes share a common internal representation.

Also, when a derived class overrides or hides members of its superclass, it can no longer refer to them directly. Java provides additional syntax and semantics that enable a subclass to access such superclass members when the need arises.

In the next section, we examine the Java semantics for accessing members from different places. Then we can return to the specifics of implementing a hierarchy of derived classes.

7.5 Scope of Access

In writing a Java class, we declare variables, constants, and methods that are given identifiers. Java defines a set of rules that specify where those identifiers can then be used, both inside and outside of the class. We say that the rules determine the **scope of access** of an identifier. The term is usually shortened to *scope*, and the rules are thus called the **scope rules** of the language.

The scope rules for access within a class (internal access scope rules) are straightforward and do not depend on the access modifiers attached to an identifier. External access scope rules determine where an identifier can be used outside of a class and depend on both the access modifiers and the location where the access takes place. We look first at internal scope and then at external scope.

Scope of access (scope) The region of program code where it is legal to reference (use) an identifier

Scope rules The rules that determine where in a program an identifier may be referenced, given the point where the identifier is declared and its specific access modifiers

▓ Internal Scope

Any identifier declared as a static or instance member of a class can be used anywhere within the class, with two exceptions. You can't use one class variable to initialize another before the first one has been defined. And, within its block, a local identifier hides a class member of the same name. Let's take a closer look at each of these exceptions.

Order of Definition Suppose you are defining a Circle class and you want to provide class variables that are initially set to pi and pi times two. The first of the following two declarations is illegal because its initialization expression uses the second identifier before it has been given a value:

```
public static double twoPI = PI * 2; // PI isn't defined yet
public static double PI = 3.14159265358979323846;
```

Reversing the order of the statements makes them both legal:

```
public static double PI = 3.14159265358979323846;
public static double twoPI = PI * 2; // PI already has a value
```

The scope rule that requires us to define a class variable's value before it is used applies only to references in expressions that initialize other class variables as part of their declaration. Otherwise, it's legal to refer to class variables before they are defined. For example, the following declarations are legal:

```
public static int circumference(Circle anyCircle)
{
  return anyCircle.radius * twoPI;
}
static double PI = 3.14159265358979323846;
static double twoPI = PI * 2;
```

In this code, the method is allowed to refer to the variable twoPI before it is defined. Why is this case different? The JVM performs all class variable declaration initializations before it starts executing statements in main, and it does so in the order that the initializations are written in the code. So an initialization expression can use only class variables that have already been given values.

The method circumference isn't executed until it is called from some point in the program, which can happen only after all of the variable declaration initializations are complete. In terms of the order of execution, all initialization expressions are executed before any other use of a variable.

Note that regular assignment statements that initialize variables in methods are distinct from declaration initialization expressions. They are executed in the normal flow of control, which starts after all of the declaration initializations take place.

Constant declarations do not follow this rule because the compiler computes constant values at compile time. That is, the compiler searches through our code to find all the constant declarations before it computes their values. As a consequence, it doesn't require us to define a constant before referring to it. The JVM isn't able to search through Bytecode in the same way, so it requires us to initialize variables before their use in initialization expressions.

To make life easier for human readers of your code, it's good form to define constants ahead of any references to them. Some programmers even make a point of writing all constant declarations before the variable declarations, just as a reminder that constants are given their values first.

Shadowing   The scope rule that says local identifiers block access to identifiers with the same name in the enclosing class is called shadowing.

> **Shadowing**   A scope rule specifying that a local identifier declaration blocks access to an identifier declared with the same name outside of the block containing the local declaration.

In Java, the scope of a local identifier is the remainder of the block follwing the point at which it is declared. The block includes all of the statements between the { and } that contain the declaration. For example:

```
public class SomeClass
{
    static int var;                // Class member var
    static final int CONST = 5;  // Class member CONST
    static Label label1;
    public static void someMethod(int param)
    {
        int var = CONST;
        final int CONST = 10;
        var = param * CONST;
        label1.setText("" + var);
    }
}
```

Scope of local constant CONST, which shadows the same identifier declared as a class member.

Scope of local variable var which shadows the same identifier declared as a class member

In this example, the scope of the local declarations extends from the point that each one appears to the end of the block. Thus, in the first use of CONST, to initialize var as part of its declaration, the initialization refers to the class version of CONST. The second use of CONST in the expression assigned to var, refers to the local constant.

Using this Refer to an Object from Within Itself   Java provides a keyword, this, which can be used within an object to refer to the object itself. With regard to their scope, formal parameters are treated as local identifiers that are declared at the beginning of the method body. Their scope thus includes the entire body of the method.

Here's an example showing the use of this to access instance fields from within a method that defines local names that shadow access to those fields:

```
public class SomeClass
{
    static int var = -1;         // Instance member var
    static final int CONST = 5; // Class member CONST
```

```
int param = 0;                            // Instance member param
public int someMethod(int param)          // Defines local param
{
    int var;                              // Defines local var
    // Define and set local CONST to instance CONST * 2
    final int CONST = this.CONST*2;
    if (param > this.param)               // Compare local and instance params
        var = param * CONST;              // Use local values
    else
        var = this.param * this.CONST;    // Use instance values
    return var;
}
}
```

Understanding the internal scope rules helps to avoid or locate errors in implementing the internal representation of the class. An example of a scope-related error is when you declare a local identifier that shadows a class member, but misspell the name in the local declaration. The compiler won't complain, but merely directs all of the references to the local identifier to its correctly spelled class member equivalent, as shown here:

```
public class SomeClass
{
    static int var;                           // Class member var
    public static void someMethod(int param)
    {
        int ver;                              // Misspelling of var
        var = param * param;                  // Accidentally refers to class member var
        System.out.println("" + var);         // Accidentally refers to class member var
        System.out.println("" + SomeClass.var); // Intentional reference to class member var
    }
}
```

This program exhibits erroneous behavior in which a class member is changed and displayed as a side effect of calling a method. Knowing the scope rules leads us to look for references to the class member within the method, and then to check the local declarations. The last line of someMethod illustrates how to intentionally access a shadowed class field. We just use the class name to refer to the field.

■ External Scope

The external access scope rules for members control their use by code that is outside of the class. Java allows class members to be accessed from three external places: derived classes, members of the same package, and code external to the package.

A package contains a set of related classes, and sometimes we want to make members of those classes accessible to each other, even if they aren't public. For example, suppose that a Date class is part of a calendar package. Another class, called ShowWeek, in the package displays a week surrounding a given date. Both of the classes use the Julian day as their internal representation. It is thus more efficient for a Date object to make its Julian day member directly accessible to ShowWeek than to require conversion of the date first to its external form and then back to a Julian day in the other object. The user is unaware of this shortcut, so the encapsulation is preserved.

Classes naturally belong together in a package if they have common internal representations. In that case, they can bypass each other's encapsulations because the common details of their implementations are already known to anyone who's working with them.

Java defines four levels of access for class members, three of which enable direct access by other package members. The four levels of access are public, protected, default (package), and private. There are keywords that we use as access modifiers for each of these levels except the package level, which is the default level. If you omit an access modifier from the declaration of a class member, it is at the package level of access by default.

public Access   A public member can be accessed from anywhere outside of the class. User code, derived classes, and other classes in the same package can all access a public member. The member may still be hidden by a declaration of the same name in another class, in which case references to it must be qualified with its class or instance name.

Here's an example of using qualified names. If the class ShowWeek defines a julianDay field and Date also defines julianDay as a static field, then ShowWeek would need to refer to

```
Date.julianDay
```

to access the static field of Date. If julianDay is an instance field of Date and the particular object is called instanceName, then ShowWeek must refer to it as follows:

```
instanceName.julianDay
```

protected Access   A protected member is accessible to classes in the same package and can be inherited by derived classes outside of the package. Code that is outside of the package can only **inherit** protected members of a class; it can't access them directly.

Inherit   To acquire a field or method from a superclass

In the following code segment, we define two packages. The second package has a class (DerivedClass) that is derived from the class in the first package (SomeClass). DerivedClass inherits the protected field someInt from SomeClass. Notice that DerivedClass doesn't include a declaration of someInt.

DerivedClass defines a method that has one parameter of the class SomeClass and another parameter of its own class. It then tries to access the someInt field in both parameters.

```
package one;
public class SomeClass
{
   protected int someInt;
}
```

```
import one.*;
package two;
public class DerivedClass extends SomeClass
{
  void demoMethod(SomeClass param1, DerivedClass param2)
  {
    param1.someInt = 1;    // Generates a compiler error
                           // Can't access member of instance of SomeClass
    param2.someInt = 1;    // This access is legal
                           // It refers to the inherited member

  }
}
```

The compiler will issue an error message for the first assignment statement because it is illegal to access the protected field of a superclass when the superclass resides in a different package. The second assignment is valid because it refers to the inherited field within DerivedClass.

The protected modifier provides the least restrictive level of access that isn't public. We use protected to enable users to extend our class with a subclass. The subclass inherits its own copies of the protected members, but cannot access the originals.

It is unusual to see protected in an application designed with CRC cards because all of the responsibilities and collaborations are known in advance. But if a package of classes is independent of an application (such as the java.util package), it is often desirable to enable users to derive their own classes from the library classes.

Package Access   When no access modifier is specified, then classes in the same package can access the member. No other external access is allowed. A member at the package level of access cannot be inherited by a derived class in another package. Up to this point, we've given only examples in which every member of a class is inherited by a subclass. With the introduction of the package level of access, we see that Java also lets us selectively restrict the members that are inherited.

A derived class in the same package retains access to the members of its superclass that are at the package level of access. All classes within the same package have access to each other's public, protected, and package members.

Here's the preceding example, but with both classes in the same package and someInt at the package level of access. In this case, both assignment statements are valid.

```
package one;
public class SomeClass
{
  int someInt;
}


package one;
public class DerivedClass extends SomeClass
```

External Access	`public`	`protected`	Default (package)	`private`
Same package	yes	yes	yes	no
Derived class in another package	yes	yes (inheritance only)	no	no
User code	yes	no	no	no

Table 7.1   Java's External Scope Rules

```
{
  void demoMethod(SomeClass param1, DerivedClass param2)
  {
    param1.someInt = 1;
    param2.someInt = 1;
  }
}
```

`private` Access   Lastly, the `private` modifier cuts off all external access, even by classes in the same package. A `private` member of a class can be referred to only by other members of the class, and only the internal scope rules apply to it. It isn't even permissible for a derived class in the same package to access a `private` member of its superclass.

Instances of a class can refer to each other's `private` members. A member is `private` to its class, which includes all instances of the class. Thus two objects, someObj and otherObj, that have `private int` fields called someInt can refer to each other's fields. That is, someObj can refer to otherObj.someInt and otherObj can refer to someObj.someInt.

Within a method, all local identifiers are automatically `private`; Java doesn't allow us to declare them with access modifiers. The reason is that the lifetime of a local identifier is limited to a particular method call, so it simply doesn't exist when external code is running. Table 7.1 summarizes the external scope rules.

So far, we have primarily used the `public` and package levels of access, keeping data members at the package level and making most methods and classes `public`. This simple scheme provides encapsulation and a consistent user interface that is strictly a set of method calls. However, this scheme is inflexible and limits our ability to provide for either extension or the construction of related classes that are grouped into a package.

Now that we have a better understanding of Java's access rules, we must consider which access modifier is most appropriate for each member of a class. Once you have identified all of its members, take a second look at each one and ask the following question:

> Do I want to access this member from other classes in the same package, from derived classes, or from user code?

Based on your answer to each part of this question, use Table 7.1 to decide which access modifier is most appropriate.

7.6 Implementing a Derived Class

Given the CRC card design for a subclass and its superclass, you can determine what you must include in the subclass to implement its responsibilities. You may find that you simply need to change the operation of an inherited method, which means that you override or hide it with a new version. Because a derived class doesn't inherit any constructors, it will probably need one or more new constructors. We often implement new constructors by calling the old ones to do much of the work, and then adding a few statements to take care of initializing any new fields that we've added. In some cases, you may find it necessary to change the internal representation of the subclass.

After you have designed the subclass interface and its internal representation, you implement it by writing the necessary field and method declarations within a class declaration that `extends` the superclass. Here are the steps in the form of a checklist:

1. Study the interfaces of the superclass and the subclass, identifying the members that are inherited.
2. Determine whether the internal representation must change in the subclass.
3. Provide constructors as needed.
4. Add fields and methods to those that are inherited, as necessary.
5. Hide any inherited fields or class methods that you wish to replace.
6. Override any instance methods that you wish to replace.

We have already seen how to read an existing class hierarchy to determine what is inherited by a subclass. When we are creating a new hierarchy, we start from a set of CRC cards. During the enactment of the scenarios, it may become clear that certain responsibilities are `public`, `private`, or package-level in their access requirements; this fact should be written on the cards. As we've noted, a CRC card design rarely results in a `protected` responsibility.

As we design the internal representation for a class, we may also notice that certain fields need an access level other than package. For example, we might define some `public` class constants. Armed with this information, we can list the members that a subclass inherits.

Next, we reconsider the choice of internal representation given the responsibilities of the subclass. Unless we have a good reason for making the representation different from the superclass, it should remain the same. Thus we begin with the inherited representation and look for any omissions. We can easily add any extra fields needed.

Sometimes an inherited field is inappropriate for the subclass. Perhaps the superclass uses an `int` field for part of its representation, and the purpose of the subclass is to extend its range by using `long`. Then we must hide the inherited field in the subclass.

Once we have the interface and internal representation, we can begin to implement the constructors. Java has some special rules regarding constructors in derived classes that we examine next.

Constructors in Derived Classes

What would happen if we forgot to include a constructor in the declaration of a derived class? Java automatically provides a default constructor that calls the superclass constructor with an empty parameter list. We mentioned this issue briefly in Chapter 5.

In fact, Java requires every constructor in a derived class to call a constructor in its superclass. That call must be the first statement appearing in the constructor even before any declarations. If it isn't the first statement, Java automatically inserts the same default call.

Java requires us to call a superclass constructor in this way because every derived class is a specialized form of its superclass. An object of the subclass can be assigned to a variable of both its own class and its superclass (and by extension, any of the classes above it in the hierarchy). The superclass may perform initialization operations to create a valid object. Rather than requiring every derived class to duplicate those operations, Java simply enforces the rule that one of the superclass constructors must be called, either explicitly in our constructor or implicitly by default.

Of course, the superclass constructor must call a constructor for its superclass, and so on until the constructor for Object is called. Thus the process of instantiating an object calls a chain of constructors that provides essential initialization all the way up to Object. Next, we examine how Java identifies methods and the Java syntax for calling a constructor in the superclass.

Overloading and Method Signatures

If you were to examine the interface of the class JTextField, you would discover that it has not one, but five constructors:

```java
public JTextField()
public JTextField(String text)
public JTextField(int columns)
public JTextField(String text, int columns)
public JTextField(Document doc, String text, int columns)
```

We've always been careful to avoid declaring duplicate identifiers in our programs, yet JTextField has five constructors, all with the same name. How is this possible? In the case of methods, Java uses more than just the name to identify them; it also uses the parameter list. A method's name, the number and types of parameters that are passed to it, and the arrangement of the different parameter types within the list combine into what Java calls the signature of the method.

Signature   The distinguishing features of a method heading; the combination of the method name with the number and type(s) of its parameters in their given order

Overloading   The repeated use of a method name with a different signature

Java allows us to use the name of a method as many times as we wish, as long as each one has a different signature. When we use a method name more than once, we are overloading its identifier. The Java compiler needs to be able to look at a method call and determine which version of the method to invoke. The five constructors in the class JTextField, for instance, all have different signatures: the first constructor takes no arguments, the second takes a String, the third takes an int, the fourth takes both a String and an int, and the fifth takes an object of class Document, a String, and an `int`. Java decides which version to call based on the arguments in the statement that invokes JTextField.

The following method headings have different signatures and thus overload each other:

```
public static void someName(int formal1, int formal2, int formal3)
public static void someName(int formal1, double formal2, int formal3)
public static void someName(double formal1, int formal2, int formal3)
public static void someName(int formal1, int formal2, String formal3)
```

Even though all of these parameters have the same names, the differences in their types enable Java to distinguish among them. For example, the statement

```
someName(1, 2.0, 3);
```

calls the second version because it has an `int` value, a `double` value, and another `int` value as its arguments. If we write the call as

```
someName(1.0, 2, 3);
```

then the `double`, `int`, `int` pattern of its arguments identifies the third version of the method as the target of the call.

The following method headings all have the same signature and cannot be declared together in a class. Their signature is the method name (aName) and the presence of three parameters of types `int`, `double`, and `String`, in that order.

```
public static void aName(int formal1, double formal2, String formal3)
public static void aName(int large, double medium, String small)
public void aName(int red, double green, String blue)
static int aName(int thing1, double thing2, String hatCat)
```

Keep in mind that the types of the parameters determine the signature of a method. The names of the parameters, the return type, and the modifiers of a method are not part of its signature.

Overloading is related to, but different from, hiding and overriding. Hiding and overriding are mechanisms whereby a name is replaced when the same name is declared in a new context. For example, an instance method identifier overrides a method with the same name in its superclass if it has the same signature. The declaration in the derived class results in an identifier that duplicates the one in the superclass. Because they are in different classes, however, the duplication is acceptable. When we use the identifiers, we indicate which one we mean. An instance identifier is associated with a specific object of one or the other class type, and a class identifier is preceded with the name of the class and a period.

If we declare a method with the same name as an inherited superclass method, but the methods have different signatures, then the new method overloads the name of the superclass method. The two identifiers are the same, but the different signatures allow them to be distinguished. Different signatures also serve to distinguish overloaded methods within the same class. The Java compiler decides which version to call by comparing the types of the arguments with the types of the parameters in each signature.

To summarize, overloading allows us to add new versions of a name that can coexist in a single context, while hiding and overriding provide a way to replace a name with a new declaration in a different context.

Accessing Overridden and Hidden Methods and Fields

Using the keyword super followed by a parameter list refers to the constructor in the superclass with the same signature. Keep in mind that you have to use super or the name of the superclass in only two cases:

- When you are accessing a method or field that has been overridden or hidden
- When you are accessing a superclass constructor

Otherwise, the name has been inherited and you can refer to it directly.

Here are some examples of using super:

```
super();                          // Call to the default constructor of the superclass
someInt = super.someInt;          // Reference to a hidden field in the superclass
super.classMethod();              // Call to a hidden class method in the superclass
SuperClassName.classMethod();     // Another way to call the same hidden method
super.instanceMethod();           // Call to an overridden instance method in the superclass
```

A Concrete Example

In the example used to present the CRC card technique in Chapter 6, the filtered list of classes included a business phone number. What distinguishes a business number from a home number is the presence of an extension in the business number. Let's extend the class Phone to include an extension number. We need to add a field in BusinessPhone to hold the extension. Should we change the methods asDigits and asString to include the extension? Yes; let's do so. Here, then, is the CRC card for BusinessPhone:

Class Name: *BusinessPhone*	Superclass: *Phone*	Subclasses:
Responsibilities	**Collaborations**	
Create itself (area code, number, extension)	*Phone*	
Know its extension 　*return int*	*None*	
asDigits 　*return long*	*Phone*	
asString 　*return String*	*Phone*	
· · ·		

The constructor can call its superclass constructor and then store the extension. knowExtension just returns the value of extension. asDigits and asString can call upon their superclass methods to help them.

```
package phone;
public class BusinessPhone extends Phone
// Adds an extension to an object of class Phone
{
  private int extension;

  public BusinessPhone(int area, int number, int exten)
  {
    super(area, number);                      // Calls superclass constructor
    extension = exten;
  }

  // Knowledge methods
  public int knowExtension()
  {
    return extension;
  }

  public long asDigits()
  {
    long digits;
    digits = super.asDigits();                // Accesses superclass method
    return (long) (digits * 10000 + extension);
  }

  public String asString()
  {
    String string = super.asString();         // Accesses superclass method
    return (string + "-" + extension);
  }
}
```

Notice that the asDigits and asString methods of BusinessPhone override the instance methods of the same name in Phone. The new class inherits all of the fields and methods of Phone and then adds some of its own. The following program is a test driver that creates a Phone object and three BusinessPhone objects, and applies the methods from both classes to them:

```
import java.io.*;
import phone.*;
public class TestDrPhone
```

```
{
  public static void main(String[] args) throws IOException
  {
    Phone firstPhone;
    BusinessPhone secondPhone;
    BusinessPhone thirdPhone;
    BusinessPhone fourthPhone;
    PrintWriter outFile;
    outFile = new PrintWriter(new FileWriter("DrPhoneOut"));
    outFile.println("Test results for class Business Phone");
    firstPhone = new Phone(523, 3733344);
    secondPhone = new BusinessPhone(713, 2233121, 1234);
    thirdPhone = new BusinessPhone(523, 3733344, 1234);
    fourthPhone = new BusinessPhone(713, 2233121, 1234);
    outFile.println("knowAreaCode: " + firstPhone.knowAreaCode());
    outFile.println("knowDigits: " + firstPhone.knowDigits());
    outFile.println("asDigits: " + firstPhone.asDigits());
    outFile.println("asString: " + firstPhone.asString());
    outFile.println("knowAreaCode business: " +
      secondPhone.knowAreaCode());
    outFile.println("knowDigits business: " + secondPhone.knowDigits());
    outFile.println("asDigits business: " + secondPhone.asDigits());
    outFile.println("asString business: " + secondPhone.asString());
    if (secondPhone.equals(thirdPhone))
      outFile.println("two business phones are equal");
    else
      outFile.println("two business phones are not equal");
    if (firstPhone.equals(secondPhone))
      outFile.println("a phone and a business phone are equal");
    else
      outFile.println("a phone and a business phone are not equal");
    if (firstPhone.equals(thirdPhone))
      outFile.println("a phone and a business phone are equal");
    else
      outFile.println("a phone and a business phone are not equal");
    if ( secondPhone.equals(fourthPhone))
      outFile.println("two business phones are equal");
    else
      outFile.println("two business phones are not equal");
    outFile.close();
  }
}
```

Here are the results of file `DrPhoneOut`:

```
Test results for class BusinessPhone
knowAreaCode: 523
knowDigits: 3733344
asDigits: 5233733344
asString: 523-373-3344
knowAreaCode business: 713
knowDigits business: 2233121
asDigits business: 71322331211234
asString business: 713-223-3121-1234
two business phones are not equal
a phone and a business phone are not equal
a phone and a business phone are equal
two business phones are equal
```

Look carefully at this driver. The method `equals`, as defined in `Phone`, is applied to objects of both `Phone` and `BusinessPhone`. The methods `knowAreaCode` and `knowDigits`, as defined in `Phone`, are applied to objects of both `Phone` and `BusinessPhone`. The overridden methods `asDigits` and `asString` are applied to objects of both `Phone` and `BusinessPhone`, with the system determining which method is appropriate.

Before we move on to the input and output of objects, we would like to introduce one more technique. In Chapter 6, we mentioned that it is sometimes useful to create constructors that take an existing instance and use its contents to build a new instance. We use these *copy constructors* to illustrate the difference between shallow and deep copying of objects.

7.7 Copy Constructors

One way to simplify the creation of a new instance of an immutable object (one with no transformer methods) from an old instance is to provide a constructor that takes an existing object as a parameter. It may also have other parameters that provide values to substitute in creating the new object. Here's an example of the heading and documentation for such a constructor:

```
public SavingsAccount(SavingsAccount oldAcct, String address)
// oldAcct must contain valid account information.
// A SavingsAccount object is created with its contents
//    equal to those of the old account except that
//    the address is set equal to the address parameter.
```

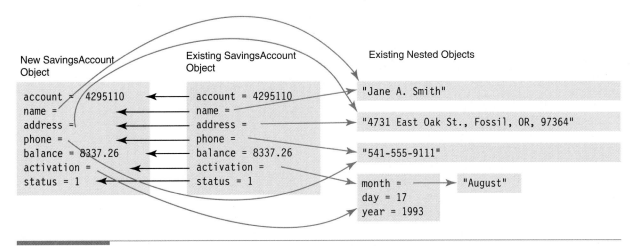

Figure 7.4 Shallow Copying

Here's an example of how it would be called, where oldAccount is an existing object of type SavingsAccount and address is a string that holds a new address value for the account:

```
account = new SavingsAccount(oldAccount, address);
```

The body of the constructor would copy every field from oldAccount to its own equivalent fields, substituting the value in its address parameter for the one in the address field of oldAccount. Note that if any of the fields in the object are themselves objects, we must use their observers to copy the actual values from the fields of the nested objects. Otherwise, the new object simply refers to the same places in memory as oldAccount.

This copy constructor is said to perform a deep copy of the object. A deep copy copies what a reference refers to, rather than the reference itself. A shallow copy ignores the presence of nested objects, treating them like fields of simple types. Figure 7.4 illustrates shallow copying, and Figure 7.5 shows deep copying. In both figures, the colored arrows indicate that a field is a reference type with an address that specifies another place in memory. The black arrows indicate copying of values.

Deep copy An operation that copies one class instance to another, using observer methods as necessary to eliminate nested references and copy only the simple types to which they refer; the result is that the two instances do not contain any duplicate references

Shallow copy An operation that copies a source class instance to a destination class instance, simply copying all references so that the destination instance contains duplicate references to values that are also referred to by the source

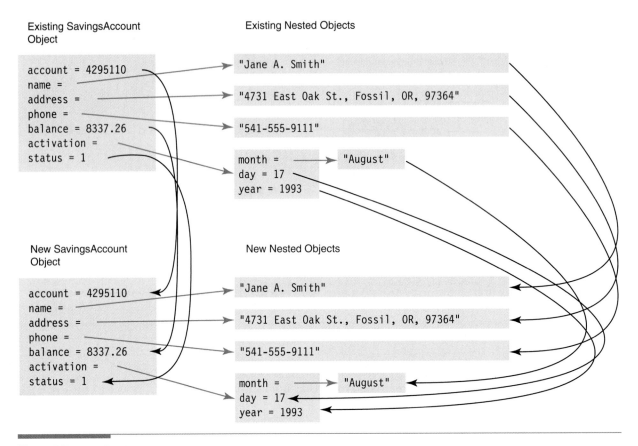

Figure 7.5 Deep Copying

7.8 Output and Input of Objects

The title of this section looks a bit strange. We usually talk about "input and output," not "output and input." However, if we are talking about objects, they cannot be created outside the application and read in. Rather, objects must be created in an application and then written to a file. Once they are on a file, we can read the data values back in and re-create the object. There are two ways to write and read objects. The first is to transform each data field of an object into a string and then output the strings individually. The reverse transformation is required to read in the strings representing data fields, convert them to the proper form, and store them in the object's fields. Transforming objects into strings and back again is a lot of work for the programmer. Fortunately, Java provides a way to save objects and read them back again without requiring all of this work. Saving an object with this approach is called *serializing* the object.

The basic unit of data in the `FileReader` and `FileWriter` classes is the character. The `BufferedReader` and `PrintWriter` classes include methods that make reading and writing strings easier, but the basic unit remains the character. Java provides two classes for which the object is the basic unit of data: `ObjectOutputStream` (derived from `OutputStream`) and `ObjectInputStream` (derived from `InputStream`). To write an object to a file, we use the `writeObject` method of the `ObjectOutputStream` class. To read objects from a file, we use the `readObject` method of the `ObjectInputStream` class.

How can this be? Java uses the Unicode character set; all the characters take up the same number of bits. Untold numbers of objects exist, whose structures vary in size and shape. Writing would seem to be easy, but how do we figure out how the bytes group when inputting the object? Fortunately, we don't have to know. One of the most important features in the java.io package is the ability to convert an object into a stream of bytes that can later be converted back into a copy of the original object. This translation from object to bytes is called serializing. The reverse translation is called deserializing. We do not need to understand how Java performs this conversion; we just have to know how to use this feature.

Serializing Translating an object into a stream of bytes

Deserializing Translating a serialized stream of bytes back into the original object

Let's examine the syntax and semantics of writing objects through the use of a pair of application programs. The first creates an object and writes it out; the second reads the object back in and writes it to the screen. Let's use the class Name from Chapter 4 for this example. Recall that Name has three data fields: `first`, `middle`, and `last`. To serialize objects of the class Name, we need to add the words `implements Serializable` beside the class name. Here is the documentation (a list of the methods) for Name to refresh your memory:

```
public class Name implements Serializable
// This class defines a name consisting of three parts
{
  // Constructors
  public Name() throws IOException
  public Name(String firstName, String lastName, String middleName)

  // Knowledge methods
  public String knowFirstName()
  public String knowMiddleName()
  public String knowLastName()

  // Additional observer methods that return a formatted name
  public String firstLast()
```

```
public String full()
public String lastFirstMI()

// Additional observer methods that compare an instance to another name
public boolean equals(Name otherName)
public int compareTo(Name otherName)
}
```

In Chapter 8 we explain the meaning of the implements clause in the class heading. For our purposes here it is sufficient to view it as a way of telling Java that objects of this class can be output and input using writeObject and readObject, respectively.

Our first application reads the data for the three fields from a file, instantiates a Name object, and then writes the Name object onto the second file. The second application reads the Name object and prints it.

```
import java.io.*;
import Name;

public class ObjectFileWrite
{

  public static void main(String[] args) throws IOException
  {
    ObjectOutputStream outObject;        // Output data file
    BufferedReader inFile;               // Input data file
    String first;
    String second;
    String last;
    Name person;

    // Prepare files
    inFile = new BufferedReader(new FileReader("infile.dat"));
    outObject =
      new ObjectOutputStream(new FileOutputStream("outObject.dat"));
    // Read names from the file
    first = new String(inFile.readLine());
    second = new String(inFile.readLine());
    last = new String(inFile.readLine());
    // Instantiate a person
    person = new Name(first, last, second);
    // Write out person
    outObject.writeObject(person);
    // Close files and quit
    outObject.close();
    inFile.close();
  }
}
```

Here is infile.dat:

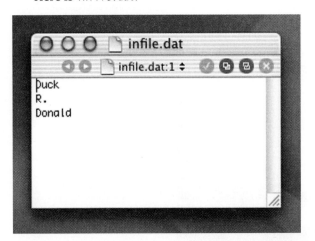

The application that reads the object back in and prints it is very straightforward. We apply readObject to the file of type ObjectInputStream, which returns an object of the class Object. Note that the object read from the file must be cast into a Name object before being assigned to the person variable. We use the methods of the class Name to access the fields so as to print them. We must also mention one more piece of syntax: readObject can throw a ClassNotFoundException. In Chapter 9, we show how to handle an exception, but for the moment we just add it to the *throws* clause of the main method.

```java
import java.io.*;
import Name;

public class ObjectFileRead
{
  public static void main(String[] args)
   throws IOException, ClassNotFoundException
  {
    ObjectInputStream inObject;       //Input file
    Name person;
    // Prepare file
    inObject = new ObjectInputStream(new FileInputStream("outObject.dat"));

    //Read Name object
    person = (Name)inObject.readObject();

    System.out.println(person.knowFirstName() + ' ' +
      person.knowMiddleName() + ' ' + person.knowLastName());
    inObject.close();
  }
}
```

Here is the screen output from the application `ObjectFileRead`:

You should note two additional points of syntax. The first is how the object files are instantiated:

```
inObject =
  new ObjectInputStream(new FileInputStream("outObject.dat"));
outObject =
  new ObjectOutputStream(new FileOutputStream("outObject.dat"));
```

This follows the pattern of `BufferedReader` and `PrintWriter`: `FileInputStream` and `FileOutputStream` objects are instantiated as arguments to the `ObjectInputStream` and `ObjectOutputStream` constructors.

The second thing to notice is that the input object has to be type cast back into a `Name` object. The object that is input is just a sequence of bits. We must indicate how to break up this sequence of bits into the proper fields by using the appropriate class name as a type cast.

```
person = (Name)inObject.readObject();
```

Now that we have seen the mechanics of implementing a derived class and discussed the method for designing a class interface, let's bring all the pieces together in a Case Study that illustrates the process.

EXTENDING THE ADDRESS BOOK

Problem: In Chapter 6, we created a file that contained a simplified version of a computerized address book. It was so successful, that we will now improve it in the following ways:

- Add a birthday to each entry.
- Replace the text file with an object file.

Brainstorming: Our problem statement implies that we should replace a `PrintWriter` object with an `ObjectOutputStream` object. We don't need to brainstorm about this change, but we do need to think about what is involved in representing a birthday. A birthday is a date, so we should have a month, day, and year. Do we need separate classes for month, day, and year? Because each can be represented by an integer, let's let month, day, and year just be fields in the Birthday class.

Do we really need a year field? It isn't polite to ask people how old they are, but there is no harm in having a year. If we don't know the year, we can just substitute a value that represents "not known."

Determining Responsibilities: Because we may be creating an entry without knowing what the birthday is, we need a nonparameterized constructor that sets all the values to "not known."

What type of scenarios can we imagine for our Birthday class? Certainly, Entry will send a message to Birthday asking for a copy, so "Know birthday" must be a responsibility. What else might Entry request of Birthday? Perhaps Entry might want to know if Birthday is within a certain time period of a date. This task implies that the birthday can be compared to another date.

We have called this class Birthday because that is its role in our Entry class. However, it is really just a general date class. We should use Birthday as the field name in Entry, but Date as the name of the class. Here, then, is the CRC card for the Date class:

Class Name: Date	Superclass:	Subclasses:
Responsibilities	**Collaborations**	
Create (month, day, year)	None	
Create ( )	None	
Know month return int	None	
Know day return int	None	
Know year return int	None	
Compare (other date) return int	None	

Notice that we made some assumptions when summarizing this class in a CRC card. We assumed that the month, day, and year were kept—or at least returned—as integers. If we implement the Date class ourselves, we might want to rethink an integer representation for these fields. But before we spend any time writing this class ourselves, we should look in the Java library. Surely, a date is such a common object that a Date class must already exist.

Library Search[1]:   Let's begin by looking for a Date class in the Java Class Library. A Date class sounds like it might be categorized as a utility, so we look there first. Success right off the bat: The class Date is a member of the java.util package. A quick scan of the methods shows that they include appropriate constructors, knowledge methods, and a compareTo method. However, the parameterized constructor and the knowledge methods are marked deprecated. "Deprecated" means that they will not be supported in future language releases. In the case of the Date methods, they are deprecated in favor of the methods in the Calendar class. So on we go to the Calendar class specification.

The class Calendar is also part of the java.util package. However, it is an abstract class; that is, some of its methods are marked abstract. Does this mean that we have to derive a class from Calendar and fill in the missing code? Maybe, but perhaps the package already offers a derived class. Yes, GregorianCalendar is listed as a subclass of Calendar. Does the combination of the concrete methods in both of these classes give us what we need? GregorianCalendar has both a parameterized and a nonparameterized constructor. It does not provide a comparison method per se, but there are Boolean methods after and before. A further examination of the documentation for these two classes shows that they provide a wide variety of class constants and operations to set and manipulate not only dates down to minutes and seconds, but also time zones.

In our problem, is it appropriate to use the class GregorianCalendar or should we build a simple Date class ourselves? We use GregorianCalendar in this Case Study and ask you to implement a new Date class in the Case Study Follow-Up exercises.

We have not yet mentioned the driver class that must read in the entries written in Chapter 6, prompt for and read the birthday, and then write out the expanded entry. *Oops!* We have forgotten that an entry as input has only three fields, but an entry that is written out now has four fields. We must derive a new class from Entry that includes the Birthday field. We can read each entry from the file and store the values into the derived class. Because we plan to write the entries as objects, we need to overload the writeToFile method. We had better summarize these observations in CRC cards.

---

[1]A listing of the Java libraries can be found in many reference books as well as on Sun's Web site.

Class Name: *EntryPlus*	Superclass: *Entry*		Subclasses:
Responsibilities		**Collaborations**	
Create (name, address, phone, date)		Name, Address, Phone, Date	
Create ( )		Name, Address, Phone, Date	
Know birthday return Date			
Write to file (outfile)		ObjectOutputStream	

Class Name: *PlusDriver*	Superclass:		Subclasses:
Responsibilities		**Collaborations**	
Prepare input files		BufferedReader	
Prepare output files		ObjectOutputStream	
Process entries		EntryPlus, Name, Address, Phone, Date	
Close files		BufferedReader ObjectOutputStream	

Responsibility Algorithms: The only responsibility that needs expanding is "Process entries". We must read the entries back in, prompt for and read a birthday, and write out the Entry object. Because we wrote the file one string per line, reading the data back in is easy. Once we have an object of the class EntryPlus, we can write it to a new file using ObjectOutputStream.

```
Process Entries
while more entries
Get an entry
Get birthday
entryPlus = new EntryPlus(Name, Address, Phone, Date)
Write entry on outFile
```

```
Get an Entry
Get Name object
Get Address object
Get Phone object
```

Get Birthday

```
Write "Enter the birthday for " + name.full()
Write "Month: "
Read and convert month to int
Write "Day: "
Read and convert day to int
Write "Year: "
Read and convert year to int
```

"Get Name object", "Get Address object", and "Get Phone object" were previously developed in Chapter 6. The only difference is that we are reading these objects from a file rather than from the keyboard, so we don't need prompts.

```java
//**********************************************************
// This class extends the Entry class with a date field.
// Method writeToFile overloads the method in the superclass.
//**********************************************************

package addressBook;
import java.util.*;
import java.io.*;
public class EntryPlus extends Entry implements Serializable
{
  private GregorianCalendar birthday;
  public EntryPlus(Name newName, Address newAddress, Phone phoneNumber,
    GregorianCalendar date)
  {
    super(newName, newAddress, phoneNumber);
    birthday = date;
  }
  // Knowledge method
  public GregorianCalendar knowBirthday()
  {
    return birthday;
  }
  public void writeToFile(ObjectOutputStream outObject) throws IOException
  {
    // The EntryPlus object is written to a file of objects
    outObject.writeObject(this);
  }
}
```

```
//****************************************************************
// This class is a driver that creates entries made up of a
// name, an address, a phone number, and a date.  The name, address,
// and phone number are read from a file.  The birthday is read
// from the screen.  Each entry is written to a file of EntryPlus
// objects.
//****************************************************************

import java.io.*;
import java.util.*;
import addressBook.*;
public class PlusDriver
{
  public static void main(String[] args) throws IOException
  {
    // Declare instance variables
    Name name;
    Address address;
    Phone phone;
    EntryPlus entry;
    GregorianCalendar birthday;
    // String and integer variables used for input
    String first, last, middle, street, city, state, zip;
    int areaCode, number, month, day, year;

    // Set up input files including screen
    BufferedReader inFile;
    inFile = new BufferedReader(new FileReader("Entries"));

    BufferedReader in;                        // To input birthday
    // Instantiate in using System.in
    in = new BufferedReader(new InputStreamReader(System.in));

    // Set up output file of objects
    ObjectOutputStream outObject;
    outObject =
      new ObjectOutputStream(new FileOutputStream("EntryObjects"));

    first = inFile.readLine();                // Read in first name
    while (first != null)
    {
```

```
        // Read in rest of name
        last = inFile.readLine();
        middle = inFile.readLine();
        name = new Name(first, last, middle);

        // Read in address
        street = inFile.readLine();
        city = inFile.readLine();
        state = inFile.readLine();
        zip = inFile.readLine();
        address = new Address(street, city, state, zip);

        // Read in phone number
        areaCode = Integer.parseInt(inFile.readLine());
        number = Integer.parseInt(inFile.readLine());
        phone = new Phone(areaCode, number);

        // Prompt for and read in birthday
        System.out.println("Enter the birthday for " + name.full()
          + " as integers.");
        System.out.println("Month: ");
        month = Integer.parseInt(in.readLine());
        System.out.println("Day: ");
        day = Integer.parseInt(in.readLine());
        System.out.println("Year: ");
        year = Integer.parseInt(in.readLine());
        birthday = new GregorianCalendar(month, day, year);

        // Instantiate and output entry
        entry = new EntryPlus(name, address, phone, birthday);
        entry.writeToFile(outObject);

        first = inFile.readLine();
    }
    outObject.close();
    inFile.close();
  }
}
```

7.9 Testing and Debugging

Testing and Debugging Hints

1. Study the entire hierarchy for a class before you try to use or extend it. Watch out for cases of overriding and hiding that change the semantics of a class member.

2. An `abstract` class cannot be instantiated as an object; instead, a derived class must be written to extend it.

3. Overriding applies to instance methods; hiding applies to class methods. You cannot hide an instance method with a class method or override a class method with an instance method. However, Java does allow `static` and instance fields to hide each other.

4. When you write a class that extends a superclass, make sure that the compilation unit (program or package) imports the superclass if it isn't one of the standard ones that is always imported.

5. The access modifiers for a method that overrides or hides a method in a superclass must grant the same level of access or greater. The most restrictive form of access is `private`, then package, then `protected`, then `public`. You can override a `private` method with a `public` one, but you can't use `private` to override a `public` method.

6. Make sure that the first statement of every constructor is a call to one of the superclass constructors. If you omit the call, Java automatically inserts a call to `super()`.

7. Overloading a method requires that the two methods have different signatures. The signature is the name of the method plus the types of its parameters in a specific order. The return type and modifiers are not part of the signature.

8. Use `super` to access fields or methods of a superclass that have been hidden or overridden by a derived class.

9. Use `this` to access instance fields that have been hidden by a local declaration.

10. Thoroughly document the interface of a class to facilitate its proper use, ensure its correct design, and simplify testing.

11. If you use any file I/O, remember that `main` must have the `throws IOException` clause appended to its heading.

12. The constructors for arguments to the `ObjectInputStream` and `ObjectOutputStream` are instances of `FileInputStream` and `FileOutputStream`, respectively.

13. For instances of a class to be written on a file, the class must implement the `Serializable` interface.

14. When an instance of a class is read from a file, the object must be type cast back into its original class. For this reason, the `main` method of an application that uses the method `readObject` must include `ClassNotFoundException` in its *throws* clause.

Learning Portfolio

Summary

Object-oriented languages such as Java organize class data types into a hierarchy. At the top of Java's hierarchy is a class called `Object` that provides a few basic operations. Using inheritance, other classes extend `Object` and are said to be derived from it. Derived classes inherit all of the `public` and `protected` fields and methods of their superclass, except for its constructors. We must explore the entire inheritance hierarchy for a class to determine its full interface.

Instance methods can override superclass instance methods, and class methods and fields can hide superclass class methods and fields. Overriding and hiding enable us to change the meaning of a method or field when extending a superclass with a derived class. In this way, the derived class can retain the same form of interface, but operate in a different manner.

Constructors are not inherited by derived classes. The first statement in a constructor must be a call to a constructor for the superclass. Otherwise, Java will automatically insert such a call to the default constructor for the superclass.

Java allows us to declare multiple methods with the same name as long as they have different signatures. The method name is then said to be overloaded. The signature consists of the method name plus the types of its parameters in a particular order. The return type and modifiers are not part of the signature. Java determines which version of an overloaded method to call by examining the types in the argument list and selecting the method with the matching parameter list.

Sometimes we need to access a method or field in a superclass that has been overridden or hidden. We can use the `super` keyword to refer to the superclass version of a field or method instead of the local version. Similarly, a method can define a local variable or parameter with the same name as a field in the class; we can then use `this` to refer to the instance version instead of the local version.

Scope rules determine the range of code that has access to an identifier. Internal scope rules specify where class members can be accessed within a class. In Java, members can be used anywhere within a class, with two exceptions: Class variables must be defined before they are used to initialize other variables, and local variables can shadow class variables (name precedence).

External scope rules specify where a member can be accessed outside of a class. Java provides four levels of external access. The default level is package, which extends access to all classes in the same package. With `protected` access, derived classes can access a member as well. A member with `public` access can be used by any code that imports the class. The `private` access level restricts access to only the class containing the member.

In this chapter, we learned how to declare derived classes. The advantage of a derived class is that we can use the interface from the superclass as the model for our design. We benefit from inheriting many fields and methods that give our derived class powerful capabilities with no extra work on our part. In some cases, however, a new object is sufficiently different from anything that exists in the standard hierarchy that we have to design it from the ground up. Now that you know how to design and implement both derived classes and top-level classes, you are prepared to explore a wide range of useful and general abstractions that computer scientists have identified as fundamental to the development of more advanced algorithms. The remainder of this text primarily examines some of these abstractions and their implementation.

Objects can be written to and read from a file. They can be written on a file of the class `ObjectOutputStream` and read from a file of the class `ObjectInputStream`. Only objects of classes that implement the `Serializable` interface can be written on object files. Object files are used when the output from one application is used as input into another application.

Quick Check

1. What is the most general class in Java? (p. 332)
2. What is the mechanism that allows one class to extend another class? (pp. 328–333)
3. What do you call a class that is an extension of another class in the hierarchy? (p. 330)
4. Overriding refers to _____ methods; hiding refers to fields and _____ methods. (p. 336)
5. What kinds of members are *not* inherited by a derived class? (pp. 333–336)
6. What is an operation that has multiple meanings depending on the object to which it is applied? (p. 337)
7. Are constructors inherited? (pp. 333–336)
8. A reference to an instance of a _____ class can be assigned to a variable of its _____ class. (p. 332)
9. Explain the meaning of the keyword `extends`. (p. 337)

10. What do we call the rules that determine where in a program an identifier can be recognized? (p. 339)

11. What keyword refers to a class's superclass? (p. 349)

12. What keyword allows an object to refer to itself? (pp. 341–342)

13. What is the name of the file class that outputs objects? (pp. 354–358)

14. What is the name of the file class that inputs objects? (pp. 354–358)

Answers

1. Object 2. Inheritance 3. Derived class 4. instance; class 5. private 6. Polymorphic operation 7. Class constructors are not inherited. 8. derived; super 9. extends tells the compiler the class from which this class is being derived. 10. Scope rules 11. super 12. this 13. ObjectOutputStream 14. ObjectInputStream

Exam Preparation Exercises

1. a. Name two kinds of scope.
   b. Do both internal and external scope depend on the access modifiers of an identifier?
   c. Define internal scope.
   d. What are the two exceptions that apply to internal access of members?
   e. What is shadowing?
   f. Is it legal to define local variables with the same identifier in nested blocks?

2. Name the three external places from which Java allows class members to be accessed.

3. a. List the four levels of access for class members.
   b. Which of the four levels is the default access?
   c. From where can a public member be accessed?
   d. From where can a member with no access modifier be accessed?
   e. From where can a private member be accessed?
   f. From where can a protected member be accessed?

4. a. What nonpublic members should be part of the inheritance interface?
   b. How do you make them part of the inheritance interface?

5. What happens if we forget to include a constructor in a new class?

6. a. Distinguish between a deep copy and a shallow copy.
   b. Under what conditions are a deep copy and a shallow copy the same?

7. To which class can all Java objects trace themselves back?

8. What modifier of a class or field indicates that it is incomplete?

9. What does the inheritance mechanism allow one class to acquire from another?

10. What do you call the class that is extended by a derived class?

11. When we examine a derived class, we have access to more than just the methods and fields defined in the class. Explain.

12. What happens if a derived class defines an instance method with the same form of heading as a method in its superclass?

13. What happens if a derived class defines a data field with the same name as a data field in the superclass?

14. Distinguish between overriding and hiding.

15. Is it possible to remove a member that is inherited?

16. Overloading, overriding, and hiding are similar, yet different. Fill in the following table showing whether the sentence describes overloading, overriding, or hiding.

Situation	Hiding	Overriding	Overloading	Shadowing
a. A class method has the same name and signature as a superclass method.				
b. An instance method has the same name and signature as a superclass instance method.				
c. A class has two methods with the same name but different signatures.				
d. A field in a derived class has the same name as a field in its superclass.				
e. An instance method has the same name but a different signature than a superclass instance method.				
f. A method declares a variable with the same name as a field in the class.				
g. A method has a parameter with the same name as a field in the class.				

17. What parts of a superclass's interface cannot be inherited?

18. Can an object file be written with a text editor? Explain.

19. Why does an object read from an object file have to be type cast back into its original class?

Programming Warm-Up Exercises

1. Declare three constructors for the class `MyClass`.

2. Fill in the blanks in the documentation in the following code segment.

```
public class MyName extends YourName
{
  int myField;                      // myField is an _____field.

  public MyName(int myField)        // _____ with a parameter
                                    // that shadows the _____ _____
  {
    this.myField = myField;         // Assign the _____ to
                                    // the _____ field.
  }
}
```

3. a. How does the syntax of a constructor differ from that of a method?
   b. How is a constructor invoked?
   c. How many constructors can a class have?
   d. What is the signature of a method?
   e. What happens if a class does not have a constructor?
   f. What must be the first statement in every constructor?

4. a. Declare a `public` class `SomeClass`.
   b. Write the heading for a `public` class method `someMethod`.
   c. Write the heading for an integer class method `someMethod` that should be accessible to the classes in the package but not to derived classes.
   d. Write the heading for an integer class method `someMethod` that should be accessible only to other methods in the class.
   e. Write the heading for a character class method `someMethod` that should be accessible to classes in the package and any derived classes.

5. a. Write the heading for a public method `someMethod`.
   b. Write the heading for an integer method `someMethod` that should be accessible to the classes in the package but not to derived classes.
   c. Write the heading for an integer method `someMethod` that should be accessible only to other methods in the class.

Learning Portfolio

6. Is the following code segment correct? If so, to what does each reference to var refer?

```java
public class SomeClass
{
  int var;                        // Class member var
  final int CONST = 3;            // Class member CONST
  public void someMethod(int param)
  {
    int var;
    var = param * CONST;
    final int CONST = 10;
      var = 5;
      System.out.println("" + this.var);
  }
}
```

7. Examine the following constructor headings and give the signature for each.

```java
public someClass()
public someClass(int a)
public someClass(double a)
public someClass(String a, int b, double c)
```

8. Examine the following method headings and give the signature for each. Could methods with these signatures all be declared within one class?

```java
public int someMethod()
public void someMethod()
public double someMethod()
public double someMethod(int a)
public double someMethod(String a)
public double someMethod(int a, int b)
```

9. Are these code segments correct? If not, why not?

a. `public double taxRate = 29.3;`
   `public double myRate = taxRate*1.1;`

b. `public double myRate = taxRate*1.1;`
   `public double taxRate = 29.3;`

10. **a.** Write the statement that declares a variable outFile, instantiates an object of the class ObjectOutputStream and assigns its address to outFile.

  b. Write the statement that writes myName, an instance of the class Name, on outFile.

  c. Write the statement that declares a variable inFile, instantiates an object of class ObjectInputStream, and assigns its address to inFile.

  d. Write the statement that reads myName, an instance of the class Name from inFile.

Programming Problem

1. Take the CRC cards used to design the Address hierarchy and complete the design and implementation of a package that contains the five classes. Design and implement a test plan for the package.

Case Study Follow-Up

1. Write an application that reads the file of objects and prints the names to the screen.

2. Write an application that reads the file of objects and prints the names and addresses in a text file in the format that is usually used for addresses. We discussed this format in Chapter 6 when we first developed the AddressBook class, but chose not to implement it because we wanted to simplify reading of the file. Now that we can write and read objects, this is no longer a concern, but it would be useful to be able to view a file with all of our entries in an easy-to-read form.

3. Design and implement a Date class that could be substituted for class GregorianCalendar in the Case Study.

Event-Driven Input and Output

goals

Knowledge Goals
- To understand the relationship of a JFrame to its content pane and the objects it contains
- To understand the Java event-handling model
- To learn the different parts of an event loop
- To understand how an event handler can receive events from multiple sources

Skill Goals
To be able to:
- Construct a code segment that creates a JFrame window on the screen
- Use a JLabel object to display a message in a JFrame on the screen
- Use a layout manager to organize labels in a window
- Write an event handler for a single button
- Register an event handler with a button
- Write an event loop using a button
- Use a JTextField to input a value
- Group user interface objects together with a JPanel
- Write an event handler that distinguishes among multiple event sources

timeline

introduction

Until now, we've used simplified screen input and output to simulate the old-fashioned printer and keyboard interface of early computers. From your use of computers, you're probably more familiar with the modern graphical user interface (GUI) based on windows. Although the GUI makes it much easier for people to use programs, it requires more work on the part of the programmer. Many older programming languages lack specific support for GUI programming and rely primarily on the style of I/O that we introduced in Chapter 2. But because Java was developed after the GUI became the standard mechanism for interactive input and output, it includes built-in features that simplify the programming of a user interface.

Java provides many different types of windows and interface components. In fact, entire books have been written just to explain all of the user interface features that Java supports. In this text, we use a very simple but adequate subset of Java's capabilities.

1970

The mobile robot Shakey uses artificial intelligence in its navigation

1970

Dennis Ritchie and Kenneth Thompson at Bell Labs develop the UNIX operating system for which they later received the U.S. National Medal of Technology

1970

IBM introduces the 8 inch floppy disk

1971

A team at Intel creates the first microprocessor, the Intel 4004

1971

Ray Tomlinson uses the @ sign, and sends the first electronic-mail message through ARPANET

1971

The programming language Pascal is developed by Niklaus Wirth

8.1 Frames

The type of window that we use in this text is called a *frame*, and it is implemented in Java by a class called JFrame. A frame has all of the features that you are used to seeing in a window on a personal computer: the ability to change size, to be closed, to be turned into an icon (a small pictorial representation of the window), and so on.

Our example applications won't support all the features of a JFrame. Instead, we focus on those features that illustrate the essential concepts of GUI programming. Supporting extra features would make our code longer, and the extra code won't illustrate new principles but just add more of the same kinds of method calls. Once you understand the underlying concepts of the GUI, you can easily read the class documentation and add support for more window features as you wish.

To use a frame for output in Java, our code must perform four steps:

1. Import classes and declare fields.
2. Instantiate frame objects and specify some of their properties.
3. Put display objects into the frame.
4. Make the frame visible on the screen.

■ Import Classes and Declare Fields

The first of these steps breaks down into three parts.

1. Import the package containing the JFrame class.
2. Declare a variable of the class JFrame.
3. Declare a variable of the class Container.

The JFrame class is contained in the swing package within a larger package called javax. So we write the following import statement:

```
import javax.swing.*;   // Supplies JFrame class for output display
```

We need to declare both a JFrame variable and a Container variable. Here's why. A JFrame object has two parts. The window frame contains the "close" button and other components. The content pane represents the main area inside the frame where we place information to be displayed. (See Figure 8.1.) The content pane is an object of the class Container, so we must provide a variable of this class so that we can refer directly to it.

Suppose that our JFrame is to be called outputFrame and we want to refer to its content pane as outputPane. Then we would write the following declarations:

```
JFrame outputFrame;       // Declare a variable of class JFrame
Container outputPane;      // Declare a variable of class Container
```

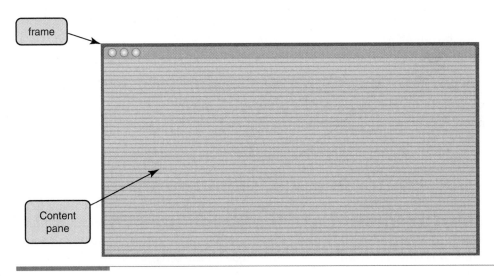

frame

Content pane

Figure 8.1 A Frame and Its Content Pane

■ Instantiate Frame Objects and Specify Some of Their Properties

The second step in using a frame has five parts.

1. Instantiate a JFrame object.
2. Ask the JFrame object to return a content pane object whose address we assign to the Container variable.
3. Specify the action to take when the window is closed.
4. Specify the size of the JFrame object (adjust its size to fit the output).
5. Specify a layout manager for the content pane object.

So far, we have imported the JFrame class and declared a variable of the class JFrame. Like any other variable, the variable called outputFrame remains empty until we assign it a value. What sort of value do we assign to a JFrame variable? The answer to this question is both trivial and deep: We assign it the address of a JFrame object. The answer is trivial because it seems so obvious, like the answer to the question, "Who is buried in Grant's tomb?" In practice, it is really that simple. We just write the following assignment statement:

```
outputFrame = new JFrame();
```

Java then instantiates an object of the class JFrame and assigns its address to outputFrame. The answer to our question is deep because the actual contents of a JFrame object are quite complex. We could read a biography of President Grant as one way of knowing who is buried in his tomb. Likewise, we could read all of the source code in the swing package to learn how JFrame objects work. Fortunately, Java makes it unnecessary for us to do this by relying on the principle of abstraction: We don't have to understand what makes JFrame objects work to use them.

Get a Content Pane   As we've just seen, the JFrame that is referenced by outputFrame consists of two parts: a window frame and a content pane. Rather than instantiate a new content pane object, we merely ask the JFrame to give us the one that was created within it automatically when we instantiated the JFrame. We send this request to the JFrame by calling one of its methods:

```
outputPane = outputFrame.getContentPane();
```

The content pane referenced by outputPane is an empty window that is waiting to be filled and then shown on the screen. Before we can do so, we need to specify some additional properties of the frame and content pane. For the frame, we need to indicate what should happen when it is closed and what its size should be on the screen. For the content pane, we need to indicate how elements should be arranged within it.

Specify the Action to Take When the Frame Is Closed   Specifying what should happen when the frame is closed by the user is done through a call to an instance method associated with the frame. This method is named setDefaultCloseOperation. We pass it an argument indicating the action that the frame should perform. The JFrame class provides several named class constants that are allowed as arguments to this method. We created class constants and used them in a similar fashion in our Student class in Chapter 4.

The only one of these actions that is appropriate for our programs is to exit the program (end execution and remove the frame from the screen). The constant for this action is called EXIT_ON_CLOSE. Because this constant is associated with the JFrame class, we must write it with the class name, separated by a period, as shown here within the parentheses:

```
outputFrame.setDefaultCloseOperation(JFrame.EXIT_ON_CLOSE);
```

Specify the Size of the Frame   We set the size of the frame by calling another instance method, named setSize. This method takes two arguments that are integer numbers. The first is the width of the frame and the second is its height. The sizes are specified in **pixels**. A typical display screen is 1,024 pixels wide by 768 pixels high, so you need to choose numbers that produce a frame that fits on the screen in a reasonable manner, with room for all of the information that it displays. Here is an example call, which sets the size of the frame to be 300 pixels wide and 200 pixels high:

Pixels   An abbreviation of "picture elements"; the individual dots that make up an image on a display screen

```
outputFrame.setSize(300, 200);
```

Specify a Layout Manager   We fill the content pane by adding display elements to it. How does Java know where the elements should be positioned within the pane? We can either tell it manually or let Java handle their layout automatically. Manual placement of elements allows us to precisely control the appearance of output within the pane, but requires us to tediously compute the coordinates of each element within the pane and specify them in our code. We will take the simpler approach of letting Java handle the layout automatically.

Because Java provides several different styles of automatic layout, we have to indicate which one to use. The style of layout is determined by specifying the name of a **layout manager** through a method associated with outputPane. This method is called setLayout.

> **Layout manager** A class that automatically manages the placement of display elements within a content pane on the screen

The setLayout method that we apply to outputPane takes one argument, a layout manager object. A layout manager is another of Java's classes that we instantiate with the use of new, just as we did to create a new JFrame object. Let's use the simplest of Java's layout managers, FlowLayout. A call to setLayout is written as follows:

```
outputPane.setLayout(new FlowLayout());
```

The FlowLayout manager's responsibility is to automatically place elements that we add to a content pane in the order that we add them. The first element goes in the upper-left corner of the window, and the next element goes to the right of it on the same line. When no more room is left on a line, the manager moves to the next line in the window and continues adding elements there. One other bit of housekeeping that we need to perform relates to the fact that the layout managers we use belong to another package, called awt. Thus, we need to import awt along with swing. The awt package is part of the java master package, as you can see from the declarations below.

Let's review the steps we have taken so far with an example code segment.

```
import java.awt.*;              // Supplies layout manager
import javax.swing.*;          // Supplies JFrame class for output display
...
JFrame outputFrame;            // Declare a variable of class JFrame
Container outputPane;          // Declare a container variable
outputFrame = new JFrame();    // Create a new JFrame object
// Get content pane
outputPane = outputFrame.getContentPane();
// Set the action to take on closing
outputFrame.setDefaultCloseOperation(JFrame.EXIT_ON_CLOSE);
// Set the size of the frame
outputFrame.setSize(300, 200);
// Apply setLayout method to outputPane;
// an object of class FlowLayout is an argument
outputPane.setLayout(new FlowLayout());
```

Notice in this example that, as we have seen in previous chapters, we can instantiate an object within an argument list. The argument of setLayout is an object of the class FlowLayout. We use new to create an instance of FlowLayout in the argument list:

```
outputPane.setLayout(new FlowLayout());
```

◼ Add Output to the Content Pane

We have now taken care of all of the steps needed to create a content pane that is ready to receive information to display. A content pane is called a container class because we can add elements into it. Java supports various specialized container classes in addition to `Container`.

Initially, we add only elements called *labels* to our panes. A label is a block of text that is placed into the pane. We add the label to the pane using the `add` instance method. Here is an example:

```
outputPane.add(new JLabel("This is the text in the label."));
```

Note that we are instantiating an anonymous object of the class `JLabel`, within the argument list. The `add` method places this new object into the pane. We could also declare a variable to be of class `JLabel`, assign it a value, and pass the variable as an argument to `add`:

```
JLabel newLabel;
newLabel = new JLabel("This is the text in the label.");
outputPane.add(newLabel);
```

Once again, because of Java's use of abstraction, we don't need to know the details of what a `JLabel` object contains. We simply accept that it has been properly defined in the Java library, and that the `add` method uses it appropriately.

◼ Make the Frame Visible on the Screen

The only step that remains to cause our frame to be displayed on the screen is to make it visible. We do this with a method call associated with the frame:

```
outputFrame.setVisible(true);
```

As you can see by the way that the call is written, it is an instance method. If we later call this method with the argument `false`, the frame will disappear from the screen.

Now let's put all the pieces together so that we can see their relationship to each other. Our list of steps is repeated here as comments in the code.

```
// Import classes
import java.awt.*;          // Supplies layout manager
import javax.swing.*;       // Supplies JFrame class for output display

public class frameExample ...
...
  public static void main(String[] args)
  {
    // Declare a variable of class JFrame
    JFrame outputFrame;
```

```
// Declare a variable of class Container
Container outputPane;

final String WORDS = "Programming and Problem Solving with Java";
...
// Instantiate a JFrame object
outputFrame = new JFrame();
// Ask the JFrame object to return a content pane Container object
outputPane = outputFrame.getContentPane();
// Specify the action to take when the window is closed
outputFrame.setDefaultCloseOperation(JFrame.EXIT_ON_CLOSE);
// Specify the size of the JFrame object
outputFrame.setSize(300, 200);
// Specify a layout manager for the content pane object
outputPane.setLayout(new FlowLayout());
// Add output to the content pane object
outputPane.add(new JLabel("The title of this book is "));
outputPane.add(new JLabel("Introduction to " + WORDS));
// Make the JFrame object visible on the screen
outputFrame.setVisible(true);
  ...
```

The ellipses (...) in this code segment indicate pieces of the Java application that are yet to be filled in. Let's now put all these steps together into a class. We can redo the program from Chapter 2 that prints a name in two formats, but use a window that the program constructs rather than System.out. Thus far, we have not seen how to input values from a window, so we just supply a name as a series of constants. If you turn back to page 71, you can compare the differences between this version and our earlier version.

```
//*****************************************************************
// PrintName application
// This application prints a name in two different formats
//*****************************************************************
import java.awt.*;        // Supplies layout manager
import javax.swing.*;     // Supplies JFrame class for output display
public class PrintName
{
  public static void main(String[] args)
  {
    final String FIRST  = "Herman";     // Person's first name
    final String LAST   = "Herrmann";   // Person's last name
    final char   MIDDLE = 'G';          // Person's middle initial
    JFrame outputFrame;                 // Declare JFrame variable
    Container outputPane;               // Declare Container variable
    String firstLast;                   // Name in first-last format
    String lastFirst;                   // Name in last-first format
```

```
// Create a JFrame object
outputFrame = new JFrame();
// Ask the JFrame object to return a content pane Container object
outputPane = outputFrame.getContentPane();
// Specify the action to take when the window is closed
outputFrame.setDefaultCloseOperation(JFrame.EXIT_ON_CLOSE);
// Specify the size of the JFrame object
outputFrame.setSize(300, 200);
// Specify a layout manager for the content pane object
outputPane.setLayout(new FlowLayout());
// Add output to the content pane
// Display name in first-last format
firstLast = FIRST + " " + LAST;
outputPane.add (new JLabel("Name in first-last format is "
    + firstLast));
// Display name in last-first-middle format
lastFirst = LAST + ", " + FIRST + ", ";
outputPane.add(new JLabel("Name in last-first-initial format is "
    + lastFirst + MIDDLE + "."));
// Make the JFrame object visible on the screen
outputFrame.setVisible(true);
  }
}
```

8.2 Formatting Output

To format a program's output means to control how it appears visually on the screen. In the last section, we used the layout manager called FlowLayout to arrange our output. In this section, we introduce another layout manager, called GridLayout, and examine how to format the output values themselves.

■ Using GridLayout for Tabular Output

We introduced FlowLayout as the simplest of Java's layout managers. The advantage of FlowLayout is that it entirely manages the placement of labels as we add them to a pane. While this simplicity is convenient, it prevents us from controlling the appearance of output on the screen. We do not have the option of telling FlowLayout to place output values on separate lines. If we use the GridLayout manager, however, we gain the ability to control the position of a label with respect to others in the pane.

GridLayout works much the same as FlowLayout in that we simply add labels to the pane, and the layout manager places them consecutively into the available space. The difference is that GridLayout partitions the pane into a fixed number of rows and columns—a rectangular grid. Starting with the top row and the leftmost column, GridLayout fills successive columns, moving to the next row when it has filled every column on the row. Every column

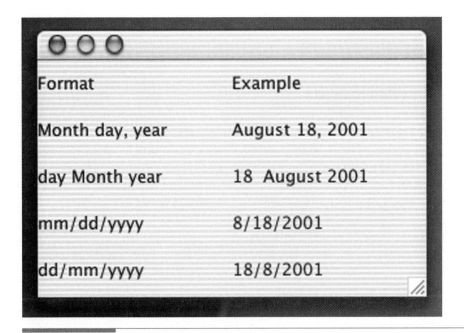

Format	Example
Month day, year	August 18, 2001
day Month year	18 August 2001
mm/dd/yyyy	8/18/2001
dd/mm/yyyy	18/8/2001

Figure 8.2   A Grid Layout with Five Rows and Two Columns

is the same size as every other column, and the rows are also equal in size. Figure 8.2 shows a frame with a 5 × 2 grid.

When we specify GridLayout as the manager for the content pane, we provide the constructor with a pair of integer arguments that determine the number of rows and columns in the pane. If one of the arguments is zero, then that dimension isn't specified and the grid grows as needed in that direction to accommodate the contents of the pane. The first argument is the number of rows and the second argument is the number of columns.

For example, the layout in Figure 8.2 is specified with a method call to setLayout.

```
datePane.setLayout(new GridLayout(5,2));   // 5 rows and 2 columns
```

If we wanted the datePane content pane to have two columns and an arbitrary number of rows, we would write the call with the first argument to the GridLayout constructor being zero:

```
datePane.setLayout(new GridLayout(0,2));   // Any number of rows of 2 columns
```

Using zero for the number of columns (the second argument) would allow GridLayout to partition the pane into any number of columns. The number it chooses depends on the size of the largest label (as all columns are equal in size) and the number of these labels that can fit horizontally on the screen. Because this setup could lead to some rather strange column configurations, it is more common for the user to specify the number of columns. GridLayout is typically used to display a table of values, often with a text label at the top of each column (called a *column heading*) that explains what the column contains. Figure 8.2 uses the column headings "Format" and "Example."

Alignment of Text Within JLabels

By default, the text within a label begins at the left edge of the label. Sometimes, however, we want to center the text within the label or have it appear as far to the right as possible within the label. Java allows us to do so by providing a second argument when calling the JLabel constructor. This argument can be any of three predefined class constants provided by the JLabel class: `JLabel.LEFT`, `JLabel.CENTER`, or `JLabel.RIGHT`. For example, if we want the column heading "Format" in Figure 8.2 to be centered, we would write

```
datePane.add(new Label("Format", JLabel.CENTER));
```

If instead we write

```
datePane.add(new Label("Format", JLabel.RIGHT));
```

then the text would be positioned as far to the right as possible within the label. Because the usual position for text is toward the left, we rarely need to use `JLabel.LEFT`. Figure 8.3 shows the result of centering the headings from the example in Figure 8.2.

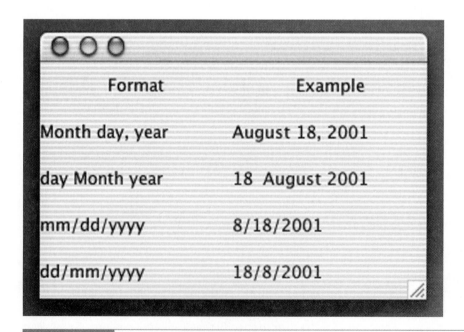

Figure 8.3 A Grid with Centered Headings in the First Row

8.3 Event Handling

Recall from Chapter 1 that one of Java's control structures is asynchronous control. A mouse click is an action that can trigger the application to perform a set of instructions at any time during its execution. For this reason, it is called asynchronous, which means "not connected with a specific moment in time." The application can be busily working away on some operation, when the user chooses that random moment to click the mouse. The application must stop what it is doing and transfer control to the instructions that take care of the mouse click. Once it has responded to the user's action, control returns to the application at the point where it was interrupted. In Java, a user action of this form is called an event, and responding to it is called event handling. Events are handled by special methods called event handlers.

The event-handling process sounds very much like calling a method, but there is a basic difference. We write a statement in our code that explicitly calls a method at a specific point in the application's execution. An event handler, on the other hand, can implicitly be called at any time, and no corresponding method call statement appears anywhere in the application. How, then, is the event handler called?

The answer is that there are objects called event listeners whose function is to watch for (that is, listen for) events to occur and respond to them. An object that generates a particular kind of event is called an event source. When an event source generates an event, we say that the source fired the event. Every event source keeps a list of the listeners that want to be notified when that kind of event occurs. Letting an event source know that the listener wants to be notified is called registering the listener. Perhaps you've filled out an online software registration form that contained a box to check beside words that said something like, "Send me e-mail notification of new products and product updates." Filling out this form and submitting it is like registering a listener (you) with an event source (the company). When the company has an update to your software (an event fires), it sends you e-mail (notifies the listener).

Each listener has an event handler method that is designed to respond to (handle) the event. When an event occurs, the appropriate listener is notified by calling its event handler method. When the event handler returns (the method finishes executing), the application continues executing. Figure 8.4 illustrates the process for a button that the user can click in a pane. If no listener is interested or if the interested listener doesn't have an event handler for that particular type of event, the event is ignored and the application continues uninterrupted.

Asynchronous Not occurring at the same moment in time as some specific operation of the computer; not synchronized with the computer's actions

Event An action, such as a mouse click, that takes place asynchronously with respect to the execution of the application

Event handling The process of responding to events

Event handler A method that responds to an event; part of the event listener that is invoked by the event source object

Event listener An object that contains event handler methods

Event source An object that generates events

Firing an event An event source generates an event

Registering a listener Adding a listener to an event source's list of interested listeners

Button A component that can be added to a frame and that fires an event (called a *button event*) when the user clicks it with the mouse

Creating a Button

Let's make the abstract concept of event handling more concrete by introducing the JButton class that allows us to put a button on the screen. We can then explore how to handle the events that it generates. Before we can handle a button event, we have to put a button object

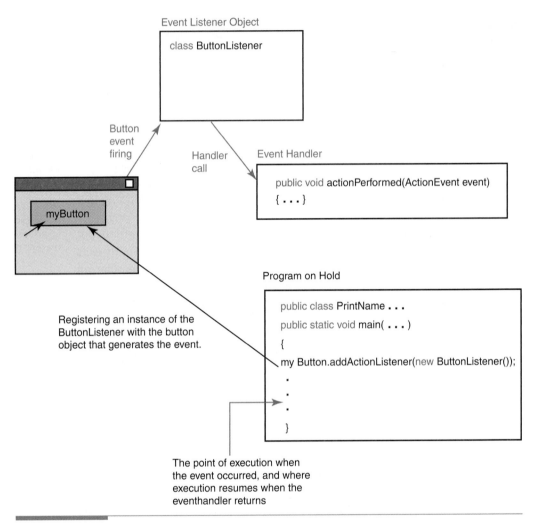

Event Listener Object

class ButtonListener

Button event firing

Handler call

Event Handler

public void actionPerformed(ActionEvent event)
{ . . . }

myButton

Registering an instance of the ButtonListener with the button object that generates the event.

Program on Hold

public class PrintName . . .

public static void main(. . .)

{

my Button.addActionListener(new ButtonListener());

.
.
.

}

The point of execution when the event occurred, and where execution resumes when the eventhandler returns

Figure 8.4 Event Handling

into the pane and register a listener with the button. First we consider how to add a button to a pane. The process is very much like adding a label.

1. Declare a variable of the JButton class.

2. Instantiate a JButton object and assign its address to the variable.

3. Add the object to the frame's content pane using the add method.

An example JButton declaration is

```
JButton done;                    // Declare a JButton variable called done
```

The call to its constructor includes the string that should appear inside the button. For example:

```
done = new JButton("Done");    // Create a JButton object
```

The call to the add method for a content pane called dataPane is written as follows:

```
dataPane.add(done);
```

When the setVisible method for the frame is called, a button is included in the frame with the word "Done" appearing inside it. Note that we use our convention of starting a variable identifier with a lowercase letter, but the string that appears in the button is capitalized. Java may not use proper English capitalization, but our user interface should! The identifier done with a lowercase "d" is the name of a button object; "Done" with a capital "D" is the string that appears in the button on the screen. Here's a code segment showing the steps we've covered so far:

```
JButton done;                 // Declare a button variable
...
done = new JButton("Done");   // Instantiate a button
...                           // Register the event listener
outPane.add(done);            // Add the button to the frame
```

This segment would appear in main, or wherever we are creating the user interface. We still need to look at how to register the event listener. First, however, we have to create one.

■ Creating and Registering a Button Event Listener

First we must declare a new class (a button event listener) to handle button events. This class is based on ActionListener, which we will describe shortly. The button event listener is registered with an event source through a method call. The method to register the event listener is called addActionListener, and it takes an object of our listener class as its argument.

We've already defined numerous classes in Java. However, ActionListener is a bit different. Rather than designing the class heading and methods ourselves, Java gives us a precise model to follow. This Java-provided model is called an **interface**. Previously, we defined an *interface* in the general sense. In Java, however, an interface is part of the language; it is a way of specifying the fields and methods that must be present in a class that is an **implementation** of the interface. Likewise, we previously defined *implementation* as the stage in the software development life cycle in which an algorithm is translated into a programming language. In Java, an implementation is a specific part of the language. The Java designers have used these general terms in a very specific way to define part of the language.

Interface (in Java) A model for a class that specifies the fields and methods that must be present in a class that implements the interface

Implementation (in Java) A class containing the definitions of the methods specified in an interface

The ActionListener interface specifies that we need to write a class that has one method called actionPerformed, with one parameter that takes the event source object as an argument. Here is the code for a class that implements the ActionListener interface:

```
class ButtonHandler implements ActionListener
{
  public void actionPerformed(ActionEvent event)  // Event handler method
  {
    // Body of button event handler method goes here
  }
}                                                  // End of ButtonHandler
```

There are only two major differences between this and the other classes that we've declared:

- The class heading includes the clause `implements ActionListener`.
- The heading of the `actionPerformed` method must have a signature that matches the example.

In Chapter 7 we saw an `implements` clause when we output objects to a file and read them back in. There, we used the clause `implements Serializable` in our class headings. `Serializable` is another interface that is defined in the Java library. Unlike `ActionListener`, however, the `Serializable` interface does not require that we implement any methods. Merely including the `implements Serializable` clause in the class heading is sufficient to tell Java that objects of that class should be prepared for input and output. Now, let's take a closer look at our implementation of `ActionListener`.

No modifiers appear in front of the heading for the class `ButtonHandler` in our example. You must decide which ones are appropriate for each situation. When the class is defined in the application class itself, you might use `private` and `static`. If the class is defined as part of a package that you import, it could be `public`. When you are handling all events from a class of event sources, for example, and all of the buttons will be registered with this one handler, then it should be `static`. If you plan to instantiate different handlers for use by different event sources, however, then the modifier should not be `static`.

Just as we get to choose the name of any other class, so we also get to choose the name (`ButtonHandler`) of the class that implements `ActionListener`. The interface specifies that `actionPerformed` has one parameter of the class `ActionEvent` (a predefined class that represents a source event). We can choose any name that we wish for the parameter; here we simply called it `event`.

The fact that our new class `implements` the `ActionListener` interface means that we can pass a `ButtonHandler` object to any method that specifies a parameter of type `ActionListener` (such as the `addActionListener` method). A class that implements an interface can be used in place of the interface that it implements.

Let's look at how this class definition is written within an application. We provide a skeleton of an application that includes just the essential parts of the two classes.

```
// Import declarations go here
public class ButtonDemo                       // Application class heading
{
                                              // Start of ButtonHandler class
  private static class ButtonHandler implements ActionListener
```

```
{
  public void actionPerformed(ActionEvent event) // Event handler method
  {
    // Body of button event handler method goes here
  }
}                                          // End of ButtonHandler class

// More declarations for the application (ButtonDemo)

public static void main(String[] args)        // main, just as usual
{
  ...                                         // Body of main starts here
  JButton done;                               // Declare a button variable
  ButtonHandler buttonAction;                 // Button listener variable
  ...                                         // Declarations, set up frame, etc.
  done = new JButton("Done");                 // Instantiate a button
  buttonAction = new ButtonHandler();         // Instantiate the listener
  done.addActionListener(buttonAction);       // Register the event listener
  outPane.add(done);                          // Add the button to the pane
  ...                                         // Remainder of application
}
}
```

As you can see, this application class is just like those we've written previously, except that it contains another class with one method inside of it. We could also declare the ButtonHandler class separately and import it into our application.

Because addActionListener is an instance method associated with done, this particular event listener is registered with the event that is generated by the button. We can register an event listener with multiple sources (different buttons) so that one handler method responds to all of those sources. Alternatively, we can register each source with a different handler. We explore both of these approaches later in this chapter.

Although we use the identifier "ButtonHandler" for the class, it is actually a listener class. Because the listener contains the method that handles the event, we use the linguistic shortcut of calling it a button handler rather than calling it "the listener that contains the method that handles the event." All we have to do to complete the ButtonHandler class definition is fill in the body of the actionPerformed method with statements to be executed when the event fires. Those statements might be, for example,

```
dataPane.add(new JLabel("Some new label text")); // Add a new label
dataLabel.setText("Replacement text");            // Change an existing label
```

From the preceding code, we can see that we need to take three steps to register the listener with the event source:

1. Declare a variable of the listener class (for example, ButtonHandler).
2. Instantiate an object of the listener class.

3. Register the listener by calling the `addActionListener` method associated with the button, and passing it the variable of the listener class.

■ An Event-Handling Example

We have seen how to create labels and buttons, how to name a button event, and how to register its listener. We now have all of the syntax that we need to write an application with a user interface dialog that responds to events. But what goes in the body of the event handler? We've been discussing the creation and handling of events in the abstract. In solving a real problem, we would know beforehand what a button in our interface should do. Then it would be clear what must happen in the handler.

Let's look at a very simple problem to illustrate how it all works. We will pick something absolutely trivial so that we can focus on the essential structure and not on how to solve the underlying problem. Suppose we want a user interface that contains a label and a button. The label begins with the number 0 in it, and each time we click the button, the number is incremented. That is, in the button handler, we add 1 to the current value of number and re-display it in the label.

```
number++;
numberLabel.setText("" + number);
```

We used the `setText` method in a previous example without mentioning it. This instance method of a `JLabel` object simply replaces the text in a label with the new string that is its argument. (Clearly, `setText` is a transformer and thus `JLabel` objects are mutable.)

Now, let's look at the code for setting up a typical frame, since we're already familiar with how to do this.

```java
//****************************************************************
// SimpleButton application
// This class displays a number and a button, and each time the
// button is clicked, the number is incremented
//****************************************************************
import java.awt.*;          // Supplies layout manager
import javax.swing.*;       // Supplies JFrame class for output display
public class SimpleButton
{
  public static void main(String[] args)
  {
    JFrame outputFrame;                 // Declare JFrame variable
    Container outputPane;               // Declare Container variable

    // Create a JFrame object
    outputFrame = new JFrame();
    // Ask the JFrame object to return a content pane Container object
    outputPane = outputFrame.getContentPane();
    // Specify the action to take when the window is closed
    outputFrame.setDefaultCloseOperation(JFrame.EXIT_ON_CLOSE);
```

```
    // Specify the size of the JFrame object
    outputFrame.setSize(200, 75);
    // Specify a layout manager for the content pane object
    outputPane.setLayout(new FlowLayout());
    // Add output to the content pane
        ⋮
    // Make the JFrame object visible on the screen
    outputFrame.setVisible(true);
  }
}
```

We need to add our label and our button to the empty content pane. In past examples, we've added a label with a statement such as the following, which instantiates an anonymous label within the method call:

```
outputPane.add(new JLabel("" + number));
```

However, our problem calls for us to change the value of this label after it has been created. We therefore need to store its address in a variable so that we can refer to the value after we create it. The same is true for the button. Here's how it should look instead, with the button code added, too:

```
JLabel numberLabel;
JButton incrementButton;
number = 0;
numberLabel = new JLabel("" + number);
incrementButton = new JButton("Increment");
outputPane.add(numberLabel);
outputPane.add(incrementButton);
```

Our label and the variable `number` should be accessible to both `main` and to the button handler. We can take care of this task by writing them as class members. They do not have to be accessible outside of the application class, so they can be `private`. And because we are not creating instances of our application class, they should be declared as `static`.

```
private static int number;
private static JLabel numberLabel;
private static JButton incrementButton;
```

Here's the button handler, which is just the skeleton we saw earlier, with our two lines of executable statements inserted:

```
private static class ButtonHandler implements ActionListener
{
  public void actionPerformed(ActionEvent event) // Event handler method
  {
    number++;
    numberLabel.setText("" + number);
  }
}                                      // End of ButtonHandler class
```

What's left to be done? Oh yes! We need to add statements to instantiate a `ButtonHandler` object and then register it with the button. We can do this locally within `main`.

```
ButtonHandler incrementListener;
incrementListener = new ButtonHandler();
incrementButton.addActionListener(incrementListener);
```

There's one more detail that we've forgotten. The event-handling classes, such as `ActionListener`, are in another package, `java.awt.event.*`, so we also need to import this package. Everything is now ready to be assembled into a working application.

```java
//*******************************************************************
// SimpleButton application
// This class displays a number and a button, and each time the
// button is clicked, the number is incremented
//*******************************************************************
import java.awt.*;         // Supplies layout manager
import java.awt.event.*;   // Supplies event classes and interfaces
import javax.swing.*;      // Supplies JFrame class for output display
public class SimpleButton
{
  // Field declarations
  private static int number;
  private static JLabel numberLabel;
  private static JButton incrementButton;
  // Start of ButtonHandler class
  private static class ButtonHandler implements ActionListener
  {
    public void actionPerformed(ActionEvent event)// Event handler method
    {
      number++;
      numberLabel.setText("" + number);
    }
  }
  // End of ButtonHandler class
  // Start of main
  public static void main(String[] args)
  {
    JFrame outputFrame;                 // Declare JFrame variable
    Container outputPane;               // Declare Container variable
    ButtonHandler incrementListener;    // Declare event listener

    // Create a JFrame object
    outputFrame = new JFrame();
    // Ask the JFrame for its content pane
    outputPane = outputFrame.getContentPane();
    // Specify the window-closing action
```

```
        outputFrame.setDefaultCloseOperation(JFrame.EXIT_ON_CLOSE);
        // Specify the frame size
        outputFrame.setSize(200, 75);
        // Specify a layout manager
        outputPane.setLayout(new FlowLayout());
        // Prepare label and button for user interface
        number = 0;
        numberLabel = new JLabel("" + number);
        incrementButton = new JButton("Increment");
        incrementListener = new ButtonHandler();
        incrementButton.addActionListener(incrementListener);
        // Add output to the content pane
        outputPane.add(numberLabel);
        outputPane.add(incrementButton);
        // Make the JFrame visible
        outputFrame.setVisible(true);
    }
}
```

Here's what the application displays after the button has been clicked repeatedly.

Event Loops

Our SimpleButton example allows us to click the button as many times as we wish. Each time the button is clicked, the number is incremented. When we finally grow tired of watching the number increase, we simply close the window to stop the application. Without explicitly intending to do so, we've implemented another control structure: an **event loop**. Recall our discussion of looping from Chapter 5, where we explicitly used a *while* loop. Here the loop is implicit—no Java statement spells it out. Figure 8.5 illustrates this loop.

> **Event loop** Repeating an action in response to repeated events

In Chapter 5, we saw that loops can be broken down into six parts: initialization, entry, repeated process, exit condition, exit condition update, and exit. Event loops have a similar breakdown. We initialized our loop by setting up the button and its event handler, and by setting number to zero and creating the label. We enter the loop when the frame is displayed on the screen. The repeated process is to increment number and redisplay it. Our exit condition is the closing of the window, which is handled independently by another event handler that is built into objects of the class JFrame. Thus we don't have to explicitly program the exit condition update. Later in the chapter, when we look at

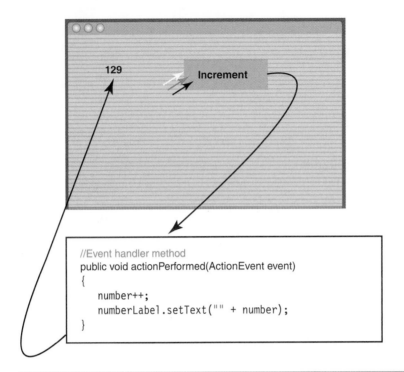

Figure 8.5 An Event Loop

handling events from multiple buttons, we can add a "Done" button for which we program a separate check.

When you write an event-handling class, it is important to be conscious of any event loops that you create. Because they are coded implicitly, it is easy to overlook the fact that they are even present. The danger arises when you create an event loop that doesn't have an exit condition. Then the only way to end the loop is to issue an operating system command to stop the application. For example, if we had forgotten to set the default closing operation, we would have no way out of the event loop. In our code, it is not at all obvious that this action is what ends the loop.

8.4 Entering Data Using Fields in a Frame

Figure 8.6 shows a frame that might be used for entering data into a company payroll application. This frame contains three labels and a button (Done) in the left column of its grid. The right column has three data entry **fields**.

It's important to clarify that a data entry field and a Java field (a declaration in a class) are not the same. One is an area on the screen, while the other is a name representing a constant or variable. In this case, the Java designers used

Field A component of a frame in which the user can type a value; the user must first place the cursor in the field by clicking inside the field

the same word to mean two different things. When discussing fields, we must clearly indicate which kind we mean. Syntactically, Java doesn't confuse them because a data entry field is an object, and a field in a class is a class member.

The user clicks within a data entry field to position the cursor there and then types a value into the field using the keyboard. In some cases, the application may display a field with an initial value that the user can delete before entering a value. Such an initial value is called a *default value*. Alternatively, an application can be written to display a field without a default value. Including a default value is one way to show users how they should type their data within the field.

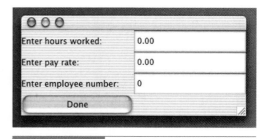

Figure 8.6 Possible Data Entry Frame for a Payroll Program

A user can enter the data into the fields in any order and then go back to any field and correct a mistyped value. None of the user's actions are seen by the code until the user clicks a button. Of course, the computer responds to the user's keystrokes and mouse clicks, so some code must be handling these actions. What is it? The JVM, working together with the operating system, handles the individual keystrokes and mouse actions.

The value that the user sees in a field on the screen is stored in the corresponding object. We can retrieve this value at any time with the instance method getText. Of course, we don't want to get the value at just any old time—we want to get it when the user has finished editing it. The user can indicate this fact by clicking on a button.

When the button event fires, the handler within the button listener is invoked. Within the event handler is our code that gets and processes the values that are currently stored in the field objects. After performing that task, our event handler code might restore the values in the fields to their default values (using setText, just as with a label). Seeing the fields return to their default values signals the user that he or she can enter another set of values. Figure 8.7 shows this process, which you should recognize as an event loop.

Entering data in the manner just described is typical of modern applications and is called a **dialog**. In a theatrical play, a dialog is an exchange between two characters. In the case of the computer, a dialog is an exchange between the user and an application. The application initiates the dialog by displaying a frame, the user replies by entering data into the fields of the frame and clicking a button, the application processes the data and responds by updating the frame, and the user replies again. This dialog continues until the user indicates that there are no more data to enter, perhaps by closing the window.

Dialog A user interface technique in which the user enters data and then performs a separate action (such as clicking a button) when the entered values are ready to be processed by the application

You should always take time to design a dialog so that it is easy to use. For example, the dialog should clearly label data entry fields and indicate the form of the data to be entered into them. Such considerations are especially important when a dialog involves entering data into multiple fields in a frame.

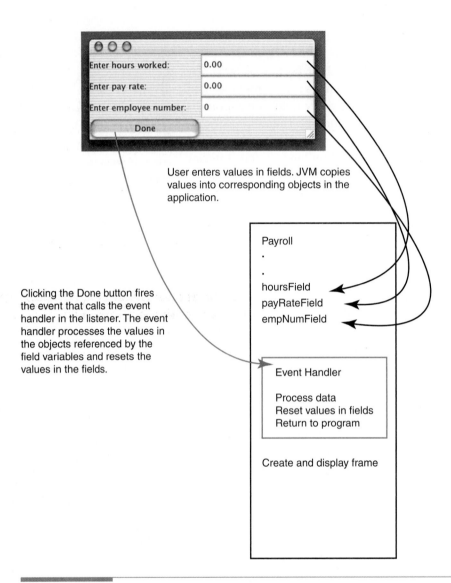

Figure 8.7 Data Entry Process

8.5 Creating a Data Entry Field

Creating a data entry field in Java is very similar to creating a label. The essential steps are the same, with only minor differences:

1. Declare a variable of the appropriate field class.
2. Instantiate an object of the class.
3. Add the object to the content pane using the add method.

A data entry field is an object of the class JTextField. For example, we would declare a variable called inputField as follows:

```
JTextField inputField;        // Declare a field for data entry
```

When creating a JLabel object with new, we pass a string to the JLabel constructor that tells it what text to display in the label. When creating a JTextField object, we provide the constructor with the size of the field. Here is an example of creating a JTextField object and assigning its address to the variable inputField:

```
inputField = new JTextField(6);
```

In this example, the object associated with inputField is specified to have space for typing six characters within it. We can give a default value to the field by including a string as the first argument to the constructor. For example,

```
inputField = new JTextField("Replace Me", 10);
```

would cause the JTextField object to be created with space for ten characters, and initially the words "Replace Me" would appear within the field.

The last step in creating a field is to add it to a content pane. Just as with a label, we use the content pane's add method. If our content pane is called dataEntryPane, then we would write the following:

```
dataEntryPane.add(inputField);
```

When we call dataEntryFrame.setVisible(true), the frame appears on the screen with a field for entering data. As you can see, creating a field is just as simple as creating a label. There is one very important difference between a JLabel and a JTextField, however: The user of the application cannot change the text written in a JLabel, but the user can change the text in the JTextField.

In some of our examples, we've instantiated anonymous labels directly within the argument list of add. Java lets us do the same thing with a JTextField, but we should never do so. Our purpose in adding a JTextField is to later access its contents for input data, so a JTextField object must have its address assigned to a variable to be useful.

Next, let's look at how to get the data from the field after the user has entered it.

8.6 Using a Field

Just as a JLabel object has methods such as setText associated with it, so a JTextField object also comes with a set of instance methods. One method that JTextField shares in common with JLabel is setText. The setText method replaces the current contents of a field with a string that is passed to it. Here is an example of calling setText:

```
inputField.setText("Replace Me");
```

If you want to clear the field so that it appears empty, you simply call `setText` with an empty string:

```
inputField.setText("");
```

A call to `setText` immediately changes the contents of the field on the screen. You do *not* call the frame's `setVisible` method again to update the field. In the last section, we saw how a field can be given a default value by its constructor. Once a field has been created and shown on the screen, it is often useful to be able to change its contents. For example, if the user enters an erroneous value into a field, we might display an error message and set the contents of the field to some value that shows the user how to type an input value correctly.

We previously mentioned the `getText` method, which is also associated with `JTextField`. It enables us to get the current value in the field as it appears on the screen. The `getText` method returns a value of the class `String` that holds a copy of the contents of the field. For example, if we declare a `String` variable called `fieldContents`, we can write

```
fieldContents = inputField.getText();
```

to store the characters currently contained in `inputField` into `fieldContents`.

Note that we have not yet said anything about when or where to call the `getText` method. We have considered the steps of creating the field and taking data from it in isolation from the rest of the application. In the following sections, we examine how these steps are related to handling a button event that tells the application when the user is ready to have it look at the data.

8.7 Reading Data in an Event Handler

Once a button fires its event, control transfers to the first statement in the event handler. But what should the event handler do? In this case, the event is the user's signal that some data has been typed into a field and is now ready for processing. Because we have just been exploring the mechanics of getting the data, rather than solving an actual problem, we don't know what the data represents or what we should do with it.

Our discussion up to this point has put the cart before the horse. In solving a real problem, we begin by identifying the input data and specifying what should happen to it. Then we design the user interface to enable the user to enter the data and generate the events that cause the code to process it. Let's once again look at a trivial problem that we can use to illustrate the design process. Suppose the user should be able to enter a string and have it appear in a label in the same frame when he or she has finished typing. Here is a definition of the problem:

Input: A string that the user enters

Output: The input string, displayed in a label

Processing: Copy the input string from the data entry field to the label

When does the code copy the input string to the label? We need an event to signal when the user has finished typing. Let's use a button called "Copy" to generate the event. What happens after the code copies the string? The problem statement doesn't answer this question. We need a second event to indicate when the user has finished looking at the output. Such an event could be generated by a second button, but instead we decide to do what we did in our SimpleButton example and let the user close the window to end execution.

The event handler for the button simply copies the data from the input field to the output label. For example:

```
fieldContents = inputField.getText();
outputLabel.setText(fieldContents);
```

We can even shorten these two lines to just one and eliminate the string variable fieldContents:

```
outputLabel.setText(inputField.getText());
```

This single line of code carries out the main action that we want to perform on the data. The button event handler that contains it is written just as before, except that we insert this line into the body of the method:

```
private static class ButtonHandler implements ActionListener
{
  public void actionPerformed(ActionEvent event)  // Event handler method
  {
    outputLabel.setText(inputField.getText());
  }
}                                                 // End of ButtonHandler
```

After this method executes, it returns control to the JVM. If the user then closes the window, the application exits.

All that remains is to declare the appropriate variables, assign object addresses to them, add them to the content pane, and show the frame on the screen. In SimpleButton, we saw that the output label must be declared as a class field to make it accessible to both main and the event handler. Do any of the other declarations here need to be declared outside of main? Yes. We want to be able to initialize and add the data entry field in main, and access it in the event handler, so we also declare it at the class level. Here is the complete application, which we call CopyString:

```
//****************************************************************************
// This application displays a frame with a data entry field and copies its
// contents to a label when the user clicks a button marked "Copy"
//****************************************************************************
import java.awt.*;                            // Layout manager
import java.awt.event.*;                      // Event-handling classes
import javax.swing.*;                         // User interface classes
```

```java
public class CopyString
{
  // Define a button handler
  private static class ButtonHandler implements ActionListener
  {
    public void actionPerformed(ActionEvent event) // Event handler method
    {
      outputLabel.setText(inputField.getText());
    }
  }                                                // End of ButtonHandler

  // Declare pieces of the user interface shared by main and CopyString
  private static JLabel outputLabel;               // Label for output
  private static JTextField inputField;            // Input field

  public static void main(String[] args)
  { // Declare pieces of the user interface accessed only by main
    JFrame dataFrame;                              // User interface frame
    Container dataPane;                            // Content pane
    JLabel entryLabel;                             // Label for input field
    JButton copy;                                  // Copy button
    ButtonHandler copyAction;                      // Declare action handler
    // Instantiate the pieces of the interface
    dataFrame = new JFrame();
    dataPane = dataFrame.getContentPane();
    dataFrame.setDefaultCloseOperation(JFrame.EXIT_ON_CLOSE);
    dataFrame.setSize(450, 75);
    dataPane.setLayout(new GridLayout(2,2));
    entryLabel = new JLabel("Enter a string:");
    outputLabel = new JLabel("");
    inputField = new JTextField("", 30);
    copy = new JButton("Copy");
    copyAction = new ButtonHandler();              // Instantiate listener
    copy.addActionListener(copyAction);            // Register listener
    // Put pieces into frame and make it visible
    dataPane.add(entryLabel);
    dataPane.add(inputField);
    dataPane.add(copy);
    dataPane.add(outputLabel);
    dataFrame.setVisible(true);
  }
}
```

The application initially displays a frame that looks like this:

After the user enters a string and clicks the copy button, the frame appears as follows:

When the user closes the window, the program removes the frame from the screen and quits. But what happens if the user doesn't close the window? What if the user types some more data and clicks the button again? The button fires another event, which dutifully calls the event handler again, and the output label is updated with the new input value. The user can keep entering new data values until he or she closes the window. We've created an event loop! In some applications, this event loop would be useful. For this problem, however, our intent is to allow the user to enter just one value.

How can we prevent the user from entering a second value? We can remove the button from the pane so that it can't be clicked again. A `Container` object supports a `remove` method that allows us to delete items that we've previously inserted with `add`. We can write a second line in our event handler that calls this method for `dataPane`, passing it the button `copy`:

```
dataPane.remove(copy);
```

Notice, however, that `dataPane` and `copy` are declared locally within `main`. If we want them to be accessible to both `main` and the event handler, then they must become class fields. Here is the revised section of the class member declarations:

```
private static JLabel outputLabel;        // Label for output
private static JTextField inputField;      // Input field
private static Container dataPane;         // Content pane
private static JButton copy;               // Copy button
```

Now, as soon as the user clicks the "Copy" button, the button disappears. At the same time, the input string appears in the output label. The only event that the user can then generate is closing the window.

Our example has demonstrated the input of a string. Just as with `System.in` and file input, `String` is the only form of input that Java supports with a field. We must use one of the `parse` methods if we wish to input a numeric value. For example:

```
amount = Double.parseDouble(dataField.getText());
```

Now, let's put together what we've seen thus far in a Case Study.

TOTALING RAINFALL AMOUNTS

Problem: You are working for a scientific research project that is keeping track of the total rainfall in your area. Observers from different stations call you to report how much rain has fallen at the end of a storm. You need to enter the values for each station as they come in and display the running total for each station.

Brainstorming: We begin by looking at the nouns in the problem statement as the start of our brainstorming. They are *you*, *project*, *total rainfall*, *observers*, *stations*, *storm*, and *values*. Going back over the list, you realize that *project* and *storm* are not really objects; they just give information about the context of the problem. Here is your first pass at the classes in the problem:

Filtering: Values and total rainfall are numeric values, so we don't need classes for them. What are observers? They are the people who provide the rainfall values, so they are not a class in our problem solution. However, this reminds us that we must have a frame to input the rainfall values. What does "you" represent? The processing that must be done. As you cannot actually do the processing within the machine, you are responsible for seeing that the values are input and the total is calculated and displayed. That is, you are responsible for developing the algorithmic solution and writing the code to carry out the tasks. Stations are the different places from which you receive values and for which you need to keep totals. They sound like actual objects, so let's make a Station class, and then we can instantiate an object for each station. Here is our filtered list:

Scenarios: What happens when an observer calls in with a rainfall amount? The user interface CRC card is raised, and it must collaborate with a station. Each station is an instance of the Station class, and we want to enter the rainfall amount for the particular station. We then click a button and see the new total. Thus a station needs to have a button, a data entry field, and a label for output. It also needs to label the field and the output with descriptions.

After a value has been entered, the user clicks the button; the station should then add the value to the total and the new total should be displayed. The data entry field should also be reset to 0.0 to indicate that the field is ready for more input. This default value has the advantage that if you accidentally click its button without entering a new value, the total isn't affected. When designing an object that is also a user interface component, it is a good idea to draw it out by hand to make sure that it is complete and understandable.

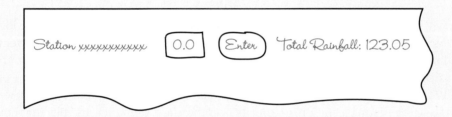

We initially state that Station collaborates with three library classes: JLabel, JButton, and JTextField. Of course, we need an event handler for the button, so it also needs to collaborate with an ActionHandler (a class we will write that implements the ActionListener interface).

Until now, we've used main to set up all of the elements in a user interface. But much of what a station does is related to its part of the user interface. Let's make a Station object be responsible for creating its own portion of the interface and returning it for main to add as a unit to the frame.

What are the responsibilities of a Station object?

1. Create each piece of the user interface when it is instantiated.
2. Return the station's portion of the user interface.
3. Handle button clicks by reading a value, updating the total, and resetting the data entry field.

The first responsibility has to be a constructor, as it takes place during instantiation. Returning the user interface components is the task of an instance method. Handling button events is the job of an event handler. So, it sounds like our Station object needs three methods. Here is the CRC card as it now stands:

Class Name: *Station*	Superclass:	Subclasses:
Responsibilities	**Collaborations**	
Create self	JButton, JLabel, JTextField	
Get user interface elements	None	
Handle button events	ActionHandler, JTextField, JLabel	
.		
.		
.		

Now that we've identified these responsibilities, the user interface card can be lowered. As part of this process, however, we've determined that the input and the event handling are part of the Station class. The user interface is not directly involved in the data entry scenario. We should also note that each Station represents a separate event loop. What initializes and terminates these loops? Each loop is initialized by the user interface instantiating a station, getting its user interface elements, and placing them in the content pane. The loops are all terminated by closing the window. All of this activity is handled in the initialization of the user interface, which occurs in the application class. Let's call it Rainfall.

Class Name: *Rainfall*	Superclass:	Subclasses:
Responsibilities	**Collaborations**	
Initialize user interface	Station, JFrame, Container	
.		
.		
.		

Responsibility Algorithms: The Station constructor should take the name of the station as a string and use it to form the first label, concatenating it with "Station" and ":". This label never changes again, so we can instantiate it anonymously. Our constructor needs to create the rest of the user interface components described previously. They include the data entry field, the button, and the output label. We want each instance of the class to have its own copy of the fields, so they should be instance fields (nonstatic). None of the fields is used outside of the class, so they all involve package-level access. The button needs an event handler, so we also declare an `ActionHandler` class, nested within the class. Of course, we need an instance field to hold the total, and it should be a `double` variable that is initialized to 0.0. Here are the class declarations that we've identified so far:

```
A text field for data entry
A button to signal when data is ready
A label to hold output
An ActionHandler to handle the button events
Total, a double variable
```

We want the user interface elements to be incorporated in a unit that can be added to a content pane. This "unit" sounds a bit like a pane, but we can't put a pane inside a pane. Browsing through your Java library reference, you discover the class `JPanel`, which is a `Container` object that can have a layout manager and hold user interface components, just like a content pane. It can also be added to a content pane so that its contents appear within the pane. This is a perfect example of the building-block approach! We can add these components to a `JPanel` that is an instance field in our `Station` object.

The job of the constructor is then to initialize all of these fields.

```
Constructor Station, takes one parameter, name, of class String

Create a JPanel object, panel
Set the layout manager for the panel to FlowLayout
Create the text field, amountField, leaving space for 10 digits, and
   initializing it to "0.0"
Create a button called enter
Create an event handler for the button
Register the handler with the button
Create a label called outputLabel and initialize it to "Total Rainfall: 0.0"
Add a label to the panel with "Station " + name + ":"
Add amountField to the panel
Add enter button to the panel
Add outputLabel to the panel
```

To get the panel from the object, we use a value-returning instance method that returns a reference to panel.

```
Instance method getPanel, has no parameters and returns a JPanel reference
return panel
```

Lastly, we have to design an `ActionListener` implementation within our `Station` class. We want the event listener to be unique to each instance of `Station`. That way, the button in each `Station` object has an event handler that can directly access the station's fields. So, we must make the event handler be an instance class (not static). What does the event handler do when the user clicks the button? It gets the string from the input field, converts it to a double value (using parseDouble), adds it to the total, updates the output label, and resets the input field to 0.0.

> Private Class ActionHandler implements ActionListener
>
> Public void method actionPerformed takes one parameter, event, of class ActionEvent
>
> ```
> Declare a local variable, value, of type double, to hold the input value
> Assign value the result of applying parseDouble to the value from
>   amountField.getText
> Set total to total plus value
> Use setText to update outputLabel with "Total Rainfall: " + total
> Use setText to reset amountField to "0.0"
> ```

We are now ready to code the Station class.

```
//*****************************************************************************
// This package provides a class for rainfall reporting stations. Each
// station is represented by a separate panel that contains its own
// user interface elements.
//*****************************************************************************
package station;
import java.awt.*;                              // Layout manager
import java.awt.event.*;                        // Event-handling classes
import javax.swing.*;                           // User interface classes
public class Station
{
  JButton enter;                               // Enter data button
  JTextField amountField;                      // Data entry field
  JLabel outputLabel;                          // Result display label
  JPanel panel;                                // Panel for user interface
  ActionHandler action;                        // Event handler
  double total = 0.0;                          // Total rainfall

  public Station (String name)                 // Station constructor
  {
    // Set up panel to hold user interface elements
    panel = new JPanel();                      // Get a panel
    panel.setLayout(new FlowLayout());         // Set layout for the panel
    // Create user interface elements
    amountField = new JTextField("0.0", 10);   // Field for data entry
    enter = new JButton("Enter");              // Enter button
    action = new ActionHandler();              // Create an event handler
    enter.addActionListener(action);           // Register handler with button
    outputLabel = new JLabel("Total Rainfall: "  // Label for output
                        + total);
    // Add user interface elements to panel
    panel.add(new JLabel("Station " + name + ":"));
```

```
    panel.add(amountField);
    panel.add(enter);
    panel.add(outputLabel);
}                                              // End Station constructor


public JPanel getPanel()                       // Instance method
{
    return panel;                              // Return the filled panel
}

// Define an event handler with an instance of a Station
private class ActionHandler implements ActionListener
{
    public void actionPerformed(ActionEvent event)
    // Handle events from the Enter button in this station's panel
    {
        double value;                                 // Holds input value
        // Convert string in amountField to a double value
        value = Double.parseDouble(amountField.getText());  // Get value from field
        total = total + value;                        // Add amount to sum
        outputLabel.setText("Total Rainfall: " + total);  // Display total
        amountField.setText("0.0");                   // Clear input field
    }
}
}
```

All that's left is to design the application class and main. Given that so much of the work is done in the Station class, main has very little to do. We need to declare and set up our frame and content pane as usual. Then we instantiate as many Station objects as there are stations, adding each one's panel to the content pane. Finally, we display the frame. Let's assume there are three stations: Austin, Amherst, and LaCrosse.

```
public static void method main, takes the usual parameters
Declare a JFrame, inputFrame
Declare a Container, inputPane
Instantiate a JFrame for inputFrame
Set inputPane to the content pane of inputFrame
Set the size of inputFrame
Set the default closing operation for inputFrame to exit
Set the layout manager for inputPane to be an N by 1 grid
Instantiate station "Austin" and add its panel to inputPane
Instantiate station "Amherst" and add its panel to inputPane
Instantiate station "LaCrosse" and add its panel to inputPane
Make the frame visible
```

Let's call the application class `Rainfall`. Here is code for the complete application:

```
//*************************************************************************
// This application keeps track of rainfall amounts for three stations
//*************************************************************************
import java.awt.*;                                // Layout manager
import java.awt.event.*;                          // Event-handling classes
import javax.swing.*;                             // User interface classes
import station.*;                                 // Rainfall station
public class Rainfall
{
  public static void main(String[] args)
  {
    JFrame inputFrame;                            // User interface frame
    Container inputPane;                          // Content pane
    // Set up the frame
    inputFrame = new JFrame();
    inputPane = inputFrame.getContentPane();
    inputFrame.setSize(500, 150);
    inputFrame.setDefaultCloseOperation(JFrame.EXIT_ON_CLOSE); // End event loops
    inputPane.setLayout(new GridLayout(0,1));
    // Add components to pane at start of event loops
    // In each case, create a station object and
    // directly get its panel to add to the frame
    inputPane.add((new Station("Austin")).getPanel());     // Station for Austin
    inputPane.add((new Station("Amherst")).getPanel());    // Station for Amherst
    inputPane.add((new Station("LaCrosse")).getPanel());   // Station for LaCrosse
    inputFrame.setVisible(true);                            // Show the frame
  }
}
```

When the application executes, the frame shown below is displayed. The contents shown in the frame are the result of entering several values, with the frame appearing as it does just before the user clicks Enter to cause a value to be processed for the Amherst station.

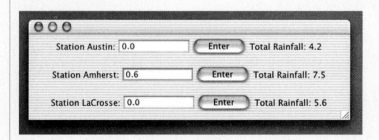

CASE STUDY

With applications that input data from fields, the most common error is to try to assign the field contents directly to an `int` or `double` variable. Remember that Java takes only `String` values as input and that you must convert the input to any other type with the appropriate `parse` method. Another common problem arises when the user enters a number that causes integer overflow. When you want a field to input an integer value, limit its size (through the constructor call) to nine characters. As noted earlier, we are not yet ready to handle errors in which the user enters nonnumeric data into such a field. Our application simply crashes with an error message if this error happens.

8.8 Handling Multiple Button Events

When we first discussed the handling of button events in a frame, we restricted our user interface to a single button. In the preceding Case Study, we created a user interface containing multiple buttons, but each button was registered with a different event handler instance. In this section, we consider the handling of events from multiple buttons with a single handler.

When we instantiate a button with `new`, we pass a string as an argument to its constructor. This string is used to label the button on the screen. However, it is also used to identify an event from the button. For example, suppose we need a user interface with two buttons, copy and done. We create one `ButtonHandler` listener object, and register it with both buttons as follows:

```
buttonAction = new ButtonHandler();        // Instantiate a ButtonHandler object,
                                           //   and assign its address to the variable
                                           //   buttonAction.
copy = new JButton("Copy");                // Instantiate a JButton object that is
                                           //   displayed with the word "Copy" and
                                           //   assign its address to the variable copy.
                                           // The string also identifies it.
copy.addActionListener(buttonAction);      // Register the button listener.
done = new JButton("Done");                // Instantiate a second JButton that
                                           //   displays the word "Done" inside it.
                                           // Assign its address to the variable done.
                                           // The string also identifies it.
done.addActionListener(buttonAction);      // Register the button listener.
```

Figure 8.8 shows a frame with these buttons in it.

When the user clicks either of these buttons, `actionPerformed` is called, just as we saw previously. How does `actionPerformed` decide which button was clicked? Recall that when we write the heading for the `actionPerformed` method, we include a parameter of type `ActionEvent`. The event source passes an object to the method through that parameter. That object has a field containing the string we gave

Figure 8.8 Frame with Two Buttons

to the button to identify it. We access the string by calling the value-returning method `getActionCommand` that is associated with the parameter object.

For example, if the heading for `actionPerformed` is written

```
public void actionPerformed(ActionEvent someButton)
```

then we obtain the string that identifies which button was clicked by using the following statement (`command` is a `String` variable):

```
command = someButton.getActionCommand();
```

Within our declaration of the method, we use string comparisons and branches to perform the necessary action for the particular button. For example, we might extend the event handler in our `CopyString` class as follows:

```
private static class ButtonHandler implements ActionListener
{
  public void actionPerformed(ActionEvent buttonEvent) // Event handler method
  {
    String command;                                  // String to hold button name
    command = buttonEvent.getActionCommand();        // Get the button's name
    if (command.equals("Copy"))                      // When the name is "Copy"
      outputLabel.setText(inputField.getText());     // Copy the field
    else if (command.equals("Done"))                 // When the name is "Done"
    {
      dataFrame.dispose();                           // Close the frame
      System.exit(0);                                // Quit the program
    }
    else                                             // Otherwise it's an error
      outputLabel.setText("An unexpected event occurred.");
  }
}
```

When the event source calls `actionPerformed`, the method gets the button's name using `getActionCommand`. It then uses an *if-else-if* structure to decide which button was clicked and execute the appropriate statements. Although `getActionCommand` should never return a name other than `"Copy"` or `"Done"`, we provide a branch for other names just to be safe. At some point in the future, the program could be changed to add another button. If the new programmer forgets to add a corresponding branch to handle that event, the program will display an error message instead of crashing.

In the preceding example, we introduced two new methods, dispose and exit. The dispose method is an instance method associated with a JFrame object. Its effect is to permanently remove the frame from the screen. We could also have called setVisible(false), but dispose does some extra work in the background that saves the JVM from having to clean up after us. The exit method is a class method associated with the System class. It causes the JVM to terminate execution of our application. Passing it an argument of 0 indicates that the application was intentionally ended in a normal manner.

We have now seen how to handle multiple button events in a single handler. In the preceding Case Study, we saw how to handle events from different buttons by using a handler for each one. How do we decide which approach to take for a given problem?

When a user interface contains buttons that perform tasks associated with a specific object, it makes sense to combine the handling of their events into a single method. If clicking a button requires processing that is unrelated to other buttons, then it should have its own event handler. For example, in our Rainfall application, each station has its own Enter button, and a handler that is dedicated to that particular button. Both the button and its handling are integral to a Station object. It would not make sense to create a single button handler that responds to the buttons for all of the stations. On the other hand, if we extend the definition of a Station object to include a Reset button, then it makes perfect sense to have the handler for a station respond to both the Enter and the Reset buttons appropriately.

A SIMPLE CALCULATOR

Problem: It's useful to have a calculator that you can display on your computer screen when you look around and can't find your handheld one. Let's write a Java application that simulates a simple calculator. Once we have the basic design, we can easily extend it to provide other functions.

Brainstorming: Rather than look at the problem statement, you pick up your pocket calculator. After all, this problem involves simulating the pocket calculator. What objects do you see? A register on the top that shows what you are entering and displays the answer, an On button, buttons for each of the 10 decimal digits, buttons for each of the four basic operations (addition, subtraction, multiplication, and division), a Clear button, and a button marked with an equals sign. There are buttons for percent and square root, but you do not use them often enough to add them to the simulation. So the first list of proposed classes is as follows:

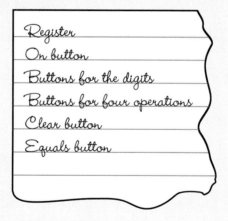

Register
On button
Buttons for the digits
Buttons for four operations
Clear button
Equals button

Filtering: We certainly need a register to show the output. Do we need an On button? No, running the application is equivalent to the On button. However, we do need some way of quitting the application. We could have a Quit button or we could let the window-closing event end the application. Window closing ... We need an object to represent the calculator itself; that is, we need a window to hold all the other objects. What about the buttons for each digit? No, we can let the user input a number into a text field rather than clicking individual buttons. This means that we need a label for the text field. Do we need an Enter button? No, we can let the button for the operation signal that the value is ready to be read. We do need a button for each operation. We certainly need a Clear button to set the register value to zero. What about the Equals button? On the calculator, it signals that we want to see the results so far in the register. Instead of an Equals button, let's just display the result of each operation in the register as we go along. Here is our filtered list of classes:

User interface window with data register, button, labels
Buttons for four operations
Clear button

Scenarios: What happens when the application begins? The user interface card is raised. It must set up the user interface on the screen. To do so, it collaborates with the JFrame, JTextField, JButton, and JLabel classes. From our experience with the last Case Study, we know that we can add the user interface components either to a panel or directly to the content pane of the frame. If we needed to instantiate multiple calculators in a window, then using a panel would make sense. Here, however, we need just one calculator, so we can directly place its components into the content pane. (Case Study Follow-Up Exercise 12 asks you to rewrite the application using a panel.) We can, therefore, use main to organize the window. Let's call the application class Calculator. We know that this application collaborates with the usual user interface library classes, and it also needs to register the button handlers with the buttons. We can lower the user interface CRC card, which is now called Calculator.

Class Name: *Calculator*	Superclass:	Subclasses:
Responsibilities		**Collaborations**
Initialize user interface		*JFrame, Container, JLabel, JButton, JTextField, Numeric Handler, ClearHandler*

What happens when the user clicks an operation button? The appropriate button handler performs a calculation and sends the value to the output register. The only collaborations that we need are with the input text field (calling its standard methods to get its contents and to set them to a new value) and with the ActionEvent class (to get the name of the event). The four operator buttons are event sources. When the user clicks one, an actionPerformed method is invoked with the event source as an argument. The processing of the buttons is embedded within this method, the responsibility for which resides in a class we call NumericHandler.

Class Name: *NumericHandler*	Superclass:		Subclasses:
Responsibilities		**Collaborations**	
Action performed		JTextField, ActionEvent	
.			
.			
.			

The clear button has a different function than the other buttons. When it is clicked, the register is set to zero; no value is input from the text field, and no arithmetic operation is performed. It makes sense to use one button handler for the four arithmetic buttons, but a separate one for the clear button.

Class Name: *ClearHandler*	Superclass:		Subclasses:
Responsibilities		**Collaborations**	
Action performed		JTextField, ActionEvent	
.			
.			
.			

Most of the objects are instances of classes provided in the Java library. Thus the only new classes are the two event handlers and `Calculator`. The main responsibility of the main method will be to set up the frame and populate it with all of the user interface objects.

Responsibility Algorithms: The first step is to identify the fields of the `Calculator` class. They are mainly the interface variables. Declaring these variables requires us to make a list of the components in the window. We need a frame and content pane to hold everything, three labels (one for input and two for the register), a field for entering a data value, four buttons for the user to click to indicate the operation when a value is ready for input, and a button for the user to click to clear the register. This same list also tells us what we need to add to the pane. This portion of the responsibility algorithms is shown below. All of the variables should be class fields, so they are static. We can give them package access, rather than making them explicitly private.

Before we go on, let's simplify the problem somewhat. We will first create a calculator with only plus and minus functions. After we verify this simplified version of the application, we can add division and multiplication operations. (See Case Study Follow-Up Exercise 10.)

```
Declare Interface Variables
Declare a JFrame, calcFrame
Declare a Container, calcPane
Declare a JLabel, resultLabel
Declare a JLabel, register
Declare a JLabel, entryLabel, for prompting
Declare a JTextField, inputField, for input
Declare a JButton, add
Declare a JButton, subtract
Declare a JButton, clear
```

The responsibility of main, creating the user interface, is similar to what we've done in several previous applications. Does this mean that we can just cut and paste the algorithms? No, the objects in the window are not the same, but the steps used to create them are the same, so we already know how to write the outline of the algorithm. The steps shown in color require further expansion. We're applying functional decomposition to simplify the problem-solving process.

```
public static main method (standard arguments)
Instantiate each interface object
Register listeners with buttons
Create the frame
Get the content pane
Size the frame
Set default close operation
Set layout manager for the pane
Add each interface object to the pane
Make the frame visible
```

```
Instantiate Each Interface Object
Set calcFrame to address of new JFrame
Get content pane from calcFrame and assign its address to calcPane
Set up calcPane as a four-row, two-column grid
Set resultLabel to address of new JLabel, "Result:"
Set register to address of new JLabel, "0.0"
Set inputField to address of new JTextField, empty with 10 spaces
Set add to address of new JButton, "+"
Set subtract to address of new JButton, "-"
Set clear to address of new JButton, "Clear"
```

CASE STUDY

> **Add Each Interface Object to the Pane**
>
> ```
> Add resultLabel to calcPane
> Add register to calcPane
> Add entryLabel to calcPane
> Add inputField to calcPane
> Add add to calcPane
> Add subtract to calcPane
> Add clear to calcPane
> ```

We still have one more step in main to flesh out.

> **Register Listeners with Buttons**
>
> ```
> Register the event listener for the arithmetic buttons
> Register the event listener for the clear button
> ```

Registering an event listener for a button involves three steps: declare a variable of the listener class, instantiate a listener object, and add the listener object to the button. The listener for the numeric operations is, of course, NumericHandler.

> **Register the Event Listener for the Arithmetic Buttons**
>
> ```
> Declare a NumericHandler, operation
> Instantiate a NumericHandler for operation
> add operation as listener for arithmetic buttons
> ```

For the clear operation, we just substitute ClearHandler.

> **Register the Event Listener for the Clear Button**
>
> ```
> Declare a ClearHandler, clearOperation
> Instantiate a ClearHandler for clearOperation
> add clearOperation as listener for clear button
> ```

We have now completed the responsibility algorithms for the application class Calculator. The remaining classes handle the buttons. First, we design the listener for the numeric buttons. We have said that the listener class is called NumericHandler. What should the actionPerformed method do when the user clicks the add or subtract button? It should get the value to be used in the calculation from the input field and convert it to a real number. If the user enters a string that does not represent a legitimate real number, a NumberFormatException may be thrown. In Chapter 9, we show you how to handle this exception; here, we assume correct input.

Next, we determine which operation should be applied to the number, addition or subtraction. Wait a minute: Addition and subtraction are binary operations! We have one value; where is the other one? Actually, the value just input is the second operand. The first operand is the value in the register. Rather than extract it from the window each time, we should keep a copy in numeric form. (We must be sure to set that value to zero originally.) Back to the question of determining which button was clicked: We use the parameter in the actionPerformed method to tell us.

Handle Numeric Button Events   *Level 1*

```
Set secondOperand to numerical value (double) of entry string
Set whichButton to name of event source
if whichButton is "+"
   Set result to result + secondOperand
else
   Set result to result — secondOperand
Display result in register
Clear inputField
```

The algorithm for handling the Clear button is even simpler; all we have to do is set the register to zero as well as the variable that contains the same value. We should also clear the input field. These actions are performed in the actionPerformed method of the class ClearHandler.

Handle Clear Button Event   *Level 1*

```
Set result to zero
Display result in register
Clear inputField
```

As in our previous applications, we must decide where each object should be declared. Because we are writing this application as just a single class that won't be instantiated by user code, we can make all of the members static and declare them at the class level.

The coding of the algorithm into Java is now easy. Here is the result:

```java
//****************************************************************************
// This application implements a simple on-screen calculator
//****************************************************************************
import java.awt.*;                          // awt interface classes
import java.awt.event.*;                    // awt event classes
import javax.swing.*;                       // User interface classes

public class Calculator
{
  static JTextField inputField;             // Data entry field
  static JLabel register;                   // Result shown on screen
  static double result;                     // Keeps current value
  static JFrame calcFrame;                  // Declare a frame
  static Container calcPane;                // Container to hold
                                            //  content pane of frame

  static NumericHandler operation;          // Declare numeric listener
  static ClearHandler clearOperation;       // Declare clear listener
  static JLabel resultLabel;                // Indicate output area
  static JLabel entryLabel;                 // Label for input field
  static JButton add;                       // Add button
```

```java
static JButton subtract;                    // Subtract button
static JButton clear;                       // Clear button

// Define event listener for numeric buttons
static class NumericHandler implements ActionListener
{
  public void actionPerformed(ActionEvent event)
  // Handle events from the buttons in calcPane
  {
    double secondOperand;                   // Holds input value
    String whichButton;                     // Holds the button's name
    // Get the operand
    secondOperand =
      Double.parseDouble(inputField.getText());
    whichButton = event.getActionCommand(); // Get the button's name

    if (whichButton.equals("+"))            // When the name is "add"
      result = result + secondOperand;      //   add the operand
    else                                    // Otherwise
      result = result - secondOperand;      //   subtract the operand

    register.setText("" + result);          // Display result
    inputField.setText("");                 // Clear input
  }
}

static class ClearHandler implements ActionListener
{
  public void actionPerformed(ActionEvent event)
  // Handle events from the Clear button in calcPane
  {
    result = 0.0;                           // Set result back to zero
    register.setText("0.0");                // Reset result in register
    inputField.setText("");                 // Clear input
  }
}

public static void main(String[] args)
{
  operation = new NumericHandler();         // Instantiate a NumericHandler
  clearOperation = new ClearHandler();      // Instantiate a ClearHandler
  result = 0.0;                             // Initialize result

  // Instantiate labels and initialize input field
  resultLabel = new JLabel("Result:");
  register = new JLabel("0.0", JLabel.RIGHT);
  entryLabel = new JLabel("Enter #:");
  inputField = new JTextField("", 10);
```

```
// Instantiate button objects
add = new JButton("+");
subtract = new JButton("-");
clear = new JButton("Clear");

// Register the button listeners
add.addActionListener(operation);
subtract.addActionListener(operation);
clear.addActionListener(clearOperation);

// Add interface elements to calcFrame
calcFrame = new JFrame();                    // Give the frame a value
calcFrame.setSize(300, 200);                 // Specify size of frame
// Set close operation to exit
calcFrame.setDefaultCloseOperation(JFrame.EXIT_ON_CLOSE);
calcPane = calcFrame.getContentPane();       // Get the content pane
calcPane.setLayout(new GridLayout(4,2));     // Set the layout manager
calcPane.add(resultLabel);
calcPane.add(register);
calcPane.add(entryLabel);
calcPane.add(inputField);
calcPane.add(add);
calcPane.add(subtract);
calcPane.add(clear);
calcFrame.setVisible(true);                  // Show the frame
    }
}
```

When we run the application, it displays a window like the one here:

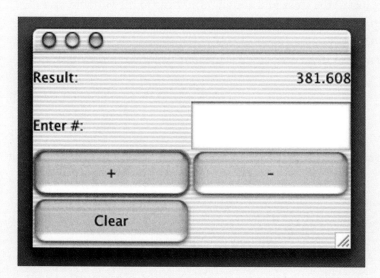

8.9 Testing and Debugging

Table 8.1 shows a partial test plan for the Calculator application. The first test case assumes that the calculator has an initial value of 0.0. Successive test cases use the preceding result as one of the two operands for a calculation. To be more thorough, we should check that the application properly handles the closing of the window, and we should include both negative and positive values.

Testing and Debugging Hints

1. Remember to label each input field with a prompting message.
2. Make certain that every field, label, and button follows the three basic steps: declare a variable, instantiate an object, and add it to the pane.
3. Remember to specify a layout manager for a pane or panel.
4. The value in a TextField is a string. If you need to input a number, you must use getText to input the string, and then convert the string to a number using methods such as Integer.parseInt and Double.parseDouble. Applying these methods to a nonnumeric value causes the application to halt with an error message such as *Number Format Exception*.
5. A button event listener declaration must follow the pattern of headings specified by the ActionListener interface. You can choose the name of the class, and its modifiers, but the rest of the class heading and the method signature must appear as shown in the examples in this book.
6. Once you have declared the button action listener class, you must perform three steps to register the event listener: declare a variable of that class, instantiate an object of the class and assign its address to the variable, and register the listener by calling the button's addActionListener method with the variable as its argument.
7. Confirm that every part of an event loop is present, especially the exit condition.

Reason for Test Case	*Input Values*	*Expected Output*	Observed Output
Test add command	12.5, +	12.500	
Test subtract command	2.5, -	10.000	
Test clear command	*none*, Clear	0.000	
Test window closing	*none*	Window disappears	

Table 8.1 Test Plan for the Calculator Application

Summary

Graphical user interfaces (GUIs) provide more convenient and intuitive input for users. However, they also take more programming effort than the simple line-oriented I/O that we've used in the past. Java is one of the first widely used languages to offer extensive support for GUI programming.

The basic window object is a JFrame; it provides a content pane in the form of a Container object that is returned by the getContentPane instance method. We add user interface objects to the content pane with the add method, and we remove them with the remove method. As part of creating a JFrame, we must specify its default closing operation, its size, and the layout manager to use for its content pane. We use setVisible(true) to make the frame appear on the screen and dispose() to remove the frame.

Objects that we can place into a content pane include a JLabel, JTextField, and JButton. We can change the contents of a JLabel or JTextField with setText, and we can retrieve the String value of a JTextField with getText. A JPanel is another class, with similarities to a content pane, that we can use to preassemble groups of interface elements. We can then add the whole JPanel as a unit to the content pane of a JFrame, so that the group of elements appears together.

We must register an event listener with an event source, such as a button, to handle events from the source. The event listener is registered with a call to addActionListener. An event handler is a method in a class definition that follows the specification of the ActionListener interface.

Event loops provide an implicit way of repeating actions in event-driven applications. We must check that an event loop is designed properly and that all of its aspects are implemented correctly.

When a user interface includes multiple buttons, we can use the string associated with each button to determine which one was clicked. The event handler is passed an ActionEvent value as a parameter, and we call its associated value-returning instance method, getActionCommand, to retrieve the string associated with the button.

Quick Check

1. What contains a content pane, and what does a content pane contain? (pp. 376–380)
2. Where is an event sent when a user clicks a button with the mouse? (pp. 385–393)
3. Where does updating of the process within an event loop occur? (pp. 393–394)
4. What is the handler method to which button events are sent? (pp. 385–393)
5. Write statements that declare a private JTextField variable called dataField, instantiate a corresponding object, and add it to a content pane called outPane. (pp. 394–398)
6. Write a statement that adds a label with the message "Quick Check" to outPane. (pp. 376–380)

7. When a dialog involves processing input from a field after a button has been clicked, what part of the code is responsible for reading the field and processing it? (pp. 394–396)

8. How do you register an event listener with a button? (pp. 387–390)

9. What Java interface does an event listener implement, and in what package is the interface found? (pp. 387–390)

10. What are the parts of an event loop? (pp. 393–394)

11. Which method provides the string that we use to identify the source of an event? (pp. 409–411)

Answers

1. A JFrame contains a content pane and the content pane contains user interface elements. 2. The button event handler 3. In the user's actions and in the event handler 4. actionPerformed
5. `private static JTextField dataField;`
   `dataField = new JTextField(10);`
   `outPane.add(dataField);`
6. `outPane.add(new JLabel("Quick Check"));` 7. The event handler 8. With the addActionListener method
9. ActionListener is found in java.awt.event. 10. Initialization of the loop exit condition and the process, loop entry, exit condition update, process update, and exit 11. getActionCommand

Exam Preparation Exercises

1. If a and b are int variables with a = 5 and b = 2, what output does each of the following statements produce?
   a. `outPane.add(new JLabel("a = " + a + "b = " + b));`
   b. `outPane.add(new JLabel("Sum:" + a + b));`
   c. `outPane.add(new JLabel("Sum:  " + a + b));`
   d. `outPane.add(new JLabel(a / b + " feet"));`

2. What does the following application display?

```
import java.awt.*;
import javax.swing.*;
public class ExamPrep
{
  public static void main(String[] args)
  {
    JFrame out;
    Container outPane;
    final int LBS = 10;
    int   price;
    int   cost;
    char ch;
    out = new JFrame();
```

```
        outPane = out.getContentPane();
        out.setSize(300, 200);
        out.setDefaultCloseOperation(JFrame.EXIT_ON_CLOSE);
        outPane.setLayout(new GridLayout(0,1));
        price = 30;
        cost = price * LBS;
        ch = 'A';
        outPane.add(new JLabel("Cost is "));
        outPane.add(new JLabel("" + cost));
        outPane.add(new JLabel("Price is " + price + "Cost is " + cost));
        outPane.add(new JLabel("Grade " + ch + " costs "));
        outPane.add(new JLabel("" + cost));
        out.setVisible(true);
    }
}
```

3. To use each of the following statements, a Java application must `import` which package(s)?

   a. `outPane.add(new JLabel("x"));`

   b. `private static class ButtonHandler implements ActionListener`

   c. `outPane.setLayout(new GridLayout(0, 2));`

4. Given the statements

   ```
   String heading;
   String str;

   heading = "Exam Preparation Exercises";
   ```

   what is the output of each of the following code segments?

   a. `outPane.add(new JLabel("" + heading.length()));`

   b. `outPane.add(new JLabel(heading.substring(6, 16)));`

   c. `outPane.add(new JLabel("" + heading.indexOf("Ex")));`

5. Name three kinds of objects that can be contained in the content pane of a `JFrame` object.

6. What are the steps in adding a data entry field to the content pane of a `JFrame` object in Java?

7. What determines the amount of information in a prompt?

8. (True or False?) A `JPanel` can hold just one user interface element.

9. Do we have to get a content pane from a JPanel as we do with a JFrame?

10. What method would you use to change the value displayed in a JTextField object?

11. When giving a value to a label with new, what is passed to the constructor?

12. What method do you use to change the text within an existing label?

13. What happens if you forget to include the statement
    dataFrame.setVisible(true);?

14. What are the three steps needed to add a button to a content pane?

15. What are the three parts of registering an event listener?

16. What happens when a user clicks a button but no listener is registered for the event?

17. How are normal classes and classes that implement the ActionListener interface different?

18. actionPerformed takes one argument of a Java class. What is the name of the class?

19. What are the parts of an event loop?

20. Why do you not have to write an event handler for window closing?

21. How do you associate a string with a button event?

22. Describe the two ways that multiple buttons can be distinguished.

Programming Warm-Up Exercises

1. a. Declare a button variable called stop.

   b. Instantiate a button object, labeling it "Stop", and assign its address to stop.

   c. Declare a button listener variable and instantiate a button listener object.

   d. Register the button listener with the button.

   e. Add the button to the content pane dataPane.

   f. Write the statements to declare a listener class.

2. Provide a user interface with two buttons, Enter and Quit.

   a. Write the statements that declare variables for the buttons and a single listener.

   b. Write the statements that instantiate the buttons and the listener.

   c. Write the statements that add the buttons to the content pane.

   d. Write the statements that register the listener with the buttons.

   e. Write the statement that accesses a button's name from within an event handler.

   f. Code a class that implements ActionListener. When each button is clicked, display its name on the screen.

3. Provide a user interface with two buttons, Enter and Quit.

   a. Write the statements that declare the variables for the buttons and two listeners.

   b. Write the statements that instantiate the buttons and the listeners.

   c. Write the statements that add the buttons to the content pane.

   d. Write the statements that register the listeners with the buttons.

   e. Code classes that implement `ActionListener` for each button. When each button is clicked, display its name on the screen.

4. a. Write the statement that stores the values entered in the field `dataField` into the `String` variable `dataValue`.

   b. Write a statement to replace the current contents of `dataField` with `"Next Value"`.

5. a. Write the declarations needed for a frame (`exampleFrame`) whose content pane has one label (`exampleLabel`), one field (`exampleField`), and one button (`exampleButton`).

   b. Write the statements that define a class (`ExampleClass`) that is an implementation of `ActionListener`. When the `exampleButton` is clicked, the contents of `exampleField` are stored into `exampleValue` and removed from `exampleField`.

   c. Write the statements that registers the button event listener `exampleHandler` with its associated event source `exampleButton`.

   d. Write the statements that define a class (`Example2Class`) that is an implementation of `ActionListener`. When the `exampleButton` is clicked, the contents of `exampleField` are copied into `exampleLabel`.

6. Write the statement that displays the number 2000 in an existing `JTextField` object, called `exampleField`.

7. Write the statement that takes the string representing an integer number in the `JTextField exampleField` and stores it into the `int` variable `data`.

8. Write the field declarations for a class whose objects each contain three labels (a data entry prompt, count, and average), a data entry field, and a button. Each of the objects also keeps a total and a count of the number of values entered.

9. Write the constructor for the class described in Exercise 8. The class is called `Exam`. The count and total should initially be zero.

10. Write the event handler for the button component of the class described in Exercises 8 and 9. When the button is clicked, the value should be read from the text field, the count and average labels should be updated, and the value in the text field should be reset to 0.

11. Write the heading for a constructor for a class called `Demo` that takes one parameter of the class `JLabel` and a second parameter of the class `String`.

12. Write the statements to declare a JPanel variable, instantiate an object for it, set its layout manager to FlowLayout, and add three labels to it.

Programming Problem

1. You have bought a car, taking out a loan with an annual interest rate of 9%. You will make 36 monthly payments of $165.25 each. You want to keep track of the remaining balance you owe after each monthly payment. The formula for the remaining balance is

$$bal_k = pmt\left(\frac{1 - (1 + i)^{k-n}}{i} \right)$$

where

bal_k = balance remaining after the kth payment

k = payment number (1, 2, 3, ...)

pmt = amount of the monthly payment

i = interest rate per month (annual rate ÷ 12)

n = total number of payments to be made

Write an application to calculate and display the balance remaining after each monthly payment. Start by showing the remaining balance after the first payment, and show each subsequent payment when a button is clicked. Display an identifying message with each numerical result that indicates which payment period is being displayed. Be sure to include appropriate comments in your code, choose meaningful identifiers, and use indentation as we do in the code in this chapter.

Case Study Follow-Up

1. Does Rainfall crash if the user enters nonnumeric values? Explain.
2. Write a test plan for Rainfall.
3. Rainfall stops when the user closes the window. How else could the application be designed to allow the user to quit? Explain.
4. What happens when a negative value is input in Rainfall?
5. Modify Rainfall to display the names of three towns in your area for its stations.
6. Modify Rainfall to handle six stations, using names of towns near you.
7. Modify Rainfall to compute and display the average rainfall for a storm for each station.

8. Most of the code in the Calculator application involves input/output. The code is long, but the concepts are simple. Examine the code below and mark the statements associated with creating the frame and content pane as *F*; the statements associated with handling buttons as *B*; and the statements that create the buttons, register the listeners with them, and place the buttons into the frame as *FB*. Notice that all the comments have been removed; you have to read and understand the actual code to answer this question and Exercise 9.

```java
import java.awt.*;
import java.awt.event.*;
import javax.swing.*;

public class Calculator
{
  static JTextField inputField;
  static JLabel register;
  static double result;
  static JFrame calcFrame;
  static Container calcPane;
  static NumericHandler operation;
  static ClearHandler clearOperation;
  static JLabel resultLabel;
  static JLabel entryLabel;
  static JButton add;
  static JButton subtract;
  static JButton clear;

  static class NumericHandler implements ActionListener
  {
    public void actionPerformed(ActionEvent event)
    {
      double secondOperand;
      String whichButton;
      secondOperand =
        Double.parseDouble(inputField.getText());
      whichButton = event.getActionCommand();

      if (whichButton.equals("+"))
        result = result + secondOperand;
      else
        result = result - secondOperand;
```

```
    register.setText("" + result);
    inputField.setText("");
  }
}

static class ClearHandler implements ActionListener
{
  public void actionPerformed(ActionEvent event)
  {
    result = 0.0;
    register.setText("0.0");
    inputField.setText("");
  }
}

public static void main(String[] args)
{
  operation = new NumericHandler();
  clearOperation = new ClearHandler();
  result = 0.0;
  resultLabel = new JLabel("Result:");
  register = new JLabel("0.0", JLabel.RIGHT);
  entryLabel = new JLabel("Enter #:");
  inputField = new JTextField("", 10);
  add = new JButton("+");
  subtract = new JButton("-");
  clear = new JButton("Clear");
  add.addActionListener(operation);
  subtract.addActionListener(operation);
  clear.addActionListener(clearOperation);
  calcFrame = new JFrame();
  calcFrame.setSize(300, 200);
```

```
        calcFrame.setDefaultCloseOperation(JFrame.EXIT_ON_CLOSE);
        calcPane = calcFrame.getContentPane();
        calcPane.setLayout(new GridLayout(4,2));
        calcPane.add(resultLabel);
        calcPane.add(register);
        calcPane.add(entryLabel);
        calcPane.add(inputField);
        calcPane.add(add);
        calcPane.add(subtract);
        calcPane.add(clear);
        calcFrame.setVisible(true);
    }
}
```

9. List the statements that relate to the Clear button, describing what each one does in English.

10. Complete the original Calculator project by adding buttons for multiplication and division.

11. Write a test plan to test the final project and implement the test plan for Calculator.

12. Rewrite the Calculator application so that a separate class contains the entire calculator object. When an object is instantiated, it should create a JPanel containing the user interface for a calculator. The class should provide a method that returns the JPanel. The function of the main method can then be simplified to creating the frame, instantiating a calculator object, getting its panel, and adding it to the content pane, similar to what we did for the Station objects in the Rainfall program.

13. After completing Exercise 12, change main to instantiate two calculators and place them into the frame. Be sure to test them thoroughly to ensure that they operate independently of each other.

Exceptions and Additional Control Structures

goals

Knowledge Goals
- To understand what is and is not an exception
- To know when throwing an exception is appropriate
- To know how an exception should be handled
- To understand the role of the *switch* statement
- To understand the purpose of the *break* statement
- To understand the distinctions among the alternative looping statements
- To be aware of Java's additional operators and their place in the precedence hierarchy with respect to each other

Skill Goals
To be able to:
- Use the Java exception-handling facilities *try*, *catch*, and *throw*
- Define an exception class
- *Throw* an exception
- Write a *switch* statement for a multiway branching problem
- Write a *do* statement and contrast it with a *while* statement
- Write a *for* statement as an alternative to a *while* statement
- Choose the most appropriate looping statement for a given problem

timeline

1972

HP introduces the hand-held scientific calculator; hand-held calculators replace the slide rule

1972

Nolan Bushnell takes his video game Pong and founds Atari, launching the computer-entertainment industry

1972

Alan Kay's ideas fuel the development of the computer language Smalltalk

1972

Dennis Ritchie develops the programming language C

1972

Alain Colmerauer develops the programming language Prolog

1972

The first programmable word processor is introduced in Canada

introduction

Several times throughout this book we have said that a construct could cause an *exception*. Until now, we have handled exceptions by forwarding them to "someone else." In this chapter, we stop passing the buck and examine how to handle exceptions within our code. We also show you how to generate exceptions of your own.

In Chapters 4 and 5, we introduced the Java statements for the selection and loop control structures. In some cases, we considered more than one way of implementing these structures. For example, selection may be implemented by an *if* structure. Although the *if-(then)* is sufficient to implement any selection structure, Java also provides the *if-else* for the sake of convenience—the two-way branch is used frequently in programming.

This chapter introduces several new statements that are also nonessential to, but nonetheless convenient for, programming. The *switch* statement makes it easier to write selection structures that have many branches. Two new looping statements, *for* and *do*, make it easier to program certain types of loops. The *break* and *continue* statements are control statements that are used as part of larger looping and selection structures.

Finally, we examine the remaining operators in Java and study their place in the precedence hierarchy.

1972
Steve Wozniak makes free phone calls using his invention, the "blue box"

1973
Xerox PARC's experimental Alto personal computer, featuring a mouse, a graphical user interface, and connection to a local area network, becomes operational

1973
Ten thousand components are placed on a 1-square-cm chip through large-scale integration

1973
Eckert and Mauchley's ENIAC patent is invalidated, and John Vincent Atanasoff is federally recognized as the inventor of the modern computer

1974
Charles Simonyi writes the first WYSIWYG ("What You See Is What You Get") program entitled Bravo

1974
The first World Computer Chess Tournament takes place in Stockholm; the winner is the program Kaissa

9.1 Exception-Handling Mechanism

In Chapter 8, we defined an *exception* as an unusual situation that is detected while an application is running. An exception halts the normal execution of a method. There are three parts to an exception-handling mechanism: defining the exception, raising or generating the exception, and handling the exception. We look first at handling exceptions and then at defining and raising them.

■ The *try-catch-finally* Statement

Ever since Chapter 2, when we introduced the BufferedReader class, we have found it necessary to forward an IOException to the JVM. We noted that the alternative to forwarding is to catch an exception.

When an error occurs in a method call, it isn't always possible for the method itself to take care of it. For example, suppose we ask the user for a file name in a dialog, get the name from a field, and then attempt to open the file (prepare it for reading by calling the FileReader constructor). The constructor discovers that the file doesn't exist and, therefore, cannot open it. Perhaps the file has been deleted, or maybe the user just mistyped the name. The constructor has no way of knowing that the proper response to the error is to ask the user to reenter the name. Because the constructor can't deal with this error appropriately, it doesn't even try. It passes the problem on to the method that called it, such as main.

> **Exception handler** A section of code that is executed when a particular exception occurs. In Java, an exception handler appears within a catch clause of a *try-catch-finally* control structure.

When a call returns with an exception, normal execution ends and the JVM looks to see whether code is available to take care of the problem. That code is called an **exception handler** and is part of a *try-catch-finally* statement.

The syntax template for a *try-catch-finally* statement follows:

```
try
        Block

catch (Exception-Type Object-Name)
        Block

    ⋮

finally
        Block
```

As the diagram shows, the statement has three main parts. The first part is the keyword try and a block (a { } pair enclosing any number of statements). The second part is an optional series of catch clauses, each consisting of the keyword catch, a single parameter declaration enclosed in parentheses, and a block. The last part is also optional and consists of the keyword finally and a block.

When a statement or series of statements in an application may result in an exception, we enclose them in the block following `try`. For each type of exception that can be produced by the statements, we write a `catch` clause. Here's an example:

```
try
{
    ...         // Statements that try to open a file
}
catch (IOException ioErr)
{
    ...         // Statements that execute if the file can't be opened
}
finally
{
    ...         // Statements that are always executed
}
```

The `try` statement is meant to sound something like the coach telling the gymnast, "Go ahead and try this move that you're unsure of, and I'll catch you if you fall." We are telling the computer to try executing some operations that might fail, and then providing code to catch the potential exceptions. The `finally` clause provides an opportunity to clean up, regardless of what happens in the `try` and `catch` blocks. We focus on the execution of a `try` statement without a `finally` clause (a *try-catch* statement) and briefly describe at the end of this section what happens when we add the `finally` clause.

Execution of *try-catch*   If none of the statements in the `try` block throws an exception, then control transfers to the statement following the entire *try-catch* statement. That is, we try some statements, and if everything goes according to plan we continue on with the succeeding statements.

When an exception occurs, control immediately transfers to the block associated with the appropriate `catch`. It is important to recognize that control jumps directly from whatever statement caused the exception to the `catch` block. If statements appear in the `try` block following the one that caused the exception, they are skipped. If the `catch` block executes without causing any new exceptions, then control transfers to the next statement outside of the *try-catch* structure.

How does the computer know which `catch` is appropriate? It looks at the class of the parameter declared in each one and selects the first one with a class that matches the thrown exception. Given how Java uses objects for just about everything, it should come as no surprise to learn that an exception is an object and has a class. We've already seen three such classes: `IOException`, `NumberFormatException`, and `ClassNotFoundException`. Another of these classes is `ArithmeticException`, which is thrown when we attempt to execute an invalid arithmetic operation (such as integer division by zero).

Let's look at an example of a *try-catch* statement to illustrate this process. In the following code, note that the first catch has a parameter of type IOException and the second has a parameter of ArithmeticException.

```
try
{
  // Some statements
}
catch (IOException ioErr)
{
  // Statements to handle IO errors
}
catch(ArithmeticException arithErr)
{
  // Statements to handle division by zero
}
```

The computer begins by executing the statements within the try block. If one of them causes an IOException, then control jumps to the first catch clause. On the other hand, if a statement causes an ArithmeticException, then control jumps to the second catch clause.

What happens if a statement throws an exception that isn't among the catch clauses? In that case, the try statement fails to catch the error, and its enclosing method throws the exception to its caller. If the caller doesn't have a handler for the error, it throws the exception to its caller, and so on, until the exception is either caught or ends up at the JVM. In the latter case, the JVM halts the application and displays an error message.

Any object that is passed to a catch clause through its parameter list must have an associated value-returning method called getMessage. The getMessage method returns a string containing a message. For example, it might contain the name of the file that could not be opened. Thus you could write the following statement in a catch clause to display a message:

```
catch (IOException ioErr)
{
  out.add(new JLabel("I/O Exception encountered for " +
    ioErr.getMessage()));
}
```

Let's look at an actual example. Suppose we have prompted the user to enter a file name into a field. When the user clicks a button, an event handler is called to open that file as a PrintWriter. We could use the following code in the button event handler to attempt to open the file. If the file can't be opened, we display an error message and clear the input field so that the user can try again.

```
filename = fileField.getText();
try
{
```

```
    outFile = new PrintWriter(new FileWriter(filename));
}
catch (IOException ioErr)
{
    errorLabel.setText("Unable to open file " + filename);
    fileField.setText("");
}
```

Execution of try-catch-finally When a `finally` clause appears in a `try` statement, the block follow-ing `finally` is always executed, no matter what happens in the `try` and `catch` blocks. Thus, even when a `catch` causes a new exception, the `finally` block executes. The `finally` block gives us an opportunity to clean up after a failed `catch`. In writing the algorithm for the `finally` block, however, it is important to realize that this block always executes, even if the `try` succeeds.

In this book we use only *try-catch* statements, and we keep our exception handlers sim-ple so that they won't produce additional exceptions. The `finally` clause is really needed only when a `catch` contains statements that might generate a new exception, and we need to undo some of its processing before throwing the exception.

■ Generating an Exception with *throw*

Standard library classes are not the only classes that can generate exceptions. Here we in-troduce the *throw* statement, which we use when raising or generating an exception.

All exceptions are thrown by a *throw* statement. Its syntax is quite simple:

Throw-Statement

> throw Object-Expression;

The Object-Expression must be either a variable or a value of a reference type that can be assigned to the class `Throwable`. That is, it must denote the address of an object of the class `Throwable` or a subclass of `Throwable` such as `Exception` (which we discuss in the next sec-tion). The class `Throwable` and all of its subclasses must have a `String`-returning `getMessage` method. When an exception is thrown, the JVM looks for a `catch` clause that can handle that specific class of exception.

The *throw* statement may be written within a *try* statement that is intended to catch it. In that case, control is transferred to the `catch` clause with the corresponding class.

More often, the *throw* occurs inside a method that is called from within a *try* statement, as shown in Figure 9.1. The JVM first looks for a `catch` within the method. When it fails to find one, it causes the method to return. The JVM then looks around the point where the method was called and finds an appropriate `catch` clause. The `catch` executes, and control transfers to the statement following the *try-catch*.

If the JVM can't find a matching `catch` when it forces the method to return, it causes the method containing the call to return as well. The JVM looks around that call point for a *try-catch*; if it can't find one, it forces another return. The series of returns can lead all the way

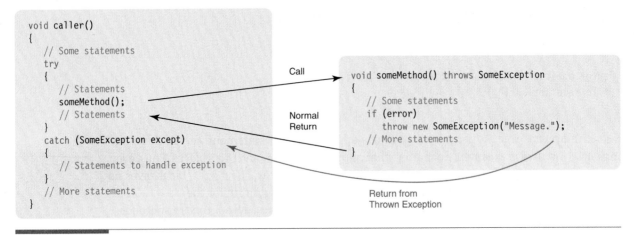

Figure 9.1 Throwing an Exception to be Caught in a Calling Method

back to `main`. If `main` fails to catch the exception, then the JVM handles it by stopping the application and displaying an error message.

As we've seen previously, we must handle each class of exception either by catching it or explicitly forwarding it with a `throws` clause in the method heading. Thus an exception can cause a chain of returns that reaches the JVM only when our code is written to allow it to do so. We can't generate an exception that is accidentally uncaught.

We can throw any of the standard exceptions that Java provides. For example:

```java
throw new FileNotFoundException(filename);
```

It's actually quite rare to throw one of the predefined exceptions. One situation where we might do so is when we've caught such an exception in a `catch` clause but some aspect of handling it must be passed to a higher-level method.

Instead of throwing a predefined exception, we typically want to define and throw a new exception class. A user of the class must then handle that class of exception. For example, in our `Address` class from Chapter 7, we could have validated the ZIP code. Basic ZIP codes are five digits or less. If a ZIP code is greater than 99,999, we can throw a `ZipCodeInvalidException` in the constructor for an `Address` object as follows:

```java
public Address(String name, String city, String state, int zipCode)
     throws ZipCodeInvalidException
{
  if (zipCode <= 99999)
    this.zipCode = zipCode;       // If valid, store value
  else                            //   throw exception
    throw new ZipCodeInvalidException("" + zipCode);
```

```
      .
      .
      .
}
```

We would call this constructor within a *try-catch* statement:

```
try
{
  myAddress = new Address("myName", "Austin", "Texas", 78744);
}
catch (ZipCodeInvalidException zip)
{
  // Exception handler
  // Print bad ZIP code
  System.out.println(zip.getMessage() + " is invalid");
}
```

Whatever method is attempting to create an Address object with an invalid ZIP code is then responsible for handling the error. Of course, we also need to define the class called ZipCodeInvalidException.

Exception Classes

A *throw* statement must have an exception object to throw. Exception objects are very simple to create. Their class name conveys the basic information that tells the JVM what sort of exception is being thrown. Typically, all we need to add is an error message or some other piece of information that helps the catch clause handle the error.

The predefined type Exception is derived from Throwable and provides a field for an error message. All we have to do is extend it with our own class name and supply a pair of constructors that call super. Here is how we define zipCodeInvalidException:

```
package addressBook;
public class ZipCodeInvalidException extends Exception
{
  public ZipCodeInvalidException()
  {
    super();
  }
  public ZipCodeInvalidException(String message)
  {
    super(message);
  }
}
```

Look at the *try-catch* in the previous section:

```
try
{
  myAddress = new Address("myName", "Austin", "Texas", 78744);
}
catch (ZipCodeInvalidException zip)
{
  // Exception handler
  // Print bad ZIP code
  System.out.println(zip.getMessge() + " is invalid");
}
```

Switch expression The expression whose value determines which *switch* label is selected. It must be an integer type other than `long`.

In the `catch` clause, we use `getMessage` to retrieve the same string that was used to instantiate the object of class `ZipCodeInvalidException`.

Whenever you design a class, you should consider whether some error conditions cannot be handled strictly within the class. Exceptions are, as their name implies, meant to be used for exceptional situations. We recommend using an exception only when no simple way to handle an error is available.

9.2 Additional Control Statements

The *switch* Statement

The *switch* statement is a selection control structure for multiway branches. A *switch* is similar to nested *if* statements. The value of a **switch expression**—an integer expression—determines which of the branches executes. Look at the following example *switch* statement:

```
switch (digit)            // The switch expression is (digit)
{
  case 1 : Statement1;    // Statement1 executes if digit is 1
           break;         // Go to Statement5
  case 2 :
  case 3 : Statement2;    // Statement 2 executes if digit is 2 or 3
           break;         // Go to Statement5
  case 4 :  Statement3;   // Statement3 executes if digit is 4
           break;         // Go to Statement5
  default: Statement4;    // Execute Statement4 and go to Statement5
}
Statement5;               // Always executes
```

In this example, `digit` is the switch expression. The statement means, "If `digit` is 1, execute Statement1 and break out of the *switch* statement and continue with Statement5. If `digit` is 2 or 3, execute Statement2 and continue with Statement5. If `digit` is 4, execute Statement3 and continue with Statement5. If `digit` is none of the values previously mentioned, execute Statement4 and continue with Statement5." Figure 9.2 shows the flow of control through this statement.

The *break* statement causes control to immediately jump to the statement following the *switch* statement. We will see shortly what happens if we omit the *break* statements.

Let's look at the syntax template for the *switch* statement and then consider what actually happens when it executes. The syntax template for the *switch* statement is

Switch-Statement

```
switch (Integral-Expression)
{
    SwitchLabel . . .Statement . . .
        .
        .
        .
}
```

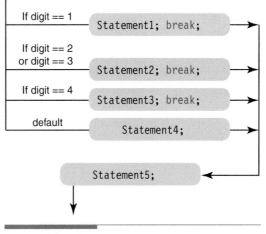

Figure 9.2 Flow of Control in the Example *switch* Statement

Here Integral-Expression is an expression of type `char`, `byte`, `short`, or `int`. The Switch-Label in front of a statement is either a *case label* or a *default label*:

Switch-Label

```
    case Constant-Expression :
    default :
```

In a case label, Constant-Expression is an expression of type `char`, `byte`, `short`, or `int`, whose operands must be literal or named constants. Following are examples of constant expressions (where `CLASS_SIZE` is a named constant of type `int`):

```
3
CLASS_SIZE
'A'
```

The data type of Constant-Expression is converted, if necessary, to match the type of the switch expression.

In our earlier example that tests the value of `digit`, the following are the case labels:

```
case 1 :
case 2 :
case 3 :
case 4 :
```

As that example shows, multiple case labels may precede a single branch.

The value resulting from each Constant-Expression within a *switch* statement must be unique. If a value appears more than once among the case labels, a syntax error results. In that scenario, the compiler simply can't determine to which of the identical cases to branch. Also, only one `default` label can appear in a *switch* statement.

Be careful: `case 1` does not mean the first case. We've listed the values in order because it makes the statement easier to read. Java, however, allows us to place them in *any* order. The following *switch* statement behaves in exactly the same way as our earlier example:

```
switch (digit)          // The switch expression is (digit)
{
  case 3  :
  case 2  : Statement2;   // Statement2 executes if digit is 2 or 3
            break;        // Go to Statement5
  case 4  : Statement3;   // Statement3 executes if digit is 4
            break;        // Go to Statement5
  case 1  : Statement1;   // Statement1 executes if digit is 1
            break;        // Go to Statement5
  default : Statement4;   // Else execute Statement4 and go to
                          // Statement5
}
Statement5;               // Always executes
```

The flow of control through a *switch* statement goes like this: First, the switch expression is evaluated. Next, each expression beside the reserved word `case` is tested to see whether it matches the switch expression. If the values match, control branches to the statement associated with that case label (the statement on the other side of the colon). From there, control proceeds sequentially until either a *break* statement or the end of the *switch* statement is encountered. If the value of the *switch* expression doesn't match any case value, then one of two things happens. If there is a `default` label, control branches to the associated statement. If there is no `default` label, the statements in the *switch* are skipped and control proceeds to the statement following the entire *switch* statement.

The following *switch* statement prints an appropriate comment based on a student's grade (`grade` is of type `char`). The switch expression can be `char`, as Java considers `char` to be an integral type because it can be converted to type `int`.

```
switch (grade)
{
  case 'A' :
  case 'B' : outFile.print("Good Work");
             break;
  case 'C' : outFile.print("Average Work");
             break;
```

```
case 'D' :
case 'F' : outFile.print("Poor Work");
           numberInTrouble++;
           break;              // Unnecessary, but a good habit
}
```

Note that the final *break* statement is unnecessary, but programmers often include it anyway. One reason is that it's easier to insert another case label at the end if a *break* statement is already present.

If grade does not contain one of the specified characters, none of the statements within the *switch* executes. It would be wise to add a default label to account for an invalid grade:

```
switch (grade)
{
  case 'A' :
  case 'B' : outFile.print("Good Work");
             break;
  case 'C' : outFile.print("Average Work");
             break;
  case 'D' :
  case 'F' : outFile.print("Poor Work");
             numberInTrouble++;
             break;
  default  : outFile.print(grade + " is not a valid letter grade.");
}
```

A *switch* statement with a *break* statement after each case alternative behaves exactly like an *if-else-if* control structure. For example, the preceding *switch* statement is equivalent to the following code:

```
if (grade == 'A' || grade == 'B')
  outFile.print("Good Work");
else if (grade == 'C')
  outFile.print("Average Work");
else if (grade == 'D' || grade == 'F')
{
  outFile.print("Poor Work");
  numberInTrouble++;
}
else
  outFile.print(grade + "is not a valid letter grade.");
```

Is either of these two versions better than the other? There is no absolute answer to this question. In this particular example, the *switch* statement is easier to understand because of its table-like form. When implementing a multiway branching structure, our advice is to use the one that you feel is easiest to read. Keep in mind that Java provides the *switch* statement as a matter of convenience. Don't feel obligated to use a *switch* statement for every multiway branch.

Finally, let's look at what happens if we omit the *break* statements inside a *switch* statement. Let's rewrite the preceding code segment as if we forgot to include the *break* statements, and see how it behaves:

```
switch (grade)     // Wrong version
{
  case 'A' :
  case 'B' : outFile.print("Good Work");
  case 'C' : outFile.print("Average Work");
  case 'D' :
  case 'F' : outFile.print("Poor Work");
             numberInTrouble++;
  default  : outFile.print(grade + " is not a valid letter grade.");
}
```

If grade happens to be 'H', control branches to the statement at the default label and the output to the file is

```
H is not a valid letter grade.
```

Unfortunately, this case alternative is the only one that works correctly. If grade is 'A', all of the branches execute and the resulting output is

```
Good WorkAverage WorkPoor WorkA is not a valid letter grade.
```

Remember that after a branch is taken to a specific case label, control proceeds sequentially until either a *break* statement or the end of the *switch* statement is encountered. Forgetting a *break* statement in a case alternative is a very common source of errors in Java code.

■ The *do* Statement

The *do* statement is a looping control structure in which the loop condition is tested at the end (bottom) of the loop. This format guarantees that the loop body executes at least once. The syntax template for the *do* statement follows:

Do-Statement

```
do
  Statement
while ( Expression );
```

As usual in Java, Statement is either a single statement or a block. Also, note that the *do*

Admiral Grace Murray Hopper

From 1943 until her death on New Year's Day in 1992, Admiral Grace Murray Hopper was intimately involved with computing. In 1991, she was awarded the National Medal of Technology "for her pioneering accomplishments in the development of computer programming languages that simplified computer technology and opened the door to a significantly larger universe of users."

Admiral Hopper was born Grace Brewster Murray in New York City on December 9, 1906. She attended Vassar and received a Ph.D. in mathematics from Yale. For the next ten years, she taught mathematics at Vassar.

In 1943, Admiral Hopper joined the U.S. Navy and was assigned to the Bureau of Ordnance Computation Project at Harvard University as a programmer on the Mark I. After the war, she remained at Harvard as a faculty member and continued work on the Navy's Mark II and Mark III computers. In 1949, she joined Eckert-Mauchly Computer Corporation and worked on the UNIVAC I. It was there that she made a legendary contribution to computing: She discovered the first computer "bug"—a moth caught in the hardware.

Admiral Hopper had a working compiler in 1952, at a time when the conventional wisdom was that computers could do only arithmetic. Although not on the committee that designed the computer language COBOL, she was active in its design, implementation, and use. COBOL (which stands for Common Business-Oriented Language) was developed in the early 1960s and remains in wide use in business data processing.

Admiral Hopper retired from the Navy in 1966, only to be recalled within a year to full-time active duty. Her mission was to oversee the Navy's efforts to maintain uniformity in programming languages. It has been said that just as Admiral Hyman Rickover was the father of the nuclear navy, Rear Admiral Hopper was the mother of computerized data automation in the Navy. She served with the Naval Data Automation Command until she retired again in 1986 with the rank of rear admiral. At the time of her death, she was a senior consultant at Digital Equipment Corporation.

During her lifetime, Admiral Hopper received honorary degrees from more than 40 colleges and universities. She was honored by her peers on several occasions, including the first Computer Sciences Man of the Year award given by the Data Processing Management Association, and the Contributions to Computer Science Education Award given by the Special Interest Group for Computer Science Education of the ACM (Association for Computing Machinery).

Admiral Hopper loved young people and enjoyed giving talks on college and university campuses. She often handed out colored wires, which she called nanoseconds because they were cut to a length of about one foot—the distance that light travels in a nanosecond (billionth of a second). Her advice to the young was, "You manage things, you lead people. We went overboard on management and forgot about leadership."

When asked which of her many accomplishments she was most proud of, she answered, "All the young people I have trained over the years."

May We Introduce

statement ends with a semicolon.

The *do* statement

```
do
{
   Statement1;
   Statement2;
      .
      .
      .
   StatementN;
} while (Expression);
```

means "Execute the statements between `do` and `while` as long as `Expression` still has the value `true` at the end of the loop." In other words, you execute the statements before you test the expression. Because `while` appears at the end of the block, this statement is sometimes called the *do-while* statement.

Let's compare a *while* loop and a *do* loop that perform the same task: They find the first line that contains just a period in a file of data. We assume that the file contains at least one such line.

while Solution

```
inputStr = dataFile.readLine();
while (!inputStr.equals("."))
   inputStr = dataFile.readLine();
```

do Solution

```
do
   inputStr = dataFile.readLine();
while (!inputStr.equals("."));
```

The *while* solution requires a priming read so that `inputStr` has a value before the loop is entered. This preliminary activity isn't required for the *do* solution because the input statement within the loop executes before the loop condition is evaluated.

We can also use the *do* statement to implement a count-controlled loop if we know in advance that the loop body should always execute at least once. Following are two versions of a loop to sum the integers from 1 through n.

while Solution

```
sum = 0;
counter = 1;
while (counter <= n)
{
   sum = sum + counter;
   counter++;
}
```

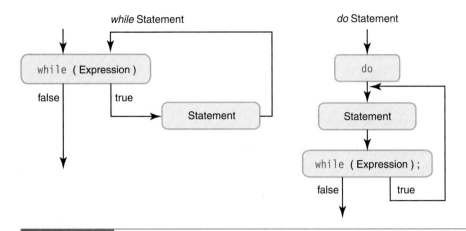

Figure 9.3 Flow of Control: *while* and *do*

do Solution

```
sum = 0;
counter = 1;
do
{
  sum = sum + counter;
  counter++;
} while (counter <= n);
```

If n is a positive number, both of these versions are equivalent. If n is 0 or negative, however, the two loops give different results. In the *while* version, the final value of sum is 0 because the loop body is never entered. In the *do* version, the final value of sum is 1 because the body executes once and *then* the loop test occurs.

Because the *while* statement tests the condition before executing the body of the loop, it is called a *pretest loop*. The *do* statement does the opposite and thus is known as a *posttest loop*. Figure 9.3 compares the flow of control in the *while* and *do* loops.

When we finish introducing all of the new looping constructs, we will offer some guidelines for determining when to use each type of loop.

■ The *for* Statement

The *for* statement is designed to simplify the writing of count-controlled loops. The following statement prints out the integers from 1 through n:

```
for (count = 1; count <= n; count++)
  outFile.println("" + count);
```

This *for* statement says, "Initialize the loop control variable count to 1. While count is less than or equal to n, execute the output statement and increment count by 1. Stop the loop after count has been incremented to n + 1."

The syntax template for a *for* statement follows:

For-Statement

```
for (Init ; Expression ; Update )
        Statement
```

Expression is the condition that continues the loop and must be of type `boolean`. Init can be any of the following: nothing, a local variable declaration, or an expression. Init can also be a series of local variable declarations and expressions separated by commas. Update can be omitted, can be an expression, or can be a series of expressions separated by commas.

Most often, a *for* statement is written such that Init initializes a loop control variable and Update increments or decrements the loop control variable. Here are two loops that execute the same number of times (50):

```
for (loopCount = 1; loopCount <= 50; loopCount++)
   .
   .
   .

for (loopCount = 50; loopCount >= 1; loopCount--)
   .
   .
   .
```

Just like *while* loops, *do* and *for* loops may be nested. For example, the nested *for* structure

```
for (lastNum = 1; lastNum <= 7; lastNum++)
{
   for (numToPrint = 1; numToPrint <= lastNum; numToPrint++)
      outFile.print("" + numToPrint);
   outFile.println();
}
```

prints the following triangle of numbers:

```
1
12
123
1234
12345
123456
1234567
```

Although *for* statements are used primarily for count-controlled loops, Java allows you to write any *while* loop by using a *for* statement. To use *for* loops intelligently, you should know the following facts:

1. In the syntax template, Init and Update are optional. If you omit Update, the termination condition is not automatically updated.
2. According to the syntax template, Expression—the continuation condition—is optional, as shown here:

```
for ( ; ; )
    outFile.println("Hi");
```

   If you omit it, the expression is assumed to be the value true, creating an infinite loop.
3. Init can be a declaration with initialization:

```
for (int count = 1; count <= 20; count++)
    outFile.println("Hi");
```

In the last example, the variable count has local scope, even though no braces in the code explicitly create a block. The scope of count extends only to the end of the *for* statement. Like any local variable, count is inaccessible outside its scope (that is, outside the *for* statement). Because count is local to the for statement, it's possible to write code like this:

```
for (int count = 1; count <= 20; count++)
    outFile.println("Hi");
for (int count = 1; count <= 100; count++)
    outFile.println("Ed");
```

This code does not generate a compile-time error (such as "MULTIPLY DEFINED IDENTIFIER"). Instead, we have declared two distinct variables named count, each of which remains local to its own *for* statement.

The syntax for Init and Update allows them to have multiple parts, separated by commas. All of the parts execute as if they form a block of statements. For example, it is sometimes useful to have a second variable in a loop that is a multiple of the iteration counter. The following loop has two variables: one that counts by one and is used as the loop control variable and another that counts by five.

```
for (int count = 1, int byFives = 5; count <= n; count++, byFives = count * 5)
    outFile.println("Count = " + count + " * 5 = " + byFives);
```

If n is 7, this loop produces the following output:

```
Count = 1 * 5 = 5
Count = 2 * 5 = 10
Count = 3 * 5 = 15
Count = 4 * 5 = 20
Count = 5 * 5 = 25
Count = 6 * 5 = 30
Count = 7 * 5 = 35
```

Guidelines for Choosing a Looping Statement

Here are some guidelines to help you decide when to use each of the three looping statements (*while*, *do*, and *for*):

1. If the loop is a simple count-controlled loop, the *for* statement is a natural choice. Concentrating the three loop control actions—initialize, test, and increment/decrement—into one location (the heading of the *for* statement) reduces the chances that you will forget to include one of them.

2. If the loop is an event-controlled loop whose body should execute at least once, a *do* statement is appropriate.

3. If the loop is an event-controlled loop and nothing is known about the first execution, use a *while* statement.

4. When in doubt, use a *while* statement.

9.3 Additional Java Operators

Java offers a rich, sometimes bewildering, array of operators that allow you to manipulate values of the primitive data types. Operators you have learned about so far include the assignment operator (=), the arithmetic operators (+, -, *, /, %), the increment and decrement operators (++, --), the relational operators (==, !=, <, <=, >, >=), the string concatenation operator (+), and the conditional (short-circuit evaluation) logical operators (!, &&, ||). In certain cases, a pair of parentheses is also considered to be an operator—namely, the type cast operator,

```java
y = (float)someInt;
```

Java also has many specialized operators that are seldom found in other programming languages. Table 9.1 lists these additional operators. As you inspect the table, don't panic—a quick scan will do.

The operators in Table 9.1, along with those you already know, comprise all of the Java operators.

Assignment Operators and Assignment Expressions

Java has several assignment operators. The equals sign (=) is the basic assignment operator. When combined with its two operands, it forms an assignment expression (*not* an assignment statement). Every assignment expression has a *value* and a *side effect*—namely, that the value is stored into the variable denoted by the left side of the expression. For example, the expression

Assignment expression A Java expression with (1) a value and (2) the side effect of storing the expression value into a memory location

```java
delta = 2 * 12
```

has the value 24 and the side effect of storing this value into delta.

Operator		Remarks
Combined Assignment Operators		
+=	Add and assign	
–=	Subtract and assign	
*=	Multiply and assign	
/=	Divide and assign	
%=	Remainder and assign	
Increment and Decrement Operators		
++	Pre-increment	Example: ++someVar
++	Postincrement	Example: someVar++
--	Pre-decrement	Example: --someVar
--	Postdecrement	Example: someVar--
Bitwise Operators		Integer operands only
<<	Left shift	
>>	Right shift with sign extension	
>>>	Right shift with zero extension	
&	Bitwise AND	
|	Bitwise OR	
^	Bitwise EXCLUSIVE OR	
~	Complement (invert all bits)	
Boolean Full Evaluation Operators		Boolean operands only
&	Boolean AND	
|	Boolean OR	
^	Boolean EXCLUSIVE OR	
More Combined Assignment Operators		Integer operands only
<<=	Shift left and assign	
>>=	Shift right with sign extension and assign	
>>>=	Shift right with zero extension and assign	
&=	Bitwise AND and assign	
|=	Bitwise OR and assign	
^=	Bitwise EXCLUSIVE OR and assign	
Other operators		
instanceof	Type comparison	object instanceof ClassName
?:	Conditional operator	Form: Expr1 ? Expr2 : Expr3

Table 9.1   Additional Java Operators

In Java, an expression consisting of a variable and an increment or decrement expression also becomes an **expression statement** when it is terminated by a semicolon. All three of the following are valid Java statements:

> **Expression statement** A statement formed by appending a semicolon to an assignment expression, an increment expression, or a decrement expression

```
alpha++;
beta--;
--gamma;
```

Each of these statements either increments or decrements the given variable.

Because an assignment is an expression and not a statement, you can use it anywhere that an expression is allowed. The following statement stores the value 20 into firstInt, the value 30 into secondInt, and the value 35 into thirdInt:

```
thirdInt = (secondInt = (firstInt = 20) + 10) + 5;
```

Although some Java programmers use this style of coding, we do not recommend it. It is hard to read and error-prone.

In Chapter 6, we cautioned against the mistake of using the = operator in place of the == operator:

```
if (alpha = 12)   // Wrong
   .
   .
   .
```

The condition in the *if* statement is an assignment expression, not a relational expression. The value of the expression is 12, which is not a boolean value, so a compiler error results.

In addition to the = operator, Java has several combined assignment operators (+=, *=, and the others listed in Table 9.1). These operators have the following semantics:

Statement	Equivalent Statement
i += 5;	i = i + 5;
pivotPoint *= n + 3;	pivotPoint = pivotPoint * (n + 3);

The combined assignment operators are another example of "ice cream and cake." They are sometimes convenient for writing a line of code more compactly, but you can do just fine without them. We do not use them in this book.

Increment and Decrement Operators

The increment and decrement operators (++ and --) operate only on variables, not on constants or arbitrary expressions. Suppose a variable someInt contains the value 3. The expression ++someInt denotes pre-incrementation. The side effect of incrementing someInt occurs first, so the expression has the value 4. In contrast, the expression someInt++ denotes postincrementation. The value of the expression is 3, and *then* the side effect of incrementing someInt takes place. The following code illustrates the difference between pre- and post-incrementation:

```
int1 = 14;
int2 = ++int1;
// At this point, int1 == 15  and  int2 == 15
int1 = 14;
int2 = int1++;
// At this point int1 == 15  and  int2 == 14
```

Some people make a game of seeing how much they can accomplish in the fewest keystrokes possible by using side effects in the middle of larger expressions. Professional software development, however, requires writing code that other programmers can read and understand. Use of side effects reduces readability.

By far, the most common use of ++ and -- is to perform the incrementation or decrementation as a separate expression statement:

```
count++;
```

Here, the value of the expression is not used, but we get the desired side effect of incrementing count.

■ Bitwise Operators

You use the bitwise operators listed in Table 9.1 (<<, >>, >>>, &, |, and so forth) to manipulate individual bits within a memory cell. This book does not explore the use of these operators; the topic of bit-level operations is most often covered in a course on computer organization and assembly language programming. However, we will draw your attention to the fact that three of the bitwise operators have a second meaning in Java: The &, | and ^ operators can also be used with boolean operands to perform logical AND, OR, and EXCLUSIVE OR operations without short-circuit evaluation.

Recall from Chapter 4 that when the first operand of && is false, the second operand need not be evaluated because the result must be false. When used in combination with boolean operands, the & operator causes the second operand to be evaluated regardless of the value of the first operand. Similar rules apply to the | and ^ operators.

Here is an example that illustrates the difference between these logical operators:

```
// This code works OK when i is 0 because m/i isn't evaluated
if (i != 0 && m/i >= 4)
  k = 20;
```

Now consider what happens if we use & in place of &&:

```
// This code fails when i is 0 because of division by zero
if (i != 0 & m/i >= 4)
    k = 20;
```

In rare cases, full evaluation is useful. We recommend, however, that you always use the relational operators && and || in your logical expressions.

Theoretical Foundations

Analysis of Algorithms

If you are given the choice of cleaning a room with a toothbrush or a broom, you probably would choose the broom. Using a broom sounds like less work than using a toothbrush. True, if the room is located in a doll house, it may be easier to use the toothbrush, but in general a broom is the faster way to clean. If you are given the choice of adding numbers together with a pencil and paper or a calculator, you would probably choose the calculator because it is usually less work. If you are given the choice of walking or driving to a meeting, you would probably choose to drive; it sounds like less work.

What do these examples have in common? And what do they have to do with computer science? In each of the settings mentioned, one of the choices seems to involve significantly less work. Measuring the amount of work precisely is difficult in each case, however, because there are unknowns. How large is the room? How many numbers must be added? How far away is the meeting? In each case, the unknown information relates to the size of the problem. With an especially small problem (for example, adding 2 plus 2), our original guess at which approach to take (using the calculator) might be wrong. Of course, our intuition is usually correct, because most problems are reasonably large.

In computer science, we need a way to measure the amount of work done by an algorithm relative to the size of a problem, because usually more than one algorithm is available to solve any given problem. We often must choose the most efficient algorithm—that is, the algorithm that does the least work for a problem of a given size.

The amount of work involved in executing an algorithm relative to the size of the problem is the algorithm's complexity. We would like to be able to look at an algorithm and determine its complexity. Then we could take two algorithms that perform the same task and determine which completes the task faster (requires less work).

How do we measure the amount of work required to execute an algorithm? We use the total number of *steps* executed as a measure of work. One statement, such as an assignment, may require only one step; another statement, such as a loop, may require many steps. We define a *step* as any operation roughly equivalent in complexity to a comparison, an I/O operation, or an assignment.

Complexity A measure of the effort expended by the computer in performing a computation, relative to the size of the computation

Given an algorithm with just a sequence of simple statements (no branches or loops), the number of steps performed is directly related to the number of statements. When we introduce branches, however, it becomes possible to skip some statements in the algorithm. Branches allow us to subtract steps without physically removing them from the algorithm because only one branch executes at a time. Because we usually want to express work in terms of the worst-case scenario, we use the number of steps in the longest branch.

Now consider the effect of a loop. If a loop repeats a sequence of 15 simple statements 10 times, it performs 150 steps. Loops allow us to multiply the work done in an algorithm without physically adding statements.

Now that we have a measure for the work done in an algorithm, we can compare algorithms. Suppose, for example, that Algorithm A always executes 3,124 steps and Algorithm B always does the same task in 1,321 steps. Then we can say that Algorithm B is more efficient—that is, it takes fewer steps to accomplish the same task.

If an algorithm, from run to run, always takes the same number of steps or fewer, we say that it executes in an amount of time bounded by a constant. Such algorithms are said to have *constant time* complexity. Be careful: *Constant time* doesn't mean small; it just means that the amount of work done does not exceed some amount from one run to another regardless of the size of the problem.

If a loop executes a fixed number of times, the work done is greater than the physical number of statements but is still constant. What happens if the number of loop iterations can change from one run to the next? Suppose a data file contains N data values to be processed in a loop. If the loop reads and processes one value during each iteration, then the loop executes N iterations. The amount of work done therefore depends on a variable, the number of data values. In this example, the variable N determines the size of the problem.

If we have a loop that executes N times, the number of steps to be executed is some factor times N. This factor is the number of steps performed within a single iteration of the loop. Specifically, the work done by an algorithm with a data-dependent loop is given by the expression

$$\overbrace{S_1 \times N}^{\substack{\text{Steps performed} \\ \text{by the loop}}} + \underbrace{S_0}_{\substack{\text{Steps performed} \\ \text{outside the loop}}}$$

where S_1 is the number of steps in the loop body (a constant for a given simple loop), N is the number of iterations (a variable representing the size of the problem), and S_0 is the number of steps outside the loop. Mathematicians call expressions of this form *linear*; hence, algorithms such as this one are said to have *linear time* complexity. Notice that if N grows very large, the term $S_1 \times N$ dominates the execution time. That is, S_0 becomes an insignificant part of the total execution time. For example, if S_0 and S_1 are each 20 steps, and N is 1,000,000, then the total number of steps is 20,000,020. The 20 steps contributed by S_0 represent only a tiny fraction of the total in this case.

What about a data-dependent loop that contains a nested loop? The number of steps in the inner loop, S_2, and the number of iterations performed by the inner loop, L, must be multiplied by the number of iterations in the outer loop:

$$\overbrace{(S_2 \times L \times N)}^{\substack{\text{Steps performed} \\ \text{by the nested loop}}} + \overbrace{(S_1 \times N)}^{\substack{\text{Steps performed} \\ \text{by the outer loop}}} + \overbrace{S_0}^{\substack{\text{Steps performed outside} \\ \text{the outer loop}}}$$

By itself, the inner loop performs $(S_2 \times L)$ steps. Because it is repeated N times by the outer loop, however, it accounts for a total of $(S_2 \times L \times N)$ steps. If L is a constant, then the algorithm still executes in linear time.

Theoretical Foundations

Now suppose that for each of the N outer loop iterations the inner loop performs N steps (L = N). Here the formula for the total steps is

$$(S_2 \times N \times N) + (S_1 \times N) + S_0$$

or

$$(S_2 \times N^2) + (S_1 \times N) + S_0$$

Because N^2 grows much faster than N (for large values of N), the inner loop term ($S_2 \times N^2$) accounts for the majority of steps executed and the work done. Thus the corresponding execution time is essentially proportional to N^2. Mathematicians call this type of formula *quadratic*. If we have a doubly nested loop, where each loop depends on N, then the complexity expression is

$$(S_3 \times N^3) + (S_2 \times N^2) + (S_1 \times N) + S_0$$

and the work and time are proportional to N^3 whenever N is reasonably large. Such a formula is called *cubic*.

The following table shows the number of steps required for each increase in the exponent of N, where N is a size factor for the problem, such as the number of input values.

N	N^0 (Constant)	N^1 (Linear)	N^2 (Quadratic)	N^3 (Cubic)
1	1	1	1	1
10	1	10	100	1,000
100	1	100	10,000	1,000,000
1,000	1	1,000	1,000,000	1,000,000,000
10,000	1	10,000	100,000,000	1,000,000,000,000
100,000	1	100,000	10,000,000,000	1,000,000,000,000,000

As you can see, each time the exponent increases by 1, the number of steps is multiplied by an additional order of magnitude (factor of 10). That is, if N is made 10 times greater, the work involved in an N^2 algorithm increases by a factor of 100, and the work involved in an N^3 algorithm increases by a factor of 1,000. To put this idea in more concrete terms, an algorithm with a doubly nested loop, in which each loop depends on the number of data values, takes 1,000 steps for 10 input values and 1 quadrillion steps for 100,000 values. On a computer that executes 1 billion instructions per second, the latter case would take more than 10 days to run.

The table also shows that the steps outside the innermost loop account for an insignificant portion of the total number of steps as N gets bigger. Because the innermost loop dominates the total time, we classify the complexity of an algorithm according to the highest order of N that appears in its complexity expression, called the *order of magnitude*, or simply the *order* of that expression. Thus we talk about algorithms having "order N squared complexity" (or "cubed" or so on) or we describe them with what is called *Big-O notation*. In Big-O notation, we express the complexity by putting the highest-order term in parentheses with a capital O in front. For example, O(1) is constant time; O(N) is linear time; O(N^2) is quadratic time; and O(N^3) is cubic time.

Determining the complexities of different algorithms allows us to compare the work they require without having to program and execute them. For example, if you had an $O(N^2)$ algorithm and a linear algorithm that performed the same task, you probably would choose the linear algorithm. We say *probably* because an $O(N^2)$ algorithm actually may execute fewer steps than an $O(N)$ algorithm for small values of N. Recall that if the size factor N is small, the constants and lower-order terms in the complexity expression may be significant.

To see how this idea works, let's look at an example. Suppose that Algorithm A is $O(N^2)$ and that Algorithm B is $O(N)$. For large values of N, we would normally choose Algorithm B because it requires less work than A. But suppose that in Algorithm B, $S_0 = 1,000$ and $S_1 = 1,000$. If N = 1, then Algorithm B takes 2,000 steps to execute. Now suppose that for algorithm A, $S_0 = 10$, $S_1 = 10$, and $S_2 = 10$. If N = 1, then Algorithm A takes only 30 steps to execute. The following table compares the number of steps taken by these two algorithms for different values of N.

N	Algorithm A	Algorithm B
1	30	2,000
2	70	3,000
3	130	4,000
10	1,110	11,000
20	4,210	21,000
30	9,310	31,000
50	25,510	51,000
100	101,010	101,000
1,000	10,010,010	1,001,000
10,000	1,000,100,010	10,001,000

From this table we can see that the $O(N^2)$ Algorithm A is actually faster than the $O(N)$ Algorithm B, up to the point where N equals 100. Beyond that point, Algorithm B becomes more efficient. Thus, if we know that N is always less than 100 in a particular problem, we would choose Algorithm A. For example, if the size factor N is the number of test scores on an exam and the class size is limited to 30 students, Algorithm A would be more efficient. On the other hand, if N is the number of scores at a university with 25,000 students, we would choose Algorithm B.

Constant, linear, quadratic, and cubic expressions are all examples of *polynomial* expressions. Algorithms whose complexity is characterized by such expressions are said to execute in *polynomial time* and form a broad class of algorithms that encompasses everything we've discussed so far.

In addition to polynomial-time algorithms, we will encounter a logarithmic-time algorithm in Chapter 11. There are also factorial $[O(N!)]$, exponential $[O(N^N)]$, and hyperexponential $[O(N^{N^N})]$ class algorithms, which can require vast amounts of time to execute and are beyond the scope of this book. For now, the important point to remember is that different algorithms that solve the same problem can vary significantly in the amount of work they do.

Theoretical Foundations

▓ The ?: Operator

The last operator shown in Table 9.1 is the ?: operator, sometimes called the conditional operator. This ternary (three-operand) operator has the following syntax:

Conditional-Expression

```
Expression1 ? Expression2 : Expression3
```

Here's how it works. First, the computer evaluates Expression1. If the value is `true`, then the value of the entire expression is Expression2; otherwise, the value of the entire expression is Expression3.

A classic example of the conditional operator's use is to set a variable max equal to the larger of two variables a and b. Using an *if* statement, we would do it this way:

```
if (a > b)
    max = a;
else
    max = b;
```

With the ?: operator, we can use the following assignment statement:

```
max = (a > b) ? a : b;
```

The ?: operator is certainly not an intuitively obvious bit of Java syntax; it's one of the unusual features that Java inherited from C. We do not use it in this book, but you should be aware of it in case you encounter it when reading code written by someone else.

▓ Operator Precedence

Table 9.2 summarizes the rules of operator precedence for the Java operators we have encountered so far, excluding the bitwise operators. (Appendix B contains the complete list.) In the table, the operators are grouped by precedence level, and a horizontal line separates each precedence level from the next-lower level.

The column labeled *Associativity* describes the grouping order. Within a precedence level, most operators are grouped from left to right. For example,

```
a − b + c
```

Operator	Associativity	Remarks
++ --	Right to left	++ and -- as postfix operators
++ --	Right to left	++ and -- as prefix operators
Unary + Unary −	Right to left	
!	Right to left	
(cast)	Right to left	
* / %	Left to right	
+ −	Left to right	
+	Left to right	String concatenation
< <= > >=	Left to right	
instanceof	Left to right	
== !=	Left to right	
&	Left to right	Boolean operands
^	Left to right	Boolean operands
|	Left to right	Boolean operands
&&	Left to right	
||	Left to right	
?:	Right to left	
= += −= *= /= %=	Right to left	

Table 9.2   Precedence (Highest to Lowest)

means

```
(a − b) + c
```

and not

```
a − (b + c)
```

Certain operators, however, are grouped from right to left—specifically, the unary operators, the assignment operators, and the ?: operator. Look at the unary "− "operator, for example. The expression

```
sum = - -1
```

means

```
sum = -(-1)
```

instead of the meaningless

```
sum = (- -)1
```

This associativity makes sense because the unary "–" operation is naturally a right-to-left operation.

A word of caution: Although operator precedence and associativity dictate the *grouping* of operators with their operands, the precedence rules do not define the *order* in which subexpressions are evaluated. Java further requires that the left-side operand of a two-operand operator be evaluated first. For example, if i currently contains 5, the statement

```
j = ++i + i;
```

stores 12 into j. Let's see why. The expression statement contains three operators: =, ++, and +. The ++ operator has the highest precedence, so it operates just on i, not on the expression i + i. The addition operator has higher precedence than the assignment operator, giving implicit parentheses as follows:

```
j = (++i + i);
```

So far, so good. But now we ask this question: In the addition operation, is the left operand or the right operand evaluated first? As we just saw, the Java language tells us that the left-side operand is evaluated first. Therefore, the result is 6 + 6, or 12. If Java had instead specified that the right-side operand comes first, the expression would have yielded 6 + 5, or 11.

In most expressions, Java's left-side rule doesn't have any surprising effects. But when side effect operators such as increment and assignment are involved, you need to remember that the left-side operand is evaluated first. To make the code clear and unambiguous, it's best to write the preceding example with two separate statements:

```
i++;
j = i + i;
```

The moral here is that it's best to avoid unnecessary side effects altogether.

MONTHLY RAINFALL AVERAGES

Problem: Meteorologists have recorded monthly rainfall amounts at several sites throughout a region of the country. You have been asked to write an application that reads one year's rainfall amounts from sites within the region from a file and that prints out the average of the 12 values for each of the sites on a separate file. The first line of a data set consists of the name of the site, and the 12 values for the site follow on the next line with exactly one blank in between each value. The data file is named `rainData.dat`.

Brainstorming: This problem sounds familiar. In Chapter 8, we wrote an application that took rainfall amounts from observers and calculated the running average. In that problem we used a window for input and output; this problem asks for file input and output. Calculating an average should be the same, but where the calculation takes place is different. In the previous problem the calculation took place in the handler for the button event. This problem does not include any buttons.

There are other nouns in the problem, but they describe the context like *region, country*, and *sites*, so they are not objects in the solution. What are the objects? The application and the file objects.

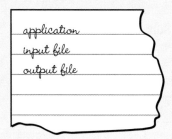

application
input file
output file

Filtering: This looks like a very sparse set of classes for a problem that includes calculating a series of averages. This problem has a process that is repeated over different data, but we do not have any objects other than numeric values and files.

What about error conditions? We can't determine what they might be at this stage, other than to say that the data might have been entered incorrectly on the file. Let's add an exception class to our list of classes.

Before we look at the responsibilities of each class, let's name them. Let's call the application class `RainFall` and the exception class `DataSetException`.

Scenarios: The processing takes place within the application class `Rainfall`: processing a data set, writing the average, and repeating the process until no more data sites remain. The class `DataSetException` should just pass the message sent to it on to its superclass to be printed if the application ends with an error. `Rainfall` has the responsibility to throw a `DataSetException` if necessary.

CRC Cards: On the CRC card, we summarize `RainFall`'s responsibilities.

Class Name: *Rainfall*	Superclass: *Object*	Subclasses:
Responsibilities	**Collaborations**	
Prepare the file for input	*FileReader, BufferedReader*	
Prepare the file for output	*FileWriter, PrintWriter*	
Process data	*BufferedReader*	
Throw exceptions if necessary	*DataSetException*	

Class Name: *DataSetException*	Superclass: *Exception*	Subclasses:
Responsibilities	**Collaborations**	
Create itself		
Pass message to super	*Super*	

Responsibility Algorithms: Preparing a file for input and output has become so routine that we do not need to write the algorithms for these operations. The third responsibility, processing data, is the heart of the problem. At the topmost level of the design, we need a loop to process the data from all the sites. Each iteration must process one site's data, then check for a new site name. The application does not know in advance how many recording sites are in the file, so the loop cannot be a count-controlled loop. Although we can make *for*, *while*, or *do* loops work correctly, we use a *do* loop under the assumption that the file definitely contains at least one site's data. Therefore, we can set up the loop so that it processes the data from a recording site and then, at the *bottom* of the loop, decides whether to iterate again.

```
Process Data
Prepare input file, inFile
Prepare output file, outFile
Read data set name
do
   Process one site
   Read data set name
while (more data)
Close files
```

Processing one site requires another loop to input 12 monthly rainfall amounts and sum them. Using the summing technique with which we are highly familiar by now, we initialize the sum to 0 before starting the loop, and each loop iteration reads another number and adds it to the accumulating sum. A *for* loop is appropriate for this task, because we know that exactly 12 iterations must occur. What if the user has keyed one of the data values incorrectly? What if a negative value is input? We had better put the *for* loop in a *try-catch* statement. Once we have the value, we should throw an exception if it is negative.

```
Process One Site
Set sum to 0.0
try to
  Get a line of values
  for months going from 1 to 12
    Get rainfall amount
      if amount is negative
        throw DataSetException("negative value found")
      else
        Set sum to sum  + amount
  Write "Average for " + data set name + " is "  + sum/12
catch and handle exceptions
```

Because all of the input values are on one line with a blank in between them, we must extract the characters that make up one value before we can convert it. We can

CASE STUDY

use the `String` methods `indexOf` and `substring` to extract a string that represents exactly one floating-point value.

> Get Rainfall Amount
>
> ```
> Set index to line.indexOf(' ')
> Set currentValue to line.substring(0, index)
> Set line to substring(index+1, line.length())
> Set amount to Double.parseDouble(currentValue)
> ```

Before we go on, we had better hand-simulate this algorithm. Let's apply it to the following string:

`"23.5 5.6 5.44"`

index	currentValue	line	amount
4	"23.5"	"5.6 5.44"	23.5
3	"5.6"	"5.44"	5.6
error	"5.44"		

There is an error in the logic. Unless a blank follows the last value rather than an end of line, the `indexOf` method returns –1, indicating that there isn't another blank. We then use the `index` in the next statement, producing an error in the method `substring`. We need to check whether a blank is found. If it is not, the remaining string is the last value in the line.

> Get Rainfall Amount (revised)
>
> ```
> Set index to line.indexOf(' ')
> if index > 0
>   Set currentValue to line.substring(0, index)
>   Set line to substring(index+1, line.length())
> else
>   Set currentValue to line
>   Set amount to Double.parseDouble(currentValue)
> ```

We now need to decide what other errors might occur, how to catch them, and how to handle them. The file can throw an `IOException`, the conversion operation can throw a `NumberFormatException`, and our own code can throw a `DataSetException`. For the `IOException`, let's catch it, print out the site name, and end the application. For the `NumberFormatException`, let's print out the site name with an error message and continue processing with the next site. We can do the same for `DataSetException`.

Catch and Handle Exceptions

```
catch IOException
  Write "I/O Exception with site " + data set name
  End application
catch NumberFormatException
  Write "NumberFormatException with site " + data set name
catch DataSetException
  Write message + data set name
```

The only abstract step left is to determine when the outer loop finishes. We could read in a new site name and quit if there are no more data, or we could use a site name of "Quit" to end the processing. Let's use the latter technique here.

More Data

```
dataSetName is not "Quit"
```

Assumptions: The file contains data for at least one site.

```
package rainfall;

// Define an Exception class for signaling data set errors
public class DataSetException extends Exception
{
  public DataSetException()
  {
    super();
  }
  public DataSetException(String message)
  {
    super(message);
  }
}


package rainfall;
import java.io.*;
public class Rainfall
// ***********************************************************************
//  Rainfall application
//  This application accepts input of 12 monthly rainfall amounts from a recording
//    site and computes the average monthly rainfall.
//  This process is repeated for as many recording sites as the user wishes.
// ***********************************************************************
```

```java
{
  static void processOneSite(BufferedReader inFile, PrintWriter outFile, String
    dataSetName)
  {
    int    count;           // Loop control variable
    double amount;          // Rainfall amount for one month
    double sum = 0.0;       // Sum of amounts for the year
    String dataLine;        // String to input amount from inFile
    String currentValue;    // Floating-point string
    int    index;           // Position of blank

    try
    {
      // Next line could produce an IOException
      dataLine = inFile.readLine();
      for (count = 1; count <= 12; count++)   // For 12 months
      {
        index = dataLine.indexOf(' ');        // Find position of blank
        if (index > 0)
        { // Blank found
          currentValue = dataLine.substring(0, index);  // Extract a number
          // Remove current value from string
          dataLine = dataLine.substring(Math.min(index+1,
                     dataLine.length()), dataLine.length());
        }
        else  // Remaining string is current value
          currentValue = dataLine;
        // Next line could produce NumberFormatException
        amount = Double.parseDouble(currentValue);  // Convert to double
        if (amount < 0.0)
          throw new DataSetException("Negative value in site ");
        else
          sum = sum + amount;
      }
      outFile.println("Average for " + dataSetName + " is " + sum/12);

    }
    catch (IOException except)
    {
      outFile.println("IOException with site " + dataSetName);
      System.exit(0);
    }
```

```
    catch (NumberFormatException except)
    {
      outFile.println("NumberFormatException in site " + dataSetName);
    }
    catch (DataSetException except)
    {
      outFile.println(except.getMessage() + dataSetName);
    }
  }

  public static void main(String[] args) throws FileNotFoundException,
    IOException
  {
    String  dataSetName;              // Name of reporting station
    BufferedReader inFile;            // Data file
    PrintWriter outFile;             // Output file

    inFile = new BufferedReader(new FileReader("rainData.dat"));
    outFile = new PrintWriter(new FileWriter("outfile.dat"));

    dataSetName = inFile.readLine();      // Get name of reporting station
    do
    {
      processOneSite(inFile, outFile, dataSetName);
      dataSetName = inFile.readLine();    // Get name of reporting station
    } while (!dataSetName.equals("Quit"));
    inFile.close();
    outFile.close();
  }
}
```

Testing: We should test two separate aspects of the Rainfall application. First, we should verify that the application works correctly given valid input data. Supplying arbitrary rainfall amounts of zero or greater, we must confirm that the application correctly adds up the values and divides by 12 to produce the average. Also, we should verify that the application behaves correctly when it reaches the sentinel value "Quit".

Second, we should test the data validation code. We should include negative numbers in the file to ensure that such data sets are not processed. Similarly, we need to include some values that are improperly formed floating-point values. Here's a sample input file that accomplishes the necessary testing:

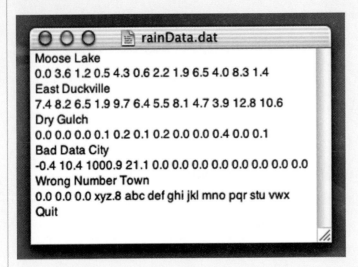

Here is the output from running the application on this data file:

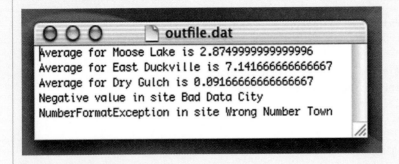

9.4 Testing and Debugging

The same testing techniques we used with *while* loops apply to *do* and *for* loops as well. There are, however, a few additional considerations with these loops.

The body of a *do* loop always executes at least once. For this reason, you should try data sets that show the result of executing a *do* loop the minimal number of times.

With a data-dependent *for* loop, it is important to test for proper results when the loop executes zero times. This situation arises when the starting value is greater than the ending value (or less than the ending value if the loop control variable is being decremented).

When an application contains a *switch* statement, you should test it with enough different data sets to ensure that each branch is selected and executed correctly. You should also test the application with a switch expression whose value is not in any of the case labels.

An application that handles exceptions must be tested to ensure that the exceptions are generated appropriately and then handled properly. Test cases must be included to cause exceptions to occur, and the expected results from handling them must be specified.

Testing and Debugging Hints

1. Make sure that all exceptions are either caught or forwarded as appropriate.

2. In a *switch* statement, make sure that a *break* statement appears at the end of each case alternative. Otherwise, control "falls through" to the code in the next case alternative.

3. Case labels in a *switch* statement consist of values, not variables. They may, however, include named constants and expressions involving only constants.

4. A switch expression must be one of the types `char`, `byte`, `short`, or `int`. It cannot be of type `long` or a floating-point or string expression.

5. The case constants of a *switch* statement cannot be of type `long` or be floating-point or string constants.

6. If the possibility exists that the value of the switch expression might not match one of the case constants, you should provide a `default` alternative.

7. Double-check long *switch* statements to make sure that you haven't omitted any branches.

8. The *do* loop is a posttest loop. If the possibility exists that the loop body might be skipped entirely, use a *while* or *for* statement.

9. The *for* statement heading (the first line) always has three parts within the parentheses. Typically, the first part initializes a loop control variable, the second part tests the variable, and the third part increments or decrements the variable. The three parts must be separated by semicolons. Any of the parts can be omitted, but the semicolons still must be present.

Summary

An exception occurs when an error condition is encountered in a method and the method cannot directly resolve the problem. The method is said to "throw an exception," which we can catch using a *try* statement. Catching an exception and handling it properly enables the application to continue executing, rather than allowing the error to be passed to the JVM, which halts the application with an error message.

Learning Portfolio

Typical exceptions include `IOException`, `NumberFormatException`, and `Arithmetic-Exception`.

The *throw* statement gives us the ability to throw exceptions when we detect them. When we create new classes derived from `Exception`, we can throw exceptions that are specific to our classes and methods. Those exceptions can then be caught and handled in ways that are more appropriate than would be possible if we were restricted to using the exception classes in the Java library.

The *switch* statement is a multiway selection statement. It allows the code to choose among a set of branches. A *switch* statement containing *break* statements can always be simulated by an *if-then-else-if* structure. If a *switch* statement can be used, however, it often makes the code easier to read and understand. It cannot be used with floating-point or string values in the case labels.

The *do* loop is a general-purpose looping statement. It works like the *while* loop except that its test occurs at the end of the loop, guaranteeing at least one execution of the loop body. As with a *while* loop, a *do* loop continues as long as the loop condition remains `true`. A *do* loop is a convenient choice for loops that test input values and then repeat if the input is not correct.

The *for* statement is another looping statement and is commonly used to implement count-controlled loops. The initialization, testing, and incrementation (or decrementation) of the loop control variable are centralized in one location, the first line of the *for* statement.

The *for*, *do*, *switch*, and *throw* statements are the "ice cream and cake" of Java. We can live without them if we absolutely must, but they are very nice to have. Similarly, the additional operators that Java supplies, such as +=, %=, and ?:, are sometimes convenient shortcuts, but we can program effectively without them. Often, the use of the less common operators results in code that is more difficult to understand. For this reason, we recommend that you avoid them. Even so, you must be aware of their meaning so that you can interpret them when you encounter code written by a programmer who values compact syntax over clarity.

Quick Check

1. Write a statement that converts a string to an integer and writes out the string if a `NumberFormatError` occurs. (pp. 432–435)

2. What is the superclass of all exceptions? (pp. 437–438)

3. Given a switch expression that is the `int` variable `nameVal`, write a *switch* statement that writes the following to the `PrintWriter` file called `outData`: your first name if `nameVal = 1`, your middle name if `nameVal = 2`, and your last name if `nameVal = 3`. (pp. 438–442)

4. How would you change the code you wrote for Question 3 so that it writes an error message if the value is not 1, 2, or 3? (pp. 438–442)

5. What is the primary difference between a *while* loop and a *do* loop? (pp. 442–445)

6. A certain problem requires a count-controlled loop that starts at 10 and counts down to 1. Write the heading (the first line) of a *for* statement that controls this loop. (pp. 445–447)

7. What Java looping statement would you choose for a loop that is both count-controlled and event-controlled and whose body might not execute even once? (p. 448)

8. What is the difference between an expression and an expression statement in Java? (pp. 448–450)

Answers

1.
```
try
{
  intValue = Integer.parseInt("123");
}
catch(NumberFormatException except)
{
  System.out.println(except.getMessage);
}
```

2. Throwable

3.
```
switch (nameVal)
{
  case 1 : outData.println("Mary");
           break;
  case 2 : outData.println("Lynn");
           break;
  case 3 : outData.println("Smith");
           break; // Not required
}
```

4.
```
switch (nameVal)
{
  case 1   : outData.println("Mary");
             break;
  case 2   : outData.println("Lynn");
             break;
  case 3   : outData.println("Smith");
             break;
  default : outData.println("Invalid name value.");
             break;   // Not required
}
```

5. The body of a *do* loop always executes at least once; the body of a *while* loop may not execute at all. 6. `for (count = 10; count >= 1; count--)` 7. A *while* (or perhaps a *for*) statement 8. An expression becomes an expression statement when it is terminated by a semicolon.

Exam Preparation Exercises

1. Which control structure should you use if you think an operation might throw an exception?

2. Which statement raises an exception?

3. What part of the *try-catch-finally* structure must have a parameter consisting of an exception object?

4. Our code can catch exceptions it throws, but not exceptions that the system throws. (True or False?)

5. Mark the following statements as true or false. If a statement is false, explain why.

   a. There can only be one `catch` clause for each `try`.

   b. The exception handler is located within the `catch` clause.

   c. The `finally` clause is optional.

   d. The `finally` clause is rarely used.

6. Define the following terms: switch expression, pretest loop, posttest loop.

7. A switch expression may be an expression that results in a value of type `int`, `float`, `boolean`, or `char`. (True or False?)

8. The values in case labels may appear in any order, but duplicate case labels are not allowed within a given *switch* statement. (True or False?)

9. All possible values for the switch expression must be included among the case labels for a given *switch* statement. (True or False?)

10. Rewrite the following code fragment using a *switch* statement.

```
if (n == 3)
    alpha++;
else if (n == 7)
    beta++;
else if (n == 10)
    gamma++;
```

11. What is printed by the following code fragment if *n* equals 3? (Be careful here.)

```
switch (n + 1)
{
    case 2  : outData.println("Bill");
    case 4  : outData.println("Mary");
    case 7  : outData.println("Joe");
    case 9  : outData.println("Anne");
```

```
      default : outData.println("Whoops!");
   }
```

12. If a *while* loop whose condition is delta <= alpha is converted to a *do* loop, the loop condition of the *do* loop is delta > alpha. (True or False?)

13. A *do* statement always ends in a semicolon. (True or False?)

14. What is printed by the following code fragment? (All variables are of type int.)

```
n = 0;
i = 1;
do
{
  outData.print(i);
  i++;
} while (i <= n);
```

15. What is printed by the following code fragment? (All variables are of type int.)

```
n = 0;
for (i = 1; i <= n; i++)
  outData.print(i);
```

16. What is printed by the following code fragment? (All variables are of type int.)

```
for (i = 4; i >= 1; i--)
{
  for (j = i; j >= 1; j--)
    outData.print(j + " ");
  outData.println(i);
}
```

17. What is printed by the following code fragment? (All variables are of type int.)

```
for (row = 1; row <= 10; row++)
{
  for (col = 1; col <= 10 - row; col++)
    outData.print("*");
  for (col = 1; col <= 2 * row - 1; col++)
    outData.print(" ");
  for (col = 1; col <= 10 - row; col++)
    outData.print("*");
  outData.println();
}
```

18. A *break* statement located inside a *switch* statement that is located within a *while* loop causes control to exit the loop immediately. (True or False?)

19. Classify each of the following as either an expression or an expression statement.

    a. `sum = 0`

    b. `sqrt(x)`

    c. `y = 17;`

    d. `count++`

20. Rewrite each statement as described.

    a. Using the `+=` operator, rewrite the statement

    ```
    sumOfSquares = sumOfSquares + x * x;
    ```

    b. Using the decrement operator, rewrite the statement

    ```
    count = count – 1;
    ```

    c. Using a single assignment statement that uses the `?:` operator, rewrite the statement

    ```
    if (n > 8)
        k = 32;
    else
        k = 15 * n;
    ```

Programming Warm-Up Exercises

1. **a.** Declare an exception of the class `MyException`.

   b. Write the class `MyException`.

   c. Write the statement that throws an exception of class `MyException`.

2. Write a *try-catch* statement that attempts to open the file `data.in` for reading and writes an error message if an exception is thrown.

3. Write a *switch* statement that does the following:

   If the value of `grade` (a variable of type `char`) is

   'A', add 4 to `sum`

   'B', add 3 to `sum`

   'C', add 2 to `sum`

   'D', add 1 to `sum`

   'F', print "Student is on probation" on the `PrintWriter` file `outData`

4. Modify the code you wrote for Exercise 3 so that an error message is printed if `grade` does not equal one of the five possible grades.

5. Write a code segment that reads and sums values until it has summed ten data values or until a negative value is read, whichever comes first. Use a *do* loop for your solution.

6. Rewrite the following code segment using a *do* loop instead of a *while* loop.

```
response = Integer.parseInt(inData.readLine());
while (response >= 0 && response <= 127)
{
  response = Integer.parseInt(inData.readLine());
}
```

7. Rewrite the following code segment using a *while* loop.

```
inInt = Integer.parseInt(inData.readLine());
if (inInt >= 0)
  do
  {
    System.out.println("" + inInt);
    inInt = Integer.parseInt(inData.readLine());
  } while (inInt >= 0);
```

8. Rewrite the following code segment using a *for* loop.

```
sum = 0;
count = 1;
while (count <= 1000)
{
  sum = sum + count;
  count++;
}
```

9. Rewrite the following *for* loop as a *while* loop.

```
for (m = 93; m >= 5; m--)
  outData.println( m + " " + m * m);
```

10. Rewrite the following *for* loop as a *do* loop.

```
for (k = 9; k <= 21; k++)
  outData.println( k + " " + 3 * k);
```

11. Write a value-returning method that accepts two int parameters, base and exponent, and returns the value of base raised to the exponent power. Use a *for* loop in your solution.

Programming Problems

1. Develop a Java application that inputs a two-letter abbreviation for one of the 50 states from a field and displays the full name of the state in a label. If the abbreviation isn't valid, the application should display an error message and ask for an abbreviation again. The names of the 50 states and their abbreviations are given in the following table. Use two buttons: one to enter an abbreviation and one to quit.

State	Abbreviation	State	Abbreviation
Alabama	AL	Montana	MT
Alaska	AK	Nebraska	NE
Arizona	AZ	Nevada	NV
Arkansas	AR	New Hampshire	NH
California	CA	New Jersey	NJ
Colorado	CO	New Mexico	NM
Connecticut	CT	New York	NY
Delaware	DE	North Carolina	NC
Florida	FL	North Dakota	ND
Georgia	GA	Ohio	OH
Hawaii	HI	Oklahoma	OK
Idaho	ID	Oregon	OR
Illinois	IL	Pennsylvania	PA
Indiana	IN	Rhode Island	RI
Iowa	IA	South Carolina	SC
Kansas	KS	South Dakota	SD
Kentucky	KY	Tennessee	TN
Louisiana	LA	Texas	TX
Maine	ME	Utah	UT
Maryland	MD	Vermont	VT
Massachusetts	MA	Virginia	VA
Michigan	MI	Washington	WA
Minnesota	MN	West Virginia	WV
Mississippi	MS	Wisconsin	WI
Missouri	MO	Wyoming	WY

(*Hint:* Use nested *switch* statements, where the outer statement uses the first letter of the abbreviation as its switch expression.)

2. Design and write a Java application that reads a date in numeric form from a set of three fields and displays it in English within a label. Use appropriate buttons. For example:

Given the date:

10   27   1942

The application displays:

`October twenty-seventh, nineteen hundred forty-two.`

Here is another example:

Given the date:

12   10   2010

The application displays:

`December tenth, two thousand ten.`

The application should display an error message for any invalid date, such as 2 29 1883 (1883 wasn't a leap year).

3. Write a Java application that reads full names from an input file and writes the initials for the names to an output file named `initials`. For example, the input

`John James Henry`

should produce the output

`JJH`

The names are stored in the input file as first name, middle name, last name, with each name separated by an arbitrary number of blanks. Only one name appears per line. The first name or the middle name could be just an initial, or there may not be a middle name.

4. Write a Java application that converts letters of the alphabet into their corresponding digits on the telephone. The application should let the user enter letters repeatedly until a "Q" or a "Z" is entered. (Q and Z are the two letters that are not on the telephone.) An error message should be printed for any nonalphabetic character that is entered.

The letters and digits on the telephone have the following correspondence:

ABC = 2	DEF = 3	GHI = 4
JKL = 5	MNO = 6	PRS = 7
TUV = 8	WXY = 9	

Here is an example:

When the user enters P, the application displays:

`The letter P corresponds to 7 on the telephone.`

When the user enters A, the application displays:

`The letter A corresponds to 2 on the telephone.`

When the user enters D, the application displays:

`The letter D corresponds to 3 on the telephone.`

When the user enters 2, the application displays:

`Invalid letter. Enter Q or Z to quit.`

When the user enters Z, the application quits.

Case Study Follow-Up

1. Rewrite the `processOneSite` method in the `Rainfall` application, replacing the *for* loop with a *do* loop.

2. Rewrite the `processOneSite` method in the `Rainfall` application, replacing the *for* loop with a *while* loop.

3. Change `main` in the `Rainfall` application so that it asks the user for the input file name using a `JFrame`, and catches the `FileNotFoundException` if the name is invalid. In the case of an invalid file name, the user should be asked to reenter the file name until a valid name is entered or the user closes the `JFrame` (signalling that he or she wants to stop the application)

4. Change the *do* loop in `main` in the `Rainfall` application to be a *while* loop.

5. Could the module Get Rainfall Amount be made a method? Explain.

One-Dimensional Arrays

goals

Knowledge Goals

- To understand the difference between atomic and composite data types
- To understand the difference between unstructured and structured composite data types
- To understand how Java implements arrays
- To understand the process of passing an array as an argument
- To understand the difference between an array and the information stored within the array
- To understand the role of an array in structuring data within a problem

Skill Goals

To be able to:

- Declare and instantiate a one-dimensional array
- Access and manipulate the individual components in a one-dimensional array where the elements are atomic types
- Access and manipulate the individual components in a one-dimensional array where the elements are composite types
- Use an initializer list to instantiate a one-dimensional array

timeline

1975
IBM introduces the first laser printer

1976
The first commercial e-mail service, OnTyme, struggles to find a market for its product because of the installation requirements for its use

1976
Steve Jobs and Steve Wozniak create the "Apple I" computer

1977
Steve Jobs and Steve Wozniak found Apple Computer Inc.; the Apple II computer sets the standard for personal computers

1977
Bill Gates and Paul Allen form a partnership and create Microsoft

1977
Commodore introduces the PET, a PC with a built-in monitor

CHAPTER 10

introduction

In Chapter 3, we showed a diagram of Java data types (repeated on the next page as Figure 10.1). Java data types are classified into primitive and reference types. Recall that in Java, a variable of a primitive type holds an actual value of that type, whereas a variable of a reference type holds the address of an object. In previous chapters, we have covered all of the primitive types and the class type. In this chapter, we extend the discussion of the Java data types by examining the array type. Before doing so, we first step back and look at data types from a general perspective, rather than a Java perspective.

1978
Epson introduces the first successful dot matrix printer, the TX-80

1978
The VAX 11/780 and the VMS operating system developed at DEC popularize the 32-bit architecture

1978
The WordStar program for word processing debuts

1978
Ron Rivest, Adi Shamir, and Leonard Adleman introduce RSA, a strong encryption algorithm for public-key cryptosystems

1979
Dan Bricklin and Bob Frankston develop VisiCalc, the first electronic spreadsheet

1979
Motorola introduces the 32-bit 68000 chip, which is later used for the Macintosh computer

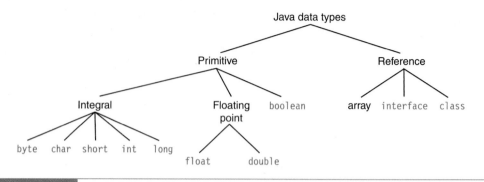

Figure 10.1 Java Data Types

10.1 Atomic Data Types

Recall that a *data type* is a set of data values, along with a set of operations on those values. The definitions of integers and real numbers come from mathematics. Integer numbers are the set of whole numbers from negative to positive infinity. The operations defined for them are the arithmetic operations [specified by +, -, / (integer division), *, and modulus], assignment, and the relational operations. Real numbers are the set of all numbers from negative to positive infinity. The operations defined for them are the same as those for the integers, except that integer division and modulus are excluded.

Because computers have finite capabilities, programming languages put limits on the range of integers and the range and precision of real numbers. Java provides four types of integer numbers that differ only in the range of values that they can represent in memory: byte, short, int, and long. Java has two real (floating-point) types that differ only in the range and precision that they can represent: float and double.

Alphanumeric characters are the symbols that we use in written language. These symbols vary from one natural language to another. The same is true of characters used to represent textual data in a computer. For many years, two character sets dominated the computer world: ASCII and EBCDIC. In these character sets, each character occupies one byte in memory, giving 256 possible characters. Some of these characters are nonprintable control characters used by the computer's hardware. Unicode is a relatively new character set that uses two bytes to represent each character. It was developed to include characters for writing text in many natural languages. Unicode, which Java uses, contains ASCII as a subset.

The operations defined on alphanumeric characters are the relational operations and assignment. The ordering used by the relational operators is the collating sequence of the character set. Although the collating sequence differs for different character sets, the letters and digits are ordered as we would expect—that is, 'A' < 'B' < 'C' ... and '1' < '2' < '3' ....

Different programming languages treat characters differently. In Pascal, for example, the data type for a character is distinct. Arithmetic operations, when applied to character data, cause compile-time errors. In C++, no real distinction is made between characters and numbers.

Arithmetic operations may be applied to character data (and often are). The only difference is that when character data is printed, the character itself is printed rather than the numeric representation of the character. In Java, applying arithmetic operations to character data causes the compiler to insert a cast operation that converts the character to a numerical value.

The Boolean data type includes two literals, true and false. The operations allowed on these values are the logical operators AND, OR, and NOT; the relational operations; and assignment. Although many languages consider Boolean values to be ordered, Java does not, so only equal and not equal can be applied to Boolean values in Java. Java calls the Boolean type `boolean` and the constants `true` and `false`.

Integers, reals, characters, and Booleans are called **atomic** or **simple elements** because they have no component parts that can be accessed separately. They are also ordered. Types that are atomic and ordered are called **scalar data types**.

For example, a single character is atomic, but the string `"Good Morning"` is not because it is composed of 12 characters. When we say that the values are ordered, we mean that exactly one of the relations less than, greater than, or equal holds true for any pair of values. For example,

```
1 < 2    'C' > 'A'    3.562 < 106.22    false == false
```

> **Atomic (simple) elements** Elements that have no component parts
>
> **Scalar data type** A data type in which the values are ordered and each value is atomic (indivisible)
>
> **Ordinal data type** A data type in which each value (except the first) has a unique predecessor and each value (except the last) has a unique successor
>
> **Composite data type** A data type that allows a collection of values to be associated with an identifier of that type

Integers, characters, and Booleans have yet another property: Each value (except the first) has a unique predecessor and each value (except the last) has a unique successor. Types with this property are called **ordinal data types**. Although theoretically Booleans are ordinal, Java's type `boolean` is not.

Real numbers are not ordinal because a real value has no unique predecessor or successor. If one more digit of precision is added, the predecessor and successor change; that is, 0.52 and 0.520 are the same, but the predecessor of 0.52 is 0.51, and the predecessor of 0.520 is 0.519. Because Java's type `boolean` is not ordered, it is not ordinal.

Although the ordinals form a subset of the scalars, the two types are quite different. Mathematicians make this same distinction when they talk about continuous values versus discrete values. Many real-life analogies demonstrate this distinction as well: the spectrum of colors in a real rainbow versus the discrete colors in a child's crayon drawing of a rainbow or the continuous tone of a violin sliding up the scale versus the discrete tones of a piano.

Java classifies the atomic types that it represents as "primitive."

10.2 Composite Data Types

Sometimes we may need to show a relationship among variables or to store and reference collections of variables as a group. For this reason, we need a way to associate an identifier with a collection of values. A data type made up of a collection of values is called a **composite data type**.

Composite data types come in two forms: unstructured and structured. In an *unstructured data type*, no relationship exists among the values in the data type other than that they are members of the same collection. A *structured data type*, on the other hand, is an organized collection of components in which a relationship exists among the items in the collection. We use this relationship to access individual items within the collection as well as to manipulate the collection as a whole.

Unstructured data type A collection of components that are not organized with respect to one another.

Structured data type An organized collection of components; the organization determines the means used to access individual components

A value in an atomic type is a single data item; it cannot be broken down into component parts. For example, in Java each `int` value is a single integer number and cannot be further decomposed. In contrast, in a composite data type, each value is a collection of component items. The entire collection is given a single name, yet each component can still be accessed individually.

The class is an example of a composite data type. A class has a name and is composed of named data fields and methods. An instance of a class, including the data fields and methods, can be passed as an argument. The data fields and methods can be accessed individually by name. A class is unstructured because the meaning does not depend on the ordering of the data fields or the methods within the source code. That is, we can change the order in which the members of the class are listed without changing the function of the class.

In Java, all composite types are either classes, interfaces, or arrays. Rather than talking about the *type* of a composite object, we talk about its *class*. An example of a composite object in Java is an instance of the `String` class, used for creating and manipulating strings. When you declare a variable `myString` to be of class `String`, `myString` does not reference just one atomic data value; rather, it references an entire collection of characters and the methods that manipulate the characters. Even so, you can access each component in the string individually by using an expression such as `myString.charAt(3)`, which accesses the `char` value at position 3. Therefore the characters within the string are ordered.

Atomic data types serve as the building blocks for composite types. A composite type gathers together a set of component values and usually imposes a specific arrangement on them (see Figure 10.2). If the composite type is a built-in type, the syntax of the language provides the accessing mechanism. If the composite type is user-defined, the accessing mechanism is built into the methods provided with the class.

In Chapters 1 through 9, we have discussed control structures and the `class`, an unstructured composite type. In the next three chapters, we focus on structured composite data types. Of course, we do not abandon the `class`, but we focus on having a structured composite type as a field in a `class`.

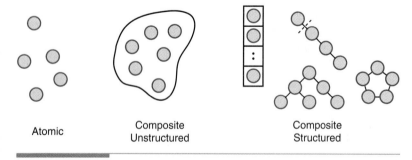

Atomic   Composite   Composite
                    Unstructured   Structured

Figure 10.2   Atomic (Simple) and Composite Data Types

10.3 One-Dimensional Arrays

How we organize our data plays an important role in the design process. If the internal data representation for a class is a composite type (that is, if it contains more than a single atomic field), we call the internal representation a **data structure**. The choice of data structure directly affects the design because it determines the algorithms used to process the data. The class gives us the ability to refer to an entire group of components by one name, which simplifies the design of many applications.

> **Data structure** The implementation of a composite data field in an abstract data type

Many problems, however, have so many components that it is difficult to process them if each one must have a unique field name. For example, if we use individually named values to read and print a file in reverse order, all the values must be read and saved before the last one can be printed. If there are 1,000 values, we must define 1,000 individual variables to hold the values and input and output each value separately—an incredibly tedious task! An array—the last of Java's built-in reference types—is the data type that allows us to program operations of this kind with ease.

Let's look at how we would have to solve this problem with simple variables.

```java
// Read 1,000 numbers and print them in reverse order
import java.io.*;
public class ArrayExample
{
  public static void main(String[] args) throws IOException
  {
    BufferedReader inFile;
    PrintWriter outFile;
    inFile = new BufferedReader(new FileReader("infile.dat"));
    outFile = new PrintWriter(new FileWriter("outfile.dat"));

    // Declare 1,000 integer variables
    int value0;
    int value1;
    int value2;
    .
    .
    .
    int value999;

    // Read 1,000 integer values
    value0 = Integer.parseInt(inFile.readLine());
    value1 = Integer.parseInt(inFile.readLine());
    value2 = Integer.parseInt(inFile.readLine());
    .
    .
    .
    value999 = Integer.parseInt(inFile.readLine());
```

```
  // Write 1,000 values
  outFile.println(value999);
  outFile.println(value998);
  outFile.println(value997);
        .
        .
        .
  outFile.println(value0);
  inFile.close();
  outFile.close();
    }
}
```

This application is more than 3,000 lines long, and we have to use 1,000 separate variables. Note that all the variables have the same name except for an appended number that distinguishes them. Wouldn't it be more convenient if we could put the number into a counter variable and use *for* loops to go from 0 through 999, and then from 999 back down to 0? For example, if the counter variable were number, we could replace the 2,000 original input/output statements with the following four lines of code (we enclose number in brackets to set it apart from value):

```
for (number = 0; number < 1000; number++)
  value[number] = Integer.parseInt(inFile.readLine());
for (number = 999; number >= 0; number--)
  outFile.println(value[number]);
```

This code fragment is correct in Java *if* we declare value to be a *one-dimensional array*. Such an array is a collection of variables—all of the same type—where the first part of each variable name is the same, and the last part is an *index value*.

The declaration of a one-dimensional array is similar to the declaration of a simple variable (a variable of a simple data type), with one exception: You must indicate that it is an array by putting square brackets next to the type.

```
int[] value;
```

Because an array is a reference type, it must be instantiated. At that time, we must specify the size of the array.

```
value = new int[1000];
```

Here value represents an array with 1,000 components, all of type int. The first component has index value 0, the second component has index value 1, and the last component has index value 999.

The following application prints out numbers in reverse order using an array. It is certainly much shorter than our first version of the application.

```java
// Read 1,000 numbers and print them in reverse order
import java.io.*;
public class ArrayExample
{

  public static void main(String[] args) throws IOException
  {
    BufferedReader inFile;
    PrintWriter outFile;
    inFile = new BufferedReader(new FileReader("infile.dat"));
    outFile = new PrintWriter(new FileWriter("outfile.dat"));

    // Declare and instantiate an array
    int[] value = new int[1000];
    for (int number = 0; number < 1000; number++)
      value[number] = Integer.parseInt(inFile.readLine());
    for (int number = 999; number >= 0; number--)
      outFile.println(value[number]);

    inFile.close();
    outFile.close();
  }
}
```

infile	*outfile*
10	9999
20	9998
30	9997
40	.
.	.
.	40
9997	30
9998	20
9999	10

In general terminology, an array differs from a class in three fundamental ways:

1. An array is a *homogeneous* data structure (all components in the structure are of the same data type), whereas classes are *heterogeneous* types (their components may be of different types).

2. A component of an array is accessed by its *position* in the structure, whereas a component of a class is accessed by an *identifier* (the field name).

3. Because array components are accessed by position, an array is a structured data type.

Let's now define Java arrays formally and look at the rules for accessing individual components.

Declaring an Array

A one-dimensional array is a structured collection of components (often called array elements) that can be accessed individually by specifying the position of a component with a single index value.

> **One-dimensional array** A structured collection of components, all of the same type, that is given a single name. Each component (array element) is accessed by an index that indicates the component's position within the collection.

Here is a syntax template describing the simplest form of a one-dimensional array declaration:

Array-Declaration

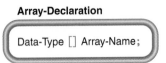

In the syntax template, Data-Type describes what is stored in each component of the array. The brackets following Data-Type indicate that this structure is an array of Data-Type elements. Array components may be of almost any type, but for now we limit our discussion to atomic components. From Figure 10.1, we know that the array is a reference type. Array-Name is a location in memory that will hold the address of an array when that array is instantiated. For example,

```
int[] numbers;
```

declares a variable that can hold the address of an array of integers. We tell the compiler how many components the array contains when we instantiate it.

Creating an Array

You create an array just like you create an object; you use new. Following is the syntax template for instantiating an array. Notice that arrays don't need to be initialized, so we don't pass a list of arguments. Instead, we put the number of slots to be in the array in brackets beside the type of the array.

Array-Creation

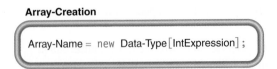

Int-Expression is an integer expression that specifies the number of components in the array. This expression must have a value greater than or equal to 0. If the value is n, the range of index values is 0 through $n - 1$, not 1 through n. For example, the declarations

```
float[] angle;              // Declares the array variable
angle = new float[4];       // Instantiates the array object
int[] testScore;            // Declares the array variable
testScore = new int[10];    // Instantiates the array object
```

instantiate the arrays shown in Figure 10.3. The `angle` array has four components, each capable of holding one `float` value. The `testScore` array has a total of ten components, all of type `int`.

An array can be declared and instantiated in separate statements or the declaration and creation can be combined into one step as shown here.

```
// Declared and instantiated in one statement
float[] angle = new float[4];
// Declared and instantiated in one statement
int[] testScore = new int[10];
```

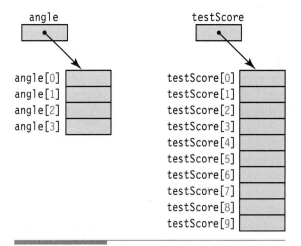

Figure 10.3   `angle` and `testScore` Arrays

Because arrays are reference types in Java, they are instantiated at run time, not at compile time. Therefore, the Int-Expression used to instantiate an array object does not have to be a constant. It can instead be a value that you have read into the application. For example, if you have read the value of `dataSize` from a file, the following declaration is legal:

```
int[] data = new int[dataSize];
```

Once instantiated, the array always has the specified number of components. For example, if `dataSize` is 10 when the array is instantiated but is later changed to 15, `data` still has 10 components.

Java provides an alternative syntax for declaring an array variable. You can place the brackets that signal an array after the array name, as shown here:

```
char letters[];
char upperCase[];
char lowerCase[];
```

We do not recommend using this syntactic form, however. It is more consistent—and safer—to place the brackets with the type of the components. It is safer because, as you may recall from Chapter 2, Java also lets us declare multiple identifiers with a statement such as this:

```
char letters[], upperCase[], lowerCase;
```

Look closely at this example: `letters` and `upperCase` are composite variables of type `char[]`, but `lowerCase` is a simple variable of type `char`. If you use the syntax that we introduced first, you cannot forget to put the brackets on one of the array identifiers:

```
char[] letters, upperCase, lowerCase;
```

Declaring and Creating an Array with an Initializer List

Java also provides an alternative way to instantiate an array. You learned previously that Java allows you to initialize a variable in its declaration:

```
int delta = 25;
```

The value 25 is called an *initializer*. You can also initialize an array in its declaration, using a special syntax for the initializer. In this case, you specify a list of initial values for the array elements, separate them with commas, and enclose the list within braces:

```
int[] age = {23, 10, 16, 37, 12};
```

In this declaration, `age[0]` is initialized to 23, `age[1]` is initialized to 10, and so on. Notice two interesting things about this syntax. First, it does not use the `new` operator. Second, it does not specify the number of components. When the compiler sees an initializer list, it determines the size by finding the number of items in the list, instantiates an array of that size, and stores the values into their proper places. Of course, the types of the values in the initializer list must match the type of the array.

What values are stored in an array when it is instantiated by using `new`? If the array components are primitive types, they are set to their default value: 0 for integral types, 0.0 for floating-point types, and `false` for Boolean types. If the array components are reference types, the components are set to `null`.

In only two situations can an object be created without using `new`: when using an array initializer list and by creating a `String` literal.

Accessing Individual Components

Recall that to access an individual field of a class, we use dot notation—the name of the class object, followed by a period, followed by the field name. In contrast, to access an individual array component, we write the array name, followed by an expression enclosed in square brackets. The expression specifies which component to access. The syntax template for accessing an array component follows:

Array-Component-Access

Array-Name [Index-Expression]

The Index-Expression may be as simple as a constant or a variable name or as complex as a combination of variables, operators, and method calls. Whatever the form of the expression, it must give an integer value as a result. Index expressions can be of type byte, char, short, or int.[1] Using an index expression of type long produces a compile-time error.

The simplest form of index expression is a constant. For example, using our angle array, the sequence of assignment statements

```
angle[0] = 4.93;
angle[1] = -15.2;
angle[2] = 0.5;
angle[3] = 1.67;
```

fills the array components one at a time (see Figure 10.4).

Each array component—angle[2], for instance—can be treated exactly the same as any simple variable of type float. For example, we can do the following to the individual component angle[2]:

```
// Assign it a value
angle[2] = 9.6;

// Read a value into it
angle[2] = Double.parseDouble(inFile.readLine());

// Write its contents
outFile.println(angle[2]);

// Pass it as an argument
y = Math.sqrt(angle[2]);

// Use it in an expression
x = 6.8 * angle[2] + 7.5;
```

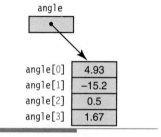

Figure 10.4 angle Array with Values

Now let's look at a more complicated index expression. Suppose we declare a 1,000-element array of int values with the statement

```
int[] value = new int[1000];
```

and execute the following statement:

```
value[counter] = 5;
```

---

[1]Java inherits the notion that char is a numeric type from C. The Java language specifications say that arrays must be indexed by int values but that values of type short, byte, or char may also be used because they are subjected to unary numeric promotion and become int values. For clarity, we type cast char values to int when using them as indexes.

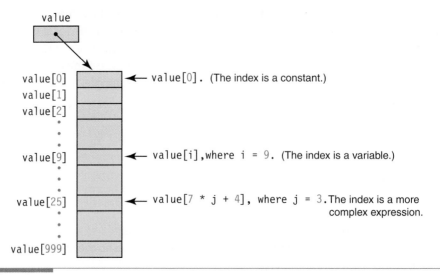

Figure 10.5   An Index as a Constant, a Variable, and an Arbitrary Expression

In this statement, 5 is stored into an array component. If counter is 0, 5 is stored into the first component of the array. If counter is 1, 5 is stored into the second place in the array, and so forth. If we execute the statement

```
if (value[number+1] % 10 != 0)
```

then the expression number+1 selects an array component. The specific array component accessed is divided by 10 and checked to see whether the remainder is nonzero. If number+1 is 0, we are testing the value in the first component; if number+1 is 1, we are testing the second place; and so on. Figure 10.5 shows the index expression as a constant, a variable, and a more complex expression.

◼ Out-of-Bounds Array Indexes

Given the declaration

```
float[] alpha = new float[100];
```

the valid range of index values is 0 through 99. Starting at 0 seems awkward, because we are used to numbering things beginning with 1. However, you should not be surprised; the positions in a string begin with 0. What happens if we try to execute the statement

```
alpha[i] = 62.4;
```

when i is less than 0 or when i is greater than 99? A memory location outside the array would be accessed, which causes an *out-of-bounds* error. Some languages—C++, for instance—

do not check for this kind of error, but Java does. If your code attempts to use an out-of-bounds array index, an ArrayIndexOutOfBoundsException is thrown. Rather than try to catch this error, you should write your code so as to prevent it.

> **Out-of-bounds array index** An index value that is either less than 0 or greater than the array size minus 1

In Java, each array that is instantiated has a `public` instance variable, called length, associated with it that contains the number of components in the array. We can use length when processing the components in the array to keep from having an out-of-bounds error. How? Array-processing algorithms often use *for* loops to step through the array elements one at a time. The following loop zeroes out the 100-element alpha array:

```
for (int index = 0; index < alpha.length; index++)
  alpha[index] = 0.0;
```

Use this pattern—initialize the counter to zero, and then use a "less than" test against the size of the array as recorded in length—and you can be sure that your counter is within the bounds of the array. If your code crashes with an ArrayIndexOutOfBoundsException, immediately verify that your relational operator is the less than operator, not the less than or equal to operator.

■ Aggregate Array Operations

We can assign one array to another and we can compare two arrays for equality—but we might not get the answer we expect. Arrays, like classes, are reference types. As a consequence, the value stored in a reference variable is not the object itself but rather the address of where the object is stored. Let's see what happens when we test two arrays for equality and assign one array to another.

```
int[] numbers = {2, 4, 6};
int[] values = new int[3];
values[0] = 2;
values[1] = 4;
values[2] = 6;

if (numbers == values)
  ...
numbers = values;
if (numbers == values)
  ...
```

The first *if* expression is false, because the variables numbers and values hold two different memory addresses. (See Figure 10.6a.) The next statement takes the contents of values (the address where the array is stored) and stores it into numbers. The next *if* expression is true, because the two variables now hold the same memory address. (See Figure 10.6b.)

You should not be surprised at this example. An assignment for reference types is a shallow assignment; an equality test for reference types is a shallow test. If you want to have a deep test, you must write a method to do the comparison, element by element.

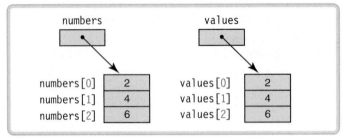

a. Result is false; *these are two different arrays.*

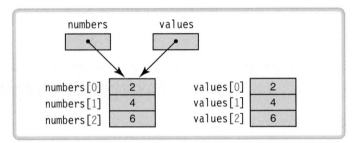

b. Result is true *after a shallow copy.*

Figure 10.6 Comparison of Array Variables

```
int[] numbers = {2, 4, 6, 9};
int[] sameNumbers = new int[numbers.length];
// Deep copy of numbers to someNumbers
for (int index = 0; index < numbers.length; index++)
  sameNumbers[index] = numbers[index];

// Compare arrays component by component
boolean compareArrays(int[] one, int[] two)
{
  if (one.length != two.length)
    return false;

  boolean result = true;
  int index = 0;
  while (index < one.length && result)
  {
    if (one[index] == two[index])
      index++;
    else
      result = false;
  }
  return result;
}
```

After the preceding deep copy code executes, what would be the result of each of the following expressions?

```
numbers == sameNumbers
. . .
compareArrays(numbers, sameNumbers)
. . .
```

The first expression is `false`. The arrays contain the same values, but the equality test is for addresses, not values. The second expression is `true`, because `compareArrays` is a method that performs a deep comparison.

10.4 Examples of Declaring and Processing Arrays

We now look in detail at some specific examples of declaring and accessing arrays. These examples demonstrate different uses of arrays in applications.

■ Occupancy Rates

An application might use the following declarations to analyze occupancy rates in an apartment building:

```
final int BUILDING_SIZE = 350; // Number of apartments

int[] occupants = new int[BUILDING_SIZE];
// occupants[aptNo] is the number of occupants in apartment aptNo
int totalOccupants;          // Total number of occupants
```

Here `occupants` is a 350-element array of integers (see Figure 10.7). `occupants[0] = 3` if the first apartment has three occupants; `occupants[1] = 5` if the second apartment has five occupants; and so on. If values have been stored into the array, then the following code totals the number of occupants in the building:

```
totalOccupants = 0;
for (int aptNo = 0; aptNo < occupants.length; aptNo++)
  totalOccupants = totalOccupants + occupants[aptNo];
```

The first time through the loop, `counter` is 0. We add the contents of `totalOccupants` (that is, 0) and the contents of `occupants[0]`, storing the result into `totalOccupants`. Next, `counter` becomes 1 and the loop test occurs. The second loop iteration adds the contents of `totalOccupants` and the contents of `occupants[1]`, storing the result into `totalOccupants`. Now `counter` becomes 2 and the loop test is made. Eventually, the loop adds the contents of `occupants[349]` to the sum and increments `counter` to 350. At this point, the loop condition is `false`, and control exits the loop.

Note how we used the named constant `BUILDING_SIZE` in the array declaration and `occupants.length` in the *for* loop. When we use a constant in this manner, it is easy to make changes. If the number of apartments changes from 350 to 400, we just need to alter the declaration of `BUILDING_SIZE`. We could also have written

```
for (int aptNo = 0; aptNo < BUILDING_SIZE; aptNo++)
```

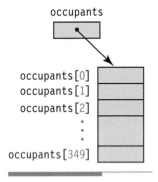

Figure 10.7 occupants Array

but we prefer to use the `length` field because it is specifically associated with the array. In the future, we might modify the application to use a different constant to set the size of `occupants`. Then `BUILDING_SIZE` would no longer be the correct value to terminate the loop, but `occupants.length` would remain valid.

■ Sales Figures

Now let's look at an example where the values stored in the array are sales figures and the indexes are the product numbers. (The products are gourmet hamburgers.) The product numbers range from 1 through 5. We can make the array contain six components and just ignore the zeroth position, or we can set up five components and make sure that we add (or subtract) one from the product number to get the proper slot. Let's use the latter strategy.

```
// Declare and instantiate an array with five real components
double[] gourmetBurgers = new double[5];
```

The data for this example consist of (hamburger number, day's sales) pairs. The data file contains a week's worth of such pairs. The first value is an integer between 1 and 5 that represents one of the gourmet hamburgers. The next value is the sales amount for that hamburger for the day. Each value appears on a line by itself. The following code segment reads in a (hamburger number, sales figure) pair:

```
inFile = new BufferedReader(new FileReader("salesIn.dat"));
outFile = new PrintWriter(new FileWriter("salesOut.dat"));
int burgerNumber;
double salesAmount;
. . .
burgerNumber = Integer.parseInt(inFile.readLine());
salesAmount = Double.parseDouble(inFile.readLine());
```

To add the sales amount to the value in the appropriate slot in the array, we use `burgerNumber − 1` as the index into the array `gourmetBurgers`:

```
gourmetBurgers[burgerNumber − 1] =
  salesAmount + gourmetBurgers[burgerNumber − 1];
```

If we put our input and processing into a loop, we can process the week's worth of sales figures. We can then write the totals out to a file with the following loop:

```
for (burgerNumber = 0; burgerNumber < gourmetBurgers.length; burgerNumber++)
{
  outFile.print("Gourmet Burger # " + (burgerNumber + 1));
  outFile.println(": " + gourmetBurgers[burgerNumber]);
}
```

Figure 10.8 shows the contents of the array gourmetBurgers after the data shown have been processed. Note that the data appear with several values on each line, with commas between pairs, to save space.

This example, where the index into the array component is one less than the number assigned to a type of hamburger, is a type of problem where the index has semantic content. That is, the index has meaning within the problem itself.

gourmetBurgers

gourmetBurgers[0]	246.41
gourmetBurgers[1]	271.04
gourmetBurgers[2]	350.13
gourmetBurgers[3]	640.69
gourmetBurgers[4]	177.42

```
Data    1 50.25, 2 44.75, 4 100.33, 3 85.12, 5 20.76
        3 75.20, 1 50.20, 4 95.12, 5 77.44, 2 44.75
        5 12.23, 4 125.12, 3 55.23, 2 70.12, 1 44.75
        1 55.66, 2 66.67, 3 77.78, 4 200.12, 5 44.75
        2 44.75, 3 56.80, 4 120.00, 5 11.12, 1 45.55
```

Figure 10.8 gourmetBurgers Array

■ Character Counts

As a final example, let's use an array to count the number of times that each letter in the English alphabet is used in text, either uppercase or lowercase. We declare an array of 26 integers, one for each letter. Note that we do not need to set the contents of the array slots to 0, because they are automatically initialized to 0 when we instantiate the array.

```
int[] letterCount = new int[26];
```

letterCount[0] is the counter for the number of times we see 'A' or 'a', letterCount[1] is the counter for the number of times we see 'B' or 'b', and letterCount[25] is the number of times we see 'Z' or a 'z'. How do we convert a letter to its position in the array? We read a character and see if it is a letter. If so, we convert it to uppercase using Character.toUpperCase. The uppercase letter (cast to int) minus 'A' (also cast to int) gives us the letter's place in the array. The following code fragment accomplishes this conversion:

```
if ((letter >= 'A' && letter <= 'Z') || (letter >= 'a' && letter <= 'z'))
{
   index = (int)Character.toUpperCase(letter) - (int)'A';
```

The following statement increments the counter for the character:

```
   letterCount [index] = letterCount [index] + 1;
}
```

All of the pieces are tied together in the following application:

```
import java.io.*;
public class CountLetters
{
```

```java
public static void main(String[] args) throws IOException
{
  BufferedReader dataFile;
  char letter;
  int index;
  int location;
  String inString;
  int[] letterCount = new int[26];
  dataFile = new BufferedReader(new FileReader("Words.in"));

  inString = dataFile.readLine();      // Priming read
  while (inString != null)
  {
    for (location = 0; location < inString.length(); location++)
    {
      letter = inString.charAt(location);
      if ((letter >= 'A' && letter <= 'Z') || (letter >= 'a' && letter <= 'z'))
      {
        // Convert letter to an index
        index =(int)Character.toUpperCase(letter) - (int)'A';
        // Increment counter
        letterCount[index] = letterCount[index] + 1;
      }

    }
    inString = dataFile.readLine();   // Get a line
  }
  // Write the character and the count on the screen
  for (index = 0; index < letterCount.length; index++)
    System.out.println("The number of " +
      (char)(index + (int)'A') + "'s is " + letterCount[index]);
  dataFile.close();
  }
}
```

Here are the first and last paragraphs of the input, followed by the output:

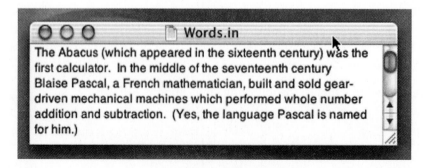

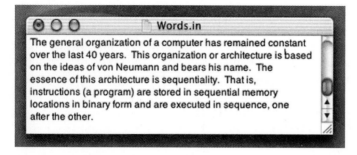

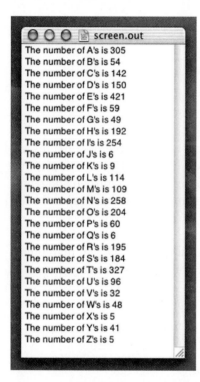

10.5 Arrays of Objects

Although arrays with atomic components are very common, many applications require a collection of composite objects. For example, a business may need a list of parts records, and a teacher may need a list of students in a class. Arrays are ideal for these applications. We simply define an array whose components are references to objects.

Arrays of Strings

Let's define an array of strings, each of which is a grocery item. Declaring and creating an array of objects is exactly like declaring and creating an array where the components are atomic types.

```
String[] groceryItems = new String[10];  // Array of references to strings
```

Here groceryItems is an array of 10 strings. How many characters appear in each string? We don't know yet. The array of strings has been instantiated, but the string objects themselves have not been created. In other words, groceryItems is an array of *references* to string objects, which are set to null when the array is instantiated. We must instantiate the string objects separately. The following code segment reads and stores references to 10 strings into groceryItems:

```
inFile = new BufferedReader(new FileReader("infile.dat"));
outFile = new PrintWriter(new FileWriter("outfile.dat"));
...
int index;    // Index into groceryItems
String[] groceryItems = new String[10];  // Provides places for 10 references

// Read strings from file inFile and store references
for (index = 0; index < groceryItems.length; index++)
{
  groceryItems[index] = inFile.readLine();
}
```

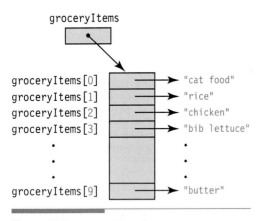

Figure 10.9 groceryItems Array

The readLine method is a value-returning method that instantiates the string, stores values into it, and returns a reference to it. That is, the reference to the string is returned and stored into groceryItems. Figure 10.9 shows what the array looks like with values in it.

An array name with no brackets is an array variable. An array name with brackets is a component. We can manipulate the component just like any other variable of that type or class.

Expression	Class/Type
groceryItems	Reference to an array
groceryItems[0]	Reference to a string
groceryItems[0].charAt(0)	A character

How would you read in grocery items if you know that there are no more than 10, but you don't know exactly how many? You would need a *while* loop that reads in a grocery item and stores it into the first place. If there were another item, it would be stored into the second place, and so on. As a consequence, you must keep a counter of how many items you read in. The following code fragment reads and stores grocery items until 10 have been read or the file is empty:

```
// Read and store strings from file inFile
int index = 0;
String anItem = inFile.readLine();
while (index < groceryItems.length  && anItem != null)
```

```
{
  groceryItems[index] = anItem;
  index++;
  anItem = inFile.readLine();
};
System.out.println(index + " grocery items were read and stored.");
```

Look carefully at Figures 10.9 and 10.10. In Figure 10.9, every slot in the array is filled with grocery items. In Figure 10.10, index items have been read in and stored. If index is equal to 10, then the two figures are the same. To process the items in Figure 10.10, you use a loop that goes from 0 through index–1.

You first saw a reference to an array of strings in Chapter 2. In the class PrintName, the following statement appears:

```
public static void main(String[] args) throws IOException
```

The parameter for the method main is an array of strings, called args by convention. You can run Java applications in ways that allow you to pass string arguments to main. Although we do not use this feature in our applications, we still have to list the parameter on the heading.

In the figures throughout this chapter, we have drawn array variables with an arrow to the object structure to which they refer. An array type is a reference type. When we declare an array variable with the name groceryItems, one location in memory is assigned to that name. When we instantiate the array, the address of the place in memory where the actual structure begins is stored into the location groceryItems. This address is called the **base address** of the array.

If the component type is an atomic type, the values are actually stored in the memory locations beginning at the base address. If the component type is a reference type, a reference to the first component is stored at the base address. We have used the arrow in our drawings as a visual reminder that the reference variable contains the address indicating where the actual object can be found.

Clearly, strings and arrays are related. You can visualize a string as an array of characters. Conversely, you can visualize an array as a string of values. Because of this similarity, the String class has methods that transform a string into an array of char and an array of char (char[]) into a string. The method toCharArray in the class String converts a string value into a char[]. The method valueOf takes a char[] and converts it into a string.

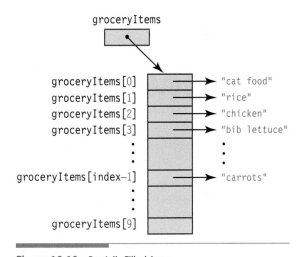

Figure 10.10 Partially Filled Array

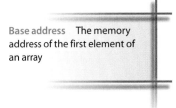

Base address The memory address of the first element of an array

▪ Arrays of User-Defined Objects

In the last example, the components of the array were strings. Now let's look at an array of user-defined objects. We have used a Name class in several Case Studies. The following code declares and instantiates an array of elements of the class Name:

```
Name[] friends = new Name[10];
```

The following table shows the types involved and indicates how to access the various components:

Expression	Class/Type
friends	Reference to an array
friends[0]	Reference to a Name object
friends[0].knowFirst()	Reference to a string
friends[0].knowLast()	Reference to a string
friends[0].knowMiddle()	Reference to a string
friends[0].knowFirst().charAt(1)	A character

10.6 Arrays and Methods

The only observer method provided for arrays is component access, which has its own special syntax: the array variable's name, followed by an index enclosed in brackets. The index specifies which component to access.

When we use an array as a field in a class, however, we may need to pass an array variable as an argument to a method or pass a component of an array to a method. Recall that a copy of each argument is sent to the method. Because an array, like a class, is a reference type, the method receives the address indicating where the object is stored.

Suppose we define a public class method (say, in the class Accounting) that takes the array as an argument and returns the sum of the components in the array:

```
public static double sumSales(double[] data)
{
  double sum = 0.0;
  for (int index = 0; index < data.length; index++)
    sum = sum + data[index];
  return sum;
}
```

The following code uses the method sumSales to sum the week's gourmet hamburger sales:

```
outFile.print("This week's sales of gourmet hamburgers: ");
outFile.println(Accounting.sumSales(gourmetBurgers));
```

What does sumSales receive as an argument? The base address of gourmetBurgers (the arrow in Figure 10.8).

We must consider two cases when passing array components as arguments to a method: (1) the component is of a primitive type or (2) the component is of a reference type. If the component is of a primitive type, the method cannot change the value of its argument. If the component is of a reference type, and the method changes its parameter, there are two possibilities. Assigning a new value to the parameter causes it to refer to a different object and doesn't affect the argument. Changing the parameter with a transformer method has the side effect of changing the argument and is considered poor programming style. Recall our house analogy: Are you just looking at the house, or are you going inside?

10.7 Special Kinds of Array Processing

Two types of problems occur frequently that use arrays. One type of problem uses only part of the defined array to store data. In the other, the index values have specific meaning within the problem.

Partial (or Sub) Array Processing

The size of an array is the declared number of array components—the number of slots set aside for the array object in memory. Java has an instance variable length associated with each array object that contains this value. In many problems, however, we do not know the number of data values, so we declare the array to be as big as it would ever need to be. As a consequence, we may not fill all of the array components with values. To avoid processing slots into which we have not stored valid data, we must keep track of how many components are actually filled.

As we put values into the array, we keep a count of how many components are filled. We then use this count to process only those components that contain valid values. The remaining places are not processed. For example, if there are 250 students in a class, an application to analyze test grades would set aside 250 locations for the grades. However, some students may be absent on the day of the test. We must therefore count the number of test grades and use that number, rather than 250, to control the processing of the array. This number becomes part of the internal representation of the class being defined. Figure 10.10 visualizes this type of processing.

Indexes with Semantic Content

In some problems, an array index has meaning beyond a simple position; that is, the index has semantic content. An example is the gourmetBurgers array discussed earlier. This array was indexed by the number of the type of hamburger minus one. That is, the sales for the hamburger that the company called #1 occupied the 0 position in the array; hamburger #2 occupied position 1 in the array; and so on.

CASE STUDY

GRADING TRUE/FALSE TESTS

Problem Statement: Your history teacher gives true/false exams. Knowing that you are studying computer science, she asks you to write an application that grades true/false questions. The answer key to the exam is on the first line of data, followed by a line with the student's name and then a line with his or her answers. Your teacher gives you the following example of the file to use as a guideline.

```
TFTFTFTFTTTFFFT
Joe Jones
TFTFTFTFTTTFFTT
Janet Jerome
TFTFTFTFTTTFFFF
Jeff Jubilee
TFTFTFTFTTTFFFT
. . .
```

As output, she wants the student's name followed by the number of questions answered correctly, written on a file with one student's data per line.

Brainstorming: The relevant objects in the problem statement are students, exam answers, and the key. The students each consist of a name. The exam answers are a series of characters (T's and F's). The key is another series of characters.

input file
output file
key
exam answer
student

Filtering: Let's look at the key object first. An exam is made up of questions, the answers to which are either T or F. Therefore, the key is an ordered collection of T's and F's that represents the correct answers to the questions. The student object contains a name and is associated with a set of exam answers, which is a sequence of T's and F's. The description of the key and the exam answers are identical. Viewed in this light, a student really isn't an important object; it is a student's *answer sheet* that is the object. An answer sheet is made up of a name and a sequence of T's and F's. If we think of the answer key as having the name "Answer Key," then the answer key and a student's answer sheet are instances of the same class: an answer sheet. Finally, we need a driver or application class that coordinates the interaction of the other classes.

CASE STUDY

input file
output file
answer sheet
application class

Scenarios: What are the responsibilities of the AnswerSheet class? The class must create instances of itself, input a name and a sequence of T's and F's from a file, and compare two AnswerSheet objects (the key and a student's answer sheet) to find the number of matching answers. There must also be a knowledge responsibility to return the name on the answer sheet. There is no need for a knowledge responsibility to return the sequence of T's and F's.

At this stage you should step back and see if anything is missing from the design. You notice that the sample data provided by your teacher has 15 questions. The test you took last week had 20 questions. Because the number of questions varies, the number of questions on the exam must be input to the constructor for the class AnswerSheet to determine the number of T's and F's.

CRC Cards:

Class Name: AnswerSheet	Superclass: Object	Subclasses:
Responsibilities	**Collaborations**	
Create itself (numQuestions)	None	
Input name and answers	BufferedReader	
Compare with another answer sheet return int	None	
Know the name return String	None	

Class Name: *GradeExams*	Superclass: *Object*	Subclasses:
Responsibilities	**Collaborations**	
Prepare files for input	*FileReader, BufferedReader*	
Prepare files for otput	*FilerWriter, PrintWriter*	
Get key	*AnswerSheet*	
Process exams	*AnswerSheet*	
Close files	*None*	

Data Representation: The exam answers are an ordered collection of T's and F's. An array is the obvious choice for holding the T's and F's. The index of an individual answer is the question number minus one. Now we are ready to design the algorithms for the two classes.

Responsibility Algorithms for AnswerSheet: We have forgotten something. How do we know how many questions were asked on this exam? We must know this information to instantiate the objects of class AnswerSheet. The user could enter it from the keyboard as an event, or the user could enter the number of questions on the file, on the line immediately before the key. Because this application does not need the user to be present to enter any other data, putting the number of questions on the data file is the better choice. The responsibility for reading this value should be in the driver.

> Answer Sheet (int numQuestions)
>
> ```
> Create responses as an array of numQuestions characters
> ```

There is another problem: A student's answer sheet contains a name that is printed along with the number correct. The key doesn't have a name to be read. We can have two input methods, one that reads a name and the sequence of T's and F's and one that reads just the T's and F's. Another alternative is to have the instructor supply "Answer Key" for the name. This second alternative is simpler because it requires only one input method. Here, then, is what the input file would look like.

```
15
Answer Key
TFTFTFTFTTTFFFT
Joe Jones
TFTFTFTFTTTFFTT
Janet Jerome
TFTFTFTFTTTFFFF
Jeff Jubilee
TFTFTFTFTTTFFFT
. . .
```

Because the name is only printed exactly as it was read in, we do not need to use the class `Name`; we can just read the line and store it into a string field, `name`. We can read the line containing the T's and F's into a string and type cast them to an array of `char` using the `String` method `toCharArray`.

```
Input name and answers (BufferedReader inFile)
Set name to inFile.readLine()
Set responses to inFile.readLine().toCharArray()
```

```
Know name
return name
```

In a by-hand algorithm, we would hold the student answers next to the key and compare them, position by position. The operational verb is "compare." To grade a student's answer, the operation must compare its ordered collections of T's and F's with the ordered collection of T's and F's of the key. The return value is the number of places where the values match.

```
int numOfMatches(AnswerSheet answer)
Set numCorrect to 0
for counter going from 0 through key.length-1
    if (key[counter] == answer[counter])
        Increment numCorrect
return numCorrect
```

Responsibility Algorithms for GradeExams (the driver) The responsibilities for the driver include the preparation of the files and reading in the number of questions, which are concrete steps. The responsibility "Get Key" is concrete as well: We simply instantiate an AnswerSheet object and apply "Input Name and Answers" to it. The work is in the "Process Exams" responsibility. There must be a loop that applies "Input Name and Answers" to an AnswerSheet object and tells it to compare itself to the key, returning the number of correct answers. The name and the number of correct answers are then written on the output file. The name "Input Name and Answers" is too long; let's simply call this method input.

```
Process exams
studentSheet = new AnswerSheet
while more exams
    studentSheet.input(inFile)
    numberCorrect = studentSheet.numOfMatches(key)
    Write studentSheet.knowName() + ": number correct  "
        + numberCorrect
```

CASE STUDY

How do we know whether there are more exams? Reading is done within the input method, so checking for the end of the data must be done there as well. If input of the line containing the name returns null, then the line with the T's and F's should not be read. How does the input method let the driver know when the end of file has been reached? We must add an additional Boolean method to the class AnswerSheet that returns true if there is more data, and false otherwise. Here is the revised algorithm for the input method and the algorithm for the moreData method.

```
input (BufferedReader inFile)  Revised
Set name to inFile.readLine()
if (name != null)
  Set responses to inFile.readLine().toCharArray()
```

```
Boolean moreData()
return name != null
```

```java
//****************************************************************
// This class provides a name object and an array of T's and F's
// representing answers on a true/false test.
//****************************************************************

package grader;
import java.io.*;
public class AnswerSheet
{
  private char[] responses;              // Contains T's and F's
  private int numItems;                  // Number of questions
  private String name;
  public AnswerSheet(int numQuestions)  // Constructor
  {
    responses = new char[numQuestions];
    numItems = numQuestions;
  }
  public void input(BufferedReader inFile) throws IOException
  // Name and sequence of T's and F's are read
  {
    name = inFile.readLine();
    if (name != null)
        responses =  inFile.readLine().toCharArray();
  }
```

```java
public int numOfMatches(AnswerSheet key)
// Return the number of matches between key and student
//   answer
{
  int numCorrect = 0;
  for (int counter = 0; counter < responses.length; counter++)
    if (responses[counter] == key.responses[counter])
      numCorrect++;
  return numCorrect;
}
public String knowName()
// Knowledge responsibility
{
  return name;
}
public boolean moreData()
{
  return name != null;
}
}


//****************************************************************
// This class is a driver that creates a key and a student
// answer sheet.  The answer sheet is compared with the key
// and the number correct is printed following the name.
//****************************************************************

import grader.*;
import java.io.*;
public class GradeExams
{
  public static void main(String[] args) throws IOException
  {
    BufferedReader inFile;
    PrintWriter outFile;

    inFile = new BufferedReader(new FileReader("Exams"));
    outFile = new PrintWriter(new FileWriter("Results"));

    AnswerSheet key;
    AnswerSheet studentSheet;
    int numItems;

    numItems = Integer.parseInt(inFile.readLine());
```

```
// Instantiate the key and student sheet objects
key = new AnswerSheet(numItems);
studentSheet = new AnswerSheet(numItems);

// Read values into the key and student answer sheet objects
key.input(inFile);
studentSheet.input(inFile);

while (studentSheet.moreData())
// Compare student answer sheets to the key and print
//    results until end of file
{
  outFile.println(studentSheet.knowName() + ": number correct " +
    studentSheet.numOfMatches(key));
  studentSheet.input(inFile);
}

inFile.close();
outFile.close();
  }
}
```

Testing: This application has one class and a driver. In the past we have used the word "driver" to refer to a simple application class that is used to test a method. Here we are using it in its other context: the main class in an object-oriented design. The driver in this Case Study is class GradeExams, the class that contains the main method. Actually, these two definitions are not dissimilar. In both cases, the driver starts the process. In a regular application, the driver implements the top-level algorithm, which might start any process. In a test driver, the process is always the same because its role is strictly to test one or more methods.

Does this mean that we need to design a test driver for this application and import class GradeExams? No, quite the contrary. We can let GradeExams test itself by carefully choosing our data sets. That is, we can use a black-box testing strategy.

There are three kinds of input to the application: an integer that specifies the number of questions, a sequence of T's and F's that represent the key and a student's answers, and a string that represents a student's name. For the moment, let's assume that the data are correct on the file, and instead concentrate on the main processing: the comparison of the key and a student exam. The following cases come immediately to mind.

1. the key and the student responses match completely (all are correct)
2. the key and the student responses do not match at all (all are wrong)
3. the key and the student responses partially match (some are correct)

CASE STUDY

Depending on the number of questions, there could be thousands of cases in the third category. How many do we have to try to convince ourselves that the application is correct? The end cases here would be that they agree in the first and last positions, they do not agree in the first and last position, they agree somewhere in the middle, and they disagree somewhere in the middle.

As the algorithm is not dependent on the number of questions, let's use 5 questions for our test cases.

Test #	Reason for Test	Input	Expected Output
	Initial input	5 Answer Key TTTTT	file
1	All correct (Also tests same in first and last position)	Jones TTTTT	Joe Jones: number correct 5
2	All wrong (also tests different in first and last position)	Janet Jerome FFFFF	Janet Jerome: number correct 0
3	Partially correct	Jeff Jubilee TFTFT	Jeff Jubilee: number correct 3
4	Test ending condition	eof on data file	application ends

Provided our input is correct, if the implemented test plan produces the expected results, we should be fairly confident that the application is correct. *Provided our input is correct?* We have not built any error checking into these classes. This omission is a serious flaw in our design. The Case Study Follow-Up questions at the end of this chapter ask you to make these classes more robust by adding error checking. The results of this test plan are shown here.

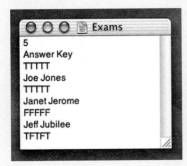

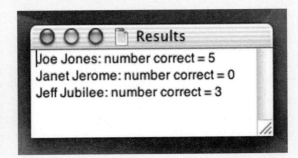

10.8 Testing and Debugging

The most common error in processing arrays is an out-of-bounds array index. That is, the application attempts to access a component by using an index that is either less than zero or greater than the array size minus one. For example, given the declarations

```
String[] line = new String[100];
int  counter;
```

the following *for* statement would print the 100 elements of the line array and then try to print a one hundred first value—the value that resides in memory immediately beyond the end of the array:

```
for (counter = 0; counter <= line.length; counter++)
  outfile.println(line[counter]);
```

This error is easy to detect, because your application will halt with an ArrayIndexOutOfBoundsException. The loop test should be counter < line.length. You won't always use a simple *for* statement when accessing arrays, however. Suppose we read data into the line array in another part of the application. Let's use a *while* statement that reads to the end of the file:

```
counter = 0;
inString = infile.readLine();
while (inString != null)
{
  line[counter] = inString;
  counter++;
  inString = infile.readLine();
}
```

This code seems reasonable enough, but what if the input file has more than 100 lines? After the one-hundredth line is read and stored into the array, the loop executes one more time and the ArrayIndexOutOfBoundsException is thrown, causing the application to crash.

The moral is this: When processing arrays, pay special attention to the design of loop termination conditions. Always ask yourself if the loop could possibly keep running after the last array component has been processed.

Whenever an array index goes out of bounds, your first suspicion should be a loop that fails to terminate properly. The second thing to check for is array access involving an index that is based on an input value or a calculation. When an array index is input as data, a data validation check is an absolute necessity.

As we have demonstrated in many examples in the last several chapters, it is possible to combine data structures in various ways: classes whose components are objects, classes whose components are arrays, arrays whose components are objects, arrays whose components are strings, and so forth. When we use arrays of objects, confusion can arise about precisely where to place the operators for array element selection ([]) and class field selection (.).

To summarize the correct placement of these operators, let's use a StudentRec class where the data fields are defined as follows:

```
class StudentRec
{
  String   stuName;                      // Student's name
  float    gpa;                          // Student's grade point average
  int[]    examScores = new int[4];      // There are four exams
  char     courseGrade;                  // A, B, C, D, or F
  ...
}
```

If we declare a variable of type StudentRec and an array of type StudentRec

```
StudentRec student = new StudentRec();
StudentRec[] members = new StudentRec[100];
```

the following chart shows how to access the fields of student. Recall that the dot operator is a binary (two-operand) operator; its left operand is a class variable or class name, and its right operand is a field. The [] operator is a unary (one-operand) operator; it comes immediately after an expression denoting an array:

Expression	Item Denoted	Meaning
student	A StudentRec object	A single student
student.stuName	A string	A name
student.gpa	A real number	A GPA
student.examScores	An array of int	
student.examScores[0]	An integer	The first exam score
student.examScores[4]	Crash!! Index out of range	
student.courseGrade	A character	
members[0]	A StudentRec object	The first student
members[0].stuName	A string	The name of the first student
members[0].gpa	A real number	The GPA of the first student
members[0].examScores	An array of int	The exam scores for the first student
members[0].examScores[1]	An integer	The second score for the first student

Testing and Debugging Hints

1. When an individual component of a one-dimensional array is accessed, the index must be within the range 0 through the array size minus 1. Attempting to use an index value outside this range will cause your application to crash.

2. The individual components of an array are themselves variables of the component type. When values are stored into an array, they should either be of the component type or be explicitly converted to the component type; otherwise, implicit type conversion occurs.

3. As with all of Java's composite data types, declaring an array variable and instantiating the array object are separate steps. We omit the size of a one-dimensional array in its declaration but *must* specify it when the array object is instantiated.

4. When an array is an argument, the reference to the array object is passed to the method. The method cannot change the reference, but it can change the elements in the array.

5. An individual array component can be passed as an argument. If the component is of a reference type, the method can change the referenced object if it is a mutable object. If the component is of an atomic type, the method cannot change it.

6. Although an object of a reference type passed as an argument can be changed if the type is mutable, it is poor programming style to do so.

7. We use subarray processing to process array components when the actual number of data items is not known until the application begins executing. The length field of the array object contains the number of slots in the array; the number of data values stored into the array may differ.

8. When methods perform subarray processing on a one-dimensional array, the array name and the number of data items actually stored in the array should be encapsulated together into a class.

9. When a one-dimensional array is instantiated without an initializer list, each of the values is automatically initialized to its default value.

10. A one-dimensional array is an object, so a reference to it may be set to null.

11. When processing the components in a one-dimensional array, we use a loop that begins at zero and stops when the counter is equal to the length field associated with the array object.

Summary

The one-dimensional array is a homogeneous data structure that gives a name to a sequential group of like components. Each component is accessed by its relative position within the group (rather than by its name, as in a class), and each component is a variable of the component type. To access a particular component, we give the name of the array and an index that specifies which component of the group we want. The index can be an expression of any integral type except `long`, as long as it evaluates to an integer ranging from 0 through the array size minus 1. Array components can be accessed in random order directly, or they can be accessed sequentially by stepping through the index values one at a time.

Quick Check

1. Declare and instantiate a one-dimensional array named `quizAnswer` that contains 12 components indexed by the integers 0 through 11. The component type is `boolean`. (pp. 486–488)

2. Given the declarations

   ```
   final int SIZE = 30;

   char[] firstName = new char[SIZE];
   ```

   a. Write an assignment statement that stores 'A' into the first component of the array `firstName`. (pp. 488–490)

   b. Write an output statement that prints the value of the fourteenth component of the array `firstName`. (pp. 488–490)

   c. Write a *for* statement that fills the array `firstName` with blanks. (p. 491)

3. Declare and instantiate a five-element one-dimensional `int` array named oddNums, using an initializer list that contains the first five odd integers, starting with 1. (p. 488)

4. Give the heading for a public void method named someFunc, where someFunc has a single parameter: a one-dimensional `float` array called `values`. (pp. 500–501)

5. Given the declaration

   ```
   studentRec[] gradeBook = new studentRec[150];
   ```

   where StudentRec is the class defined on page 511 in this chapter, do the following:

   a. Write an assignment statement that records the fact that the tenth student has a grade point average of 3.25. (p. 500)

   b. Write an assignment statement that records the fact that the fourth student scored 78 on the third exam. (p. 500)

6. Given the declarations in Question 2 and the following code fragment, which reads characters into the array firstName until a blank is encountered, write a *for* statement that prints out the portion of the array that is filled with input data. (p. 000)

```
n = 0;
line = infile.readLine();
letter = line.charAt(n);
while (letter != ' ')
{
    firstName[n] = letter;
    n++;
    letter = line.charAt(n);
}
```

Answers

1. `boolean[] quizAnswer = new boolean[12];`
2. **a.** `firstName[0] = 'A';` **b.** `outFile.println(firstName[13]);`
   c. `for (int index = 0; index < firstName.length; index++)`
   `firstName[index] = ' ';`
3. `int[] oddNums = {1, 3, 5, 7, 9};`
4. `public void someFunc(float[] values)`
5. **a.** `gradeBook[9].gpa = 3.25;` **b.** `gradeBook[3].examScores[2] = 78;`
6. `for (int index = 0; index < n; index++)`
   `outFile.print(firstName[index]);`

Exam Preparation Exercises

1. Every component in an array must have the same type, and the number of components is fixed at creation time. (True or False?)

2. The components of an array must be of a primitive type. (True or False?)

3. Declare and instantiate one-dimensional arrays according to the following descriptions.

   a. A 24-element `float` array

   b. A 500-element `int` array

   c. A 50-element double-precision floating-point array

   d. A 10-element `char` array

4. Write a code fragment to perform the following tasks:

   a. Declare a constant named `CLASS_SIZE` representing the number of students in a class.

   b. Declare a one-dimensional array `quizAvg` whose components will contain floating-point quiz score averages.

   c. Instantiate the array with size `CLASS_SIZE`.

5. Write a code fragment to do the following tasks:

   a. Declare a one-dimensional `int` array named `birdSightings`.

   b. Instantiate the array with 20 components.

6. Given the declarations

   ```
   final int SIZE = 100;
   int[] count = new int[SIZE];
   ```

   write code fragments to perform the following tasks:

   a. Set `count` to all zeros.

   b. Read values into the array.

   c. Sum the values in the array.

7. What is the output of the following code fragment? The input data for the code are given below it.

   ```
   int[] a = new int[100];
   int[] b = new int[100];
   int j;
   int m;
   int sumA = 0;
   int sumB = 0;
   int sumDiff = 0;
   m = Integer.parseInt(inFile.readLine());

   for (j = 0; j < m; j++)
   {
      a[j] = Integer.parseInt(inFile.readLine());
      b[j] = Integer.parseInt(inFile.readLine());
      sumA = sumA + a[j];
      sumB = sumB + b[j];
      sumDiff = sumDiff + (a[j] - b[j]);
   }
   ```

```
for (j = m - 1; j >= 0; j--)
    outFile.println(a[j] + " " + b[j] + " " + (a[j] - b[j]));
outFile.println();
outFile.println(sumA + " " + sumB + " " + sumDiff);
```

Data

    5
   11
   15
   19
   14
    4
    2
   17
    6
    1
    3

8. A person wrote the following code fragment, intending to print 10 20 30 40:

```
int[] arr = {10, 20, 30, 40};
int index;
for (index = 1; index <= 4; index++)
    outFile.println(" " + arr[index]);
```

Instead, the application halted with an exception. Explain the reason for this output.

9. Given the declarations

```
int[] sample = new int[8];
int i;
int k;
```

show the contents of the array sample after the following code segment executes. Use a question mark to indicate any undefined values in the array.

```
for (k = 0; k < 8; k++)
    sample[k] = 10 - k;
```

10. Using the declarations and array contents of Exercise 9, show the contents of the array sample after the following code segment executes.

```
for (i = 0; i < 8; i++)
    if (i <= 3)
        sample[i] = 1;
    else
        sample[i] = -1;
```

11. Using the declarations and array contents of Exercise 9 and the new values stored in Exercise 10, show the contents of the array `sample` after the following code segment executes.

```
for (k = 0; k < 8; k++)
    if (k % 2 == 0)
        sample[k] = k;
    else
        sample[k] = k + 100;
```

12. What are the two basic differences between a class and an array?

13. If an array is passed as an argument, can the method change the array?

14. For each of the following descriptions of data, determine which general type of data structure (array of primitive values, class, array of class objects, class containing class objects) is appropriate.

   a. A payroll entry with a name, address, and pay rate

   b. A person's address

   c. An inventory entry for a part

   d. A list of addresses

   e. A list of hourly temperatures

   f. A list of passengers on an airliner, including names, addresses, fare classes, and seat assignments

   g. A departmental telephone directory with last name and extension number

15. What happens in Java if you try to access an element that is outside the extent of the array?

16. To what are the array components initialized when you instantiate an array using `new`?

17. To what are the array components initialized when you instantiate an array using an initializer list?

Programming Warm-Up Exercises

Use the following declarations in Exercises 1–7. You may declare any other variables that you need.

```
public class Grades
{
    final int NUM_STUDENTS = 100;  // Number of students
```

```
boolean[] failing = new boolean[NUM_STUDENTS];
boolean[] passing = new boolean[NUM_STUDENTS];
int[] score = new int[NUM_STUDENTS];
}
```

1. Write a Java instance method that initializes all components of `failing` to `false`.

2. Write a Java instance method that sets the components of `failing` to `true` wherever the corresponding value in `score` is less than 60.

3. Write a Java instance method that sets the components of `passing` to `true` wherever the corresponding value in `score` is greater than or equal to 60.

4. Write a Java value-returning instance method `passTally` that reports how many components in `passing` are `true`.

5. Write a Java value-returning instance method `error` that returns `true` if any corresponding components in `passing` and `failing` are the same.

6. Write a Java value-returning instance method that takes an integer `grade` as a parameter and that reports how many values in `score` are greater than or equal to `grade`.

7. Write a Java instance method that reverses the order of the components in `score`; that is, score[0] goes into score[score.length – 1], score[1] goes into score[score.length – 2], and so on.

8. Write a code segment to read in a set of part numbers and associated unit costs, separated by blanks. Use an array of class objects with two members, `number` and `cost`, to represent each pair of input values. Assume the end-of-file condition terminates the input.

Programming Problems

1. The local baseball team is computerizing its records. The team has 20 players, identified by the numbers 1 through 20. Their batting records are coded in a file. Each line in the file contains four numbers: the player's identification number and the number of hits, walks, and outs he or she made in a particular game. Here is a sample:

   3   2   1   1

   This example indicates that during a game, player number 3 was at bat four times and made two hits, one walk, and one out. For each player, there are several lines in the file. To compute each player's batting average, one adds the player's total number of hits and divides by the total number of times at bat. A walk does not count as either a hit or an at-bat when the batting average is being calculated.

Design and implement an application that prints a table showing each player's identification number, batting average, and number of walks. (Be careful: The players' identification numbers are 1 through 20, but Java array indexes start at 0.)

2. Design, implement, and test a class that calculates the mean and standard deviation of integers stored in a file. The output should be of type `float` and should be properly labeled. The formula for calculating the mean of a series of integers is to add all the numbers, then divide by the number of integers. Expressed in mathematical terms, the mean $\overline{X}$ of N numbers $X_1, X_2, \ldots X_N$ is

$$\overline{X} = \frac{\sum_{i=1}^{N} X_i}{N}$$

To calculate the standard deviation of a series of integers, subtract the mean from each integer (you may get a negative number) and square the result, add the squared differences, divide by the number of integers minus 1, then take the square root of the result. Expressed in mathematical terms, the standard deviation S is

$$S = \sqrt{\frac{\sum_{i=1}^{N} \left(X_i - \overline{X}\right)^2}{N-1}}$$

The methods of the class that access the input data should take a file as a parameter.

3. A local bank is gearing up for a big advertising campaign and would like to see how long its customers are waiting for service at its drive-up windows. Several employees have been asked to keep accurate records for the 24-hour drive-up service. The collected information, which is read from a file, consists of the time the customer arrived in hours, minutes, and seconds; the time the customer actually was served; and the teller's ID number. Design and implement a class with the following responsibilities:

   a. Reads in the wait data.

   b. Computes the wait time in seconds.

   c. Calculates the mean, standard deviation (defined in Programming Problem 2), and range.

   d. Prints a single-page summary showing the values calculated in part (c).

Input

The first data line contains a title.

The remaining lines each contain a teller ID, an arrival time, and a service time. The times are broken up into integer hours, minutes, and seconds according to a 24-hour clock.

Processing

Calculate the mean and the standard deviation.

Locate the shortest wait time and the longest wait time for any number of records up to 100.

Output

The input data (echo print).

The title.

The following values, all properly labeled: number of records, mean, standard deviation, and range (minimum and maximum).

4. Your history professor has so many students in her class that she has trouble determining how well the class does on exams. She has discovered that you are a computer whiz and has asked you to write an application to perform some simple statistical analyses on exam scores. Your application must work for any class size up to 100.

Write and test a computer application that does the following:

a. Reads the test grades from the file inData.

b. Calculates the class mean, standard deviation (defined in Programming Problem 2), and percentage of the test scores falling in the ranges < 10, 10–19, 20–29, 30–39, ... , 80–89, and ≥ 90.

c. Prints a summary showing the mean, the standard deviation, and a histogram of the percentage distribution of test scores.

Input

The first data line contains the number of exams to be analyzed and a title for the report.

The remaining lines have 10 test scores on each line until the last line, and 1–10 scores on the last line. The scores are all integers.

Output

The input data as they are read.

A report consisting of the title that was read from the data, the number of scores, the mean, the standard deviation (all clearly labeled), and the histogram.

5. Write an application that, within an event loop, reads an apartment number and the number of occupants in the apartment. The apartment number serves as an index into an array of apartments. The components in the array represent the number of people who live in the apartment. Use the data structure described in this chapter. Use window input, and when the user presses the Quit button print the number of people in the building, the average number of people per apartment, the number of apartments with above-average occupancy, and the number with below-average occupancy.

Case Study Follow-Up

1. The exam-grading application contains no error checking.
   a. What happens if a letter other than a T or F is entered in the key?
   b. What happens if a letter other than a T or F is entered for a student?
   c. It is easy to include a check that each input value is a T or F, but what should the application do if an error occurs?

2. Redesign and rewrite the exam-grading application to incorporate error checking based on the answers in Exercise 1. Use an exception class.

3. Using the solution of reading the sequence of T's and F's as a string means that the user doesn't really have to enter the number of questions. Why? Because the array created from the string also has a `length` field. Rewrite this application so as to take advantage of this information.

Array-Based Lists

goals

Knowledge Goals

- To understand the list abstraction and basic list operations
- To know how to use a key to establish the order of a sorted list
- To recognize the difference between an array and a list
- To understand how to use an array to represent a list
- To understand the role of abstract classes
- To understand the principle of "divide and conquer" as expressed in the binary search algorithm
- To understand the role of the Comparable interface

Skill Goals

To be able to:

- Insert an item into a list
- Delete an item from a list
- Search for an item in a list
- Define a class that extends an abstract class
- Sort the items in a list into ascending or descending order
- Build a list in sorted order
- Search for an item in a sorted list using a linear search
- Search for an item using a binary search
- Use Java's Comparable interface

timeline

1979
Cellular phone systems are developed and tested in Tokyo and Chicago

1980
IBM chooses to use PC-DOS, an operating system created by the little-known company Microsoft, for its new PC

1980
Jean Ichbiah is instrumental in the development of the programming language Ada, released on December 10, 1980, the anniversary of Ada Lovelace's birthday

1980
Based on his program Vulcan, Wayne Ratliff develops dBase II, the original PC database program

1981
IBM creates a PC and does not patent the architecture, leaving the door open for competition

1982
Columbia Data Products develops its own PC, modeled after IBM's

introduction

Chapter 10 introduced the array, a structured reference type that holds a collection of components of the same type or class. Typically, a one-dimensional array holds a list of items. We all know intuitively what a "list" is; in our everyday lives we use lists all the time—grocery lists, lists of things to do, lists of addresses, lists of party guests. In computer applications, lists are very useful and popular ways to organize the data. In this chapter, we examine algorithms that build and manipulate a list implemented using a one-dimensional array to hold the items.

1982
AutoCAD, a computer-assisted design software package, is released by Autodesk

1982
John Warnock and Charles Geschke found Adobe Systems Inc., and develop software to improve the relationship between the PC and the printer

1982
Time magazine selects the computer as its "Man of the Year" signifying the incredible growing impact of computer technology on society

1982
Commercial e-mail service is up and running in 25 cities

1983
Lotus 1-2-3, one of the most important early applications for the IBM PC, integrates graphics with the spreadsheet, like VisiCalc did for the Apple II.

1983
DARPA (Defense Advanced Research Projects Agency) makes TCP/IP the primary Internet protocol, setting the framework for a globally connected network

11.1 Lists

From a logical point of view, a list is a homogeneous collection of elements, with a linear relationship between elements. Here *linear* means that, at the logical level, every element in the list except the first one has a unique predecessor, and every element except the last one has a unique successor.[1] The number of items in the list, which we call the length of the list, is a property of a list. That is, every list has a length.

Lists can be unsorted—their elements may be placed into the list in no particular order—or they can be sorted in a variety of ways. For instance, a list of numbers can be sorted by value, a list of strings can be sorted alphabetically, and a list of addresses could be sorted by ZIP code. When the elements in a sorted list are of composite types, one of the members of the structure, called the key member, determines their logical (and often physical) order. For example, a list of students on a class roll can be sorted alphabetically by name or numerically by student identification number. In the first case, the name is the key; in the second case, the identification number is the key. (See Figure 11.1.)

If a list cannot contain items with duplicate keys, we say that it has *unique keys*. (See Figure 11.2.) This chapter deals with both unsorted lists and lists of elements with unique keys, sorted from smallest to largest key value. The items on the list can be of any type, atomic or composite. In the following discussion, "item," "element," and "component" are synonyms; they refer to what is stored in the list.

Linear relationship Every element except the first has a unique predecessor, and every element except the last has a unique successor

Length The number of items in a list; it can vary over time

Unsorted list A list in which data items are placed in no particular order with respect to their content; the only relationships between data elements consist of the list predecessor and successor relationships

Sorted list A list whose predecessor and successor relationships are determined by the content of the keys of the items in the list; a semantic relationship exists among the keys of the items in the list

Key A member of a class whose value is used to determine the logical and/or physical order of the items in a list

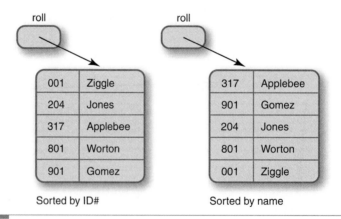

Figure 11.1   List Sorted by Two Different Keys

---

[1]At the implementation level, a relationship also exists between the elements, but the physical relationship may not be the same as the logical one.

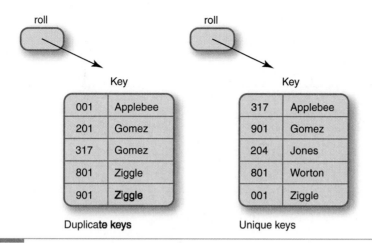

Figure 11.2 List with Duplicate Keys and List with Unique Keys

11.2   List **Class**

In this section, we will design and implement a general-purpose class that represents a list of items. Let's think in terms of a to-do list. Before we begin to brainstorm, however, we must ask an important question: For whom are we designing the class? We may be designing it for ourselves to keep in our library of classes. We may be designing it for others to use in a team project. When we create a class, the software that uses it is called the client of the class. In our discussion, we will use the terms *client* and *user* interchangeably, as we sometimes think of them as referring to the people writing the software that uses the class, rather than the software itself.

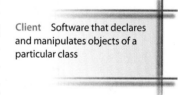

Client   Software that declares and manipulates objects of a particular class

▪ Brainstorming the List **Class**

Because we are designing a general-purpose class, our brainstorming must be more speculative. We don't have a specific problem to solve; we have to think in terms of what we currently do with our to-do lists as well as what other things we might like to do if we could. Ideally, we will start with an empty list each morning and add things to it. As we accomplish a task on the list, we will cross it off. We will check whether an item is already on the list. We will check whether we can add one more item to the list. We will check whether the list is empty (we wish!). We will go through the list one item at a time.

Let's translate these observations into responsibilities for the list, in the form of a CRC card. Notice that constructors are obvious because they are prefaced by "create," and observers have a "returns" shown. Likewise, the choice of identifier for transformers gives their type away: insert and delete. Note that this is our first experience with an iterator.

CRC Card

Class Name: *List*	Superclass: *Object*	Subclasses:
Responsibilities	**Collaborations**	
Create itself (max Items)	*None*	
Is list full? *return boolean*	*None*	
Is list empty? *return boolean*	*None*	
Know length *return int*	*None*	
Is an item in the list? *return boolean*	*None*	
Insert into list (item)	*None*	
Delete from list (item)	*None*	
Set up for iteration	*None*	
Know next item	*None*	

Although we have designed our CRC card for a to-do list, the responsibilities outlined remain valid for any kind of list. For example, if we are creating a list of people to invite to a wedding, all of these operations are valid. We add names to the list, check whether a name is already on the list, count the names on the list, check whether the list is full (that is, the length is equal to the number of invitations bought), delete names, and review the names one at a time.

To make the rest of the discussion more concrete, let's first assume that the items on the list are strings. Later, we will see how the items can be made even more general.

Refining the Responsibilities

Let's go back through the responsibilities, refining them, and converting them into method headings. Because we are designing a general-purpose class, we do not have any specific scenarios that we can use. Instead, we will consider a variety of simplified scenarios that exemplify how we believe the class may be employed. Because the class is intended for widespread use, we should pay special attention to the documentation right from the design stage.

The observers, testing for full and empty, returning the number of items, and checking whether an item is in the list, need no further discussion. Here are their method headings:

```
public boolean isFull()
// Returns true if no room to add a component; false otherwise

public boolean isEmpty()
// Returns true if no components in the list; false otherwise

public int length()
// Returns the number of components in the list

public boolean isThere(String item)
// Returns true if item is in the list; false otherwise
```

In designing the transformers, we must make some decisions. For example, do we allow duplicates in our list? This choice has implications for deleting items as well as inserting items. If we allow duplicates, what do we mean by "removing an item"? Do we delete just one copy or all of them? Because this chapter focuses on algorithms, for now we just make a decision and design our algorithms to fit. We will examine the effects of other choices in the exercises.

Let's allow only one copy of an item in the list. This decision means that deleting an item just removes one copy. However, do we assume that the item to be removed is in the list? Is it an error if it is not? Or does the delete operation mean "delete, if there"? Let's use the last meaning.

We now incorporate these decisions into the documentation for the method headings.

```
public void insert(String item)
// Adds item to the list
// Assumption:  item is not already in the list

public void delete(String item)
// item is removed from the list if present
```

The iterator allows the user to see each item in the list one at a time. Let's call the method that implements the "Know next item" responsibility getNextItem. The list must keep track of the next item to return when the iterator is called. It does so with a state variable that records the position of the next item to be returned. The constructor initializes this position to 0, and it is incremented in getNextItem. The client can use the length of the list to control a loop, asking to see each item in turn. As a precaution, we should reset the current position after accessing the last item. In an actual application, we might need a transformer iterator that goes through the list applying an operation to each item; for our general discussion here, we simply provide an observer iterator.

What happens if a user inserts or deletes an item in the middle of an iteration? Nothing good, you can be sure! Adding and deleting items changes the length of the list, invalidating the termination condition of our iteration-counting loop. Depending on whether an addition or deletion occurs before or after the iteration point, our iteration loop could end up skipping or repeating items.

We have several choices in how we handle this possibly dangerous situation. The list can throw an exception, reset the current position when inserting or deleting, or disallow transformer operations while an iteration is taking place. We choose the latter option here by way of an assumption in the documentation. In case the user wants to restart an iteration, let's provide a resetList method that reinitializes the current position.

```java
public void resetList()
// The current position is reset

public String getNextItem()
// Assumption:  No transformers are called during the iteration
```

Before moving on to the implementation phase, let's consider how we might use getNextItem. Suppose the client code wants to print out the items in the list. The client application cannot directly access the list items, but it can use getNextItem to iterate through the list. The following code fragment prints the string values in list:

```java
String next;
for (int index = 1; index <= list.length(); index++)
{
  next = list.getNextItem();   // Get an item
  System.out.println(next + " is still in the list");
}
```

Now is also the time to review the CRC card and see whether we need to add any responsibilities. For example, do we need to provide an equals test? If we want to perform a deep comparison of two lists, we must provide equals; however, comparing lists is not a particularly useful operation, and we can provide the client with the tools needed to write a comparison operation if necessary. In fact, here is the algorithm to compare two lists. It determines whether the lengths match; if they do, it iterates through the lists checking whether corresponding items are the same.

```
isDuplicate
if lengths are not the same
  return false
else
  Set counter to 1
  Set same to true
  Set limit to length of first list
  while they are still the same AND counter is less than or equal to limit
    Set next1 to next item in the first list
    Set next2 to next item in the second list
    Set same to result of seeing if next1.compareTo(next2) is 0
    Increment counter
return same
```

We can implement this algorithm without having to know anything about the list. We just use the instance methods supplied in the interface.

```java
public boolean isDuplicate(List list1, List list2)
// Returns true if the lists are identical
{
  if (list1.length() != list2.length())
    // Number of items is not the same
    return false;
  else
  {
    String next1;                   // An item from list1
    String next2;                   // An item from list2
    int counter = 1;                // Loop control variable
    boolean same = true;            // True if lists are equal
    int limit = list1.length();     // Number of items in list
    list1.resetList();              // Set up for iteration
    list2.resetList();
    while (same && counter <= limit)
    {
      next1 = list1.getNextItem();  // Get an item from list1
      next2 = list2.getNextItem();  // Get an item from list2
      same = next1.compareTo(next2) == 0;
      counter++;
    }
  }
  return same;
}
```

This method was included in the following driver, which was run twice with two different versions of list1.dat. We can write this driver without knowing anything about the list's implementation. All we have to do is import the package list, where the class List is stored.

```java
import list.*;
import java.io.*;
public class ListDriver
{
  public static void main(String[] args) throws IOException
  {
    BufferedReader inFile;
    BufferedReader inFile2;
    inFile = new BufferedReader(new FileReader("list1.dat"));
    inFile2 = new BufferedReader(new FileReader("list2.dat"));

    // Instantiate the lists
    List list1 = new List(20);
```

```
    List list2 = new List(20);
    String line;          // Used for reading input

    // Read values and insert into lists
    line = inFile.readLine();
    while (line != null)
    {
      list1.insert(line);
      line = inFile.readLine();
    }

    line = inFile2.readLine();
    while (line != null)
    {
      list2.insert(line);
      line = inFile2.readLine();
    }

    if (isDuplicate(list1, list2))
      System.out.println("Lists are the same.");
    else
      System.out.println("Lists are not the same.");

    inFile.close();
    inFile2.close();

  }
  public boolean isDuplicate(List list1, List list2)
  // Returns true if the lists are identical
  { ... }
}
```

Result from the first run:

```
Lists are the same.
```

Result from the second run:

```
Lists are not the same.
```

Internal Data Representation

How will we represent the items in the list? An array of strings is the obvious answer. What other data fields do we need? We have to keep track of the number of items in our list, and we need a state variable that tells us where we are in the list during an iteration.

```
public class List
{
  // Data fields
  protected String[] listItems;   // Array to hold list items
  protected int numItems;         // Number of items in the list
  protected int currentPos;       // State variable for iteration
  ...
}
```

In Chapter 10, we introduced the concept of subarray processing. At that time, we pointed out that every Java array object has a final field called length that contains the number of components defined for the array object. The literature for lists uses the identifier "length" to refer to the number of items that have been put into the list. Faced with this ambiguity in terminology, we still talk about the length of the list, but we refer to the field that contains the number of items in the list as numItems.

It is very important to understand the distinction made between the array object that contains the list items and the list itself. The array object is listItems[0]..listItems[listItems.length − 1]; the items in the list are listItems[0]..listItems[numItems − 1]. Figure 11.3 illustrates this distinction. In the figure, six items have been stored into the list, which was created with the following statement:

```
List myList = new List(10);
```

For simplicity, the figure shows the list items as integers rather than strings.

Responsibility Algorithms for Class List

As Figure 11.3 shows, the list exists in the array elements listItems[0] through listItems[numItems − 1]. To create an empty list, it is sufficient to set the numItems field to 0. We do not need to store any special values into the data array to make the list empty, because the list algorithms process only those values stored in listItems[0] through listItems[numItems − 1]. We will explain why currentPos is set to 0 when we look more closely at the iterator.

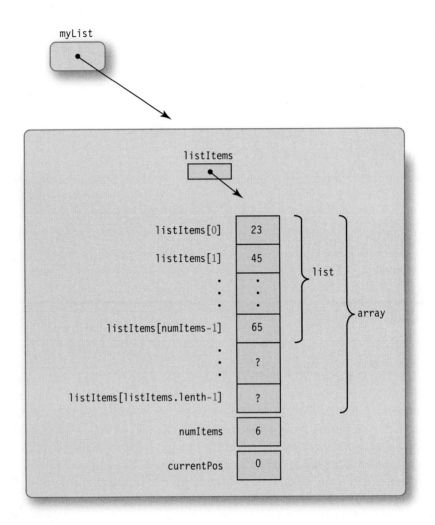

Figure 11.3 An Instance of Class List

```
public List(int maxItems)
// Instantiates an empty list object with room for maxItems items
{
  numItems = 0;
  listItems = new String[maxItems];
  currentPos = 0;
}
```

Should the class provide a default constructor? Let's do so as a precaution.

```java
public List()
// Instantiates an empty list object with room for 100 items
{
  numItems = 0;
  listItems = new String[100];
  currentPos = 0;
}
```

The observers isFull, isEmpty, and length are very straightforward. Each is only one line long, as is so often the case in methods within the object-oriented paradigm.

```java
public boolean isFull()
// Returns true if no room to add a component; false otherwise
{
  return (listItems.length == numItems);
}
```

```java
public boolean isEmpty()
// Returns true if no components in the list; false otherwise
{
  return (numItems == 0);
}
```

```java
public int length()
// Returns the number of components in the list
{
  return numItems;
}
```

We have one more observer to implement: isThere. Because isThere is an instance method, it has direct access to the items in the list. We just loop through the items in the list looking for the one specified in the parameter list. The loop ends when we find the matching item or have looked at all items in the list. Our loop expression has two conditions: The index is within the list, and the corresponding list item is not equal to the one for which we are searching. After exiting the loop, we return the assertion that the index is still within the list. If this assertion is true, then the search item was found.

```
isThere

Set index to 0
while more to examine and item not found
    Increment index
return (index is within the list)
```

We can code this algorithm directly into Java, using the compareTo method of String.

```
public boolean isThere(String item)
// Returns true if item is in the list; false otherwise
{
  int index = 0;
  while (index < numItems && listItems[index].compareTo(item) != 0)
    index++;
  return (index < numItems);
}
```

This algorithm is called a *sequential* or *linear search* because we start at the beginning of the list and look at each item in sequence. We halt the search as soon as we find the item we are seeking (or when we reach the end of the list, concluding that the desired item is not found in the list).

We can use this algorithm in any application requiring a list search. In the form shown, it searches a list of String components, but the algorithm works for any class that has a compareTo method.

Let's look again at the heading for the operation that puts an item into the list.

```
public void insert(String item)
// Adds item to the list
// Assumption:  item is not already in the list
```

Does anything in the documentation say where each new item should go? No, this is an unsorted list. Where we put each new item is up to the implementer. In this case, let's put each new item in the easiest place to reach: the next free slot in the array. Therefore, we can store a new item into listItems[numItems] and then increment numItems.

This algorithm brings up a question: Do we need to check whether the list has room for the new item? We have two choices. The insert method can test numItems against listItems.length and throw an exception if there isn't room, or we can let the client code make the test before calling insert. Our documentation is incomplete because it does not specify what occurs in this situation. Let's test for isFull and leave the list unchanged if the list is full. The client can check before the call if he or she wishes to do something else in this situation.

This algorithm is so simple, we just go directly to code.

```
public void insert(String item)
// If the list is not full, puts item in the last position in the
//  list; otherwise list is unchanged.
{
  if (!isFull())
  {
    listItems[numItems] = item;
    numItems++;
  }
}
```

Deleting a component from a list consists of two parts: finding the item and removing it from the list. We can use the same algorithm we used for isThere to look for the item. We know from the documentation that the item may or may not be in the list. If we find it, how do we re-move it? We shift each item that comes after the one being deleted forward by one array slot.

```
delete

Set index to location of item to be deleted if found
if found
    Shift remainder of list up
    Decrement numItems
```

```
shiftUp

(index is the location of the item to be deleted)
Set listItems[index] to listItems[index + 1]
Set listItems[index + 1] to listItems[index + 2]
    .
    .
    .
Set listItems[numItems − 2] to listItems[numItems − 1]
```

```java
public void delete(String item)
// Removes item from the list if it is there
// Implements "delete if there" semantics
{
  int index = 0;
  boolean found = false;
  while (index < numItems && !found)
  {
    if (listItems[index].compareTo(item) == 0)
      found = true;
    else
      index++;
  }
  if (found)
  {
    for (int count = index; count < numItems-1; count++)
      listItems[count] = listItems[count+1];
    numItems--;
  }
}
```

The resetList method is analogous to the open operation for a file in which the file pointer is positioned at the beginning of the file, so that the first input operation accesses the first component of the file. Each successive call to an input operation gets the next item in the file. Therefore resetList must initialize currentPos to the first item in the list. Where is the first item in an array-based list? In position 0. The getNextItem operation is analogous to an input operation; it accesses the current item and then increments `currentPos`. When `currentPos` reaches `numItems`, we reset it to 0.

We mentioned earlier that we need to keep the client from performing deletions and insertions during an iteration. Let's review how methods within a class might interact to change the state of the list and thus cause problems. In Chapter 5, we discussed the concept of state and mutable and immutable objects. Clearly, a `List` object is a mutable object, because transformer methods are defined for it. `resetList` changes the state variable `currentPos`. `insert` and `delete` change not only the contents of the list structure, but also the state variable `numItems`. Likewise, `getNextItem` changes the internal state of `currentPos`.

We need to monitor the interactions of these transformers carefully. If `currentPos` is reset during successive calls to `getNextItem`, the iteration just begins again. If `insert` or `delete` is invoked during an iteration, however, several things could happen. For example, `currentPos` could now be greater than `numItems`, causing `getNextItem` to send back an item no longer in the list. To solve this problem of interacting transformers, we have chosen to place a precondition on the method `getNextItem`: No transformer methods have been called since the last call to `getNextItem`.

```
public void resetList()
// The iteration is initialized by setting currentPos to 0
{
  currentPos = 0;
}


public String getNextItem()
// Returns the item at the currentPos position; resets
//   current position to first item after the last item is returned
// Assumption:  no transformers have been invoked since last call
{
  String next = listItems[currentPos];
  if (currentPos == numItems-1)
    currentPos = 0;
  else
    currentPos++;
  return next;
}
```

Both of the methods change `currentPos`. Shouldn't we consider them to be transformers? We could certainly argue that they are, but their *intention* is to set up an iteration through the items in the list, returning one item at a time to the client.

■ Test Plan

The documentation for the methods in the class `List` determines the tests necessary for a black-box testing strategy. The code of the methods indicates a need for a clear-box testing strategy. Thus, to test the `List` class implementation, we use a combination of black-box and clear-box strategies. We first test the constructor by seeing whether the list is empty (in which case a call to `length` returns 0).

The methods length, insert, and delete must be tested together. That is, we insert several items and check the length; we delete several items and check the length. How do we know that the insert and delete operations work correctly? We must write an auxiliary method printList that iterates through the list using length and getNextItem to print out the values. We call printList to check the status of the list after a series of insertions and deletions. To test the isFull operation, we must test it when the list is full and when it is not. We must also call insert when the list is full to confirm that the list remains unchanged.

Do we need to test any special cases for delete and isThere? We look first at the end cases. What are the end cases in a list? The item is in the first position in the list, the item is in the last position in the list, and the item is the only one in the list. We must verify that delete can correctly delete items in these positions. We must check that isThere can find items in these same positions and correctly determine that values are not in the list.

These observations are summarized in the following test plan. The tests are shown in the order in which they should be performed.

Operation to Be Tested and Description of Action	Input Values	Expected Output	Observed Output
Constructor (4)			
print length		0	
insert			
insert four items and print	mary, john, ann, betty	mary, john, ann, betty	
insert item and print	sarah	mary, john, ann, betty	
isThere			
isThere susy and print whether found		item is not found	
isThere mary and print whether found		item is found	
isThere ann and print whether found		item is found	
isThere betty and print whether found		item is found	
isFull			
invoke (list is full)		list is full	
delete ann and invoke		list is not full	
delete			
print		mary, john, betty	
delete betty and print		mary, john	
delete mary and print		john	
delete john and print		(empty)	
isEmpty		yes	

But what about testing `length`, `resetList`, and `getNextItem`? They do not appear explicitly in the test plan, but they are tested each time we call the auxiliary method `printList` to print the contents of the list. We do, however, have to add one test involving the iterator: We must print out `length` items to test whether the current position is reset after the last item is returned.

To implement this test plan, we must construct a test driver that carries out the tasks outlined in the first column of the preceding plan. We might make the test plan be a document separate from the driver, with the last column filled in and initialed by a person running the application and observing the screen output. Alternatively, we might incorporate the test plan into the driver as comments and have the output go to a file. The key to properly testing any software lies in the plan: It must be carefully thought out and it must be written.

Here is the output from a test driver that implements this test plan:

```
Unsorted.out

Constructor test
Length of the list is 0
insert test
mary
john
ann
betty
insert into full list test
mary
john
ann
betty
isThere test
susy is not there
mary is there
ann is there
betty is there
isFull test
List is full
List is not full
delete test
mary
john
betty
betty deleted
mary
john
mary deleted
john
john deleted
isEmpty test
List is empty
```

11.3 Sorting the List Items

getNextItem presents the items to the user in the order in which they were inserted. Depending on how we are using the list, sometimes we might want to rearrange the list components into a certain order before an iteration. For example, if the list holds names for wedding invitations, we might want to see the names in alphabetic order. Arranging list items into order is a very common operation and is known in software terminology as **sorting.**

Sorting Arranging the components of a list into order (for instance, words into alphabetical order or numbers into ascending or descending order)

If you were given a sheet of paper with a column of 20 names on it and were asked to write them in ascending order, you would probably do the following:

1. Make a pass through the list, looking for the lowest name (the one that comes first alphabetically).
2. Write it on the paper in a second column.
3. Cross the name off the original list.
4. Repeat the process, always looking for the lowest name remaining in the original list.
5. Stop when all names have been crossed off.

We could implement this algorithm as client code, using getNextItem to go through the list searching for the lowest value. When we found it, we could insert it into another list and delete it from the original. However, we would need two lists—one to hold the original list and a second to hold the sorted list. In addition, the client would have destroyed the original list. If the list is large, we might not have enough memory to maintain two copies, even if one is empty. A better solution is to derive a class from List that has a sort method that rearranges the values in the list. Because the data fields in List are declared protected, we can inherit them. By accessing the values directly within the list, we can avoid maintaining two lists.

Let's call our derived class ListWithSort.

Class Name: *ListWithSort*	Superclass: *List*	Subclasses:
Responsibilities	**Collaborations**	
Create itself (maxItems)	*super*	
Sort the items in the list	*String*	

■ Responsibility Algorithms for Class ListWithSort

The constructor takes the maximum number of items and calls List's constructor. None of the other methods needs to be overridden.

Going back to our by-hand algorithm, we can search listItems for the smallest value, but how do we "cross off" a list component? We could simulate crossing off a value by replacing it with null. In this way, we set the value of the crossed-off item to something that doesn't interfere with the processing of the rest of the components. However, a slight variation of our hand-done algorithm allows us to sort the components *in place*. We do not have to use a second list; we can, instead, put a value into its proper place in the list by having it swap places with the component currently in that list position.

We can state the algorithm as follows: We search for the smallest value in the array holding the items and exchange it with the component in the first position in the array. We search for the next-smallest value in the array and exchange it with the component in the second position in the array. This process continues until all components are in their proper places.

```
selectSort

for count going from 0 through numItems − 2
  Find the minimum value in listItems[count]..listItems[numItems − 1]
  Swap minimum value with listItems[count]
```

Figure 11.4 illustrates how this algorithm works.

Observe that we perform numItems − 1 passes through the list because count runs from 0 through numItems − 2. The loop does not need to be executed when count equals numItems − 1 because the last value, listItems[numItems − 1], is in its proper place after the preceding components have been sorted.

This algorithm, known as the *straight selection sort,* belongs to a class of sorts called selection sorts. Many types of sorting algorithms exist. Selection sorts are characterized by finding the smallest (or largest) value left in the unsorted portion at each iteration and swapping it with the value indexed by the iteration counter. Swapping the contents of two variables requires a temporary variable so that no values are lost (see Figure 11.5).

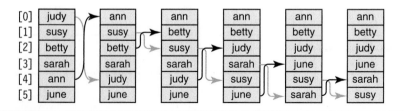

Figure 11.4 Straight Selection Sort

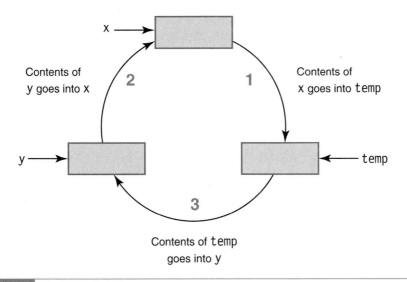

Figure 11.5   Swapping the Contents of Two Variables, *x* and *y*

■ Class ListWithSort

We are now ready to code our derived class. In the documentation, we need to include a note stating that the alphabetic order may be lost with future insertions.

```
public class ListWithSort extends List
{
  // The items in the list can be rearranged into ascending order
  //   This order is not preserved in future insertions

  public ListWithSort()
  { // Default constructor
    super();
  }

  public ListWithSort(int maxItems)
  { // Constructor
    super(maxItems);
  }

  public void selectSort()
  // Arranges list items in ascending order;
  //   selection sort algorithm is used
```

```
{
  String temp;            // Temporary variable
  int passCount;          // Loop control variable for outer loop
  int searchIndex;        // Loop control variable for inner loop
  int minIndex;           // Index of minimum so far

  for (passCount = 0; passCount < numItems - 1; passCount++)
  {
    minIndex = passCount;
    // Find the index of the smallest component
    //   in listItems[passCount]..listItems[numItems - 1]
    for (searchIndex = passCount + 1; searchIndex < numItems; searchIndex++)
      if (listItems[searchIndex].compareTo(listItems[minIndex]) < 0)
        minIndex = searchIndex;
    // Swap listItems[minIndex] and listItems[passCount]
    temp = listItems[minIndex];
    listItems[minIndex] = listItems[passCount];
    listItems[passCount] = temp;
  }
}
}
```

With each pass through the outer loop in selectSort, we look for the minimum value in the rest of the array (listItems[passCount] through listItems[numItems − 1]). Therefore, minIndex is initialized to passCount and the inner loop runs from searchIndex equal to passCount + 1 through numItems − 1. Upon exit from the inner loop, minIndex contains the position of the smallest value. (Because the *if* statement is the only statement in the loop, we do not have to enclose it in a block.)

This method may swap a component with itself, which occurs if no value in the remaining list is smaller than listItems[passCount]. We could avoid this unnecessary swap by checking whether minIndex is equal to passCount. Because this comparison would occur in every iteration of the outer loop, it is more efficient not to check for this possibility and just to swap something with itself occasionally. For example, if our list contains 10,000 elements, then making this comparison adds 10,000 operations to the execution of the loop, yet we might save just a few dozen unnecessary swap operations as a result. Table 11.1 shows an input file and the results of sorting the file.

This algorithm sorts the components into ascending order. To sort them into descending order, we must scan for the *maximum* value instead of the *minimum* value. Simply changing the test in the inner loop from "less than" to "greater than" accomplishes this goal. Of

Original File	Sorted File
red	black
blue	blue
yellow	brown
brown	crimson
black	green
pink	orange
green	pink
orange	red
white	rose
violet	violet
crimson	white
rose	yellow

Table 11.1 File Sorting

course, in this case minIndex would no longer be an appropriate identifier and should be changed to maxIndex.

11.4 Sorted List

ListWithSort does not provide the user with a true sorted list class. That is, the insert and delete algorithms do not preserve ordering by value. The insert operation places a new item at the end of the list, regardless of its value. After selectSort has been executed, the list items remain in sorted order only until the next insertion or deletion takes place. Of course, the client could sort the list after every insertion, but this technique is inefficient. Let's now look at a sorted list design in which all the list operations cooperate to preserve the sorted order of the list components.

■ Brainstorming the Sorted List

The design for the class List says nothing about the order of its items. If we want to keep the list items in sorted order, we need to specify this criterion. Let's go back to the CRC card design for List and indicate that we want the list to be sorted.

Class Name: *List*	Superclass: *Object*	Subclasses:
Responsibilities	**Collaborations**	
Create itself (maxItems)	None	
Is list full? return boolean	None	
Is list empty? return boolean	None	
Know length return int	None	
Is an item in the list? return boolean	None	
Insert into list (item), keeping list sorted	None	
Delete from list (item), keeping list sorted	None	
Set up for iteration	None	
Know next item in sorted order	None	

The first thing we notice is that the observers do not change. They remain the same whether the list is sorted by value or not. The transformers insert and delete and the iterator now have additional constraints, however. Rather than designing an entirely new class, we can derive SortedList from List, overriding those methods whose implementations need changing.

Class Name: *SortedList*	Superclass: *List*	Subclasses:
Responsibilities	**Collaborations**	
Create itself (maxItems)	None	
Insert into list (item), keeping the list sorted	String	
Delete from list (item), keeping the list sorted	String	
Look at each item in sorted order	String	

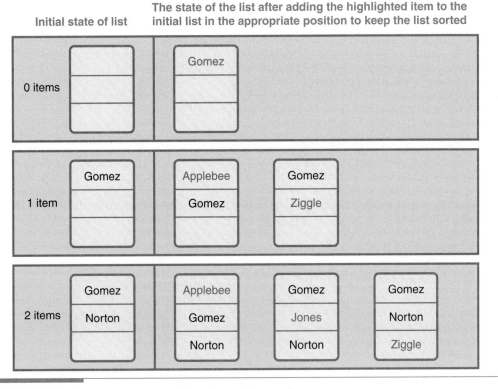

Figure 11.6   Inserting Items into a List So That Ordering Is Preserved

▣ Responsibility Algorithms for Class SortedList

Let's look first at insert. Figure 11.6 illustrates how it should work.

The first item inserted into the list can go into the first position. Because there is only one item, the list is sorted. If a second item being inserted is less than the first item, the first item must be moved into the second position and the new item put into the first position. If the second item is larger, it goes into the second position. If we add a third item that is smaller than the first item, the other two items shift down by one and the third item goes into the first position. If the third item is greater than the first item but less than the second, the second shifts down and the third item goes into the second position. If the third item is greater than the second item, it goes into the third position.

To generalize, we start at the beginning of the list and scan until we find an item greater than the one we are inserting. We shift that item and the rest of the items in the list down by one position to make room for the new item. The new item goes in the list at that point.

```
insert

if (list is not full)
    while place not found AND more places to look
        if item > current item in the list
            Increment current position
        else
            Place found
    Shift remainder of the list down
    Insert item
    Increment numItems
```

Assuming that index is the place where item is to be inserted, the algorithm for shifting the remainder of the list down is as follows:

```
shiftDown
Set listItems[numItems] to listItems[numItems – 1]
Set listItems[numItems – 1] to listItems[numItems – 2]
  .
  .
  .
Set listItems[index + 1] to listItems[index]
```

This algorithm is illustrated in Figure 11.7.

This algorithm is based on how we would accomplish the task by hand. Often, such an adaptation is the best way to solve a problem. However, in this case, further thought reveals a slightly better approach. Notice that we search from the front of the list (people always do), and we shift down from the end of the list upward. We can, in fact, combine the searching and shifting operations by beginning at the *end* of the list.

If item is the new item to be inserted, we can compare item to the value in listItems[numItems – 1]. If item is *less*, we put listItems[numItems – 1] into listItems[numItems] and compare item to the value in listItems[numItems – 2]. This process continues until we find the place where item is greater than or equal to the list item. We then store item directly after it. Here is the algorithm:

```
insert (revised)

if (list is not full)
    Set index to numItems – 1
    while index >= 0 && (item.compareTo(listItems[index]) < 0)
        Set listItems[index + 1] to listItems[index]
        Decrement index
    Set listItems[index + 1] to item
    Increment numItems
```

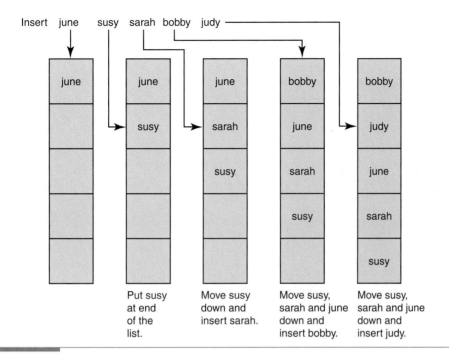

Figure 11.7   Inserting into a Sorted List

Notice that this algorithm works even if the list is empty. When the list is empty, numItems is 0 and the body of the *while* loop is not entered. Thus item is stored into listItems[0], and numItems is incremented to 1. Does the algorithm work if item is the smallest value? What about the largest value? Let's see. If item is the smallest value, the loop body executes numItems times and index is −1. Thus item is stored into position 0, where it belongs. If item is the largest value, the loop body is not entered. The value of index remains numItems − 1, so item is stored into listItems[numItems], where it belongs.

Are you surprised that the general case also takes care of the special cases? This situation does not happen all the time, but it occurs sufficiently often that it is good programming practice to start with the general case. If we begin with the special cases, we may still generate a correct solution, but we may not realize that we don't need to handle the special cases separately. Thus we have this guideline: Begin with the general case, then treat as special cases only those situations that the general case does not handle correctly.

The methods delete and getNextItem must maintain the sorted order—but they already do! An item is deleted by removing it and shifting all of the items larger than the one deleted up by one position; getNextItem merely returns a copy of an item—it does not change an item. Only insert needs to be overridden in the derived class SortedList.

```
package list;
public class SortedList extends List
{
```

```java
public SortedList()
{
  super();
}
public SortedList(int maxItems)
{
  super(maxItems);
}
public void insert(String item)
// If the list is not full, puts item in its proper place in
//   the list; otherwise list is unchanged
// Assumption:  item is not already in the list
{
  if (!isFull())
  {
    int index = numItems - 1;              // Loop control variable
    while (index >= 0 && (item.compareTo(listItems[index]) < 0))
    { // Find insertion point
      listItems[index+1] = listItems[index];
      index--;
    }
    listItems[index+1] = item;           // Insert item
    numItems++;                          // Increment number of items
  }
}
}
```

■ Test Plan

We can use the same test plan for the sorted list that we used for the unsorted version. The only difference is that in the expected output, the list items should appear in sorted order. Alternatively, we could use the same input file that was used to test ListWithSort to test SortedList.

11.5 The List Class Hierarchy and Abstract Classes

We have created a hierarchy with the class List at the top and two derived classes. We can visualize this hierarchy as follows:

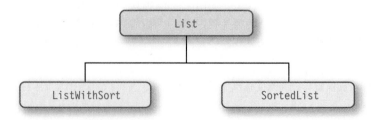

ListWithSort is a List. SortedList is a List. ListWithSort is not a SortedList, and SortedList is not a ListWithSort.

We could have organized the hierarchy using an abstract class. Recall from Chapter 7 that an abstract class is a class that is headed by the word abstract and leaves one or more methods incomplete. We cannot instantiate an abstract class. Rather, another class must extend the abstract class and implement all of the abstract methods. In the preceding example, we could have implemented the observers and iterator in the abstract class and left the implementation of the transformers to the derived class. Then the unsorted and sorted versions of the list could both inherit from the abstract class. The documentation for the classes would be as follows:

```java
public abstract class List
{
  public List()
  public List(int maxItems)
  public boolean isFull()
  public boolean isEmpty()
  public int length()
  public boolean isThere(String item)
  public void resetList()
  public String getNextItem()
  public abstract void delete(String item)
  public abstract void insert(String item)
}

public class UnsortedList extends List
{
  public UnsortedList()
  public UnsortedList(int maxItems)
  public void delete(String item)
  public void insert(String item)
}

public class SortedList extends List
{
  public SortedList()
  public SortedList(int maxItems)
  public void delete(String item)
  public void insert(String item)
}

public class ListWithSort extends UnsortedList
{
  public ListWithSort()
  public ListWithSort(int maxItems)
  public void selectSort()
}
```

Under these conditions, the class hierarchy would look like this:

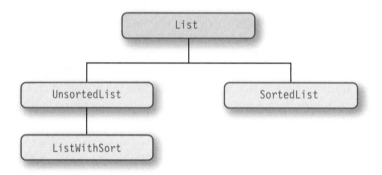

11.6 Searching

In our SortedList class, we overrode the insert method—the only method that we had to rewrite to keep the list in sorted order. However, if the list is already sorted, we can perform a more efficient search. In this section, we look at two searching algorithms that depend on the list items being in sorted order.

■ Sequential Search

The isThere algorithm assumes that the list to be searched is unsorted. A drawback to searching an unsorted list is that we must scan the entire list to discover that the search item is not present. Think what it would be like if your city telephone book contained people's names in random rather than alphabetical order. To look up Marcus Anthony's phone number, you would have to start with the first name in the phone book and scan sequentially, page after page, until you found it. In the worst case, you might examine tens of thousands of names, only to find out that Marcus's name is not in the book.

Of course, telephone books *are* alphabetized, and the alphabetical ordering makes searching easier. If Marcus Anthony's name is not in the book, you can discover this fact quickly by starting with the A's and stopping the search as soon as you pass the place where his name should be. Although the sequential search algorithm in isThere works in a sorted list, we can make the algorithm more efficient by taking advantage of the fact that the items are sorted.

How does searching in a sorted list differ from searching in an unordered list? When we search for an item in an unsorted list, we won't discover that the item is missing until we reach the end of the list. If the list is already sorted, we know that an item is missing when we pass the place where it should be in the list. For example, if a list contains the values

and we are looking for judy, we need simply compare judy with becca, bobby, and june to know that judy is not in the list.

If the search item is greater than the current list component, we move on to the next component. If the item is equal to the current component, we have found the desired element. If the item is less than the current component, then we know that it is not in the list. In either of the last two cases, we stop looking. In our original algorithm, the loop conditions stated that the index was within the list and the corresponding list item was not the one sought. In this algorithm, the second condition must be that the item being sought is less than the corresponding list item. However, determining whether the item is found is a little more complex. We must first assert that the index is within the list and, if that is true, assert that the search item is equal to the corresponding list item.

```
isThere (in a sorted list)
Set index to 0
while index is within the list AND item is greater than listItems[index]
    Increment index
return (index is within the list AND item is equal to listItems[index])
```

Why can't we just test whether item is equal to listItems[index] after we exit the loop? This strategy works in all cases but one: if item is larger than the last element in the list. In that case, we would exit the loop with index equal to numItems. Trying to access listItems[index] would then cause the code to crash with an "index out of range" error. Therefore, we must check the value of index first.

```
public boolean isThere(String item)
// Returns true if item is in the list; false otherwise
// Assumption:  List items are in ascending order
{
  int index = 0;
  while (index < numItems
      && item.compareTo(listItems[index]) > 0)
    index++;
  return (index < numItems && item.compareTo(listItems[index]) == 0);
}
```

On average, searching a sorted list in this way takes the same number of iterations to find an item as searching an unsorted list. The advantage of this new algorithm is that we find out sooner if an item is missing. Thus it is slightly more efficient. Another search algorithm exists that works only on a sorted list, but it is more complex: a binary search. However, the extra complexity is worth the trouble.

■ Binary Search

The *binary search* algorithm on a sorted list is considerably faster both for finding an item and for discovering that an item is missing. A binary search is based on the principle of successive approximation. The algorithm divides the list in half (divides by 2—that's why it's called a *binary* search) and decides which half to look in next. Division of the selected portion of the list is repeated until the item is found or it is determined that the item is not present in the list.

This method is analogous to the way in which we look up a name in a phone book (or word in a dictionary). We open the phone book in the middle and compare the desired name with one on the page that we turned to. If the name we're seeking comes before this name, we continue our search in the left-hand section of the phone book. Otherwise, we continue in the right-hand section of the phone book. We repeat this process until we find the name. If it is not present, we realize that either we have misspelled the name or our phone book isn't complete. See Figure 11.8.

With this approach, we start with the whole list (indexes 0 through numItems − 1) and compare our search value to the middle list item. If the search item is less than the middle list item, we continue the search in the first half of the list. If the search item is greater than the middle list item, we continue the search in the second half of the list. Otherwise, we have found a match. We keep comparing and redefining the part of the list in which to look (the search area) until we find the item or the search area is empty.

Let's write the algorithm bounding the search area by the indexes first and last. See Figure 11.9.

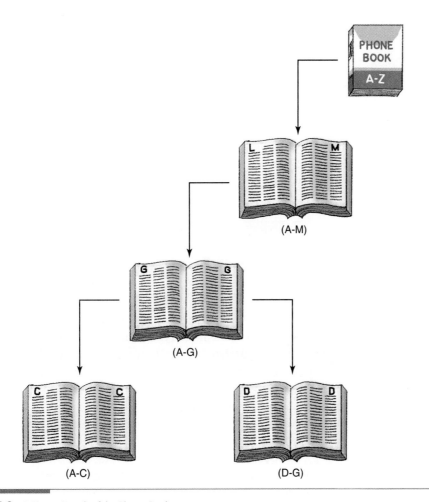

(A-M)

(A-G)

(A-C)   (D-G)

Figure 11.8 A Binary Search of the Phone Book

```
Binary Search

Set first to 0
Set last to numItems – 1
Set found to false
while search area is not empty and !found
  Set middle to (first + last) divided by 2
  if (item is equal to listItems[middle])
    Set found to true
  else if (item is less than listItems[middle])
    Set last to middle – 1      // look in first half
  else
    Set first to middle + 1      // look in last half
```

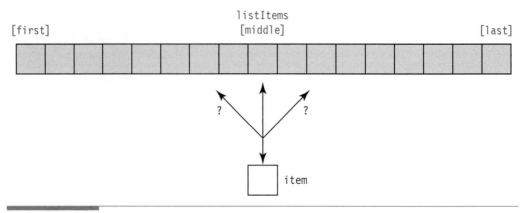

Figure 11.9 Binary Search

This algorithm should make sense. With each comparison, at best, we find the item for which we are searching; at worst, we eliminate half of the remaining list from consideration. Before coding this algorithm, we need to determine when the search area is empty. If the search area is between `listItems[first]` and `listItems[last]`, then the area is empty if `last` is less than `first`.

Let's do a walk-through of the binary search algorithm. The item we are searching for is `"bat"`. Figure 11.10a shows the values of `first`, `last`, and `middle` during the first iteration. In this iteration, `"bat"` is compared with `"dog"`, the value in `listItems[middle]`. Because `"bat"` is less than (comes before) `"dog"`, `last` becomes `middle – 1` and `first` stays the same. Figure 11.10b shows the situation during the second iteration. This time, `"bat"` is compared with `"chicken"`, the value in `listItems[middle]`. Because `"bat"` is less than (comes before) `"chicken"`, `last` becomes `middle – 1` and `first` again stays the same.

In the third iteration (Figure 11.10c), `middle` and `first` are both 0. The item `"bat"` is compared with `"ant"`, the item in `listItems[middle]`. Because `"bat"` is greater than (comes after) `"ant"`, `first` becomes `middle + 1`. In the fourth iteration (Figure 11.10d), `first`, `last`, and `middle` are all the same. Again, `"bat"` is compared with the item in `listItems[middle]`. Because `"bat"` is less than `"cat"`, `last` becomes `middle – 1`. Now that `last` is less than `first`, the process stops; `found` is `false`.

The binary search is the most complex algorithm that we have examined so far. Table 11.2 shows `first`, `last`, `middle`, and `listItems[middle]` for searches for the items `"fish"`, `"snake"`, and `"zebra"`, using the same data as in the previous example. Examine the results in this table carefully.

Notice in the table that whether we searched for `"fish"`, `"snake"`, or `"zebra"`, the loop never executed more than four times. It never executes more than four times in a list of 11 components

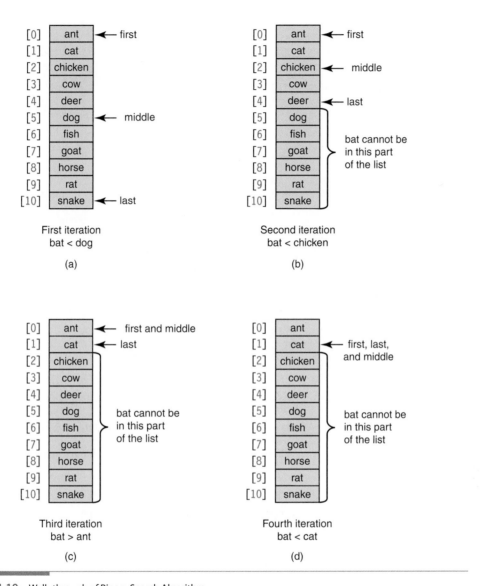

Figure 11.10 Walk-through of Binary Search Algorithm

Iteration	first	last	middle	listItems[middle]	Terminating Condition
item : fish					
First	0	10	5	dog	
Second	6	10	8	horse	
Third	6	7	6	fish	found is true
item : snake					
First	0	10	5	dog	
Second	6	10	8	horse	
Third	9	10	9	rat	
Fourth	10	10	10	snake	found is true
item : zebra					
First	0	10	5	dog	
Second	6	10	8	horse	
Third	9	10	9	rat	
Fourth	10	10	10	snake	
Fifth	11	10			last < first

Table 11.2   Binary Searching

because the list is cut in half each time through the loop. The following table compares a sequential search and a binary search in terms of the average number of iterations needed to find an item:

	Average Number of Iterations	
Length	**Sequential Search**	**Binary Search**
10	5.5	2.9
100	50.5	5.8
1,000	500.5	9.0
10,000	5000.5	12.0

If the binary search is so much faster, why not use it all the time? It certainly is faster in terms of the number of times through the loop, but it requires more computations within the binary search loop than in the other search algorithms. Thus, if the number of components in the list is small (say, less than 20), the sequential search algorithms are faster because they perform less work at each iteration. As the number of components in the list increases, the binary search algorithm becomes relatively more efficient.

Here is the code for isThere that uses the binary search algorithm:

```
public boolean isThere(String item)
// Returns true if item is in the list; false otherwise
//   Binary search algorithm is used
// Assumption:  List items are in ascending order
```

```
{
  int first = 0;                // Lowest position in search area
  int last = numItems-1;        // Highest position in search area
  int middle;                   // Middle position in search area
  boolean found = false;
  while (last >= first && !found)
  {
    middle = (first + last)/2;
    if (item.compareTo(listItems[middle]) == 0)
      found = true;
    else if (item.compareTo(listItems[middle]) < 0)
      // item not in listItems[middle]..listItems[last]
      last = middle - 1;
    else
      // item not in listItems[first]..listItems[middle]
      first = middle + 1;
  }
  return found;
}
```

Complexity of Searching and Sorting

We introduced Big-O notation in Chapter 9 as a way of comparing the work done by different algorithms. Let's apply it to the algorithms that we've developed in this chapter and see how they compare with each other. In each algorithm, we start with a list containing some number of items, N.

In the worst case, the isThere sequential-search method scans all N components to locate an item. That is, it requires N steps to execute. On average, isThere takes roughly N/2 steps to find an item; however, recall that in Big-O notation, we ignore constant factors (as well as lower-order terms). Thus the method isThere is an order N—that is, an O(N)—algorithm.

What about the algorithm we presented for a sequential search in a sorted list? The number of iterations is decreased for the case in which the item is missing from the list. However, we have simply taken a case that would require N steps and reduced its time, on average, to N/2 steps. Therefore, this algorithm is also O(N).

Now consider isThere when we use the binary search algorithm. In the worst case, it eliminates half of the remaining list components on each iteration. Thus the worst-case number of iterations equals the number of times N must be divided by 2 to eliminate all but one value. This number is computed by taking the logarithm, base 2, of N (written $\log_2 N$). Here are some examples of $\log_2 N$ for different values of N:

Theoretical Foundations

N	Log$_2$N
2	1
4	2
8	3
16	4
32	5
1024	10
32,768	15
1,048,576	20
33,554,432	25
1,073,741,824	30

As you can see, for a list of more than 1 billion values, the binary search algorithm takes only 30 iterations. It is definitely the best choice for searching large lists. Algorithms such as the binary search algorithm are said to be of *logarithmic order*.

Now let's turn to sorting. The method `selectSort` contains nested *for* loops. The total number of iterations is the product of the iterations performed by the two loops. The outer loop executes $N - 1$ times. The inner loop also starts out executing $N - 1$ times, but steadily decreases until it performs just one iteration: The inner loop executes N/2 iterations. The total number of iterations is thus

$$\frac{(N - 1) \times N}{2}$$

Ignoring the constant factor and lower-order term, this is N^2 iterations, and `selectSort` is an $O(N^2)$ algorithm. Whereas `isThere`, when coded using the binary search algorithm, takes only 30 iterations to search a sorted array of 1 billion values, putting the array into order takes `selectSort` approximately 1 billion times 1 billion iterations!

Our `insert` algorithm for a sorted list forms the basis for an *insertion sort,* in which values are inserted into a sorted list as they are input. On average, `insert` must shift down half of the values (N/2) in the list; thus, it is an $O(N)$ algorithm. If we call `insert` for each input value, we execute an $O(N)$ algorithm N times; therefore, an insertion sort is an $O(N^2)$ algorithm.

Is every sorting algorithm $O(N^2)$? Most of the simpler ones are, but $O(N \times \log_2 N)$ sorting algorithms exist. Algorithms that are $O(N \times \log_2 N)$ are much closer in performance to $O(N)$ algorithms than are $O(N^2)$ algorithms. For example, if N is 1 million, then an $O(N^2)$ algorithm takes 1 million times 1 million (1 trillion) iterations, but an $O(N \times \log_2 N)$ algorithm takes only 20 million iterations—that is, it is 20 times slower than the $O(N)$ algorithm but 50,000 times faster than the $O(N^2)$ algorithm.

11.7 Generic Lists

In generic lists, the operations are defined, but the types of the objects on the list are not. Although we called the components of our lists "items," they are actually Strings. Is it possible to construct a truly general-purpose list where the items can be of any type? For example, could we have a list of Name objects as defined in Chapter 4 or a list of Address objects as defined in Chapter 6? Yes, we can. All we have to do is declare the objects on the list to be Comparable. What is Comparable? It's a Java interface. Let's see how we can use it to make our lists generic.

■ Comparable Interface

In Chapter 5, we defined the Java construct interface as a model for a class that specifies the constants (final fields) and instance methods that must be present in a class that implements the interface. The Comparable interface is part of the standard Java class library. Any class that implements this interface must implement the method compareTo. This method compares two objects and returns an integer that determines the relative ordering of the two objects (the instance to which it is applied and the method's parameter).

```
intValue = item.compareTo(listItems[index]);
```

intValue is negative if item comes before listItems[index], is 0 if they are equal, and is positive if item comes after listItems[index]. We have used this method to compare strings in the classes designed in this chapter because the String class implements the Comparable interface.

To make our List class as generic as possible, we replace String with Comparable throughout the class. As a consequence, any object of a class that implements the Comparable interface can be passed as an argument to insert, delete, or isThere. In addition, the type of the array elements must be declared as implementing Comparable and getNextItem must return a value of type Comparable. Here is the complete abstract class List:

```java
public abstract class List
{
  protected Comparable[] listItems;    // Array to hold list items
  protected int numItems;              // Number of items in the list
  protected int currentPos;            // State variable for iteration

  public List(int maxItems)
  // Instantiates an empty list object with room for maxItems items
  {
    numItems = 0;
    listItems = new Comparable[maxItems];
    currentPos = 0;
  }

  public List()
  // Instantiates an empty list object with room for 100 items
```

```
  {
    numItems = 0;
    listItems = new Comparable[100];
    currentPos = 0;
  }

  public boolean isFull()
  // Returns true if there is no room for another component;
  //   false otherwise
  {
    return (listItems.length == numItems);
  }

  public boolean isEmpty()
  // Returns true if there are no components in the list;
  //   false otherwise
  {
    return (numItems == 0);
  }

  public int length()
  // Returns the number of components in the list
  {
    return numItems;
  }

  public abstract boolean isThere(Comparable item);
  // Returns true if item is in the list; false otherwise

  // Transformers
  public abstract void insert(Comparable item);
  // If list is not full, inserts item into the list;
  //   otherwise list is unchanged
  // Assumption:  item is not already in the list

  public abstract void delete(Comparable item);
  // Removes item from the list if it is there

  // Iterator pair
  public void resetList()          // Prepare for iteration
  {
    currentPos  = 0;
  }
  public Comparable getNextItem()
  // Returns the item at the currentPos position; resets current
  //   position to first item after the last item is returned
  // Assumption:  no transformers have been invoked since last call
```

```
  {
    Comparable next = listItems[currentPos];
    if (currentPos == numItems-1)
      currentPos = 0;
    else
      currentPos++;
    return next;
  }
}
```

Notice that we have made the `isThere` method be abstract. This way, the derived class can determine which searching algorithm to use.

■ Polymorphism

We have discussed polymorphism several times, as it is a major feature of object-oriented programming. In a hierarchy of classes, polymorphism enables us to override a method name with a different implementation in a derived class. Thus multiple forms of a given method can appear within the hierarchy (literally, polymorphism means *having multiple forms*).

The Java compiler decides which form of a polymorphic instance method to use by looking at the class of its associated instance. For example, if `compareTo` is associated with a `String` variable, then the version of `compareTo` defined in the class `String` is called.

Thus far, this is all straightforward. But consider the case where we apply `compareTo` to an object that has been passed as a parameter declared to be `Comparable`. The abstract `insert` method that we defined in the last section is precisely the example we have in mind.

```
public abstract void insert(Comparable item);
```

An instance of any class that implements `Comparable` can be passed as an argument to this parameter. The class of the argument object determines which form of `compareTo` is actually called within `insert`. At compile time, however, the Java compiler does not have any way to determine the class of the argument object. Instead, it must insert Bytecode that identifies the argument's class at run time and then calls the appropriate method. Programming language designers call this approach **dynamic binding**. When the compiler can identify the appropriate form of the method to use, it is called **static binding**.

Dynamic binding Determining at run time which form of a polymorphic method to call

Static binding Determining at compile time which form of a polymorphic method to call

The practical implication of dynamic binding is that it allows us to define a generic `List` class that works with items that are of any class that implements `Comparable`. Whenever a method in the `List` class needs to compare two items, the appropriate form of `compareTo` is called—even when the class of the items isn't known until run time.

The other practical implication of dynamic binding is that it is slower than static binding. With static binding, the JVM transfers control directly to the appropriate method. In dynamic binding, the JVM must first identify the class of the object and then look up the address of the associated method before transferring control to it.

CASE STUDY

MERGING ADDRESS BOOKS

Problem: In earlier chapters we created an electronic address book in which each entry contains a name, an address, a phone number, and a birthday. We have stored the entries on a file of objects. The electronic address book has been so successful that we have shared it with others. Now we want to combine the entries from two address books and print address labels in alphabetical order. If the same name appears in both address books, the appropriate label should be printed only once. We also want to save the combined address books.

Brainstorming: The processing seems very straightforward. We create a new address book object made up of all the entries in both address books, removing duplicate entries along the way. The combined address book must then be sorted and labels printed on a text file. In addition to the classes involved in the class Entry, we have three instances of an object file (two input and one output), a text file, and a driver:

ObjectInputStream
ObjectOutputStream
PrintWriter
Driver

Filtering: To this point, we have been working with files. The restriction that the list of labels be alphabetized may lead to a different solution. We could read the two files of entries and store them into two SortedList objects. Then we could merge the two lists and the output would be sorted. Let's revise our list of classes:

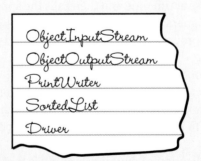

ObjectInputStream
ObjectOutputStream
PrintWriter
SortedList
Driver

Determining Responsibilities: This problem is somewhat different in that all of the responsibilities are in the driver, and they are clearly spelled out in the problem description. At this point, we switch from an object-oriented view and look at the tasks outlined in the problem statement. By using SortedList objects, we have already taken care of sorting the output: We will create the addresses in sorted order.

Class Name: *LabelDriver*	Superclass: *Object*	Subclasses:
Responsibilities	**Collaborations**	
Prepare files for input	*ObjectInputStream*	
Prepare files for output	*PrintWriter ObjectOutputStream*	
Read first file into SortedList	*SortedList*	
Read second file into SortedList	*SortedList*	
Merge two lists into third SortedList	*SortedList*	
Print labels	*PrintWriter*	
Write combined file	*ObjectOutputStream*	

Responsibility Algorithms: The first two responsibilities are concrete. The next two responsibilities are identical except for the name of the SortedList object and the file name. Let's set up this processing as a helper method called "Generate lists".

```
Generate lists(SortedList list, ObjectInputStream inFile)
Set more data to true
while more data
  try
    Read an entry from inFile
    list.insert(entry)
  catch EOFException
    Set more data to false
```

The fifth responsibility poses a greater challenge. When faced with a complex problem, a good strategy is to consider how you might solve the problem by hand (that is, to look for things that are familiar). One algorithm might be to take the first name on the first list, write it to the new list, and search the second list to see if it is found there. If the name is present, it would be a duplicate, so we would cross it off the second list. When we finish going through the first list, we then add to the new list all of the names that remain on the second list. For each item on the first list, we must search the entire second list.

This by-hand algorithm serves as a good model for a computer solution. Because the lists are ordered alphabetically, however, a more efficient algorithm is possible. Let's pretend that the names are on index cards in two stacks rather than in two lists. If we pick up the first card in each stack and compare them, three possibilities arise:

1. The name on the first stack comes alphabetically before the name on the second stack.
2. The name on the second stack comes alphabetically before the name on the first stack.
3. The names are the same.

If the name on the first stack comes first, we would put the card in the output stack face down. If the name on the second stack comes first, we would put that card in the output stack face down. If the names are the same, we would put one of the cards on the output stack face down and tear up the other card. The stack from which the card was removed now has a new card on the top (or both stacks have new cards on top), and we repeat the comparing process. This algorithm allows us to look at only one name from each list at a time, so we do not search the second list.

"Picking up the first card in each stack" is equivalent to examining the name from the first entry in each list. "Compare them" is a call to the Name class method compareTo. Recall that compareTo returns a negative value if the object comes before the parameter, zero if the two are the same, and a positive value if the parameter comes before the object.

"Put a card on the output stack face down" translates into inserting the entry into the combined list. "Tear up" translates into not processing the entry. "New card" translates into getting the next entry.

What halts the processing? In our by-hand algorithm, we stopped comparing names when one or both of the stacks became empty. A stack is "empty" when one or both lists run out of entries. Because we know how many items are in each list, we can count how many times we get a new item from each list and stop when we have accessed the last one in one of the lists. One list may run out of entries before the other, in which case those remaining entries must be inserted into the result.

```
Merge
Set up for processing firstList
Set up for processing secondList
while moreData1 AND moreData2
    Set compareResult to 'firstEntry comes before secondEntry'
    if compareResult < 0
      Put firstEntry in resultList
    else if compareResult > 0
      Put secondEntry in resultList
    else
      Process both entries
if moreData1
    Insert rest of firstList into resultList
else if moreData2
    Insert rest of secondList into resultList
```

Set up for processing firstList

```
Reset firstList
Set firstEntry to next entry in firstList
Set firstCount to 1
Set firstLimit to length of firstList
Set moreData1 to firstCount <= firstLimit
```

Set up for processing secondList

```
Reset secondList
Set secondEntry to next entry in secondList
Set secondCount to 1
Set secondLimit to length of secondList
Set moreData2 to secondCount <= secondLimit
```

firstEntry comes before secondEntry

```
compareResult =
   firstEntry.knowName().compareTo(secondEntry.knowName())
```

Put firstEntry in resultList

```
resultList.insert(firstEntry)
if firstCount equals firstLimit
   Set moreData1 to false
else
   Set firstEntry to next item in firstList
   firstCount++
```

Put secondEntry in resultList

```
resultList.insert(secondEntry)
if secondCount equals secondLimit
   Set moreData2 to false
else
   Set secondEntry to next item in secondList
   secondCount++
```

```
Process both entries
resultList.insert(firstEntry)
if firstCount equals firstLimit
    Set moreData1 to false
else
    Set firstEntry to next entry in firstList
    firstCount++
if secondCount equals secondLimit
    Set moreData2 to false
else
    Set secondEntry to next item in secondList
    secondCount++
```

```
Insert rest of firstList into resultList
while firstCount <= firstLimit
    resultList.insert(firstEntry)
    firstCount++
    if firstCount <= firstLimit
        Set firstEntry to next entry in firstList
```

```
Insert rest of secondList into resultList
while secondCount <= secondLimit
    resultList.insert(secondEntry)
    secondCount++
    if secondCount <= secondLimit
        Set secondEntry to next entry in secondList
```

This algorithm is by far the most complex we have examined to date. You are well advised to study it until you completely understand it. The merging of two ordered lists is one of those familiar algorithms that appears in many different places. For example, the union of two sets is calculated in exactly the same way.

Now we must simply examine the "Print labels" and "Write combined file" responsibilities. We have all the entries in alphabetical order in resultList. We can use a *for* loop to iterate through the list, printing out the address labels. We can also use a *for* loop to write out the entries in resultList. In fact, as both these responsibilities require *for* loops to process the combined list of entries, we can combine the processing into the same loop.

```
//***************************************************************
// This application merges two address books into one and
// prints out address labels.
//***************************************************************
```

```java
import java.io.*;
import addressBook.*;
import list.*;

public class MergeBooks
{
  public static void main(String[] args) throws IOException
  {
    // Declare files and lists
    ObjectInputStream firstFile;
    ObjectInputStream secondFile;
    ObjectOutputStream outFile;
    PrintWriter labelFile;
    SortedList firstList;        // First list of entries
    SortedList secondList;       // Second list of entries
    SortedList resultList;       // Combined list of entries

    // Declare an entry for each list
    EntryPlus firstEntry;
    EntryPlus secondEntry;
    EntryPlus resultEntry;

    // Declare a counter for each list
    int firstCount;
    int secondCount;

    boolean moreData1;           // More data in firstList
    boolean moreData2;           // More data in secondList

    // Declare variables for the number of entries in each list
    int firstLimit;
    int secondLimit;
    int resultLimit;

    int compareResult;           // Result from a comparison

    // Prepare files
    firstFile = new ObjectInputStream(new FileInputStream("adBook1.dat"));
    secondFile = new ObjectInputStream(new FileInputStream("adBook2.dat"));
    outFile = new ObjectOutputStream(new FileOutputStream("adBook3.dat"));
    labelFile = new PrintWriter(new FileWriter("labels.out"));

    // Create the two lists of entries
    firstList = new SortedList();
    secondList = new SortedList();
```

```
try
{
  generateLists(firstFile, firstList);
  generateLists(secondFile, secondList);
}
catch(ClassNotFoundException except)
{
  System.out.println("problems reading in objects");
}

// Set up for processing first list
firstList.resetList();
firstEntry = firstList.getNextItem();
firstCount = 1;
firstLimit = firstList.length();
moreData1 = firstCount <= firstLimit;

// Set up for processing second list
secondList.resetList();
secondEntry = secondList.getNextItem();
secondCount = 1;
secondLimit = secondList.length();
moreData2 = secondCount <= secondLimit;

resultList = new SortedList(200);   // Instantiate combined list
// Merge loop
while (moreData1 && moreData2)
{
  compareResult = firstEntry.knowName().compareTo(secondEntry.knowName());
  if (compareResult < 0)    // firstEntry comes first
  {
    resultList.insert(firstEntry);
    if (firstCount == firstLimit)
      moreData1 = false;
    else
    {
      firstEntry = firstList.getNextItem();
      firstCount++;
    }
  }
  else if (compareResult > 0)        // secondEntry comes first
  {
    resultList.insert(secondEntry);
    if (secondCount == secondLimit)
      moreData2 = false;
```

```
    else
    {
      secondEntry = secondList.getNextItem();
      secondCount++;
    }
  }
  else      // Duplicates
  {
    resultList.insert(firstEntry);
    if (firstCount == firstLimit)
      moreData1 = false;
    else
    {
      firstEntry = firstList.getNextItem();
      firstCount++;
    }
    if (secondCount == secondLimit)
      moreData2 = false;
    else
    {
      secondEntry = secondList.getNextItem();
      secondCount++;
    }
  }
}

// Loops to add remaining entries to combined list
if (moreData1)
  while (firstCount <= firstLimit)
  {
    resultList.insert(firstEntry);
    firstCount++;
    if (firstCount <= firstLimit)
      firstEntry = firstList.getNextItem();
  }
else if (moreData2)
  while (secondCount <= secondLimit)
  {
    resultList.insert(secondEntry);
    secondCount++;
    if (secondCount <= secondLimit)
      secondEntry = secondList.getNextItem();
  }

// Print labels and write combined file
resultList.resetList();
resultLimit = resultList.length();
for (int counter = 1; counter <= resultLimit; counter++)
```

```
        {
          Address resultAddress;
          resultEntry = resultList.getNextItem();     // Get an entry
          outFile.writeObject(resultEntry);           // Write the entry
          resultAddress = resultEntry.knowAddress();
          labelFile.println(resultEntry.knowName().full());
          labelFile.println(resultAddress.knowStreet());
          labelFile.println(resultAddress.knowCity() + ","
            + resultAddress.knowState() + " " + resultAddress.knowZip());
          labelFile.println();
        }

        // Close files and exit
        firstFile.close();
        secondFile.close();
        outFile.close();
        labelFile.close();
    }
    static void generateLists(ObjectInputStream inFile, SortedList list)
      throws IOException, ClassNotFoundException
    {
      EntryPlus entry;
      boolean moreData = true;
      while(moreData)
      {
        try
        {
          entry = (EntryPlus)inFile.readObject();
          list.insert(entry);
        }
        catch(EOFException except)
        {
          moreData = false;
        }
      }
    }
}
```

Because EntryPlus does not implement Comparable, we need to change our List class to call the compareTo method associated with the Name field in an item. We can access this field using the knowName method for the EntryPlus object. Of course, sortedList was also written to use String items, and must be changed so that items are EntryPlus objects.

Testing MergeBooks required that we write a small program to enable us to create data files and another program to view the name fields in the files. When you work with files of serialized objects it is often necessary to write such helper programs as part of the testing process. Recall that serialized object files cannot be viewed or created with an editor.

Here are the names for the entries on files adBook1.dat and adBook2.dat:

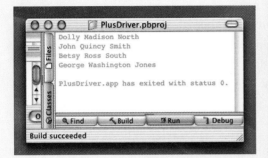

Here are the name fields from file adBook3.dat and the labels printed on file labels.out:

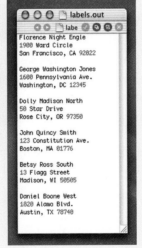

11.8 Testing and Debugging

We have written a test plan for the unsorted list and the sorted list. However, we have not tested the sort method that was used in the class ListWithSort. The method selectSort takes an array of items and rearranges the items so that they are in ascending order. If we write a black-box testing plan, which end cases should we test in addition to the general case? These cases fall into two categories, based on the length of the list of items and on the order of the items in the original list:

1. The list is empty.
2. The list contains one item.
3. The list contains more than one item.
4. The list contains the maximum number of items.
5. The list is already sorted in ascending order.
6. The list is already sorted in descending order.

We leave it as an exercise to convert this list into a complete test plan.

Testing and Debugging Hints

1. Review the testing and debugging hints from Chapter 10.
2. When the objects on the list are of simple types, their type names must be on the parameter lists for `isThere`, `insert`, and `delete`.
3. When the objects on the list are of composite types, use `Comparable` in the parameter lists for the class name.
4. Verify that any argument to a list method with a `Comparable` parameter belongs to a class that has implemented the `Comparable` interface.
5. Be careful: arguments of primitive types cannot be passed to a method whose parameter implements the `Comparable` interface.
6. Test general-purpose methods outside the context of a particular application, using a test driver.
7. Choose test data carefully so that you test all end conditions and some conditions in the middle. End conditions reach the limits of the structure used to store them. For example, a list test plan should include test data in which the number of components is 0, 1, and the array size, as well as somewhere in between.

Learning Portfolio

Summary

This chapter provided practice in working with lists, where the items on the list are stored in a one-dimensional array. We examined algorithms that insert, delete, and search data stored in an array-based unsorted list, and we wrote methods to implement these algorithms. We also examined an algorithm that takes the array in which the list items are stored and sorts them into ascending order.

We examined several search algorithms: sequential search in an unsorted list, sequential search in a sorted list, and binary search. The sequential search in an unsorted list compares each item in the list to the one being searched for. All items must be examined before it can be determined that the search item is not present in the list. The sequential search in a sorted list can determine that the search item is not in the list when it passes the place where the item belongs. The binary search looks for the search item in the middle of the list. If it is not there, then the search continues in the half where the item should be. This process continues to cut the search area in half until either the item is found or the search area is empty.

We also examined the insertion algorithm that keeps the items in the list sorted by value. We generalized the list in an abstract class called List, leaving the insert, delete, and isThere methods abstract. Finally, we demonstrated the use of the Comparable interface as a way to make the list items generic.

Quick Check

1. What is the difference between a list and an array? (pp. 523–524)
2. If the list is unsorted, does it matter where a new item is inserted? (p. 543)
3. The following code fragment implements the "delete, if it's there" meaning for the delete operation in an unsorted list. Change it so that the other meaning is implemented; that is, there is an assumption that the item is in the list. (pp. 525–536)

```
while (index < numItems && !found)
{
  if (listItems[index].compareTo(item) == 0)
    found = true;
  else
    index++;
}
if (found)
{
  for (int count = index; count < numItems-1; count++)
    listItems[count] = listItems[count+1];
  numItems--;
}
```

4. In a sequential search of an unsorted array containing 1,000 values, what is the average number of loop iterations required to find a value? What is the maximum number of iterations? (pp. 557–558)
5. The following code fragment sorts list items into ascending order. Change it to sort into descending order. (pp. 542–543)

```
for (passCount = 0; passCount < numItems; passCount++)
{
  minIndex = passCount;
```

```
      for (searchIndex = passCount + 1; searchIndex < numItems;
          searchIndex++)
        if (listItems[searchIndex].compareTo(listItems[minIndex]) < 0)
          minIndex = searchIndex;
      temp = listItems[minIndex];                    // Swap
      listItems[minIndex] = listItems[passCount];
      listItems[passCount] = temp;
    }
```

6. Describe how the insert operation can be used to build a sorted list from unsorted input data. (pp. 545–548)

7. Describe the basic principle behind the binary search algorithm. (pp. 552–557)

Answers

1. A list is a variable-sized structured data type; an array is a built-in type often used to implement a list.
2. No.
3.
```
    index = 0;
    while (listItems[index].compareTo(item) != 0)
      index++;
    for (int count = index; count < numItems-1; count++)
      listItems[count] = listItems[count+1];
    numItems--;
```
4. The average number is 500.5 iterations. The maximum is 1,000 iterations. **5.** The only required change is to replace the < 0 with > 0 in the inner loop. As a matter of style, the name minIndex should be changed to maxIndex. **6.** The list initially has a length of 0. Each time a value is read, insert adds the value to the list in its correct position. When all the data values have been read, they are in the array in sorted order. **7.** The binary search takes advantage of sorted list values, looking at a component in the middle of the list and deciding whether the search value precedes or follows the midpoint. The search is then repeated on the appropriate half, quarter, eighth, and so on, of the list until the value is located.

Exam Preparation Exercises

1. A binary search can be applied to integers as well as to objects. Suppose the following values are stored in an array in ascending order:

   28   45   97   103   107   162   196   202   257

   Applying the binary search algorithm to this array, search for the following values and indicate how many array-component comparisons are required to either find the number or find that it is not present in the list.

   a. 28

   b. 32

   c. 196

   d. 194

2. Repeat Exercise 1, applying the algorithm for a sequential search in a sorted list.

3. The following values are stored in an array in ascending order:

   29 57 63 72 79 83 96 104 114 136

   Apply the binary search algorithm looking for 114 in this list, and trace the values of `first`, `last`, and `middle`. Indicate any undefined values with a U.

4. A binary search is always a better choice than a sequential search. (True or False?)

5. If `resetList` initializes `currentPos` to −1 rather than 0, what corresponding change would have to be made in `getNextItem`?

6. We have said that arrays are homogeneous structures, yet Java implements them with an associated integer. Explain.

7. Why does the outer loop of the sorting method run from 0 through `numItems − 2` rather than `numItems − 1`?

8. A method that returns the number of days in a month is an example of (a) a constructor, (b) an observer, (c) an iterator, or (d) a transformer.

9. A method that adds a constant to the salary of everyone in a list is an example of (a) a constructor, (b) an observer, (c) an iterator, or (d) a transformer.

10. A method that stores values into a list is an example of (a) a constructor, (b) an observer, (c) an iterator, or (d) a transformer.

11. What Java construct is implemented using the keyword `implements`?

12. What kind of class cannot be instantiated?

13. Which interface contains the method `compareTo`? What does `compareTo` return?

14. The class `List` assumes that no duplicate items appear in the list.

   a. Which method algorithms would have to be changed to allow duplicates?

   b. Would there still be options for the `delete` operation? Explain.

Programming Warm-Up Exercises

1. Complete the implementation of `UnsortedList` as a class derived from the abstract class `List`.

2. Complete the implementation of `ListWithSort` as a class derived from `UnsortedList`.

3. Derive a subclass of `UnsortedList` that has the following additional methods.

   a. A value-returning instance method named `occurrences` that receives a single parameter, `item`, and returns the number of times `item` occurs in the list.

b. A Boolean instance method named greaterFound that receives a single argument, item, and searches the list for a value greater than item. If such a value is found, the method returns true; otherwise, it returns false.

c. An instance method named component that returns a component of the list given a position number (pos). The position number must be within the range 0 through numItems − 1.

d. A copy constructor for the List class that takes an argument that specifies how much to expand the array holding the items. Implement the copy constructor by creating a larger array and copying all of the items in the list into the new array.

4. Complete the implementation of SortedList as a class derived from the abstract class List.

5. Derive a subclass of SortedList that has the additional methods outlined in Programming Warm-Up Exercise 3.

6. Write a Java Boolean method named exclusive that takes three arguments: item, list1, and list2 (both of class List as defined in this chapter). The method returns true if item is present in either list1 or list2 but not both.

7. The insert method in the class SortedList inserts items into the list in ascending order. Derive a new class from List that sorts the items into descending order.

8. Exam Preparation Exercise 14 asked you to examine the implication of a list with duplicates.

   a. Design an abstract class ListWithDuplicates that allows duplicate keys.

   b. How does your design differ from List?

   c. Implement your design where the items are unsorted and delete deletes all of the duplicate items.

   d. Implement your design where the items are sorted and delete deletes all of the duplicate items.

   e. Did you use a binary search in part (d)? If not, why not?

9. Rewrite the method insert in the class SortedList so that it implements the first insertion algorithm discussed for sorted lists. That is, the place where the item should be inserted is found by searching from the beginning of the list. When the place is found, all of the items from the insertion point to the end of the list shift down by one position.

Programming Problems

1. A company wants to know the percentages of total sales and total expenses attributable to each salesperson. Each person has a pair of data lines. The first line contains his or her name, with the last name coming first. The second line contains his or her sales (int) and expenses (float). Write an application that produces a report with a header line containing the total sales and total expenses. Follow this header with a table containing each salesperson's name, percentage of total sales, and percentage of total expenses, sorted by the salesperson's name. Use one of the list classes developed in this chapter to implement your solution.

2. Only authorized shareholders are allowed to attend a stockholders' meeting. Write an application to read a person's name from the keyboard, check it against a list of shareholders, and print a message on the screen saying whether the person may attend the meeting. The list of shareholders is in a file called owners, with one name per line, in the following format: first name, blank, last name. Use the end-of-file condition to stop reading the file. The maximum number of shareholders is 1,000.

   As a stockholder enters the meeting, he or she enters his or her name. If the name does not appear on the list, the code should repeat the instructions on how to enter the name and then tell the user to try again. A message saying that the person may not enter should be printed only after he or she has been given a second chance to enter the name.

3. Enhance the application in Problem 2 as follows:

   a. Print a report file showing the number of stockholders at the time of the meeting, the number present at the meeting, and the number of people who tried to enter but were denied permission to attend.

   b. Follow this summary report with a list of the names of the stockholders, with either *Present* or *Absent* after each name.

4. An advertising company wants to send a letter to its clients announcing a new fee schedule. The clients' names appear on several different lists in the company. The various lists are merged to form one file, called clients, but the company does not want to send a letter twice to anyone.

   Write an application that removes any names appearing on the list more than once. Each data line contains a four-digit code number, followed by a blank, and then the client's name. For example, Amalgamated Steel is listed as

   ```
   0231 Amalgamated Steel
   ```

   Your code should output each client's code and name, but no duplicates should be printed. Use one of the list classes developed in this chapter to implement your solution.

Case Study Follow-Up

1. What changes would be required for the application MergeBooks to:
   a. Count the number of names on the first file?
   b. Count the number of names on the second file?
   c. Count the number of names on the combined file?
   d. Print these counts on the screen using System.out?

2. Develop data files to test the six cases outlined in the Testing and Debugging section.

3. Change the application so that the resulting address book and printed labels contain only those entries that appear in both address books.

4. Change the application so that the resulting address book and printed labels contain only those entries that appear in the first address book but not the second.

Multidimensional Arrays and Numeric Computation

goals

Knowledge Goals

- To understand the role of a two-dimensional array in representing a table with rows and columns
- To know how floating-point numbers are represented in the computer
- To know how the limited numeric precision of the computer can affect calculations
- To understand the relationship between an array and a matrix
- To understand how a two-dimensional array is constructed as an array of arrays

Skill Goals

To be able to:

- Declare a two-dimensional array
- Perform fundamental operations on a two-dimensional array:
  - Access a component of the array
  - Initialize the array
  - Print the values in the array
  - Process the array by rows
  - Process the array by columns
- Declare a two-dimensional array as a parameter
- Declare and process a multidimensional array
- Use the class DecimalFormat to format output

timeline

1983

Bjarne Stroustrup works on the development of the programming language C++ at AT&T Bell Labs

1984

Apple introduces its 32-bit Macintosh computer through a famous Orwellian-themed advertising campaign that premiers during the Super Bowl

1984

Sony and Philips introduce the CD-ROM, a new means of storing digital data that far exceeds the floppy disk's potential

1984

The Last Starfighter revolutionizes the use of supercomputer-generated graphics in movies, and the term "cyberspace" is coined by William Gibson

1984

Intel's 16-bit 80286 chip, created in 1982, will be installed in 15 million PCs within 6 years

1985

The Cray 2 and Thinking Machines' parallel processor Connection Machine take speed to a new level: 1 billion operations per second

introduction

The structures that we choose to hold a collection of data objects play an important role in the design process. In the last two chapters, we discussed the one-dimensional array and its use in problems where the logical representation of the data is a list of objects. The choice of data structure directly affects the design, because it determines the algorithms used to process the data objects. For example, if the data items are stored in sorted order within the array, we can apply a binary search algorithm to them rather than a linear search.

In many problems, however, the relationships between data items are more complex than can be represented in a simple list. For example, we need a more sophisticated data structure when simulating board games (such as chess, Tic-Tac-Toe, or Scrabble), computer graphics (where points on the screen are arranged as a two-dimensional object), or matrix operations in mathematics. In this chapter we examine the two-dimensional array, which is useful when we need to organize data in two dimensions. We usually call these dimensions *rows* and *columns*.

In addition, we extend the definition of an array to allow arrays with any number of dimensions, called multidimensional arrays. Each dimension represents a different feature of the data objects in the structure. For example, we might use a three-dimensional array to store objects representing sales figures by (1) store number, (2) month, and (3) item number.

Finally, we take a closer look at the limitations of the computer in doing calculations, noting how these limitations can cause numerical errors and how we can avoid such errors. This discussion relates directly to the Case Study, in which we examine arrays as implementation structures for two mathematical objects, vector and matrix.

1985

Microsoft releases Windows 1.0. It is their first in a series of widely-used operating systems

1985

Intel introduces the 80386, a 32-bit processing chip with on-chip memory management

1985

Paul Brainard creates PageMaker, and launches the world of PC desktop publishing

1986

The Cray XMP supercomputer executes 713 million floating-point calculations per second

1988

Microprocessor speeds reach 17 million instructions per second with Motorola's 88000 chip

1988

Robert Morris Jr. releases a worm program into the Internet, demonstrating the need for greater network security

12.1 Two-Dimensional Arrays

A one-dimensional array is used to represent items in a list or a sequence of values. A two-dimensional array is used to represent items in a table with rows and columns, provided each item in the table is of the same type or class. We access a component in a two-dimensional array by specifying the row and column indexes of the item in the array. This task is a familiar one. For example, if you want to find a street on a map, you look up the street name on the back of the map to find the coordinates of the street, usually a number and a letter. The number specifies a row, and the letter specifies a column. You find the street where the row and column intersect.

Two-dimensional array A collection of components, all of the same type, structured in two dimensions. Each component is accessed by a pair of indexes that represent the component's position in each dimension.

Figure 12.1 shows a two-dimensional array with 100 rows and 9 columns. The rows are accessed by an integer ranging from 0 through 99; the columns are accessed by an integer ranging from 0 through 8. Each component is accessed by a row–column pair—for example, (0, 5).

■ Array Declaration and Instantiation

We declare a two-dimensional array variable in exactly the same way that we declare a one-dimensional array variable, except that we use two pairs of brackets. Likewise, we instantiate a two-dimensional array object in exactly the same way, except that we must specify sizes for two dimensions. Below is the syntax template for declaring an array with two dimensions:

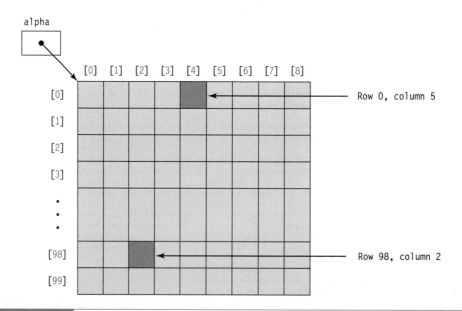

Figure 12.1 alpha Array

Two-Dimensional-Array-Declaration

> Data-Type[][] Array-Name;

The first two lines of the following code fragment would create the two-dimensional array shown in Figure 12.1, where the data in the table are floating-point numbers.

```
double[][] alpha;
alpha = new double[100][9];
String[][] beta;
beta = new String[10][10];
```

The first dimension specifies the number of rows, and the second dimension specifies the number of columns. Once the two-dimensional array has been created, alpha.length and beta.length give the number of rows in each array.

Accessing Individual Components

To access an individual component of the alpha array, we use two expressions (one for each dimension) to specify its position. We place each expression in its own pair of brackets next to the name of the array:

alpha[0][5] = 36.4;

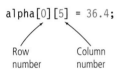

The syntax template for accessing a two-dimensional array component follows:

Two-Dimensional-Array-Component-Access

> Array-Name [Index-Expression] [Index-Expression]

As with one-dimensional arrays, each index expression must result in an integer value between 0 and the number of slots in that dimension minus one.

Let's look now at some examples. Here is the declaration of a two-dimensional array with 364 integer components ($52 \times 7 = 364$):

```
int[][] hiTemp;
hiTemp = new int[52][7];
```

Here hiTemp is an array with 52 rows and 7 columns. Each place in the array (each component) can contain an int value. Our intention is that the array hold high temperatures for each day

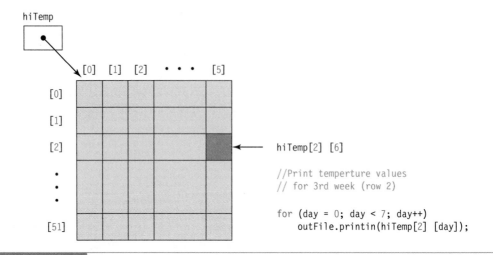

Figure 12.2 hiTemp Array

in a year. Each row represents one of the 52 weeks in a year, and each column represents one of the 7 days in a week. (To keep the example simple, we ignore the fact that there are 365— and sometimes 366—days in a year.) The expression hiTemp[2][6] refers to the int value in the third row (row 2) and the seventh column (column 6). Semantically, hiTemp[2][6] is the temperature for the seventh day of the third week. The code fragment shown in Figure 12.2 would print the temperature values for the third week.

To obtain the number of columns in a row of an array, we access the length field for the specific row. For example, the statement

```
midYear = hiTemp[26].length;
```

stores the length of row 26 of the array hiTemp, which is 7, into the int variable midYear.

■ Using Initializer Lists

Just as we can create a one-dimensional array with a list of values, so we can create a two-dimensional array with a list of a list of values. For example, the following statement instantiates a two-dimensional array of baseball hits. This array represents the hits for a five-day period for your four favorite baseball players.

```
int[][] hits = {{2, 1, 0, 3, 2},
                {1, 1, 2, 3, 4},
                {1, 0, 0, 0, 0},
                {0, 1, 2, 1, 1}};
```

As in the case of a one-dimensional array, you do not use new with an initializer list. Now what would happen if one of your favorite players went into a slump, and the manager gave him a rest for a few days? How could you represent that scenario in your array? Suppose that the third player sat out three games. Here is how you would represent this situation:

```
int[][] hits = {{2, 1, 0, 3, 2},
                {1, 1, 2, 3, 4},
                {1, 0},
                {0, 1, 2, 1, 1}};
```

The third row in the table would have only two columns, not five like the others. In such a *ragged array*, the lengths of the rows are not all the same. In fact, we could instantiate the same ragged array as follows:

```
int[][] hits;
hits = new int[4][];
hits[0] = new int[5];
hits[1] = new int[5];
hits[2] = new int[2];
hits[3] = new int[5];
```

If we then access the lengths of rows 1 and 2 with the code

```
one = hits[1].length;
two = hits[2].length;
```

we would find that variable one has been assigned a value of 5 and variable two contains 2.

The moral here is that in Java, each row of a two-dimensional array is itself a one-dimensional array. Many programming languages directly support two-dimensional arrays; Java doesn't. In Java, a two-dimensional array is an array of references to array objects. Because of the way that Java handles two-dimensional arrays, the drawings in Figures 12.1 and 12.2 are not quite accurate. Figure 12.3 shows how Java actually implements the array hiTemp.

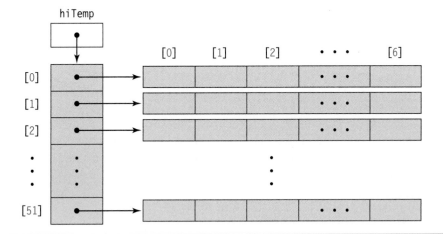

Figure 12.3 Java Implementation of hiTemp Array

From the Java programmer's perspective, however, the two views are synonymous in the majority of applications. We typically instantiate arrays with the same number of columns in every row, rarely creating a ragged array. For this reason, we continue to use the stylized version.

12.2 Processing Two-Dimensional Arrays

Processing data in a two-dimensional array generally means accessing the array in one of four patterns: randomly, along rows, along columns, or throughout the entire array. Each of these strategies may also involve subarray processing.

The simplest way to access a component is to look directly in a given location. For example, a user might enter map coordinates that we use as indexes into an array of street names to access the desired name at those coordinates. This process is referred to as *random access* because the user may enter any set of coordinates at random.

In many cases, we might want to perform an operation on all the elements of a particular row or column in an array. Consider the `hiTemp` array defined previously, in which the rows represent weeks of the year and the columns represent days of the week. If we wanted the average high temperature for a given week, we would sum the values in that row and divide by 7. If we wanted the average for a given day of the week, we would sum the values in that column and divide by 52. The former case is access by row; the latter case is access by column.

Now suppose that we want to determine the average high temperature for the year. We must access every element in the array, sum them, and divide by 364. In this case, the order of access—by row or by column—is not important. (The same is true when we initialize every element of an array to some constant, such as −1.) This approach involves access throughout the array.

Sometimes, however, we must access every array element in a particular order, either by rows or by columns. For example, if we wanted the average high temperature for every week, we would run through the entire array, taking each row in turn. However, if we wanted the average high temperature for each day of the week, we would run through the array one column at a time.

Let's take a closer look at these patterns of access by considering three common examples of array processing:

1. Sum the rows.
2. Sum the columns.
3. Initialize the array to all zeros (or some special value).

In the following discussion, we use the generic identifiers `row` and `col`, rather than problem-dependent identifiers, and look at each algorithm in terms of generalized two-dimensional array processing. The array that we use is declared and instantiated by the following statement:

```
int[][] data = new int[50][30]; // A two-dimensional array
```

In the following discussion we assume that `data` contains valid information.

Sum the Rows

Suppose we want to sum row number 3 (the fourth row) in the array and print the result. We can do this easily with a *for* loop:

```
int total = 0;
for (int col = 0; col < data[3].length; col++)
  total = total + data[3][col];
outFile.println("Row sum: " + total);
```

This *for* loop runs through each column of data, while keeping the row index fixed at 3. Every value in row 3 is added to total.

Now suppose we want to sum and print two rows—row 2 and row 3. We can use a nested loop and make the row index be a variable:

```
for (int row = 2; row <= 3; row++)
{
  int total = 0;
  for (int col = 0; col < data[row].length; col++)
    total = total + data[row][col];
  outFile.println("Row sum: " + total);
}
```

The outer loop controls the rows, and the inner loop controls the columns. For each value of row, every column is processed; then the outer loop moves to the next row. In the first iteration of the outer loop, row is held at 2 and col goes from 0 through data[2].length. Therefore, the array is accessed in the following order:

```
data[2][0]    [2][1]    [2][2]    [2][3]    . . .    [2][29]
```

In the second iteration of the outer loop, row is incremented to 3, and the array is accessed as follows:

```
data[3][0]    [3][1]    [3][2]    [3][3]    . . .    [3][29]
```

We can generalize this row processing to run through every row of the array by having the outer loop run from 0 through data.length-1. However, if we want to access only part of the array (subarray processing), given variables declared as

```
int rowsFilled;   // Data is in 0..rowsFilled − 1
int colsFilled;   // Data is in 0..colsFilled − 1
```

then we write the code fragment as follows:

```
for (int row = 0; row < rowsFilled; row++)
{
```

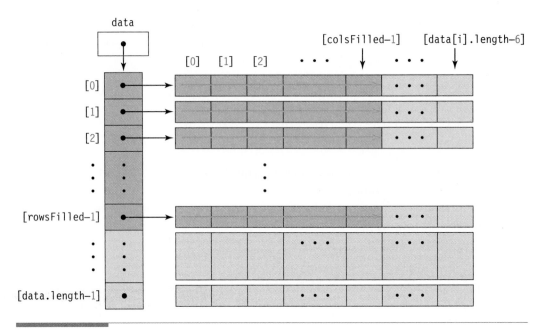

Figure 12.4 Subarray Processing by Row.

```
  // Array is not ragged
  total = 0;
  for (int col = 0; col < colsFilled; col++)
    total = total + data[row][col];
  outFile.println("Row sum: " + total);
}
```

This is an example of subarray processing by row. Figure 12.4 illustrates subarray processing by row.

Sum the Columns

Suppose we want to sum and print each column. The code to perform this task follows. Again, we have generalized the code to sum only the portion of the array that contains valid data.

```
for (int col = 0; col < colsFilled; col++)
{
  // Array is not ragged
  total = 0;
  for (int row = 0; row < rowsFilled; row++)
    total = total + data[row][col];
  outFile.println("Column sum: " + total);
}
```

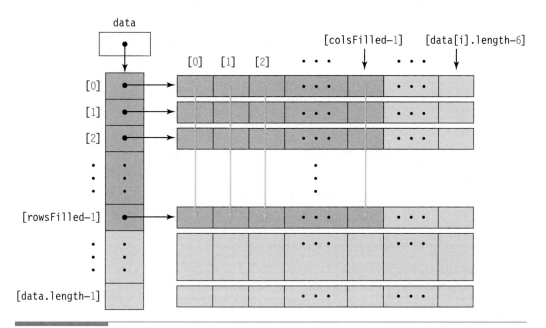

Figure 12.5 Subarray Processing by Column.

In this case, the outer loop controls the column, and the inner loop controls the row. All the components in the first column are accessed and summed before the outer loop index changes and the components in the second column are accessed. Figure 12.5 illustrates sub-array processing by column.

Initialize the Array

Instantiating an array with initializer lists is impractical if the array is large. For a 100-row by 100-column array, you don't want to list 10,000 values. If the values are all different, you should store them into a file and input them into the array at run time. If the values are all the same, the usual approach employs nested *for* loops and an assignment statement. Here is a general-purpose code segment that sets every item in the array to −1:

```
for (int row = 0; row < data.length; row++)
  for (int col = 0; col < data[row].length; col++)
    data[row][col] = -1;
```

In this case, we initialized the array a row at a time, but we could just as easily have run through each column instead. The order doesn't matter as long as we access every element.

Almost all processing of data stored in a two-dimensional array involves either processing by row or processing by column. The looping patterns for row processing and column processing are so useful that we summarize them next. To make them more general, we use minRow for the first row number and minCol for the first column number. Remember that row processing has the row index in the outer loop, and column processing has the column index in the outer loop.

Row Processing

```
for (int row = minRow; row < rowsFilled; row++)
   for (int col = minCol; col < colsFilled; col++)
      // Whatever processing is required
```

Column Processing

```
for (int col = minCol; col < colsFilled; col++)
   for (int row = minRow; row < rowsFilled; row++)
      // Whatever processing is required
```

■ Two-Dimensional Arrays and Methods

A two-dimensional array can be a parameter in a method, and it can be the return value type for a method. The syntax and semantics are identical to those for one-dimensional arrays except we use an additional pair of brackets. Let's enclose the array initialization code fragment within a method:

```
void initialize(int[][] data)
// Set every cell in data to -1
{
   for (int row = 0; row < data.length; row++)
      for (int col = 0; col < data[row].length; col++)
         data[row][col] = -1;
}
```

Because Java has a field associated with each array that contains the number of slots defined for the array, we do not have to pass this information as a parameter as we do in many other languages. This ability is a consequence of the object orientation of the language. The array is an object and the information about the object is encapsulated with it.

As an example of a value-returning method, let's design one that returns a copy of the array passed as a parameter. All the information we need to instantiate the new array is present in the array passed as a parameter. We just instantiate it and copy in the values.

```
int[][] copy(int[][] data)
// Returns a deep copy of data, assuming data is not ragged
{
   int[][] copyData = new int[data.length] [data[0].length];
   for (int row = 0; row < data.length; row++)
      for (int col = 0; col < data[row].length; col++)
         copyData[row][col] = data[row][col];
   return copyData;
}
```

12.3 Multidimensional Arrays

Java does not place a limit on the number of dimensions that an array can have. We can generalize our definition of an **array** to cover all cases.

You might have guessed that you can have as many dimensions as you want. How many should you use in a particular case? As many as there are features that describe the components in the array.

Take, for example, a chain of department stores. Monthly sales figures must be kept for each item by store. There are three important pieces of information about each item: the month in which it was sold, the store from which it was purchased, and the item number. We can declare an array to summarize this data as follows:

> **Array** A collection of components, all of the same type, ordered on *N* dimensions (*N* >= 1). Each component is accessed by *N* indexes, each of which represents the component's position within that dimension.

```java
int[][][] sales;      // Declare array of sales figures
// First dimension represents number of stores;
//   second dimension represents months;
//   third dimension represents items
sales = new int[100][12][10];   // Instantiate array
```

Figure 12.6 provides a graphic representation of the `sales` array.

The number of components in `sales` is 12,000 (10 × 12 × 100). If sales figures are available only for January through June, then half of the array is empty. If we want to process the data in the array, we must use subarray processing. The following code fragment sums and prints the total number of each item sold this year to date by all stores:

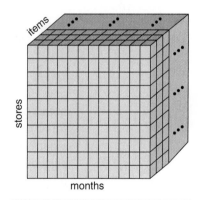

Figure 12.6 `sales` Array

```java
int currentMonth = 6;    // Range: 1..12

for (int item = 0; item < sales[0][0].length; item++)
{
  numberSold = 0;
  for (int store = 0; store < sales.length; store++)
    for (int month = 0; month < currentMonth; month++)
      numberSold = numberSold + sales[store][month][item];
  outFile.println("Item # " + item + " Sales to date = "
                  + numberSold);
}
```

Because `item` controls the outer *for* loop, we are summing each item's sales by `month` and `store`. If we want to find the total sales for each store, we use `store` to control the outer *for* loop, summing that location's sales by `month` and `item` with the inner loops.

```java
int currentMonth = 6;

for (int store = 0; store < sales.length; store++)
```

```
{
  numberSold = 0;
  for (int item = 0; item < sales[0][0].length; item++)
    for (int month = 0; month < currentMonth; month++)
      numberSold = numberSold + sales[store][month][item];
  outFile.println("Store # " + store + " Sales to date = "
                  + numberSold);
}
```

It takes two loops to access each component in a two-dimensional array; it takes three loops to access each component in a three-dimensional array. The task to be accomplished determines which index controls the outer loop, the middle loop, and the inner loop. If we want to calculate monthly sales by store, month controls the outer loop and store controls the middle loop. If we want to calculate monthly sales by item, month controls the outer loop and item controls the middle loop.

A multidimensional array can be a parameter and can serve as the return type of a method. Just be sure that you have as many pairs of brackets as you have dimensions following the type or class name.

12.4 Vector Class

We cannot end our discussion of arrays without mentioning a class that is available in the java.util package: the Vector class. The Vector class offers functionality similar to that of the one-dimensional array. In fact, the array is the underlying implementation structure used in this class. In contrast to an array, however, a vector can grow and shrink; its size is not fixed for its lifetime. The Vector class provides methods to manipulate items at specified index positions. In many ways, the vector resembles the general-purpose list classes that we designed in Chapter 11. We explore the Vector class in more detail in the exercises.

12.5 Floating-Point Numbers

We have used floating-point numbers off and on since we introduced them in Chapter 2, but we have not examined them in depth. Floating-point numbers have special properties when used on the computer. Thus far, we've tended to ignore these properties, but now it's time to consider them in detail.

Representation of Floating-Point Numbers

As we know, Java represents numbers in the binary number system and its different numeric types use different numbers of bits. To simplify the following discussion, let's assume that we have a computer in which each memory location is the same size and is divided into a sign plus five decimal digits. When we define a variable or constant, the location assigned to it consists of five digits and a sign. When we define an integral variable or constant, the interpretation of the number stored in that place is straightforward. When we define a floating-point variable or constant, the number stored there has both a whole-number part and a fractional part, so we must code it to represent both parts.

Let's see what such coded numbers might look like. The range of whole numbers we can represent with five digits is −99,999 through +99,999:

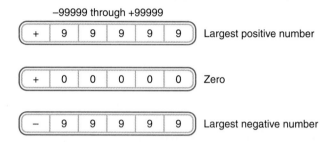

−99999 through +99999

| + | 9 | 9 | 9 | 9 | 9 | Largest positive number

| + | 0 | 0 | 0 | 0 | 0 | Zero

| − | 9 | 9 | 9 | 9 | 9 | Largest negative number

Our **precision** (the number of digits we can represent) is five digits, and each number within that range can be represented exactly.

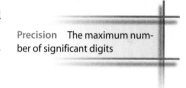

Precision The maximum number of significant digits

What happens if we allow one of those digits (the leftmost one, for example) to represent an exponent?

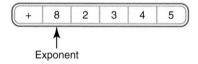

| + | 8 | 2 | 3 | 4 | 5 |

Exponent

Then +82345 represents the number $+2345 \times 10^8$. The range of numbers we now can represent is much larger:

$$-9999 \times 10^9 \text{ through } 9999 \times 10^9$$

or

$$-9{,}999{,}000{,}000{,}000 \text{ through } +9{,}999{,}000{,}000{,}000$$

However, our precision is now only four digits; that is, only four-digit numbers can be represented exactly in our system. What happens to numbers with more digits? The four leftmost digits are represented correctly, and the rightmost digits, or least significant digits, are lost (assumed to be 0). Figure 12.7 shows the result. Note that 1,000,000 can be represented exactly but −4,932,416 cannot, because our coding scheme limits us to four **significant digits.**

Significant digits Those digits from the first nonzero digit on the left to the last nonzero digit on the right (plus any 0 digits that are exact)

To extend our coding scheme to represent floating-point numbers, we must be able to represent negative exponents. Examples are

$$7394 \times 10^{-2} = 73.94$$

and

$$22 \times 10^{-4} = .0022$$

NUMBER	POWER OF TEN NOTATION	CODED REPRESENTATION (Sign Exp)	VALUE
+99,999	+9999 × 10^1	+ 1 9 9 9 9	+99,999
−999,999	−9999 × 10^2	− 2 9 9 9 9	−999,999
+1,000,000	−1000 × 10^3	+ 3 1 0 0 0	+1,000,000
−4,932,416	−4932 × 10^3	− 3 4 9 3 2	−4,932,416

Figure 12.7   Coding Using Positive Exponents

Because our scheme does not include a sign for the exponent, let's change it slightly. The existing sign becomes the sign of the exponent, and we add a sign to the far left to represent the sign of the number itself (see Figure 12.8).

We can now represent all the numbers between -9999×10^9 and 9999×10^9 accurately to four digits. Adding negative exponents to our scheme allows us to represent fractional numbers as small as 1×10^{-9}.

Figure 12.9 shows how we would encode some floating-point numbers. Note that our precision remains four digits. The numbers 0.1032, −5.406, and 1,000,000 can be represented exactly. The number 476.0321, however, has seven significant digits but is represented as 476.0;

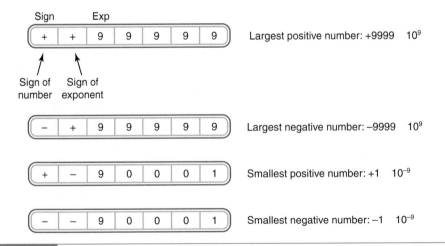

Figure 12.8   Coding Using Positive and Negative Exponents

NUMBER	POWER OF TEN NOTATION	CODED REPRESENTATION (Sign, Exp)	VALUE
0.1032	+1032 10^{-4}	+ − 4 1 0 3 2	0.1032
−5.4060	−5406 10^{-3}	− − 3 5 4 0 6	−5.406
−0.003	−3000 10^{-6}	− − 6 3 0 0 0	−0.0030
476.0321	+4760 10^{-1}	+ − 1 4 7 6 0	476.0

Figure 12.9 Coding of Some Floating-point Numbers

the 321 cannot be represented in our system. (Some computers, including all JVMs, perform *rounding* rather than simple truncation when discarding excess digits. Using our assumption of four significant digits, rounding would store 476.0321 as 476.0 but would store 476.0823 as 476.1. We continue our discussion assuming simple truncation rather than rounding.)

Arithmetic with Floating-Point Numbers

When we use integer arithmetic, our results are exact. Floating-point arithmetic, however, is seldom exact. To understand why, let's add three floating-point numbers x, y, and z using our coding scheme.

First we add x to y, and then we add z to the result. Next, we perform the operations in a different order, first adding y to z, and then adding x to that result. The associative law of arithmetic says that the two answers should be the same—but are they? Let's use the following values for x, y, and z:

$$x = -1324 \times 10^3 \qquad y = 1325 \times 10^3 \qquad z = 5424 \times 10^0$$

Here is the result of adding z to the sum of x and y:

$$\begin{array}{ll} (x) & -1324 \times 10^3 \\ (y) & \underline{\;\;1325 \times 10^3} \\ & \qquad 1 \times 10^3 \quad = \quad 1000 \times 10^0 \end{array}$$

$$\begin{array}{ll} (x+y) & 1000 \times 10^0 \\ (z) & \underline{5424 \times 10^0} \\ & 6424 \times 10^0 \quad \leftarrow \; (x+y)+z \end{array}$$

Here is the result of adding x to the sum of y and z:

$$
\begin{array}{lr}
(y) & 1325000 \times 10^0 \\
(z) & \underline{5424 \times 10^0} \\
& 1330424 \times 10^0 \quad = \quad 1330 \times 10^3 \text{ (truncated to four digits)}
\end{array}
$$

$$
\begin{array}{lr}
(y+z) & 1330 \times 10^3 \\
(x) & \underline{-1324 \times 10^3} \\
& 6 \times 10^3 \quad = \quad 6000 \times 10^0 \leftarrow x + (y + z)
\end{array}
$$

These two answers are the same in the thousands place but are different thereafter. This discrepancy results from a representational error.

Representational error makes it unwise to use a floating-point variable as a loop control variable. Because precision may be lost in calculations involving floating-point numbers, it is difficult to predict when (or even *if*) a loop control variable of type `float` (or `double`) will equal the termination value. As a consequence, a count-controlled loop with a floating-point control variable can behave unpredictably.

Representational error An arithmetic error that occurs when the precision of the true result of an arithmetic operation is greater than the precision of the machine

Also because of representational errors, you should never compare floating-point numbers for exact equality. Rarely are two floating-point numbers exactly equal, and thus you should compare them only for near equality. If the difference between the two numbers is less than some acceptable small value, you can consider them equal for the purposes of the given problem.

■ Implementation of Floating-Point Numbers in the Computer

All computers limit the precision of floating-point numbers, although modern machines use binary rather than decimal arithmetic. In our representation, we used only five digits to simplify the examples. In fact, some computers really are limited to only four or five digits of precision. Other systems provide 6 significant digits, 15 significant digits, and 19 significant digits, respectively, for three sizes of floating-point types. We have shown only a single-digit exponent, but most systems allow two digits for the smaller floating-point type and up to four-digit exponents for a longer type.

Some languages leave the range and precision of floating-point types to each individual compiler. Java, however, states the range and precision in the language specification in the following formula:

$$s \times m \times 2^e$$

where s is $+1$ or -1, m is a positive integer less than 2^{24}, and e is between -126 and 127, inclusive, for values of type `float`. For values of type `double`, m is less than 2^{53} and e is between $-1{,}022$ and $1{,}023$. No, we don't expect you to calculate this value. Each Java numeric class (such as `Integer` or `Double`) provides two constants, `MAX_VALUE` and `MIN_VALUE` that contain those values..

When you declare a floating-point variable, part of the memory location contains the exponent, and the number itself (called the *mantissa*) is assumed to be in the balance of the location. The name "floating-point" refers to the concept that the decimal point is allowed to float (move to different positions as necessary). In our coding scheme, every number is stored as four digits, with the leftmost digit being nonzero and the exponent adjusted accordingly. Numbers in this form are said to be *normalized*. For example, the number 1,000,000 is stored as

+	+	3	1	0	0	0

and 0.1032 is stored as

+	+	4	1	0	3	2

Normalization provides the maximum precision possible.

In Java, values of type `float` use 32 bits with an approximate range of $-3.4E+38$ to $3.4E+38$ with 6 significant digits. Values of type `double` use 64 bits with an approximate range of $-1.7E+308$ to $1.7E+308$ with 15 significant digits.

Model Numbers   Any real number that can be represented exactly as a floating-point number in the computer is called a *model number*. A real number whose value cannot be represented exactly is approximated by the model number closest to it. In our system with four digits of precision, 0.3021 is a model number. The values 0.3021409, 0.3021222, and 0.30209999999 are examples of real numbers that are represented in the computer by the same model number. The following table shows all of the model numbers for an even simpler floating-point system that has one digit in the mantissa, no sign (all mantissas are positive or zero), and an exponent that can be $-1, 0$, or 1.

0.0×10^{-1}	0.0×10^{0}	$0.0 \times 10^{+1}$
0.1×10^{-1}	0.1×10^{0}	$0.1 \times 10^{+1}$
0.2×10^{-1}	0.2×10^{0}	$0.2 \times 10^{+1}$
0.3×10^{-1}	0.3×10^{0}	$0.3 \times 10^{+1}$
0.4×10^{-1}	0.4×10^{0}	$0.4 \times 10^{+1}$
0.5×10^{-1}	0.5×10^{0}	$0.5 \times 10^{+1}$
0.6×10^{-1}	0.6×10^{0}	$0.6 \times 10^{+1}$
0.7×10^{-1}	0.7×10^{0}	$0.7 \times 10^{+1}$
0.8×10^{-1}	0.8×10^{0}	$0.8 \times 10^{+1}$
0.9×10^{-1}	0.9×10^{0}	$0.9 \times 10^{+1}$

The difference between a real number and the model number that represents it is a form of representational error called *rounding error*. We can measure rounding error in two ways. The *absolute error* is the difference between the real number and the model number. For example, the absolute error in representing 0.3021409 by the model number 0.3021 is 0.0000409. The *relative error* is the absolute error divided by the real number; it is sometimes stated as a percentage. For example, 0.0000409 divided by 0.3021409 is 0.000135, or 0.0135%.

The maximum absolute error depends on the *model interval*—the difference between two adjacent model numbers. In our example, the interval between 0.3021 and 0.3022 is 0.0001. The maximum absolute error in this system, for this interval, is less than 0.0001. Adding digits of precision decreases the model interval (and thus the maximum absolute error).

The model interval is not a fixed number, but rather varies with the exponent. To see why the interval varies, consider that the interval between 3021.0 and 3022.0 is 1.0, which is 10^4 times larger than the interval between 0.3021 and 0.3022. This makes sense, because 3021.0 is simply 0.3021 times 10^4. As a consequence, a change in the exponents of adjacent model numbers has an equivalent effect on the size of the interval between them. Stated in practical terms, we give up significant digits in the fractional part to represent numbers with large integer parts. Figure 12.10 illustrates this idea by graphing all of the model numbers listed in the preceding table.

We also can use the relative and absolute error to measure the rounding error resulting from calculations. For example, suppose we multiply 1.0005 by 1,000. The correct result is 1,000.5, but because of rounding error, our four-digit computer produces 1,000.0 as its result. The absolute error of the computed result is 0.5, and the relative error is 0.05%. Now suppose we multiply 100,050.0 by 1000. The correct result is 100,050,000, but the computer produces 100,000,000 as its result. If we look at the relative error, it remains a modest 0.05%, but the absolute error has grown to 50,000. This example is another case in which we change the size of the model interval.

Whether it is more important to consider the absolute error or the relative error depends on the situation. It is unacceptable for an audit of a company to discover a $50,000 accounting error; the fact that the relative error is only 0.05% is not important. On the other hand, a 0.05% relative error is acceptable in representing prehistoric dates because the error in measurement techniques increases with age. That is, if we are talking about a date roughly 10,000 years ago, an absolute error of 5 years is acceptable; if the date is 100,000,000 years ago, then an absolute error of 50,000 years is equally acceptable.

Comparing Floating-Point Numbers   Earlier, we cautioned against comparing floating-point numbers for exact equality. Our exploration of representational errors in this chapter reveals why calculations may not produce the expected results even though it appears that they should. In

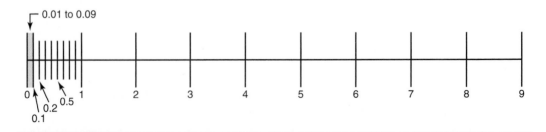

Figure 12.10   A Graphical Representation of Model Numbers

Chapter 4, we wrote an expression that compares two floating-point variables r and s for near equality using the floating-point absolute-value method `Math.abs`:

```
Math.abs(r - s) < 0.00001
```

From our discussion of model numbers, you now can recognize that the constant 0.00001 in this expression represents a maximum absolute error. We can generalize this expression as

```
Math.abs(r - s) < ERROR_TERM
```

where `ERROR_TERM` is a value that must be determined for each programming problem.

What if we want to compare floating-point numbers with a relative error measure? We must multiply the error term by the value in the problem to which the error is relative. For example, if we want to test whether r and s are "equal" within 0.05% of s, we write the following expression:

```
Math.abs(r - s) < 0.0005 * s
```

Keep in mind that the choice of the acceptable error and the determination of whether it should be absolute or relative depends on the particular problem at hand. The error terms we have shown in our example expressions are completely arbitrary and may not be appropriate for most problems. In solving a problem that involves the comparison of floating-point numbers, you typically want to keep the error term as small as possible. Sometimes the choice is specified in the problem description or is reasonably obvious. Some cases require careful analysis of both the mathematics of the problem and the representational limits of the particular computer. Such analyses fall within the domain of a branch of mathematics called *numerical analysis* and are beyond the scope of this text.

Underflow and Overflow   In addition to representational errors, we must watch out for two other problems in floating-point arithmetic: *underflow* and *overflow*.

Underflow is the condition that arises when the value of a calculation is too small to be represented. Going back to our decimal representation, let's look at a calculation involving small numbers:

$$
\begin{array}{r}
4210 \times 10^{-8} \\
\times\ 2000 \times 10^{-8} \\
\hline
8420000 \times 10^{-16} = 8420 \times 10^{-13}
\end{array}
$$

We cannot represent this value in our scheme because the exponent -13 is too small; our minimum is -9. One way to resolve this problem is to set the result of the calculation to 0.0. Obviously, any answer depending on this calculation will not be exact.

Overflow is a more serious problem because we have no logical recourse available when it occurs. For example, the result of the calculation

$$\begin{array}{r} 9999 \times 10^9 \\ \times\ 1000 \times 10^9 \\ \hline 9999000 \times 10^{18} = 9999 \times 10^{21} \end{array}$$

cannot be stored in our system, so what should we do? To be consistent with our response to underflow, we could set the result to 9999×10^9 (the maximum representable value in this case). Yet this strategy seems intuitively wrong. The alternative is to stop with an error message.

In Java, if an overflow occurs, the result is set to a special value called a *signed infinity*. If an underflow occurs, the result is set to a signed zero. No exception is thrown in either case.

Although here we are discussing problems with floating-point numbers, note that integer numbers can also overflow both negatively and positively. All implementations of Java ignore integer overflow and underflow. To see how your system handles this situation, try adding 1 to a `byte` variable that has been set to 127 and adding -1 to a `byte` variable that has been set to -128.

Sometimes you can avoid overflow by arranging computations carefully. Suppose you want to know how many different five-card poker hands can be dealt from a deck of cards. Here we are looking for the number of *combinations* of 52 cards taken 5 at a time. The standard mathematical formula for the number of combinations of n things taken r at a time is

$$\frac{n!}{r!(n-r)!}$$

We could write a method `factorial` and place this formula in an assignment statement:

```
hands = factorial(52) / (factorial(5) * factorial(47));
```

The only problem is that 52! is a very large number (approximately 8.0658×10^{67}), as is 47! (approximately 2.5862×10^{59}). Both of these numbers are well beyond the capacity of the JVM to represent exactly (52! requires 68 digits of precision). Even though we can represent them as floating-point numbers, most of the precision will be lost. By rearranging the calculations, however, we can achieve an exact result with any integral type with nine or more digits of precision (with `int` in Java). How? Consider that most of the multiplications in computing 52! are canceled when the product is divided by 47!

$$\frac{52!}{5!\times 47!} = \frac{52 \times 51 \times 50 \times 49 \times 48 \times 47 \times 46 \times 45 \times 44 \times \ldots}{(5 \times 4 \times 3 \times 2 \times 1) \times (47 \times 46 \times 45 \times 44 \times \ldots)}$$

So, we really have to compute only

```
hands = 52 * 51 * 50 * 49 * 48 / factorial(5);
```

which means the numerator is 311,875,200 and the denominator is 120. If we have nine or more digits of precision, we get an exact answer: 2,598,960 poker hands.

Cancellation Error   Another type of error that can happen with floating-point numbers is a *cancellation error*, a form of representational error that occurs when we add or subtract numbers of widely differing magnitudes. Let's look at an example:

$$(1 + 0.00001234 - 1) = 0.00001234$$

The laws of arithmetic say this equation should be true. But is it true if the computer does the arithmetic?

$$
\begin{array}{r}
100000000 \times 10^{-8} \\
+\quad\;\; 1234 \times 10^{-8} \\
\hline
100001234 \times 10^{-8}
\end{array}
$$

To four digits, the sum is $1,000 \times 10^{-3}$. Now the computer subtracts 1:

$$
\begin{array}{r}
1000 \times 10^{-3} \\
-1000 \times 10^{-3} \\
\hline
0
\end{array}
$$

The result is 0, not .00001234.

Sometimes you can avoid adding two floating-point numbers that are drastically different in size by carefully arranging the calculations. Suppose a problem requires many small floating-point numbers to be added to one large floating-point number. The result will be more accurate if the code first sums the smaller numbers to obtain a larger number and then adds the sum to the large number.

Software Engineering Tip

Choosing a Numeric Data Type

A first encounter with all the numeric data types of Java may leave you feeling a bit overwhelmed. To help in choosing an alternative, you may even feel tempted to toss a coin. You should resist this temptation, because each data type exists for a reason. Here are some guidelines:

1. In general, `int` is preferable.

    As a rule, you should use floating-point types only when absolutely necessary—that is, when you definitely need fractional values. Not only is floating-point arithmetic subject to representational errors, but it is also significantly slower than integer arithmetic on most computers.

    For ordinary integer data, use `int` instead of `byte` or `short`. It's easy to make overflow errors with these smaller data types.

2. Use `long` only if the range of `int` values is too restrictive. Compared to `int`, the `long` type requires twice as much memory space.

3. The default floating-point type in Java is `double`. It should be used unless you are certain that a problem can be solved with the lower precision of the `float` type.

By following these guidelines, you'll find that the simple types you use most often are `int` and `double`, along with `char` for character data and `boolean` for Boolean data. Only rarely do you need the longer or shorter variations of these fundamental types.

12.6 Decimal Format Type

To give more precise control over the formatting of numbers, Java provides a class called `DecimalFormat` that is part of a package called `java.text`. The `DecimalFormat` class allows us to create patterns that can be used to format numbers for output. These patterns take the form of strings, which are made up of characters that represent the parts of a formatted number. For example, the pattern

```
"###,###"
```

indicates that a number should be formatted with a maximum of six decimal digits. When the number contains more than three digits, a comma should be used to separate the thousands from the rest of the number.

We must follow four steps to use `DecimalFormat` patterns to format numbers:

1. `import java.text.*;`

Practical Implications of Limited Precision

A discussion of representational, overflow, underflow, and cancellation errors may seem purely academic. In fact, these errors have serious practical implications in many problems. We close this offer three examples illustrating how limited precision can have costly or even disastrous effects.

During the Mercury space program, several of the spacecraft splashed down a considerable distance from their computed landing points. Each mishap delayed the recovery of the spacecraft and the astronaut, putting both in some danger. Eventually, the problem was traced to an imprecise representation of the Earth's rotation period in the code that calculated the landing point.

As part of the construction of a hydroelectric dam, a long set of high-tension cables had to be constructed to link the dam to the nearest power distribution point. The cables were to be several miles long, and each one was to be a continuous unit. (Because of the high power output from the dam, shorter cables couldn't be spliced together.) The cables were constructed at great expense and strung between the two points. It turned out that they were too short, however, so another set had to be manufactured. The problem was traced to errors of precision in calculating the length of the catenary curve (the curve that a cable forms when hanging between two points).

An audit of a bank turned up a mysterious account with a large amount of money in it. The account was traced to an unscrupulous programmer who had used limited precision to his advantage. The bank computed interest on its accounts to a precision of a tenth of a cent. The tenths of cents were not added to the customers' accounts, so the programmer had the extra tenths for all the accounts summed and deposited into an account in his name. Because the bank had thousands of accounts, these tiny amounts added up to a large amount of money. And because the rest of the bank's applications did not use as much precision in their calculations, the scheme went undetected for many months.

The moral of this discussion is twofold: (1) The results of floating-point calculations are often imprecise, and these errors can have serious consequences; and (2) if you are working with extremely large numbers or extremely small numbers, you need more information than this book provides and should consult a numerical analysis text.

Background Information

2. Declare a variable of type DecimalFormat for each number format we wish to use.

3. For each format, create an object of class DecimalFormat that contains the pattern.

4. Format a number using the format method of one of the DecimalFormat objects.

Let's examine each of these steps in turn. You are already familiar with writing import declarations, so all you need to do for the first step is to remember to put the declaration at the beginning of your code. Declaring variable of class DecimalFormat is done in the same way as declaring other kinds of object variables. For example:

```
DecimalFormat dollar;      // Format for dollar amounts
DecimalFormat percent;     // Format for percentages
```

The third step involves using new and the DecimalFormat constructor to create a value we can assign to the variable. The call to the constructor contains the string representing the pattern. The following statements associate patterns with each of the variables declared above. In these patterns, the # sign and 0 represent the places that digits should be placed. Other characters ($, comma, period, %) are to be inserted directly into the formatted number. A 0 indicates a digit that is requred (a 0 is to be inserted if the number doesn't have a nonzero digit in that place), and # is for optional digits..

```
dollar = new DecimalFormat("$###,##0.00");
percent = new DecimalFormat("##0.00%");
```

The last step is to format the number using a method called format, which is a value-returning method associated with each of the DecimalFormat objects. The format method takes as its parameter a numerical value and returns a value of type String that contains the formatted number. For example, if we write

```
out.add(new JLabel(dollar.format(2893.6723)));
out.add(new JLabel(percent.format(0.142)));
```

then labels are added to the content pane called out, which contain strings of the form

```
$2,893.67      and      14.20%
```

The first string matches the format pattern associated with dollar. Note that the use of the % sign in the percent pattern causes the value to be multiplied by 100 before it is formatted.

See Appendix E for more information on writing the patterns themselves.

MATRIX MANIPULATION

Problem: Many mathematical problems, such as rotations in graphics, require the addition, subtraction, and multiplication of two matrices. Design and implement a general-purpose `Matrix` class that provides the operations addition, subtraction, and multiplication for real matrices.

Brainstorming: We are not asked to solve a problem in this Case Study; rather, we are asked to produce a class for the library. We have to create a test driver to be sure the class works properly, but we do not need to deliver it to the client. Thus our usual pattern of object-oriented problem solving is not appropriate here.

Background: You reach for your algebra book to refresh your memory on what matrices are and how matrix addition, subtraction, and multiplication work. You find that a matrix is just like an array data type—well, not exactly. A matrix is a mathematical object; an array is a structured data type. A more accurate statement is that an array is a perfect structure to implement a matrix.

Before we start to design the user interface for the `Matrix` class, we review what the operations on matrices mean. To add two matrices, you add the values in the corresponding positions: result[i][j] = A[i][j] + B[i][j]. To subtract one matrix from another, you subtract the values in the corresponding positions: result[i][j] = A[i][j] − B[i][j]. A + B and A − B are only defined on matrices with the same dimensions.

$$A = \begin{bmatrix} 5 & 0 & 1 & 4 \\ 2 & 1 & 3 & 2 \\ 1 & 1 & 0 & 0 \\ 1 & 2 & 3 & 4 \\ 2 & 3 & 1 & 0 \end{bmatrix} \qquad B = \begin{bmatrix} 1 & 1 & 1 & 2 \\ 2 & 1 & 0 & 3 \\ 1 & 2 & 4 & 1 \\ 0 & 0 & 4 & 5 \\ 0 & 0 & 1 & 1 \end{bmatrix}$$

$$A + B = \begin{bmatrix} 6 & 1 & 2 & 6 \\ 4 & 2 & 3 & 5 \\ 2 & 3 & 4 & 1 \\ 1 & 2 & 7 & 9 \\ 2 & 3 & 2 & 1 \end{bmatrix} \qquad A - B = \begin{bmatrix} 4 & -1 & 0 & 2 \\ 0 & 0 & 3 & -1 \\ 0 & -1 & -4 & -1 \\ 1 & 2 & -1 & -1 \\ 2 & 3 & 0 & -1 \end{bmatrix}$$

Matrix multiplication is slightly more complex. If matrix E is the result of multiplying matrices C and D, then

$$E[i][j] = C[i][1]^*D[1][j] + C[i][2]^*D[2][j] + \cdots + C[i][n]^*D[n][j].$$

Why didn't we use the same matrices, A and B, for multiplication that we used for addition and subtraction? Well, matrices A and B cannot be multiplied. Look carefully at the formula: The first row of C is multiplied item by item by the first column of D and the values summed. Therefore, the number of columns in C must be equal to the number of rows in D. Here is an example:

$$C = \begin{bmatrix} 1 & 2 & 3 & 4 \\ 0 & 2 & 1 & 3 \\ 1 & 1 & 0 & 0 \end{bmatrix} \qquad D = \begin{bmatrix} 1 & 1 \\ 0 & 1 \\ 2 & 3 \\ 4 & 2 \end{bmatrix}$$

$$C * D = \begin{bmatrix} 23 & 20 \\ 14 & 11 \\ 1 & 2 \end{bmatrix}$$

The sum obtained by multiplying a row by a column is called the *dot product*. Another way of stating multiplications is that

$$E[i][j] = \text{dot product of row } i \text{ and column } j$$

Now that we understand the semantics of the operations, we are ready to determine the responsibilities

Scenarios: If we were the users of the class, what facilities would we need? First, of course, we would need to create the matrix itself, by telling it how many rows and columns there should be. Next, we would need a way to put values into the slots of the matrix. We would probably want to print out the matrix after it is constructed to confirm that the values are correct. At that point, we would be ready to apply one of the binary operations—say, addition. We would send the message to one matrix to add itself to the matrix in the message parameter and return the result to us. We would follow the same process for subtraction and multiplication.

Are there any states of the matrix object we might want to know about? Well, it might be useful to view the value at a particular matrix position, so let's add that task to the list of responsibilities. We also might want to access the number of rows and columns in a matrix.

What about error conditions? Matrix addition and subtraction require that the matrices have the same dimensions, and matrix multiplication requires that the number of columns in the first matrix equal the number of rows in the second matrix. It makes sense for the matrix that is told to perform an operation to confirm that the operation is legal before complying with the request. If the operation is not legal, the matrix can throw an exception.

CRC Card: We can summarize our observations in a CRC card:

CASE STUDY

Class Name: *Matrix*	Superclass: *Object*	Subclasses:
Responsibilities	Collaborations	
Create itself (rows, columns)	*None*	
Know value at (row, col) *return double*	*None*	
Know number of rows *return int*	*None*	
Know number of columns *return int*	*None*	
Set a value at (row, col, value)	*None*	
Print (outFile)	*PrintWriter*	
Add self to (two) *return Matrix*	*None*	
Subtract (two) from self *return Matrix*	*None*	
Multiply self times (two) *return Matrix*	*None*	

Internal Data Representation: Earlier, we said that an array is the ideal implementation structure for a matrix. In many languages, we would have to include the number of rows and number of columns as data fields in the Matrix class. Java, however, provides them automatically as instance variables in the array object. Let's represent the numeric values in the matrices as double; this strategy allows us to handle the largest range of values.

```
public class Matrix
{
  // Private data field
  private  double[][] matrix;
  . . .
}
```

CASE STUDY

Responsibility Algorithms: To create the matrix, we need a constructor that takes the number of rows and the number of columns as parameters and creates the array.

```java
public Matrix(int rows, int columns)
// Create empty matrix
{
  matrix = new double[rows][columns];
}
```

Now that we know the internal structure is an array, we can give the client an alternative constructor that takes the array of values as data rather than having to input one value at a time. This constructor makes a shallow copy of the array. Case Study Follow-up Exercise 5 asks you to rewrite this constructor to make a deep copy.

```java
public Matrix(double[][] data)
// Stores the reference argument into matrix
{
  matrix = data;
}
```

The next method simply asks the object to return a copy of an item at a particular slot in the array.

```java
public double knowValueAt(int row, int col)
// Returns the value at matrix[row][col]
{
  return matrix[row][col];
}
```

The next two observer methods return the number of rows and the number of columns. Because Java implements a two-dimensional array as an array of references to arrays and each one-dimensional array object has an instance variable that contains the number of slots in the array, we have direct access to this information. The length field of the two-dimensional array gives the number of rows; the length of each row gives the number of columns in that row. We do not need to worry about ragged arrays because of the way that we have implemented the constructor.

```java
public int knowRows()
// Returns the number of rows in matrix
{
  return matrix.length;
}

public int knowColumns()
// Returns the number of columns in matrix
```

```
{
  return matrix[0].length;
}
```

The main transformer method takes a value and a row and column number. The value is stored into the matrix at the [row][column] position.

```
public void setValue(double dataItem, int row, int col)
// Sets matrix[row][col] to dataItem
{
  matrix[row][col] = dataItem;
}
```

The remaining observer is printMatrix. We want to print the matrix by row. We have a pattern that we can follow exactly from our general discussion about arrays. Because we don't know how many columns the matrix has, we should print a blank line between rows.

```
public void printMatrix(PrintWriter outFile)
// Prints matrix on outFile by row
{
  for (int row = 0; row < matrix.length; row++)
  {
    for (int col = 0; col < matrix[0].length; col++)
      outFile.print(matrix[row][col] + "  ");
    outFile.println();
    outFile.println();
  }
}
```

The last three methods lie at the heart of this problem: adding, subtracting, and multiplying matrices. One matrix is the one to which the method is applied and the other matrix is a parameter.

```
add(two)
if the addition is not legal
  throw MatException
else
  Create result matrix with the same dimensions as matrix
  for row going from 0 through matrix.length – 1
    for col going from 0 through matrix[0].length – 1
      Set result[row][col] to matrix[row][col] + two.matrix[row][col]
return result
```

Each of these steps is concrete. Determining if the addition is legal is a matter of checking the dimensions of matrix against the dimensions of the parameter. The string that goes with the exception can simply state that the addition is not legal.

```
public Matrix add(Matrix two) throws MatException
// Returns the sum of matrix and two.matrix
{
  if (matrix.length != two.matrix.length ||
      matrix[0].length != two.matrix[0].length)
    throw new MatException("Illegal matrix add.");
  else
  {
    Matrix result = new Matrix(matrix.length, matrix[0].length);
    for (int row = 0; row < matrix.length; row++)
      for (int col = 0; col < matrix[0].length; col++)
      {
        result.matrix[row][col] = matrix[row][col] +
            two.matrix[row][col];
      }
    return result;
  }
}
```

```
sub(two)

  if the subtraction is not legal
    throw MatException
  else
    Create result matrix with the same dimensions as matrix
    for row going from 0 through matrix.length − 1
      for col going from 0 through matrix[0].length − 1
        Set result[row][col] to matrix[row][col] − two.matrix[row][col]
  return result
```

```
public Matrix sub(Matrix two) throws MatException
// Returns two.matrix subtracted from matrix
{
  if (matrix.length != two.matrix.length ||
      matrix[0].length != two.matrix[0].length)
    throw new MatException("Illegal matrix subtract.");
  else
  {
    Matrix result = new Matrix(matrix.length, matrix[0].length);
    for (int row = 0; row < matrix.length; row++)
      for (int col = 0; col < matrix[0].length; col++)
      {
        result.matrix[row][col] = matrix[row][col] -
            two.matrix[row][col];
      }
    return result;
  }
}
```

```
multiply (two)

if multiplication is not legal
   throw MatException
else
   Create result matrix with number of rows in matrix and number of columns in
      two.matrix
   for row going from 0 through matrix.length − 1
      for col going from 0 through two.matrix[0].length − 1
         Set result[row][col] to dot product of row of matrix
            and col of two.matrix
```

```
dotProduct(row,col,two)

Set total to 0
for index going from 0 through number of rows of two
   Set total to matrix[row][index] * two.matrix[index][col]+ total
```

Let's make dotProduct be a helper function.

```java
public Matrix multiply(Matrix two) throws MatException
// Returns matrix times two.matrix
{
  if (matrix[0].length != two.matrix.length)
    throw new MatException("Illegal matrix multiplication.");
  else
  {
    Matrix  result =
      new Matrix(matrix.length, two.matrix[0].length);
    for (int row = 0; row < matrix.length; row++)
      for (int col = 0; col < two.matrix[0].length; col++)
      {
        result.matrix[row][col] = dotProduct(row,col,two);
      }
    return result;
  }
}

private double dotProduct(int row, int col, Matrix two)
// Returns the dot product of row of matrix and column of two.matrix
{
  double total = 0;
  for (int index = 0; index < two.matrix.length; index++)
    total = total + matrix[row][index]*two.matrix[index][col];
  return total;
}
```

CASE STUDY

Before we collect these methods into a complete class, have we forgotten anything? The class has two constructors, three knowledge methods, a transformer that sets a value in a specified row and column—but what happens if the specified row and column are not within the bounds of the matrix? The class should check for this error and throw an exception. What about the binary matrix operations? We know that these numeric operations can cause underflow and overflow. If underflow occurs, the values are automatically set to zero; if overflow occurs, the values are set to signed infinity. In the case of overflow, the operation should throw an exception. The Double class has a boolean class method called isInfinite that we can use to determine if overflow has occurred. In the following class, overflow is checked, but the other error conditions are left to a Case Study Follow-Up exercise.

```java
//**********************************************
// Class MatException is thrown from class Matrix
// under certain error conditions.
//**********************************************

package matrix;
public class MatException extends Exception
{
  public MatException()
  {
    super();
  }

  public MatException(String message)
  {
    super(message);
  }
}


//*******************************************************************
// This class provides a basic matrix object. There are two
// constructors, one transformer, three knowledge methods, a
// print, and three binary operations.  Certain errors are
// checked and MatException is thrown if they arise.
//*******************************************************************
package matrix;
import java.io.*;

public class Matrix
{
  // Private data field
  private double[][] matrix;

  public Matrix(int rows, int columns)
```

```java
// Creates empty matrix
{
  matrix = new double[rows][columns];
}

public Matrix(double [][] data)
// Stores the reference argument into matrix
{
  matrix = data;
}

public double knowValueAt(int row, int col)
// Returns the value at matrix[row][col]
{
  return matrix[row][col];
}

public int knowRows()
// Returns the number of rows in matrix
{
  return matrix.length;
}

public int knowColumns()
// Returns the number of columns in matrix
{
  return matrix[0].length;
}

public void setValue(double dataItem, int row, int col)
// Sets matrix[row][col] to dataItem
{
  matrix[row][col] = dataItem;
}

public void printMatrix(PrintWriter outFile)
// Writes matrix on outFile by row
{
  for (int row = 0; row < matrix.length; row++)
  {
    for (int col = 0; col < matrix[0].length; col++)
      outFile.print(matrix[row][col] + "  ");
    outFile.println();
    outFile.println();
  }
}
```

```java
public Matrix add(Matrix two) throws MatException
// Returns the sum of matrix and two.matrix
// Throws MatException if the matrices cannot be added
//   or overflow occurs
{
  if (matrix.length != two.matrix.length ||
      matrix[0].length != two.matrix[0].length)
    throw new MatException("Illegal matrix add.");
  else
  {
    Matrix result =
      new Matrix(matrix.length, matrix[0].length);
    for (int row = 0; row < matrix.length; row++)
      for (int col = 0; col < matrix[0].length; col++)
      {
        result.matrix[row][col] = matrix[row][col] +
          two.matrix[row][col];
        if (Double.isInfinite(result.matrix[row][col]))
          throw new MatException("Addition overflow");
      }
    return result;
  }
}

public Matrix sub(Matrix two) throws MatException
// Returns two.matrtix subtracted from matrix
// Throws MatException if the matrices cannot be subtracted
//   or overflow occurs
{
  if (matrix.length != two.matrix.length ||
      matrix[0].length != two.matrix[0].length)
    throw new MatException("Illegal matrix subtract.");
  else
  {
    Matrix result =
      new Matrix(matrix.length, matrix[0].length);
    for (int row = 0; row < matrix.length; row++)
      for (int col = 0; col < matrix[0].length; col++)
      {
        result.matrix[row][col] =
          matrix[row][col] — two.matrix[row][col];
        if (Double.isInfinite(result.matrix[row][col]))
          throw new MatException("Subtraction overflow");
      }
```

```
      return result;
   }
}


public Matrix multiply(Matrix two) throws MatException
// Returns matrix times two.matrix
// Throws MatException if the matrices cannot be multiplied
//    or overflow occurs
{
  if (matrix[0].length != two.matrix.length)
    throw new MatException("Illegal matrix multiplication.");
  else
  {
    Matrix  result =
      new Matrix(matrix.length, two.matrix[0].length);
    for (int row = 0; row < matrix.length; row++)
      for (int col = 0; col < two.matrix[0].length; col++)
      {
        result.matrix[row][col] = dotProduct(row,col,two);
        if (Double.isInfinite(result.matrix[row][col]))
          throw new MatException("Multiplication overflow");
      }
    return result;
  }
}


private double dotProduct(int row, int col, Matrix two)
// Returns the dot product of row of matrix and column of two.matrix
{
  double total = 0;
  for (int index = 0; index < two.matrix.length; index++)
    total = total + matrix[row][index]*two.matrix[index][col];
  return total;
}
}
```

Testing: Because the branching statements only check for errors and throw exceptions if they occur, a clear- or white-box testing strategy is appropriate. The end cases for addition and subtraction would be for sizes of one by one and something larger. For multiplication, the outer dimensions should be one and the inner dimensions should be something else, and the inner dimensions should be one and the outer dimensions should be something else. Then the error conditions must all be checked. A fuller test plan is left as a Case Study Follow-Up exercise.

CASE STUDY

Shown below is a test driver that carries out the addition, subtraction, and multiplication operations.

```java
//******************************************************************
// Class MatrixDriver is a test driver for class Matrix. The four
// matrices that are defined are those used in the Background
// section of the Case Study.  The same operations are performed.
// One additional operation is performed: An illegal multiply
// operation is requested and an exception is thrown.
//******************************************************************
import matrix.*;
import java.io.*;

public class MatrixDriver
{
  public static void main(String[] args) throws IOException
  {
    PrintWriter outFile;
    outFile = new PrintWriter(new FileWriter("Matrix.out"));

    Matrix result;
    int row, col;
    // Set up arrays and instantiate four objects of class Matrix
    double[][] data1 =
               {{5.0, 0.0, 1.0, 4.0},
                {2.0, 1.0, 3.0, 2.0},
                {1.0, 1.0, 0.0, 0.0},
                {1.0, 2.0, 3.0, 4.0},
                {2.0, 3.0, 1.0, 0.0}};
    double[][] data2 =
               {{1.0, 1.0, 1.0, 2.0},
                {2.0, 1.0, 0.0, 3.0},
                {1.0, 2.0, 4.0, 1.0},
                {0.0, 0.0, 4.0, 5.0},
                {0.0, 0.0, 1.0, 1.0}};
    double[][] data3 =
               {{1.0, 2.0, 3.0, 4.0},
                {0.0, 2.0, 1.0, 3.0},
                {1.0, 1.0, 0.0, 0.0}};
    double[][] data4 =
               {{1.0, 1.0},
                {0.0, 1.0},
                {2.0, 3.0},
                {4.0, 2.0}};
```

```
Matrix one = new Matrix(data1);
Matrix two = new Matrix(data2);
Matrix three = new Matrix(data3);
Matrix four = new Matrix(data4);

try
{
  outFile.println("Matrix one:");
  one.printMatrix(outFile);

  outFile.println("Matrix two:");
  two.printMatrix(outFile);

  outFile.println("Result of adding one and two:");
  result = one.add(two);
  result.printMatrix(outFile);

  outFile.println("Result of subtracting two from one:");
  result = one.sub(two);
  result.printMatrix(outFile);

  outFile.println("Matrix three:");
  three.printMatrix(outFile);

  outFile.println("Matrix four:");
  four.printMatrix(outFile);

  outFile.println("Result of multiplying three by four:");
  result = three.multiply(four);
  result.printMatrix(outFile);

  outFile.println("Result of multiplying four by three:");
  result = four.multiply(three);
}
catch(MatException except)
{
  outFile.println(except.getMessage());
}
```

CASE STUDY

```
        outFile.close();
    }
}
```

Output from partial test of class Matrix:

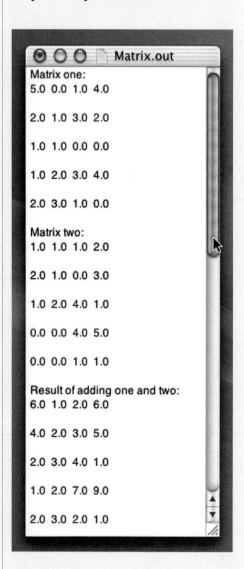

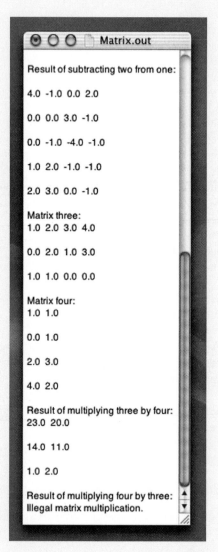

12.7 Testing and Debugging

Errors with multidimensional arrays usually fall into two major categories: index expressions that are out of order and index range errors. We have been very careful to use an array object's own `length` value in loop expressions so as to minimize range errors. However, inadvertent switching of indexes can cause index range errors.

Take a look at the code for `dotProduct`. What happens if we reverse the indexes in the following statement?

```
total = total + matrix[row][index]*two.matrix[index][col];
```

That is, what happens if we code the statement as follows?

```
total = total + matrix[index][row]*two.matrix[col][index]; // Wrong
```

If the first matrix is a 3 × 5 and the second is a 5 × 2, `index` goes from 0 through 4 while `row` and `col` remain at 0. `matrix[0][0]` and `two.matrix[0][0]` are accessed; then `matrix[1][0]` and `two.matrix[0][1]` are accessed; then `matrix[2][0]` and `two.matrix[0][2]` are accessed. This last access causes an `ArrayIndexOutOfBoundsException` to be thrown: `two.matrix[0][2]` doesn't exist.

How can you avoid such errors? This question has no simple answer. You just have to be careful and thoroughly test your code.

Testing and Debugging Hints

1. With multidimensional arrays, use the proper number of indexes when referencing an array component, and make sure the indexes are in the correct order.

2. In loops that process multidimensional arrays, double-check the upper and lower bounds on each index variable to verify that they are correct for that dimension of the array.

3. When declaring a multidimensional array as a parameter, confirm that you have the proper number of brackets beside the type on the parameter list.

4. When passing an array object as an argument, be sure that it has the same number of dimensions as the parameter of the method to which it is being passed.

5. Be wary of representational, cancellation, overflow, and underflow errors. If possible, try to arrange calculations in your code to keep floating-point numbers from becoming too large or too small.

6. If your code increases the value of a positive integer and the result suddenly becomes a negative number, suspect integer overflow.

7. Avoid mixing data types in expressions, assignment operations, argument passing, and the return of a method value. If you must mix types, explicit type casts can prevent unwelcome surprises caused by implicit type conversion.

Summary

Two-dimensional arrays are useful for processing information that is represented naturally in tabular form. Processing data in two-dimensional arrays usually takes one of two forms: processing by row or processing by column. Java implements a two-dimensional array as an array of references to one-dimensional arrays. Associated with each two-dimensional array is a final instance variable length that contains the number of rows. Associated with each row of the table is a final instance variable length that contains the number of items in the row (the column length). The number of items in a row is usually the same for each row, but does not need to be. If the rows are uneven, the array is called a ragged array.

A multidimensional array is a collection of like components that are ordered on more than two dimensions. Each component is accessed by a set of indexes, one for each dimension, that represents the component's position on the various dimensions. Each index may be thought of as describing a feature of a given array component.

The floating-point types built into the Java language are float and double. Floating-point numbers are represented in the computer with a fraction and an exponent. This representation permits numbers that are much larger or much smaller than those that can be represented with the integral types. Floating-point representation also allows us to perform calculations on numbers with fractional parts.

Using floating-point numbers in arithmetic calculations does have some drawbacks. Representational errors, for example, can affect the accuracy of compu- tations. When using floating-point numbers, keep in mind that if two numbers are vastly different from each other in size, adding or subtracting them can produce the wrong answer. Remember, also, that the computer has a limited range of numbers that it can represent. If your code tries to compute a value that is too large or too small, it may result in unusual or unexpected values.

The class DecimalFormat provides methods that allow the user to specify the appearance of numeric output.

Quick Check

1. Declare a two-dimensional array named plan, and create an array object with 30 rows and 10 columns. The component type of the array is float. (pp. 582–583)

2. Given the array created in Question 1, answer the following questions.

   a. Assign the value 27.3 to the component in row 13, column 7 of the array plan from Question 1. (pp. 583–584)

   b. We can use nested *for* loops to sum the values in each row of the array plan. What range of values would the outer *for* loop count through to do this? (pp. 587–589)

c. We can use nested *for* loops to sum the values in each column of the array plan. What range of values would the outer *for* loop count through to do this? (pp. 588–589)

d. Write a code fragment that initializes the array plan to all 1s. (pp. 589–590)

e. Write a code fragment that prints the contents of the array plan, one row per line of output. (pp. 589–590)

3. Suppose the array plan is passed as an argument to a method in which the corresponding parameter is named someArray. What would the declaration of someArray look like in the parameter list? (p. 590)

4. Given the declarations

```
final int SIZE = 10;
char[][][][] quick = new char[SIZE][SIZE][SIZE][SIZE-1];
```

a. How many components does the array quick contain? (pp. 591–592)

b. Write a code fragment that fills the array quick with blanks. (pp. 591–592)

5. Why is it inappropriate to use a variable of a floating-point type as a loop control variable? (pp. 595–596)

6. If a computer has four digits of precision, what would be the result of the following addition operation? (pp. 595–596)

400400.000 + 199.9

7. Given that the pattern "$#,##0.00" has been stored into the object referenced by the DecimalFormat variable num, what is the result of each of the following calls to format? (pp. 602–604)

```
num.format(39144932.109)
num.format(-27.0)
```

8. What pattern would you use to display a numerical value as a percentage with three leading blanks, at least one digit in the integer part, and exactly two fractional digits? (pp. 602–604)

Answers

```
1. float[][] plan;
   plan = new float[30][10];
2. a. plan[13][7] = 27.3;
   b. for (row = 0; row < 30; row++)
   c. for (col = 0; col < 10; col++)
   d. for (row = 0; row < 30; row++)
        for (col = 0; col < 10; col++)
          plan[row][col] = 1.0;
   e. for (row = 0; row < 30; row++)
      {
          for (col = 0; col < 10; col++)
            outFile.print(plan[row][col]);
          outFile.println();
      }
```

3. `float[][] someArray`
4. **a.** Nine thousand ($10 \times 10 \times 10 \times 9$)
   b. `for (dim1 = 0; dim1 < SIZE; dim1++)`
       `for (dim2 = 0; dim2 < SIZE; dim2++)`
         `for (dim3 = 0; dim3 < SIZE; dim3++)`
           `for (dim4 = 0; dim4 < SIZE − 1; dim4++)`
             `quick[dim1][dim2][dim3][dim4] = ' ';`
5. Representational errors can cause the loop termination condition to be evaluated with unpredictable results.
6. 400500.000 (actually, 4.005E+5)
7. $39,144,932.11 $–27.00
8. `"   #0.00%"`

Exam Preparation Exercises

1. Given the declarations

   ```
   final int NUM_SCHOOLS = 10;
   final int NUM_SPORTS = 3;
   int[][]  kidsInSports = new int[NUM_SCHOOLS][NUM_SPORTS];
   double[][] costOfSports = new double[NUM_SPORTS][NUM_SCHOOLS];
   ```

   answer the following questions:
   a. What is the number of rows in `kidsInSports`?
   b. What is the number of columns in `kidsInSports`?
   c. What is the number of rows in `costOfSports`?
   d. What is the number of columns in `costOfSports`?
   e. How many components does `kidsInSports` have?
   f. How many components does `costOfSports` have?
   g. What kind of processing (row or column) would be needed to total the amount of money spent on each sport?
   h. What kind of processing (row or column) would be needed to total the number of children participating in sports at a particular school?

2. Given the following code segments, draw the arrays and their contents after the code is executed. Indicate any undefined values with the letter U.
   a. `int[][] exampleA;`
      `exampleA = new int[4][3];`
      `int i, j;`
      `for (i = 0; i < 4; i++)`
        `for (j = 0; j < 3; j++)`
          `exampleA[i][j] = i * j;`

b.
```
int[][] exampleB;
exampleB = new int[4][3];
int i, j;
for (i = 0; i < 3; i++)
  for (j = 0; j < 3; j++)
    exampleB[i][j] = (i + j) % 3;
```

c.
```
int[][] exampleC;
exampleC = new int[8][2];
int i, j;
exampleC[7][0] = 4;
exampleC[7][1] = 5;
for (i = 0; i < 7; i++)
{
  exampleC[i][0] = 2;
  exampleC[i][1] = 3;
}
```

3. **a.** Define an `int` variable `teamType` and an `int` variable `resultType`.

   b. Define a two-dimensional array variable `outcome`.

   c. This array will be used to keep track of the wins and losses for a baseball season. `teamType` represents the classes: freshman (0), sophomore (1), junior (2), and senior (3). `resultType` represents the outcome for the team: won (0), tied (1), or lost (2). Instantiate an array object for the variable `outcome`.

   d. Write a code fragment that increases the number of freshman wins by 1.

   e. Write a code fragment that determines which class won the most games.

   f. Write a code fragment that determines the total number of wins for all classes.

4. The number of rows in the array must be specified on the parameter list of a method that takes the array as a parameter. (True or False?)

5. Declare and instantiate the two-dimensional arrays described below.

   a. An array with five rows and six columns that contains `boolean` values

   b. An array, indexed from 0 through 39 and 0 through 199, that contains `double` values

   c. An array, indexed from 0 through 3 and 0 through 2, that contains `char` values

6. A logging operation keeps records of 37 loggers' monthly production for purposes of analysis, using the following array structure:

```
final int NUM_LOGGERS = 37;

int[][] logsCut;  // Logs cut per logger per month
logsCut = new int[NUM_LOGGERS][12];
int monthlyHigh;
int monthlyTotal;
int yearlyTotal;
int high;
int month;
int bestMonth;
int logger;
int bestLogger;
```

a. The following statement assigns the January log total for logger number 7 to monthlyTotal. (True or False?)

```
monthlyTotal = logsCut[7][0];
```

b. The following statements compute the yearly total for logger number 11. (True or False?)

```
yearlyTotal = 0;
for (month = 0; month < NUM_LOGGERS; month++)
  yearlyTotal = yearlyTotal + logsCut[month][10];
```

c. The following statements find the best logger (most logs cut) in March. (True or False?)

```
monthlyHigh = 0;
for (logger = 0; logger < NUM_LOGGERS; logger++)
  if (logsCut[logger][2] > monthlyHigh)
  {
    bestLogger = logger;
    monthlyHigh = logsCut[logger][2];
  }
```

d. The following statements find the logger with the highest monthly production and the logger's best month. (True or False?)

```
high = -1;
for (month = 0; month < 12; month++)
  for (logger = 0; logger < NUM_LOGGERS; logger++)
    if (logsCut[logger][month] > high)
```

```
        {
            high = logsCut[logger][month];
            bestLogger = logger;
            bestMonth = month;
        }
```

7. Declare and instantiate the `double` arrays described below.

   a. A three-dimensional array in which the first dimension is indexed from 0 through 9, the second dimension is indexed from 0 through 6 representing the days of the week, and the third dimension is indexed from 0 through 20

   b. A four-dimensional array in which the first two dimensions are indexed from 0 through 49, and the third and fourth have 20 and 30 slots, respectively

8. If a system supports 10 digits of precision for floating-point numbers, what are the results of the following computations?

   a. 1.4E+12 + 100.0

   b. 4.2E–8 + 100.0

   c. 3.2E–5 + 3.2E+5

9. Define the following terms:

   a. mantissa

   b. exponent

   c. representational error

   d. significant digits

   e. overflow

10. Show precisely the output of the following Java application. Use a □ to indicate each blank.

```java
import java.awt.*;
import java.text.*;
import javax.swing.*;


public class ExamPrep
{
    public static void main(String args[])
    {
        DecimalFormat decimal;
        DecimalFormat integral;
        JFrame dataFrame;              // User interface frame
```

```
            Container dataPane;              // Content pane
            dataFrame = new JFrame();
            dataPane = dataFrame.getContentPane();
            dataFrame.setDefaultCloseOperation(JFrame.EXIT_ON_CLOSE);
            dataFrame.setSize(450, 75);
            dataPane.setLayout(new GridLayout(2,1));
            decimal = new DecimalFormat("#0.0");
            integral = new DecimalFormat("#0");
            String ch;
            int    n;
            double y;

            ch = "A";
            dataPane.add(new JLabel(ch));
            ch = "B";
            dataPane.add(new JLabel(ch));
            n = 413;
            y = 21.8;
            dataPane.add(new JLabel(integral.format(n) + " is the value of n"));
            dataPane.add(new JLabel(decimal.format(y) + " is the value of y"));
            dataFrame.setVisible(true);
        }

    }
```

11. Given that x is a double variable and x = 2314.3827, show the output of each pair of statements below. Use a ☐ to indicate each blank.

    a. num = new DecimalFormat("#0.00");

    out.add(new JLabel("x is " + num.format(x)));

    b. num = new DecimalFormat("#,##0.00");

    out.add(new JLabel("x is " + num.format(x)));

    c. num = new DecimalFormat("0.0");

    out.add(new JLabel("x is " + num.format(x)));

    d. num = new DecimalFormat("#,##0.000");

    out.add(new JLabel("x is " + num.format(x)));

Programming Warm-Up Exercises

1. Using the declarations in Exam Preparation Exercise 1, write code fragments to do the following tasks. Assume sport 0 is football, 1 is basketball, and 2 is volleyball.

   a. Determine which school spent the most money on football.

   b. Determine which sport the last school spent the most money on.

   c. Determine which school had the most students playing basketball.

   d. Determine in which sport the third school had the most students participating.

   e. Determine the total amount spent by all the schools on volleyball.

   f. Determine the total number of students who played any sport. (Assume that each student played only one sport.)

   g. Determine which school had the most students participating in sports.

   h. Determine which was the most popular sport in terms of money spent.

   i. Determine which was the most popular sport in terms of student participation.

2. Examine the following documentation of a class:

```
public class TwoDimensions
{
    // Private data
    private int[][] data;
    private int rowsUsed;        // Number of rows that contain data
    private int columnsUsed;     // Number of columns that contain data
    // Methods
    public TwoDimensions(int maxRows, int maxColumns)
    // Constructor: creates a maxRows x maxColumns array
    public void inputData(BufferedReader inFile)
    // Reads data into the array
    // Data are on the file as follows:
    // First line: number of rows (rowsUsed)
    // Second line: number of columns (columnsUsed)
    // Data are stored one value per line in row order.
    // That is, the first columnsUsed values go into row 0; the
    // next columnsUsed values go into row 1; etc.
    public void print(PrintWriter outFile)
    // Prints the values in the array on outFile, one row per line
```

```
public int maxInRow(int row)
// Returns the maximum value in the specified row
public int maxInCol(int column)
// Returns the maximum value in the specified column
public int maxInArray()
// Returns the maximum value in the entire array
public int sum()
// Returns the sum of the values in the array
public int sumInRow(int row)
// Returns the sum of the values in the specified row
public int sumInCol(int column)
// Returns the sum of the values in the specified column
public boolean allPlus()
// Returns true if all the values are positive; false otherwise
```

    a. Write the code for the constructor TwoDimensions.

    b. Write the code for the method inputData.

    c. Write the code for the method print.

    d. Write the code for the method maxInRow.

    e. Write the code for the method maxInCol.

    f. Write the code for the method maxInArray.

    g. Write the code for the method sum.

    h. Write the code for the method sumInRow.

    i. Write the code for the method sumInCol.

    j. Write the code for the method allPlus.

3. Write a code segment that finds the largest value in a two-dimensional double array of 50 rows and 50 columns.

4. Given the following declarations

```
final int NUM_DEPTS = 100;
final int NUM_STORES = 10;
final int NUM_MONTHS = 12;
```

    a. Declare an array variable sales that will be indexed by the number of departments, number of stores, and number of months and that contains double values.

    b. Instantiate an array object for the variable sales.

    c. What values do the components in the array have after it is created?

d. Write a code segment to calculate the sum of the sales for January.

e. Write a code segment to calculate the sum of the sales for store 2.

f. Write a code segment to calculate the sum of the sales for department 33.

5. In an application you are writing, a `double` variable `beta` potentially contains a very large number. Before multiplying `beta` by 100.0, you want the code to test whether it is safe to do so. Write an *if* statement that tests for a possible overflow *before* multiplying by 100.0. Specifically, if the multiplication would lead to overflow, print a message and don't perform the multiplication; otherwise, go ahead with the multiplication.

6. The `Vector` class in `java.util` provides functionality very similar to that offered by an array. In fact, the underlying data structure is an array. The advantage of a `Vector` is that it can grow and shrink; the disadvantage is that this capability is time-consuming. To grow beyond the initial size requires the system to create a larger array and move the objects into it. Listed below are some of the useful methods in the `Vector` class and the corresponding array operations.

Method	Array Equivalent/Explanation
`Vector myVector;`	`Object[] myVector;`
`myVector = new Vector(10);`	`myVector = new Object[10];`
`myVector.setElementAt(item, 9);`	`myVector[9] = item;`
`item = myVector.elementAt(5);`	`item = myVector[5];`
`myVector.addElement(item);`	`myVector[numItems] = item;`
	`numItems++;`
`myVector.size()`	Returns the number of items in `myVector`
`myVector.capacity()`	`myVector.length`

a. Run an experiment to determine how many slots are added to a `Vector` object when you add one more item than you originally stated should be in the vector.

b. Make a table like the one shown in this exercise showing five other useful methods in the class.

Programming Problems

1. Write an application that plays Tic-Tac-Toe. Represent the board as a 3 × 3 character array. The array is initialized to blanks, and each player is asked in turn to input a position. The first player's position is marked on the board with an O, and the second player's position is marked with an X. Continue the process until a player wins or the game is a draw. To win, a player must have three marks in a row, in a column, or on a diagonal. A draw occurs when the board is full and no one has won.

Each player's position should be input as indexes into the Tic-Tac-Toe board—that is, a row number, a space, and a column number. Make the application user-friendly.

After each game, print out a diagram of the board showing the ending positions. Keep a count of the number of games each player has won and the number of draws. Before the beginning of each game, ask each player if he or she wishes to continue. If either player wishes to quit, print out the statistics and stop. Use buttons as appropriate.

2. Photos taken in space by the Galileo spacecraft are sent back to earth as a stream of numbers. Each number represents a level of brightness. A large number represents a high brightness level, and a small number represents a low level. Your job is to take a matrix (a two-dimensional array) of these numbers and print it as a picture.

One approach to generating a picture is to print a dark character (such as a $) when the brightness level is low, and to print a light character (such as a blank or a period) when the level is high. Unfortunately, errors in transmission sometimes occur. Your photo-generation code should first attempt to find and correct these errors. Assume a value is in error if it differs by more than 1 from each of its four neighboring values. Correct the erroneous value by giving it the average of its neighboring values, rounded to the nearest integer.

Example:

	5		The 2 would be regarded as an error and
4	2	5	would be given a corrected value of 5.
	5		

Note that you must process values on the corners or boundaries of the matrix differently than the values on the interior. Your application should print an image of the uncorrected picture and then an image of the corrected picture.

3. The following diagram represents an island surrounded by water (shaded area).

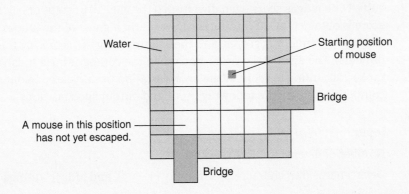

Two bridges lead out of the island. A mouse is placed on the green square. Write an application to make the mouse take a walk across the island. The mouse is allowed to travel one square at a time, either horizontally or vertically. A random number from 1 through 4 should be used to decide which direction the mouse is to take. The mouse drowns when he hits the water; he escapes when he enters a bridge.

You may generate a random number up to 100 times. If the mouse does not find his way by the hundredth try, he will die of starvation. In that case, restart the mouse in a reinitialized array and repeat the whole process. Count the number of times he escapes, drowns, and starves.

Input

First input line—the size of the array, including border of water and bridges (not larger than 20 × 20)

Next N input lines—the rows of the two-dimensional array, where the positions containing negative numbers represent the water, the positions in the edge containing a 0 represent the bridges, the position containing a 1 represents the starting position of the mouse, and all other positions contain 0s

Output

A line stating whether the mouse escaped, drowned, or starved

A line showing the mouse's starting position and the position of the two bridges

A map showing the frequency of the mouse's visits to each position

You should print these items (double-spaced between trips) for each trip by the mouse.

4. In competitive diving, each diver makes three dives of varying degrees of difficulty. Nine judges score each dive from 0 through 10 in steps of 0.5. The total score is obtained by discarding the lowest and highest of the judges' scores, adding the remaining scores, and then multiplying the scores by the degree of difficulty. The divers take turns, and when the competition is finished, they are ranked according to score. Write an application to calculate the outcome of a competition, using the following input and output specifications.

Input

Number of divers

Diver's name (ten characters), difficulty (`double`), and judges' ratings (nine `doubles`)

There is a line of data for each diver for each dive. All the data for Dive 1 are grouped together, then all the data for Dive 2, then all the data for Dive 3.

Output

The input data, echo-printed in tabular form with appropriate headings—for example, Name, Difficulty, Judge's number (1–9)

A table that contains the following information:

Name   Dive 1   Dive 2   Dive 3   Total

where Name is the diver's name; Dive 1, Dive 2, and Dive 3 are the total points received for a single dive; and Total is the overall total

5. You are to test what happens when overflow occurs. Write a simple application that does the following tasks:

   Calculate the factorial of an integer number

   Embed the factorial in a loop that goes from 1 to 100

   Print out the result of each factorial within the loop

   Run your application with the factorial calculated using each of the integer types. Record the results of each run.

   Redo the experiment taking the factorial of a real number. Record the results of each run.

   Write a report describing what you learned about overflow and Java.

6. Extend the class `UnsortedList` so that the `insert` method creates a new array that is twice the size of the current one when the list is full and moves the elements into it. Test your new class.

Case Study Follow-Up

1. There are no checks for row and column parameters being in bounds in the Matrix Manipulation Case Study. List the methods where this error might occur.

2. Implement checks for the out-of-bounds error described in Exercise 1 and recode the solution.

3. Design and implement a test plan for the class `Matrix` as modified in Exercise 2.

4. The `java.math` package contains the `BigInteger` and `BigDecimal` classes, which allow you to work with arbitrary-size and arbitrary-precision integers and floating-point values. How would you have to change the class `Matrix` to define the operations using `BigInteger` rather than `double`?

5. Write a derived class of `Matrix` that overrides the constructor which takes an array as a parameter. The new version of the constructor should make a deep copy of the array rather than a shallow copy.

Recursion

goals

Knowledge Goals
- To understand the concept of a recursive definition
- To understand the difference between iteration and recursion
- To understand when recursion is appropriate

Skill Goals
To be able to:
- Identify the base cases and the general case in a recursive definition
- Identify the size of the problem, that aspect that must decrease
- Write a recursive algorithm for a problem involving only simple variables
- Write a recursive algorithm for a problem involving structured variables

timeline

1989
Tim Berners-Lee proposes his idea for the World Wide Web, an internet-based hypermedia initiative for global information sharing

1989
Intel releases its latest microchip, the 80486, which contains 1.2 million transistors

1990
The launching of Windows 3.0 furthers the legal debate between Microsoft and Apple; the operating system has a marked resemblance to the Macintosh's operating system

1990
Intel releases the i486 with its built-in math coprocessor and the iPSC/860. Motorola introduces the 68040 with its on-chip floating point unit

1990
Berners-Lee develops the first web-client and server, the prototype for the WWW, which uses URLs, HTML, and HTTP

1992
The widely publicized computer virus Michelangelo is expected to destroy 1 of 4 hard drives on March 6th, but proves to have little effect

introduction

In Java, any method can call another method. A method can even call itself! When a method calls itself, it makes a **recursive call**. The word *recursive* means "having the characteristic of coming up again, or repeating." In this case, a method call is repeated by the method itself. Recursion is a powerful technique that can be used in place of iteration (looping).

Recursive solutions are generally less efficient than iterative solutions to the same problem. However, some problems lend themselves to simple, elegant, recursive solutions and are exceedingly cumbersome to solve iteratively. Some programming languages, such as early versions of FORTRAN, BASIC, and COBOL, do not support recursion. Other languages are especially oriented to recursive algorithms—LISP, for example. Java lets us take our choice: We can implement both iterative and recursive algorithms.

> **Recursive call** A method call in which the method being called is the same as the one making the call

Our examples are broken into two groups: problems that use only simple variables and problems that use structured variables. If you are studying recursion before reading Chapter 10 on structured data types, then cover only the first set of examples and leave the rest until you have completed Chapters 10 through 12.

Rather than examine one large Case Study at the end of the chapter, we solve several small problems using recursion throughout the chapter.

1992
The first 64-bit chip is introduced by DEC

1993
Apple Computer announces the Newton, a personal digital assistant (PDA) with handwriting recognition capabilities

1993
Intel introduces the Pentium Chip

1994
Jim Clark and Marc Andreesen create Netscape Communications (their first browser), contributing to a growing population of web surfers

1995
Toy Story is produced from the Pixar division of Disney and is the first full-length computer-generated feature film. It receives rave reviews

1995
Sun Microsystems introduces the object-oriented programming language Java™

JAVA

13.1 What Is Recursion?

You may have seen a set of gaily painted Russian dolls that fit inside one another. Inside the first doll is a smaller doll, inside of which is an even smaller doll, inside of which is yet a smaller doll, and so on. A recursive algorithm is like such a set of Russian dolls. It reproduces itself with smaller and smaller examples of itself until a solution is found—that is, until no more dolls remain. The recursive algorithm is implemented by using a method that makes recursive calls to itself.

Power Function Definition

Let's examine a method that calculates the result of raising an integer to a positive power. If x is an integer and n is a positive integer, then

$$x^n = \underbrace{x * x * x * x * \cdots * x}_{n \text{ times}}$$

We could also write this formula as

$$x^n = x * \underbrace{(x * x * x * \cdots * x)}_{n - 1 \text{ times}}$$

or even as

$$x^n = x * x * \underbrace{(x * x * \cdots * x)}_{n - 2 \text{ times}}$$

In fact, we can write the formula most concisely as

$$x^n = x * x^{n-1}$$

This definition of x^n is a classic recursive definition—that is, a definition given in terms of a smaller version of itself.

x^n is defined in terms of multiplying x times x^{n-1}. How is x^{n-1} defined? Why, as $x * x^{n-2}$, of course! And x^{n-2} is $x * x^{n-3}$; x^{n-3} is $x * x^{n-4}$; and so on. In this example, "in terms of smaller versions of itself" means that the exponent is decremented each time.

When does the process stop? When we reach a case for which we know the answer without resorting to a recursive definition. In this example, it is the case

Recursive definition A definition in which something is defined in terms of smaller versions of itself

where n equals 1: x^1 is x. The case (or cases) for which an answer is explicitly known is called the base case. The case for which the solution is expressed in terms of a smaller version of itself is called the recursive or general case. A recursive algorithm expresses the solution in terms of a call to itself, a recursive call. A recursive algorithm must terminate; that is, it must have a base case.

■ Power Function Implementation

We use an *if* statement to determine which case is being executed. The following method implements the power function with the general case and the base case marked in the comments.

Base case   The case for which the solution can be stated non-recursively

General case   The case for which the solution is expressed in terms of a smaller version of itself; also known as the *recursive case*

Recursive algorithm   A solution that is expressed in terms of (1) smaller instances of itself and (2) a base case

```
public static int power(int x, int n)
// Returns x raised to the power n
// Assumption:  x is a valid integer and n is greater than 0
// Note: Large exponents may result in integer overflow
{
  if (n == 1)
    return x;                 // Base case
  else
    return x * power(x, n - 1); // Recursive call
}
```

We can think of each recursive call to power as creating a completely new copy of the method, each having its own copies of the parameters x and n. The value of x remains the same for each version of power, but the value of n decreases by 1 for each call until it becomes 1.

Let's trace the execution of this recursive method, with the following initial call:

```
xToN = power(2, 3);
```

We will use a new format to trace recursive routines: We number the calls and then discuss what is happening in paragraph form. This trace is also summarized in Figure 13.1, where each box represents a call to the power method. The values for the parameters for that call are shown in each box. Refer to the figure while you work through the trace in paragraph form.

Call 1: power is called with the number equal to 2 and the exponent equal to 3. Within power, the parameters x and n are initialized to 2 and 3, respectively. Because n is not equal to 1, power is called recursively with x and n − 1 as arguments. Execution of Call 1 pauses until an answer is sent back from this recursive call.

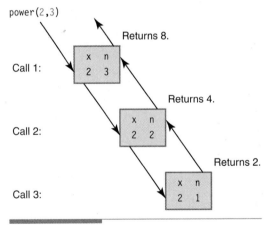

Figure 13.1 Execution of power(2, 3)

Call 2: x is equal to 2 and n is equal to 2. Because n is not equal to 1, the method power is called again, this time with x and n − 1 as arguments. Execution of Call 2 pauses until an answer is sent back from this recursive call.

Call 3: x is equal to 2 and n is equal to 1. Because n equals 1, the value of x is returned. This call to the method has finished executing, and the method return value (which is 2) is passed back to the place in the statement from which the call was made in Call 2.

Call 2: This call to the method can now complete the statement that contained the recursive call because the recursive call has returned. Call 3's return value (which is 2) is multiplied by x. This call to the method has finished executing, and the method return value (which is 4) is passed back to the place in the statement from which the call was made in Call 1.

Call 1: This call to the method can now complete the statement that contained the recursive call because the recursive call has returned. Call 2's return value (which is 4) is multiplied by x. This call to the method has finished executing, and the method return value (which is 8) is passed back to the place in the statement from which the call was made. Because the first call (the nonrecursive call) has now completed, 8 is the final value of the method power.

What happens if no base case exists? We have **infinite recursion**, the recursive equivalent of an infinite loop. For example, if the condition

Infinite recursion The situation in which a method calls itself over and over endlessly

```
if (n == 1)
```

were omitted, power would be called over and over again forever. Infinite recursion also occurs if we call power with n less than or equal to 0.

In actuality, recursive calls can't go on forever. Here's why. When we call a method, either recursively or nonrecursively, the computer system creates temporary storage for the parameters and the method's (automatic) local variables. This temporary storage is a region of memory called the *run-time stack*. When the method returns, its parameters and local variables are released from the run-time stack. With infinite recursion, the recursive method calls never return. Each time the method calls itself, a little more of the run-time stack is used to store the new copies of the variables. Eventually, the memory space on the stack runs out. At that point, the program crashes with an error message such as "RUN-TIME STACK OVERFLOW" (or the application may simply freeze).

13.2 More Examples with Simple Variables

For some people, thinking recursively is intuitive; for others, it is a mysterious process verging on the supernatural. The objective of the rest of this chapter is to demystify the recursive process by working through a collection of examples.

Calculating the Factorial Function

Let's look at another example: calculating a factorial. The factorial of a number n (written $n!$) is n multiplied by $n - 1, n - 2, n - 3$, and so on. Another way of expressing a factorial is

$$n! = n * (n - 1)!$$

This expression looks like a recursive definition. The term $(n - 1)!$ is a smaller instance of $n!$—that is, it takes one less multiplication to calculate $(n - 1)!$ than it does to calculate $n!$

If we can find a base case, we can write a recursive algorithm. Fortunately, we don't have to look too far: 0! is defined in mathematics to be 1.

```
factorial(number)
if number is 0
   return 1
else
   return number * factorial(number − 1)
```

We can code this algorithm directly as follows:

```
public static int factorial(int number)
// Returns the factorial of number
// Assumption: number is greater than or equal to 0
// Note: Large values of number may cause integer overflow
{
  if (number == 0)
    return 1;                            // Base case
  else
    return number * factorial(number − 1); // General case
}
```

Let's trace this method with an original number of 4.

Call 1: number is 4. Because number is not 0, the else branch is taken. The *return* statement cannot be completed until the recursive call to factorial with number − 1 as the argument has been completed.

Call 2: number is 3. Because number is not 0, the else branch is taken. The *return* statement cannot be completed until the recursive call to factorial with number − 1 as the argument has been completed.

Call 3: number is 2. Because number is not 0, the else branch is taken. The *return* statement cannot be completed until the recursive call to factorial with number − 1 as the argument has been completed.

Call 4: number is 1. Because number is not 0, the else branch is taken. The *return* statement cannot be completed until the recursive call to factorial with number − 1 as the argument has been completed.

Call 5: number is 0. Because number equals 0, this call to the method returns, sending back 1 as the result.

Call 4: The *return* statement in this copy can now be completed. The value to be returned is number (which is 1) times 1. This call to the method returns, sending back 1 as the result.

Call 3: The *return* statement in this copy can now be completed. The value to be returned is number (which is 2) times 1. This call to the method returns, sending back 2 as the result.

Call 2: The *return* statement in this copy can now be completed. The value to be returned is number (which is 3) times 2. This call to the method returns, sending back 6 as the result.

Call 1: The *return* statement in this copy can now be completed. The value to be returned is number (which is 4) times 6. This call to the method returns, sending back 24 as the result.

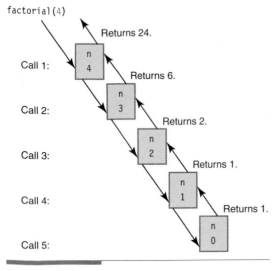

factorial(4)

Call 1: n 4   Returns 24.

Call 2: n 3   Returns 6.

Call 3: n 2   Returns 2.

Call 4: n 1   Returns 1.

Call 5: n 0   Returns 1.

Figure 13.2   Execution of factorial(4)

Because this is the last of the calls to factorial, the recursive process ends. The value 24 is returned as the final value of the call to factorial with an argument of 4.

Figure 13.2 summarizes the execution of the factorial method with an argument of 4.

Let's organize what we have done in the preceding examples into an outline for writing recursive algorithms:

1. Understand the problem. (We threw this task in for good measure; it is always the first step.)
2. Determine the base case(s). A base case is one to which you know the answer. It does not involve any further recursion.
3. Determine the recursive case(s). A recursive case is one in which you can express the solution in terms of a smaller version of itself.

We have used the factorial and power algorithms to demonstrate recursion because they are easy to visualize. In practice, we would never want to calculate either of these values using the recursive solution. That is, in both cases, the iterative solutions are simpler and much more efficient because starting a new iteration of a loop is a faster operation than calling a method. Let's compare the code for the iterative and recursive versions of the factorial problem.

Iterative Solution

```
public static int factorial(int number)
{
   int factor;
   int count;

   factor = 1;
   for (count = 2; count <= number; count++)
      factor = factor * count;
   return factor;
}
```

Recursive Solution

```
public static int factorial(int number )
{


   if (number == 0)
      return 1;
   else
      return number * factorial(number − 1);
}
```

The iterative version has two local variables, whereas the recursive version has none. A recursive method usually includes fewer local variables than does an iterative method. Also, the iterative version always has a loop, whereas the recursive version always has a selection statement—either an *if* or a *switch*. A branching structure serves as the main control structure in a recursive method; a looping structure is the main control structure in an iterative method.

■ Converting Decimal Integers to Binary Numbers

You enter integer data in decimal form, and the computer converts these decimal numbers to binary form for use within a program. Do you know how decimal integers are converted to binary numbers? The algorithm for this conversion follows:

1. Take the decimal number and divide it by 2.
2. Make the remainder the rightmost digit in the answer.
3. Replace the original dividend with the quotient.
4. Repeat, placing each new remainder to the left of the previous one.
5. Stop when the quotient is 0.

This algorithm is clearly meant for a calculator and paper and pencil. Certainly, we cannot implement expressions such as "to the left of" in Java as yet. Let's do an example—convert 42 from base-10 to base-2—to get a feel for the algorithm before we try to write a computer solution. Remember, the quotient in one step becomes the dividend in the next step.

Step 1

$$
\begin{array}{r}
21 \quad \leftarrow \text{Quotient} \\
2\overline{)42} \\
\underline{4} \\
2 \\
\underline{2} \\
0 \quad \leftarrow \text{Remainder}
\end{array}
$$

Step 2

$$
\begin{array}{r}
10 \quad \leftarrow \text{Quotient} \\
2\overline{)21} \\
\underline{2} \\
1 \\
\underline{0} \\
1 \quad \leftarrow \text{Remainder}
\end{array}
$$

Step 3

$$
\begin{array}{r}
5 \quad \leftarrow \text{Quotient} \\
2\overline{)10} \\
\underline{10} \\
0 \quad \leftarrow \text{Remainder}
\end{array}
$$

Step 4

$$
\begin{array}{r}
2 \quad \leftarrow \text{Quotient} \\
2\overline{)5} \\
\underline{4} \\
1 \quad \leftarrow \text{Remainder}
\end{array}
$$

Step 5

$$
\begin{array}{r}
1 \quad \leftarrow \text{Quotient} \\
2\overline{)2} \\
\underline{2} \\
0 \quad \leftarrow \text{Remainder}
\end{array}
$$

Step 6

$$
\begin{array}{r}
0 \quad \leftarrow \text{Quotient} \\
2\overline{)1} \\
\underline{0} \\
1 \quad \leftarrow \text{Remainder}
\end{array}
$$

The answer is the sequence of remainders from last to first. Therefore, the decimal number 42 is 101010 in binary.

It looks as though we can implement the solution to the problem with a straightforward iterative algorithm. Each remainder is obtained from the remainder operation (% in Java), and each quotient is the result of the / operation.

```
convert(number)

while number > 0
  Set remainder to number % 2
  Print remainder
  Set number to number / 2
```

Let's do a walk-through to test this algorithm.

Number	Remainder
42	0
21	1
10	0
5	1
2	0
1	1

(remainder from step	1	2	3	4	5	6)
Answer:	0	1	0	1	0	1

The answer is backwards! An iterative solution (using only simple variables) doesn't work. We need to print the last remainder first. The first remainder should be printed only after the rest of the remainders have been calculated and printed.

In our example, we should print 42 % 2 after (42 / 2) % 2 has been printed. This, in turn, means that we should print (42 / 2) % 2 after ((42 / 2) / 2) % 2 has been printed. Now our solution begins to look like a recursive definition. We can summarize by saying that, for any given number, we should print number % 2 after (number / 2) % 2 has been printed.

What is the base case? We know the answer when number is zero: We have finished and have nothing left to do. What is the recursive case? Convert number divided by 2. When this conversion is complete, print the remainder of number divided by 2 (number % 2). This solution leads to the following algorithm:

```
convert (number)

if number > 0
  convert(number / 2)
  Print number % 2
```

If number is 0, we have called convert as many times as necessary and can begin printing the answer. The base case occurs when we do nothing. The recursive solution to this problem is encoded in the following convert method.

```
public static void convert(int number)
// Converts number to binary and prints it
// Assumption:  number >= 0
{
  if (number > 0)
  {
    convert(number / 2);    // Recursive call
    outFile.print(number % 2);
  }
  // Empty else clause is the base case
}
```

Let's do a code walk-through of convert(10). We pick up our original example at step 3, where the dividend is 10.

Call 1: convert is called with an argument of 10. Because number is not equal to 0, the *then* clause is executed. Execution pauses until the recursive call to convert with an argument of (number / 2) has completed.

Call 2: number is 5. Because number is not equal to 0, execution of this call pauses until the recursive call with an argument of (number / 2) has completed.

Call 3: number is 2. Because number is not equal to 0, execution of this call pauses until the recursive call with an argument of (number / 2) has completed.

Call 4: number is 1. Because number is not equal to 0, execution of this call pauses until the recursive call with an argument of (number / 2) has completed.

Call 5: number is 0. Execution of this call to convert is complete. Control returns to the preceding call.

Call 4: Execution of this call resumes with the statement following the recursive call to convert. The value of number % 2 (which is 1) is printed. Execution of this call is complete.

Call 3: Execution of this call resumes with the statement following the recursive call to convert. The value of number % 2 (which is 0) is printed. Execution of this call is complete.

Call 2: Execution of this call resumes with the statement following the recursive call to convert. The value of number % 2 (which is 1) is printed. Execution of this call is complete.

Call 1: Execution of this call resumes with the statement following the recursive call to convert. The value of number % 2 (which is 0) is printed. Execution of this call is complete. Because this is the nonrecursive call, execution resumes with the statement immediately following the original call.

Figure 13.3 shows the execution of the convert method with the values of the parameters.

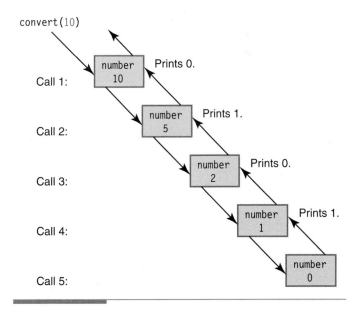

Figure 13.3   Execution of convert(10)

Next, we examine a more complicated problem—one in which the recursive solution is not immediately apparent.

■ Towers of Hanoi

One of your first toys may have been a board with three pegs holding colored circles of different diameters. If so, you probably spent countless hours moving the circles from one peg to another. If we put some constraints on how the circles or discs can be moved, we have an adult game called the Towers of Hanoi.

When the game begins, all the circles are on the first peg in order by size, with the smallest on the top. The object of the game is to move the circles, one at a time, to the third peg. The catch is that a circle cannot be placed on top of one that is smaller in diameter. We can use the middle peg as an auxiliary peg, but it must be empty at the beginning and end of the game.

To get a feel for how this problem might be resolved, let's look at some sketches of what the configuration must be at certain points if a solution is possible. We use four circles or discs. The beginning configuration is

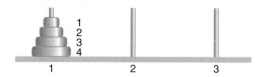

To move the largest circle (circle 4) to peg 3, we must move the three smaller circles to peg 2. Then we can move circle 4 into its final place:

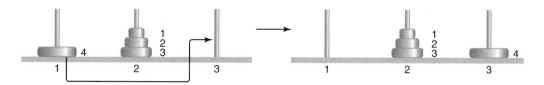

Let's assume we can do this. Now, to move the next largest circle (circle 3) into place, we must move the two circles on top of it onto an auxiliary peg (peg 1, in this case):

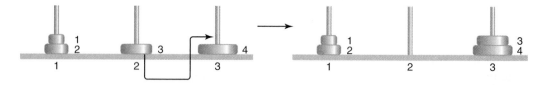

To get circle 2 into place, we must move circle 1 to another peg, freeing circle 2 to be moved to its place on peg 3:

The last circle (circle 1) can now be moved into its final place, and we are finished:

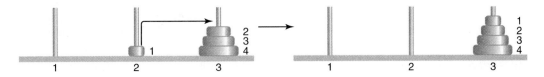

Get n Circles Moved from Peg 1 to Peg 3

```
Get n - 1 circles moved from peg 1 to peg 2
Move nth circle from peg 1 to peg 3
Get n - 1 circles moved from peg 2 to peg 3
```

This algorithm certainly sounds simple; surely, there must be more to it! But this solution really is all there is.

Let's write a recursive method that implements this algorithm. We can't actually move discs, of course, but we can print out a message to do so. Notice that the beginning peg, the ending peg, and the auxiliary peg keep changing during the algorithm. To make the algorithm easier to follow, we call the pegs beginPeg, endPeg, and auxPeg. These three pegs, along with the number of circles on the beginning peg, are the parameters of the method.

We have the recursive (general) case, but what about a base case? How do we know when to stop the recursive process? The clue lies in the expression "Get n circles moved." If we don't have any circles to move, we don't have anything to do. We are finished with that stage. Therefore, when the number of circles equals 0, we do nothing (that is, we simply return).

```
public static void doTowers(
    int circleCount,    // Number of circles to move
    int beginPeg,       // Peg containing circles to move
    int auxPeg,         // Peg holding circles temporarily
    int endPeg     )    // Peg receiving circles being moved
// Moves are written on file outFile
{
  if (circleCount > 0)
  {
    // Move n - 1 circles from beginning peg to auxiliary peg
```

```
    doTowers(circleCount - 1, beginPeg, endPeg, auxPeg);
    outFile.println("Move circle from peg " + beginPeg
            + " to peg " + endPeg);
    // Move n - 1 circles from auxiliary peg to ending peg
    doTowers(circleCount - 1, auxPeg, beginPeg, endPeg);
  }
}
```

It's difficult to believe that such a simple algorithm actually works, but we can prove it. We enclose the method within a driver class that invokes the doTowers method. Output statements have been added so that we can see the values of the arguments with each recursive call. Because two recursive calls are made within the method, we have indicated which recursive statement issued the call.

```java
// Driver class for doTowers method
// Reads the number of circles from a file and calls doTowers
import java.io.*;              // File types

public class Towers
{
  PrintWriter outFile;         // Output data file
  BufferedReader inFile;       // Input data file
  public static void main(String[] args) throws IOException
  {
    // Prepare files
    inFile = new BufferedReader(new InputStreamReader(System.in));
    outFile = new PrintWriter(new FileWriter("recursion.out "));
    int circleCount;           // Number of circles on starting peg
    System.out.println("Input the number of circles: ");
    circleCount = Integer.parseInt(inFile.readLine());
    outFile.println("Input number of circles: " + circleCount);
    outFile.println("OUTPUT WITH " + circleCount + " CIRCLES");
    outFile.print("From original: ");
    doTowers(circleCount, 1, 2, 3);
    infile.close();
    outFile.close();
  }
```

```
public static void doTowers(
    int circleCount,     // Number of circles to move
    int beginPeg,        // Peg containing circles to move
    int auxPeg,          // Peg holding circles temporarily
    int endPeg     )     // Peg receiving circles being moved
// Moves are written on file outFile.
// This recursive method moves circleCount circles from beginPeg
// to endPeg. All but one of the circles are moved from beginPeg
// to auxPeg, then the last circle is moved from beginPeg to
// endPeg, and then the circles are moved from auxPeg to endPeg.
// The subgoals of moving circles to and from auxPeg involve recursion.
{
    outFile.println("#circles: " + circleCount + " Begin: " +
      beginPeg + " Auxil: " + auxPeg + " End: " + endPeg);
    if (circleCount > 0)
    {
        // Move n - 1 circles from beginning peg to auxiliary peg
        outFile.print("From first:    ");
        doTowers(circleCount-1, beginPeg, endPeg, auxPeg);

        outFile.println("Move circle " +  circleCount + " from peg "
          + beginPeg + " to peg " + endPeg);

        // Move n - 1 circles from auxiliary peg to ending peg
        outFile.print("From second:    ");
        doTowers(circleCount - 1, auxPeg, beginPeg, endPeg);
    }
  }
}
```

The output from a run with three circles follows. "Original" means that the parameters listed beside it are from the nonrecursive call, which is the first call to doTowers. "From first" means that the parameters listed are for a call issued from the first recursive statement. "From second" means that the parameters listed are for a call issued from the second recursive statement. Notice that a call cannot be issued from the second recursive statement until the preceding call from the first recursive statement has completed its execution.

```
 ● ● ●           recursion.out
Input number of circles: 3
OUTPUT WITH 3 CIRCLES
From original: #circles: 3 Begin: 1 Auxil: 2 End: 3
From first:    #circles: 2 Begin: 1 Auxil: 3 End: 2
From first:    #circles: 1 Begin: 1 Auxil: 2 End: 3
From first:    #circles: 0 Begin: 1 Auxil: 3 End: 2
Move circle 1 from peg 1 to peg 3
From second:   #circles: 0 Begin: 2 Auxil: 1 End: 3
Move circle 2 from peg 1 to peg 2
From second:   #circles: 1 Begin: 3 Auxil: 1 End: 2
From first:    #circles: 0 Begin: 3 Auxil: 2 End: 1
Move circle 1 from peg 3 to peg 2
From second:   #circles: 0 Begin: 1 Auxil: 3 End: 2
Move circle 3 from peg 1 to peg 3
From second:   #circles: 2 Begin: 2 Auxil: 1 End: 3
From first:    #circles: 1 Begin: 2 Auxil: 3 End: 1
From first:    #circles: 0 Begin: 2 Auxil: 1 End: 3
Move circle 1 from peg 2 to peg 1
From second:   #circles: 0 Begin: 3 Auxil: 2 End: 1
Move circle 2 from peg 2 to peg 3
From second:   #circles: 1 Begin: 1 Auxil: 2 End: 3
From first:    #circles: 0 Begin: 1 Auxil: 3 End: 2
Move circle 1 from peg 1 to peg 3
From second:   #circles: 0 Begin: 2 Auxil: 1 End: 3
```

13.3 Recursive Algorithms with Structured Variables

In our definition of a recursive algorithm, we identified two cases: the recursive (or general) case and the base case for which an answer can be expressed nonrecursively. In the general case for all our algorithms so far, we expressed one argument in terms of a smaller value each time. When we use structured variables, however, we often state the recursive case in terms of a smaller structure rather than a smaller value; the base case occurs when there are no values left to process in the structure.

Printing the Values in an Array

Let's write a recursive algorithm for printing the contents of a one-dimensional array of n elements to show what we mean. What is the base case? We have no elements left to print. What is the general case? We print the item in the first position in the array, and print the rest of the items.

```
Print Array

if more elements
   Print the item in the first position
   Print the rest of the array
```

The recursive case is to print the values in an array that is one element "smaller"; that is, the size of the array decreases by 1 with each recursive call. The base case occurs when the size of the array becomes 0—that is, when we have no more elements left to print.

Our arguments must include the index of the first element (the one to be printed). How do we know when no more elements are left to print (that is, when the size of the array to be printed is 0)? We have printed the last element in the array when the index of the next element to be printed is beyond the index of the last element in the array. Therefore, we must pass the index of the last array element as an argument. We call the indexes `first` and `last`. When `first` is greater than `last`, we are finished. The name of the array is `data`.

```
public static void print(
                        int[] data,   // Array to be printed
                        int first,    // Index of first element
                        int last  )   // Index of last element
// Prints an array
{
  if (first <= last)
  {                              // Recursive case
    outFile.println(data[first]+ " ");
    printArray(data, first + 1, last);
  }
  // Empty else clause is the base case
}
```

Here is a code walk-through of the method call

```
print(data, 0, 4);
```

using the pictured array.

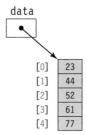

data

Call 1: `first` is 0 and `last` is 4. Because `first` is less than `last`, the value in `data[first]` (which is 23) is printed. Execution of this call pauses while the array from `first` + 1 through `last` is printed.

Call 2: `first` is 1 and `last` is 4. Because `first` is less than `last`, the value in `data[first]` (which is 44) is printed. Execution of this call pauses while the array from `first` + 1 through `last` is printed.

Call 3: `first` is 2 and `last` is 4. Because `first` is less than `last`, the value in `data[first]` (which is 52) is printed. Execution of this call pauses while the array from `first` + 1 through `last` is printed.

Call 4: `first` is 3 and `last` is 4. Because `first` is less than `last`, the value in `data[first]` (which is 61) is printed. Execution of this call pauses while the array from `first` + 1 through `last` is printed.

Call 5: `first` is 4 and `last` is 4. Because `first` is equal to `last`, the value in `data[first]` (which is 77) is printed. Execution of this call pauses while the array from `first` + 1 through `last` is printed.

Tail recursion A recursive algorithm in which no statements execute after the return from the recursive call

Call 6: first is 5 and last is 4. Because first is greater than last, the execution of this call is complete. Control returns to the preceding call.

Call 5: Execution of this call is complete. Control returns to the preceding call.

Calls 4, 3, 2, and 1: Each execution is completed in turn, and control returns to the preceding call.

Notice that once the deepest call (the call with the highest number) was reached, each of the calls before it returned without doing anything. When no statements execute after the return from the recursive call to the method, the recursion is known as tail recursion. Tail recursion often indicates that we could solve the problem more easily using iteration. We used a recursive solution in the array example because it made the recursive process easy to visualize; in practice, an array should be printed iteratively.

Figure 13.4 shows the execution of the print method with the values of the parameters for each call. Notice that the array becomes smaller with each recursive call (data[first]

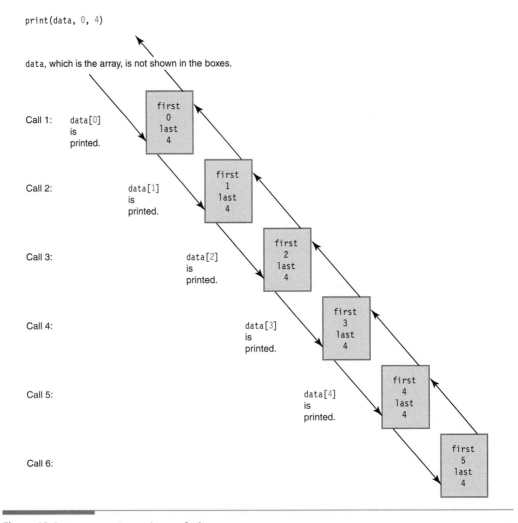

Figure 13.4 Execution of print(data, 0, 4)

through data[last]). If we want to print the array elements in reverse order recursively, we simply swap the two statements within the *if* statement.

Binary Search

Do you remember the binary search in Chapter 11? Here is the description of the algorithm: "The algorithm divides the list in half (divides by 2—that's why it's called a *binary* search) and decides which half to look in next. Division of the selected portion of the list is repeated until the item is found or it is determined that the item is not in the list." There is something inherently recursive about this description.

Although the method that we wrote in Chapter 11 was iterative, it really is a *recursive algorithm*. The solution is expressed in terms of smaller versions of the original problem: If the answer isn't found in the middle position, perform a binary search (a recursive call) to search the appropriate half of the list (a smaller problem). In the iterative version, we kept track of the bounds of the current search area with two local variables, first and last. In the recursive version, we call the method with these two values as arguments. We must call the recursive binary search method from the isThere method of the SortedList class rather than writing it as part of that method.

```
private boolean binIsThere(int first, int last, int item)
// Returns true if item is in the list
{
  if (first > last)      // Base case 1
    return false;
  else
  {
    int midPoint;
    midPoint = (first + last) / 2;
    if (item < listItems[midPoint])
      return binIsThere(first, midPoint-1, item);
    else if (item == listItems[midPoint])
      return true;      // Base case 2
    else
      return binIsThere(midPoint+1, last, item);
  }
}

public boolean isThere(int item)
// Returns true if item is in the list
{
  return binIsThere(0, numItems-1, item);
}
```

13.4 Recursion or Iteration?

Recursion and iteration are alternative ways of expressing repetition in an algorithm. When iterative control structures are used, processes are made to repeat by embedding code in a looping structure such as a *while*, *for*, or *do*. In recursion, a process is made to repeat by having a method call itself. A selection statement controls the repeated calls.

Which is better to use—recursion or iteration? This question has no simple answer. The choice usually depends on two issues: efficiency and the nature of the problem at hand.

Historically, the quest for efficiency, in terms of both execution speed and memory usage, has favored iteration over recursion. Each time a recursive call is made, the system must allocate stack space for all parameters and local variables. The overhead involved in any method call is time-consuming. On early, slow computers with limited memory capacity, recursive algorithms were visibly—sometimes painfully—slower than the iterative versions. On modern, fast computers, however, the overhead associated with recursion is often so small that the increase in computation time is almost unnoticeable to the user. Except in cases where efficiency is absolutely critical, then, the choice between recursion and iteration more often depends on the second issue—the nature of the problem at hand.

Consider the factorial and power algorithms discussed earlier in the chapter. In both cases, iterative solutions were obvious and easy to devise. We imposed recursive solutions on these problems merely to demonstrate how recursion works. As a rule of thumb, if an iterative solution is more obvious or easier to understand, use it; it is probably more efficient. For other problems, the recursive solution is more obvious or easier to devise, such as the Towers of Hanoi problem. (It turns out that the Towers of Hanoi problem is surprisingly difficult to solve using iteration.) Computer science students should be aware of the power of recursion. If the definition of a problem is inherently recursive, then a recursive solution should certainly be considered.

13.5 Testing and Debugging

Recursion is a powerful technique when used correctly. Improperly used, it can result in errors that are difficult to diagnose. The best way to debug a recursive algorithm is to construct it correctly in the first place. To be realistic, however, we give a few hints about where to look if an error crops up.

Testing and Debugging Hints

1. Be sure a base case exists. If there is no base case, the algorithm will continue to issue recursive calls until all memory has been used. Each time the method is called, either recursively or nonrecursively, stack space is allocated for the parameters and local variables. If no base case is available to end the recursive calls, the run-time stack eventually overflows. An error message such as "STACK OVERFLOW ERROR" indicates that the base case is missing.

2. Be sure you have not used a *while* structure. The basic structure in a recursive algorithm is the *if* statement. At least two cases must be provided: the recursive case and the base case. If the base case does nothing, the *else* clause is omitted. The selection structure, however, must be present. If a *while*

statement is used in a recursive algorithm, it usually should not contain a recursive call.

3. Use your system's debugger program (or use debug output statements) to trace a series of recursive calls. Inspecting the values of parameters and local variables often helps to locate errors in a recursive algorithm.

Summary

A recursive algorithm is expressed in terms of a smaller instance of itself. It must include a recursive (or general) case, for which the algorithm is expressed in terms of itself, and a base case, for which the algorithm is expressed in nonrecursive terms.

In many recursive problems, the smaller instance refers to a numeric argument that is reduced with each call. In other problems, the smaller instance refers to the size of the data structure being manipulated. In the base case, the size of the problem (value or structure) reaches a point for which an explicit answer is known.

In the conversion of decimal integers to binary numbers, the size of the problem is the number to be converted. When it is 0, the conversion is finished. In the Towers of Hanoi game, the size of the problem is the number of discs to be moved. When only one is left on the beginning peg, it can be moved to its final destination.

In the example of printing an array using recursion, the size of the problem is the size of the array being printed. When the array size reaches 1, the solution is known. In the binary search algorithm, the size of the problem is the size of the search area. There are two base cases in this algorithm: (1) when the search item is found and (2) when the search area becomes empty and you know that the search value is not there.

Quick Check

1. What is the essential ingredient in a recursive definition? (pp. 636–637)
2. What distinguishes the base case from the recursive case in a recursive algorithm? (pp. 636–637)
3. What is the size of the problem in the recursive power algorithm? (pp. 636–638)
4. What is the base case in the Towers of Hanoi algorithm? (pp. 644–648)

Learning Portfolio

5. In working with simple variables, the recursive case is often stated in terms of a smaller value. What is typical of the recursive case in working with structured variables? (pp. 648–651)

6. Which control structures are used to implement recursion? (pp. 651–652)

7. Which control structures are used to implement iteration? (pp. 651–652)

8. In the binary search algorithm, what is the base case? (p. 651)

9. Which of the algorithms presented in this chapter are better implemented using iteration? (pp. 651–652)

Answers

1. The essential ingredient in a recursive definition is the repetition of the problem in terms of a smaller version of itself. **2.** The base case is the simplest case—that is, the case for which the solution can be stated nonrecursively. **3.** The size of the problem is the power to which the number is taken. It is decreased by one in each call. **4.** There are no more circles left to move. **5.** It is often stated in terms of a smaller structure. **6.** Selection **7.** Looping **8.** The search area is empty or the item is found. **9.** Factorial, power, printing values in an array

Exam Preparation Exercises

1. Recursion is an example of
   a. Selection
   b. A data structure
   c. Repetition
   d. Data-flow programming

2. A void method can be recursive, but a value-returning method cannot. (True or False?)

3. When a method is called recursively, the arguments and local variables of the calling version are saved until its execution resumes. (True or False?)

4. Given the recursive formula $F(N) = -F(N - 2)$, with a base case of $F(0) = 1$, what are the values of $F(4)$, $F(6)$, and $F(5)$? (If any of the values are undefined, say so.)

5. What algorithm error(s) leads to infinite recursion?

6. What control structure appears most commonly in a recursive method?

7. If you develop a recursive algorithm that employs tail recursion, what should you consider?

8. A recursive algorithm depends on making something smaller. When the algorithm works on a data structure, what may become smaller?
   a. Distance from a position in the structure
   b. The data structure
   c. The number of variables in the recursive method

9. What is the name of the memory area used by the computer system to store a method's parameters and local variables?

10. Given the following input:

```
15
23
21
19
```

What is the output of the following method?

```java
public void printNums()
{
  int n;
  String line;
  line = inFile.readLine();
  if (line != null)                 // If not EOF ...
  {
    n = Integer.parseInt(line);
    outFile.print(n + " ");
    printNums();
    outFile.print(n + " ");
  }
}
```

Programming Warm-Up Exercises

1. Write a Java value-returning method that implements the recursive formula $f(n) = f(n - 1) + f(n - 2)$ with base cases of $f(0) = 1$ and $f(1) = 1$.

2. Add whatever is necessary to fix the following method so that func(3) equals 10.

```java
public static int func(int n)
{
  return func(n - 1) + 3;
}
```

3. Rewrite the following printSquares method using recursion.

```java
public static void printSquares()
{
  int count;
  for (count = 1; count <= 10; count++)
    outFile.println(count + " " + count * count);
}
```

4. Modify the `factorial` method discussed in this chapter to print its parameter and returned value indented two spaces for each level of call to the method. The call `factorial(3)` should produce the following output on `System.out`:

```
3
  2
    1
      0
      1
    1
  2
6
```

5. Write a recursive value-returning method that sums the integers from 1 through n.

6. Rewrite the following method so that it is recursive.

```java
public static void printSqRoots(int n)
{
    int i;
    for (i = n; i > 0; i--)
        outFile.println(i + " " + Math.sqrt((double)i));
}
```

7. The `print` method discussed in this chapter prints the contents of an array from first element to last. Write a recursive method that prints from last element to first.

8. Write an `isThere` method that takes an array as a parameter and performs a recursive linear search.

9. Rewrite the `power` method using another base case.

10. Rewrite the `power` method using the following formula.

if n == 0, return 1

if n == 1, return x

if n is even, return power(x*x, n/2)

else return x*power(x, n–1)

Programming Problems

1. Use recursion to solve the following problem.

   A *palindrome* is a string of characters that reads the same forward and backward. Write a program that reads in strings of characters and determines if each string is a palindrome. Each string appears on a separate input line. Echo-print each string, followed by "Is a palindrome" if the string is a palindrome or "Is not a palindrome" if the string is not a palindrome. For example, given the input string

   `Able was I, ere I saw Elba.`
   the program should print "Is a palindrome." In determining whether a string is a palindrome, consider uppercase and lowercase letters to be the same and ignore punctuation characters.

2. Write a program to place eight queens on a chessboard in such a way that no queen attacks any other queen. This classic problem lends itself well to a recursive solution. Represent the chessboard as an 8 × 8 Boolean array. If a square is occupied by a queen, the value is `true`; otherwise, the value is `false`. The status of the chessboard when all eight queens have been placed is the solution.

3. A maze is to be represented by a 10 × 10 array of characters: P (for path), H (for hedge), or E (for Exit). The maze has one exit. Write a program to determine if it is possible to exit the maze from a given starting point. You may move vertically or horizontally in any direction to a square that contains P; you may not move to a square that contains H. If you move into a square that contains E, you have exited.

   The input data consists of two parts: the maze and a series of starting points. The maze is entered as 10 lines of 10 characters (P, H, and E). Each succeeding line contains a pair of integers that represents a starting point (that is, row and column numbers). Continue processing entry points until end-of-file occurs.

Applets

goals

Knowledge Goals
- To understand the differing roles of applications and applets
- To understand how a browser operates
- To understand the role of HTML

Skill Goals
To be able to:
- Write an applet to perform a simple task
- Embed Bytecode within a Web page
- Construct a simple HTML Web page that executes an applet

timeline

1995
E-commerce sites Ebay and Amazon.com open, forecasting a revolution in the way goods are bought and sold

1995
Microsoft releases the Windows 95 operating system and sells 600,000 units in the first month

1997
In a legendary match, IBM's Deep Blue computer defeats Garry Kasparov, the world champion chess player

1999
Membership to the Internet Service Provider AOL exceeds 20 million, signifying an explosion of personal computer use for the Internet

1999
Shawn Fanning, while at Northeastern University, founds Napster. The easy trading of music in MP3 format raises copyright issues

2000
The Y2K crisis costs millions to fix, yet the new millennium was ushered in with few glitches

introduction

So far in this text, we have written all of our programs as Java applications. That is, we have written a class that contains a method called `main` that acts as the driver for whatever set of responsibilities our objects support. Java provides a second type of program called an *applet*. As its name implies, it is intended to be a small application that doesn't stand on its own but rather is run in a Web browser.

From an educational viewpoint, we have presented only applications to this point because they enable us to use all of Java's features. They also do not require the use of a browser or a separate program (called an applet viewer) to run compiled code. Now that you are comfortable with Java, we end this book with a chapter on applets. We describe what they are, how to write them, and how to run them.

2000
The dot-com business model proves faulty, start-up companies fail, tech stock plummets, and the dot-com bubble bursts

2000
Judge rules that Microsoft is a monopoly and is in violation of anti-trust laws. Microsoft appeals.

2000
The Human Genome Project completes a draft of the DNA sequence for humans

2001
Dell Computer Corporation becomes the leading global maker of computer systems, targeting both PC owners and businesses

2002
Hitachi's super-computer, Earth Simulator, at 40 trillion operations per second, performs 5-times faster than the former leading supercomputer, IBM's ASCI White

2002
Microsoft releases the .NET development environment partially in response to the success of Java

14.1 What Is an Applet?

Applets are a kind of mini-application designed to be distributed along with Web pages and run under a browser or applet viewer. They are used as elements of Web pages. Most Web browsers include a special JVM that can execute the Bytecode version of an applet. When the browser encounters a link to an applet Bytecode file, it copies the file into memory and calls its JVM to execute the Bytecode.

The browser's ability to execute applets enables us to create Web pages that are as sophisticated as almost any program we can write in Java. We say "almost" because applets are subject to certain limitations that do not apply to Java applications. For example, you would not want your browser to run an applet that destroys the files on your computer. Thus applets are prohibited from accessing files.[1] Likewise, an applet cannot send messages to other computers from your computer (except the one from which it was loaded). These security restrictions are included in Java to prevent the creation of harmful applets by malicious programmers.

Applets differ from applications in several ways:

- An applet doesn't have a `main` method. It is much more like a windowing component than a stand-alone application.

- An applet is not invoked in the same fashion as an application. Instead, it is embedded within an HTML document. HTML is the language used to create Web pages. We describe HTML briefly later in this chapter.

- Applets are subjected to more security constraints than an application because they are distributed over the Web.

- Applets are not in control of their own execution. They simply respond when told to do so by the browser or viewer.

Because of the way that applets are executed, they do not have constructors. Instead, the operations that we would normally place into a constructor (such as initializing fields or setting up the user interface) should be written in the applet's `init` method. When a browser first downloads an applet, its JVM executes this method. In this chapter we use the `init` method not only to serve as a constructor but also to play the role of `main` in an application. It contains the main block of code that begins the work of the applet.

Whereas all applications are usually derived implicitly from `Object`, applets must be explicitly derived from the `Applet` or `JApplet` class, both of which are descendants of the class `Container`. These classes contain additional methods called `start`, `stop`, and `destroy` that are used with more sophisticated applets that employ features of Java not covered in this text. For example, if an applet is showing a graphics animation, we may want it to stop when the user moves to a different Web page and resume (start) when the user returns to the page with the applet.

---

[1] Later versions of Java ease this restriction to allow special cases of file access when a user permits it.

In Chapter 8, you learned how to create GUIs using the swing package. Swing is a GUI toolkit provided as a core part of the Java 2 platform. It is not a new set of tools, but rather an enhancement of the AWT toolkit that was used on previous platforms. Many of the Swing classes that you used in Chapter 8 have the letter "J" in front of them: JButton, JLabel, and JTextField. The "J" distinguishes the class from the AWT class of the same name. Both AWT and Swing support applets. Figure 14.1 shows the inheritance hierarchy. As you can see, the JApplet class is derived from Applet.

In our applications, we had to instantiate a JFrame into whose content pane we added our user interface components. Because an applet is itself a container, we simply call methods such as add and setLayout directly. Thus writing applets is easier than writing applications with frames.

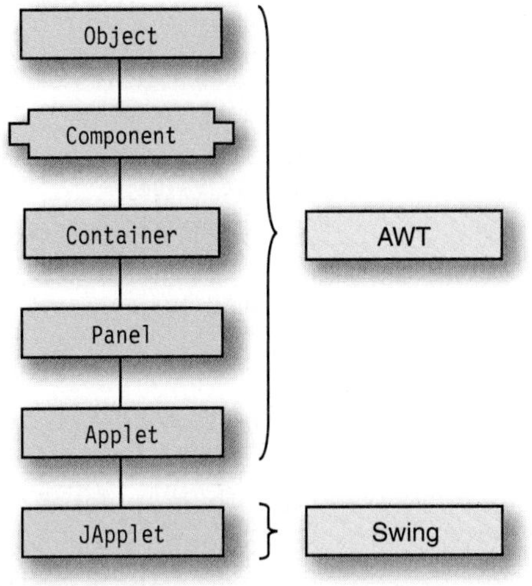

14.2   How Do You Write an Applet?

We demonstrate how to write an applet through the use of two previous examples. The first is the factorial function, which originally did not use a GUI, and the second is the calculator application, which did use such an interface.

Figure 14.1   Applet Inheritance Hierarchy for AWT and Swing

Factorial

Let's consider how to write an applet in the context of a specific problem. In Chapter 13, we wrote the factorial function. What we didn't mention there is that the factorial of a number becomes very large very fast. Let's write an applet that lets us enter a number and then displays the factorial of that number. This process continues until the user closes the window in the browser. Thus an event loop is set up, allowing the user to continue to enter a value for which the factorial is computed.

We display the code for the applet and intersperse discussion of this code at the different parts. Note that we are removing the "J" from in front of the class names of the window components. That is, we are presenting AWT applets rather than Swing applets. The reason for doing so is that many older browsers are not set up to accept Swing applets, and those that are can still run AWT applets.

```
// Applet FactInt on file FactInt.java computes the factorial of
//   its input and stores it in a variable of type int, which is
//   displayed on the screen.

import java.applet.Applet;
import java.awt.*;          // Supplies user interface classes
import java.awt.event.*;    // Supplies event classes
```

```java
public class FactInt extends Applet implements ActionListener
{
  public void actionPerformed(ActionEvent event)
  // Event handler method
  {
    int value;
    value = Integer.parseInt(inputField.getText());
    inputField.setText("");
    outLabel.setText(value + " factorial is " + factorial(value));
  }
```

The main heading is just like that of an application, except the phrase extends Applet implements ActionListener follows the class name. This phrase tells the compiler that we are working with an applet and not an application: Our class is derived from Applet. This applet also
implements the ActionListener interface, so we should expect a public method actionPerformed
to be part of the class. The event handler takes a string as input, converts it to an integer value,
resets the text field to the empty string, and invokes the factorial function within the output statement. The factorial function that follows is identical to the one from Chapter 13.

```java
private int factorial(int n)
// Assumption:  n is not negative
{
  if (n == 0)
    return 1; // Base case
  else
    return (n * factorial(n-1));        // General case
}
```

The next sections of code set up a button, a label, and a text input field.

```java
// Set up a button, label, and input field
private TextField inputField;
private Label label;
private Label outLabel;
private Button button;
```

In an application, the method where execution begins is main. In an applet, execution begins in the init method. The initializations that are carried out in main in an application are
carried out in init in an applet.

```java
public void init()
{
  // Instantiate components
  label = new Label("Enter an integer; click Enter.");
  outLabel = new Label("Answer");
  button = new Button("Enter");
  button.addActionListener(this);
```

```
inputField = new TextField("Value here");

// Add components
add(label);
add(inputField);
add(button);
add(outLabel);

// Specify a layout manager for the window
setLayout(new GridLayout(4,1));

    }
}
```

Here is a series of screen shots showing the initial window and the results from various input values.

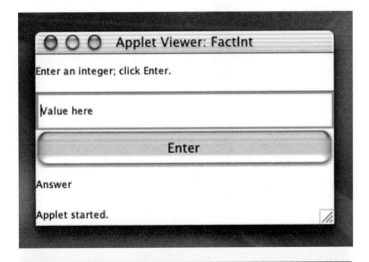

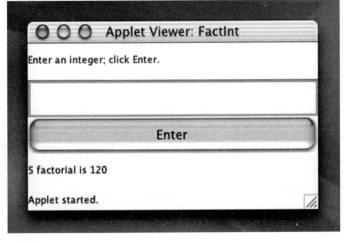

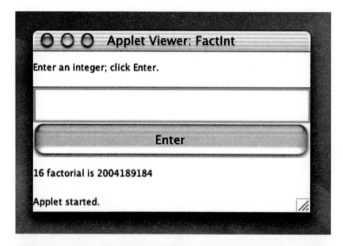

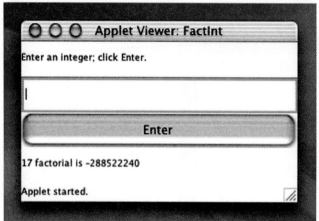

To stop execution, the user closes on the applet window (or browser window).

See what we mean about the factorial becoming very large very fast? 16! is 10 digits. 17! cannot possibly be a negative number. What happened? The result was too large to store in an integer variable, so overflow occurred. The JVM just kept going with a "garbage" value for the number, which in this case was displayed as a negative number.

■ Calculator

Now let's look at a little more complex example. In Chapter 8, we created a calculator that performs addition and subtraction. Let's convert it into an applet. Look back at that program as you read through this code. As before, we embed textual comments at important places.

```
import java.applet.Applet;          // Applet class
import java.awt.event.*;            // Event-handling classes
import java.awt.*;                  // User interface classes
```

The outer `public` class both extends the class `Applet` and implements the `ActionListener` interface. Thus `Calculator2` is its own listener class. This fact is reflected here in the heading and in the code where `this` is the argument for the `addActionListener` method. Notice that within the event handler, the code is enclosed within a *try-catch* statement that handles numeric input errors.

```java
import java.applet.Applet;    // Applet class
import java.awt.event.*;      // Event handling classes
import java.awt.*;            // Uer interface classes

public class Calculator2 extends Applet implements ActionListener
{
  public void actionPerformed(ActionEvent event)
  //Handles events from the buttons in the applet
  {
    double secondOperand;              // Holds input value
    String whichButton;                // Holds the button's name
    // Get the operand, checking for numeric format error
    try
    {
      secondOperand = Double.parseDouble(inputField.getText());
    }
    catch (NumberFormatException except)
    {
      secondOperand = 0.0;                   // If error, set to zero
    }

    whichButton = event.getActionCommand();  // Get the button's name

    if (whichButton.equals("+"))             // When the name is "+"
      result = result + secondOperand;       //  add the operand
    else if (whichButton.equals("-"))        // When the name is "-"
      result = result - secondOperand;       //  subtract operand
    else
      result = 0.0;                          // Clear result to zero

    register.setText("" + result);           // Display result
    inputField.setText("");                  // Clear input
  }
```

Because we are extending Applet rather than JApplet, the J's have all been removed from class names in the following declarations.

```java
  private TextField inputField;      // Data field
  private Label register;            // Result shown on screen
  private double result;             // Keeps current value

  public void init()
  {
    Label resultLabel;                        // Indicates output area
```

```
    Label entryLabel;                          // Label for input field
    Button add;
    Button subtract;
    Button clear;
    result = 0.0;

    // Instantiate labels and initialize input field
    resultLabel = new Label("Result:");
    register = new Label("0.0", Label.RIGHT);
    entryLabel = new Label("Enter #:");
    inputField = new TextField("", 10);
```

Notice that no Frame (or JFrame) items have been declared or instantiated. The applet already has its own window.

```
    // Instantiate button objects
    add = new Button("+");
    subtract = new Button("-");
    clear = new Button("Clear");

    // Register the button listener with the buttons
    add.addActionListener(this);
    subtract.addActionListener(this);
    clear.addActionListener(this);

    // Add interface elements to applet window
    setLayout(new GridLayout(4,2));             // Set the layout manager
    add(resultLabel);
    add(register);
    add(entryLabel);
    add(inputField);
    add(add);
    add(subtract);
    add(clear);
  }
}
```

Here is how this applet appears on the screen.

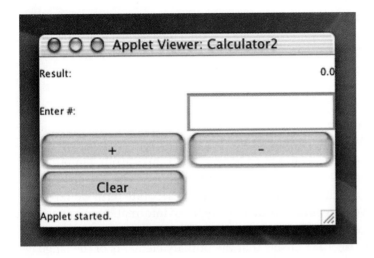

14.3 How Do You Run an Applet?

As we said earlier, the applet must be run within a Web browser or an applet viewer. The browser recognizes a link to a Bytecode file and the JVM within the browser executes the code. Most Java systems provide an applet viewer that runs the Bytecode version of the applet so that you can see the results. Although each system is different, there is usually an HTML file associated with each applet that gives the name of the compiled class to the viewer. The name of the class is typically the name of the `public` class with a `.class` extension. Remember that the JVM executes Bytecode, not Java code or machine language code.

Let's first review a few fundamental facts about Web browsers. We will then look at HTML, the language in which Web pages are written.

■ Web Browsers

The terms *Internet* and *Web* are often used as synonyms, but they are not. The Internet is a network. A network is a collection of computing devices connected so that they can communicate and share resources. A local area network (LAN) is a network that connects a small number of nodes in a close geographic area. A wide area network (WAN) is a network that connects two or more local area networks. The Internet is a wide area network that spans the planet. In contrast, the Web is an infrastructure of information and the network software used to access it.

A Web page is a document that contains or references various kinds of data as well as contains links to other Web pages. Web pages are referenced by their Uniform Resource Locator (URL), such as `http://www.jbpub.com`. When you access a

Network A collection of connected computing devices that communicate and share resources

Local area network (LAN) A network in a close geographic area

Wide area network (WAN) A network that connects two or more local area networks

Internet A wide area network that spans the planet

Web An infrastructure of information and the network software used to access it

Uniform Resource Locator (URL) The address of a Web page on the Internet

Web page in your browser by entering a URL, the browser goes to that page and brings a copy back to you. Thus the expression "visit a Web page" is somewhat misleading. Your browser actually visits the other site and brings back a copy for you to view. If the Web page contains a link to an applet, the code is brought to your browser and run on your browser's JVM.

■ HTML

Hypertext Markup Language (HTML) The language used to create or build Web pages

Markup language A language that uses tags to annotate the information in a document

Tag The syntactic element in a markup language that indicates how information should be displayed

Both browsers and applet viewers read Web pages. To create or build Web pages, we use the Hypertext Markup Language (HTML). The term *hypertext* means that the information is not organized linearly, like a book. Instead, links to other information are embedded within the text so that the viewer can jump from one place to another as needed within the text. These days, a more accurate term would be *hypermedia*, because Web pages deal with many types of information in addition to text, including images, audio, and video.

The term markup language means that the primary elements of the language take the form of tags that we insert into a document to annotate the information stored there. In the case of HTML, the tags indicate how the information should be displayed. It's as if you took a printed document and marked it up with extra notation to specify other details, as shown in Figure 14.2.

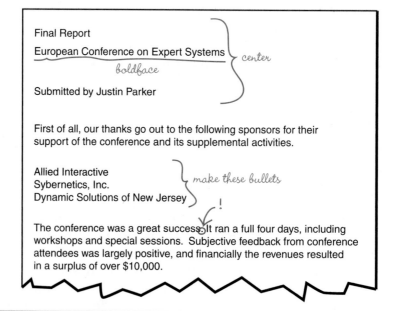

Figure 14.2 A Marked-up Document

```
<HTML>
<HEAD>
<TITLE>Factorial Labs</TITLE>
</HEAD>
<BODY>
<H1>Factorial with Int Result</H1>
<P>Enter increasing values beginning with 0 and record the results of the factorial of
your input. At some point, the answer will seem strange. Record what seems strange about
the answer and return to the previous page. </P>
<P><HR></P>
<P><APPLET code = "FactInt.class" width=250 height=150></APPLET></P>
</BODY>
</HTML>
```

Figure 14.3   An HTML Document That Causes the Applet Fact Int to be Executed

Factorial

Figure 14.3 shows the HTML document that has the link to the Bytecode version of FactInt.

Although this chapter will not try to teach you HTML, we do want to point out the features that cause the execution of the applet. Tags are enclosed in angled brackets and are not case-sensitive. Most of them come in pairs, with the second or closing tag preceded by a "/". At the beginning and the end of the document, you will see <HTML> ... </HTML>; at the beginning and the end of the title, you will see <TITLE> ... </TITLE>. The body of the HTML code is enclosed in <BODY> ... </BODY>. <H1> ... </H1> indicates that the information between the tags is a type 1 heading, and <P> ... </P> encloses a paragraph. <HR> inserts a horizontal rule (line) and has no ending tag.

The following HTML code runs the applet:

```
<APPLET code = "FactInt.class" width=250 height=150></APPLET>
```

Between <APPLET and </APPLET> lie the keywords that cause the applet to be executed. The JVM starts executing the Bytecode at the file FactInt.class. The applet is in an event loop that keeps executing as long as the browser remains on the Web page containing the applet.

```
<title>Calculator2.class</title>
<hr>
<applet codebase="Java Classes" code="Calculator2.class" width=200 height=200>
</applet>
<hr>
<a href="Calculator2.java">The source.</a>
```

Figure 14.4 .html file for running the calculator applet

◼ Calculator

We ran the calculator applet within a viewer provided by our particular Java system. Figure 14.4 shows the .html file that was automatically generated by our Java system when the calculator applet was compiled.

Although this HTML document is a little different, the important element is: the applet tag with the name of the file with a .class extension. Notice the two-stage process:

1. Compile the Java code into Bytecode.
2. Create an HTML document with a link to the Bytecode file in the Web page.

CASE STUDY

SEARCHING EXPERIMENTS

Problem Write an applet that lets the user experiment with looking for items in a list and trying to determine which searching algorithm is being used. The number of comparisons is a metric that is often employed to measure searching efficiency, so the applet should display the number of comparisons performed in determining whether the value was present in the list.

Background In Chapter 11, three searching algorithms were presented and discussed: a sequential search in a sorted list, a sequential search in an unsorted list, and a binary search. A sequential search begins by looking at the first item in the list and continues looking at each successive item until it finds the item or reaches the end of the list. A sequential search in a sorted list can recognize when the search has reached the place where the item would be if it were present and thus can stop at that point. A binary search assumes that the list items are sorted; it begins looking in the middle of the list and successively throws away half of the list with each comparison until it finds the item or there is nowhere else to look.

Brainstorming The problem doesn't state which of the three algorithms is used. We can wait to decide that later, because the primary processing does not depend on the algorithm. The classes in this solution are found in the problem statement: a list of items, an item, and a counter to keep track of the number of comparisons. Because the applet runs from a web page, we know that the input and output will be from the GUI components on the screen. Thus we must have an input text field and an output label. Where there is an input text field, a button is always lurking nearby.

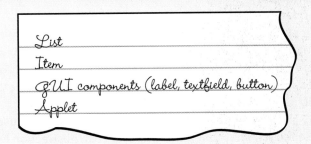

List
Item
GUI components (label, textfield, button)
Applet

Scenarios The user enters an item, and the applet reports whether the item is in the list and how many comparisons were required to make that determination. Where there is a button, there is a listener and an event loop. What actions must be executed within the event handler? The item must be read, the list must be searched, and the results must be given to the user. The user may input another item or quit the process by closing the applet window (if an applet viewer is being used) or going to another Web page.

What must the applet do to set up this situation within the event handler? For one thing, it must generate a list to be searched. Because the problem statement says nothing about the types of items in the list, let's make them be integers. We can then use a random-number generator to create the items in the list.

Class Name: *Search*	Superclass: *Applet*	Subclasses:
Responsibilities	**Collaborations**	
Prepare GUI components	*Label, TextField, Button*	
Generate list values	*Random*	
Get an item		
Search the list (item) *return boolean*	*List*	
Report results		

Responsibility Algorithms The first responsibility, preparing the GUI components, is very straightforward. We need an input label, an output label, a text field, and a button. Generating the list requires a little more thought. The CRC card says that this operation collaborates with the class Random. This Java class supplies a method that generates a random number. We can call this method to give us an integer, say, between 0 and 999. Here is how the method works:

```
Random rand = new Random();
value = Math.abs(rand.nextInt()) % 1000;
```

The first line initializes the random-number generator. Each time it is called, the nextInt method returns a random number within the range of the int data type. The Math.abs method converts the result to a nonnegative integer, and the % 1000 limits the values to three digits. Random is in java.util.

Which list ADT shall we use? Does the list need to be sorted? It must be sorted only if we decide to use the searches that require a sorted list. Abstraction lets us write the primary algorithms without having to decide right away. What size shall we make the list? Let's set a constant SIZE to be 100. This way it would be easy to change later.

```
Generate values

for counter going from 1 to SIZE
    Generate random number
    Insert number into list
```

CASE STUDY

The next three responsibilities are within the event handler and can be grouped together.

```
Event handler
Get item
Search list for item
if found
  Write item, " is in list found with ", count, " comparisons"
else
  Write item, " is not in list, determined with ", count, " comparisons"
```

Have we forgotten anything? Yes—how are we going to count the number of comparisons? We can derive a class from one of the list classes and have it override the isThere method. Before we do that, let's spend a minute thinking about the processing that we need to do. We don't delete an item, and we don't use any of the observers. In fact, we aren't really dealing with a list at all, because the number of items is a constant. It would be much more efficient to just generate the random numbers directly into an array, and then write an isThere method that searches the array and counts the number of comparisons. We can borrow the code from one of our list classes. We use the linear search because the array items are not in sorted order.

```
Generate list (revised)
for counter going from 0 to SIZE − 1
  values[counter] = Math.abs(rand.nextInt()) % 1000
```

```
Is there (item)
Set location to 0
Set found to false
Set count to 0
Set moreToSearch to (location less than SIZE)
while moreToSearch and !found
  Increment count
  if item equals values[location]
    Set found to true
  else
    Increment location
    Set moreToSearch to (location less than SIZE)
return found
```

We have to make count be a field in the applet class. We need two outputs from our isThere method (found and count), yet the *return* statement can only return one value.

Therefore, we must make count be a field that other methods can access. Here is the code for our applet, followed by a picture showing execution by the applet viewer:

```java
//************************************************************
// This applet prompts a user to input an integer value and
//  reports if the value is in a list and how many comparisons
//  it took to make that determination.
//************************************************************
import java.applet.Applet;
import java.awt.*;          // Supplies user interface classes
import java.awt.event.*;    // Supplies event classes
import java.util.*;         // Supplies Random class

public class Search extends Applet implements ActionListener
{

  private int[] values;         // Values to be searched
  private int count = 0;        // Comparison count
  private final int SIZE = 100; // Size of the array

  // Event handler method
  public void actionPerformed(ActionEvent event)
  {
    int value;
    value = Integer.parseInt(inputField.getText());
    inputField.setText("");
    if (isThere(value))
      outLabel.setText(value + " is in list found with "
        + count + " comparisons");
    else
      outLabel.setText(value + " is not in list determined with "
      + count + " comparisons");
  }

  private boolean isThere (int item)
  // Returns true if the item is in the array;
  //  otherwise, returns false
  {
    boolean moreToSearch;
    int location = 0;
    boolean found = false;
    count = 0;
    moreToSearch = (location < SIZE);
```

```
    while (moreToSearch && !found)
    {
      count++;
      if (item == values[location])
        found = true;
      else
      {
        location++;
        moreToSearch = (location < SIZE);
      }
    }
    return found;
}

private void generateValues(int size)
// Initializes the values array with random integers
//  from 0 to 999
{
  values = new int[size];
  Random rand = new Random();
  for (int index = 0; index < size; index++)
    values[index] = Math.abs(rand.nextInt()) % 1000;
}

private static TextField inputField;
private static Label label;
private static Label outLabel;
private static Button button;


public void init()
{
  // Instantiate the GUI components
  label = new Label("Enter a value between 0 and 999; click Enter.");
  outLabel = new Label("Results");
  button = new Button("Enter");
  inputField = new TextField("Value here");

  // Finish processing GUI components
  button.addActionListener(this);
  add(label);
  add(inputField);
```

```
    add(button);
    add(outLabel);

    // Generate the array of integers
    generateValues(SIZE);
    setLayout(new GridLayout(4,1));
  }
}
```

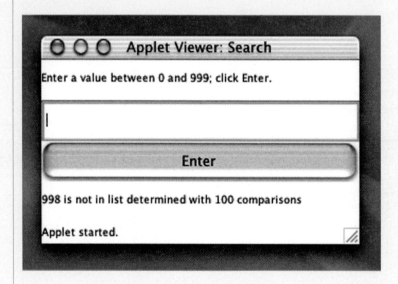

14.4 Testing and Debugging

Testing an applet is much like testing an application. Because an applet is usually much smaller, however, there is less code to test. In contrast, the steps involved in getting an applet to run are more involved because you have to set up a Web page.

Testing and Debugging Hints

1. Be sure that all of your initialization is within the `init` method.
2. An applet is often its own event listener. In such a case, confirm that the `addActionListener` method has `this` as its argument.
3. The spelling of the file name in the viewer or Web page must be identical to the name of the file containing the Bytecode version of the applet.

Summary

A Java application must have a method named `main`, and the included classes should all have constructors. A Java applet, on the other hand, is a class derived from the class `Applet` that implements `ActionListener`; here, the class is its own listener, and initializations are done within the `init` method. Most applets are in event loops that continue running until the applet window is closed or you exit the Web page within which the applet is embedded.

The link to the Bytecode version of the applet is found within a Web page. An example of HTML code that provides the link is `<APPLET code = "FactInt.class" width=250 height=150></APPLET>`. Using the keyword `code` followed by the equals sign and a file name with a `.class` extension says to execute the Bytecode stored in that file.

Quick Check

1. How do applications and applets differ in terms of how they are used? (pp. 660–661)

2. How does a Web page get loaded into your browser? (pp. 667–668)

3. What is HTML used for? (pp. 668–669)

4. In an applet class heading, what phrase must follow the applet class name? (pp. 661–667)

5. How is an applet linked within a Web page? (pp. 668–669)

6. What is the meaning of the `.class` extension? (p. 667)

Answers

1. An application is a stand-alone program that solves a problem. An applet is a small piece of code that runs under a browser.
2. When you enter a URL into your browser, the browser goes to that place and brings back a copy of what is there for you to see, including any applets to which it links.
3. HTML is the language used to write Web pages.
4. `extends Applet implements ActionListener`
5. `<APPLET code = "AppletName.class" ... ></APPLET>` links the applet whose Bytecode is stored in the file `AppletName.class` into the Web page.
6. `.class` means that the file contains the Bytecode version of an applet.

Exam Preparation Exercises

1. Name four ways in which applets differ from applications.

2. Because applets do not have constructors, where are their initializations carried out?

3. Because applets do not have a main method, where does execution begin?

4. From which class must your applet be derived?

5. Why do we not need to instantiate a Frame or JFrame with an applet?

6. Why do you not need to append an object name to add components to the window?

7. What happens when an int variable overflows in Java?

8. What distinguishes a Swing component from an AWT component?

9. How do you run an applet?

10. What is HTML?

11. What is a markup language?

12. What is a tag?

13. What is the HTML tag that encloses a Web page?

14. What does <P> ··· </P> enclose?

15. Distinguish between the Internet and the Web.

16. Describe what happens when you enter a URL in your browser.

17. Distinguish between a LAN and a WAN.

Programming Warm-Up Exercises

1. Write the Java statement that provides access to the Applet class.

2. Write the class heading for an applet class named Sorts.

3. For the applet of Exercise 2, write the statements that declare, instantiate, and place a text field into the window.

4. For the applet of Exercise 2, write the statements that declare, instantiate, and place into the window a label with the phrase: "Enter a real number between 0.0 and 1.99".

5. For the applet of Exercise 2, write the statements that declare, instantiate, and place a button object into the window.

6. Write the statement that registers a listener with the button of Exercise 5.

7. For the applet of Exercise 2, write the statement that sets the layout of the window.

8. Write the HTML tags that must appear in a Web page to execute the following applets:

   a. Sorts

   b. Search

   c. Calculator

9. Write the HTML statements that create the following title: Now is the time!

10. Write the HTML tag(s) to place a horizontal rule on the page.

11. What HTML symbols enclose a paragraph?

Programming Problems

1. Write an applet that calculates the factorial of a number using `byte` arithmetic. That is, the input value is a `byte`, and the value returned by the factorial function is a `byte`. Execute your applet by inputting increasing values beginning with 0. What is the largest factorial value that can be calculated? What happens when you enter a larger value?

2. Write an applet that calculates the factorial of a number using `short` arithmetic. That is, the input value is a `short`, and the value returned by the factorial function is a `short`. Execute your applet by inputting increasing values beginning with 0. What is the largest factorial value that can be calculated? What happens when you enter a larger value?

3. Write an applet that calculates the factorial of a number using `long` arithmetic. That is, the input value is a `long`, and the value returned by the factorial function is a `long`. Execute your applet by inputting increasing values beginning with 15. What is the largest factorial value that can be calculated? What happens when you enter a larger value?

4. Write an applet that calculates the factorial of a number using `float` arithmetic. That is, the input value is a `float`, and the value returned by the factorial function is a `float`. Execute your applet by inputting increasing values beginning with 50. What is the largest factorial value that can be calculated? What happens when you enter a larger value?

5. Write an applet that calculates the factorial of a number using `double` arithmetic. That is, the input value is a `double`, and the value returned by the factorial function is a `double`. Execute your applet by inputting increasing values beginning with 100. What is the largest factorial value that can be calculated? What happens when you enter a larger value?

6. Write an applet that counts the number of comparisons required to sort a list of integers using the selection sort algorithm. Have the user enter the size of the list, and report back the number of comparisons. Run your applet five times and record the size of the list and the number of comparisons required. Relate your findings to the discussion of Big-O complexity in Chapter 11.

Case Study Follow-Up

1. Rather than having the number of elements be a constant, ask the user to input the number of elements to be searched.

2. Create another applet exactly like the altered version of Search in Case Study Follow-Up Exercise 1, but replace the linear search with a linear search in a sorted list. Don't forget to sort the values before you search.

3. Create another applet exactly like the one in Exercise 2, but replace the linear search with a binary search. Be sure to sort the values before you search.

4. The output from each applet should give the user enough information to determine which search algorithm is being used. After the user runs the applet for a number of times, have the user enter which of the three algorithms he or she thinks is being used. If the answer is correct, congratulate the user; otherwise, suggest that he or she run the applet again at another time.

Appendix A

Java Reserved Words

These words appear in red when used in this book.

abstract	else	interface	super
boolean	extends	long	switch
break	false	native	synchronized
byte	final	new	this
case	finally	null	throw
catch	float	package	throws
char	for	private	transient
class	goto	protected	true
const	if	public	try
continue	implements	return	void
default	import	short	volatile
do	instanceof	static	while
double	int	strictfp	

Appendix B

Operator Precedence

In the following table, the operators are grouped by precedence level (hightest to lowest), and a horizontal line separates each precedence level from the next.

Precedence (highest to lowest)

Operator	Assoc.*	Operand Type(s)	Operation Performed
.	LR	object, member	object member access
[]	LR	array, int	array element access
(args)	LR	method, arglist	method invocation
++, --	LR	variable	post-increment, decrement
++, --	RL	variable	pre-increment, decrement
+, -	RL	number	unary plus, unary minus
~	RL	integer	bitwise complement
!	RL	boolean	boolean NOT
new	RL	class, arglist	object creation
(type)	RL	type, any	cast (type conversion)
*, /, %	LR	number, number	multiplication, division, remainder
+, -	LR	number, number	addition, subtraction
+	LR	string, any	string concatenation
<<	LR	integer, integer	left shift
>>	LR	integer, integer	right shift with sign extension
>>>	LR	integer, integer	right shift with zero extension
<, <=	LR	number, number	less than, less than or equal
>, >=	LR	number, number	greater than, greater than or equal
instanceof	LR	reference, type	type comparison
==	LR	primitive, primitive	equal (have identical values)
!=	LR	primitive, primitive	not equal (have different values)
==	LR	reference, reference	equal (refer to the same object)
!=	LR	reference, reference	not equal (refer to different objects)
&	LR	integer, integer	bitwise AND
&	LR	boolean, boolean	boolean AND
^	LR	integer, integer	bitwise XOR
^	LR	boolean, boolean	boolean XOR

Precedence (highest to lowest)

Operator	Assoc.*	Operand Type(s)	Operation Performed
`|`	LR	integer, integer	bitwise OR
`|`	LR	boolean, boolean	boolean OR
`&&`	LR	boolean, boolean	conditional AND (short-circuit evaluation)
`||`	LR	boolean, boolean	conditional OR (short-circuit evaluation)
`?:`	RL	boolean, any, any	conditional (ternary) operator
`=`	RL	variable, any	assignment
`*=`, `/=`, `%=`, `+=`, `-=`, `<<=`, `>>=`, `>>>=`, `&=`, `^=`, `|=`	RL	variable, any	assignment with operation

*LR means left-to-right associativity; RL means right-to-left associativity.

Appendix C

Primitive Data Types

Type	Value Stored	Default Value	Size	Range of Values
char	Unicode character	Character code 0	16 bits	0 to 65535
byte	Integer value	0	8 bits	−128 to 127
short	Integer value	0	16 bits	−32768 to 32767
int	Integer value	0	32 bits	−2147483648 to 2147483647
long	Integer value	0	64 bits	−9223372036854775808 to 9223372036854775807
float	Real value	0.0	32 bits	±1.4E-45 to ±3.4028235E+38
double	Real value	0.0	64 bits	±4.9E-324 to ±1.7976931348623157E+308
boolean	true or false	false	1 bit	NA

Appendix D

ASCII Subset of Unicode

The following chart shows the ordering of characters in the ASCII (American Standard Code for Information Interchange) subset of Unicode. The internal representation for each character is shown in decimal. For example, the letter A is represented internally as the integer 65. The space (blank) character is denoted by a "□".

Left Digit(s) \ Right Digit	ASCII									
	0	1	2	3	4	5	6	7	8	9
0	NUL	SOH	STX	ETX	EOT	ENQ	ACK	BEL	BS	HT
1	LF	VT	FF	CR	SO	SI	DLE	DC1	DC2	DC3
2	DC4	NAK	SYN	ETB	CAN	EM	SUB	ESC	FS	GS
3	RS	US	□	!	"	#	$	%	&	'
4	(	)	*	+	,	-	.	/	0	1
5	2	3	4	5	6	7	8	9	:	;
6	<	=	>	?	@	A	B	C	D	E
7	F	G	H	I	J	K	L	M	N	O
8	P	Q	R	S	T	U	V	W	X	Y
9	Z	[	\	]	^	_	`	a	b	c
10	d	e	f	g	h	i	j	k	l	m
11	n	o	p	q	r	s	t	u	v	w
12	x	y	z	{	|	}	~	DEL		

Codes 00–31 and 127 are the following nonprintable control characters:

NUL	Null character	VT	Vertical tab	SYN	Synchronous idle
SOH	Start of header	FF	Form feed	ETB	End of transmitted block
STX	Start of text	CR	Carriage return	CAN	Cancel
ETX	End of text	SO	Shift out	EM	End of medium
EOT	End of transmission	SI	Shift in	SUB	Substitute
ENQ	Enquiry	DLE	Data link escape	ESC	Escape
ACK	Acknowledge	DC1	Device control one	FS	File separator
BEL	Bell character (beep)	DC2	Device control two	GS	Group separator
BS	Back space	DC3	Device control three	RS	Record separator
HT	Horizontal tab	DC4	Device control four	US	Unit separator
LF	Line feed	NAK	Negative acknowledge	DEL	Delete

Appendix E

Decimal Format Type*

To give more precise control over the formatting of numbers, Java provides a class called `DecimalFormat` that is part of a package called `java.text`. The `DecimalFormat` class allows us to create patterns that can be used to format numbers for output. These patterns are in the form of strings, made up of characters that represent the parts of a formatted number. For example, the pattern

```
"###,###"
```

indicates that a number should be formatted with up to six decimal digits, and when there are more than three digits in the number, a comma should be used to separate the thousands from the rest of the number.

There are four steps we must follow to use `DecimalFormat` patterns to format numbers:

- `import java.text.*;`
- Declare a variable of type `DecimalFormat` for each number format we wish to use.
- For each variable, instantiate a `DecimalFormat` object that contains the pattern.
- Format each number using the `format` method associated with each of the `DecimalFormat` class.

Let's examine each of these steps in turn. You are familiar with writing `import` declarations, so all you need to do for the first step is remember to put the declaration at the start of your program. Declaring variables of type `DecimalFormat` is done in the same way as declaring variables of type `String` or `JFrame`. For example:

```
DecimalFormat dollar;          // Format for dollar amounts
DecimalFormat percent;         // Format for percentages
DecimalFormat accounting;      // Format for negative values in ()
```

The third step involves using `new` and the `DecimalFormat` constructor to create an object whose address we can assign to the variable. The call to the constructor contains the string representing the pattern. Here are statements that associate patterns with each of the variables declared previously. Don't be concerned yet with trying to interpret the specific patterns shown; we explain them shortly.

```
dollar = new DecimalFormat("$###,##0.00");
percent = new DecimalFormat("##0.00%");
accounting = new DecimalFormat("$###,##0.00;($###,##0.00)");
```

---

*This appendix repeats and expands upon the discussion in Chapter 12.

Appendix E

The last step is to format the number using a method called `format`, which is a value-returning method associated with each of the `DecimalFormat` objects. The `format` method takes as its parameter a numerical value and returns a value of type `String` that contains the formatted number. For example, if we write

```
out.add(new JLabel(dollar.format(2893.67)));
```

then a label is added to the content pane called `out`, which contains a string of the form

```
$2,893.67
```

Now that we have seen the process for using patterns to format numeric values, let's look at how to write the patterns themselves. The following table shows the characters that can appear in a pattern string and their meanings.

Character	Meaning
0	Display one digit here. If no digit is present in this place, display a zero.
#	Display one digit here. If no digit is present in this place, display nothing here (not even a blank).
,	If there are digits on both sides of this place, insert a comma to separate them. The comma is only meaningful in the integer part of the pattern (the part to the left of the decimal point).
.	Put the decimal point here. If the pattern doesn't have any digit symbols (0 or #) to the right of the period, and the number doesn't have a fractional part, don't insert the decimal point.
%	When used anywhere to the right of the rightmost digit in the pattern, this indicates that the number is a percentage. Multiply it by 100 before displaying it, and put the % sign here.
;	The pattern to the left of ; is for nonnegative numbers. The pattern to the right is for negative numbers.
'	The character following is one of the special pattern characters, but should be printed literally (For example, use '# to show a # in the formatted number.)
other	Anything else is inserted exactly as it appears.

Now we can interpret the patterns we associate with the `DecimalFormat` variables. The pattern we gave to `dollar` is `"$###,##0.00"`, which means the number should have a decimal point with at least two fractional digits and one digit in the integer part. When the integer part has more than three digits, use a comma as a separator. The number should start with a dollar sign to the left of the first digit.

We use the pattern "##0.00%" to tell format that the number is a percentage that should first be multiplied by 100. After that, it is formatted with fractional digits and at least two digits in the integer part. The percent sign is to be placed to the right of the last digit.

The third pattern, "$###,##0.00;($###,##0.00)", is the most complex of the three, but is really just a minor variation on the dollar format. The semicolon indicates that the pattern on the left, which is the same as the pattern we gave to dollar, is to be used when the number is nonnegative. The pattern on the right (the same pattern but in parentheses) is to be used when the number is negative.

Here is a code segment that shows the definition and use of these patterns. Note that we are also using JLabel.RIGHT to align the numbers to the right within their labels.

```
dollar = new DecimalFormat("$###,##0.00");
percent = new DecimalFormat("##0.00%");
accounting = new DecimalFormat("$###,##0.00;($###,##0.00)");

out.add(new JLabel(dollar.format(2893.67), JLabel.RIGHT));
out.add(new JLabel(dollar.format(-2893.67), JLabel.RIGHT));
out.add(new JLabel(dollar.format(4312893.6), JLabel.RIGHT));
out.add(new JLabel(dollar.format(0), JLabel.RIGHT));
out.add(new JLabel(percent.format(0.23679), JLabel.RIGHT));
out.add(new JLabel(percent.format(1), JLabel.RIGHT));
out.add(new JLabel(accounting.format(2893.67), JLabel.RIGHT));
out.add(new JLabel(accounting.format(-2893.67), JLabel.RIGHT));
```

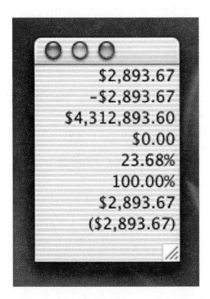

Let's take a closer look at each of the labels in this frame. The first label demonstrates what happens when a positive floating-point value is formatted with the dollar format. Only as many digits are used as are necessary, and the dollar sign is immediately adjacent to the leftmost digit. The second label shows the result of formatting a negative number. The format is the same as in the first case, but a minus sign precedes the dollar sign.

The third label is an example of formatting a number with more digits than the pattern specifies. Notice that the pattern is expanded to fit. The separation between the decimal point (or the rightmost digit, in the case of an integer) and the comma closest to it are used as a guide to the placement of additional commas. In this case, the comma is three places to the left of the decimal point, so additional commas are inserted every three places. We can't split up the fractional part of a number with a separator character such as a comma or period. If you try to use a comma in the fractional part, it simply ends up being pushed to the right end of the number. It is also interesting to compare the value in the code segment with the value displayed—this is a perfect example of what we said earlier about the kind of minor inaccuracies you often encounter with floating-point numbers!

The fourth label demonstrates that an integer value can be formatted to look like a floating-point value. It also shows that placing a zero in the pattern forces a zero to appear in the resulting string when there is no corresponding digit in the number.

The fifth label shows the use of the percent format. Notice that the value is multiplied by 100 before it is formatted. This example also shows that when there are more digits of precision in the fractional part than in the pattern, it is not expanded to show the additional fractional digits. The sixth label shows the application of the percent format to an integer.

The last two labels in the frame demonstrate the use of the pattern we associated with accounting. When the number is nonnegative, it is formatted normally, and when it is negative, it is enclosed in parentheses. Using two different patterns separated by a semicolon suppresses the automatic insertion of the minus sign and allows us to use other characters to indicate that the number is negative. As a safeguard, however, if we mistakenly use the same pattern on both sides of the semicolon, format ignores the semicolon and reverts to using the minus sign.

DecimalFormat gives us a powerful mechanism to format numbers in the patterns we typically use in our programs. However, it has some limitations. For example, when printing a dollar amount on a check, it is typical to fill the extra space around the number with asterisks or dashes to prevent tampering. DecimalFormat doesn't enable us to do this directly. However, because the format method returns its value as a string, we can store a formatted number into a String object and then use string operations to further refine its formatting.

Suppose we write the assignments

```
dollar = new DecimalFormat("###,##0.00");
value = 8239.41;
```

then the expression

```
dollar.format(value)
```

has the value "8,239.41". Further suppose that we want to display this in a fixed space of thirteen character positions, where the first character is the dollar sign and the spaces between the dollar sign and the first digit are filled with stars: "$****8,239.41". If the number has more digits, fewer stars are needed, and if it has fewer digits then more stars must be concatenated. The number of stars to add is

```
12 - dollar.format(value).length
```

because the dollar sign takes up one of the thirteen character positions. The maximum value of this expression is 8, because the format requires at least three decimal digits and a decimal point. Thus, if we use a string constant called STARS that contains eight stars, we can write

```
STARS.substring(0, 12 - dollar.format(value).length)
```

to get a string with the proper number of stars. All we have left to do is to concatenate the pieces to form the desired string.

```
"$" + STARS.substring(0, 12 - dollar.format(value).length) + dollar.format(value)
```

Look closely at this expression to be certain that you understand how it works. Many programming problems require that output values be precisely formatted. In such cases, you may need to use complex combinations of the string operations that Java provides. Breaking an output format into its component pieces and deciding how to format each piece before concatenating them together is a common strategy for dealing with this complexity.

Appendix F

Program Style, Formatting, and Documentation

Useful programs have very long lifetimes, during which they must be modified and updated. Good style and documentation are essential if another programmer is to understand and work with your program.

General Guidelines

Style is of benefit only for a human reader of your programs—differences in style make no difference to the computer. Good style includes the use of meaningful identifiers, comments, and indentation of control structures, all of which help others to understand and work with your program. Perhaps the most important aspect of program style is consistency. If the style within a program is not consistent, it then becomes misleading and confusing.

Comments

Comments are extra information included to make a program easier to understand. You should include a comment anywhere the code is difficult to understand. However, don't overcomment. Too many comments in a program can obscure the code and be a source of distraction.

In our style, there are four basic types of comments: headers, declarations, in-line, and sidebar.

Header comments appear at the top of a class, method, or package and should include your name, the date that the code was written, and its purpose. It is also useful to include sections describing the input, output, and assumptions that form the basis for the design of the code. The header comments serve as the reader's introduction to your program. Here is an example:

```
// This method computes the sidereal time for a given date and solar time
//
// Written by: Your Name
//
// Date completed: 4/8/03
//
// Input: java.util.calendar object for the date and solar time
//
// Output: a java.util.calendar object containing the corresponding
//   sidereal time
//
// Assumptions: Solar time is specified for a longitude of 0 degrees
```

Declaration comments accompany the field declarations in a class. Anywhere that an identifier is declared, it is helpful to include a comment that explains its purpose. For example:

```
// Class constants
static final String FIRST  = "Herman";     // Person's first name
static final String LAST   = "Herrmann";   // Person's last name
static final char   MIDDLE = 'G';          // Person's middle initial
// Instance variables
JFrame outputDisplay;                       // Output frame
String firstLast;                           // Name in first-last format
String lastFirst;                           // Name in last-first format
int studentCount;                           // Number of students
int sumOfScores;                            // Sum of their scores
long sumOfSquares;                          // Sum of squared scores
double average;                             // Average of the scores
float deviation;                            // Standard deviation of scores
char grade;                                 // Student's letter grade
String stuName;                             // Student's name
```

Notice that aligning the comments gives the code a neater appearance and is less distracting.

In-line comments are used to break long sections of code into shorter, more comprehensible fragments. It is generally a good idea to surround in-line comments with blank lines to make them stand out. In this text we save space by printing the in-line comments in color rather than using blank lines. Some editors also color comments automatically, which makes it easier to spot them on the screen. However, blank lines are still helpful because code is often printed on paper in black and white. Here is an example:

```
// Instantiate labels and input field

resultLabel = new JLabel("Result:");
register = new JLabel("0.0", Label.RIGHT);
entryLabel = new JLabel("Enter #:");
inputField = new JTextField("", 10);

//Instantiate button objects

add = new JButton("+");
subtract = new JButton("-");
clear = new JButton("Clear");

// Register the button listeners

add.addActionListener(operation);
subtract.addActionListener(operation);
clear.addActionListener(clearOperation);
```

Even if comments aren't needed, blank lines can be inserted wherever there is a logical break in the code that you would like to emphasize.

Sidebar comments appear to the right of executable statements and are used to shed light on the purpose of the statement. Sidebar comments are often just pseudocode statements from your responsibility algorithms. If a complicated Java statement requires some explanations, the pseudocode statement should be written to its right. For example:

```
while ((line = dataFile.readLine()) != null) // Get a line if not EOF
```

Because the page of a textbook has a fixed width, it is sometimes difficult to fit a sidebar comment next to a long line of code. In those cases, we place the sidebar comment before the statement to which it refers. Most computer screens can now display more characters on a line than fit across a page, so this situation is less common in practice. However, if lines of code become too long, they are hard to read. It is then better to place the sidebar comment before the line of code.

In addition to the four main types of comments that we have discussed, there are some miscellaneous comments that we should mention. Although we do not do this in the text, to conserve space, we recommend that classes and methods be separated in a compilation unit file by a row of asterisks.

```
//**********************************************************************
```

Programmers also sometimes place a comment after the right brace of a block to indicate which control structure the block belongs to. This is especially helpful in a package file where there may be multiple classes. Indicating where a class or long method ends helps readers keep track of where they are looking in scanning the code.

```
        return noCorrect;
    }
} // End of class TheKey
```

Identifiers

The most important consideration in choosing a name for a field or method is that the name convey as much information as possible about what the field is or what the method does. The name should also be readable in the context in which it is used. For example, the following names convey the same information, but one is more readable than the other:

```
datOfInvc      invoiceDate
```

Although an identifier may be a series of words, very long identifiers can become quite tedious and can make the program harder to read. The best approach to designing an identifier is to try writing out different names until you reach an acceptable compromise—and then write an especially informative declaration comment next to the declaration.

Formatting Lines and Expressions

Java allows you to break a long statement in the middle and continue onto the next line. The split can occur at any point where it would be possible to insert spaces without affecting the behavior of the code. When a line is so long that it must be split, it's important to choose a breaking point that is logical and reasonable. Compare the readability of the following code fragments:

```
outFile.println(" for a radius of " + radius + " the diameter of the cir"
              + "cle is " + diameter);
outFile.println(" for a radius of " + radius +
               " the diameter of the circle is " + diameter);
```

When writing expressions, keep in mind that spaces improve readability. Usually you should include one space on either side of the == operator as well as most other operators. Occasionally, spaces are left out to emphasize the order in which operations are performed. Here are some examples:

```
if (x+y > y+z)
   maximum = x + y;
else
   maximum = y + z;
hypotenuse = Math.sqrt(a*a + b*b);
```

Indentation

The purpose of indenting statements in a program is to provide visual cues to the reader and to make the program easier to debug. When a program is properly indented, the way the statements are grouped is immediately obvious. Compare the following two program fragments:

```
while (count <= 10)
{
num = Integer.parseInt(in.readLine());
if (num == 0)
{
count++;
num = 1;
}
out.println(num);
out.println(count);
}
```

```
while (count <= 10)
{
   num = Integer.parseInt(in.readLine());
   if (num == 0)
   {
     count++;
     num = 1;
   }
   out.println(num);
   out.println(count);
}
```

As a basic rule in this text, each nested or lower level item is indented by two spaces. Exceptions to this rule are parameter declarations and statements that are split across two or more lines. Indenting by two spaces is a matter of personal preference. Some people prefer to indent by more spaces.

In this text, we prefer to place the braces on separate lines so that it is easy to scan down the left edge of a block of code and find them. Placing them on separate lines also reminds us to consider whether the beginning or the end of a block would benefit from an in-line comment and automatically gives us a place to write one. This is just one style of placement, and you will encounter other styles as you examine code written by other programmers.

As we noted at the beginning of this appendix, the most important aspect of code formatting is consistency. You may frequently find it necessary to adopt the style of another programmer in order to update his or her code in a consistent manner. Even when you believe your own favorite style to be superior, resist the temptation to mix your style with a different, existing style. The mixture is likely to be more confusing than either style alone.

Abstract A modifier of a class field that indicates it is incomplete and must be fully defined in a derived class

Abstract step A step for which some implementation details remain unspecified

Abstraction The separation of the logical properties of an object from its implementation

Access modifiers Reserved words in Java that specify where a class, method, or field may be accessed

Algorithm Instructions for solving a problem in a finite amount of time using a finite amount of data

Anonymous object An object that is instantiated but not assigned to an identifier and, therefore, lacks a name

Argument An expression used for communicating values to a method

Arithmetic/logic unit (ALU) The component of the central processing unit that performs arithmetic and logical operations

Array A collection of components, all of the same type, ordered on N dimensions (N>=1). Each component is accessed by N indexes, each of which represents the component's position within that dimension

Assembler A program that translates an assembly language program into machine code

Assembly language A low-level programming language in which a mnemonic represents each machine language instruction for a particular computer

Assignment expression A Java expression with (1) a value and (2) the side effect of storing the expression value into a memory location

Assignment statement A statement that stores the value of an expression into a variable

Asynchronous Not occurring at the same moment in time as some specific operation of the computer; not synchronized with the computer's actions

Atomic (simple) elements Elements that have no component parts

Auxiliary storage device A device that stores data in encoded form outside the computer's main memory

Base address The memory address of the first element of an array

Base case The case for which the solution can be stated non-recursively

Binary operator An operator that has two operands

Button A component that can be added to a frame and that fires an event (called a *button event*) when the user clicks it with the mouse

Bytecode A standard machine language into which Java source code is compiled

Call A statement that causes a method to be executed; in Java we call a method by writing its name, followed by a list of arguments enclosed in parentheses

Caught exception An exception in Java that must either be caught with a *catch* statement or explicitly thrown to the next level

Central processing unit (CPU) The part of the computer that executes the instructions (object code) stored in memory; made up of the arithmetic/logic unit and the control unit

Character stream file A file that is stored as a sequence of characters

Class A description of the representation of a specific kind of object, in terms of data and operational behaviors

Class A definition for an object or an application in Java

Class field A field that belongs to a class rather than its object instances; identified as such with the modifier

Class method   A method that belongs to a class rather than its object instances; identified as such with the modifier

Client   Software that declares and manipulates objects of a particular class

Code   Instructions for a computer that are written in a programming language

Collaboration   An interaction between objects in which one object requests that another object carry out one of its responsibilities

Compiler   A program that translates code written in a high-level language into machine code

Complexity   A measure of the effort expended by the computer in performing a computation, relative to the size of the computation

Composite data type   A data type that allows a collection of values to be associated with an identifier of that type

Computer   A programmable device that can store, retrieve, and process data

Computer program   Instructions defining a set of objects and orchestrating their interactions to solve a problem

Computer programming   The process of specifying objects and the ways in which those objects interact to solve a problem

Concrete step   A step for which the implementation details are fully specified

Constructor   An operation that creates a new instance of a class

Container class   A class into which you can add other elements

Control abstraction   The separation of the logical properties of the operations on an object from their implementation

Control structure   A statement used to alter the normally sequential flow of control

Control unit   The component of the central processing unit that controls the actions of the other components so that instructions (the object code) execute in the correct sequence

Copy constructor   An operation that creates a new instance of a class by copying an existing instance, possibly altering some or all of its state in the process

Count-controlled loop   A loop that executes a specified number of times

Data   Information in a form that a computer can use

Data abstraction   The separation of the logical representation of an object's range of values from their implementation

Data structure   The implementation of a composite data field in an abstract data type

Data type   The specification in a programming language of how information is represented in the computer as data and the set of operations that can be applied to it

Declaration   A statement that associates an identifier with a field, a method, a class, or a package so that the programmer can refer to that item by name

Deep copy   An operation that copies one class instance to another, using observer methods as necessary to eliminate nested references and copy only the simple types to which they refer; the result is that two instances do not contain any duplicate references

Derived   A class that is created as an extension of another class in the hierarchy

Deserializing   Translating a serialized stream of bytes back into the original object

Desk checking   Tracing an execution of a design or code on paper

Glossary

Dialog   A technique of user interface in which the user enters data and then performs a separate action (such as clicking a button) when the entered values are ready to be processed by the application

Direct execution   The process by which a computer performs the actions specified in a machine language program

Documentation   The written text and comments that make an application easier for others to understand, use, and modify

Dynamic binding   Determining at run time which form of a polymorphic method to call

Editor   An interactive program used to create and modify source programs or data

Encapsulation   Designing a class so that its implementation is protected from the actions of external code except through the formal interface

Evaluate   To compute a new value by performing a specified set of operations on given values

Event counter   A variable that is incremented each time a particular event occurs

Event counter   An action, such as a mouse click, that takes place asynchronously with respect to the execution of the application

Event handling   the process of responding to events

Event listener   An object that contains event handler methods

Event loop   Repeating an action in response to repeated events

Event source   An object that generates events

Event-controlled loop   A loop that terminates when something happens inside the loop body to signal that the loop should be exited

Exception   An unusual condition that is indicated by a method using a throw statement; the method's caller must either catch the exception or explicitly throw it to the next level

Exception handler   A section of code that is executed when a particular exception occurs. In Java, an exception handler appears within a clause of a *try-catch-finally* control structure

Execution trace   Going through the code with actual values, recording the state of the variables

Expression   An arrangement of identifiers, literals, and operators that can be evaluated to compute a value of a given type

Expression statement   A statement formed by appending a semicolon to an assignment expression, an increment expression, or a decrement expression

Field   A named place in memory that holds a data object; a component of a frame in which the user can type a value; the user must first place the cursor in the field by clicking inside the field

File   A named area in a secondary storage that is used to hold a collection of data; the collection of data itself

Firing an event   An event source generates an event

Flow of control   The order in which the computer executes statements

Functional decomposition   A technique for developing software in which the problem is divided into more easily handled subproblems, the solutions to which create a solution to the overall problem

General case   The case for which the solution is expressed in terms of a smaller version of itself; also known as the *recursive case*

Hardware   The physical components of a computer

Hide   To provide a field in a derived class that has the same name as a field in its superclass; to provide a class method that has the same form of heading as a class method in its superclass. The field or class method is said to hide the corresponding component of the superclass

Hypertext Markup Language (HTML)   The language used to create or build Web pages

Identifier   A name associated with a package, class, method, or field and used to refer to that element

Immutable object   An object whose state cannot be changed once it is created

Implementation (in Java)   A class containing the definitions of the methods specified in an interface

Infinite recursion   The situation in which a method calls itself over and over endlessly

Information   Any knowledge that can be communicated

Inherit   To acquire a field or method from a superclass

Inheritance   A mechanism that enables us to define a new class by adapting the definition of an existing class; a mechanism by which one class acquires the properties - the data fields and methods - of another class

Input/output (I/O) devices   The parts of the computer that accept data to be processed (input) and present the results of that processing (output)

Inspection   A verification method in which one member of a team reads the code or design line-by-line and the other team members point out errors

Instantiate   To create an object based on the description supplied by a class

Interactive system   A system that supports direct communication between the user and the computer

Interface   A connecting link at a shared boundary that allows independent systems to meet and act on or communicate with each other

Interface (in Java)   A model for a class that specifies the fields and methods that must be present in a class that implements the interface

Internet   A wide area network that spans the planet

Interpretation   The translation, while a program is running, of nonmachine-language instructions (such as Bytecode) into executable operations

Iteration   An individual pass through, or repetition of, the body of a loop

Iteration counter   A counter variable that is incremented in each iteration of a loop

Iterator   An operation that allows us to process - one at a time - all of the components in an object

Key   A member of a class whose value is used to determine the logical and/or physical order of the items in a list

Layout manager   A class that automatically manages the placement of display elements within a content pane on the screen

Length   The number of items in a list; it can vary over time

Linear relationship   Every element except the first has a unique predecessor, and every element except the last has a unique successor

Glossary

Literal value   Any constant value written in Java

Local Area Network (LAN)   A network in a close geographic area

Loop   A control structure that causes a statement or group of statements to be executed repeatedly

Loop entry   The point at which the flow of control reaches the first statement inside a loop

Loop exit   The point at which the repetition of the loop body ends and control passes to the first statement following the loop

Loop test   The point at which the *while* expression is evaluated and the decision is made either to begin a new iteration or to skip to the statement immediately following the loop

Machine language   The language, made up of binary-coded instructions, that is used directly by the computer

Markup language   A language that uses tags to annotate the information in a document

Member   A field or method within a class

Memory unit   Internal data storage in a computer

Metalanguage   A language that is used to write the syntax rules for another language

Method   A subprogram in Java

Mixed type expressions   An expression that contains operands of different data types; also called a mixed mode expression

Modifiability   The property of an encapsulated class definition that allows the implementation to be changed without having an effect on code that uses it (except in terms of speed or memory space)

Module   A self-contained collection of steps that solves a problem or subproblem; it can contain both concrete and abstract steps

Mutable Object   An object whose state can be changed after it is created

Named constant (symbolic constant)   A location in memory, referenced by an identifier, that contains a data value that cannot be changed

Narrowing conversion   A type conversion that may result in a loss of some information, as in converting a value of type `double` to type `float`

Network   A collection of connected computing devices that communicate and share resources

Object   A collection of data values and associated operations

Object code   A machine language version of a source code

Object-oriented design   A technique for developing software in which the solution is expressed in terms of objects - self-contained entities composed of data and operations on that data that interact by sending messages to one another

Observer   An operation that allows us to observe the state of an object without changing it

One-dimensional array   A structured collection of components, all of the same type, that is given a single name. Each component (array element) is accessed by an index that indicates the component's position within the collection

Operating system   A set of programs that manages all of the computer's resources

Ordinal data type   A data type in which each value (except the first) has a unique predecessor and each value (except the last) has a unique successor

Out-of-bounds array index   An index value that is either less than zero or greater than the array size minus one

Overloading   The repeated use of a method name with a different signature

Override   To provide an instance method in a derived class that has the same form of heading as an instance method in its superclass. The method in the derived class redefines (overrides) the method in its superclass. We cannot override class methods

Package   A collection of related classes

Package   A named collection of object classes in Java that can be imported by a program

Peripheral device   An input, output, or auxiliary storage device attached to a computer

Pixel   An abbreviation of "picture elements"; the individual dots that make up an image on a display screen

Polymorphic   An operation that has multiple meanings depending on the class of object to which it is bound

Precision   The maximum number of significant digits

Programming   Developing instructions for carrying out a task involving a set of objects

Programming language   A set of rules, symbols, and special words used to construct a computer program

Public interface   The members of a class that can be accessed outside of the class, together with the modes of access that are specified by other modifiers

Recursive algorithm   A solution that is expressed in terms of (1) smaller instances of itself and (2) a base case

Recursive call   A method call in which the method being called is the same as the one making the call

Recursive definition   A definition in which something is defined in terms of smaller versions of itself

Registering a listener   Adding a listener to an event source's list of interested listeners

Representational error   An arithmetic error that occurs when the precision of the true result of an arithmetic operation is greater than the precision of the machine

Reserved word   A word that has special meaning in Java; it cannot be used as a programmer-defined identifier

Responsibility   An action that an implementation of an object must be capable of performing

Reuse   The ability to import a class into code that uses it without additional modification to either the class or the user code; the ability to extend the definition of a class

Scalar data type   A data type in which the values are ordered and each value is atomic (indivisible)

Scope of access (scope)   The region of program code where it is legal to reference (use) an identifier

Scope rules   The rules that determine where in a program an identifier may be referenced, given the point where the identifier is declared and its specific access modifiers

Self-documenting code   Program code containing meaningful identifiers as well as judiciously used clarifying comments

Semantics   The set of rules that determines the meaning of instructions written in a programming language

Serializing   Translating an object into a stream of bytes

Shadowing   A scope rule specifying that a local identifier declaration blocks access to an identifier declared with the same name outside of the block containing the local declaration

Shallow copy   An operation that copies a source class instance to a destination class instance, simply copying all references so that the destination instance contains duplicate references to values that are also referred to by the source

Short-circuit (conditional) evaluation   Evaluation of a logical expression in left-to-right order with evaluation stopping as soon as the final Boolean value can be determined

Signature   The distinguishing features of a method heading; the combination of the method name with the number and type(s) of its parameters in their given order

Significant digits   Those digits from the first nonzero digit on the left to the last nonzero digit on the right (plus any 0 digits that are exact)

Software   Computer programs; the set of all programs available on a computer

Software engineering   The application of traditional engineering methodologies and techniques to the development of software

Software piracy   The unauthorized copying of software for either personal use or use by others

Sorted list   A list whose predecessor and successor relationships are determined by the content of the keys of the items in the list; a semantic relationship exists among the keys of the items in the list

Sorting   Arranging the components of a list into order (for instance, words into alphabetical order or numbers into ascending or descending order)

Source code   Instructions written in a high-level programming language

Standard (built-in) type   A data type that is automatically available for use in every Java program

State   The information stored in an object at any given time

Static binding   Determining at compile time which form of a polymorphic method to call

Strongly typed   A property of a programming language in which the language allows variables to contain only values of the specified type or class

Structured data type   An organized collection of components; the organization determines the means used to access individual components

Subclass   A class that is derived from another class (its superclass)

Superclass   A class that is extended by one or more derived classes (its subclasses)

Switch expression   The expression whose value determines which *switch* label is selected. It must be an integer type other than long

Syntax   The formal rules governing how valid instructions are written in a programming language

Tag   The syntactic element in a markup language that indicates how information should be displayed

Tail recursion   A recursive algorithm in which no statements execute after the return from the recursive call

Termination condition   The condition that causes a loop to be exited

Test plan   A document that specifies how an application is to be tested

Test plan implementation   Using the test cases specified in a test plan to verify that an application outputs the predicted results

Transformer   A method that changes the state of a mutable object

Transformer   An operation that changes the internal state of an object

Two-dimensional array   A collection of components, all of the same type, structured in two dimensions. Each component is accessed by a pair of indexes that present the component's position in each dimension

Type casting   The explicit conversion of a value from one data type to another

Type conversion   The implicit (automatic) conversion of a value from one data type to another

Unary operator   An operator that has just one operand

Uncaught exception   An exception in Java that can optionally be caught or allowed to propagate automatically to the next level

Uniform Resource Locator (URL)   The address of a web page on the Internet

Unsorted list   A list in which data items are placed in no particular order with respect to their content; the only relationships between data elements consist of the list predecessor and successor relationship

Unstructured data type   A collection of components that are not organized with respect to one another

Value-returning method   A method that is called from within an expression and returns a value that can be used in the expression

Variable   A location in memory, referenced by an identifier, that contains a data value that can be changed

Virtual machine   A program that makes one computer act like another

Virus   Code that replicates itself, often with the goal of spreading to other computers without authorization, and possibly with the intent of doing harm

Void method   A method that is called as a separate statement; when it returns, processing continues with the next statement

Walk-through   A verification method in which a team performs a manual simulation of the code or design

Web   An infrastructure of information and the network software used to access it

Wide Area Network (WAN)   A network that connects two or more local area networks

Widening conversion   A type conversion that does not result in a loss of information

Chapter 1 Exam Preparation Exercises

1. The steps keep repeating forever, because there is no way for the algorithm to stop. (Also, it is a poor algorithm because the last action is lathering—you wouldn't want to leave the lather in your hair.) Corrected algorithm:

```
1. Wet hair
2. Lather
3. Rinse
4. Repeat Steps 2 and 3 once
```

3. In the following recipe for chocolate pound cake, the statements that are branches, loops, or subalgorithm references are marked.

```
Preheat the oven to 350 degrees
Line the bottom of a 9-inch tube pan with wax paper
Sift 2 3/4 c flour, 3/4 t cream of tartar, 1/2 t baking soda, 1 1/2 t salt, and
    1 3/4 c sugar into a large bowl
Add 1 c shortening to the bowl
If [BRANCH] using butter, margarine, or lard, then
    add 2/3 c milk to the bowl,
else
    (for other shortenings) add 1 c minus 2 T of milk to the bowl
Add 1 t vanilla to the mixture in the bowl
If [BRANCH] mixing with a spoon, then
    see [SUBALGORITHM REFERENCE] the instructions in the introduction to the
    chapter on cakes,
else
    (for electric mixers) beat the contents of the bowl for 2 minutes at medium
    speed, scraping the bowl and beaters as needed
Add 3 eggs plus 1 extra egg yolk to the bowl
Melt 3 squares of unsweetened chocolate and add it to the mixture in the bowl
Beat the mixture for 1 minute at medium speed
Pour the batter into the tube pan
Put the pan into the oven and bake for 1 hour and 10 minutes
Perform [SUBALGORITHM REFERENCE] the test for doneness described in the
    introduction to the chapter on cakes
Repeat [LOOP] the test once each minute until the cake is done
Remove the pan from the oven and allow the cake to cool for 2 hours
Follow [SUBALGORITHM REFERENCE] the instructions for removing the cake from the
    pan, given in the introduction to the chapter on cakes
Sprinkle powdered sugar over the cracks on top of the cake just before serving
```

7. Means-ends analysis

9. Look for things that are familiar

Answers

Chapter 1 Programming Warm-Up Exercises

1. Each student will come up with a different answer for this problem, depending on where he or she finds the recipe and how the cookbook is written. A correct answer would identify most or all of the nouns in the problem as objects—for example, individual ingredients, bowls, tube pan, and oven. Loops in recipes are often things like "Beat the mixture 300 strokes" or "sift the mixture three times." Many angel food cake recipes specify different actions to take when cooking at a high altitude, which provides an example of a branch. Choosing to add an optional ingredient is another case of a branch. Some recipes include a complicated series of steps that are set off from the rest of the process or that are simply divided into stages such as preparing different mixtures. These represent candidates for subprograms. Each step or group of steps in the recipe should thus be identified as a sequence, branch, loop, or subprogram.

2. Each student will come up with a different answer for this problem, depending on what type of appliance he or she chooses. A correct answer would identify most or all of the nouns in the directions as objects. For example, setting the time and date on a computer would probably involve working with a window that has boxes for data values and buttons. Each text box and button would be an object. There might be check boxes where you could set an option to be on or off. Such checks would correspond to branching statements. There might be instructions to click an arrow repeatedly to set a data value, which would correspond to a looping statement. A button that brings up a separate window might represent a subprogram, depending on what action clicking the button might generate. Each instruction should correspond to a sequence, branch, loop, or subprogram.

Chapter 2 Exam Preparation Exercises

2. Dwits
   a. XYZ   Invalid—must end with 1, 2, or 3
   b. 123   Invalid—must start with X, Y, or Z
   c. Xl   Valid
   d. 23Y   Invalid—must start with X, Y, or Z
   e. XY12   Valid
   f. Y2Y   Invalid—must end with 1, 2, or 3
   g. ZY2   Valid
   h. XY23Xl   Valid

5. False; reserved words cannot be used as variable names.

9. Only one character can be stored into a variable of type `char`.

12. True; a literal string can be assigned to a variable of type `String`.

15. This program may be corrected in several ways. Here is one correct version:

```
public class LotsOfErrors
```

```
  {
    public static void main(String[] args)
    {
      final String FIRST = "Martin";
      final String MID = "Luther";
      final String LAST = "King";
      String name;
      name = FIRST + ' ' + MID + ' ' + LAST + " Jr.";
      System.out.println(name);
    }
  }
```

20. "Sending a message" means telling a method to apply itself to the object or class to which it is attached—that is, invoking a method.

22. An application

25. The name of a constructor must be identical to the name of the class. Because we begin class names with uppercase letters, the constructor must also begin with an uppercase letter.

Chapter 2 Programming Warm-Up Exercises

2.
```
System.out.println("The moon ");
System.out.println("is ");
System.out.println("blue.");
```

4.
```
System.out.println("Make: " + make);
System.out.println("Model: " + model);
System.out.println("Color: " + color);
System.out.println("Plate type: " + plateType);
System.out.println("Classification: " + classification);
```

5.
```
//****************************************************************
// PrintName application
// This program prints a name in two different formats
//****************************************************************
public class PrintName
{
  public static void main(String[] args) throws IOException
  {
    String FIRST  = "Herman";    // Person's first name
    String LAST   = "Herrmann";  // Person's last name
    String MIDDLE = "G";         // Person's middle initial
    String firstLast;            // Name in first-last format
    String lastFirst;            // Name in last-first format
    String firstInitialLast      // Name in first, initial, last format
    BufferedReader in;           // Input stream for strings
    in = new BufferedReader (new InputStreamReader(System.in));
    System.out.print("Enter first name: ");      // Prompt for first name
```

```
        first = in.readLine();                    // Get first name
        System.out.print("Enter last name: ");    // Prompt for last name
        last = in.readLine();                      // Get last name
        System.out.print("Enter middle initial: "); // Prompt for middle initial
        middle = in.readLine();                    // Get middle initial
        firstLast = first + " " + last;            // Generate first format
        System.out.println("Name in first-last format is " + firstLast);
        lastFirst = last + ", " + first + ", ";    // Generate second format
        System.out.println("Name in last-first-initial format is " +
                        lastFirst + middle + ".");
        firstInitialLast = first + " " + middle + ". " + last;
        System.out.println("Name in first-initial-last format is " +
                        firstInitialLast):
    }
}
```

8.
```
public class Date
{
    String month;                    // Month in string form
    String year;                     // Year in string form
    String day;                      // Day in string form

    public Date(String newMonth, String newYear, String newDay)
    {  // Constructor
        month = newMonth;
        year = newYear;
        day = newDay;
    }

    public String monthDayYear()     // Returns mm/dd/yyyy format
    {
        return month + "/" + day + "/" + year;
    }

    public String yearMonthDay()     // Returns yyy-mm-dd format
    {
        return year + "-" + month + "-" + day;
    }
} // End of Date class
```

Chapter 3 Exam Preparation Exercises

2. **a.** 27

  b. 13

  c. 5

 d. 0

 e. 3

 f. 8

 g. 3

5. **a.** a = 5b = 2

  b. Sum:52

  c. Sum: 52

  d. 2 feet

7. $y = -b + \sqrt{b^2 - 4ac}$

10. **a.** 26

  b. reparation

  c. 0

  d. 15

  e. 15

  f. 15

Chapter 3 Programming Warm-Up Exercises

2. ```
int sum;
sum = n*(n+1)/2;
```

4. **a.** `Math.abs(i)`

  **b.** `Math.abs(n)`

  **c.** `Math.abs(x + y)`

  **d.** `Math.abs(x) + Math.abs(y)`

  **e.** `Math.pow(x, 3.0)/(x + y)`

  **f.** `Math.sqrt(Math.pow(x, 6.0) + Math.pow(y, 5.0))`

  **g.** `Math.pow((x + Math.sqrt(y)), 7.0)`

7. This is a laboratory exercise for the student, but it requires that appropriate documentation be added.

```
// Programming Assignment 2
// William T. Verts
// June 27, 2003
// This application computes the cost per ounce given a total
// cost and a weight expressed in pounds and ounces.

public class WarmUp2
{
  public static void main(String[] args)
  {
    final int TOT_COST = 1376; // Total cost
```
```

```
      final int POUNDS = 10;        // Weight in pounds
      final int OUNCES = 12;        // Additional ounces
      int    totOz;        // Total weight in ounces
      double uCost;        // Computed cost per ounce
      // Calculations
      totOz = 16 * POUNDS;
      totOz = totOz + OUNCES;
      uCost = TOT_COST / totOz;
      System.out.println("Cost per unit: " + uCost);
    }
  }
```

8.
```
  //***********************************************
  // Rectangle application
  // This application finds the perimeter and the area
  // of a rectangle, given the length and width
  //***********************************************
  public class Rectangle
  {
    public static void main(String[] args)
    {
      double length;              // Length of the rectangle
      double width;               // Width of the rectangle
      double perimeter;           // Perimeter of the rectangle
      double area;                // Area of the rectangle

      length = 10.7;
      width = 5.2;
      perimeter = length * 2.0 + width * 2.0;  // Calculate perimeter
      area = length * width;                   // Calculate area
      // Print perimeter
      System.out.println("The perimeter of a rectangle with length " +
        length + " and width " + width + " is " + perimeter);
      // Print area
      System.out.println("The area of the rectangle is " + area);
    }
  }
```

11.
```
  //***************************************************************
  // This application computes the sum and product of two integers
  //***************************************************************
  public class SumProd
  {
    public static void main(String[] args)
    {
      final int INT2 = 8;
      final int INT1 = 20;
```

```
        System.out.println("The sum of " + INT1 + " and "
            + INT2 + " is " + (INT1+INT2));
        System.out.println("Their product is " + (INT1*INT2));
      }
    }
```

Chapter 4 Exam Preparation Exercises

1. A control structure changes the sequential execution of the statements in a program.

2. A logical expression is an expression made up of logical values and operations. The logical values may take the form of relational operators applied to numeric values.

7. **a.** xyxy

   b. `The value of x is 3`

   c. 376z

      (Despite the indentation, the final output statement is not part of the *else* clause.)

10. **a.** x < y && y <= z

    b. x > 0 && y > 0 && z > 0

    c. x != y && x != z

    d. x == y && x == z

14. ```
if (typeA || typeB)
{
  if (typeA && typeB)
    System.out.print("Type AB");
}
else
  System.out.print("Type 0");
    ```

15.

| Data Set | ch1, ch2, ch3 | Expected Output |
|----------|---------------|-----------------|
| Set 1 | A, A, A | All initials are the same. |
| Set 2 | A, A, B | First two are the same. |
| Set 3 | B, A, A | Last two are the same. |
| Set 4 | A, B, A | First and last are the same. |
| Set 5 | A, B, C | All initials are different. |
    ```

18. a. The `String` class provides methods that can be used to compare two strings.

b.

Method Name	Argument	Returns	English Description
equals	String	boolean	Returns `true` if the two strings are equal, `false` otherwise.
equalsIgnoreCase	String	boolean	Returns `true` if the two strings are equal, ignoring case of letters; `false` otherwise.
compareTo	String	int	Returns 0: the two strings are equal. Returns <0: object's string comes before argument's string. Returns >0: object's string comes after argument's string.
toUpperCase	none	String	Returns object's string in all uppercase letters.
toLowerCase	none	String	Returns object's string in all lowercase letters.

Chapter 4 Programming Warm-Up Exercises

4.
```
if (pageNumber % 2 == 0)
    leftPage = true;
```
We have to use the *if* form here because the problem does not say to set `leftPage` to `false` if `pageNumber` is odd.

5.
```
if (i > j)
  if (i > k)
    biggest = i;
  else
    biggest = k;
else
  if (j > k)
    biggest = j;
  else
    biggest = k;
```

or

```
biggest = i;
if (j > biggest)
  biggest = j;
if (k > biggest)
  biggest = k;
```

7.
```
if (age > 64)
    System.out.print("Senior voter");
else if (age < 18)
    System.out.print("Under age");
else System.out.print("Regular voter");
```

```
9. // This is a nonsense program segment
   if (a > 0)
     if (a < 20)
     {
       System.out.print("A is in range.");
       b = 5;
     }
     else
     {
       System.out.print("A is too large.");
       b = 3;
     }
   else
     System.out.print("A is too small.");
   System.out.print("All done.")
11. discriminant = b * b - 4.0 * a * c;
    if (discriminant < 0.0)
        System.out.println("No real roots.");
    else
    {
        root1 = (-b - discriminant) / (2.0 * a);
        root2 = (-b + discriminant) / (2.0 * a);
    }
```

Chapter 5 Exam Preparation Exercises

1.

```
Import the library package java.io.*
Declare a file variable
Instantiate the file object and assign its address to the file variable
Use methods associated with the file object to read or write
Call a method to close the file
```

4. It skips the next 1,000 characters in the file. If EOF is reached first, an exception is thrown.

7. Loops are segments of code that are repeated from zero to many times as long as an expression is true. Branches are segments of code that may be executed zero or one time, depending on the value of an expression.

9.
```
number = 1;
while (number < 11)
{
  out.println(number);
  number++;
}
```

13. a. The output is BCDE.

b.
```
inLine = inFile.readLine();
count = 0;
while (count < inLine.length())
{
  outFile.print(inLine.charAt(count));
  count++;
}
outFile.println();
```

14. Yes, this code segment needs a priming read.

```
datum = inFile.readLine();
while (datum != null)
{
  letter = datum.charAt(0);
  count = 0;
  while (count < datum.length())
  {
    outFile.print(letter);
    count++;
    letter = datum.charAt(count);
  }
  outFile.println();
  datum = inFile.readLine();
  outFile.println("Another line read...");
}
```

18. Written

20. a. Count-controlled and event-controlled.

b. A count-controlled loop executes a predetermined number of times. An event-controlled loop executes as long as an event is true and exits the loop when the event becomes false.

c. The loop runs forever (or until the program is manually terminated by the operating system).

d. The loop runs forever (or until the program is manually terminated by the operating system).

e. Sentinel-controlled, end-of-file-controlled, and flag-controlled.

22. a. An assignment expression is an expression containing an assignment operator.

b. `((line = dataFile.readLine())!=null)`

Answers

Chapter 5 Programming Warm-Up Exercises

5. W
   88
      This is a string.

7.
```
line = fileInBuf.readLine();
fileOutPr.println();
fileOutPr.println(line);
fileOutPr.println();
```

9.
```
dangerous = false;
while (!dangerous)
{
  pressure = Float.parseFloat(inFile.readLine());
  if (pressure > 510.0)
    dangerous = true;
}
```

or

```
dangerous = false;
while (!dangerous)
{
  pressure = Float.parseFloat(inFile.readLine());
  dangerous = (pressure > 510.0);
}
```

11.
```
count28 = 0;
loopCount = 1;
while (loopCount <= 100)
{
  number = Integer.parseInt(inFile.readLine());
  if (number == 28)
    count28++;
  loopCount++;
}
```

13.
```
count = 0;
sum = 0;
scoreLine = scoreFile.readLine();
while (scoreLine != null)
{
  score = Integer.parseInt(scoreLine);
  sum = sum + score;
  count++;
  scoreLine = scoreFile.readLine();
}
if (count > 0)
  average = (float)sum / (float)count;
```

16.
```
count++;
if (count == 13)
  count = 0;
```

or

```
count = (count+1) % 13;
```

18.
```
hour = 1;
tenMinute = 0;
am = true;
done = false;
while (!done)
{
  timeOut.print(hour + ":");
  timeOut.print(tenMinute + "0");
  if (am)
    timeOut.println(" A.M.");
  else
    timeOut.println(" P.M.");
  tenMinute++;
  if (tenMinute > 5)
  {
    tenMinute = 0;
    hour++;
    if (hour == 13)
      hour = 1;
    else if (hour == 12)
      am = !am;
  }
  done = (hour == 1 && tenMinute == 0 && am);
}
```

20.
```
String fpString;
int places;
int position;
float fpNumber;

fpString = String.valueOf(fpNumber);
position = fpString.indexOf(".");
fpString = fpString.substring(0, Math.min(position + 5, fpString.length()));
places = (fpString.substring(position + 1, fpString.length())).length();
while (places < 4)
{
  fpString = fpString + "0";
  places++;
}
  outFile.println(fpString);
```

Answers

Chapter 6 Exam Preparation Exercises

1. Object-oriented design focuses on the data objects in the problem; functional decomposition focuses on the tasks in the problem.

4. Class method

6. The public interface of a class consists of the members of a class that can be accessed outside of the class, together with the modes of access that are specified by other modifiers.

7. To protect the class members from being accessed directly by a client application

13. The goal of brainstorming is to come up with a potential list of classes.

16. Built-in or library classes may be identified during the brainstorming phase. We do not need to make CRC cards for them or the classes removed during the filtering phase.

19. When a class has no unfilled responsibilities, it becomes inactive.

22. To indicate that a class is just a variation, the original class is listed as the superclass.

25. Absolutely

28. A computer virus is code that replicates itself, often with the goal of spreading to other computers without authorization, and possibly with the intent of doing harm.

30. Self-documenting code is application code containing meaningful identifiers as well as judiciously used clarifying comments.

31. a. A compilation unit is made up of optional package and import statements and a class declaration(s).

    b. No

    c. In a file

    d A file containing a compilation unit is named by the public class with a .java extension.

    e. Yes

Answers

Chapter 6 Programming Warm-Up Exercises

1.

Class Name: Car	Superclass:	Subclasses:
Responsibilities	**Collaborations**	
Create Car (make, model, color, license)	None	
Know make return String	None	
Know model return String	None	
Know color return String	None	
Know license return String	None	

3.

Class Name: Book	Superclass:	Subclasses:
Responsibilities	**Collaborations**	
Create Book (title, author, call numbrr)	None	
Know title return String	None	
Know author return Name	None	
Know call number return String	None	

6.

Class Name: Cow	Superclass:	Subclasses:
Responsibilities		**Collaborations**
Create Cow (name, ID number, birth date, recent calving date)		None
Know name return Name		None
Know ID number return String		None
Know birth date return Date		None
Know calving date return Date		None

7.

Class Name: MilkProduced	Superclass: Cow	Subclasses:
Responsibilities		**Collaborations**
Create MilkProduced (name, ID number, birth date, recent calving date)		None
Set milk amount (quantity)		
Average is return double		None
Total output is return double		None
Set total to zero		None

9. There are actually only two classes in the proposed list in Exercise 8 in addition to the file: "Participant" and "Time." All of the other classes listed in Exercise 8 can be represented as primitive types. However, there does need to be a "User Interface," which will be represented by the driver.

10. Here is a CRC card for the participant class of Exercise 9:

Class Name: Participant	Superclass:		Subclasses:
Responsibilities		**Collaborations**	
Create Participant (name, weight, jog, jump, bench)		None	
Set current statistics (weight, jog, jump, bench)		Name	
Know weight return double		None	
Know jog return Time		None	
Know jump return double		None	
Know bench return double		None	

12. What happens if:

a name to be processed doesn't exist?

a participant wants to quit the program?

the user wants to determine who has the fastest jogging time?

the user wants to determine who has the best long-jump distance?

the user wants to determine who has the highest bench-press weight?

the user wants to determine who has the most improved jogging time? long-jump record? bench-press weight?

15. All the compilation units of a package must be kept in one directory with the same name as the package.

Chapter 7 Exam Preparation Exercises

1. a. Internal scope and external scope

b. No. Internal scope does not depend on the access modifiers.

c. Internal scope refers to the scope within a class. Any identifier declared in a class can be used anywhere within the class.

d. You can't use a class variable to initialize another variable before it has been defined. A local identifier shadows a class member with the same name.

e. Shadowing is a scope rule that specifies that a local identifier has precedence over a class identifier with the same name.

f. Yes.

4. a. Protected members

    b. They are automatically part of the interface.

9. Data fields and methods that are `public` or `protected`

12. The method in the derived class overrides the method in the superclass.

15. No, you cannot remove a member, but you can hide it by covering it with a member of the same name.

16.

Situation	Hiding	Overriding	Overloading	Shadowing
A class method has the same name and signature as a superclass method.	X			
An instance method has the same name and signature as a superclass instance method.		X		
A class has two methods with the same name but different signatures.			X	
A field in a derived class has the same name as a field in its superclass.	X			
An instance method has the same name but a different signature than a superclass instance method.			X	
A method declares a variable with the same name as a field in the class.				X
A method has a parameter with the same name as a field in the class.				X

Chapter 7 Programming Warm-Up Exercises

```
2. public class MyName extends YourName
   {
     int myField;        // myField is an instance field

     public MyName(int myField)      // Constructor with a parameter
                                     //  that shadows the instance field

     {
       this.myField = myField;       // Assign the parameter to
                                     //  the instance field

     }
   }
```

Answers

4. a. `public class SomeClass`

    b. `public static void someMethod()`

    c. `static int someMethod()`

    d. `private static int someMethod()`

    e. `protected static char someMethod()`

6.
```
public class SomeClass
{
  int var;                         // Class member
  final int CONST = 3;             // Class member CONST
  public void someMethod(int param)
  {
    int var;                       // Local variable
    var = param * CONST;
    final int const = 10;
    var = 5;                       // Local variable
    System.out.println("" + this.var); // Class member
  }
}
```

8. The code segment is not correct because the signatures are not distinct.
```
public int someMethod()              // someMethod
public void someMethod()             // someMethod
public double someMethod()           // someMethod
public double someMethod(int a)      // someMethod, int
public double someMethod(String a)   // someMethod, String
public double someMethod(int a, int b) // someMethod, int, int
```

Chapter 8 Exam Preparation Exercises

2. `Cost is`
`300`
`Price is 30Cost is 300`
`Grade A costs`
`300`

4. a. `26`

    b. `reparation`

    c. `0`

9. No. We just instantiate a `JPanel` object.

13. Nothing appears on the screen.

14. Declare a variable of the JButton class, instantiate a JButton object and assign its address to the variable, and add the object to the frame's content pane using the add method.

17. Classes that implement the ActionListener interface must have an actionPerformed method with an ActionEvent parameter.

20. There is a default event handler provided for the window closing.

Chapter 8 Programming Warm-Up Exercises

2. a.
```
ButtonHandler action;
JButton enter;
JButton quit;
```
   b.
```
enter = new JButton("Enter");
quit = new JButton("Quit");
action = new ButtonHandler();
```
   c.
```
outPane.add(enter);
outPane.add(quit);
```
   d.
```
enter.addActionListener(action);
quit.addActionListener(action);
```
   e.
```
String name;
name = event.getActionCommand();
```
   f.
```
private class ButtonHandler implements ActionListener
{
  public void actionPerformed(ActionEvent event)
  {
    String name;
    name = event.getActionCommand();
    if (name.equals("Enter"))
      out.add(new JLabel("Enter was pressed."));
    else if (name.equals("Quit"))
      out.add(new JLabel("Quit was pressed."));
    else
      out.add(new JLabel("An unexpected event occurred.")):
  }
}
```

5. a.
```
JFrame exampleFrame;
JLabel exampleLabel;
JTextField exampleField;
static JButton exampleButton;
container outPane;
```

    b.
```
private static class ExampleClass implements ActionListener
{
   public void actionPerformed(ActionEvent event)
   {
      exampleValue = exampleField.getText();
      exampleField.setText("");
   }
}
```
    c. `exampleButton.addActionListener(exampleHandler);`

    d.
```
private class Example2Class implements ActionListener
{
   public void actionPerformed(ActionEvent event)
   {
      exampleLabel.setText(exampleField.getText());
   }
}
```

6. `exampleField.setText("2000");`

8.
```
JLabel promptLabel;
JLabel countLabel;
JLabel averageLabel;
JTextField inField;
JButton button;
int count;
int total;
```

12.
```
JPanel myPanel;
myPanel = new JPanel();
myPanel.setLayout(new FlowLayout());
myPanel.add(new JLabel("one"));
myPanel.add(new JLabel("two"));
myPanel.add(new JLabel("three"));
```

Chapter 9 Exam Preparation Exercises

1. Use a *try-catch* statement.

4. False

6. A *switch* expression is the expression in a *switch* statement whose value determines which case label is selected.

A pretest loop is a loop in which the test occurs before the body of the loop. If the loop expression is false, the loop body is not executed.

A posttest loop is a loop in which the test occurs after the loop body. The body of a posttest loop always executes at least once.

10.
```
switch (n)
{
  case 3 : alpha++;
          break;
  case 7 : beta++;
          break;
  case 10: gamma++;
          break;
}
```

15. Nothing is printed. A *for* loop is a pretest loop.

17.
```
********* *********
********   ********
*******     *******
******       ******
*****         *****
****           ****
***             ***
**               **
*                 *
```

19. a. expression

b. expression

c. expression statement

d. expression

Chapter 9 Programming Warm-Up Exercises

1. a. `MyException anException;`

b.
```
public class MyException extends Exception
{
  public MyException()
  {
    super();
  }
  public MyException(String message)
  {
    super(message);
  }
}
```

c. `throw new MyException("Error somewhere.");`

4.
```
switch (grade)
{
  case 'A' : sum = sum + 4;
            break;
```

```
        case 'B' : sum = sum + 3;
                   break;
        case 'C' : sum = sum + 2;
                   break;
        case 'D' : sum++;
                   break;
        case 'F' : outData.println("Student is on probation");
                   break;
        default  : outData.println("Invalid letter grade");
                   break;    // Not required
   }
```

6.
```
   response = Integer.parseInt(inData.readLine());
   if (response >= 0 && response <= 127)
   do
      {
         response = Integer.parseInt(inData.readLine());
      } while (response >= 0 && response <= 127);
```

10.
```
   k = 9;
   do
   {
      outData.println(k + " " + 3 * k);
      k++;
   } while (k <= 21);
```

11.
```
   public int power(int base, int exponent)
   // Return base raised to the exponent power
   {
      int powerValue = 1;
      for (int i = 1; i <= exponent; i++)
         powerValue = powerValue * base;
      return powerValue;
   }
```

Chapter 10 Exam Preparation Exercises

3. **a.** `float[] floatArray = new float[24];`

   b. `int[] intArray = new int[500];`

   c. `double[] doubleArray = new double[50];`

   d. `char[] charArray = new char[10];`

6.

   a. Because the array is of type `int`, the values are automatically set to 0 by the constructor.

   b.
   ```
   for (int index = 0; index < count.length; count++)
      count[index] =
         Integer.parseInt(inFile.readLine());
   ```

c.
```
int sum = 0;
    for (int index = 0; index < count.length; count++)
      sum = sum + count[index];
```

9.

[0]	[1]	[2]	[3]	[4]	[5]	[6]	[7]
10	9	8	7	6	5	4	3

11.

[0]	[1]	[2]	[3]	[4]	[5]	[6]	[7]
0	101	2	103	4	105	6	107

14. a. class containing class objects

   b. class

   c. class

   d. array of class objects

   e. array of primitive values

   f. array of class objects containing class objects

   g. array of class objects

16. The default value of the component type

Chapter 10 Programming Warm-Up Exercises

2.
```
public void setFailing()
{
  for (int index = 0; index < failing.length; index++)
    if (score[index] < 60)
      failing[index] = true;
}
```

3.
```
public void setPassing()
{
  for (int index = 0; index < passing.length; index++)
    if (score[index] >= 60)
      passing[index] = true;
}
```

6.
```
public int scoreCt(int grade)
{
  int count = 0;
  for (int index = 0; index < score.length; index++)
    if (score[index] >= grade)
      count++;
  return count;
}
```

```
7. public void reverse()
   {
     int tempScore;
     int halfLength = score.length/2;
     for (int index = 0; index < halfLength; index++)
     {
       tempScore = score[index];
       score[index] = score[score.length - (index + 1)];
       score[score.length - (index + 1)] = tempScore;
     }
   }
8. public class Parts
   {
     int number;
     double cost;
     Parts(int howMany, double howMuch)
     {
       number = howMany;
       cost = howMuch;
     }
   }
   .
   .
   Parts[] inventory = new Parts[100];
   String inLine;
   int index;
   int number;
   double cost;
   int count = 0;
   // File has been declared and instantiated
   while ((inLine = inFile.readLine()) != null)
   {
     index = inLine.indexOf(' ');          // Find position of blank

     number = Integer.parseInt(inLine.substring(0, index));  // Extract a number

     // Remove the first part of the string
     inLine = inLine.substring(index+1, inLine.length());
     cost = Double.parseDouble(inLine);
     inventory[count] = new Parts(number, cost);
     count++;
   }
```

Answers

Chapter 11 Exam Preparation Exercises

2. **a.** 1

   b. 2

   c. 7

   d. 7

3.

item	first	last	middle	Result
114	0	9	4	
	5	9	7	
	8	9	8	found is true

6. At the logical level, an array is a homogeneous data type. Java implements an array object with an extra integer variable that contains the number of cells in the array.

9. An iterator/transformer

13. The `Comparable` interface has only one method, `compareTo`, that returns a value less than 0 if the object comes before the parameter, 0 if the object and the parameter are equal, and a value greater than 0 if the parameter comes first.

14. **a.** If the class allows duplicates and no constraints restrict where the duplicates can be placed, then only the `delete` operation needs to be changed. If the implementation is sorted, a requirement might state that the duplicate item must be placed before or after the last copy inserted. In such a case, the `insert` operation might need to be altered.

   b. There would still be options for the `delete` operation. If there are duplicates, does *delete* mean "delete the first one found," "delete the last one inserted," or "delete all copies"?

Chapter 11 Programming Warm-Up Exercises

```
1. public class UnsortedList extends List
   {
     public UnsortedList()
     {
       super();
     }
     public UnsortedList(int maxItems)
     {
       super(maxItems);
     }
     public boolean isThere(String item)
     // Return true if item is in the list
```

```
      {
        int index = 0;
        while (index < numItems && listItems[index].compareTo(item) != 0)
          index++;
        return (index < numItems);
      }
      public void insert(String item)
      // If the list is not full, put item in the last position in the list;
      //  otherwise, list is unchanged
      {
        if (!isFull())
        {
          listItems[numItems] = item;
          numItems++;
        }
      }
      public void delete(String item)
      // Remove item from the list if it is there
      {
        int index = 0;
        boolean found = false;
        while (index < numItems && !found)
        {
          if (listItems[index].compareTo(item)== 0)
            found = true;
          else
            index++;
        }
        if (found)
        {
          for (int count = index; count < numItems-1; count++)
            listItems[count] = listItems[count+1];
          numItems--;
        }
      }
    }
2.  public class ListWithSort extends UnsortedList
    {
      // Allows the items in the list to be rearranged into ascending order.
      // This order is not preserved in future insertions.
```

```java
    public ListWithSort()
    {
      super();
    }

    public ListWithSort(int maxItems)
    {
      super(maxItems);
    }

    public void selectSort()
    // Arrange list items into ascending order;
    //   selection sort algorithm is used.
    {
      String  temp;            // Temporary variable
      int passCount;           // Loop control variable for outer loop
      int searchIndex;         // Loop control variable for inner loop
      int minIndex;            // Index of minimum so far

      for (passCount = 0; passCount < numItems - 1; passCount++)
      {
        minIndex = passCount;
        // Find the index of the smallest component
        //   in listItems[passCount]..listItems[numItems - 1]
        for (searchIndex = passCount + 1; searchIndex < numItems;
              searchIndex++)
          if (listItems[searchIndex].compareTo(listItems[minIndex]) < 0)
            minIndex = searchIndex;

        // Swap listItems[minIndex] and listItems[passCount]

        temp = listItems[minIndex];
        listItems[minIndex] = listItems[passCount];
        listItems[passCount] = temp;
      }
    }
  }
```

8. **a.**
```java
  public abstract class ListWithDuplicates
  {
    protected String[] listItems;      // Array to hold list items
    protected int numItems;            // Number of items in the list
    protected int currentPos;          // State variable for iteration
```

```java
public ListWithDuplicates()
// Instantiate an empty list object with room for 100 items
{
  numItems = 0;
  listItems = new String[100];
  currentPos = 0;
}

public ListWithDuplicates(int maxItems)
// Instantiate an empty list object with room for
//  maxItems items
{
  numItems = 0;
  listItems = new String[maxItems];
  currentPos = 0;
}

public boolean isFull()
// Return true if there is not room for another component;
//  false otherwise
{
  return (listItems.length == numItems);
}

public boolean isEmpty()
// Return true if there are no components in the list;
//  false otherwise
{
  return (numItems == 0);
}

public int length()
// Return the number of components in the list
{
  return numItems;
}
public abstract boolean isThere(String item);
// Return true if item is in the list

// Transformers
public abstract void insert(String item);
// If the list is not full, insert item into the list;
//  otherwise, list is unchanged
```

```
      public abstract void delete(String item);

      public void resetList()            // Prepare for iteration
      {
        currentPos = 0;
      }

      public String getNextItem()        // Return an unvisited item
      {
        String next = listItems[currentPos];
        if (currentPos == numItems-1)
          currentPos = 0;
        else
          currentPos++;
        return next;
      }
    }
```

b. The only design changes are in the name of the class and the documentation on the insert method.

c.
```
    public class UnsortedListWithDuplicates extends ListWithDuplicates
    {
      public UnsortedListWithDuplicates()
      {
        super();
      }
      public UnsortedListWithDuplicates(int maxItems)
      {
        super(maxItems);
      }
      public boolean isThere(String item)
      // Return true if item is in the list
      {
        int index = 0;
        while (index < numItems && listItems[index].compareTo(item) != 0)
          index++;
        return (index < numItems);
      }

      public void insert(String item)
      // If the list is not full, put item in the last position in the list;
      //  otherwise, list is unchanged
```

```
  {
    if (!isFull())
    {
      listItems[numItems] = item;
      numItems++;
    }
  }
  public void delete(String item)
  // Remove all copies of item from the list
  {
    int index = 0;
    while (index < numItems)
    {
      if (listItems[index].compareTo(item) == 0)
      {
        for (int count = index; count < numItems-1; count++)
          listItems[count] = listItems[count+1];
        numItems--;
      }
      else
        index++;
    }
  }
}
```

d. Only the insert and delete operations are shown because they are the only ones that would change with respect to part c.

```
  public void insert(String item)
  // If the list is not full, put item in its proper position in
  //   the list; otherwise, list is unchanged
  {
    if (!isFull())
    {
      int index = numItems - 1;                // Loop control variable
      while (index >= 0 && (item.compareTo(listItems[index]) < 0))
      {
        listItems[index+1] = listItems[index]; // Find insertion point
        index--;
      }
      listItems[index+1] = item;               // Insert item
      numItems++;                              // Increment number of items
    }
  }
  public void delete(String item)
```

```
        // Remove all copies of item from the list
        {
          int index = 0;
          while (index < numItems && item.compareTo(listItems[index]) <= 0)
          {
            if (listItems[index].compareTo(item) == 0)
            {
              for (int count = index; count < numItems-1; count++)
                listItems[count] = listItems[count+1];
              numItems--;
            }
            else
              index++;
          }
        }
```

   e. If a binary search is used to find the item to delete, you do not know whether
      the one found is the first duplicate, the last duplicate, or one in the middle. The
      method would have to search both before and after the item to look for
      duplicate copies. It is easier to use a linear search.

9.
```
public void insert(String item)
// If the list is not full, put item in its proper position in the
//  list; otherwise, list is unchanged
{
  boolean placeFound = false;
  int index = 0;
  if (!isFull())
  {
    while (!placeFound && index < numItems)
      if (item.compareTo(listItems[index]) > 0)
        index++;
      else
        placeFound = true;
    for (int count = numItems; count > index; count--)
      listItems[count] = listItems[count - 1];
    listItems[index] = item;
    numItems++;
  }
}
```

Answers

Chapter 12 Exam Preparation Exercises

2. a.

col	0	1	2
row			
0	0	0	0
1	0	1	2
2	0	2	4
3	0	3	6

b.

col	0	1	2
row			
0	0	1	2
1	1	2	0
2	2	0	1
3	U	U	U

c.

col	0	1
row		
0	2	3
1	2	3
2	2	3
3	2	3
4	2	3
5	2	3
6	2	3
7	4	5

5. a. `boolean[][] myArray = new boolean[5][6];`

   b. `double[][] MyArray = new double[40][200];`

   c. `char[][] myArray = new char[4][3];`

8. a. 1.4E+12

   b. 100.0

   c. 3.2E+5

9. a. The *mantissa* is the part of the floating-point number that contains the representable significant digits.

   b. The *exponent* is the part of the floating-point number that determines where the decimal point is placed relative to the mantissa.

   c. *Representational error* is an arithmetic error that occurs when the precision of the true result of an arithmetic operation is greater than the precision of the machine.

   d. *Significant digits* are those digits from the first nonzero digit on the left to the last nonzero digit on the right (plus any zero digits that are exact).

e. *Overflow* is the condition that occurs when the result of a calculation is greater than the maximum number that can be represented in the computer.

11. **a.** x is 2314.38

   b. x is 2,314.38

   c. x is 2314.4

   d. x is 2,314.383

Chapter 12 Programming Warm-Up Exercises

1.
```
final int NUM_SCHOOLS = 10;
final int NUM_SPORTS = 3;
//  row/column 0 is football; row/column 1 is basketball;
//  row/column 2 is volleyball
int[][]  kidsInSports = new int[NUM_SCHOOLS][NUM_SPORTS];
double[][] costOfSports = new double[NUM_SPORTS][NUM_SCHOOLS];
```
a.
```
int mostSoFar = 0;
for (int column = 1; column < NUM_SCHOOLS; column++)
  if (costOfSports[0][column] > costOfSports[0][mostSoFar])
    mostSoFar = column;
// mostSoFar is the school that spent the most on football
```
b.
```
int whichSport = 0;
int last = NUM_SCHOOLS - 1;
for (int row = 1; row < NUM_SPORTS; row++)
  if (costOfSports[row][last] > costOfSports[whichSport][last])
    whichSport = row;
// whichSport contains the sport that the last school spent the
//  most on
```
c.
```
int mostStudents = 0;
for (int row = 1; row < NUM_SCHOOLS; row++);
  if (kidsInSports[row][1] > kidsInSports[mostStudents][1])
    mostStudents = row;
// mostStudents is the school with the most students playing
//  basketball
```
d.
```
int whichSport = 0;
for (int column = 1; column < NUM_SPORTS; column++)
  if (kidsInSports[2][column] > kidsInSports[2][whichSport])
    whichSport = column;
// whichSport is the sport that the third school has the most
//  students in
```
e.
```
int sum = 0;
for (int column = 0; column < NUM_SCHOOLS; column++)
  sum = sum + costOfSports[2][column];
// sum contains the total amount spent on volleyball
```

f.
```
int totalKids = 0;
int bestSchool = 0;
for (int row = 0; row < NUM_SCHOOLS; row++)
  for(int column = 0; column < NUM_SPORTS; column++)
    totalKids = totalKids + kidsInSports[row][col];
// totalKids contains the total of all the kids in sports
```

g.
```
int bestTotal= 0;
int bestSchool = 0;
for (int row = 0; row < NUM_SCHOOLS; row++)
{
  int totalKids = 0;
  for (int column = 0; column < NUM_SPORTS; column++)
    totalKids= totalKids + kidsInSports[row][column];
  if (totalKids > bestTotal)
  {
    bestTotal = totalKids;
    bestSchool = row;
  }
}
// bestSchool contains the number of the school with the
//  most kids participating in sports
```

h.
```
double bestTotal = 0.0;
int bestSport;
for (int row = 0; row < NUM_SPORTS; row++)
{
  double totalMoney = 0.0;
  for (int column = 0; column < NUM_SCHOOLS; column++)
    totalMoney = totalMoney + costOfSports[row][column];
  if (totalMoney > bestTotal)
  {
    bestTotal = totalMoney;
    bestSport = row;
  }
}
// bestSport contains the most popular sport in terms of
//  money spent
```

i.
```
int numberOfKids = 0;
int bestSport = 0;
for (int column = 0; column < NUM_SPORTS; COLUMN++)
{
  int totalKids  = 0;
  for (int row = 0; row < NUM_SCHOOLS; row++)
    totalKids = totalKids + kidsInSports[row][column];
```

```
        if (totalKids    > numberOfKids)
        {
          numberOfKids = totalKids;
          bestSport = column;
        }
        // bestSport contains the sport in which the most students
        //   participated
      }
```

4. Given the following declarations:

```
final int NUM_DEPTS = 100;
final int NUM_STORES = 10;
final int NUM_MONTHS = 12;
```

a. `double[][][] sales;`

b. `sales = new double[NUM_DEPTS][NUM_STORES][NUM_MONTHS];`

c. `0.0 (double)`

d.
```
sum = 0.0;
for (int depts = 0; depts < NUM_DEPTS; depts++)
  for (int stores = 0; stores < NUM_STORES; stores++)
    sum = sum + sales[depts][stores][0];
// sum contains the sum of the sales for January
```

e.
```
sum = 0.0;
for (int depts = 0; depts < NUM_DEPTS; depts++)
  for (int months = 0; months < NUM_MONTHS; months++)
    sum = sum + sales[depts][1][months];
// sum contains the sum of the sales for store 2
```

f.
```
sum = 0.0;
for (int stores = 0; stores < NUM_STORES; stores++)
  for (int months = 0; months < NUM_MONTHS; months++)
    sum = sum + sales[32][stores][months];
// sum contains the sum of the sales for department 33
```

Chapter 13 Exam Preparation Exercises

1. c. repetition

4. $F(4) = 1$, $F(6) = -1$, and $F(5)$ is undefined

6. *if* is the control structure used most often in recursion.

9. Run-time stack

Chapter 13 Programming Warm-Up Exercises

1.
```java
public static int f(int n)
{
  if (n == 0 || n == 1)
    return 1;
  else
    return f(n - 1) + f(n - 2);
}
```

4.
```java
public static int factorial(int n, int level)
{
  int tempFactorial;
  int loopCount;
  for (loopCount = 1; loopCount <= level; loopCount++)
    System.out.print("  ");
  System.out.println(n);
  if (n == 0)
    tempFactorial = 1;
  else
    tempFactorial = n * factorial(n - 1, level + 1);
  for (loopCount = 1; loopCount <= level; loopCount++)
    System.out.print("  ");
  System.out.println(tempFactorial);
  return tempFactorial;
}
```

6.
```java
public static void printSqRoots(int n)
{
  if (n > 0)
  {
    outFile.println(n + " " + Math.sqrt((double)n));
    printSqRoots(n - 1);
  }
}
```

7.
```java
public static void print(
  int[] data,    // Array to be printed
  int first,     // Index of first element
  int last  )    // Index of last element
  // Print an array
```

```
    {
      if (first <= last)
      {                                 // Recursive case
        outFile.println(data[last]+ " ");
        print(data, first, last - 1);
      }
      // Empty else clause is the base case
    }
9.  public static int power(int x, int n)
    // Returns x raised to the power n
    // Assumption:  x is a valid integer and n is greater
    //   than or equal to 0
    // Note: Large exponents may result in integer overflow
    {
      if (n == 0)
        return 1;                       // Base case
      else
        return x * power(x, n - 1); // Recursive call
    }
```

Chapter 14 Exam Preparation Exercises

1. An applet doesn't have a main method. An applet is not invoked in the same fashion as an application. Applets are subjected to more security constraints than an application because they are distributed over the Web. Applets are not in control of their own execution.

4. Applet class

6. The add method is not applied to a pane object in the case of an applet.

9. The applet must be run within a Web browser or an applet viewer. The browser recognizes a link to a Bytecode file, and the JVM within the browser executes the code.

12. A tag is the syntactic element in a markup language that indicates how information should be displayed.

15. The Internet is a wide area network that spans the planet, while the Web is an infrastructure of information and the network software used to access it. Thus the Internet is the hardware and the Web makes it usable by providing the appropriate software.

17. A LAN is a local area network of nodes in a close geographic area. A WAN is a network made up of two or more other networks.

Chapter 14 Programming Warm-Up Exercises

3. ```
   TextField myField;
   myField = new TextField("My data");
   add(myField);
   ```

8. **a.** `<APPLET code = "Sorts.class" width=250 height=150></APPLET>`

   b. `<APPLET code = "Search.class" width=250 height=150></APPLET>`

   c. `<APPLET code = "Calculator.class" width=250 height=150></APPLET>`

10. `<HR>`

11. `<P></P>`
   ```

Index

Index

Index

Credits

We would like to thank the following people and organizations who generously contributed the photographs and images found in our Timeline. We also thank the IEEE Computing Society for publishing their Timeline of Computing History, which proved a valuable resource as we created a chronology of significant events and developments in the history of computer technology.

Chapter 1
Abacus – Getty Images/ PhotoDisk 2003
Typewriter – Getty Images/ PhotoDisk 2003

Chapter 2
Herman Hollerith Tabulating Machine – IBM Corporate Archives
Punched Card – Courtesy of Douglas W. Jones at the University of Iowa
Computer Chip – Getty Images/ PhotoDisk 2003
1924 IBM Logo – IBM Corporate Archives

Chapter 3
Television – Getty Images/ PhotoDisk 2003
Service Technicians – IBM Corporate Archives
George Stibitz – Lucent Technologies Inc. / Bell Labs
ENIAC – U.S. Army Photo

Chapter 4
EDVAC – U.S. Army Photo
Grace Murray Hopper (also appears on page 443) – Naval Historical Center
World's First Transistor – Lucent Technologies Inc. / Bell Labs
UNIVAC Computer Console – Lawrence Livermore National Laboratory

Chapter 5
EDVAC – U.S. Army Photo
First Silicon Transistor – Courtesy of Texas Instruments
Dartmouth College – © Trustees of Dartmouth College
Sputnik I – NASA Photo

Chapter 6
Integrated Circuit – Courtesy of Texas Instruments
John McCarthy – Courtesy of Stanford University
Xerox Copier – Courtesy of Xerox. Reprinted with Permission
IBM 7030 – IBM Corporate Archives

Chapter 7
Telstar Communications Satellite – IBM Corporate Archives
Bob Bemer – Courtesy of Bob Bemer
Englebart's Mouse – Courtesy of Bootstrap Institute
Electronic Calculator – Courtesy of Texas Instruments

Chapter 8

Edsger Dijkstra – Courtesy of The University of Texas at Austin

Grove, Noyce, and Moore – Courtesy of Intel Corporation, Reprinted with Permission

Unix Creators – Lucent Technologies Inc. / Bell Labs.

Microprocessor – Getty Images/ PhotoDisk 2003

Chapter 9

Pong Image - Pong Image provided by *www.atarimuseum.com*

Vincent Atanasoff – Courtesy Iowa State University

Chess - Getty Images/ PhotoDisk 2003

Chapter 10

Original Apple II - 1978- Photo courtesy of Apple Computer, Inc.

PET Commodore Computer – Courtesy of the Commodore History Web Site,
   www.commodore.ca

Key - Getty Images/ PhotoDisk 2003

Dan Bricklin – Louis Fabian Bachrach / Dan Bricklin

Chapter 11

Cell Phone - Getty Images/ PhotoDisk 2003

IBM PC – IBM Corporate Archives

John Warnock and Charles Geschke – Courtesy of Adobe Systems, Inc. Reprinted with
   permission

Chapter 12

CD-ROM - Getty Images/ PhotoDisk 2003

Intel 286 Microprocessor – Courtesy of Intel Corporation, Reprinted with Permission

Intel 386 Microprocessor – Courtesy of Intel Corporation, Reprinted with Permission

Seymour Cray – Courtesy of Cray Inc.

Chapter 13

Tim Berners-Lee – Photo Courtesy of Donna Coveney, MIT

Intel Pentium Chip – Courtesy of Intel Corporation, Reprinted with Permission

Java Logo - Java, and the Java Coffee Cup Logo are trademarks or registered
   trademarks of Sun Microsystems, Inc. in the U.S. and other countries, and are
   used under permission

Chapter 14

.COM – Credit AbleStock

Kasparov and Deep Blue – Courtesy of IBM

.COM – Credit AbleStock

Earth Simulator – Courtesy of the Earth Simulator Center

Sun Microsystems, Inc.
Binary Code License Agreement

READ THE TERMS OF THIS AGREEMENT AND ANY PROVIDED SUPPLEMENTAL LICENSE TERMS (COLLECTIVELY "AGREEMENT") CAREFULLY BEFORE OPENING THE SOFTWARE MEDIA PACKAGE, YOU AGREE TO THE TERMS OF THIS AGREEMENT. INDICATE YOUR ACCEPTANCE OF THESE TERMS BY SELECTING THE "ACCEPT" BUTTON AT THE END OF THIS AGREEMENT. IF YOU DO NOT AGREE TO ALL THESE TERMS, PROMPTLY RETURN THE UNUSED SOFTWARE TO YOUR PLACE OF PURCHASE, OR IF THE SOFTWARE IS ACCESSED ELECTRONICALLY, SELECT THE "DECLINE" BUTTON AT THE END OF THIS AGREEMENT.

1. LICENSE TO USE. Sun grants you a non-exclusive and non-transferable license for the internal use only of the accompanying software and documentation and any error corrections provided by Sun (collectively "Software"), by the number of users and the class of computer hardware for which the corresponding fee has been paid.

2. RESTRICTIONS Software is confidential and copyrighted. Title to Software and all associated intellectual property rights is retained by Sun and/or its licensors. Except as specifically authorized in any Supplemental License Terms, you may not make copies of Software, other than a single copy of Software for archival purposes. Unless enforcement is prohibited by applicable law, you may not modify, decompile, or reverse engineer Software. Software is not designed or intended for use in the design, construction, operation or maintenance of any nuclear facility. Sun disclaims any express or implied warranty of fitness for such uses. No right, title or interest in or to any trademark, service mark, logo or trade name of Sun or its licensors is granted under this Agreement.

3. LIMITED WARRANTY. Sun warrants to you that for a period of ninety (90) days from the date of purchase, as evidenced by a copy of the receipt, the media on which Software is furnished (if any) will be free of defects in materials and workmanship under normal use. Except for the foregoing, Software is provided "AS IS". Your exclusive remedy and Sun's entire liability under this limited warranty will be at Sun's option to replace Software media or refund the fee paid for Software.

4. DISCLAIMER OF WARRANTY. UNLESS SPECIFIED IN THIS AGREEMENT, ALL EXPRESS OR IMPLIED CONDITIONS, REPRESENTATIONS AND WARRANTIES, INCLUDING ANY IMPLIED WARRANTY OF MERCHANTABILITY, FITNESS FOR A PARTICULAR PURPOSE OR NON-INFRINGEMENT ARE DISCLAIMED, EXCEPT TO THE EXTENT THAT THESE DISCLAIMERS ARE HELD TO BE LEGALLY INVALID.

5. LIMITATION OF LIABILITY. TO THE EXTENT NOT PROHIBITED BY LAW, IN NO EVENT WILL SUN OR ITS LICENSORS BE LIABLE FOR ANY LOST REVENUE, PROFIT OR DATA, OR FOR SPE-CIAL, INDIRECT, CONSEQUENTIAL, INCIDENTAL OR PUNITIVE DAMAGES, HOWEVER CAUSED REGARDLESS OF THE THEORY OF LIABILITY, ARISING OUT OF OR RELATED TO THE USE OF OR INABILITY TO USE SOFTWARE, EVEN IF SUN HAS BEEN ADVISED OF THE POSSIBILITY OF SUCH DAMAGES. In no event will Sun's liability to you, whether in contract, tort (including negligence), or otherwise, exceed the amount paid by you for Software under this Agreement. The foregoing limitations will apply even if the above stated warranty fails of its essential purpose.

6. Termination. This Agreement is effective until terminated. You may terminate this Agreement at any time by destroying all copies of Software. This Agreement will terminate immediately without notice from Sun if you fail to comply with any provision of this Agreement. Upon Termination, you must destroy all copies of Software.

7. Export Regulations. All Software and technical data delivered under this Agreement are sub-ject to US export control laws and may be subject to export or import regulations in other countries. You agree to comply strictly with all such laws and regulations and acknowledge that you have the responsibility to obtain such licenses to export, re-export, or import as may be required after delivery to you.

8. U.S. Government Restricted Rights. If Software is being acquired by or on behalf of the U.S. Government or by a U.S. Government prime contractor or subcontractor (at any tier), then the Government's rights in Software and accompanying documentation will be only as set forth in this Agreement; this is in accordance with 48 CFR 227.7201 through 227.7202-4 (for Department of Defense (DOD) acquisitions) and with 48 CFR 2.101 and 12.212 (for non-DOD acquisitions).

9. Governing Law. Any action related to this Agreement will be governed by California law and controlling U.S. federal law. No choice of law rules of any jurisdiction will apply.

10. Severability. If any provision of this Agreement is held to be unenforceable, this Agreement will remain in effect with the provision omitted, unless omission would frustrate the intent of the parties, in which case this Agreement will immediately terminate.

11. Integration. This Agreement is the entire agreement between you and Sun relating to its subject matter. It supersedes all prior or contemporaneous oral or written communications, proposals, representations and warranties and prevails over any conflicting or additional terms of any quote, order, acknowledgment, or other communication between the parties re-lating to its subject matter during the term of this Agreement. No modification of this Agreement will be binding, unless in writing and signed by an authorized representative of each party.

Java Naming and Directory Interface (TM), Version 1.1

SUPPLEMENTAL LICENSE TERMS

These supplemental terms ("Supplement") add to the terms of the Binary Code License Agreement (collectively the "Agreement"). Capitalized terms not defined herein shall have the same meanings ascribed to them in the Agreement. The Supplement terms shall supersede any inconsistent or conflicting terms in the Agreement, either above or contained within the Software.

1. License to Distribute. You are granted a royalty-free right to reproduce and distribute the Software provided that you: (i) distribute the Software complete and unmodified, provided that the Software is distributed with your Java applet or application ("Program"); (ii) do not distribute additional software intended to replace any component(s) of the Software; (iii) do not remove or alter the Agreement, any proprietary legends or notices contained in the Software; (iv) only distribute the Software under terms no less protective of Sun than this Agreement; (v) may not create, or authorize your licensees to create additional classes, interfaces, or subpackages that are contained in the "java", "javax", or "sun" packages or similar as specified by Sun in any class file naming convention; (vi) agree to indemnify, hold harmless, and defend Sun and its licensors from and against any claims or lawsuits, including attorneys' fees, that arise or result from the use or distribution of the Program.

2. Trademarks and Logos. You acknowledge as between you and Sun that Sun owns the Java trademark and all Java-related trademarks, logos and icons including the Coffee Cup and Duke ("Java Marks") and agrees to comply with the Java Trademark Guidelines at http://java.sun.com/trademarks.html.

For inquiries please contact: Sun Microsystems, Inc. 901 San Antonio Road, Palo Alto, California 94303

BORLAND-AUTHORIZED TEXTBOOK PUBLISHER LICENSE STATEMENT AND LIMITED WARRANTY FOR TITLES

IMPORTANT – READ CAREFULLY

This license statement and limited warranty constitutes a legal agreement ("License Agreement") for the software product ("Software") identified above (including any software, media, and accompanying on-line or printed documentation supplied by Borland) between you (either as an individual or a single entity), the Book Publisher from whom you received the Software ("Publisher"), and Borland® Software Corporation. ("Borland").

BY INSTALLING, COPYING, OR OTHERWISE USING THE SOFTWARE, YOU AGREE TO BE BOUND BY ALL OF THE TERMS AND CONDITIONS OF THE LICENSE AGREEMENT. If you are the original purchaser of the Software and you do not agree with the terms and conditions of the License Agreement, promptly return the unused Software to the place from which you obtained it for a full refund.

Upon your acceptance of the terms and conditions of the License Agreement, Borland grants you the right to use the Software solely for educational or training purposes. *No rights are granted for deploying or distributing applications created with the Software.*

This Software is owned by Borland or its suppliers and is protected by copyright law and international copyright treaty. Therefore, you must treat this Software like any other copyrighted material (e.g., a book), except that you may either make one copy of the Software solely for backup or archival purposes or transfer the Software to a single hard disk provided you keep the original solely for backup or archival purposes.

You may transfer the Software and documentation on a permanent basis provided you retain no copies and the recipient agrees to the terms of the License Agreement. Except as provided in the License Agreement, you may not transfer, rent, lease, lend, copy, modify, translate, sublicense, time-share or electronically transmit or receive the Software, media or documentation. You acknowledge that the Software in source code form remains a confidential trade secret of Borland and/or its suppliers and therefore you agree not to modify the Software or attempt to reverse engineer, decompile, or disassemble the Software, except and only to the extent that such activity is expressly permitted by applicable law notwithstanding this limitation.

Though Borland does not offer technical support for the Software, we welcome your feedback.

This Software is subject to U.S. Commerce Department export restrictions, and is intended for use in the country into which Borland sold it (or in the EEC, if sold into the EEC).

LIMITED WARRANTY

The Publisher warrants that the Software media will be free from physical defects in materials and workmanship for a period of ninety (90) days from the date of receipt. Any implied warranties on the Software media are limited to ninety (90) days. Some states/jurisdictions do not allow limitations on duration of an implied warranty, so the above limitation may not apply to you.

The Publisher's, Borland's, and the Publisher's or Borland's suppliers' entire liability and your exclusive remedy shall be, at the Publisher's or Borland's option, either (a) return of the price paid, or (b) repair or replacement of the Software media that does not meet the Limited Warranty and which is returned to the Publisher with a copy of your receipt. This Limited Warranty is void if failure of the Software has resulted from accident, abuse, or misapplication. Any replacement Software will be warranted for the remainder of the original warranty period or thirty (30) days, whichever is longer. **Outside the United States, neither these remedies nor any product support services offered are available without proof of purchase from an authorized non-U.S. source.**

TO THE MAXIMUM EXTENT PERMITTED BY APPLICABLE LAW, THE PUBLISHER, INPRISE, AND THE PUBLISHER'S OR BORLAND'S SUPPLIERS DISCLAIM ALL OTHER WARRANTIES AND CONDITIONS, EITHER EXPRESS OR IMPLIED, INCLUDING, BUT NOT LIMITED TO, IMPLIED WARRANTIES OF MERCHANTABILITY, FITNESS FOR A PARTICULAR PURPOSE, TITLE, AND NON-INFRINGEMENT, WITH REGARD TO THE SOFTWARE, AND THE PROVISION OF OR FAILURE TO PROVIDE SUPPORT SERVICES. THIS LIMITED WARRANTY GIVES YOU SPECIFIC LEGAL RIGHTS. YOU MAY HAVE OTHERS, WHICH VARY FROM STATE/JURISDICTION TO STATE/JURISDICTION.

LIMITATION OF LIABILITY

TO THE MAXIMUM EXTENT PERMITTED BY APPLICABLE LAW, IN NO EVENT SHALL THE PUBLISHER, INPRISE, OR THE PUBLISHER'S OR INPRISE'S SUPPLIERS BE LIABLE FOR ANY SPECIAL, INCIDENTAL, INDIRECT, OR CONSEQUENTIAL DAMAGES WHATSOEVER (INCLUDING, WITHOUT LIMITATION, DAMAGES FOR LOSS OF BUSINESS PROFITS, BUSINESS INTERRUPTION, LOSS OF BUSINESS INFORMATION, OR ANY OTHER PECUNIARY LOSS) ARISING OUT OF THE USE OF OR INABILITY TO USE THE SOFTWARE PRODUCT OR THE PROVISION OF OR FAILURE TO PROVIDE SUPPORT SERVICES, EVEN IF INPRISE HAS BEEN ADVISED OF THE POSSIBILITY OF SUCH DAMAGES. IN ANY CASE, INPRISE'S ENTIRE LIABILITY UNDER ANY PROVISION OF THIS LICENSE AGREEMENT SHALL BE LIMITED TO THE GREATER OF THE AMOUNT ACTUALLY PAID BY YOU FOR THE SOFTWARE PRODUCT OR U.S. $25. BECAUSE SOME STATES AND JURISDICTIONS DO NOT ALLOW THE EXCLUSION OR LIMITATION OF LIABILITY, THE ABOVE LIMITATION MAY NOT APPLY TO YOU.

HIGH RISK ACTIVITIES

The Software is not fault-tolerant and is not designed, manufactured or intended for use or resale as on-line control equipment in hazardous environments requiring fail-safe performance, such as in the operation of nuclear facilities, aircraft navigation or communication systems, air traffic control, direct life support machines, or weapons systems, in which the failure of the Software could lead directly to death, personal injury, or severe physical or environmental damage ("High Risk Activities"). The Publisher, Borland, and their suppliers specifically disclaim any express or implied warranty of fitness for High Risk Activities.

U.S. GOVERNMENT RESTRICTED RIGHTS
The Software and documentation are provided with RESTRICTED RIGHTS. Use, duplication, or disclosure by the Government is subject to restrictions as set forth in subparagraphs (c)(1)(ii) of the Rights in Technical Data and Computer Software clause at DFARS 252.227-7013 or subparagraphs (c)(1) and (2) of the Commercial Computer Software-Restricted Rights at 48 CFR 52.227-19, as applicable.

GENERAL PROVISIONS.
This License Agreement may only be modified in writing signed by you and an authorized officer of Borland. If any provision of this License Agreement is found void or unenforceable, the remainder will remain valid and enforceable according to its terms. If any remedy provided is determined to have failed for its essential purpose, all limitations of liability and exclusions of damages set forth in the Limited Warranty shall remain in effect.

This License Agreement shall be construed, interpreted and governed by the laws of the State of California, U.S.A. This License Agreement gives you specific legal rights; you may have others which vary from state to state and from country to country. Borland reserves all rights not specifically granted in this License Agreement.